TWENTIETH CENTURY OPERA

D1329505

A GUIDE

By George Martin

Limelight Editions, *New York*

First Limelight Edition   June 1999

Copyright ©1999, 1979 by George Martin
All rights reserved.
No part of this book may be reproduced in any form
without permission in writing from the publisher.
Published by Proscenium Publishers Inc.,
118 East 30th Street, New York, NY 10016.

Much of this book was originally published under the title
The Companion to Twentieth-Century Opera

Library of Congress Cataloging-in-Publication Data

Martin, George Whitney.
       Twentieth century opera : a guide / by George Martin.
              p.   cm.
       Includes bibliographical references (p.   ) and index.
       ISBN 0-87910-275-6
       1. Operas--20th century Stories, plots, etc.   I. Martin, George
Whitney. Companion to twentieth-century opera.   II. Title.
III. Title: 20th century opera.
MT95.M253   1999
782.1'09'04--dc21   99-27953
                                                           CIP

Acknowledgement is made to the following for permission to use selections from their copyrighted publications indicated below:

The Yale Review: the author's essay *Stravinsky and the Natures of Ballet and Opera* was published first in *The Yale Review,* copyright Yale University, in Winter 1972.

Opera News: the synopses for *Lulu, The Turn of the Screw* and *Albert Herring* are adapted from articles by the author that first appeared in *Opera News,* a publication of The Metropolitan Opera Guild, Inc., in September 1963, March 1970, and September 1971.

Artia: for the quotations from *Leoš Janáček: Letters and Reminiscences,* edited by Bohumir Štědroň and translated by Geraldine Thomsen, copyright 1955 by Artia Prague—Czechoslovakia.

Theodore Presser Co: for the quotation from *Webern, Briefe an Hildegarde Jone und Josef Humplik,* edited by Josef Polnauer, and translated by Cornelius Cardew, copyright 1967 by Theodore Presser Co., Bryn Mawr.

Boosey and Hawkes, Inc: for permission to quote the Ronsard sonnet, translated by Clemens Krauss, from the libretto of *Capriccio.* Copyright © 1942 by Richard Strauss. Renewed 1969. Reprinted by permission of Boosey and Hawkes, Inc. Sole Agents. For permission to quote four lines from the libretto by Eric Crozier for *Albert Herring.* Copyright © 1948 by Hawkes & Son (London) Ltd. Renewed 1975. Reprinted by permission of Boosey and Hawkes, Inc.

And for the use of musical quotations to:

Boosey and Hawkes, Inc: for Bartok's *Duke Bluebeard's Castle:* Copyright © 1921 by Universal Edition. Renewed 1948. Copyright and Renewal assigned to Boosey & Hawkes, Inc. for the U.S.A. Reprinted by permission of Boosey & Hawkes, Inc. For Strauss's *Capriccio:* Copyright © 1942 by Richard Strauss. Renewed 1969. Reprinted by permission of Boosey & Hawkes, Inc. Sole Agents. For Stravinsky's *The Rake's Progress* (including text): *The Rake's Progress*—Igor Stravinsky. Libretto by W. H. Auden and Chester Kallman. Copyright 1949, 1959, 1951 by Boosey & Hawkes, Inc. Reprinted by permission. For Britten's *The Turn of the Screw:* Copyright © 1955 by Hawkes & Son (London) Ltd. Reprinted by permission of Boosey & Hawkes, Inc. For Britten's *A Midsummer Night's Dream:* Copyright © 1960 by Hawkes & Son (London) Ltd. Reprinted by permission of Boosey & Hawkes, Inc.

Universal Edition Music Publishers, Inc: for Schoenberg's *Moses und Aron.* Copyright 1957 by Mrs. Gertrud Schoenberg. For Berg's *Lulu.* Copyright 1936 by Universal Edition A. G., Wien.

OLIVIER: Prima le parole—dopo la musica!

FLAMAND: Prima la musica—dopo le parole!

The Poet and the Musician in Strauss's
Capriccio argue the eternal question of opera:
Which comes first, the words or the music?

CONTENTS

V · PROKOFIEV'S OPERAS: BAD LUCK AND
POLITICS   55

Youth. Misfortunes of the early operas. His departure and return
to Russia. Political bias in criticism of his operas. Three about invasions of Russia: *Semyon Kotko, War and Peace, The Story of a
Real Man*. Their extraordinary histories. Gradual emergence.

VI · SOME ASPECTS OF TWENTIETH-CENTURY
OPERA, 1976-99   71

Revolution in music of electrical instruments. Rock opera fails to
grow. Its deficiencies. Glass succeeds with *Einstein on the Beach*.
His subsequent operas. Competing styles. What the future may hold.

P A R T I I   SYNOPSES   87

For chronological index by composer, see pages 89-92.

PART III   COMPENDIUM AND GLOSSARY   631
OF COMPOSERS, A FEW OTHERS, AND TERMS
PERTINENT TO TWENTIETH-CENTURY OPERA.

PREFACE

Before I speak of the book's purpose and contents, a word about its revision for this Limelight Edition. In its first three editions (1979-1989, titled the *Companion to Twentieth Century Opera*), the book surveyed seventy-five years of opera, noting trends and accomplishments as well as offering synopses of seventy-eight works, and then speculated on trends and styles likely to flourish in the final quarter. Now, from the threshold of the new century, it is possible to report on the entire twentieth century, replacing speculation with operas composed and trends established. To that end much of the book has been newly written: Besides small changes here and there, two introductory chapters have been dropped, and one added; the synopses have been increased by twelve; and a large section of statistics on the number of performances replaced by a new "Compendium and Glossary" of composers, critical terms, and miscellanea pertinent to twentieth century opera. In sum, a major revision; and hence, the new title: *Twentieth Century Opera, A Guide*.

I have written chiefly for those who like opera, go to performances, perhaps occasionally buy a recording, but are not musically trained. These good people sometimes lament they are at sea in twentieth-century opera; and my aim is to help turn that sea into dry, familiar land.

I think a book entirely devoted to twentieth-century opera is needed. Too often the century and its operas are relegated to a final chapter where discussion is skimped and the few synopses offered merely reinforce the myth that in some fashion during the century opera lost its audience and all but died.

That myth should be declared dead, and buried with a stake driven through its heart, for it never was true. Many twentieth-century operas have been astonishingly popular. Kurt Weill's *Down in the Valley* (1948), for example, in its first nine years had 1600 productions, roughly 6,000 performances. And consider such works as *Amahl and the Night Visitors, The Medium, Porgy and Bess, The Threepenny Opera,* or *Einstein on the Beach.* Take *Amahl.* First presented on television on Christmas Eve 1951, and for many years re-run on that date, thirty-five years later in opera houses in the United States it was still playing more than 500 performances a season (1985-86, 531); or take *Porgy and Bess,* which regularly plays in opera houses both here and abroad, is revived periodically on Broadway, and has more than once been taken on a world tour. Or consider the career of Philip Glass, whose first opera, *Einstein on the Beach,* playing through the summer of 1976 in Europe and then to sold-out performances in New York, stimulated a new style of opera and new audience to appreciate it. In recordings his works sold to thousands and by the mid-1980s and three operas later he was enjoying a career in opera that for size of audience rivaled Puccini or Strauss at the start of the century.

As before, I have divided the book into three parts with its core in Part II: synopses, some long, some short, of ninety operas. These, I hope, will prove so readable that a person turning to one will be tempted to browse through others, or at least through their introductory paragraphs. For one way to grasp the richness of twentieth-century opera is to relish its diversity in subject, view, and style.

The book's other two parts also aim to reveal that diversity. Part I consists of six Introductory Essays: The first surveys in general terms twentieth-century opera in its initial seventy-five years, with emphasis on Alban Berg and Benjamin Britten; then four biographical essays on Janáček, Puccini, Stravinsky, and Prokofiev illustrate different aspects of twentieth-century opera; while the sixth discusses the trends and accomplishments of the century's final quarter. Part III, a Compendium and Glossary of composers, critical terms, and miscellanea pertinent to twentieth-century opera, may help operagoers find some meaning in many of the names and terms that critics often toss about.

My choice for the ninety operas of Part II, the synopses, cannot please everyone. I based it on several considerations: operas most often performed (primarily in the United States), most often recorded, or stylistically important, or seemingly gaining rather than losing popularity. The last favored Janáček, whose operas are joining the international repertory, and slighted Wolf-Ferrari, whose works were once, but are no longer (alas!), much performed. With several of the greater composers, such as Puccini and Strauss, I included their less well-known operas in order to complete the picture of their personalities. And for most purposes I defined the century stylistically, starting it about 1910, when Puccini, with *La fanciulla del West,* and Strauss, with *Ariadne auf Naxos,* shifted their styles.

The form of the synopsis varies, depending on the detail with which the opera is presented and to some extent on its structure. In the longer synopses clearly defined arias, choruses, interludes, ballets, etc., are indicated by a heading or an indented side note; in others, the paragraphing and internal comments reflect the structure. In every case the scenes, acts, and settings are as the composer indicated, and the synopsis presents the opera uncut, while indicating where any usual cuts are made. Where there are versions of scenes, such as in the finale of Janáček's *From the House of the Dead,* the synopsis follows the version the operagoer is likely to hear while stating the others. Matters of interest chiefly to scholars are ignored.

In all synopses I have given timings for scenes and acts, so that the operagoers can pace themselves: "Only half through!" (whether thought in delight or despair). The timings, of course, are averages. A two-hour opera may vary as much as fifteen minutes depending on the conductor, and tempos on a recording are apt to be faster than those in an opera house. Where composers, or others, have drawn suites from the operas that turn up in concert or recorded performances I have noted briefly what they contain.

Throughout, in whatever way seemed best, I have tried to reveal the opera's substance and musical structure. By substance I mean what the opera is about as well as its surface events, the story. Sometimes the two, because of symbolism or bad staging, are hard to relate, and with some operas, such as Prokofiev's *Fiery Angel,* Berg's *Lulu,* or Strauss's *Egyptian Helen,* I have taken a strong stand on meaning. My ideas may be wrong, but at least they should stimulate operagoers to some of their own—and that would be good! For most composers intend their audiences to think as well as feel.

With regard to the opera's musical structure, though the theatrical and technical aspects of its music are not truly divisible, in the synopses I have stressed the music's more obviously theatrical aspects: not the sequence of keys or tone rows, which I think few in an audience can follow, but the association of an instrument with a character or a theme, or for dramatic purposes the use of a particular musical form, such as the passacaglia in *Peter Grimes.* In short, nothing complicated, yet the sort of detail a casual operagoer might miss unless alerted to it.

With one short opera, *The Turn of the Screw,* in which the sounds of individual instruments are projected with unusual clarity, I have listed the instruments dominating each scene or interlude. The opera's sound is very sensual, and anyone taking the time to listen closely in the theatre, or at home, will have not only pleasure but the equivalent of a master class on instrumentation.

PART ONE

Introductory Essays

"Almighty God touched me with His little finger and said: 'Write for the theatre—mind, only for the theatre.' And I have obeyed the supreme command."

PUCCINI

In a letter to his librettist,
Giuseppe Adami (Spring, 1920)

I·

SOME ASPECTS OF
TWENTIETH CENTURY OPERA, 1900-75

Tracing the history of twentieth-century opera is like trying to follow all the streaks of light in a starburst. Something relatively whole, at least to the distant eye, begins to spark and send burning coals across the sky. Then suddenly it explodes into hundreds of smaller shooting stars. Some burn out quickly; others, slowly; while some survive to form a galaxy in place of the single brilliant originator. Diversity, with a different beauty, has replaced unity—and all a short essay can do is touch on several of the more noticeable features.

The explosion was World War I, after which life, thought, art, politics were all changed. Even before it, however, as the nineteenth century came to an end, there were signs that the relative unity in point of view from which opera had drawn strength throughout the century was breaking up. The vigor in the old forms was beginning to fail, and composers had new ideas to present and were seeking new forms in which to present them

What was breaking up was a European tradition of opera which in its subject matter and music divided roughly into four styles or ways of apprehending life. There was an Italian style, personified in Verdi: operas about real people in real situations with an emphasis on man and his potential for nobility in the face of suffering; a German style, dominated by Wagner: operas about mythical people involved in situations that were highly symbolic; a French style, a weaker version of the Italian and led by Massenet, which presented real people in real situations but aimed more at charm and pathos than passion and tragedy; and finally, a Slavic style, chiefly Russian and Czech, which had two important, distinct traditions: one nationalistic, presenting historical figures or events, the other fantastic, presenting elaborate fairy tales in which the symbolism was often satiric. Slavic opera, however, was rather isolated. Even *Boris Godunov* was not well known in the West until Diaghilev staged it in Paris with Chaliapin in 1908.

The divisions, of course, were not rigid. Wagner introduced historical figures into *Die Meistersinger* and created a profoundly human story that also had nationalistic overtones. Tchaikovsky, the most Western of the Russians, in *Eugene Onegin* sentimentalized Pushkin's story as Massenet might have done, yet composed to it with greater passion. Nevertheless, at the turn of the century in a rough way the designations Italian, German, French, and Slavic comprised the whole of opera, and each in itself offered a fairly clear definition of a style. German opera, for example, included Wagner, Humperdinck, and the young Richard Strauss and Pfitzner. In their subject matter and music the four were related. But fifty years later the term could not comfortably contain Strauss, Berg, Orff, and Weill. And Italian opera, which had seemed so strong with Puccini, Mascagni, Leoncavallo, Giordano, Cilea, Zandonai, and others, was all but dead.

One strain or substyle of the nineteenth century that continued strong through the first quarter of the twentieth was *verismo* opera. The composers chiefly were Italian, and they claimed to present life as it truly was. What they offered was the passion of Verdi with the nobility left out. Their characters, from whatever level of society, though often drawn from the lowest, were spurred only by the rawest of emotions: love, hate, fear, revenge. Confrontations among them were frequent and, as no character could control his temper, these constantly led to violence, the preferred solution to any problem. *Carmen* (1875) with its death in the marketplace was one of the first operas to point the direction. *Cavalleria Rusticana* (1890) established the genre; *I Pagliacci* (1892) confirmed it; and with *La Navarraise* (1894) Massenet imitated it. Then, after the century turned, there was *Tiefland* (1903) by D'Albert, a German; Janáček's *Jenůfa* (1904) was influenced by the style; and Puccini, whose *Tosca* (1900) owes much to it, in his one-act *Il Tabarro* (1918) composed one of its masterpieces.

The style's success, however, bred a reaction, particularly among the younger Italian composers known as *La Generazione dell' 80,* the Generation of the 1880s. These were chiefly Ildebrando Pizzetti (1880–1968), Gian Francesco Malipiero (1882–1973), and Alfredo Casella (1883–1947). They were led by the critic and musicologist Fausto Torrefranca (1883–1955), who in 1912 published an extraordinary attack on Puccini (1858–1924), stating that he represented "all the decadence of present Italian music, all its cynical commercialism, all its pious impotence . . . in a few decades hardly anything will be remembered of Puccini's works."

The composers were scarcely more restrained. They championed instrumental music, certainly a reasonable cause, but they condemned vocalism and asked for a ban on all those composers who had devoted themselves exclusively to opera. Plainly, much of the young men's anger was no more than resentment at the success of others and at the near monopoly that opera held in Italian musical life.

The charge of decadence so furiously launched was not, however, without some justification. In Verdi the characters, besides dying for love, die also for great causes: Italy, freedom, oppressed people. *Don Carlos* poses the issue of church versus state; *Simon Boccanegra* puts statesmanship in musical terms; and Aida betrays her lover for reasons not purely personal. It sometimes is said that Verdi is a battle cry and Puccini only a mating call—and Puccini is the best of the *verismo* composers. To hear a succession of these operas, in the profusion with which they held Italian stages from 1900 to 1940, is to become aware of how constantly mayhem and murder are tied to the most trivial causes. Jealousy, that most unworthy of all emotions, is everywhere, and compared to Otello most of those who feel it have accomplished so little and are so self-indulgent that there is no height from which to fall. Nevertheless, at their best *verismo* operas are valid musical works presented in a tradition that is particularly strong in theatrical values.

From a purely operatic point of view the Generation of the 1880s was a misfortune. Its members, instead of trying to reform opera, directed attention and energies away from it, and with Torrefranca they were influential in the conservatories. Later, when the three composers turned to opera, only Pizzetti had much success and in an unmelodic declamatory style that neither filled the theatres nor, being difficult to translate, traveled easily. After Puccini's death in 1924 Italian contemporary opera, for lack of good composers among the young and lingering hostility in academic and intellectual circles, declined to its present position of slight importance.

A somewhat similar misfortune befell opera in France. Here it was the success of Diaghilev's Ballets Russes seasons (1909–1929) that attracted away from opera the attention and energies of the best composers. Debussy's *Pelléas et Mélisande* was produced in 1902, and despite its great success he thereafter completed no more operas though contributing *Jeux* to Diaghilev's repertory and working on two other unfinished ballets. Ravel composed two one-act operas, *L'Heure espagnole* (1911) and *L'Enfant et les sortilèges* (1925), both perhaps with better music than his more famous ballets, *Daphnis et Chloé* (1912), *Ma Mère L'Oye* (1915), and *La Valse* (1920). Among the younger French composers working for Diaghilev were Auric, Satie, and Poulenc, who later showed a strong talent for opera; and among the Russians, Stravinsky and Prokofiev.

But if opera suffered in the first part of the century by losing the attention of some of the best composers, in the area of subject matter, through its ability to express the felt but unspoken, it soon was in a position to extend its range enormously. Like spoken drama, opera always had employed symbols—the crown for which Macbeth murdered Duncan or the more complicated system in Wagner's *Ring*, Wotan's missing eye, his spear, etc.—but opera could do more with symbols than spoken drama, for it was opera's peculiar quality that the orchestra could contradict a singer's expressed thoughts or indicate his subconscious fears and hopes. Opera, more than most art forms, therefore, was in a position to absorb easily the discoveries of the century's most startling new science, psychoanalysis.

Freud's theories, most of which he published in the century's first quarter, became common knowledge only slowly, but independently opera approached them through an increasing interest in symbolism. One strain of this style derived from Wagner, and an example of it is Strauss's *Die Frau ohne Schatten* (1919). The librettist, Hugo von Hofmannsthal, created a myth to extol the sanctity of marriage, the need for sexual satisfaction between partners, and the importance of children. Symbols are everywhere—the shadow representing the ability to conceive, the marriage bed that splits in two, and the voices of unborn children crying from the fire—and Strauss projects them through the orchestra, through his themes, and through the color and weight of the instruments used. The opera is of Wagnerian proportion—large orchestra and cast and three acts, each lasting more than an hour, with many changes of scene—and if only because of the cost of production most composers, including Strauss, did not press further in this direction.

Debussy, however, in *Pelléas et Mélisande* already had started symbolism on a different course, toward simplification, and it led further. In the opera, as in the play by Maeterlinck on which it is based, the story is stripped of the details that in a realistic drama would have been introduced to give the characters particularity. Debussy was reacting against both the Italian and German styles dominant at the turn of the century, disliking in *verismo* opera the excessive emotionalism of its big scenes and in Wagner the constant rhetoric of the orchestra. In *Pelléas* the story with its vague location and uncomplicated events is deliberately ambiguous. The characters seem almost to have no will of their own—so different from the characters of Verdi or of Wagner in *Die Meistersinger*—and to be merely pawns of forces that surround them in a half-perceived real world. The drama is less in the outward than the inward life.

Bartók in *Duke Bluebeard's Castle* (1918) carried the style still further. Here there is no action at all—only a married couple standing in a castle hall somewhere. The drama is entirely in their changes of mood and the modification of their relationship as the wife insists on opening the hall's seven doors. As she unlocks each and thrusts it open, a different colored light streams into the hall, and she discovers a new aspect of Bluebeard's personality. The music reflects each change of mood and, ultimately, the destruction of the relationship.

This kind of symbolist drama came into the theatre chiefly through Maeterlinck, and it quickly spread, taken up by playwrights, poets, and novelists as an antidote to the preceding generation's realism. The artists by intuition anticipated many of the conclusions of Freud and his colleagues, and much of what at the time was called symbolist drama, and some, too, of German expressionism, seems in hindsight to be primarily psychological studies. Berg's opera *Lulu* (1935) examines female sexuality and its effect on others, and is based on two plays by Frank Wedekind written in 1895 and 1903, well before Freud was known. Yet the plays read like a psychiatric case history, and the opera is most effective when played as such. Similarly, Prokofiev's *The Fiery Angel* (1955, but composed 1919–1927) is based on a symbolist novel published in 1907 and in its bare bones is a case history of a sexual hysteric. Even Puccini's *Turandot* (1926) owes something to the gradual merger of symbolism and psychoanalysis, and with Strauss's and Hofmannsthal's *Die Ägyptische Helena* (1928) that merger becomes complete and conscious. Here Hofmannsthal, to depict the effect of war fatigue and guilt on a marriage, combines the older tradition of Wagnerian myth, personified in Helen of Troy and her war-weary husband Menelaus, with the new techniques of psychoanalysis and therapy. In the opera Menelaus is cured of his war neuroses, including a desire to murder Helen for her guilt in causing the war, by acting out his inner feelings.

Even operas that do not deal primarily with sexual themes were touched by the new ways of apprehending a personality and adopted new methods of telling their stories. Both Verdi and Wagner, for example, in *Falstaff* (1893) and *Die Meistersinger* (1868), respectively, presented the problem of aging and the need for a man to accept it and to adjust his behavior. Both told their stories by creating a man in every way real and by putting him through a series of realistic events. Janáček, on the other hand, in *The Makropulos Affair* (1926) took over from Karel Čapek's drama (1923) a more intellectual approach. Elena Makropulos, with the aid of a secret drug, has lived almost three hundred years, and in the opera she questions the desirability of such long life and decides against it. The presentation is primarily conceptual.

Or consider how Benjamin Britten and William Plomer retold the parable of *The Prodigal Son* (1968). The boy is tempted by the Devil not from outside but from within his own personality. Says the Devil: "I am no stranger to you. You know me very well. I am your inner voice, your very self. . . ." People today have become so used to this kind of interiorizing what used to be exterior that they no longer notice it. But it has become one of the most distinctive qualities of twentieth-century art in almost all forms and has affected almost every artist's view of man and man's fate.

Even without the new science of psychoanalysis the impact of World War I would have caused many artists to search for a new concept of a hero and of tragedy. But the war was for most Europeans a tremendous shock, and the tragedy of an individual, as it had been understood formerly, now seemed, as Strauss wrote to his librettist, Hugo von Hoffmansthal, "rather idiotic and childish." What was one man's striving and failing against a background of millions slaughtered for so little purpose?

One response was to create a representative hero who might suffer a common tragedy. Alban Berg's Wozzeck is such a hero. In the nineteenth century's operatic world Wozzeck, at the bottom of the social order, without any accomplishment or cause to engage attention, would not have been a potentially tragic figure. At the turn of the century the story of his wife's infidelity, his murder of her in the public park, and his return there later to kill himself might have made a *verismo* opera. Berg constructed out of it something greater. Wozzeck, the lowly soldier, is the representative common man pushed this way and that by social forces over which he has no control and unsettled by subconscious fears and urges that he does not understand. At the opera's end, if the performance has been good, a large part of the audience will feel in some way responsible for Wozzeck's harried life and purposeless death. It is society's callousness that robs the common man's life of its joys and meaning.

That jab at the audience, or kick in its shins, though muted in *Wozzeck* is a distinctive quality of twentieth-century tragedy. Instead of the audience feeling purged by watching a great hero fail in some ambitious undertaking, it is made to feel engaged in the failure of some quite ordinary man. In the theatre the quality is most obvious in the political plays of Bertolt Brecht and his imitators; in opera it is plainest in the works on which Brecht collaborated with Kurt Weill, *The Threepenny Opera* (1928) and *The Rise and Fall of the City of Mahagonny* (1930). It is also part of the success of Britten's *Peter Grimes* (1945), in which the audience is equated more or less, depending on the production, with the townspeople who expel Grimes from their society and hound him to suicide. And there is a similar identification of the audience with society in Hans Werner Henze's *The Young Lord* (1965).

In contrast consider Ralph Vaughan Williams' *Riders to the Sea* (1937) based on John Millington Synge's play (1911). Here a woman living in a small fishing village on the west coast of Ireland loses not only her husband but her six sons to the sea. When the drowned body of the last son is laid before her, she finds a dignity and courage that will give her an unshakable peace: "No man at all can be living for ever, and we must be satisfied."

Neither Synge nor Vaughan Williams gave the story political or social overtones, but Brecht, in copying it closely in his *Señora Carrar's Rifles* (1937) and transferring it to the Spanish Civil War, ended it with the woman taking up a gun to fight the fascist enemy. Few operas that last more than a season have such a crude message, but in this century the kick in the audience's shins is often there.

Any trend if long continued, however, will breed a countertrend. In 1937 Vaughan Williams' opera in offering a personal religious response to death rather than a social or political program had seemed out of step with the times. But after World War II it was joined by others. Menotti's *Saint of Bleecker Street* (1954) opposed a sickly sister who wished to become a nun to a healthy brother who considered religion to be superstition. And the strong one, healthy in spirit, proved to be the sister. Poulenc's *Dialogues des Carmélites* (1957) showed a young woman, immobilized with fear during the French Revolution, achieving the power through religious grace to join her spiritual sisters at the guillotine. Britten's *Billy Budd* (1951) touched the same theme and through symbolism presented the conflict in the world between good and evil and the compromises society must make between them in order to survive.

Britten's interest in religion was profound, and it penetrates most of his operas. In an extraordinary number, considering the alleged irrelevance of religion in today's world, it and its postulates are the chief theme. Besides *Billy Budd*, there are *The Rape of Lucretia, Noye's Fludde, Curlew River, The Burning Fiery Furnace, The Prodigal Son,* and *Owen Wingrave*. Probably the one-act *Curlew River* is the most concentrated and intense of all his operas, and it concerns a madwoman's return to sanity—that is, her reconciliation with reality through the granting of God's grace revealed in a miracle.

This theme is very like that of the psychological dramas, such as Menelaus' return to sanity through a reconciliation with reality. In fact, of course, as the many jokes about the antipathy between priest and psychiatrist suggest, they are competitors. For many persons religion and psychoanalysis perform much the same function: they take past events that are proving troublesome in a person's life and by rearranging his attitudes toward them liberate him to a more effective life in the future. That, to be sure, is not the only purpose of religion, but it is one much to the fore in this century.

Both the religious and psychoanalytical operas, therefore, tend to have the same kind of protagonist—a person who is divided against himself. In the nineteenth century the hero battled forces outside himself; in the twentieth he battles those within. In Britten's *Albert Herring* (1947), a comedy, the timid young man gives in to his suppressed desires and emerges the stronger for it. In Britten's *Peter Grimes* (1945), a tragedy, Grimes fails to reconcile his opposing drives and creates a situation from which his only exit is suicide. The opera is one of the most universally successful to appear after World War II, and a reason surely is that Grimes is the quintessential protagonist of the period: within himself he is both hero and villain.

In operatic music, as opposed to subject matter, the century thus far has seen two revolutions. The first, foreshadowed by Wagner's extensive use of chromatics in *Tristan und Isolde* (1865), led to atonalism, twelve-tone techniques, and serial music. Its chief figures were Arnold Schoenberg (1874-1951), Anton Webern (1883-1945), and Alban Berg (1885-1935), the so-called Second Viennese School. Webern wrote no operas, but the other two composed some of their chief works in the form: Berg *Wozzeck* and *Lulu,* and Schoenberg *Moses and Aron.*

The second revolution, less clear cut and slower to develop, was fore-shadowed in the 1920s in the need of vocalists and certain instrumentalists in jazz bands to make themselves heard above the noise of the dance hall. They experimented with amplification, boosting their volume electrically. Techniques were continually improved, but real momentum came only with the rise of rock music in the mid-1950s. Suddenly in a few years entirely new sounds and ways of making them were developed and made familiar to the public by popular musicians. By the mid-1970s some opera composers were beginning to make use of these new instruments and sounds, and suddenly, in the summer of 1976, Philip Glass, in collaboration with the designer Robert Wilson, presented the world with *Einstein on the Beach,* a four-and-a-half hour, intermissionless, spectacle of light, shapes, dance, and music that seemed to create a wholly new kind of opera—discussed further in Chapter VI, dealing with the final quarter of the century.

The earlier revolution, however, is still probably the most examined, condemned, and cheered development in music in this century. Critical writing about it runs on, and on. Essentially, the music of the three Viennese composers and of those who have followed their style ceased to be a language of emotion and became a language of structure—at first architecture, the broad design, and then engineering, down to the smallest detail.

Perhaps the best way to grasp the essence of it in words, without struggling over musical notation, is through a letter Webern wrote to a freind on March 11, 1931. The parentheses and arrows are his, and the clue to reading his example is that you do not read evey line from left to right but alternately left-right, right-left, etc., reading "tenet," a palindrome, first one direction and then the other.

Dear, dear Frau Jone,

. . . I think I have laid a good foundation for something new (for orchestra). I have found a "row" (that's the 12 notes) that contains already in itself very extensive relationships (of the 12 notes amongst themselves). It is something similar to the old proverb: SATOR AREPO TENET OPERA ROTAS*

* A literal translation would be: Sator (farmer or sower) Arepo (proper name) tenet (holds or guides) opera (by his hand or work) rotas (the wheels or plough)

↓ → ↓
S A T O R
    ←
↓ A R E P O ↑   The sower controls the work
→
T E N E T
    ←
O P E R A   The work controls the sower
   ←
R O T A S
↑ ↑ ↑

To read horizontally;
So: Sator opera (retrograde of arepo)
   tenet, tenet
   opera sator (retrograde of rotas)
Then vertically from top to bottom; upwards; downwards, upwards (tenet twice over); downwards; upwards. Then vertically again: starting at the bottom right: upwards, downwards, etc. . . .

Serial music is the twelve white and black notes of an octave on the piano arranged in any order—the "row"—that suits the composer and then put through these upward, downward, backward, forward movements. In the ostinato of *Lulu,* for example, the four-minute interlude between Scenes 1 and 2 of Act II, Berg runs the material forward through a climax to a point of rest, and then note for note runs it backward. Furthermore, the row can be more than just differences in pitch: it can be the order in which instruments enter, the loudness with which they sound, rhythms, silences, and so on.

For opera there are several difficulties with the style. Even at its simplest the great majority of any audience cannot follow it. (If you cannot discern from what you hear that the row is in backward order, take heart: you are normal!) So for most persons the intellectual excitement of working out the puzzle does not arise and in its place are confusion, irritation, and boredom.

Also, the row, with its preestablished relationships, provides a very rigid tool and frame for telling a story, and in fact all composers using the style for opera have allowed the "row" to vary considerably. Even so the effort to fit a story and a row together must be exhausting, and it perhaps is significant that the two greatest operas in this style, Berg's *Lulu* and Schoenberg's *Moses und Aron,* were both left incomplete, though each man would seem to have had time to finish his work.

Lastly, there seems to be a difficulty arising out of man's nature. Certain relationships of pitch seem to be innate in all animals, including man. The distress peeps of little chickens, for example, are composed of descending phrases while rising phrases predominate in peeps of pleasure. The same general contours are present in man's sounds of distress and pleasure, and a style of music that too frequently ignores such a basic postulate of communication through sound seems unlikely to succeed for long. Serial opera, in fact, has had its day, failed to establish itself, and is receding into history, leaving behind many interesting ideas and techniques and two truncated monuments, *Lulu* and *Moses und Aron.*

With the retreat of serial music in the theatre and the failure of its claim to be the future's dominant style, multiplicity of styles continued to be a feature of twentieth-century opera. In the 1950s, for example, Luigi Dallapiccola (1904–1975) had a success with a one-act opera in serial style, *Il Prigioniero* (1950). Menotti with *The Consul* (1950) presented an important contemporary theme with all the theatrical effectiveness of *verismo* opera. Stravinsky in *The Rake's Progress* (1951) went back to an eighteenth-century style of set numbers, recitative, and harpsichord. Douglas Moore (1893–1969) succeeded with *The Ballad of Baby Doe* (1956) in a style that might be called "homespun American." Poulenc in *Dialogues des Carmélites* (1957) and *La Voix Humaine* (1958) developed a graceful style of lyric declamation that seemed suited to both operas, though the first required a large cast and chorus and the second was a forty-minute monologue for soprano. The catalog could be extended endlessly, for by 1950 the traditional styles of the previous century no longer bound composers. Each worked in his own way, and some worked in several styles. Stravinsky made the most famous switch of the period when after *The Rake's Progress* he adopted the serial style for *The Flood* (1962).

Benjamin Britten (1913–1976), however, the most successful operatic composer in the century's third quarter, had a consistent style that he developed through his sixteen operas and that in any one of them is immediately recognizable. Because he was the most successful he is the composer against whom others most often are measured, and his style may be taken as the most representative of the century's third quarter.

One nonmusical aspect of it is immediately apparent. His operas are based on excellent literary sources such as Shakespeare *(A Midsummer Night's Dream)*, Henry James *(The Turn of the Screw* and *Owen Wingrave)*, Thomas Mann *(Death in Venice)*, Herman Melville *(Billy Budd)*, Guy de Maupassant *(Albert Herring)*, and Lytton Strachey *(Gloriana)*. This emphasis on literary quality is a characteristic of twentieth-century opera generally. There seldom has been a time when contemporary literary figures took such an interest in opera. Just a partial list of some who worked in the form would include: W. H. Auden, Stephen Vincent Benét, Bertolt Brecht, Jean Cocteau, Colette, Hugo von Hofmannstal, E. M. Forster, Gertrude Stein, and Stefan Zweig.

Literary sources, of course, or even literary librettists cannot guarantee a good opera, but they do insure a libretto with some ideas worked into it. Britten's choice of stories was typical of his generation in that he was drawn again and again to stories with religious or psychological overtones. Even in Shakespare's *A Midsummer Night's Dream,* which might seem to have none, as set by Britten its dream quality and the therapy of dreams is greatly emphasized.

Britten's musical style, like that of most composers today, is weak in melody, though not always so. Some of his phrases, such as the Madwoman's cry in *Curlew River,* are instantly unforgettable, and so, too, are some of his arias, such as Billy Budd's "Billy in the darbies." But he could not, or would not, spin out melodies in the style of Mozart, Verdi, or Puccini. He did not organize his operas by melody but by structure in its broadest sense: dramatic, thematic, orchestral, and symbolic. For Britten, as for most composers today, the structure is too important to be halted or broken for lyrical effusions.

His success with structure is one of his greatest strengths. His operas are always very clearly plotted, and the audience can see why this scene follows that, why an aria or chorus is here and not there, and how all the parts build to the whole. Musically, too, his structure is clear and always closely tied to the opera's symbolism. In *Billy Budd* the fog that obscures vision and clear thinking lifts and descends to rising and falling phrases. Billy's stammer is a series of agonized gasps on the woodwinds over a muted trumpet trill. The Madwoman's insanity is flutter-tongued on the flute, and Peter Grimes's inability to merge in a group is shown by his breaking the round "Old Joe has gone fishing." In *A Midsummer Night's Dream* the theme of the wood in which the couples are lost binds Act I, the theme of sleep Act II, and both are so clearly projected in memorable sounds that audiences do not mistake them. This kind of structure is one feature of twentieth-century opera, and it is often very well done.

Then there is Britten's orchestration, which is superb. Even in his earliest operas he began to demonstrate a remarkable ability to translate his musical imagination into effects in the theatre. These are often achieved very simply, by the sudden crack of a whip, glissandi on the double bass, or the combination of trumpet and drum. His tendency which developed early in his career, was to use the orchestra as a group of solo instruments, not blending their sounds but making the most of their individual qualities. That is a very sensuous approach to music, and one of the delights of Britten's operas is the chance to savor sounds.

It is possible to see in this style, which requires only a relatively small orchestra, a response to the high cost of personnel. And there is some truth in that. But it is also part of a trend throughout the century that began in 1912 when Strauss, after the 100-men orchestras of *Salome, Elektra,* and *Der Rosenkavalier,* used only thirty-six for *Ariadne auf Naxos* (1912). Though for later operas he enlarged the orchestra again, the sound often is less blended. *Arabella* (1933) is a slimmer, more transparent score than *Rosenkavalier.* This tendency to trim the orchestra's size and to emphasize its solo qualities turns up in many composers throughout the century and probably represents a reaction against the late nineteenth-century large symphonic orchestra.

Another shift in the world of opera, almost a third revolution, looms increasingly large: The importance to contemporary opera of recordings. With the inventions of the long-play record, the cassette, and the compact disc, to say nothing of those that combine sound with pictures, opera has been released from its point of performance. It can be preserved, packaged, and transported to be played again and again; most importantly, at home.

At first everyone thought of a recording as a way to preserve a great moment of the past, but in the last fifty years it also has become a way to launch a contemporary opera into its future. In the nineteenth century opera travelled, often quickly, by new productions in other cities. Today, when production costs have risen so high, a new opera that seems successful may meet its largest audience through a recording. And in the last fifty years these have become outstanding, not only in musical quality but in the literature accompanying them. The descriptive essays are often the best critical writing available on the music, and the composers are beginning to novelize their librettos for home consumption. In Michael Tippet's *The Knot Garden* (1970), for example, where the stage direction in traditional form might have said only "Enter Mel," it now reads: "Under the influence of Dov's music the rose garden begins to form. By the last verse of the song it is all there: the enclosing walls, the fountain, the girl, the lover, the music. As the song ends a shadow enters the garden. It is Mel. He taps the lover on the shoulder."

With this kind of rubric on the scene, or even better a video cassette or laser disc that joins scene to sound, listening to a new opera at home begins to offer something like the experience in the opera house—though never matching the excitement of being present at the creation.

II·

LEOŠ JANÁČEK: A LIFE IN MUSIC

If individuality of sound, style, and subject matter as well
as the creation of a substantial body of work are the marks
of a great operatic composer, then Puccini and Richard Strauss are
among this century's greatest. Are there others to rank with them or
even close behind? Over the decades several candidates have been put
forward, but now, as the century ends, opinion seems sure of two—
Britten and Janáček. Like Puccini and Strauss, each has built an international audience, succeeding not with one or two operas but four or
five, and each appeals as much to musicologists, who want to analyze
scores, as to more theatrically minded operagoers, who want an interesting evening in the thrcatre.

Of the two Janáček is the less well known, at least in the western
hemisphere, though his operas preceded Britten's by half a century.
Czech, however, is a difficult operatic language to translate, the music
at first seemed strange, and popularity even in his country developed
slowly. Only in the years since World War II have his operas entered
the international repertory, led generally by *Jenůfa* and *Kát'a Kabanová*.
Interest in the others continues to grow, but he himself, because so little
about him has been published in English, remains for most persons a
shadowy figure.

He was born on July 3, 1854, in the village of Hukvaldy, in the district of Ostrava, then a part of the Austro-Hungarian Empire, today in
northern Czechoslovakia near the Polish border. The countryside is
semimountainous, and the hills then were covered by forests of lime
trees with the valleys cleared for agriculture. On a hill at Hukvaldy
were the ruins of a castle with a trout stream flowing through its park;
below was the small, neat village with its Catholic church dedicated to
St. Maximilian the Martyr. Janáček's father, Jiří, was the village schoolteacher, and Janáček was born in the school building, which also served
as the family's home, a solid house of stone and whitewashed plaster
with a steeply pitched roof. Close by was the summer house of the
district's archbishop.

Janáček was the tenth of fourteen children, nine of whom lived to maturity, and the family frequently was enlarged by the presence of Jiří's mother, Anna, whose calm, quiet personality often protected the children from their father's severity and short temper. Not far distant was the family of Jiří's younger brother Vincenc, who served as Janáček's godfather and was the schoolteacher of the village of Albrechtičky.

Life in Hukvaldy was simple, and so were its pleasures, most of them involving the open air, woods, and fields. In addition, however, there was music. Janáček's father started a reading and singing club with himself as choirmaster, and soon he, his choristers, and their few instrumentalists were trudging on invitation to neighboring parishes, often to celebrate High Mass. At the richer parish of Rychaltice, Janáček later recalled, "there were collapsible music stands and a gilded organ ornamented with acanthus leaves on both sides of the keyboard, and at the back, close to the window, were two enormous drums as big as flour-bins—tympani."*

Then in 1866, when Janáček was eleven, his father died, and his mother, left with a large family and little with which to support it, entered him in the Old Brno Monastery Foundation in Brno, the chief city of Hukvaldy's province, Moravia. The Foundation was a school of general education with a strong emphasis on music, and its director was Pavel Křížkovský, a family friend and former student of Janáček's father. It seems likely, therefore, that he arranged for some kind of scholarship. For Janáček, however, school in Brno, whatever its advantages, meant separation from his family. His mother accompanied him to Brno, and his last night with her before entering the school was sleepless and tearful. The next morning he watched her depart for Hukvaldy with despair.

At the Foundation, where Janáček stayed nine years, the students wore uniforms of pale blue with white trim, flat caps—Janáček wore his curly hair shoulder length—and high felt boots. In the town they were known as "Blue Boys" or "The Blues" and were a common sight, for they played or sang at balls, receptions, churches, theatres, and public concerts. Yet despite the joys of the music, which for Janáček were very real, he disliked the regimentation. Years later he wrote, "Neglected but guarded; in moments of loneliness we looked out of the

---

* Unless otherwise stated, the longer quotations are based on the translations by Geraldine Thomsen in *Leoš Janáček: Letters and Reminiscences,* ed. by Bohumír Stědroň, Prague: Artia, 1955.

barred windows. From the Prelate's garden, the birds flew for the crumbs which we threw to them. Small blue birds, blue as well, but freer than our kind."

Nevertheless the musical education was good. Křížkovský, who composed choral music in a folk song style, took an interest in Janáček, and a number of the students were sufficiently talented to keep him stimulated. While at the Foundation, apparently, Janáček first felt the urge to compose and wrote some simple songs. A friend remembered that when Janáček sang them "His eyes would shine— yes, really shine."

At age twenty he left the Foundation to study at the Prague School of Organists. He was so poor that for practice in his room he could afford only a keyboard drawn with chalk on his tabletop. But one day when he returned home, there stood a piano—and he ascribed the miracle to a priest who cared for music and seemed to have a sly smile on his face. At the end of the school year, the piano one day disappeared.

Thereafter he alternated more study at Leipzig and Vienna with teaching music at two schools in Brno, the Teachers Training Institute and the Old Brno Grammar School, and in 1882, his studies finished, he founded what today is called the Brno Conservatory but was then the Brno School of Organists. Unlike the Teachers Training Institute, where he taught relative beginners—a "torture"—the School of Organists was for professionals, and it opened in borrowed rooms with nine students and a faculty of three. Its chief purpose was to train organists and choirmasters, to place them in country churches and thereby to raise the level of music throughout the province. By 1919 when the school became the Brno Conservatory, still with Janáček as its leader, it had its own building, 186 pupils, and thirteen teachers. When he retired from the faculty in 1925, he had given forty-three years of his life to the institution, and it was one of the major accomplishments of his career.

By the time he founded the Brno School of Organists Janáček was twenty-eight and his personality formed. He had inherited his father's gift for teaching and love of music, and also his short temper. Indeed, often Janáček's actions seemed to spring from a personality that lacked some restraints innate for most persons. While a student in Prague, for example, he published a sharp criticism of a performance of a choral work led by one of his professors, and for a time it seemed as if he might have to leave the school. In Vienna, disliking the piano professor, he dropped the course. He also disliked the composition professor, and when one of his compositions, though approved by the professor, was rejected by a committee for entry in a competition, he abandoned the school. Always with Janáček, he was right, the other man wrong; he, being sensitive, should not be criticized, but the other man, presumably rhinoceros-skinned, was an appropriate object for the most sarcastic assaults. Almost anyone in a position of authority, simply because of it, was to be attacked.

Yet as a teacher—himself in the position of authority—he was for many of his students a unique and wonderful experience, even granting that their accounts, written after he became famous, may be exaggerated. Here is a man recalling the rehearsals of a boys' choir:

[Janáček] was known for his great kindness. Whoever saw his charming smile or the kind expression in his eyes never forgot them. He had, however, a fiery temper, was irritable and liable to fits of uncontrollable anger. If a chorister made a mistake, Janáček knew immediately which unfortunate creature had sung the wrong note, and pounced on him with baton or pencil, both of which were equally dangerous weapons in his hands. But we soon accustomed ourselves to such treatment and even became proud of it. "I say! He certainly went for me today!" Or, "Did you see how his baton bounced off my skull!"

A student at the School of Organists remembered:

He seemed to be everywhere and knew all that went on. His harmony lessons were far from pleasant for those who lacked talent. . . . Slow thinking irritated him, also prolonged, unadventurous compositions. He liked us to express ourselves in short, concise terms, his own method of self-expression. . . . His lessons never became dry lectures, given according to some well-tried pedagogical system. On the contrary, they gave us glimpses of a higher plane of thought which was, for some, hard to understand. It therefore often happened that, on discovering no one able to keep up with his momentary mood or flight of artistic thought, he would abruptly leave the class. . . . His lessons on musical form were utter enjoyment. When I compare them to my lessons with Max Reger, I realize that they were far more gripping and inspiring.

Such a fiery, undisciplined nature was not likely to have an easy time with love, and Janáček's marriage in 1881 with Zdeňka Schulz led for both to long periods of unhappiness. She was only fifteen at the time, twelve years younger than he and one of his pupils. The imbalance in their age and experience by itself might have caused difficulties in the marriage, but to it were added several aggravations. Her father, Emilian Schulz, as director of the Teachers Training Institute, was not only Janáček's employer but a man of position in Brno. Janáček, who counted himself a man of the people, apparently deeply resented the bourgeois status and attitudes in which Zdeňka was nurtured. And in the cultural and political struggle that was developing in the Austrian provinces of Bohemia and Moravia Schulz was pro-Austrian, favoring the continuation of the Austro-Hungarian Empire, whereas Janáček hoped for its dissolution and the founding of an independent Czechoslovakian state. In his immoderate manner he pressed his views of what he considered patriotism to a point that his father-in-law considered madness. Family life was not easy, and despite what seems to have been genuine love on both sides, the couple separated. Later they returned to life together, and a shared love for their children, a son and daughter, helped to cement, or at least to conceal, the deep divisions in their marriage.

Always Janáček composed, but perhaps because recognition came slowly and with it the stimulation of success, most of his famous works come from the final third, even the final decade of his life. Of his early works possibly the best known is the *Tema con variazioni* for piano (1880), popularly called the *Zdeňka Variations* because dedicated to her and composed while they were engaged. Though not so original as his later works, it still is attractive music, and Janáček considered it "my first completely correct work, my Opus 1." But his first success with an opera would not come until 1904 with the premiere of *Jenůfa* at Brno, and even then the success was only local. No other opera house took up the work, and it was not until its first production in Prague in 1916, when Janáček was sixty-two, that his countrymen realized that in him they had a successor to Smetana and Dvořák. Meanwhile he had his teaching at the School of Organists and another project dear to him that would greatly influence his music.

From his childhood in Hukvaldy Janáček had been interested in the folk songs he heard around him, and during his summer holiday there in 1888 he began to experiment with Moravian songs and dances. His interest quickly grew, and for the next fifteen years collecting, analyzing, and publishing the songs and dances became his chief preoccupation. He was just in time. Moravia then was a kind of bridge between a new urban, industrial way of life, already well planted in Bohemia, and the older feudal, rural culture that once had existed throughout Europe. In the west it had been extinguished by the effects of the French Revolution; to the east, in parts of southern Poland and Hungary, its last vestiges still lingered.

To find the songs Janáček travelled to the most rural parts of the province. He often would hire a driver and a farm cart and disappear for days. Once in two consecutive nights he heard a trio of peasants sing 600 verses of fifty-eight songs. "It seemed as though one song prepared the way for the next. If the atmosphere can be enchanted by the perfume of lime trees and wild thyme, these evenings surely were enchanted by the songs."

He discovered that the peasants, most of whom were illiterate, had a song for every occasion, and as the songs were reserved for the apt moment, their freshness was not staled by repetition. He estimated that the peasant oral culture had at its command to express its feelings about 3,000 songs.

The songs originated, Janáček concluded, in words. No peasant singer invented a tune and then cast about for a sentiment to fit it. The proof of this, he believed, lay in the special character of a song's rhythm, which "can be put in order only by the words." And because the words of the Moravian peasants were short and rather chunky, their sentences brief and disjointed, so, too, were their musical phrases. This style of short, pithy phrases sank deep into Janáček's subconscious, and his music began to reflect it. His vocal line, short and disjointed, is the extreme opposite of Bellini's long, flowing melody.

An important reason is the difference in the Czech and Italian language. Czech words have few vowels, and it is possible (though not often useful!) to make a sentence without any vowels at all: Strč prst skrg krk! (strrch prrst skrrz krrk)—Put your finger through your throat! Further, Czech words generally are accented on the first syllable and often much lengthened on the second: for example, Janáček. This causes phrases almost invariably to have a weak ending, whereas the interior, short prepositions and conjunctions still receive a strong accent. As a consequence Czech sounds craggy, full of small explosions, and with a frequent drooping final tone. In Italian, on the other hand, such accents and weak endings often can be elided (*amore-amor*); vowels not consonants prevail, and the accent within words falls far more variably. For all these reasons an Italian vocal line is easier than a Czech to translate without breaking the line's rhythm.

The difficulty of translation is further compounded by Janáček's orchestral style and points to a facet of his method of composition. Much of the accompaniment underlying the vocal line is made up of short phrases similar to or even identical with the singers' phrases. In the orchestra these are differentiated and contrasted by the color of the instrument for which they are scored, and in repetition they are constantly varied with trills, turns, arpeggios, and arabesques. But their rhythm generally remains the same. Any translation, therefore, that changes the rhythm of the vocal phrases literally tears the opera apart by its roots. For rhythm is for Janáček what melody is for Bellini—the organizing principle.

Besides his teaching and research, one other activity kept Janáček to some extent in the public eye: he continued to publish criticism of musical performances. In this he was not wise. The composer-critic plies a dangerous trade, for he constantly risks offending the very performer who might champion his music, and little that he writes is free of a suspicion of bias. Wise artists, though they have their opinions, do not publish them, and they suffer bad reviews in silence.

Janáček seemed not to recognize the problem. Once, in response to an unfavorable review, he wrote the editor of the magazine: "Why do you and Mr. Zázvorka wrong me so . . . ? I feel sure that you will agree that every work must be performed as the composer intended, and that it should be judged also from that point of view." A good rule, but one that he himself did not always observe.

He sometimes wrote savage reviews. In 1887 in the magazine *Hudební listy* he greeted the premiere at Brno of *The Bridegrooms,* a comic opera by a young composer, Karel Kovařovic:

Can you remember any tunes from this comic-opera, this so-called original novelty? Can you call it dramatic in any sense whatsoever? Story and music are "staged simultaneously," but in reality each is quite independent of the other. One of two things can be done—either write new music to the libretto, or write a new libretto to the music—this so-called music, filled with menacing obscurities, desperate screams and dagger stabs. It is true that one sometimes laughed, but this was at the absurdity of the story, nothing more. The Overture, with its instability of key sense and wavering harmony gave proof of the composer's genius—to induce deafness. [Trans. by Erik Chisholm]

The opera was not a success, but Kovařovic went on to compose two operas that are still in the Czech repertory, *The Dog-Heads* and *At the*

Old Bleaching House, and to become the outstanding Czech conductor, particularly of opera, in the period 1900 to 1920. And for all of that period he was the director of the National Theatre in Prague, the showcase to the world of Czech opera. For a little easy sarcasm, a little puffing of his own ego, Janáček offended the man whose sympathy in the coming years he would need most.

By 1900 he was investing all his hopes, skills, and theories as a composer in a new opera, *Jenufa,* a story of Moravian peasants in which the characters would wear Moravian costumes and sing music often similar in structure and style to Moravian folk songs. But the composition of it went slowly, harassed by his daughter's illness. His son had died at two years old in 1890, and now his twenty-year-old daughter Olga developed an ailment in her joints and slowly sickened. *"Jenufa,"* wrote Janáček later, "is tied with the black ribbon of the long illness, pains, and cries of my daugher Olga," and he dedicated the score to her.

He sent the opera to the director of the National Theatre in Prague, Karel Kovařovic, and it was rejected. Janáček lovers are quick to see prejudice at work, but as yet there is no evidence that Kovařovic's opinion was not sincerely held. His report was that the opera was badly structured. Janáček, now in his fiftieth year and still without much success as a composer, was profoundly shaken. His wife Zdeňka later remembered:

We were in the room where Olga was dying. My husband sat at his desk and suddenly clutched his head in his hands and tears started streaming down his face. In this sharp fit of depression, he began to blame himself for knowing nothing. This was more than I could stand. I had always believed in him as an artist, and I believed especially in the beauty and greatness of *Jenufa.* I took his head in my arms and, crying myself, tried to comfort him. My great faith in his work enabled me to find the right words of comfort. They must have been convincing because he gradually calmed himself. After that, I kept watch over him so as to avoid the recurrence of such a shock.

Olga died on February 26, 1903, and the grieving parents fled from Brno to Hukvaldy. After their return, one day in October a clerk from the Brno Opera House called to pick up the score of *Jenufa.* The management had decided to produce it. "When the clerk took it," Janáček wrote a friend, "he certainly carried a great weight on his shoulders; it seemed to me as though he carried many sad years of my life. . . . At last I see times on the horizon for which I have waited my whole life."

The first full rehearsal nearly ended in disaster. The trumpet player was scolded by the conductor so severely that he went out and, in Janáček's phrase, "got himself into a critical state of drunkenness." Then he returned and "cursed at everyone as though they had been dogs." Nevertheless the first performance, on January 21, 1904, went well, and overnight, locally at least, Janáček was recognized to be an exceptional composer. His theories of musical speech, which might or might not be correct, dwindled in importance before the impact of what he had fashioned on the stage. In the theater, as a critic later recalled, "Everyone felt that a great rainbow of faith in eternal love arched over the whole work. Everything small and futile, earthly and materialistic, fell into insignificance."

During the next twelve years the Brno opera produced *Jenůfa* in 1906–07, 1910–11, and 1916–17, and many persons counted it a scandal that the opera was not produced more often. But it stretched to the limit the resources of the company, which then was small, and the performances often were not good. Still, a sympathetic listener could get a sense of the work. The true scandal was that the National Theatre in Prague did not produce it.

Kovařovic was invited again and again to Brno for performances and on the ninth invitation he came—and still did not like the work. But by now others from Prague had heard it, including one of Kovařovic's librettists, Karel Šípek, and a talented writer and singer, Maria Calma-Veselý. Both were among Kovařovic's close friends and in a position to question his judgment. Meanwhile Janáček, chiefly on the opera's success and a cash award from the Czech Academy for his work on the Moravian folk song, resigned from the uncongenial job at the Teachers Training Institute in order to devote more time to composing.

His most successful works of this decade, 1905 to 15, were large-scale choral works for men's voices and the piano pieces *On an Overgrown Path* and *In the Mist*. His one effort at an opera, *Osud (Fate)*, foundered on its libretto and was not staged until the Brno Festival in 1958, thirty years after his death. Such a complete failure suggests that his touch with opera was very uncertain and the fact perhaps should be considered in judging what was about to happen to *Jenůfa*.

In the last months of 1915 Kovařovic decided to produce the opera the following spring. Unquestionably his friends had influenced him to change his mind, and probably of equal importance was a growing sense within the Czechoslovakian provinces of the Austro-Hungarian Empire that following the war might come independence. It was a time for Czechs to pull together, the moment to produce an opera closely tied to national feelings and customs. But he demanded changes in the score, and these have produced a storm among scholars—are they improvements or desecrations? As yet there is insufficient evidence available on which to form an opinion. Further, on each of the opera's revivals at Brno Janáček made alterations, so that there is confusion about which or what is the definitive original version. In any event Janáček agreed to all of Kovařovic's requests, which in Maria Calma-Veselý's opinion concerned "the production more than music." Apparently some cuts were made in Laca's part, the final duet was lengthened, the orchestration was smoothed in places, and, in general, the stagecraft of the work tightened. In this version the opera now is heard.

The Prague premiere on May 26, 1916, produced and conducted by Kovařovic, was a great success, and German and Austrian companies quickly began to negotiate for the work. At sixty-two Janáček finally had arrived at the threshold of an international career and recognition within his own country as one of its outstanding composers.

What followed is one of the most extraordinary late flowerings in the history of music. In the twelve years before his death, on August 12, 1928, he composed an astonishing string of masterworks in all forms: *The Diary of One Who Vanished,* song cycle with piano; *Glagolic Mass,* a cantata; *Capriccio,* for piano and small wind orchestra; *Concertino,* for piano and small orchestra; *Sinfonietta,* for full orchestra; two string quartets; and five operas, *The Excursions of Mr. Brouček, Kát'a Kabanová, The Cunning Little Vixen, The Makropulos Affair,* and *From the House of the Dead.* Though all the operas are not masterworks, all are good, and probably most critics would argue that at least one or two are masterworks though unable to agree on which. The five with *Jenůfa* form the canon of Janáček's operas.

For such an artistic harvest to be possible the seeds, of course, had to be sown earlier, and apparently what caused them now to sprout was a mixture of love, patriotism, and success. To take these in reverse order: there was the stimulation of success. Not only was there a constant request for new works—they were all but guaranteed numerous performances. It takes a very robust personality to survive lack of recognition continued into late life. The artistic confidence and with it the urge to create dries up. Within a month after the Prague premiere of *Jenůfa* Janáček excitedly wrote a friend: "I compose and compose, as though something were urging me on. I no longer saw any worth in my work, and scarcely believed what I said. I had become convinced that no one ever would notice anything of mine. I was quite down—my pupils had begun to advise me how to compose, and how to orchestrate. I laughed at it all, nothing else remained to me." But now with success, he worked furiously.

Politically, too, his time had come. At the end of World War I the three provinces of Bohemia, Moravia, and Slovakia, together with Czech Silesia, formed the new state of Czechoslovakia, and within its borders there was a tremendous resurgence of interest in Czech history, custom, and language. Just as Verdi rode a wave of nationalistic feeling to artistic heights, so now did Janáček. One of Mr. Brouček's excursions is to fifteenth-century Prague, where the spiritual successors of Jan Hus defeated a Habsburg emperor, and the *Glagolic Mass* is based on old Slavonic liturgy. But more important than the nationalistic subjects was the fact that Janáček's style was by now so thoroughly based on the Moravian folk style. The very grain of his music was almost pure Czech at a time when foreign influences, whether for better or worse, were out of favor.

Lastly, and the most difficult to evaluate, there was love. After their daughter Olga died in 1903 the bonds of affection between Janáček and his wife Zdeňka gradually loosened. They lived together until his death but emotionally, particularly in these last twelve years, they drifted apart. She continued to take an interest in his music, however, and ran the house in a way that encouraged him to compose, and he, perhaps more than he realized, relied on her. Nevertheless he evidently felt a need to focus his affections on someone, someone other than Zdeňka.

Late in 1903, while at the spa of Luhačovice, he found himself attracted to a beautiful woman, Kamila Urválek, with whom he had many pleasant conversations. On parting, though she was married, he started a correspondence, addressing her as "Dear Madame." Apparently nothing more serious came of this friendship than the exchange of several letters except that he made an incident of her life the basis of the ill-conceived libretto for his opera *Osud*.

In 1915, however, while vacationing at Hukvaldy he was drawn to another married woman, Mrs. Kamila Stössel, and two years later he met her again at the Luhačovice spa. She was thirty-eight years younger then he and lived with her husband and son in the Bohemian town of Písek. Again Janáček started a correspondence, moving from "Dear Madame" to "Dear Kamila" and ultimately to what read like love letters: "You were the one I thought of when writing this work *(The Diary of One Who Vanished)*. You were the gypsy, Zefka. Zefka, with the child in her arms and he following her. They all know you in Písek in the quarter down by the mill-bank, where you clothed and fed the gypsy children. The little ones fell into the trap of your heart." Besides often visiting Písek, where he saw the family, Janáček also met them from time to time in Hukvaldy and at the spa.

It is hard to know what to make of the relationship, which seems to have existed mostly in his mind. Though many of his letters to her had been published before 1990, not until then were hers to him, and in them she reveals herself as a somewhat simple woman, indifferent to his fame and music, and only gradually coming to appreciate that he was an extraordinary man. Yet for him their intimacy, enriched by his longing and fantasy, was real, and he talked of himself and his works to her more openly than to anyone else, even entitling his second String Quartet *Intimate Letters*. In his will he referred to her as his honorary wife.

Possibly more revealing, however, is a letter he wrote to her in 1921 about his life with Zdeňka:

I warned her before she took the step. She brought her father to Brno without sufficient consideration. Her father, who has a son that is certainly more close to him. I also had a mother. Poor, destitute—and she was not able to live with me. It is not a question of her father, it is a question of me and my living arrangements, my activities, my work, of all my such very modest happiness, my domestic peace and quiet which I have built up with such difficulty. It is not a question of physical comfort, it is my spiritual balance that is at stake.

There bluntly speaks the ruthless, self-centered artist. Before all else comes work, particularly for an old man with not much time. Janáček never was about to run off with Mrs. Stössel or act in any way to break his routine. It may well be that there was never any physical intimacy between them and that he was more in love with the idea of love than with Kamila. But whatever the truth of the odd relationship, it was satisfactory to him and a great stimulus.

In fact, the speed with which he completed works in this last decade began to be a stumbling block to the appreciation of them. They came too fast for the public or even musicians to digest. The opera houses no sooner would get one new work mounted than another would be on hand. But by the end of his life Janáček must have enjoyed the knowledge that he would leave behind him a sizable body of work not only as a teacher and a scholar but chiefly as a composer.

He died not far from where he had been born. He had gone for a holiday to Hukvaldy. The Stössel family also was there, and one day he went for a picnic with Kamila and her son. When time came to return to town, the boy had wandered off, and Janáček went in search of him. Walking fast, he became heated and caught a chill. It soon developed into pneumonia, and he was rushed to the hospital in Ostrava. He died there, aged seventy-four, on August 12, 1928.

III·

PUCCINI PSYCHOANALYZED:
A TWENTIETH-CENTURY APPROACH
TO MUSICAL BIOGRAPHY

It is one of the niceties of history that Freud, whose theories contributed so greatly to the distinctive stamp of twentieth-century culture, should have published his most important book, *The Interpretation of Dreams,* on November 4, 1899—so close to the start of the century. Nicer still that the publisher chose, for reasons of his own, to put on the title page the date 1900.

Still, the book's ideas were slow to spread. Only six hundred copies were printed, and it took eight years to sell them. But by 1929 it had reached its eighth edition and been translated into English, Russian, Spanish, French and Swedish. By then Freud had published many other works including his *Three Essays on the Theory of Sexuality* (1905), perhaps his second most influential book. So the gathering momentum by 1930 was great. The ideas, at least among the younger generation of the day, were widespread and generally accepted.

Not that they were entirely new. Before the Oedipus Complex there was Oedipus; Wordsworth with a line of poetry had made common the concept "the child is father of the man"; and everyone was aware that strong fathers often produced weak sons and that among siblings there was rivalry. Much of what Freud discussed was embedded in the maxims of folklore and in the intuitions of artists.

He himself, differing perhaps from his disciples, never thought otherwise. Of his startling theory of infantile sexuality he once observed that it was common knowledge among nursemaids. And he rested the claim for the importance of psychoanalysis less on its originality than on its application. "Many thinkers and students of mankind have said similar things, but our science has worked them out in detail and employed them to unravel many psychological riddles."

In the world of music such riddles coalesce chiefly around the creative artists—the composers—and after World War II, when the younger generation of the 1930s had reached maturity, biographies began to appear that attempted through psychoanalytical theories and methods to unravel the mysteries of such unusual and complicated men as Beethoven, Wagner, Puccini and even the apparently well-adjusted Brahms. Beethoven in particular has attracted such treatment for there seems so much in his behavior that must spring from just those deep and concealed tensions that psychoanalysis claims to reach and explain: his dirtiness of person, his frequent dishonesty in business, his difficult relations with servants and friends, his attachments to married women, and above all—two incidents crucial in his life—his almost deranged loveletters to an unidentified "Immortal Beloved" in which he finally rejects the woman, and his treatment of his nephew Karl that led to Karl's attempted suicide. Yet the biographers, while complimentary to each other, disagree on their theories and explanations and the fact suggests that the "science," at least when practiced on the dead, is very uncertain, though not without insights into the complexities of human behavior.

Among this century's operatic composers, the one most susceptible to this kind of probing seems to be Puccini. His life was far more orderly than Beethoven's, but it is not without incident, and as every opera-lover has observed, there is a marked pattern in his choice of subjects, his dramatic imagery—the kind of scenes he puts on the stage—and the kind of music that he composes. Leaving aside his two little-known early operas, consider the heroines in seven of his ten mature works: Manon, Mimi, Tosca, Butterfly, Magda (*La Rondine*), Giorgetta (*Il Tabarro*) and Angelica. All suffer for love, are made to suffer for it in scenes that range from pathetic to sadistic. All but Magda and Giorgetta die for it, and of the other five, three are suicides.

Even the three operas outside the pattern upset it very little. In *La Fanciulla del West* the one who suffers for love is the tenor, Johnson, and though he does not die for it, he is saved only at the last minute and after considerable mental torture. The comedy *Gianni Schicchi* falls outside the pattern, but in *Turandot* there is Liù, the slave girl, whose love for Calaf is unrequited and who, during physical torture endured to save him, kills herself.

All of Puccini's biographers, or at least those worthy of their subject, have had to face this pattern if only because Puccini himself did. He saw that he was stimulated by young women suffering for love and was at his best musically when, as he wrote to a friend, "I act as executioner to these poor frail creatures. The Neronian instinct manifests and fulfills itself."

Most biographers also have noticed a second pattern: that the typical Puccini heroine is in some way tarnished or a social outcast. Manon, Mimi, Musetta, Butterfly and Magda are kept women—indeed, Puccini's peasant neighbors at Torre del Lago referred to him as *il maestro cuccumeggiante,* "the composer of harlots' music." Tosca, socially suspect as an artist, revels in sensuality; Giorgetta is unfaithful to her husband, and the nun, Angelica, though an aristocrat, has given herself to an unsuitable man. Only Liù is pure, and she is a slave. For the most part the women are obscure, socially inferior and sensual.

In presenting Puccini's life three of his biographers, writing out of different times and backgrounds, approach these patterns quite differently. Vincent Seligman, the eldest, who published his *Puccini Among Friends* in 1938, formed his ideas and attitudes before World War I and before Freud's theories were well known. He returns often to Puccini's need to find heroines who were "lovable" and with "human" traits and, quoting the peasant neighbors, notes without comment that the heroines need not be "spotless." But chiefly, he builds his picture of Puccini from the composer's outward and visible actions, primarily through his relations with his family, friends and publisher. Only occasionally does he venture a surmise about the inner subconscious man, and generally it is so well grounded that it appears as a fact rather than a theory.

Writing a generation later George Marek in his *Puccini* (1951) is more blunt: The basis of Puccini's life and art is "erotic." Essentially, however, Marek's technique is like Seligman's, though he is far more aware of Freud: "Neither am I especially interested . . . in attempting to explain Puccini's behavior toward women in psychoanalytic terms. (It can't be done well: dead men tell no psychoanalytical tales.)"

Mosco Carner has no such hesitancy. He starts his *Puccini* (1958; 2nd ed., 1974) with the assertion "no modern biographer can afford to ignore the results of 'depth psychology' " (defined by Freud as "the science of unconscious mental processes"), and he subjects Puccini's life to a search for clues to the secret of his psyche. The emphasis falls steadily on the inner rather than the outer man, and where facts in Puccini's life are rare, Carner turns to the operas, for "where psychology leaves off, aesthetics must begin."

From the pattern of heroines who suffer for love, Carner deduces that for Puccini love was a guilt that must be expiated by suffering. The stronger the love the heavier the guilt, and those characters with the strongest love—Tosca, Butterfly, Angelica and Liù—can atone for it only by self-destruction. Where Seligman sees Puccini's repeated success with these heroines as an example of his compassion for others, Carner sees it as essentially unrelated to others, springing from a deep quirk in Puccini's psyche that in true Freudian fashion he traces back to Puccini's childhood.

About that childhood, not much is known. Puccini's family lived in Lucca, and he was born there, December 22, 1858. When he was five, his fifty-one-year-old father died, leaving a thirty-three-year-old widow, Albina, with seven children. The fifth and seventh were boys, the elder being Puccini. Times were hard, but the family had an apartment, interested relatives, and Albina was energetic and competent. Puccini was a lazy boy, did poorly at school, especially in mathematics, and passed much time with other boys playing on the walls of Lucca or in the fields catching birds. His education was aimed at qualifying him for his father's post as church organist, and his first music teacher after his father was an uncle. All his subsequent music teachers were men. By sixteen he was playing for church services, giving music lessons and contributing to the family's income. While eighteen, he walked one night to Pisa, heard a performance of *Aida* and knew that he would compose for the theatre, not the church. At twenty-one he graduated from Lucca's music school and enrolled in the conservatory at Milan, meeting the cost partly by a state scholarship secured for him by his mother and partly by a loan from a great uncle, also arranged by his mother. Once in Milan, though continuing fond of his family, he saw less of it.

When he was twenty-six, after the success of his first opera, *Le Villi* (1884), his mother died. Later that same year he eloped with Elvira Gemignani, the wife of a former schoolmate. She was two years younger than Puccini, tall, handsome, and of her two children by Gemignani, she took with her the elder, her daughter Fosca. Until Gemignani died, in 1903, Elvira's marriage to him in Catholic eyes was not dissolved, and she lived with Puccini "in sin." When he went into Lucca, she often stayed outside, and their child Tonio, born in 1886, was illegitimate until she and Puccini were able to marry, in January, 1904. The situation cannot have been easy, and it doubtless contributed to her jealousy, which at times flared into morbid aberrations. But she had some cause, for after their first six or eight years of living to-gether Puccini began to have affairs, generally with insignificant women, at least one of whom tried to gouge money out of him. By 1903 these affairs had grown sufficiently notorious and time consuming to draw a scolding letter from his publisher.

Seligman, the earliest of the three biographers, hurries over these early years, partly perhaps because not much more about them is known but also because he does not see any close connection between them and Puccini's art and adult behavior. Marek, writing later, is aware of Freudian theories about the importance of childhood but not inclined to follow them: "Speaking in psychoanalytic terms, we might say that his erotic instinct—which was purely masculine—was condi-tioned by a childhood lived among women in a fatherless home. But I am rather chary of so diagrammatic an explanation."

Carner is not, and makes it the basis of an interesting hypothesis. He proposes: Puccini, a boy of five when his father died, grew up "in a wholly feminine environment" dominated by a strong mother. "He was surrounded by five sisters, who, psychologically speaking, repre-sented so many duplications of the mother-image. He was his mother's favorite child . . . and his sorrow at her death was altogether excep-tional. Such an atmosphere was likely to establish a particularly strong fixation on the mother."

In such a situation, he continued, if Puccini had been "passive of temperament and weak in his natural instincts," he might have turned from the female sex. But he was "a boy full of vigour and resilience, given to asserting his personality and charged with a high degree of maleness. Yet, it would appear that a strong bondage to the Mother remained."

Carner finds symptoms of the bondage in the tensions disrupting Puccini's marriage, though admitting that Elvira contributed a large share to their unhappiness. Puccini's affairs were an "attempt to escape from his fixation" by bedding with women less strong than either his mother or his wife. He chose submissive, socially inferior partners who "represented the obverse of the powerful Mother" because they al-lowed him "a feeling of dominance and mastery."

The price, however, was a feeling of guilt, "since in his unconscious such a relationship would seem to bear the stigma of incest." So, he chose a woman inferior to his mother in order to be able to denigrate her in his fantasies. "It now becomes clear why Puccini was never able to form a close and absorbing attachment to women, why no women could ever inspire him in his creative life, and why he never allowed his wife to share in it."

Before going further with what Carner calls "Puccini's essential psychology," consider for a moment the supposed fixation on his mother. There are some points here that may slip by an opera-lover who is not fresh from reading Freud and several other biographies of Puccini. Indeed, the problem is endemic to this kind of biography where the writer has a jargon with which to keep the reader off balance and discusses as crucial those events so private in the subject's life that no reader can question them.

First, therefore, the fatherless house. Freud, whose theories and techniques Carner follows, taught that the essential foundations of character are laid down by the age of three and that later events can modify but not alter the traits then established. Puccini, however, had reached five before his father died. Then the "wholly feminine environment." But Puccini had a younger brother of whom he was fond, schoolmates with whom he roamed the city and countryside, uncles who concerned themselves with his life, and an unbroken succession of male teachers in his chosen field. Next, the five sisters who "represented so many duplications of the mother image." But why? Such is hardly the common feeling about sisters, yet Carner offers no evidence to show how Puccini's feelings over the years differed from the usual. And finally, "He was his mother's favorite child. . . . His sorrow at her death was altogether exceptional." Again Carner offers no evidence to support either assertion, not a letter, not an episode, not a quotation from an observer. The thesis of mother fixation, therefore, seems inadequately supported by evidence and in the circumstances, even unlikely.

On a more general point, again a problem endemic to psychoanalytical biographies, consider the terms in which Carner expresses his ideas. If Puccini had been "passive of temperament . . . [but he was] a boy full of vigour and resilience, given to asserting his personality." Later, suggesting that Puccini in *Gianni Schicchi* was beginning to work free of his mother fixation, Carner talks of him returning to the Mother "as an adult man, as master in his own home." And he ascribes to Puccini "a feminine sensibility," stating that unlike Verdi he could not create characters of "authoritative masculinity."

This equation of maleness with freedom, aggression and authority—the master in his home—and conversely femaleness with subjection, meekness and obedience—the *Hausfrau*—permeates Freud's thinking and is typical of the cultural and social ideas in Vienna at the turn of the century. Many persons today, following the Kinsey Reports and the movement for women's liberation, find this equation of gender with psychological traits misleading and even, perhaps, downright wrong. An authoritative woman is not untrue to her sex, nor is a passive boy. Freud too readily accepted as eternal verities the stereotypes of his time and place. Symptomatic of that was his dislike of G. B. Shaw, who was propagating a far more radical view of womanhood.

Carner, born in Vienna in 1904 and educated there, accepts those stereotypes without question. He remarks, for example, that "no woman could ever inspire Puccini in his creative life" and that "he never allowed his wife to share in it." In contrast, he offers the relationship of Byron and Teresa Guiccioli and of Wagner and Mathilde Wesendock, implying that these represent the best relationship between an artist and a woman. It is a highly romantic, Germanic point of view and fails to accommodate many first-rank artists. Verdi, for one, loved both his first and second wife passionately, but neither can be said in the Wesendock sense to have inspired any of his operas or had much part in his creative life. There simply are more sources of creativity than Carner's terms allow, and he often seems to measure Puccini against standards that are culturally inappropriate. That is a failing to which psychoanalytical biographies in particular seem prone, because of their concentration on the inner man. Both Seligman and Marek, focusing more on Puccini in relation to other people, his exterior behavior, give a better sense of the society in which he lived, and of what it considered natural in a man.

Returning now to Puccini's "essential psychology" and focusing on his relations with his wife Elvira. For the first six or eight years that they lived together they were happy. Puccini's letters constantly refer to "the beautiful intimacy" of that time, and Elvira's first recorded twinge of jealousy does not occur until May, 1891. He was working on *Manon Lescaut,* had gone to Lucca without her, and then to Milan to discuss the opera with his publisher, Giulio Ricordi. Apparently, a relative alarmed Elvira with gossip, and Puccini by letter tried to calm her: "You are my only and true, holy love."

But her fears only increased. As the years passed, he was away more and at some point began to have affairs. He seldom took her with him on these business trips. They were not yet married, and she had no part to play in the discussions with his publisher, librettists or theatrical producers. Thus, she was excluded from his creative life and, though proud of his success and of her position as his mistress and, later, wife, she revenged herself by expressing contempt for his art. This wounded him: "You always sneer when the word 'art' is pronounced. This has always offended me and offends me still."

Elvira, a passionate woman, was by all accounts difficult: willful, assertive, haughty, narrow-minded. With success and maturity, Puccini became a man of the world; Elvira remained provincial. She was a faithful wife, a good mother, and a loyal family member. In a letter Puccini laments the number of her relatives in the house, for "their continuous presence in our midst has expelled our intimacy." But he acknowledged that he partly had created the problem by placing her in the country at Torre del Lago. She did not like country living and wanted people around her, whereas he, whose favorite sport was shooting waterfowl, loved the isolation. By 1904, when they were able to marry, they seem mismatched, but neither had ever considered life apart, and none of his affairs, however upsetting to her, had caused them to separate.

The most important, which began in London in October, 1905, was with Sybil Seligman, married and with a nine-year-old son Vincent who later would write Puccini's biography. The affair was untypical in every way. Sybil Seligman was Puccini's social equal, or perhaps even superior, highly intelligent and artistic. She and her husband David, both of whom spoke Italian, kept an open house for Italian artists in London and were close friends of Puccini's friends, the Tostis, Paolo the song-writer and his Belgian wife, Berthe. When the affair's passion cooled, it developed into a close friendship that lasted until Puccini's death. It is not clear how much everyone knew or guessed, but the Seligman family visited the Puccinis in Italy, met them on holiday in Nice, and Sybil corresponded with Elvira as well as with Puccini. Though Carner states as part of his thesis of a mother fixation that Puccini "was never able to form a close and absorbing attachment to women," he in fact seems to have succeeded twice, with Elvira and Sybil.

Then in 1908 began the affair that was not an affair and yet became the most traumatic episode in Puccini's marriage. Elvira, incited by a relative, accused Puccini of "immoral conduct" with their housemaid,

Doria Manfredi, whose family lived in Torre del Lago. Both Puccini and Doria, whom Elvira dismissed, denied the charge, but Elvira was unable to stop there. She repeatedly went through the village telling all and sundry that Doria was a slut and, when she met her, hurling threats and abuse in her face. Despite the passage of time and the remonstrances of many, Elvira continued her campaign of slander until finally in its fourth month Doria killed herself. The village was angry at Puccini and outraged at Elvira, who, unrepentant, self-righteous, departed for their apartment in Milan. Puccini retreated temporarily to Rome and then returned to Torre del Lago.

Meanwhile, the town authorities ordered an autopsy, and it revealed that Doria had died a virgin. The Manfredi family promptly sued Elvira for public defamation, refusing Puccini's offer to settle out of court. The case went to trial at Pisa, and Elvira, who on her lawyers' advice had stayed in Milan, lost. The lawyers appealed, but before the decision could be reviewed, Puccini and the Manfredi family came to an agreement, and the charges were dropped.

For six months the "Affaire Doria" was the newspaper sensation of Italy, and the gutter press reported it in lurid detail. For Puccini, a shy man, it was a time of agony, as it was also for the children and presumably for Elvira who still managed, however, to maintain that she was the one wronged. For several weeks after the autopsy Puccini considered separating from her, but soon he was writing to Sybil Seligman that "Elvira too deserves pity," implying that she had been misled by her relatives. But his first effort at reunion foundered on her self-righteousness, and not until after the court's decision could Elvira face reality and adjust to it. After six months apart they resumed life together, but a long time passed before he began again to write about her with the affectionate warmth of the early years.

All three biographers see the protracted scandal, which stopped Puccini's work on *La Fanciulla del West* for a year, as a reason for that opera's fitful inspiration. Marek feels that he never fully recovered from its effects and that none of the later operas match *Bohème, Tosca* and *Butterfly.* Seligman, on the other hand, feels that in *Il Tabarro* (1918), *Gianni Schicchi* (1918) and *Turandot* (1926), Puccini fully recovered his powers. Carner, agreeing, ranks *Turandot* as Puccini's greatest work, not only for its superb orchestration but because it fuses best the four elements of his style: the lyric-sentimental (Liù), the heroic-grandiose (Calaf and Turandot), the comic-grotesque (the masks), and the exotic. All the biographers hear in Puccini's music for Liù, the slave girl who kills herself, an echo of the tragedy of Doria Manfredi.

As might be expected, from the three biographers' accounts of the Doria affair a rather different picture of Puccini emerges. For Seligman and Marek, with their emphasis on Puccini's outward behavior, he seems quite admirable in his efforts to settle the court suit, regardless of cost; to protect Elvira in whatever way he could; to prevent his son, who was very upset, from acting rashly; and to keep the family together. Plainly, he cared for these people; in fact, loved them; and Marek, growing passionate himself, rhapsodizes that Puccini in his life loved truly, deeply only one woman, Elvira.

Carner has all the facts in his chapter, but because of the order and emphasis given them they are muted. What emerges is less a picture of Puccini in relation to others than a further step in his interior, psychic maturity. Not only does Carner hear echoes of the tragedy in Puccini's music for Liù but also in the characters of the Aunt in *Suor Angelica* and in the Princess in *Turandot*. To these, he suggests, Elvira contributed traits, for both re-enact precisely the role she played against Doria Manfredi, "the role of the persecutor."

Still more interesting he associates Elvira in her role as persecutor with Puccini's alleged mother fixation, and to see how he does that it is necessary to return to the pattern of Puccini's earlier operas, *Manon Lescaut, Bohème, Tosca* and *Butterfly*. In these, love is guilt and the tarnished heroine must atone for it by death. And the heroines, like most women of Puccini's affairs, were weaker and less dominating than his mother, so that he could denigrate them in his fantasies and punish them on stage with torture and death.

For Carner, in these operas "the real antagonist of Puccini's frail heroines is the cruel Mother." She is cruel because Puccini with his alleged mother fixation cannot love another woman without incurring the stigma of incest, and the Mother avenges normal moral precepts by requiring the other women to die. "In the majority of his operas she exercises her baneful influence from behind the scenes, as it were, but in *Suor Angelica* and *Turandot* she is presented with her 'rival' in what are the most dramatic solo scenes in these two operas."

Conceivably *Bohème,* if staged in the style of German expressionistic theatre, as a sort of Italian *Lulu,* might be made to suggest this idea. But it is hardly conceivable that the public would accept such an interpretation, and the public would be right. For despite Carner's theorizing, all the evidence indicates that Puccini and his librettists intended just the sort of lyric-sentimental drama that commonly is presented.

But with *Suor Angelica* and even more with *Turandot,* the theory begins to seem more reasonable, if only because the operas could be presented in this guise with less violence done to them. In *Suor Angelica,* the "Mother-cum-Wife image," as Carner calls it, is projected in the cold, haughty Aunt who tortures Angelica mentally about the death of her illegitimate child. In *Turandot,* it is the Princess who will have no man for a husband and setting her suitors three riddles, which they fail to solve, executes them. She personifies for Carner Freud's theory of the love-hate impulse in which, in Freud's words, "I should like to enjoy your love" may also mean "I should like to murder you." The opera's underlying theme is to present love as a liberating force: how, under the influence of true love, the hateful, murderous Princess is transformed into a warm, loving woman.

There is evidence, chiefly in Puccini's letters to his librettists, that following *Butterfly* he consciously sought to strengthen his operas with underlying themes. A constant criticism of his operas was that though passionate, they were merely sentimental, lacking any profundity. Toscanini once harshly remarked: "Puccini was very clever, but only clever. Look at Cio-Cio-San. She thinks he (Pinkerton) is returning at last. Listen to the music. Sugary. Look at Verdi in *Traviata.* Listen to the music's agitation, its passion, its truthfulness." With this kind of criticism in mind Puccini in *La Fanciulla del West* took tentative but conscious steps to extend his artistic range, not only musically but dramatically.

For Carner *La Fanciulla* is "the first opera in which love is no longer represented as a disruptive force." Puccini's pattern of love as guilt has begun to change. In the opera, the tarnished heroine is replaced by the tarnished hero, the bandit Johnson, who is redeemed morally by Minnie's love and also saved from lynching by her last-minute intervention. Together they ride off into the sunset and to a better life. For Carner, the final scene "finds no responsive echo in Puccini's music and could not find it if we recall what has been said on his psychological make-up."

Seligman, too, finds the final scene disappointing, but for a different reason. Puccini's musical talents were particularly suited for *un*happy endings: "Those pathetic little glimpses, fluttering to and fro in the music, of a former happiness now gone beyond recall, those evocations of a passionate love now turned to ashes, which lend to Mimi's death-scene an almost intolerable poignancy." For Seligman, the limitation on Puccini's art was not psychological but artistic.

Carner consistently carries forward through the later operas his thesis of Puccini's increasing psychic maturity and finds it most directly displayed in the shaping of the libretto for *Turandot*. Here at last, in an almost perfect fusion of story, music and theme, Puccini would show love triumphant with a profound statement about its power for good in human life.

Only, as all the operatic world knows, Puccini died before completing the opera's final duet and scene, roughly fifteen minutes of music. In the duet Calaf's love for the Princess, symbolized by his kiss and trust in giving her his name, power over his life, is intended to transform her into a warm, loving woman. And in the closing scene she is to exhibit that transformation by proclaiming before the assembled court that his name is "Amor" (Love), thus saving him from execution and publicly acknowledging that she loves him.

On Puccini's death, November 29, 1924, he left behind sketches for the duet and scene that on Toscanini's suggestion were completed by Franco Alfano. But why did Puccini fail to complete the opera? By the end of March, 1924, he had finished it to that point, and not until early October was his sore throat diagnosed as cancer of the larynx. In the six months, April through September, there would seem to have been time.

One answer is the tardiness of his librettists. Although constantly requested to provide the necessary verses, they dawdled, and Puccini did not receive the text until the first of September. In the opinion of the scholar William Ashbrook: "Although his throat bothered him a great deal and he passed through periods when his will to work evaporated, there was ample time between March and September 1924 for him to have written the final scene." Seligman, on the other hand, stresses "that fatal lethargy" with which the cancer seemed to infect him. And for Carner, of course, the cause was not the tardiness of the librettists or the cancer but a psychological block. Was there not, he asks rhetorically, some "inner difficulty Puccini experienced in identifying himself with the spiritual kernel of this scene?" And at the end of his book, he concludes: "It was Puccini's tragedy that, for all his wonderful gifts, his flashes of true genius, something in the deepest layer of his psyche prevented him from soaring to the empyrean, as he attempted in his last opera."

In the face of such differences of opinion over what seems a simple question of the calendar, how is a reader to arrive at a balanced judgment of Puccini? Or of Beethoven? Or of any composer who is the subject of a psychoanalytical biography? Two thoughts, started by this foray into Puccini's life and psyche, may be applicable to the general question.

Unquestionably, psychoanalysis, even when practiced on the dead, can be a useful tool to uncover the reasons and motives that underlie human behavior and, in the case of creative artists, the origins of their works. Yet, there is an obvious danger to such psychoanalytic theorizing. The data, if the term is not too dignified, must not be taken as more than supplementary information to what is gleaned by the more traditional methods of studying a person's outward behavior.

Unfortunately today, when psychoanalysis is very much in fashion, there is a tendency to take its findings not as supplementary but alternative to the outward behavior. There is the constant suggestion that the inner man is more real than the outer man. That is nonsense. However a man may appear, he will reveal himself in his deeds, and what they are is always a significant part of what he is.

To probe a composer's psyche, his works and the rather meager information about his childhood for unconscious causes of behavior and then to define his personality almost entirely in terms of those casues., ignoring the more obvious reasons to be deduced from his overt behavior, probably distorts the personality more than to ignore the subconscious altogether.

Yet, no writer today can altogether ignore the subconscious. Even in 1951, Marek's efforts to do so have about them an air of desperation.

In 1936, on Freud's eightieth birthday, a goup of writers and artists presented him with an Address, apparently written by Thomas Mann, that was signed by Mann, Romain Rolland, Jules Romains, H. G. Wells, Virginia Woolf, Stefan Zweig and 191 others. After congratulating him on his work, the Address states, ". . . his gains for knowledge cannot be permanently denied or obscured . . . We . . . cannot imagine our mental world without Freud's bold life-work."

There is no going back. In this century, for readers and writers alike, the resonance of Wordsworth's line has been permanently changed: "The child is the father of the man. . . ."

IV·

STRAVINSKY AND THE NATURES OF BALLET AND OPERA

As a boy in St. Petersburg Stravinsky spent much of his time in the Maryinsky Theatre where his father was a leading bass in the Imperial Opera Company. Later as a composer the chief thrust of his work, not surprisingly, was for the musical theatre. In ballet for fifty years he was supreme: prolific, varied, and almost always successful. In opera he was less preeminent. Though he succeeded twice—with *Oedipus Rex* and *The Rake's Progress*—he more often failed.

The contrast is still more curious. In ballet the more revolutionary he was, generally the greater his success: *Petrushka, Apollo,* and *Agon* are better scores than *Pulcinella, Le Baiser de la Fée,* and *The Card Game.* In opera the reverse was true: his most successful works, including his attractive first opera, *Le Rossignol,* were his most conservative; whereas some of his attempted revolutions in the form—*Renard, Persephone,* and *The Flood*—were among his greatest failures.

The reasons for this lie partly in himself, partly in the differing natures of ballet and opera, and partly in the spirit of the times. There is the uniqueness of his genius—the particular kind of music he composed; there is the fact, which he always seemed reluctant to grasp, that opera and ballet cannot do all things equally well; and finally, as an example of the spirit of the times, if modern architecture is a guide, his audience wanted clean, functional lines with perpendiculars stabbing the air and horizontals, unadorned as a knife's edge, turning always in aggressive right angles. These characteristics—cold, hard and impersonal—can be displayed in ballet but are almost irrelevant in opera. No singer yet has been able to fashion a career out of a cold, impersonal voice.

Stravinsky himself is not a reliable guide to the essentials of these causes. Like Wagner, whose music and theories he detested, he talked too much, too irresponsibly, and too often merely to advance his works, regardless of merit, fact, or theory. In 1939, for example, in defending his opera *Mavra* during a series of lectures at Harvard (later published as *Poetics of Music*), he described Verdi's *Falstaff* as a capitulation to Wagnerism and "the deterioration of a genius." Then in 1958, aware perhaps that he was on record with a ludicrously foolish musical analysis, he announced in *Conversations with Igor Stravinsky* that he was "struck by the force, especially in *Falstaff*, with which Verdi resisted Wagnerism."

A man's taste for any particular opera may change, but whether or not Verdi composed *Falstaff* on the operatic theories practiced by Wagner is a fact capable of being ascertained. That Stravinsky at age fifty-seven, lecturing at a great university, should have misrepresented that fact in support of one of his works is disturbing, and a self-executing penalty arises. Though all his statements are not insincere or self-serving, a suspicion attaches to all. For example, in a newspaper interview in 1913 he asserted, "opera is in a backwater"; and asking, "What operas have been written since *Parsifal?*" gave as an answer, "Only two that count—*Elektra* and Debussy's *Pelléas*." Then in 1962 he revealed that actually at the time, "I thought *Pelléas* a great bore." Why, then, the original statement? Perhaps because in 1913 Debussy was alive and powerful in Paris?

Besides the suspicion, in many instances there is a complication. During the last twenty years of his life Stravinsky had as a close friend and secretary a fellow musician, Robert Craft, with whom he published six books of memoirs and musical comment. Craft, however, has strong musical ideas of his own, and the extent of his influence on Stravinsky's opinions is hard to gauge. Who wanted to change Stravinsky's recorded analysis of *Falstaff*—Craft, who raised the question, or Stravinsky, who replied? Fortunately, though Stravinsky's prose is suspect, his music is unambiguous, and it should have the first—and last—word.

Taken altogether its most obvious characteristic is its brevity: with a single exception all his works are unusually short for their forms. His *Fireworks*, which in 1909 started his international career by drawing Diaghilev's attention to him, is "a fantasy for a large orchestra," but it lasts only four minutes. His ballets, despite the example of Glazunov's and Tchaikovsky's "full-length" works such as *Raymonda* and *Swan Lake*, last never more than forty-five and often less than thirty minutes. In old age his inclination to be brief became even more pronounced, and he published a number of works of less than two minutes each. (For some people one of these, *Elegy for J.F.K.* (1964), raised a question: Can length ever be an absolute measure of worth? The piece lasts ninety seconds. At that length, regardless of its beauties, can it possibly be adequate to the event it attempts to commemorate?)

The exception to Stravinsky's rule of brevity is *The Rake's Progress*, the leviathan among his works. At 150 minutes it is almost three times as long as anything else he composed. Significantly his next longest work, at fifty-two minutes, is also an opera, *Oedipus Rex*. His two most successful operas, therefore, are also his two longest works. By contrast three of his operatic failures, *Mavra, Renard,* and *The Flood,* are all very short, twenty-five minutes or less.

Brevity, no doubt, is a virtue, but it can also be a structural defect, and experience indicates that the latter is more likely to be the case in opera than in ballet. An audience's eye can absorb information and sensation faster than its ear, and a dancer with his body can project acts or emotions faster than a singer with his voice. (On the coin's same side, a dancer tires faster than a singer.) A dancer with just a twitch of a shoulder or a foot turned in rather than out can signal an audience that he has begun to make fun of his material. In opera the same effect, even as achieved by Mozart in *Così fan tutte,* takes longer to project. Ballet, therefore, can tell a simple story—boy meets girl, they flirt, they go off together—faster than opera. Puccini, in the first act of *La Bohème,* gives seventeen minutes to this, but many a choreographer has told it, without any sense of hurry, in half the time.

Stravinsky's eight operas are so unrelated in style there is little loss in taking them out of chronological order, and on this point of brevity *Mavra,* his fourth, and *The Flood,* his eighth and last, are the most interesting. *Mavra,* which had its premiere in Paris in 1922, is an *opera buffa* based on a story by Pushkin. A girl introduces her boyfriend, a Hussar, into her house by disguising him as a cook and persuading her mother to hire him. But the mother discovers "the cook" shaving, screams "thief," and faints, and the Hussar, abandoning the girl, leaps out the window. Curtain.

Stravinsky set out to compose this bit of froth in the "Russo-Italian" style of opera of the previous century, in the style of Glinka and Dargomizhsky. It was an academic idea and ignored developments in *opera buffa* which only three years earlier Puccini had worked into a masterpiece with *Gianni Schicchi.* Stravinsky, nevertheless, went his own way and constructed *Mavra* with an overture and thirteen set numbers (arias, duets, etc.) connected by declamation over an orchestra. Other composers have allowed themselves fifty or sixty minutes for such an undertaking; Stravinsky allowed himself only twenty-five and had a resounding flop. He seems to have been surprised; certainly he was hurt, for he could not forget it.

The opera is paced too fast. Despite some attractive moments the music much of the time seems relentless and the voices incessant. Though *Gianni Schicchi* need not be the model for every *opera buffa,* Stravinsky might have learnt much from it. Puccini's story also is about a man introduced into a house in disguise, and when a neighbor enters, Puccini has the man sing in disguised voice. This natural operatic point Stravinsky missed, though his story, too, has a neighbor who calls. He might also have noticed that although *Gianni Schicchi* is twice as long as *Mavra,* Puccini wastes no time on an overture, frequently interrupts the complicated action with moments of repose, and ends slowly so the audience has a chance to collect its wits. In *Mavra* the ending is extraordinarily abrupt; it is less a climax than a sudden, unexpected vanishment. Stravinsky, however, did not simply misjudge the final curtain. The opera throughout is hurried.

In slightly different fashion his inclination to be brief misled him with his last opera, *The Flood* (1962). This was commissioned for television, and the musical world awaited the premiere with a double excitement, for the opera would be Stravinsky's first in a serial style of composing. The television production was a disaster. The music was not allowed to speak for itself. The performance was preceded by a lecture on the significance of Flood Myths, by a long dissertation on Stravinsky's collaboration with Balanchine, who had choreographed two of the opera's scenes, and by a number of Breck Shampoo musical commercials. After all of this came the opera, only twenty-four minutes long, in which Stravinsky attempted to tell the story not only of Noah and the Flood but also of chaos, the creation of the world, the fall of Lucifer, the tempting of Eve, and the expulsion from the Garden.

He counted on the television pictures to allow him to move so fast through so much. In his *Dialogues and a Diary* (1963), written together with Craft, he stated:

Because the succession of visualisations can be instantaneous, the composer may dispense with the afflatus of overtures, connecting episodes, curtain music. I have used only one or two notes to punctuate each stage in The Creation, for example [a narrator recounts it in reduced and simplified King

James language], and so far, I have not been able to imagine the work on the operatic stage because the musical speed is so uniquely cinematographic.

On the basis of the inadequate television performance his theory, perhaps, should have the Scottish verdict of "not proven." Concert performances at Santa Fe, New York, and London, and a staged version by the Hamburg Opera, however, tended to confirm his fear, at least for others, that the speed of some scenes was indeed too great for either the concert or operatic stage. Besides the mere "one or two notes" in the Creation, chaos is only seven bars, the tempting of Eve six, and the incidents pass too quickly to project much significance. As a result the first half of the opera, until it reaches the building of the Ark, seems padded and at the same time, paradoxically, musically sparse. It was a noble experiment, perhaps, but both Britten's *Noye's Fludde* and Boito's Prologue to *Mefistofele* are more successful partly because both attempt less at greater length.

Besides brevity, another of Stravinsky's characteristics which fits more comfortably into ballet than opera was his preference for a suite rather than a symphonic form of composition. In a suite, a succession of short pieces only loosely linked by theme, rhythm, or orchestration, each piece has its own structure and climax, and often the contrast between the succeeding pieces is as important as any of their similarities. The symphonic style, toward which operatic style in the nineteenth century had steadily grown closer, is more tightly organized. Themes are developed, harmonic relationships emphasized, and the climaxes fewer, more carefully prepared and, therefore, apt to be more pronounced.

Stravinsky generally used rhythyms as the contrasting link to bind the sections of his suites. He seemed to avoid stressing themes, perhaps because once a composer begins to relate one theme to another he has taken a long step toward the symphonic style of composing. In a typical Stravinsky suite, theme or melody will play the least important part, and each successive piece will have its own rhythm and often, as he was such an extraordinary orchestrator, its own harmonic texture. *The Rite of Spring,* for example, is a suite of thirteen pieces, and an audience leaves a performance of it not so much whistling its tunes, though some phrases are haunting, as registering the impact of the successive harmonies and rhythms.

Besides a suite's tradition of offering a series of dances, the form in still other respects is more suitable for ballet than opera. Ballet can tell.

a simple story faster than opera, but it cannot tell it with so much detail or depth. In ballet "the girl" is seldom more than that, be she princess, peasant, or sacrificial victim. Aurora in *Sleeping Beauty*, Giselle, or Elue in *The Rite of Spring* do not ring with the individual resonance of Isolde, Desdemona, or Carmen. In ballet the characters are primarily representative—a reason why ballets run to puppets, swans, and class distinctions: dance of the peasants, of the nobles, or of the bridesmaids. Or they are quite unimportant individually as in the Balanchine–Stravinsky ballets of recent years in which one set of girls rushes off as another comes on, faces and personalities irrelevant.

From his first ballets to his last Stravinsky has preceded the world in this direction of dehumanization, always a step ahead of the spirit of the times. In *Firebird,* Prince Ivan is a simple, unheroic man who survives the evil in the world only with supernatural aid. In *Petrushka,* though the mood is kept ambiguous, the chief individual is the toy of the masses and killed by a bully. In *The Rite of Spring,* the chief individual is brought to sacrifice herself, without protest from anyone, for the supposed good of the community. Even in the concert hall there is no escape or dissent from the score's rhythms. But at least in these early ballets the characters, though cardboard, still have names and costumes. By the time of *Agon,* 1957, the characters are nameless and the dancers dressed only in leotards. The dancers, further, are treated as though they were replaceable parts coming off an assembly line, being moved about in groups of three or four as needed and being substituted one for another not at the end of an act or a scene but sometimes even in the middle of a measure.

For this kind of ballet the suite style of composition is excellent. The successive pieces can be short, varied, and unencumbered with the necessities of building characters or of working slowly to a climax. When the dancers tire or the composer or choreographer runs out of ideas, the music can stop. Even *The Rite of Spring* does not so much climax as simply stop, exhausted.

None of this succeeds as well in opera, however, for opera is the world of the passionate individual. It had its origin in the Renaissance and thereafter flourished whenever individualism was in the ascendant. The characters best suited to the operatic world, as W. H. Auden in *Secondary Worlds* has noted, must be "not only passionate but willfully so, persons who insist upon their fate, however tragically dreadful or comically absurd." Stravinsky's Oedipus or Donizetti's

Don Pasquale are the types, and even Berg's Wozzeck, after starting as the most passive character in opera, in the end takes action, killing first his wife and then himself.

A suite, unless its pieces are in some way closely integrated, is ill-suited to build the musical portrait of an individual. Its contrasts are seldom useful in creating a consistent character, and its many small climaxes tend to diffuse the music's effect rather than to concentrate it in three or four big scenes.

Stravinsky's second opera, *L'Histoire du Soldat,* suffers in this way. It has many problems, such as the fact that no character in it sings—the story is advanced by the characters and a narrator talking—yet it is an opera in that the drama is intended to be conveyed through and heightened by the music. Among the opera's eleven independent pieces, of which not one lasts more than four minutes, are a march for the Soldier, a tango, waltz, and ragtime for the Princess, and a song and triumphal march for the Devil, when he succeeds in winning the Soldier's soul. None of these, however, go very far in establishing a character. Prokofiev in his *Peter and the Wolf,* also a musical drama advanced by a narrator, organized his music more carefully. Aside from whether or not his themes for his characters are better, he did more with them, carrying them forward and developing them as the drama proceeds—the wolf gobbles the duck—and building the piece steadily to its single climax in which Peter captures the Wolf. In *L'Histoire du Soldat,* the pieces are not always well chosen for the characters—ragtime, for example, has nothing to do with this particular Princess except that Stravinsky happened to be interested in both at the same time. Also, by keeping the pieces rigidly independent—he wanted the dances to be easily excerpted—he has kept them insufficiently cumulative. In performance, when the work succeeds it is because of the theatrical skill of the talking performers, not because of the music.

Perhaps the most famous of all Stravinsky's characteristics, however, is his emphasis on asymmetric rhythms. Where most composers before him tended to keep rhythms regular—4/4 was a march, or 3/4 a waltz—he mixed them so that the accented beats came irregularly. In *L'Histoire du Soldat,* for example, the Devil's triumphal march begins 4/4, 5/8, 5/4, 3/4, 3/4, 2/4, and continues in this patternless fashion.

For both ballet and opera this was an innovation, and one which quickly led to others. Traditionally in ballet the chorus moved symmetrically. The swans in *Swan Lake* are always balanced, and the corps de ballet is judged by its ability to make a perfect circle or to line up straight. With *Petrushka,* however, Stravinsky and his choreographers began to take this symmetry apart. In the crowd scenes Fokine unbalanced and fragmentized the corps de ballet, requiring different members to do different steps, often at the same time. The effect in 1913 was quite new.

In later ballets the asymmetry was pushed further, to the solo dancers, and because too much asymmetry was merely confusion, the corps de ballet was either reduced or excluded altogether. In a typical Balanchine–Stravinsky ballet of recent years a few couples will fill the stage, arms and legs going in every direction at once. In a pas de deux each dancer may reverse his partner's position: one bent at the elbow arm up, the other bent at the elbow arm down; or straight lines may oppose right angles, each joint allowing a choice. But constant asymmetry is exhausting to watch, and Balanchine intersperses it with moments of symmetrical repose in which the dancers move together. Though this kind of tension and release had always been a part of ballet, the new, asymmetrical rhythms greatly stimulated the amount of asymmetrical motion.

In opera, on the other hand, the rhythmic variety was less useful. A vocal line, because of the words, has a rhythm of its own. If the rhythm of the music varies from that too much, the words become gibberish. At the very least there is confusion, and in the audience, ultimately, irritation. In his ballet *Les Noces,* sometimes called a dance cantata, Stravinsky resolved this problem by having the words unintelligible. The singers and the small percussive orchestra generally are put at the back of the stage, and the ballet is danced between them and the audience. In performance the audience cannot distinguish the words and does not care. Despite Stravinsky's description of the work as "a suite of typical wedding episodes told through quotations of typical talk," not the voice but dance carries the message. The singers are instruments, merely providing a vocal timbre to the orchestral sound. The effect on their words of the complicated rhythms is unimportant.

It becomes crucial, though, in Stravinsky's third opera, *Renard,* composed in the same years as *Les Noces.* In *Renard,* "a burlesque story about the fox, the cock, the cat, and the goat," it is not clear which of dance or voice is to carry the message. The singers here are reduced from a chorus with solo singers to four soloists, and an audience at the start begins to identify particular voices with the animals. It is a mistake, for Stravinsky switches the voices among the animals. In *Les Noces,* where the story essentially was ritual, this had not mattered; in *Renard,* where the story is drama, it is confusing. "Save me," cries the cock. His friends come in and, seeing the fox in a compromising situation, begin to chuckle, "Ha, ha, ha, my good fellow Renard." The audience, its eyes on the dancers, struggles also to grasp the words, and most of the time it cannot because of the complicated rhythms which cut the words into syllables.

In his two most successful operas, *Oedipus Rex* and *The Rake's Progress,* Stravinsky resolved the problem the other way, by writing many fewer asymmetrical rhythms. This was a conservative solution, and though it is a joy to have the operas, it is also possible to regret those other, unrealized operas that somehow might have made use of one of his greatest gifts.

Even in these two operas, however, he did not altogether resolve his problems of composing for the voice. To most ears he probably seems less successful in *The Rake's Progress* than in *Oedipus Rex* if only because, the language being English rather than Latin, the rough places are more noticeable. For example, he sets the title "cardinal" so that it must be sung in four syllables, "cah-har-dee-nal" and he sets a chorus to a rhythm which, cutting across the natural rhythm of the words, chops their line into pieces: "Many (stop) a Duchess (stop) divested of gems, Has crossed the (stop) dread Styx (stop) by way (stop) of the Thames." It's enough to sprain a singer's jaw.

In *Oedipus Rex* he goes further. In the final chorus in successive bars the very same words are accented differently: "in VES.ti.BU.lo, IN ves.TI.bu.LO." Verdi in all of *Falstaff* is said to have only a single mis-accentuation: when Falstaff in an aria describes his slender waist as a young page to the Duke of Norfolk, he pronounces the place name as would an Italian, "nor.FOLK." By comparison Stravinsky is either sloppy, which would be out of character, or interested in something else.

He had theories about composing for the voice, but he had difficulty in stating them clearly. In a passage on vocal composition in his lectures at Harvard he ended with the extraordinary statement: "From the moment song assumes as its calling the expression of the meaning of discourse, it leaves the realms of music and has nothing more in common with it." Farewell Schubert!

The ideas which had led up to this he expressed better in his *An Autobiography* (1936) when writing about the Latin text of *Oedipus Rex:*

What a joy it is to compose music to a language of convention, almost of ritual, the very nature of which imposes a lofty dignity! One no longer feels dominated by the phrase, the literal meaning of the words. Cast in an immutable mold which adequately expresses their value, they do not require further commentary. The text thus becomes purely phonetic material for the composer. He can dissect it at will and concentrate all his attention on its primary constituent element—that is to say, on the syllable. Was not this method of treating the text that of the old masters of austere style? This, too, has for centuries been the Church's attitude towards music, and has prevented it from falling into sentimentalism, and consequently into individualism.

There is a quarrel in every sentence, almost in every phrase, but skipping over all of them to the final sentence: If he means what he seems to mean, then opera is an alien medium for him, not only because it must be about individuals and their personal deeds but also because it puts a large premium on individuality in the music. Fortunately, in *Oedipus Rex* Stravinsky did not practice what he seemed to preach.

His ideas on this subject had boiled to an emotional froth in conjunction with the premiere of his sixth opera, *Persephone,* when he had issued a manifesto on the subject. It was the result of what may have been the unhappiest collaboration of his career, with Gide, the author of the text. At the early rehearsals when Gide had begun to realize how Stravinsky intended to set some of the lines, he had protested, been harshly rebuffed, and had withdrawn to Sicily. When it became evident that he would not attend the premiere, Stravinsky prepared his manifesto and had it published the night before the opening and again a week later. The heart of it read:

In music, which is tempo and pitch controlled, as opposed to the confused sound which is in nature, there is always the syllable. Between the syllable and the general sense . . . there is the word, which channels the scattered thought to create the discursive sense. But the word, rather than an aid, is a hindrance to the musician . . . for music is not thought. One writes *crescendo,* one writes *diminuendo:* but the music that is true music does not swell or contract according to the heat of the action.

Then, perhaps feeling that he had not made himself clear, he closed with one of his most famous statements.

I am on a perfectly sure road. There is nothing to discuss or to criticise. One does not criticise anyone or anything that is functioning. A nose is not manufactured—a nose just *is*. Thus, too, my art.

The manifesto was noisy, and it advertised the show; but it was neither clear nor, in its treatment of Gide, creditable. Gide, for his part, continued to grieve over his text in silence. Years later, in *Memories and Commentaries* (1960), Stravinsky probably came closer to the simple truth when he stated (and Craft recorded):

[Gide] had expected the *Persephone* text to be sung with exactly the same stresses as he would use to recite it. He believed my musical purpose should be to imitate or underline the verbal pattern; I would simply have to find pitches for the syllables, since he considered he had already composed the rhythm.

Though that is exactly how Verdi approached Boito's great librettos—and neither man's greatness was thereby diminished—Stravinsky never would consider it. His indignation at the very thought is large and plain—like the nose on his face. Yet he was quite prepared to work in true collaboration with a choreographer. He composed ballets with both Fokine and Balanchine of stopwatch precision, adding and subtracting music as needed. Only in opera did he become implacable. There, it seems, in normal collaboration he would begin to feel dominated.

Again the reasons, though now more speculatively, seem to lie in himself and in the time and place in which he grew up. He was a lonely, hostile child, consumed apparently with a desire to show himself better than others. He did not like his parents, or his elder brothers or almost anyone who had a position in life ahead of his own. Though he was grateful to his teacher, Rimsky-Korsakov, he did not greatly admire the man's music. Rather, he made a musical hero of Glinka, a St. Petersburg artist long dead, and of Tchaikovsky, a Moscow artist. When in his *Autobiography* he described the musical scene in St. Petersburg at the turn of the century, the same indignation that had scorched Gide flared again.

[I want] to give the reader a short account of the place which the ballet and ballet music occupied in intellectual circles and among so-called "serious" musicians in the period immediately preceding the appearance of the Diaghilef group. Although our ballet shone then, as always, by reason of its technical perfection, and although it filled the theatre, it was only rarely that these circles were represented among the audience. They considered this form of art as an inferior one, especially as compared with opera, which, though mishandled and turned into musical drama (which is not at all the same thing), still retained its own prestige. This was particularly the point of view in regard to the music of the classical ballet, which contemporary opinion considered to be unworthy of a serious composer. These poor souls had forgotten Glinka and his splendid dances in the Italian style in *Russlan and Ludmilla*. It is true that Rimsky-Korsakov appreciated them—or, rather, forgave Glinka for them—but he himself, in his numerous operas, definitely gave the preference to character or national dances. We must not forget that it was these very pages of Glinka which inspired the great Russian composer, who was the first to bring about the serious recognition of ballet music in general—I refer to Tchaikovsky.

This intensity of feeling with its animus against opera, the world of his father, of his teacher, and of other "so-called 'serious' musicians," continued all his life. It may explain in part why he had such difficulty with the form. Whenever he attempted an opera, there seemed to be extra emotional hurdles to be cleared. In ballet he was the leader, both prophet and god, and the certainty of it gave him extraordinary confidence. As he observed to Craft in *Expositions and Developments* (1962), "The success of *Petrushka* was good for me in that it gave me the absolute conviction of my ear, just as I was about to begin *The Rite of Spring*." Unfortunately for the development of opera, no similar moment of conviction occurred.

V·

PROKOFIEV'S OPERAS:
BAD LUCK AND POLITICS

Prokofiev's operas are among the least performed of his works—which is odd, because critics in writing of his ballets, symphonies, concertos, solo violin and piano works are apt to state that he is a very theatrical composer. What then is the difficulty with his operas, for which his theatrical talent would seem to be ideally suited? With seven operas completed and as many more seriously contemplated, he clearly was drawn to the form, and the difficulties seem to be less with the music, for which there is a growing appreciation, than with his bad luck in getting the works produced. That bad luck, chance mixed with artistic and political problems, accompanied him from his first effort in 1916 through his death in 1953, and a glance at the table on p. 56 will suggest the magnitude of it.

To casual operagoers, some of the titles may be unfamiliar, for most persons probably have not seen more than two of the operas and even the assiduous not more than four. Two, the so-called "Soviet" operas, *Semyon Kotko* and *The Story of a Real Man*, rarely as yet have been performed outside of Russia, and a third, the comedy *Betrothal in a Monastery*, has emerged only slowly.

For a composer as famous in his lifetime as Prokofiev to have three of his seven operas posthumously premiered (four if *Semyon Kotko*, because of its live burial, is counted) is quite extraordinary. In memory no other operatic composer of comparable stature has had such a difficult time, and nothing perhaps so clearly suggests the strength of the artistic and political pressures upon Prokofiev, or, despite them, the strength of his urge to compose operas.

This urge revealed itself while he was still a child, an only child, living with his parents on a large Ukrainian estate that his father managed for an absentee landlord. His mother was an excellent pianist, and in 1900 when he was nine his parents took him on a trip to Moscow, where he saw *The Sleeping Beauty, Prince Igor,* and *Faust.* He was familiar with the famous passages and, as he later recalled, bored by

	Composed	World Premiere	Theatre and City	Production History
The Gambler	1915–16	April 29, 1929	Théâtre de la Monnaie, Brussels	Withdrawn at Maryinsky (later Kirov) Theatre, Feb. 1917 after reaching rehearsals. Artistic row.
The Love of Three Oranges	1919	Dec. 30, 1921	Chicago Opera Co., Chicago	Scheduled for 1919. Postponed twice. Artistic problems.
The Fiery Angel	1919–27	Posthumous, Sept. 29, 1955	La Fenice, Venice	In 1926 plans for a production at Berlin under Bruno Walter abandoned. Presumably artistic problems.
Semyon Kotko	1939	Sept. 20, 1940	Stanislavsky Theatre, Moscow	Dropped from the repertory in 1941 and not performed again until 1959. Political problems.
The Betrothal in a Monastery or The Duenna	1940	Nov. 3, 1946	Kirov Theatre, Leningrad	Composed for Stanislavsky Theatre, Moscow; reached private showings in 1941. Cancelled because of war.
War and Peace	1941–52	Posthumous, Nov. 8, 1957	Stanislavsky Theatre, Moscow	Parts of the opera performed 1944–47 and 1953–57. Artistic and political problems.
The Story of a Real Man	1947–48	Posthumous, Oct. 8, 1960	Bolshoi Theatre, Moscow	Closed preview of the staged opera at the Kirov Theatre, Dec. 3, 1948; production cancelled. Political problems.

the music between: "How slow everything was!" But the staging excited him, particularly the duel scene in *Faust* and the death of Valentin. Returning home he composed an opera of his own, *The Giants,* and six months later started another, *On Desert Islands.* In this, after an overture, the first act presented a sea voyage, a storm, and a shipwreck. Then, not knowing what to do with his castaway characters, he stopped.

Impressed by his efforts, his parents consulted the composer and teacher Sergi Taneyev and on his suggestion hired a conservatory student to teach Prokofiev harmony, counterpoint, instrumentation, and piano technique. The man was not a success. As Prokofiev recalled the lessons: "I wanted to compose operas with marches, storms, complicated scenes, and here I was tied hand and foot with tedious rules." The next man, the composer Reinhold Glière, was apparently a natural teacher, able to spark interest while eliciting discipline, and Prokofiev studied with him until entering the St. Petersburg conservatory in 1904. By then he had developed efficient work habits that he continued for life and had attempted another opera, *A Feast in Time of Plague,* based on Pushkin.

At the conservatory, where he completed his studies in the spring of 1914, he became a brilliant pianist, an adequate but heavy-handed conductor, and a composer whose works attracted attention and achieved occasional public performance. Three "student" works still performed today are his First Piano Concerto, Opus 10, Toccata for piano, Opus 11, and Second Piano Sonata, Opus 14. Meanwhile he had not abandoned opera. He had rewritten *A Feast in Time of Plague* and composed two more: *Undine,* on a story by E. T. A. Hoffman, and *Maddalena,* on a one-act play by M. Lieven. The last is a story of courtesan love in fifteenth-century Venice. At its climax the lady's two lovers engage in a duel and to great claps of thunder kill each other, much to her delight.

The director of the Free Theatre in Moscow heard a piano runthrough of *Maddalena* and was impressed by it, but before a production could be mounted the theatre closed. Nevertheless, *Maddalena* was never performed publicly or published until the 1980s, long after Prokofiev's death; in his later years he numbered it Opus 13, and it is sometimes listed among his works.

From all the evidence Prokofiev emerged from the conservatory with the temperament of a spoilt child. Understandably so. His mother consistently had preferred his needs over those of her husband, his teachers because of his brilliance had put up with his tantrums, and in St. Petersburg he was one of an avant-garde circle of artists that delighted in backing him and his works against any old-guard criticism. He was aggressive, self-centered, willful, arrogant, and until the last decade of his life, when he softened considerably, his personality was a cause of his difficulties. It was also a source of strength.

In these years the musical life of St. Petersburg and Moscow was a volcanic ferment with talent erupting in all divisions of the art—performers, composers, conductors, and patrons. Imagine the musical world of the next forty years without Heifetz, Milstein, Chaliapin, Rachmaninoff, Scriabin, Stravinsky, Koussevitzky, and Diaghilev. Among such giants Prokofiev scrambled to establish himself.

Regarding his operas, he was unfortunate in that the two great patrons of the era, Diaghilev and Koussevitzky, had little interest in the form. When Prokofiev one time proposed an opera, Diaghilev retorted: "Opera is passé. Contemporary taste demands ballet and pantomime." Nevertheless Prokofiev continued, while composing ballets and piano and symphonic works, to make an opera of Dostoyevsky's novel *The Gambler*. Albert Coates, an English conductor at the Maryinsky Theatre, promised to produce it, and Prokofiev, to avoid serving in the army, reenrolled in the conservatory in order to gain a student's deferment, a subterfuge that he and his artistic friends accepted as honorable. By May 1916 the opera was completed.

Encouraged by the interest in his very modern *Scythian Suite,* Prokofiev chose for *The Gambler* the most radical language possible. He eschewed melody altogether except for fragments in the orchestra; he piled dissonance upon dissonance until even his sympathetic mother complained; and he set Dostoyevsky's prose, which he felt was "more vivid, more graphic, and more convincing than any verse," as unbroken declamation. To the extent that he had a model, it was Mussorgsky's unfinished opera *The Marriage,* particularly its prose recitative.

Later, in revising the orchestration, he concluded that much of it was "tiresome modernist padding that added nothing and simply confused the vocal line." That was exactly how the original scoring impressed the singers and orchestra at the Maryinsky Theatre, and in February 1917 they refused to continue the rehearsals and forced the cancellation of the production. Prokofiev and his supporters were unable to interest any other theatre in the opera, and it was shelved until its premiere at Brussels in a revised version twelve years later.

Doubtless the opera was improved by the delay and revision. But Prokofiev might have gained more by a production, whether successful or not, that allowed him to study his work on the stage. As the opera now is, it may be judged a qualified success. It is constructed in a style even today rare in opera and then quite revolutionary—in fact, the delay in production cost the opera a footnote in history. The action proceeds for the most part by snatches of dialogue among characters who fade in and out onstage as they might in a film. The vocal lines follow the natural cadences of speech but greatly exaggerated, while underneath the orchestra provides a continuous flow of dramatic comment. These miniscenes build in each of three short acts to a more extended finale, while the final act, with the gambling scene, is in effect a finale throughout. This cinematic style apparently was instinctive with Prokofiev, for films were not yet common, and his affinity for it may explain his later great success in composing for films, most notably for Eisenstein's *Alexander Nevsky* and *Ivan the Terrible.* But as a technique for opera it has its problems. For most of any audience the exposition in *The Gambler,* especially when delivered in a foreign tongue, is confusing and consequently boring. On the other hand, its several scenes of grotesque comedy come off well, and the final act in which the Gambler's obsession takes hold is exciting. But because of the structure the opera needs translation, twentieth-century techniques of staging, and also, alas, much preperformance study by the audience; with these, it succeeds.

His second opera, the first to be produced, was *The Love of Three Oranges,* commissioned by the Chicago Opera Company in 1919 when Prokofiev was on a concert tour of the United States. He had left Russia in 1918—he seems to have had no understanding of the revolution's significance or feeling for or against it—and did not return permanently until 1932. The long absence is the basis of an idiocy in which Russian critics tend to disparage his works composed abroad and Western critics those following his return to Russia. The bias has attached particularly to criticism of his operas and unfortunately still continues.

Though commissioned in Chicago, *The Love of Three Oranges* was entirely a product of his St. Petersburg years, which may partly explain its history in the United States. In St. Petersburg before the war the

Italian *commedia dell'arte* and fables of Carlo Gozzi had been much in vogue, and the great stage director Vsevolod Meyerhold had discussed with Prokofiev the possibility of an opera on *The Love of Three Oranges*. In Chicago that background was lacking, and the idea was accepted apparently almost entirely on the enthusiasm of the company's Italian director, Cleofonte Campanini. "Gozzi! Our dear Gozzi!" he said. "Wonderful!"

But soon after rehearsals began, Campanini died, and the opera's premiere was postponed a year. Then it was postponed again when Prokofiev demanded an indemnity for the delay. Whatever his legal rights, he was foolish, spoiling any chance for another commission, and later he had the grace to say, "I was to blame."

When the twice-delayed premiere took place, nothing in American theatre at the time prepared the audience for the kind of comedy it heard. The opera is a sort of farcical improvisation, a parody on opera and theatre with as much mime, dancing, and parade as singing and lots of theatrical magic intended to deceive no one. The melodies, as usual with Prokofiev at this time, are mostly in the orchestra, and the singers seldom move from declamation into song. In Chicago the opera, though composed in Russian,was performed in French and had a moderate success. Taken by the company to New York, it was dismissed by the critics with jeers, perhaps as much out of municipal rivalry as lack of understanding. Its first real success in the United States came only after World War II, when it was revived, this time in English, by the New York City Opera. Perhaps because of the translation or because by then the *commedia dell'arte* style was better understood by everyone, the production released the opera's antic spirit and until the scenery wore out was a repertory staple.

Of all of Prokofiev's operas, *The Love of Three Oranges* has had the easiest acceptance, yet even it has its troubles. Though in Western countries it now is frequently performed, in Russia it is not. Whatever music lovers there may think of it privately—the march is universally known—official opinion holds that the opera is "only a brilliant humoresque," an example of the brittle artificiality popular in decadent societies and with little interest for more wholesome Soviet audiences. To Prokofiev such arguments were beside the point: "All I tried to do was to write an amusing opera."

With his third, *The Fiery Angel,* composed 1919–27 while living in Ettal, Bavaria, and in Paris, he turned as in *The Gambler* to an obsession, this time sexual, and as with *The Love of Three Oranges* to a source in his St. Petersburg background. In 1907 the Russian symbolist poet Valery Bryussov published his novel *The Fiery Angel* in which, anticipating Freud with a poet's imagination, he probed the behavior of a sexual hysteric, a woman whose fierce desire for sexual intercourse and equally fierce revulsion from it drove her into erratic behavior and at times reduced her to convulsions ending in a catatonic fit. Bryussov, an expert in medieval spiritualism, set the story in sixteenth-century Germany, combining with the sensuality magic and religion. At one extreme Renata seeks her imaginary, perfect lover through the black arts, and at the other chastity through the church. But not only can she find no peace, she infects the convent in which she seeks refuge. In the final scene half the nuns writhe on the floor in hysterics as an Inquisitor condemns Renata to death for carnal intercourse with the devil.

Though in five acts, seven scenes, the opera is only a few minutes longer than Strauss's one-act *Elektra* and, though less concentrated, has much the same kind of power. Prokofiev, as always, delighted in the theatrical magic, seething cauldrons, knocks on the walls and possession by devils; and he also made the most of the moments of humor, chiefly at the expense of doctors, witch or medical. A scene involving Mephistopheles and Faust, the most intellectualized part of the novel, fails or at best is enigmatic and is sometimes cut; and Renata's opening aria, the opera's exposition, though faithful to the novel, is theatrically clumsy. These flaws aside, the opera is extraordinarily vital. Prokofiev, setting prose in his declamatory style, created vocal lines full of tension, and the underlying music crackles with energy. In the opinion of some critics, Western not Russian, it is his finest opera.

He worked on it for eight years and, for reasons which are obscure, never succeeded in getting it produced. Plans for a production in Berlin in 1926 under Bruno Walter fell through; though Koussevitzky two years later at a concert in Paris presented the second act, no European house rose to the bait; and in 1930 negotiations with the Metropolitan failed, apparently because the management felt the house was too large for the work. Prokofiev meanwhile had used materials from it for his Third Symphony (1929), which is still performed. The opera's unpublished score languished in the archives of Koussevitzky's Paris publishing house, where Prokofiev left it on his return to Russia. There after his death it was discovered; a concert performance followed and finally, in 1955, its first staged performance, in Venice. Since then it has been done in Western countries with some frequency, but it is not easy to produce. It requires a good translation, imaginative staging, and an exceptional soprano. Renata is onstage for roughly eighty-six of the opera's 115 minutes. Russian critics generally disapprove of it as another example of decadent Western influence.

In November 1932 during a concert tour of Russia Prokofiev told reporters, "It gives me the greatest joy to be home again in the Soviet land." The statement often is taken to mark his spiritual return to Russia, though he continued through 1939 to give concerts in the West. Why did he return? He told a friend in Paris, Serge Moreux, "Foreign air does not suit my inspiration, because I am a Russian, and that is to say the least suited of men to be an exile, to remain in a psychological climate that isn't that of my race. . . . I've got to hear the Russian language echoing in my ears, I've got to talk to people who are my own flesh and blood, so that they can give me back something I lack here—their songs—my songs. Here I'm getting enervated. I risk dying of academism." He saw that Rachmaninoff in self-imposed exile had lost the ability to compose, and for Prokofiev composition was the purpose of life. And to Victor Seroff, after explaining that he wanted his two sons to be educated in Russia, he added, "Here I have to kowtow to publishers, managers, all sorts of committees, sponsors of productions, patronesses of art, and conductors each time I wish my work to be performed. A composer doesn't have to do that in Russia. And as for 'politics,' they don't concern me. It is none of my business."

Once back in Russia, Prokofiev began to search for another libretto, and Russian music lovers eagerly awaited him to find one. In the present century, when Italians for the most part have turned their backs on their great vocal tradition, the Russians have a good claim to be the world's most avid opera lovers. Besides the tradition, there is the expectation that a composer to be significant must accomplish something in the form. The pure symphonist does exist in modern Russian music—for example, Nikolai Miaskovsky—but Prokofiev was not one. Finally, after two highly successful theatrical works, the ballet *Romeo and Juliet* and the film *Alexander Nevsky,* he settled on a popular novel about one of the great experiences of his generation, the German invasion of the Ukraine in World War I and the subsequent civil war there between White and Red Russians. In *I, Son of the Working People* by Valentin Katayev he found what he sought: "living people, with their true passions, love, hatreds, happiness, and sorrow which were caused naturally by the 'new' events."

The story, based in part on Katayev's experiences, concerns a soldier, Semyon Kotko, who on his discharge from the tsarist army returns to his village in the Ukraine. There the local Soviet committee awards him as his share of the rich landowner's estate a plot of land, a horse, a cow, and six sheep. Kotko wants to marry Sophia (Sonya) whose father, Tkachenko, a rich peasant, is unenthusiastic about the match. Under pressure from Sophia and the village Soviet leaders he consents, but during the engagement party a German regiment invades the village, killing, burning, and forcing all Communists and many others to flee. Out on the steppes Kotko joins a band of partisans formed by the village Soviets to fight the Germans. Meanwhile in the village Tkachenko collaborates with the invaders and prepares to marry Sophia to the landowner who now is likely to recoup his lands. On the wedding day Kotko leads a patrol into the village, rescues Sophia from the church, but is captured by the Germans. Before he can be executed the partisans arrive to save him, and behind them comes the Red Army to drive the Germans away. Amid the general happiness Kotko and Sophia are reunited.

Some western critics, inflamed by the words "Red" and "Soviet," have dismissed the opera as propaganda—which is nonsense. It is a border tale of love, violence, and divided loyalty of the kind that Walter Scott wove into his novels, and as in them, though great impersonal forces sometimes loom in the background, the focus is on individuals and their fates.

Katayev, who served as librettist, imagined an opera in traditional style with arias, choruses, and Ukrainian dances. Prokofiev did not: "The subject of my opera is 'new,' therefore the method of composing it should be new." Yet in the end, perhaps because of his Ukrainian childhood, he yielded more than he first may have intended. Though he stuck to his usual declamatory style, it is more graceful and melodic. The orchestration is less thick, and the voices have a greater share of the musical interest. He worked in several Ukrainian songs, wrote some serenely lyrical love music and a number of fine ensembles of such varied character as a Ukrainian engagement party, a village going up in flames, and a service for the dead. As he completed the score, the opera's prospects seemed bright, but then Soviet politics in their most fearful aspect began to impinge.

The premiere production was to be at Stanislavsky's Opera Theatre and directed by Prokofiev's friend Vsevolod Meyerhold. He, however, was in disfavor with the country's political leaders, and in a speech touching on the opera he offended them further by disparaging "socialist realism" in the theatre. He was arrested and sent to a labor camp, where several years later he apparently was murdered for political reasons. His wife was murdered three weeks after his arrest. In this tense atmosphere the opera was reassigned to another director, Serafima Birman, who seems to have had little sympathy with it.

The audience's reaction at the premiere was ambiguous, and for six months the opera, which was played in repertory, was discussed in musical and political circles. In the former it was increasingly referred to as "Prokofiev's unsuccessful experiment," though such musicians as Miaskovsky and the pianist Sviatoslav Richter admired it. Richter later concluded that it was one of Prokofiev's "most successful works," worthy to stand beside Mussorgsky's *Boris Godunov* and *Khovanshchina.* "While listening to it, one begins to experience the life, the period of history which is depicted." But the political decision went against it, apparently because it was not in traditional operatic style and because it emphasized individuals rather than the Party. The next season it was dropped from the repertory and not revived until a concert performance in 1959, six years after Prokofiev's death.

Not many Westerners have seen *Semyon Kotko.* Czechoslovakians at Brno on May 16, 1959, gave the first performance outside of Russia; at Prague in 1963 it was part of a Prokofiev festival; and in 1973 the Bolshoi presented it on tour in Milan. Though a recording exists, most writers (I'm one) discuss the opera without having seen it onstage. Someday perhaps the lingering chill of the war will cool sufficiently for Western houses to mount it. Meanwhile it is the only opera by a major composer attempting to deal directly with the emotions and ideas of World War I. For that alone it is interesting.

Prokofiev's reaction to the political purge—even before Meyerhold, the woman who had helped him with *Peter and the Wolf* had been sent to a labor camp—was to work even harder. "Work is the only thing, the only salvation," he told the journalist Ilya Ehrenburg, and while *Semyon Kotko* was in rehearsal he completed his Sixth Sonata for Piano and another opera, *Betrothal in a Monastery,* or *The Duenna.*

Based on Richard Brinsley Sheridan's "comic opera" *The Duenna* (1775), really a play larded with songs, the structure was already set, and the opera is Prokofiev's most conventional. It is also his most lyrical and perhaps lighthearted. Even more than in *The Love of Three Oranges* the comedy is in the music as well as on the stage, chiefly because of Prokofiev's greater skill in suggesting character. Composed for Moscow's smaller theatre, the Stanislavsky, it is lightly scored and needs good singing actors.

Of all Prokofiev's operas it had the fewest problems of production. At the Stanislavsky Theatre in 1941 it reached the point of private showings when the production was cancelled because of the war. But that happened to many composers. As soon as the war ended, the Kirov Theatre in Leningrad presented the opera, and since then in Russia it has been steadily in the repertory. Why it has taken so long to emigrate to other countries is a mystery. A reason may be that by 1946 in the West Prokofiev was generally considered to be an unsuccessful operatic composer: *The Love of Three Oranges* still had its real success ahead of it; *The Gambler* was remembered as a failure; *The Fiery Angel* and *Semyon Kotko* were both unknown. Even the ballets *Cinderella* and *Romeo and Juliet* were merely names, the latter's United States premiere, for example, not occurring until the Royal Danish Ballet presented it in New York on September 26, 1956. In the years immediately after World War II Prokofiev's Western reputation rested almost entirely on his nontheatrical works—the symphonies, violin and piano concertos, and solo works. Half the man. As the other half emerges, *Betrothal in a Monastery* shows signs of entering the international repertory.

In the final decade of Prokofiev's life, 1943–1953, the project to which he devoted most of his energy was to achieve a full, uncut production of his opera *War and Peace*. "I am willing to reconcile myself to the failure of any of my works," he said to the composer Kabalevsky, "but if you only knew how much I wish for a production of *War and Peace.*" But when it came, Prokofiev was dead.

He made his first sketch of a libretto in April 1941, and then when the Germans invaded Russia in June Tolstoy's classic suddenly again was contemporary. Prokofiev worked on it steadily and a year later completed the opera, or, as it turned out, the first version of it. He promptly sent the vocal score to the Committee on Art Affairs, whose approval was necessary for a production in any state opera house. The Committee approved the work in principle but recommended that the role of the Russian people in 1812 be strengthened and that the lyrical sections, which were admired, be expanded.

Prokofiev's operatic ideal always had been short, cinematic scenes with prose dialogue set in natural speech cadence over a continuous orchestral symphony. Miaskovsky, after hearing the score, wrote a friend: "Although the music is exceptional, the opera probably will never come out: again the usual thing—scene after scene (in short like a play), wordy, etc., and almost no singing. Besides, there are many superfluous episodes." The changes that Prokofiev now made, ultimately through three revisions, were all aimed to meet these criticisms.

Meanwhile at the Bolshoi the director, Samuel Samosud, who was a steadfast believer in the opera, planned a production for late 1943 and persuaded the film director Sergei Eisenstein to act as stage director; and in New York the Metropolitan announced that it would produce the opera the following year. Though the war slightly delayed the Bolshoi production, it reached rehearsals and then was cancelled when Samosud suddenly was relieved of his post, apparently more because of theatre than state politics. The Metropolitan sought to continue with the opera, but the Russians not unnaturally insisted on the world premiere, and the New York production was indefinitely postponed. Think what a wartime production at the Metropolitan would have done for Prokofiev's reputation in the United States and the Western world: the broadcast performances, the tapes turned later into recordings, the thousands of librettos distributed, and the immediate interest in his other operas! But none of this was to be.

In January 1945 Prokofiev fell, sustaining a brain concussion from which he never fully recovered. For months he was in a hospital, then later in a sanitarium, and even when released suffered constantly from hypertension and headaches. The doctors sometimes forbade him to work, but even in his periodic relapses he continued composing, if only in his head.

Samosud soon was offered a post at the Maly Theatre in Leningrad and made as a condition of acceptance a production of *War and Peace*. One was promised, and on June 12, 1946, the first or "peace" half of the opera was produced. It had an astonishing success—105 performances in the 1946–47 season—and excited everyone to see the second or "war" half.

While Prokofiev was making revisions, however, the political atmosphere of the country changed drastically. In August and September 1946 three resolutions designed to enforce an ideological discipline on literature, theatre, and films were enacted by the Central Committee of the Communist Party. Eisenstein, for one, was charged with "distortions of historic fact" in Part II of *Ivan the Terrible,* and the film, with music by Prokofiev, was banned. Perhaps remembering Meyerhold, Eisenstein made an abject confession to all charges and died two years later without resuming work. Suddenly there was a question whether Party officials would like Prokofiev's work. After two closed rehearsals held chiefly for them the production was postponed indefinitely.

Then on February 10, 1948, the Party issued a Resolution on music in which Prokofiev, Shostakovich, Miaskovsky, Khachaturian, and several other composers were declared guilty of "formalistic distortions and anti-democratic tendencies which are alien to the Soviet people and its artistic taste" (i.e., too modern, too complicated, too Western, too individualistic). After that there was no chance of a production until the political climate changed, which seemed unlikely for there was evidence that it was determined personally by Stalin. He had gone to the Bolshoi to see an opera, *The Great Friendship,* by Vano Muradeli, and he had not been pleased. His cultural assistant and perhaps he himself had expressed his disapproval after the performance to the Bolshoi's director, who had a heart attack and within two days died. The resolution on music was entitled "On V. Muradeli's Opera *The Great Friendship*" and set up as the Party's standard for composers music that could be easily understood by the masses, music that was melodious and in the traditional styles. Presumably what was meant was music in the styles that had pleased Stalin and his generation when they were young, or Russian music as it was about 1895.

The subject was not open for debate, but Prokofiev had made a statement in 1937 that may be taken for an answer: "In the music written during this productive year, I have striven for clarity and melodiousness. But at the same time I have not tried to get by with hackneyed melodies and harmonies. This is what makes it so difficult to compose clear music: the clarity must be new, not old." Though the Maly Theatre periodically petitioned the Committee on Art Affairs to produce *War and Peace,* either part, the requests were rejected.

In addition to *War and Peace* Prokofiev had another opera caught in the political storm. Stirred by the German invasion in World War II, he had sought a contemporary story by which to celebrate the Russian defense and victory and had found it in *The Story of a Real Man,* a novel by Boris Polevoi based on a wartime incident. A Russian aviator is shot down behind the German lines. Crippled in his legs, he crawls for miles, often in delirium, until found by village partisans, old folks and children, operating behind the lines. They keep him alive and concealed, while sending word of his whereabouts, and one day a Russian plane lands to carry him out to a hospital. There his legs are amputated, and he becomes emotionally depressed, alienated, feeling there is no longer any role he can play in society. The nurses and doctors worry about him, but the clue to health is offered by an old Commissar who is in the hospital dying. With the prerogative of age he chaffs the young man, refuses to be put off, urges him to be "a true Soviet man," and gives him a goal: to fly again. The aviator learns to walk on his wooden legs and proves himself fit to return to the front by dancing a waltz and a rumba. In the final scene his plane is presumed lost but makes it back to the airfield. There he is reunited with his fiancée, who has appeared in several flashbacks and from whom he has concealed the truth about his legs. She already knows of it, however, from a friend, and embracing they look forward to life together. The chorus frames the opera, start and finish, with a majestic chorale about a young oak tree that did not break in the storm.

Though there is some sloshy sentiment in the scenes with the fiancée and perhaps some propaganda in the appeal to be "a Soviet man," the story's main thrust, which inspired Prokofiev's best music, concerns an individual's decision to rejoin the human race. And perhaps besides the general political climate of 1948 it was just that emphasis on an individual's decision that turned the political officials so severely against the opera. After hearing a closed rehearsal on December 3, 1948, they ordered the production cancelled and publicly condemned Prokofiev. "In the modernistic, anti-melodic music of his opera, in the treatment of the Soviet people, the composer remains on his old positions, condemned by the Party and by Soviet Society." The opera's premiere, in Moscow, did not take place until October 8, 1960.

Perhaps in 1948 the opera's structure could still seem "modernistic," though after thirty years of films it is hard to see how. Prokofiev returned once again to short scenes that fade in and out, connecting them with musical interludes. In the aviator's delirium in the hospital his doctor, mother, and fiancée appear before him, and as each has a few lines—a tiny scene—the staging is almost forced into quick-lighting techniques. Similarly the plane crash and his efforts to crawl back to his unit almost demand a blackout and spotlighting. At the opera's premiere and later in Prague the stage was bare except for a ramp and the minimum of props. The chorus, whose role apart from the choral frame is small, stood at the back, dressed in wartime "austerity" clothing and gazing sympathetically or expectantly at the individuals whose drama unfolded before it. Unquestionably, this kind of staging, as opposed to literal realism for *War and Peace,* was what Prokofiev wanted.

The music is neither "modernistic" nor "anti-melodic." In fact, musically it is the most traditional of all Prokofiev's operas. In addition to dramatic recitative there are many attractive tunes, some perilously close to "pop" songs, set in easily recognized numbers: arias, duets, and the waltz and the rumba. At its worst the music is conventional, chiefly the rumba and the scenes with the fiancée. At its best—the opening scenes, the partisans, the hospital, and the old Commissar—it is moving, simply but skillfully scored, and surprisingly unsentimental. There are no mock heroics.

Plainly Prokofiev tried hard to make the music melodious, clear, easily understood. But did he simplify his style only because of the political pressures or in part or whole out of artistic maturity? The question is one of the most fascinating and arguable in modern criticism, with the door wide open for bias to enter. Only one point will be made here: Prokofiev's basic characteristics all were formed and visible before he left St. Petersburg in 1918, and among them, when he wanted, were clarity and melody: for example, the *Classical Symphony* or, in his piano works, the *Visions Fugitives.* It is conceivable therefore that, despite all the anguish of the political persecution, following his return to Russia he began to emphasize melody and clarity purely as an artistic decision.

So there they are: seven operas by a major twentieth-century composer, all of which had some delay in getting started. Except for *The Love of Three Oranges* they are not yet well known in the West, but several are becoming so, chiefly *War and Peace.* Since 1964 the Bolshoi has performed it in Vienna, Milan, Montreal, New York, and Washington; in 1973 the Australians selected it to open their new opera house in Sydney; the English National Opera had a solid success with it; and so did companies in Boston, Seattle, and San Francisco. Recently, the Metropolitan announced it for the near future. Still a considerable distance behind it in number of performances but coming on are *The Gambler, The Fiery Angel,* and *Betrothal in a Monastery.*

As for *Semyon Kotko* and *The Story of a Real Man,* one or both may yet assume an honorable place in the extraordinary pageant of Russian history created by the country's composers. That pageant is a kind of continuing national epic without parallel in the operatic literature of other countries. It begins with *Prince Igor* (Borodin) and the first Tartar invasions; continues through *Boris Godunov* (Mussorgsky) and *Ivan Susanin* or *A Life for the Tsar* (Glinka), each dealing with aspects of the Polish invasions; and passes to *Khovanshchina* (Mussorgsky) and the troubles at the end of the seventeenth century. To these now must be added *War and Peace* with the story of the French invasion. The opera, in its episodic structure, large role for chorus, and somewhat uneasy yoking of individual and national stories, is squarely in the tradition.

So, too, if Richter's judgment is right, is *Semyon Kotko,* bringing the pageant down to the German invasion of World War I. Perhaps even the more individual, smaller-scaled *The Story of A Real Man,* with the German invasion of World War II, someday will seem part of it. Though probably not significant, it is interesting that much of the criticism of both operas, and until recently of *War and Peace,* repeats the contemporary criticism of *Boris Godunov:* the episodic structure, lack of melody, clipped recitatives, and lack of connection between musical ideas. When the day comes that Western audiences can see these two operas, perhaps in this historical perspective they will seem very little "Soviet" and very much Russian.

One final postponement because of politics was reserved for Prokofiev. He died on March 5, 1953, but the date sometimes is given as the 7th. As a Soviet journal explained: "Prokofiev died, alas, on the day of the tragic announcement of the death of the great Stalin. As a result it was not possible to announce his death in the press until a few days later. . . ."

VI·

SOME ASPECTS OF
TWENTIETH CENTURY OPERA, 1976-99

Rock music, through its development of electronic instruments, restricted melody and repetitive style has had an enormous influence on some kinds of opera, yet rock itself as yet has been the opera bud that will not bloom. Though rock groups in the 1960s, playing to huge audiences, astonished the world with their rhythmic vitality, amplification, and strange, new electronic sounds, they seemed unable, despite several notable attempts, to fashion a viable rock opera. Some of their works, such as *Tommy* (1967) and *Jesus Christ Superstar* (1971), were highly successful commercially, but none was at its best artistically as a staged drama. All had greater impact in other forms, as ballets, films, concerts, or, as often conceived, a succession of songs on a record.

There are discernable reasons for the fact and some interesting speculations, but none that suggests an insuperable obstacle to a rock drama that would be at its best on the stage. Meanwhile, in various ways composers of the 1970s began to tap for opera some of the potential that seemed so evident.

What is that potential? Or, put another way, what makes music "rock" as opposed to classical, primitive, or contemporary? There is no accepted definition, and to avoid a bog of argument I will leap to a conclusion. It is not only the noise: some operas are very noisy; many rock songs are quiet. It is not only the rhythm or repetition: both occur in classical and primitive music. It is not only the use of electronic sounds for contemporary "serious" music often uses laboratory-created sounds that reach performance via tape. It is chiefly the use of electric instruments.

Rock artists have made the sound of electric instruments familiar the world over. And the sight of them, too. Though the Beatles, for example, created many of their songs in a recording studio, unlike the "serious" composers they gave hundreds of public performances. Through them, other rock groups, and individuals, a large working

71

knowledge has been accumulated about electric instruments in the studio and onstage. It is that knowledge that is waiting to be exploited in an opera house.

The revolution in music caused by electric instruments—for it is that—started as early as the 1920s when the possibility of them was understood. By the late 1930s all those of a typical small rock group were in existence—the electric guitar, electric double bass, and electric organ. But with the exception of the organ, which as the Mighty Wurlitzer found a place in large, baroque movie halls, they were not much used. Then with the rise of rock in the mid-1950s the others began to dominate popular music, particularly the electric guitar. Displacing the piano, it became the era's representative instrument.

Of all the new electric instruments the guitar has proved the most expressive and versatile. In a band it can play almost any role: it can sustain a long melodic line, provide a background of percussive rhythm, or, like a harp, wash broad harmonic textures through the music. And as a solo instrument in the hands of a skillful player it can do all three at once, and more.

An electric guitar is not an ordinary acoustic guitar electrically amplified. It is a different kind of instrument, creating its sound in a different way. In the older acoustic guitar the sound is made by causing a string to vibrate. The sound produced by the string is slight—to most ears inaudible. The string's vibrations cause the surrounding air to vibrate sympathetically, and the air conducts the vibrations through the air hole under the strings into the body of the guitar, into a cavern lined with wood that acts as a sounding board. The wood resonates with the string's vibrations, emitting a sound at the same pitch as the string but considerably louder. The amplification—dread word!—is achieved entirely in the wood, without electricity.

Think for a moment of the musical qualities of the acoustic guitar. It is an outstanding instrument for intimate expression, for the folk singer's ballad or the lover's soft serenade. Even flamenco playing is relatively small scaled: for the big concert hall Tchaikovsky's piano concerto: for the small nightclub the flamenco singer and guitar. In a large hall the impression left by a guitar, when played by a master, is of an extrordinary clarity, sharp pins of light jetting from the stage into the hall's darkness.

Because of its close ties to folksinging, and perhaps, too, because it is relatively cheap and easy to carry, the guitar always has been a popular instrument and from the start had a place in jazz and dance bands—but, because of its quiet tone, a weak place. In hard times, band lore declared, the guitarist was the first to be fired.

Most of the time in a dance band of the 1920s the guitarist was relegated to the rhythm section, sounding the music's harmonic changes with a steady strum-strum. During this period steel strings began to replace gut for band instruments, and the soft sound of the classic guitar evolved into the louder, brasher tone of the steel guitar. But still any solo passage, to be heard above the piano, brass, and percussion, had to be orchestrated very carefully, and as soon as microphones became available, the guitarist, like the vocalist, would step forward for his solo to the microphone.

The physics of the microphone system was that the microphone would take the sound of the guitar, created as described above, and change it within the microphone into an electrical signal. That signal, very weak, would be conducted by a wire to an amplifier where its power would be boosted electrically. The more powerful electric signal then would pass over wires to a loudspeaker, where it would be transformed back into a sound much louder.

The aim of the system was to achieve an electric signal that perfectly represented the sound of the guitar, and of course in the early days of electric systems there was much distortion. One of the worst problems was with the microphone. The more sensitive it was, the more extraneous noise it picked up: the guitarist's breathing, the bandsmen talking, and the shuffle of the dancers' feet.

Over the years guitarists experimented with various ways of padding the microphone, fastening it to the guitar and even putting it inside the sound box. The last cut out most of the extraneous noise, but broadcast any bump of the guitar, a belt buckle hitting it, a sleeve scraping it, or the slap of a hand. But note: even with the microphone inside the guitar, with a wire running from the instrument to an amplifier, there still had to be an acoustic sound created loud enough for the microphone to pick up before the electrical system could begin to amplify it.

Finally, in the mid-1930s, some guitarists began to replace the microphone with magnetic pickup, also called a "bobbin" or sometimes a "transducer." It is a permanent magnet wound many times with a fine insulated wire. From it a wire leads directly to an amplifier. A pickup—they can be very small—is placed under each guitar string, or sometimes two are placed under different parts of the string. When the string vibrates, the magnetism in the wound wire vibrates in sympathy and develops a small alternating voltage or electric signal. This signal will be at the same number of vibrations per second, the frequency, at which the string vibrates. The electric signal goes to the amplifier, is boosted electrically, and at the loudspeaker is turned into sound.

Note what has happened. The guitar string no longer must activate a sound loud enough to be picked up by a microphone. The guitar can dispense altogether with its sound box, and some, "solid body" guitars, do. The electric signal now no longer starts with a sound caused by a string's vibration amplified by wood but with the vibration itself. That is the distinction between a true electric guitar and an acoustic guitar electrically amplified.

In one respect the guitarists had solved their problem. The pickup, despite its name, unlike the microphone did not pick up extraneous noise. It responded only to the string directly above it. On the other hand, the sound it produced was not exactly like that of an acoustic guitar, and for several reasons. Pickups require strings that will affect the magnetic field efficiently, and only steel, with its relatively harsh sound, can do it. Nylon, gut, and even bronze cannot. Furthermore, the kind of wood used in the sound box, now bypassed, had contributed to the acoustic guitar's sound. Stiff woods had given a relatively bright sound; dense, heavy woods had helped to sustain the note. The pickup lost these nuances. So some guitarists used pickups and others microphones, which were constantly improved. This was the situation roughly throughout the late 1940s and early 1950s.

Here follows a slight digression. It is also possible to create a sound from a purely electronic source, without a sounding board or even a string. A box of electronic equipment powered by electricity, such as an audio frequency oscillator or a synthesizer, can produce an electric signal which, if amplified, can be turned into a sound wave at a loudspeaker. The sound, depending on how the signal is treated (described below) before it is amplified, may sound like an oboe, a trumpet, or a guitar, or any instrument at all. Contemporary electric organs create their own sounds in this fashion. Some "preset" the treatment of the signal so that the player need only pull a tab marked "oboe" or "trumpet"; others leave the treatment of the signal to the player.

The question arises: if a player can sound a guitar from an organ, why learn to play a guitar? Why have a group or a band? Why not one man doing it all from an electric organ? The reasons are many. First, the sounds are not *exactly* equivalent, and the organ's synthetic tone coloring, no matter how good, tends—though this is controversial—to become boring. A "liveness" is missing. Then, personal skills are involved: some persons have a facility for keyboards and others for strings. And there are psychological factors: the visual impact of a guitarist, calm or running wild, is quite different from that of an organist, and in group playing there are tensions—his entry, her repeat, the chorus together—that are lost when combined in a single instrument. But practically, within the limits of ten fingers and two feet, an organist can reproduce the sound, though not the visual impact, of a small group.

With the rise of rock music in the mid-1950s, the guitarists' purpose in amplification began to change. Previously their aim had been to reproduce the guitar's sound exactly, only louder, so that the guitar could match in volume the piano, brass, and percussion. With success a new soundscape of orchestral balance had become possible: a guitar could match percussion or even four trombones. Then, as electric instruments became more common, players discovered that by "treating" the electric signal before it was amplified they could create entirely new sounds. Besides the revolution in orchestral balance, there was now a revolution in orchestral sound.

To traditional effects, such as staccato, pizzicato, or sforzando, were now added many new electronic possibilities, such as the Wahwah effect, treble boost, envelope shaping, reverberation, tremolo, vibrato, and feedback, as well as what could be done with a ring modulator or a fuzz box (for descriptions, see Glossary). Where Beethoven in his symphonic "Wellington's Victory" added a cannon and musket fire to his orchestra, a rock guitarist could accomplish as much, and more, on a single instrument.

With so many treatments possible, it is not surprising that even outside a recording studio most rock groups have a sound engineer to balance and mix the effects wanted before they are passed to an amplifier for boosting through loudspeakers. At a public performance the engineer with a portable version of a studio control desk can be put anywhere that wires can run, but the logical place is the rear of the hall. He must know exactly what effects the instrumentalists intend. In fact, the band is his instrument, and the more he rehearses with it the better will be the performance. Rock's seeming spontaneity, unlike that of jazz, is usually a highly technical, highly rehearsed result.

The skill of rock artists in putting together their treatments soon became very great, and in the early 1970s there were many attempts to create rock opera. But none, whatever its success in other forms, managed onstage, in an opera house or concert hall, to become something more than a sequence of separate numbers; scenes did not bind into drama.

One immediately noticeable fact was that the numbers—into songs, dances, and finales—were by operatic standards extremely short. In *Hair* (1968), which billed itself as *The American Tribal Love-Rock Musical,* of the twenty-two numbers on the recording seventeen are three minutes or less; in *Tommy,* of twenty-one, eleven; and in *Jesus Christ Superstar,* of twenty-three, seven. The longest number in *Hair* is five minutes; in *Tommy,* seven; and in *Jesus Christ Superstar,* seven.

The length of a number, of course, does not necessarily determine its success in an opera. Mozart's "Champagne" aria for Don Giovanni lasts only a minute, but beside the brilliance of its music it succeeds partly by contrast with the longer, surrounding scenes. As a rule, the rock numbers are too short to allow a dramatic scene to develop. Verdi's sleepwalking scene for Lady Macbeth, for example, is twelve minutes; the opening scene of *Don Giovanni,* through the Commendatore's death, thirteen minutes; and Boris Godunov's final monologue—his farewell, prayer, and death—twelve minutes. Rock artists thus far seem unable to compose at this greater length, to expand their music from numbers into scenes. Musically *Hair* gave up on drama altogether and simply offered a concert of isolated, short numbers.

Two other areas in which rock operas seem to founder, perhaps facets of a single problem, are the endings of the numbers (or scenes) and moving from one to the next. On records the "fadeaway" has become a cliché of rock endings: a melodic phrase of the number and its beat is repeated continually until its volume, by turning a knob, has been decreased gradually to silence.

Onstage the technique works passably for scenes of agreement— a love duet or soldiers marching down a road—but badly for any kind of confrontation. After an argument, say, if the drama keeps the winner onstage, then the music seemingly should turn triumphant; or if the loser, despondent. Or perhaps the composer can comment musically. But the music in some manner must reflect what has happened. It must change *within* the number, not merely at its end.

In operatic terms this raises the problem of recitative: how to move from one number to the next. On a record the rock artist or group moves from a loud, fast-beat number to a soft ballad by some blank grooves and a few moments of silence. Transferred to the stage, the technique works better for ballet than for film or opera. In *Tommy* as a ballet, for example, the dancers could end a number by some movement of physical excitement, a leap into a partner's arms or off into the wings. The stage lights then would black out the stage and, after a few moments of silence and darkness, would slowly brighten with a new color and atmosphere. But in *Tommy* as a film, the singing actors had no such inherently dramatic exit as a leap into the wings, and the scenes separated by a few seconds of darkness and silence jolted one after another. They remained isolated numbers.

In a different way the problem was demonstrated in the New York (1972) production of *Jesus Christ Superstar*. At the end of one number, to get Jesus off the stage the director put him on a carpet and had him dragged off. A joke, perhaps? Then he did it again. No joke. The fault was in the music. It did not carry the character on and off stage. It was merely a record number.

Mozart moved from aria to aria by recitative. Verdi often constructed scenes out of emotional contrast that allowed the music with the scene to vary: introductory recitative, slow aria, interruption, fast aria. Wagner through-composed; that is, he changed the scene symphonically, in the music—a technique that takes longer than recitative. Debussy and Berg connected their short scenes, often presenting a single idea or emotion, by musical interludes that reflected and even advanced the drama. Getting from one high point to another has always been one of opera's hurdles and thus far rock artists have not found a way to clear it.

In one interesting failure, *The Survival of St. Joan, A Medieval Rock Opera* (1971), the four-man rock group "Smoke Rise," visible onstage, sang all the songs. Actors mimed the songs' action and spoke the scenes of dialogue. Where there was a break between spoken scenes the group led from one to the next with an interlude, generally a solo on the electric organ with an electric guitar sometimes joining it with a Scarlatti-like tone and figuration. These connecting links were attractive. The opera foundered elsewhere, chiefly in its book and in the division between actors and singers, but the interludes were a conscious effort by four rock artists to take a long step toward opera.

Can rock artists ever take that step? Perhaps not. Rock is closely tied to folk music, and despite the complication of the electronic equipment, the music is basically simple and orgiastic, rather than dramatic: one song, one emotion pushed to an extreme, and no confrontations among characters that might lead to drama, or, musically, to counterpoint, sextets, and extended finales.

Once again the difficulty is particularly noticeable in the endings, the finales. An orgy concludes not in a climax but in exhaustion, and *Jesus Christ Superstar,* for example, had no musical climax. It succeeded dramatically as well as it did because it had in reserve a visual climax: an onstage crucifixion. But after so much all-out singing and dancing in so many of the earlier numbers no musical climax was possible; and the music merely stopped. Viewed this way, a rock artist is a primitive, opera an extremely sophisticated musical form, and rock opera, perhaps, a contradiction in terms.

Leonard Bernstein, certainly no primitive, tried to reconcile the two in his *Mass, A Theatrical Piece for Singers, Players, and Dancers,* which inaugurated The Kennedy Center, Washington, D.C., on September 8, 1971. He used electric instruments, amplified the voices, and skillfully mortised together almost every style of popular and serious music—folk, ballad, blues, rock, Broadway song and dance, Lutheran chorale, plain chant, and even twelve-tone music. But the piece, though it perfectly represented the mood and manner of the moment, has not lasted well.

Meanwhile, another classically-trained musician, nineteen years younger than Bernstein, Philip Glass (b. 1937), had been developing a style of music that was electronic, personal, largely tonal in harmony, and repetitive in its patterns, or, better, additive, for the patterns continually changed, though slowly. These patterns typically were brief, melodic fragments, a sequence of four or five chords played as arpeggios or scales, increasing or decreasing in number of notes to the bar, which altered accent, while slowly shifting time values and harmony. The style was more sophisticated in technique than most rock and had roots in Glass's work with the sitar player Ravi Shankar and in his subsequent study of Indian music. Though Glass disliked the term, his style often was described as "minimalist," by which most who used the word meant the music sounded simple, repetitious, and undramatic. It seemed to these critics to lack beginning, middle, or end; it had no narrative. It was less a piece of music than a stretch of sound, cut from a seemingly endless roll. It was not dramatic like Beethoven, or architectural like Schoenberg; besides a debt to India, it perhaps owed something to the opening of Wagner's *Das Rheingold,* in which Wagner depicts the origin of the physical world, at the bottom of the Rhine, by slowly weaving patterns on a single chord for 136 bars.

Glass honed his style in the decade 1965-75, polishing it to a high perfection by ceaseless touring with his Philip Glass Ensemble: seven players on electronic and amplified instruments, with one player, perhaps the most important, in charge of "sound mix." The others, with Glass himself at an organ played a variety of electronic keyboards and wind instruments (saxophones, clarinets, flutes), and included a soprano who sang wordlessly—all amplified. They made a sound quite different from that usuallly heard in an opera house and played a kind of music that ignored all the so-called advances of the serialists and the traditional composers. And because of the constant touring, often as many as ninety concerts in a year, Glass had built an audience for his music, particularly among the young.

Then on 25 July 1976, at Avignon, in close collaboration with the stage designer Robert Wilson, he produced his first opera, *Einstein on the Beach,* which in the following months they took to Venice, Belgrade, Paris, Brussels, Hamburg, Rotterdam, and Amsterdam. In November, in conjunction with the Metropolitan but outside the company's regular season, they brought it to New York for two performances, both of which sold out the huge house. To the amazement of many musicians and operagoers who had scarcely heard of Glass, he became with one work a famous and highly controversial composer, with an audience apparently numbering in the millions. He promptly received commissions from companies in Rotterdam and Stuttgart for two more operas, and produced *Satyagraha* (1980) and *Akhnaten* (1984). In each case, though no longer working with

Wilson, he had a success, with productions following on both sides of the Atlantic; and, after several more operas and theatre works, he composed for the Metropolitan, at a fee of $325,000, *The Voyage* (1992). And with Wilson again, in the spring of 1998, he presented as "a work in progress," *Monsters of Grace,* much of it three-dimensional film created on computers. Whatever rank posterity may award his music, among contemporaries duing the century's final quarter Glass dominated opera; for richness of commissions, operas composed, and tickets sold, he had no equal.

The Wilson-Glass *Einstein on the Beach,* however, remained a unique effort (at least until *Monsters of Grace* reaches final form); and possibly because its length, staging, and lighting made it very difficult and expensive to reproduce, it has seldom been revived in full (a studio recording of the music, almost complete, was issued in 1979.) The two chief revivals were in Brooklyn in 1984 and in Stuttgart, 1990, with the latter presenting a wholly new staging by Achim Freyer. In the Brooklyn production, faithful to Wilson, the opera ran four and a half hours without intermission, and the program invited the audience "to leave and reenter the auditorium quietly. . . The food service in the lobby will remain open during performance." And whether or not expected by the management, there was much eating, drinking, and perhaps smoking in the auditorium.

Onstage the opera presented a company of twenty-five actors, singers, dancers, and a violinist representing Einstein, in four acts, nine scenes, and five connecting "knee plays" (which more traditional artists might have called "entr'actes"), and two dances. All the scenes, in their very slow succession, were clean, trim, and gloriously lit. One, "the Bed Scene," showed the narrow side of a mattress, a long bar of light floating a few feet above the stage and held in space, or so it began to seem, only by an organ solo and a wordless soprano voice. Gradually, very gradually it began to tilt from horizontal to upright. Some persons found the effect stunning, others, monotonous; but beyond any disagreement Wilson's use of light was resplendently beautiful.

On the music opinion divided. The Glass Ensemble played, and the singers sang only numbers, "one, two, three, four. . ." or syllables, "do, re, mi. . ." The numbers represented the passage's rhythmic structure; the syllables, the pitch of the notes. The effect, depending on the listener, was hypnotic, or boring. The visual images, meanwhile, maintained only a tenuous connection with the opera's examination of Einstein and his ideas. There were trains because as a child he had played with trains, and later used them to explain his theory of relativity. There was the bed, or so some critics surmised, to suggest that Einstein at night may have pondered the threat of atomic disaster; and in the final scene a spaceship seemed somehow linked to survival as the world perhaps ended in nuclear explosion. For many the opera offered a spiritual reward, much as Wagner's *Parsifal* in the nineteenth century had given to those who had journeyed to Bayreuth to hear it. John Rockwell, the critic for the New York *Times,* found the Brooklyn revival of *Einstein,* "constantly involving and almost religiously moving," an experience "to cherish for a lifetime."

Though Glass sometimes speaks of his first three operas as a trilogy on science (*Einstein*), politics (Gandhi, in *Satyagraha*) and religion (*Akhnaten*), the two later works are quite different from the first; and with them, as requested by those who commissioned them, he took several long steps towards a more usual operatic structure. He bound scenes together with a tighter narrative, introduced intermissions and reduced running time to less than three hours; and besides his Glass Ensemble, or replicas of it, made use of a standard orchestra and operatically trained soloists and chorus. Details of some ways in which *Satyagraha* and *Akhnaten* differ from *Einstein* are discussed in the introductory paragraphs to the synopses of the two operas.

Other musicians, of course, continued to compose operas in more familiar styles, but in Germany, not surprisingly, the influence of the Second Viennese School, particularly of Alban Berg's *Wozzeck* and *Lulu,* was strong. And at Cologne in 1965, an heir to the style, Bernd Alois Zimmermann's *Die Soldaten* (perhaps best translated as *The Military*), having previously been declared unplayable, finally achieved its premiere. Since then it has been the standard-bearer of German expressionistic opera, but despite critical praise and frequent productions in Germany, as yet it has not been able to establish itself in other countries. It is, for any opera house, a very expensive, complicated undertaking. Zimmermann once described his purpose as "to concentrate and intellectually coordinate the new discoveries of recent years" so that "architecture, sculpture, painting, musical theatre, spoken theatre, ballet, film, microphone, television, tape, and sound techniques, electronic music, concrete music, circus, the musical, and all forms of motion theatre combine to form the phenomenon of pluralistic opera."

In its "unplayable" form, Zimmermann wanted twelve acting areas, each with its own musical ensemble. Most productions have made do with one huge orchestra, two or three acting areas and as many screens for film or television clips. Zimmermann's aim was to have two or three actions proceed separately but simultaneously, so that the meaning of each would be enhanced by the overlay of the others.

The story, which he drew from the play by J. M. R. Lenz, published in 1776 (See Compendium, Rihm), tells of Marie, a merchant's daughter, who breaks her engagement to a suitable man to dally with a titled army officer. Rejecting advice from an older woman on how to extricate herself from a relationship likely to end in ruin, she goes to join the officer, is raped by his gamekeeper, and becomes an army whore. In the play Marie, walking the streets, is recognized by her father and saved. In the opera, the father fails to recognize her, and in the final stage-picture she is seen abandoned on the street, weeping. Zimmermann apparently meant to portray militarism as the scourge of the world and wanted, though his wishes were not always followed, to end with images on the screens of the atomic bomb exploding over Hiroshima. Some productions have ended with Marie alone on stage, while on screens above her are films of soldiers marching, and from microphones on all sides of the theatre boom the sound of marching feet.

Zimmermann's vocal lines follow Berg's style, pushing often to expressionistic extremes. In the orchestra, as in *Wozzeck,* the music for each scene is cast in a specific musical form, such as chaconne, toccata, or rondo. Unquestionably, the opera was constructed with the greatest care and intelligence, and German audiences have found the music and drama moving. But others, though certainly not all, find the story unsympathetic and Zimmermann too pretentious both in text and music. He tends to weighty questions, such as "Can only wrong-doers be happy?"; to which the music screams a comment. The story further lacks the steady tension of quarreling brothers that helps to humanize Schoenberg's conceptual *Moses und Aron;* and in part because this girl is so clearly responsible for her fate, her story is less cathartic than *Wozzeck.* As for the music, taken alone it has not won a large audience.

Like Glass's *Einstein,* Zimmermann's *Die Soldaten* probably can never be played in small houses; the forces needed are simply too great. Strangely, in the last half of the twentieth century that giantism became a chronic symptom, perhaps of artistic decadence.

Examples of it occur in all countries. In England Harrison Birtwistle's *The Mask of Orpheus* (1986) ran four hours, presenting in its reconsideration of the Orpheus legend 126 "events," many simultaneously, and required triple casting (singer, actor, and puppet) for the principal roles as well as a large orchestra with a six-man team to control the electronic elements. In France there was Olivier Messiaen's *Saint François d'Assise,* which despite a premiere in Paris in 1983, was not fully realized until a production at the Salzburg Festival in 1992. It runs almost six hours, with two intermissions, three acts and eight scenes. It asks for a chorus of 150 and an orchestra of 120, including three ondes martenots, a kind of synthesizer capable of varying timbres as well as shifting pitch in microtones and providing effects of vibrato and glissando. The opera offers eight scenes from the saint's life, such as receiving the stigmata, and each is independent and self-contained. The pace is slow. Deconstructing an audience's usual expectation of time is an idea that has fascinated many artists of the last fifty years, and techniques such as slow-motion, flash-back, fast-forward, and action from different periods presented simultaneously on stage or screen are now common features of opera.

Messiaen, a devout Roman Catholic, was for many years an organist at La Trinité in Paris, and while playing there he developed his own style of music, one that uses many Indian scales and rhythms, serial techniques, bird calls, and vivid orchestral color, much of it provided by the ondes martenots. The opera, his only one and composed toward the end of his life, has been called a pageant, a liturgy, a statement of religious belief, its scenes like stained-glass windows, bright, colorful, and requiring contemplation to absorb fully. Messiaen is often said to be the most important French composer of recent years, and parts of the opera have appeared in concerts where musicians and possibly some of the audience attempted to plumb the depths for riches. And rewards presumably are there, for the editor of *Opera,* Rodney Milnes, in reviewing the Salzburg production, compared the opera to *Parsifal* and declared it "a masterpiece of comparable spiritual potential." (But see Compendium, Messiaen.)

Yet, as surely as in 1666 none but the rich and high-born enjoyed the fabulous baroque opera *Il pomo d'oro,* produced by the Viennese Emperor to celebrate his son's marriage to a Princess of Spain, today none but the international corps of critics (who get seats free), and the jet-set rich (who can afford them) are likely ever to see or hear a complete *Saint François d'Assise.*

Possibly, just as baroque court opera proved a musical dead end, while vitality flourished in the less grand forms playing in the small, public theatres of Venice, today's huge complicated extravaganzas will soon seem dodos while the simpler works that drew an audience to the theatre round the corner are still full of life.

One last generality of opera production in the last twenty-five years need mentioning, for controversy swirls about its examples. This is the increasing importance of the stage picture. It sometimes is said that not till the stark, symbolic productions of Wieland Wagner (See Compendium), at Bayreuth in mid-century, did critics begin their reviews with comments on the scenery rather than on the singers. And with the increasing use of light, now capable of subtleties unimagined fifty years ago, the break with the romantic, realistic tradition of older generations seemed final.

Robert Wilson, the American stage designer, playwright, and director, in the years since *Einstein on the Beach* has carried this revolution further than most, and in the last decade has begun to design and direct operas by composers of previous centuries. But as yet without the success he has achieved in his own works or in close collaboration with contemporary composers. At the Metropolitan in 1998, for example, he designed and directed a production of Wagner's *Lohengrin,* and in it, as usual, he presented a stark stage, with characters in slow motion, and much of the action portrayed in the lighting. During curtain calls after the premiere, though many applauded, he was also booed. Yet all seemed to agree the lighting was beautiful and often aptly symbolic. Then why the booing?

The trouble perhaps lay in some persons' resentment of Wilson's forcing on them his interpretation of the opera rather than allowing them time and freedom to form their own. Wagner, for example, starts the opera with a Prelude, to be played with the curtain closed, and which in its divided strings is soft, mystical, and thought-provoking. Depending on the listener, the thought may be a vision of the Grail, or perhaps of something more individual. Wagner doesn't insist; he lets the music sound, and leaves the listener to his or her response.

Wilson, with a strong stage picture, curtailed that freedom. He raised the curtain during the Prelude, revealing a backstage curtain suffused with blue light, on which a shimmering band of white light moved slowly upward, and before the Prelude was over he had begun to bring on characters. By grabbing the audience's eye he imposed on listeners *his* thought during the Prelude while preventing them from forming thier own. Or consider a non-Wilsonian example from a production of Britten's *Turn of the Screw,* at the New York City Opera in 1997. The opera concerns a Victorian household in which some vague evil soon seems afoot, and a part of the opera's fascination lies in the listener's gradual perception that the Governess telling the story, may be either imagining the evil or herself, in some way, responsible for it.

Both Britten and Henry James, on whose story the opera is based, intended that idea to occur to each listener or reader in his or her own time. But in the City Opera setting, the Governess in her first scene was so racked by physical tics she already appeared psychotic, and when she arrived at the house, its floor was raked, its walls tilted, its window askew, nothing normal. The powerful visual scenes wiped away all ambiguity.

At the time of *Einstein* Wilson had said he aimed to have his audiences "hear the picture." What may have distressed many at his *Lohengrin* was a feeling of being forced to "see the music." In a vision not theirs. But music, they might argue, is to be heard, not seen, and one of its chief glories is that each individual may hear it in his own way.

The turns opera will take in the new century cannot be forecast. They probably depend on the arrival of some strong composer, who produces a large body of work that can play to full houses around the world. This much, however, seems likely. That composer will use electronic instruments not just for special effects, but to reduce the size of the orchestra and the cost of productions, and he or she will make the sound of a traditional opera orchestra seem old-fashioned. That composer must succeed in luring large audiences into thousands of local opera houses; there is no health in composing just for the few critics and the very rich. Further, if opera is to be true to itself, emphasizing through the human voice human conditions and problems, and not become something quite different, such as a stage or television spectacular, or a light show, or something not yet imagined, it must stress music and the silent, individual act of listening over allied arts such as ballet, which is watching movement, and special effects combined with scenery, which is watching spectacle. What seems likely? Will opera, in something like its traditional form, survive?

Surely. For to quote its most distinguished critic in this last quarter century, Andrew Porter.

"Once opera had been invented, there was no stopping it. It changed musical history. It changed the appearance of our cities, in some of which the opera house is a more prominent monument than the cathedral. For nearly four centuries, it has claimed the chief attention of most composers and has swallowed up huge sums of private and public money." (*Musical Events, A Chronicle, 1980-1983,* 440).

There is no stopping it because humanity has an insatiable curiosity about itself, an irrepressible desire to imagine itself in this situation or that, and in the presence of others to weep, to laugh, to commiserate over the human condition. No doubt, too, opera will continue to swallow money, for that strand seems never to break. Meanwhile, the clarity of the nineteenth century, when opera was defined by country and culture, French opera, Italian, or German, has transformed into a period of doubt and confusion, in which old definitions have blurred while new ones are not yet certain. Yet that, too, has its reward, for the diversity of competing styles today, in music, staging, and instrumental sound, is extraordinary. From Scott Joplin's ragtime *Treemonisha* to Puccini's exotic *Turandot,* from Zimmermann's expressionistic *die Soldaten* to Glass's abstract *Einstein on the Beach,* there are styles and works for every taste.

PART TWO

Synopses

A musical experience needs three human beings at least. It requires a composer, a performer, and a listener; and unless these three take part together there is no musical experience. . . . Music demands more from a listener than simply the possession of a tape-machine or a transistor radio. It demands some preparation, some effort, a journey to a special place, saving up for a ticket, some homework on the programme perhaps, some clarification of the ears and sharpening of the instincts. It demands as much effort on the listener's part as the other two corners of the triangle, this holy triangle of composer, performer and listener.

BENJAMIN BRITTEN
On Receiving the First Aspen Award
July 31, 1964—Aspen, Colorado

SYNOPSES

The operas are listed by composer, in order of birth date, and thereunder by the year of premier. Details of premieres, librettists and sources are presented at the start of each synopsis.

JEJÍ PASTORKYŇA

(Her Step-daughter)

or

JENŮFA

Opera in three acts. World premiere, Brno, January 21, 1904 (but it remained almost unknown until its prem. in Prague, May 26, 1916); American prem. (in German), Metropolitan, New York, Dec. 6, 1924; British prem. (in English), Covent Garden, London, Dec. 10, 1956. Music and text by Leoš Janáček, based on the play *Její Pastorkyňa* (later rewritten as a novel) by Gabriela Preissová first produced at Brno in February 1892.

PRINCIPAL CHARACTERS

Grandmother Buryja, housekeeper in the mill	contralto	
Števa Buryja, her grandson by her first son and owner of the mill	tenor	shtay.vah
Laca Klemeň, her step-grandson and Števa's older half-brother	tenor	lah.tsah
Jenůfa, her granddaughter by her second son and the step-daughter of	soprano	yen.OOF.ah
Kostelnička, the second wife and widow of Grandmother Buryja's second son	soprano	kos.tell.nish.kah

The action takes place during the late nineteenth century in eastern Moravia (central Czechoslovakia; chief city Brno). Janáček intended the singers to be costumed in Moravian folk dress.

The family relationships, by blood and personality, are important. The dominant member by position and education is not the grandmother but Kostelnička, the widow of the grandmother's younger son and the only member of the middle generation to survive.

The grandmother's elder son married a widow who already had a child, Laca Klemeň, who consequently is not related by blood to the Buryja family. This elder son and his wife had a child, Števa, who on his parents' death inherited the family property. He is young, irresponsible and inclined to drink; his house is managed for him by his grandmother, and the mill and farm by a foreman. His elder half-brother, Laca, was also raised by the grandmother, but Laca's place in her affections and in the family is equivocal.

The grandmother's younger son married and had a daughter, Jenůfa. Then on his wife's death he married Kostelnička, who as the widow of the verger of the town church was a highly respected member of the community. In addition Kostelnička has, in the grandmother's words, "a man's head." Between them the two women raised Jenůfa, and Kostelnička is devoted to her step-daughter.

Jenůfa, as the opera begins, is in love with Števa and three months pregnant with his child. No one but Števa knows of her condition, and she hopes, if only he is not taken into the army, that he will marry her promptly. Števa has half-promised, but his eye wanders to other girls. Laca is deeply in love with Jenůfa and wracked by jealousy.

Janáček composed an overture for the opera but decided instead on the present forty-two-bar introduction. The overture, "Žárlivost" or "Jealousy" (5 min.), is played sometimes at concerts.

ACT I (40 min.)

The farmhouse and mill. Late afternoon. Jenůfa, holding a pot of rosemary, stands near the stream gazing up the path toward town; the grandmother sits on the porch peeling potatoes, and Laca, on a tree trunk, whittling. The music begins with the mill wheel turning, turning (xylophone) while they wait to learn whether Števa has been conscripted or excused from army service.

Jenůfa. Evening comes, and Števa has not yet returned. Fearful, she

prayer prays to the Virgin, "O Panno Maria." If Števa is conscripted and the wedding prevented, she will die of shame. "O Panno Maria" have mercy.

Laca. When the grandmother complains that Jenůfa is not helping her who is old and losing her sight, Laca replies ironically: There's much you can no longer see. These days you mistake me for a hired hand. But then, he adds bitterly, you always did prefer Števa, your own blood, though our mother's death left me as much an orphan.

Jenůfa. From the stream where she is watering the rosemary she scolds him for his tone. How can Grandmother love him when he is so disrespectful? And she promises her grandmother, "Staŕenko," to help with the chores. It is only that her rosemary, "rozmaryju," was drooping, and as folk say, if the rosemary dies all the luck in the world dies with it.

Shepherd Boy (soprano). Running out of the mill he exclaims that he has done it: he has deciphered what Jenůfa has written. He has learned to read! He wants more to read! Later, she promises. Now she must help Grandmother, "Staŕenka," who comments that Jenufa has the brains of a teacher. Sadly Jenůfa replies, thinking of Števa, that she lost her brains somewhere about the mill.

The Foreman (baritone). Admiring Laca's whittling, he undertakes to sharpen the knife. (Because Laca, the leading male role, is generally sung by a middle-aged tenor, his youth is often obscured, but he is addressed by the Foreman as "youngster.") (As the Foreman starts to work the knife against the oilstone, the xylophone, in the same phrase that began the opera, sounds alone. It is not clear what Janáček meant by this association of the mill wheel and the knife: merely continuous, repeated motion or, because the phrase recurs at a crisis in the story, something more profound.)

Jenůfa, Laca and the Foreman. While the Foreman whets the knife, Laca tweaks Jenůfa's scarf, saying, when she glowers at him, that she would like it if Števa had done it. But Jenůfa tells him to mind his business and goes to help Grandmother with the potatoes.

The Foreman admires her, whispering to Laca that her eyes could make a man lose his head—as Laca well knows.

Me (Já) never! says Laca, adding that he put worms in the flowerpot to make the rosemary, "rozmaryju," wither. The Foreman disbelieves him: Laca is not so mean as he makes out and his color changes whenever he meets Jenůfa.

Laca hotly denies the implication but betrays himself by remarking too eagerly that if Števa is conscripted then the marriage is off. But, says the Foreman, Števa was *not* taken, "neodvedli." The postman has brought the news: nine were taken but not Števa. "Neodvedli," he repeats.

Jenůfa, the grandmother and Laca all exclaim, "Neodvedli," and Kostelnička, entering, is told the news. All go into the house except Jenůfa and Laca.

Števa, Conscripts, Musicians and Townspeople. In the distance they
song   sing: the one with money can stay home, the one without

must go. At their head Števa enters, drunk. When Jenůfa softly reproves him, he snorts, "Já, já, napilý?" (Me, me drunk?) "To ty mně?" (You say that to me?). He owns a mill and a farm, and all the girls **song and** smile at him. He tells the fiddlers to play Jenůfa's fa-**dance** vorite song, "It's a long way to Nove Zamky," and between verses the people dance. As the music grows wilder, Števa tries to dance with Jenůfa but is too drunk.

Kostelnička. She orders the fiddlers to stop. Intending all to hear she tells Jenůfa that she will not consent to a marriage with Števa until he has remained sober for a year. The crowd, except for Laca, murmurs that she is too harsh but disperses as she goes off.

The Grandmother, Foreman, Laca and Townspeople. All young couples, **ensemble** they sing, must endure troubles, "svoje trápeni přestat." As all but Jenůfa and Števa depart, the xylophone rattles.

Jenůfa and Števa. She says, in a low voice, that she can understand his celebrating but still, in their position, it would be better not to cross Kostelnička. With increasing urgency she insists that they must marry at once, or "I don't know (nevím) what I might do"—"Nevím, nevím."

Števa complains that Kostelnička is always underrating him. Look how all the girls run after him.

But he should have eyes only for her, says Jenůfa, and in growing irritation she seizes his shoulder. "My God," she cries, "what a ridiculous weakling (takový směšný)." Don't worry, says Števa: of them all you have the prettiest cheeks.

Grandmother calls him into the house, and Jenůfa is left alone. As Laca enters from the other side, the xylophone sounds.

Jenůfa and Laca. He laughs at how quickly Števa was deflated by Kostelnička and offers Jenůfa a discarded flower given to Števa by one of his adoring girls. Jenůfa snatches it, insisting "I can take pride in it (mohu, mohu se pýšit)," and Laca retorts that Števa cares only for her pretty cheeks. To himself, looking at his knife, he murmurs, "This knife could make them even prettier" (xylophone).

A housemaid comes out just in time to see Laca attempt to kiss Jenůfa. When she resists him, he cuts her cheek.

At her cry the Grandmother and Foreman rush out. While Laca hysterically embraces Jenůfa, "I have loved you (Já tá lúbil) since we were children," the maid describes "the accident." Jenůfa, fainting, is led into the house, and as Laca runs off, the Foreman shouts after him: "You did it on purpose, on purpose (naschvál!)."

Vocabulary, Act I

O Panno Maria	oh pahn.no mah.REE.ah	Oh, Virgin Mary
stařenko,-a	stah.RHEN.koh,-ah	old woman (with affection)
rozmaryju	roz.mah.ree.you	rosemary
Já	yah	me
neodvedli	neh.odd.vehd.lee	not taken
Já, já, napilý?	. . . nah.peel.ee	me, me drunk?
to ty mně?	toh tee me.nyay	you say that to me?
svoje trápeni přestat	svoy.yeh TRAH.pen.ny pres.stat	to stop his worries (of love)
nevím	neh.VIM	I don't know
takový směšný	TAH.koh.vee smesh.nee	ridiculous weakling
mohu, mohu se pýšit	mo.hoo . . . say pee.shit	I can be proud (of it)
Já tá lúbil	. . . tah LOO.beel	I have loved you
naschvál	NAHSH.vahl	on purpose

ACT II (48 min.)

Six months later. Main room of Kostelnička's house. Jenůfa, pale, with an ugly scar on her cheek, is sewing. Her week-old baby is in the adjoining room where for more than five months Kostelnička kept Jenůfa concealed, telling everyone that she was visiting a relative in Vienna.

Kostelnička and Jenůfa. Questioned by her step-mother, Jenůfa confesses that she is unhappy. Kostelnička, too, has found no peace. She is filled with shame at Jenůfa's predicament and anger at Števa, who has never come to ask about Jenůfa or their child.

Jenůfa, thinking the baby has stirred, runs to the bedroom door (viola and clarinet sound a soft melody associated with her love for her child). Kostelnička protests that Jenůfa instead of fussing over the baby should pray for release from it. "A ne" (ah, no), murmurs Jenůfa; he is no trouble; he never cries. He whimpers all the time, Kostelnička snaps. Jenůfa, weak and tired, in order to sleep better takes a hot drink (drugged by Kostelnička) and retires: "Dobrou noc, mamičko" (good night, dear mother).

Kostelnička. Alone, she rants at Števa and the baby. How she prayed for it to die! But it has lived a week, and now she must humble herself and give Jenůfa to Števa. She has summoned him, and he is at the door.

Kostelnička and Števa. He is hesitant, and she, reproachful. He often had thought, he says, of asking about Jenůfa and the child but was afraid of Kostelnička. And, after Jenůfa lost her looks, "I just couldn't" (nemohl).

Kostelnička opens the door to the bedroom explaining that Jenůfa has been hidden there for the past five months, and she invites Števa to look on his son. But he won't enter. He will support them, but secretly.

She urges him to go in. He caused Jenůfa's disgrace: he must marry her. When he does not move, she kneels before him, pleading. When he covers his face, she asks softly, "You cry?" (Ty pláčes?). Rising, she takes him by the hand: "Come to them, Števa." But he pulls away.

He will not marry Jenůfa. He is afraid of her. She used to be gay and lovely but after the accident she became more and more like her stepmother, violent and moody. He is afraid of them both, and anyway, he is engaged to marry the Mayor's daughter, Karolka.

"Števa!" bursts out Kostelnička, and in the bedroom Jenůfa cries out in her sleep that a stone is falling on her.

As Kostelnička at the bedroom door reports that Jenůfa is still asleep, Števa lets himself out the front.

Kostelnička. At first indignant and then furious that Števa refused even to look at his child, his own flesh and blood, she rages that she would like to kill "the little worm" and throw its corpse at Števa's feet. But the front door opens. It is Laca, and she tries to compose herself.

Kostelnička and Laca. He saw Števa leaving and thought perhaps there was news of Jenůfa. Has she returned? She has. Will she now marry Števa? No. Laca's heart leaps. Will you give her to me who will never give her up? Never, never!

Laca, you must know everything, says Kostelnička, and swiftly she tells him of Jenůfa's confinement and the birth of the child. Laca is incredulous and then grim. To have Jenůfa will he have to take Števa's child? His face and tone indicate he will not.

Kostelnička pacing the room buries her face in her hands till, finally, in great agitation she says, the child has died, "Zemřel."

Laca asks if Števa knows, and Kostelnička nods, cursing Števa. Then to be rid of Laca, she sends him to ask the date of Števa's wedding. He goes, promising to be "back soon" (co chvíla).

Kostelnička. "Co chvíla . . . co chvíla," she mutters, and in the meantime she must live through an eternity. Perhaps she could take the baby somewhere. No. It is the obstacle to a decent life for Jenůfa. Putting on a shawl, she declares excitedly: "I will give the boy to God. Until spring, when the ice melts, all trace of him will disappear. Innocent, he will be received in Heaven."

Then in the greatest excitement, losing her mental balance, she has a **vision** vision that she interprets to be what will happen if the child is allowed to live (though in fact it is prophetic of what happens when the child is discovered dead): "They will come and attack us, Jenůfa and me, saying, look at her, look at her (vidíte ji), Kostelnička" (high C flats). She enters the bedroom, picks up the child and leaves the house.

(In the first half of this act, the heart of the opera, Kostelnička has dialogues with Jenůfa, Števa and Laca that are followed by soliloquies of increasing agitation. A test of performance is whether the conductor and singer can make of these a crescendo of emotional intensity rather than merely a repetition.)

Jenůfa. She enters, half-dazed with sleep. (Her scene, in contrast to the heavy orchestration that has gone before, is punctuated by a solo violin.) She calls to her mother, "mamičko," and is frightened to discover herself alone and the baby missing. Growing distracted, she imagines the townspeople attacking the baby and exposing him to the cold. With a scream she runs to the front door and discovers that Kostelnička has locked it. Then, thinking that Kostelnička perhaps is showing the baby to Števa, she becomes more calm and, kneeling beside an icon, **prayer** prays that the Virgin, "Panno Maria," will watch over the child. As she finishes, there is a knock at the window. It is Kostelnička, whose hands are too cold and trembling to manage the key. Jenůfa opens the door.

Kostelnička and Jenůfa. To Jenůfa's excited questions about the baby, Kostelnička tells her that she has been sick, delirious for two days, and in that time the child died, "umřel." Jenůfa, falling to her knees, buries her head in her mother's lap. "So he died (tož umřel)," she repeats brokenly. Without him her heart will break. Rather, says Kostelnička, thank God for your freedom, "svobodná!"

And Števa? asks Jenůfa. He must be told. He is fit only for curses, says Kostelnička. He offered only money, not marriage, and plans to wed the Mayor's daughter. Pay heed instead to Laca who knows all and has forgiven you.

Kostelnička, Jenůfa and Laca. Entering, Laca reports that no one was at the Mayor's house. Seeing Jenůfa he offers his hand, saying that in time she will be well again. Life, she remarks quietly, has not turned out as she had hoped. He asks her to marry him, and Kostelnička bursts in "She will, Laco, she will" (Laco, půjde). Jenůfa, however, suggests that she is no longer much of a catch. Laca embraces her, kissing her cheek and murmuring that he wants her. Jenůfa softly assents, and Kostelnička gives her blessing though it ends as a curse of Števa.

The wind pulls open the window, and Kostelnička, though no one else, hears a cry. She shrieks, and begs Laca to hold her. Jenůfa closes the window. Kostelnička gasps that it seems as though "Death were peering in."

Vocabulary, Act II

A ne	ah.neh	ah, no
dobrou noc, mamičko	doe.broh nots mah.mich.ko	good night, dear mother
nemohl	neh.moh.hl	I just couldn't
ty pláčes	tee plah.chesh	you are crying
zemřel	zem.zhel	died
co chvíla	tso 'hveel.ah	presently
vidíte ji	vee.dee.teh yee	do you see her
Panno Maria	pahn.no mah.REE.ah	Virgin Mary
umřel	oom.zhel	he died
tož umřel	tosh oom.shjel	so he died
svobodná	'svoh.boh.d'nah	(you are) free
Laco, půjde	lah.tsoh POO.ee'deh	Laco, she will go (to the altar)

ACT III (31 min.)

Two months later. Kostelnička's house, the room modestly decorated for a wedding. On a dining table covered with a white cloth is a pot of rosemary, and at each place are sprigs of rosemary tied with white ribbon. Laca and Grandmother watch a shepherdess help Jenůfa with her head scarf while Kostelnička, looking tired and ill, paces the room.

The Shepherdess, Jenůfa, Kostelnička and others. Jenůfa, though she denies it, seems sad, and the Shepherdess attempts to cheer her. A knock on the door startles Kostelnička, but it is only the Mayor and his wife. Given a drink he toasts Kostelnička, hoping she soon will be free of worry and restored to health.

Kostelnička starts bravely in response: "I am giving Jenůfa to a good man and have no cause to worry. Yet," she concludes, "I feel I am dying, dying (hynu, hynu)." Putting her hand to her head she sighs, "Sleep (spánek) no longer rests me." Ignoring Jenůfa's efforts to calm her, she says that she does not wish to get well. Long life would be a horror, "byl by hrůzou," and (sudden solo violin) after life, what then? "A jak tam?" Then, recollecting the guests, she adds, "Today is your wedding, Jenůfa. I rejoice."

The Mayor's wife, making conversation, comments on the simplicity of Jenůfa's dress: no ribbons, no flowers. "I wouldn't go to the altar without them. I wouldn't, I wouldn't (nešla). Kostelnička leads the guests into the bedroom to see the trousseau.

Laca and Jenůfa. (Dialogue introduced and dominated by cellos and solo bassoon.) He offers her some flowers, and she pins them on her dress, sighing that he deserved a better bride. He brushes aside as already forgiven all faults on her side, whereas on his, he has his whole life, "celý svůj život," to repair the harm he did her. And on her urging he even was able to overcome his jealousy and invite Števa to the wedding, and he could do it only because she was with him, "že tys se mnou." Now Števa will bring Karolka to our wedding, to our wedding, "na naši svatbu." Here they are now. (The first of two dialogues in this act between Laca and Jenůfa. Here it is still only Laca who loves.)

Karolka, Števa, Jenůfa and others. Karolka bubbles with happiness, wishing Jenůfa well, looking forward to her own wedding and teasing Števa. When she suggests that she might postpone their wedding, Števa replies, more seriously than expected, that then he would have to kill himself. Sadly Jenůfa congratulates him on finding his true love, hoping that it will never cause him grief.

Kostelnička and the guests return from admiring the trousseau, and **wedding song**   some girls enter to sing a wedding song. At its end Laca and Jenůfa kneel before Grandmother to receive her blessing (delivered against a repeated descending chromatic scale), and then kneel before Kostelnička.

Discovery of the child. As Kostelnička raises her hands, there is a cry outside. Voices call, and Jano, the cowhand, runs in with news that a dead baby has been found under the ice. All but Števa, Kostelnička and Grandmother run out. Desperately Kostelnička calls to Jenůfa not to leave her, but outside Jenůfa can be heard claiming the baby.

Laca pulls her in, urging her to be quiet, and the Mayor and the crowd pour in after them. As Jenůfa, almost in hysterics, identifies the baby's hat and embroidered blanket, the crowd begins to murmur of stoning her for murdering her child. Laca puts Jenůfa behind him and warns that he will kill to protect her.

In the moment of silence that follows Kostelnička comes forward. "I am still here" (ještě jsem tu já!), and kneeling she confesses the crime, how she did it and why. Everyone is aghast, and Jenůfa responds to her step-mother's gesture of appeal with "Don't touch me." "Jenůfa is innocent," repeats Kostelnička. "Stone me. Judge me."

Karolka, clutching her mother, abandons Števa, who stands isolated. The Shepherdess, remarking that no girl will take him now, leads Grandmother off, while Laca blames himself for initiating the tragedy by deliberately making Jenůfa unattractive to Števa.

Jenůfa helps Kostelnička to her feet. "You will have pain and humiliation enough."

"Why do you help me?" asks Kostelnička. "Do you realize the police will take me away?" And as she thinks of the humiliations of the trial, she screams and starts for the bedroom. Then stopping (the implication is that she rejects suicide), she says, "I must not! They would hold you responsible, Jenůfa."

"Now I understand," cries Jenůfa to the crowd. "The Savior will yet turn His face to her." Kostelnička, saying "Now I realize I loved myself more than you," asks Jenůfa to forgive her. And Jenůfa twice repeats, "God be with you (Panbůh vás potěš)." Sustained by Jenůfa's moral strength, Kostelnička tells the Mayor, "Take me away."

Laca and Jenůfa. She urges him to go. He is the best man she has known, and she long ago forgave him for disfiguring her. He sinned from love, as she did. "You are entering a new life," he says. "Won't you take me with you?" But the trial will lead to more scorn and suffering. "For your sake," he says, "I can bear that. What do we care for the world if we have each other?"

Suddenly the love which has been growing in her heart suffuses her and, convinced at last, she cries: "Oh, Laca, come! Love led me to you, that great love on which God smiles!" (The dialogue's success, which seems never to fail, surely is in the music. As theatre, lacking music and following the tremendous scene of Kostelnička's confession, it would require superlative acting to save it from anticlimax. Within the music the secret of success seems to lie in the aptness to the situation of the clarity and throb of the harps after the noise of Kostelnička's exit and the long-held, swelling phrase for the violins.)

Vocabulary, Act III

hynu, hynu	he.noo he.noo	I am dying, dying
spánek	spah.nek	sleep
byl by hrůzou	bill bee hrew.zow	would be a horror
a jak tam?	ah jahk tahm	and what then?
nešla	nesh.lah	I wouldn't go
celý svůj život	tsell.eee svoy zhee.vot	all my life
že tys se mnou	zhe tes seh mnow	you are with me
na naši svatbu	nah nah.shee svaht.boo	to our wedding
ještě jsem tu já	yesh.teh 'eesem too jah	I am still here
Pánbůh vás potěš	pahn.boo vahs po.t'yesh	God be with you

VÝLETY PÁNĚ BROUČKOVY

(The Excursions of Mr. Brouček)

Opera in two parts. World premiere, National Theatre, Prague, April 23, 1920; British radio prem., BBC, March 1, 1970; stage premiere, Edinburgh Festival, Sept. 9 1970; American prem. (in Eng.), Bloomington, Nov. 21, 1981. Music by Leoš Janáček, text Part 1 by Viktor Dyk, Part 2 by F. S. Procházka, after two short novels by Svatopluk Čech: *The Excursion of Mr. Brouček to the Moon* (1887) and *A New Sensational Excursion of Mr. Brouček, this time back to the Fifteenth Century* (1888).

PRINCIPAL CHARACTERS

Prague 1888	*The Moon*	*Prague 1420*	
Mr. Matěj (Matthew) Brouček, householder			tenor
Mazal, a painter	Blankytný	Petřik	tenor
The Verger at St. Vitus Cathedral	Lunobor	Domšík	bass-baritone
Málinka, his daughter	Etherea	Kunka	soprano
Würfl, the innkeeper at the Vikárka	Čaroskvouci	A Town-Councillor	bass
Potboy at the Vikárka	Child-prodigy	The Student	soprano

The action starts on a summer night in Prague, 1888, and moves in Part 1 to the Moon and in Part 2 to Prague, 1420.

Despite the implication of seriousness and length—"opera in two parts"—the work runs only 117 minutes and is a satirical comedy. In his novels Svatopluk Čech, the creator of Mr. Brouček (Mr. "Beetle"), chiefly by contrast and exaggeration scolded the small shopkeepers and householders of his day for their antagonism toward art and lack of idealism in daily life and politics. Life was more than eating sausage, drinking beer, begetting children and making money.

Operas are seldom based on satirical novels, for in these the words are often more important than the situations or structure and, to an opera public accustomed to the works of Smetana, Verdi and Wagner, Janáček's choice of Čech's novels seemed ill-fated. The opera, however, has gradually worked its way into the Czech repertory, and in the 1960s it was increasingly produced abroad. But its progress outside of Czechoslovakia has been slow because in addition to good singing-actors and an imaginative production it needs a better-than-average translation.

In the transformation from novel to opera one curious and perhaps unexpected change took place. Both Čech and Janáček intended to satirize Brouček mercilessly, but in the opera his character is ambiguous; mixed with the bad is considerable good. Though often vulgar, abusive, drunken or cowardly, he is also at times realistic about himself and others, undeceived by cant or fad, and if unrewarding to others also undemanding. Apparently as Janáček worked on the score, he was overcome by his sympathy for humanity in whatever form and instead of a caricature created an intriguing, exasperating, typical human being.

The opera's two parts are well contrasted. In the first, on the Moon, the music is light and lyric, interspersed with dances, and with some short, beautiful orchestral passages as Prague sinks into night under a full moon. In this part though Brouček comes off badly, the artists fare even worse. In the second part, Prague during the Husite wars, the music is all chorales and clashing swords, and Brouček fails utterly to rise to the occasion. But even here the Husites are not perfect, inclining toward a fanaticism and religious bickering that Brouček, out of fear or laziness, avoids.

PART 1 (Excursion to the Moon—64 min.)

ACT I (32 min.)

There is a prelude (3 min.) in which a theme associated with Brouček, a walking, staccato figure first heard on the bassoon, mixes with another associated with the lovers, Mazal and Málinka. On stage, to the left is the Vikárka Inn (still exists), from which a long flight of stairs concealed by the castle wall mounts to Hradčany Castle, in back center. On the right, in shadow, is St. Vitus Cathedral and the Verger's house. Full moon, occasionally covered by clouds.

Málinka, the Verger's daughter, runs out of the inn closely followed by Mazal, and the lovers quarrel. To goad him she threatens to marry Mr. Brouček, to which Mazal replies with laughter and a kiss. Her father, emerging from his house at that moment, is indignant, but all three promptly are distracted by the sudden appearance at the inn's door of Mr. Brouček, householder and landlord, demanding that Mr. Würfl, the innkeeper, keep the streetlight up straight. "Ah," they exclaim, "Mr. Brouček in a rosy mood!"

He is now indignant, and harsh words are spoken, among them that Mazal must pay his back rent or be evicted and, more gaily in retort, that Mr. Brouček in his rosy mood should return to the moon from which he has fallen. To end the argument Mazal and the Verger retreat into the inn, and Brouček is left with Málinka. Playing on his gallantry and insisting with feigned tears that no one will marry her, she succeeds in extracting from him a promise of marriage, but her father, not Mazal, reemerges from the inn, and Brouček adds hastily, **chorus** "But only on the moon!" While artists inside the inn sing a chorus about love, he escapes up the street, followed later by the inn's potboy trying to return to him sausages he had left behind.

Mazal joins Málinka in the street, and the lovers are beginning to make up when Brouček reappears, his feet having led him in a circle. He is gazing at the moon, thinking aloud that moon-people must be happier without artists who fail in their rent, taxes, lawyers, thieves and bankrupts. His eyes and mind in the sky he stumbles, and his short fall seems to him an infinite flight. Distant voices call and, lying on the pavement, he dreams of the moon.

Following an orchestral interlude (40 sec.), a lunar landscape appears. To the rear, in place of Hradčany Castle, a castle on a fowl's leg. To the front, Brouček asleep. An artist flies in on Pegasus, alighting near Brouček. Hitching his ethereal steed to a flower stem he strikes his lyre. Brouček awakes: "Mazal, what clothes!"

"Touch not my corporeal casing," cries the artist. "You are a vulgar sack of flesh. I am a poet whose name resounds throughout the moon: Blankytný!"

Brouček, momentarily frightened, wonders if Mazal is mad: "Not to know his landlord! When I have a three-storey house. Without mortgage!" But soon he is merely bored as Blankytný sings ecstatically of his love for Etherea. An old man materializes, Lunobor, "resembling a bundle of white hair from which stretches a hand with a butterfly net." While Blankytný extols the purity of his love and Lunobor announces the arrival of Etherea, Brouček asks bluntly: how, if love is so pure on the moon, are children made? But his question is lost in the glory of Etherea's entrance.

Sounding very much like Málinka, she emerges from the castle in **waltz**   full song, surrounded by maidens. They advance on Brouček, who is ordered by Blankytný to kneel to Etherea. He refuses, and his bold words inflame her heart. To Blankytný's dismay she hurries Brouček to Pegasus and flies away with him as Lunobar, his head in a book, instructs him on how to behave on the moon.

ACT II (32 min.)

At the lunar Temple of Arts where Čaroskvouci presides, a splendid magician with a strong resemblance to the innkeeper Würfl.

Čaroskvouci explains that, lacking any talent and too kind-hearted to be a critic, he became a patron of the arts and inspires the creations of others. Artists on all sides are singing his praise when Pegasus arrives with Etherea and Brouček. Kneeling before Čaroskvouci, she begs protection for herself and her lover. "Lover!" gasps Brouček, and much to his relief Lunobor rushes in and catches Etherea in the butterfly net.

The artists, led by a child-prodigy "with an ever-playing piccolo at **Moon Anthem**   its lips," sing the Moon Anthem and prepare to eat, which on the Moon is done by smelling flowers. Etherea, having escaped, runs to sit by Brouček, fondling him passionately. He pushes her away—"You cobweb!"—and soon, as a poet starts on a long song, falls asleep. He is waked by the prodigy thrusting flowers beneath his

nose and loudly protests that his nose has had enough. Offended at the
Czech dance   blunt reference to the nasal member, the artists dance
away.

One, Duhoslav (Rainbowglory), seizes the opportunity to show
Brouček a painting, a huge structure with colors so strong that he can
climb upon them. He suggests that Brouček will want to gaze on it till
evening. Brouček, however, takes a sausage from his pocket and, concealing his face with a handkerchief, begins to eat. The artists, returning, are pleased that he should weep over art and then furious to
discover that he merely is eating. Worse still, instead of smelling flowers he is eating meat, and they accuse him of animal murder. Etherea
dance   even more than before is drawn to him and dances madly
about him. But Brouček in his exasperation breathes his sausage
breath directly on her, and she dissolves.

While the artists dance and sing, "Sláva, sláva" (glory), he escapes on
chorus   Pegasus and fog envelops the scene. When it lifts (2.5 min.)
the Vikárka Inn is again on stage right and the last carousers, artists,
are bidding Würfl good night, "Sláva." Mazal is walking Málinka to
her door, their quarrel reconciled, and the potboy runs in with the
news that Mr. Brouček is being carried home in the "truhle," a wicker
basket specially constructed for carrying drunkards.

PART 2 (Excursion to Prague, 1420—53 min.)

(Jan Hus, the Bohemian religious reformer, was burned at the stake
in 1415. He had gone to the Council of Constance with a safe conduct
pass issued by the Holy Roman Emperor Sigismund, who broke his
word and allowed Hus to be executed. Thereafter the followers of Hus
divided into the Ultraquists, based in Prague, and the more radical
Taborites, based in Tabor. When Sigismund invaded Bohemia in 1420,
the Hus factions joined forces under Jan Žižka and defeated the Emperor at the battle of Vitkov Hill, outside Prague, July 14, 1420.)

ACT I (20 min.)

After a prelude (2 min.) of vigorous, forthright music the curtain
opens on a dark stage. The voices of Brouček and his friends, as if
above, are heard discussing secret passages that once supposedly connected Hradčany Castle with the Old-Town across the river. Brouček
believes in them, but the others laugh and say good night.

In a moment Brouček is crying for help. (The stage is still dark, although sometimes the preceding conversation is played in a set denoting the Vikárka Inn.) He has fallen into some kind of a cellar. Help! (The stage lights sufficiently to show the treasure chamber of King Wenceslas IV, who preceded Sigismund as King of Bohemia and protected Hus.) A portrait of Wenceslas suddenly turns, and Brouček falls into the chamber. Calling and cursing, he concludes that he must be in one of the old secret passages. As he examines a large portrait of Queen Sophie, it swings aside revealing a distant view of Old-Town Square across the river. He starts down the tunnel.

The lights darken, and an apparition of "The Poet" (i.e., Svatopluk **Poet's monologue**   Čech) sings that Czech patriotism must once again become what it was in 1420. (This refers to the turmoil and bickering that attended the birth of the Czechoslovakian state at the end of World War I. Janáček dedicated the opera to Masaryk, the first president of the new state and "liberator of the Czech Nation." The scene, 4 min., is sometimes played as a Prologue to Part 2.)

Brouček emerges in Old-Town Square. It is early morning, July 14, 1420. Recognizing the buildings, he speculates that the people in costume are either theatrical "extras" or on the way to a masquerade. Rudely accosting one, he is soon in an argument. The man, a Town Councillor (Würfl), and the crowd that collects promptly decide that Brouček with his strange clothes and accent is a spy for Sigismund. Brouček insists that the year is 1888, not 1420, but the crowd grows menacing and he faints.

A burgher steps forward, Domšík (the Verger), and questions him. Brouček, to avoid another altercation, says that he has been in Turkey, forgotten much of the Czech tongue and so uses strange words. Behind **chorale**   him people with pikes and halberds enter the square. Singing a chorale they enter the Tyn Church to pray before the battle. Domšík offers shelter to Brouček because the Husites will need him as a soldier. From the church the chorale fills the square.

ACT II (33 min.)

Later that morning. In Domšík's house. Full sunlight floods an upper room. Brouček, on the edge of the bed, surveys the medieval furnishings.

"Well," he concludes, "if I didn't see it, I wouldn't believe it. But if I can go to the Moon, I can go to 1420. Still, no need to fight and maybe die. No"—and he calls loudly for breakfast.

Domšík enters with proper clothes, which Brouček reluctantly puts on. In the church the people solemnly repeat the chorale.

Domšík's daughter Kunka (Málinka) leads in townspeople, including Petřik (Mazal), who loves her. They welcome Brouček to Prague.

arietta   She recounts the sermon in the church, an exhortation to fight, and Domšík ends it with: "Beat and kill, and kill, without mercy." The men drink to it, though Brouček has to be urged.

Asked what foreigners think of Czechs, he replies that abroad they are not popular. But before he can explain, Domšík, the men and a young student (soprano) begin a wrangle about doctrine that almost comes to blows. Brouček, the peace-maker, says that inasmuch as Sigismund has not injured him, he will not fight. Domšík is incredulous, but the others are violent and seize Brouček.

Just then comes the call to arms, and the men rush out, forcing Brouček to accompany them. Kunka against her will is made to stay, and she and the housemaid intone the Lord's Prayer while the armed **chorale**   crowd in the square outside sing the chorale. As the people cry for all good Czechs to "Rise Up!" Brouček, stealing into the room, changes quickly into his own clothes. "Rise up! Rise up!" the people cry, and Kunka, seizing a weapon, rushes from the room. Brouček lights his cigar and sneaks out.

The scene changes without break to the Old-Town Square. The battle has been won, and the victorious Husites, led by Jan Žižka, parade to the church. Two Taborite soldiers discover Brouček cowering before Domšík's house. Questioned about his part in the battle, he is inventing a story to his credit when Petřik calls him a liar. The interrogation is interrupted, however, by Kunka, who has learned of her father's death in battle. Sadly she accepts it as a death well died. The cause was good, and "my father lives in heaven." Alone she enters his house.

Petřik, returning to Brouček, describes how the coward begged the first of the enemy he met to spare him, saying that he was neither a Praguer nor a Husite. The Town Councillor recommends a court martial, and the townspeople cry for Brouček's death. Desperately he pleads for mercy. He is not one of them. He is a son of the future, not yet born. But the people put him in a barrel, which they ignite, and the flames crackle and blaze.

A transparent curtain falls and the burning barrel slowly diminishes to the light of a candle in Würfl's hand as he stands outside the Vikárka Inn peering into darkness to find the source of a wailing voice. It is Brouček, in a garbage barrel but delighted to be home, home, once more at home. "Where were you?" asks Würfl. "I talked with Žižka," says Brouček, "and helped to liberate Prague—but don't tell anyone."

KÁŤA KABANOVÁ

Opera in three acts. World premiere, Brno, Oct. 23, 1921; British prem., London, April 10, 1951; American prem., Cleveland, Nov. 26, 1957. Music by Leoš Janáček; also the text, based on a Czech translation by Vincenc Červinka of Alexander Ostrovsky's play *Burya,* or *The Storm,* first performed, 1860.

PRINCIPAL CHARACTERS

Dikoj (Dikoy), a merchant	bass
Boris, his nephew	tenor
Marfa Kabanová (Kabanicha), a rich merchant's widow	contralto
Tichon (Tee.'hon), her son	tenor
Katěrina Kabanová (Katya), his wife	soprano
Varvara (Barbara), Kabanicha's foster-daughter	mezzo-soprano
Kudrjáš (Kudriash), a school-teacher	tenor

The action takes place about 1860 in the small town of Kalinov, on the Volga.

Ostrovsky's play presents a clash between generations in the merchant class with the conflict colored and finally resolved by Katya Kabanová's religiosity—which is very different in kind from that of her mother-in-law. Dikoy and Kabanicha are the older, more authoritarian generation; Barbara and her lover Kudriash, the younger. Caught between, unable to settle firmly into the mores of either, are Katya and Boris. He ultimately capitulates and allows his uncle to determine his fate; Katya, stronger but also perhaps more foolish, determines her own fate, which is death.

The opera both in text and music is very concise, requiring for its three acts (90 min.) a quarter-hour less than Strauss's one-act *Elektra.* Yet dramatically nothing of importance is skimped, and the swiftness contributes to the impact. Musically, the concision on first hearing makes the opera difficult to grasp. There are fewer repeated words than in *Jenůfa,* and though the events are as broadly drawn their underlying psychology is more delicately probed. Janáček here comes closer to his ideal of setting speech musically rather than composing arias or trios to marches or other recognizable forms.

OVERTURE (4 min.)

It sets the mood, using themes from the opera, of which the most prominent is a phrase on the tympani: four taps in triple time, 1-2-3-1, followed by four more, three and a half tones higher. The phrase recurs throughout the opera, chiefly at the close of Act I; during Act III, Scene 1 (Katya's confession); and at the opera's end.

ACT I (29 min.)

SCENE 1 (12 min.)

A public park overlooking the Volga. Wide view. Benches, shrubbery and to the right the Kabanov house. Afternoon sun.

Kudriash and Glasha, a servant of the Kabanovs. He sits gazing at the river. When Glasha steps out of the house, he exclaims, pointing to the Volga, "Zázrak!" (a wonder). Always new and different! Glasha is unimpressed, and when he talks of beauty, she says, "Just what you'd expect of a teacher."

In the distance they see Dikoy waving his arms and shouting at Boris. To avoid the family quarrel Glasha reenters the house and Kudriash retreats into the park.

Dikoy and Boris. Dikoy berates his nephew for wasting the day, ignoring Boris's protest that it is a holiday. Enjoying his own anger, he tells Boris to go to hell. At the door of the Kabanov house he asks Glasha for Mme Kabanová. Told that she is in the park, he spits derisively before Boris and goes in search of her.

Kudriash and Boris. Kudriash asks how Boris can put up with his uncle, and Boris explains that he must: his uncle controls his inheritance. As Boris laments a wasted youth, churchgoers appear in the park. One, Feklusha, is greeted by Glasha and enters the house, exclaiming how good and pious are the Kabanovs. (The play makes clearer than the opera that she enjoys a pensioner's status in the household because of her many pilgrimages.) Kudriash, overhearing her, comments that Kabanicha is a hypocrite, giving alms to beggars but driving her own folk crazy with her hatreds. Boris, still pitying himself, adds that to top his troubles he has fallen in love. "Who with?" asks Kudriash. "A married woman. Truly, am I not an idiot?" (Nejsem-li hlupák?), says Boris. With his eyes he indicates it is Katya who with the Kabanov family is returning from church. Kudriash warns him curtly, "Stay away from her, or you will ruin her," and he and Boris disappear behind the house.

The Kabanovs. Kabanicha is urging Tichon to leave for the market at Kazan at once, and though he agrees, she charges him with lack of respect. Marriage has changed his manner. When he protests, she cuts him short. Katya says calmly that both she and Tichon love Kabanicha, only to be told to hold her tongue. As Kabanicha expands on her grievance, Barbara sighs, "What a place for a sermon!"

When Kabanicha stops to draw breath, Katya interjects that there is no reason to speak to her like that. Her behavior in public and private has given no cause for offense. Proudly she enters the house.

Kabanicha rounds on Tichon, saying he is too soft with his wife, loves her too much. Suppose she had a lover? He should warn her against it, harshly. Tichon protests weakly, "Ale maminko! (But dear mother)." Angrily she calls him "Idiot! (Hlupáku)" and with a large sigh enters the house.

Tichon says to Barbara, "There you are! All because of Katya." But Barbara disagrees. Katya is persecuted by Kabanicha and by Tichon. When he gapes in surprise, she cries angrily, "I see in your eyes what you would like: to get drunk! (zpít se)." He slinks off, and Barbara at the doorway, turning to the empty park, says, "I feel sorry for her! Yes, sorry for her!"

SCENE 2 (17 min.)

Later that day. A room in the Kabanov house. Katya and Barbara are embroidering. (The first half of the scene is a kind of aria in which Katya with an occasional interjection by Barbara reveals herself to Barbara and the audience. The aria divides roughly into four parts of increasing intensity with the last very short and very intense.)

aria *Katya.* 1: Putting aside her sewing, she asks, "Guess what I'm thinking?" "What?" says Barbara. "Why is it people cannot fly?" Sometimes she imagines she is a bird, and she makes some birdlike gestures. "Nonsense," says Barbara.

2: Katya's mood grows more melancholic (oboe, followed by horn).

In her childhood she lived in freedom like the birds. She washed at an outdoor fountain, carried water indoors for the flowers—"We do that here," says Barbara—and there was church. She loved church. When the sun shone, when the shafts of light crossed the rising waves of incense, she sometimes saw angels and mixed her prayers with tears. And what dreams she dreamt! Of towering cathedrals, great forests and herself flying. . . .

"Katya," asks Barbara anxiously, "what's wrong with you?"

3: Catching Barbara's hand, Katya cries, "I am succumbing to sin." She confesses vague longings that overcome her during the day and shameful dreams at night. "What dreams?" asks Barbara, beginning to understand. "I cannot sleep (Nemohu spát)," Katya cries. A man hugs her with ardor, with passion, and. . . . "And?" asks Barbara. Ecstatically Katya cries, "And I go, and I go with him (A já jdu, a jdu za ním!)"

4: Suddenly sensible, she wonders if she should talk like this to Barbara, a maiden. "I'm worse than you," says Barbara. "Go on." She loves, Katya confesses, someone other than her husband. "Who knows?" says Barbara. "You may be able to meet him." "No, no, no (ne, ne, ne)," Katya screams. And at that moment Tichon enters dressed to go to Kazan.

Katya and Tichon. She violently embraces him, begging him to stay or take her with him. (Throughout this exchange she calls him Tíšo, a diminutive of Tichon.) He breaks from her embrace, saying that men need to get away from their wives. She weeps and embraces him again. If he goes, she fears that something dreadful will happen. She suggests that he ask her to swear to be faithful to him. He can see no reason for it, and when she falls to her knees mumbling the prescribed preamble of an oath, he lifts her up. From offstage Kabanicha calls, and for a moment they face each other in silence.

Kabanicha, Katya and Tichon. He is ready to go, but Kabanicha insists that in the traditional manner he instruct his wife how to behave in his absence. His protest is promptly overruled and he begins the litany: obey my mother, be kind in speech. . . . Katya throughout remains silent and the usual answer and response becomes Tichon's mild protests and Kabanicha's stern injunctions. Finally on his mother's insistence Tichon concludes, "Don't cast your eyes on young men." Katya, her shoulders slumping, moves to the door, and Kabanicha, disappearing, snaps, "Now you two may have a talk."

"Are you angry?" asks Tichon. "No," says Katya harshly. "Goodbye (sBohem)."

Kabanicha returns, orders the household to sit closely together for a moment (another Russian custom) and makes Tichon kneel to kiss her hand. And when Katya, though silent, emotionally embraces Tichon, Kabanicha calls her shameless. Tichon with a last word to Glasha, the servant, departs.

Vocabulary, Act I

zázrak	zahs.zrahk	a wonder
nejsem-li hlupák?	nay.sem.lee 'hloo.pahk	am I not an idiot?
ale maminko	ah.leh mah.mink.oh	but (dear) mommy
hlupáku!	'hloo.pahk.oo	idiot!
zpít se	zpit seh	to get drunk
nemohu spát	nehm.oh.hoo spaht	I cannot sleep
a já jdu, a jdu za ním	ah yah'ee doo . . . zah nim	and I go, and I go with him
ne, ne, ne	neh, neh, neh	no, no, no
Tíšo	tee.show	diminutive of Tikhon
sBohem	'sboh.em	goodbye (with God)

ACT II (29 min.)

(In the play—but only between acts in the opera—Katya tells Barbara that the man she loves is Boris. Barbara promptly proposes that with Tichon away she and Katya should sleep in the summer house in the garden. And then, who knows what may follow?)

SCENE 1 (11min.)

The evening of Tikhon's departure. A room in the Kabanov house. The women are sewing.

Katya, Kabanicha and Barbara. Kabanicha berates Katya for her silence. She should noisily lament Tichon's departure. Katya replies that she is not one for such a show. But it is the custom, insists Kabanicha, and if you truly loved your husband, you would follow it. And she goes to another room.

Barbara puts on a kerchief. Glasha, she says, will make the beds in the summer house. At the end of the garden behind the raspberries is a gate opening to the public park. Kabanicha keeps it locked, but Barbara has taken the key, substituting another for it. She will now go for a walk. If she sees Boris, she will tell him to come to the gate. Handing Katya the key, she refuses to listen to protests. "There is no time for talking." She departs.

Katya looks at the key. "There it is! My unlucky fate! (Vida! Neštětí)." Going to the window, she urges herself to "throw it away (Zahodit)." But hearing a noise, she pockets it. Offstage Kabanicha loudly tells someone to talk properly: "Don't shout!"

Katya cries excitedly, "No! No! No one! (ne, ne, nikdo)" has come to stop her, and she has kept the key. It is Fate. "I will see him, see Boris (uvidím, uvidím Borise!)." Taking a shawl, she goes out a back door.

Kabanicha and Dikoy. Carrying a lamp and some cookies, she leads him in. He has no special purpose, he says; in fact, he's a little tipsy. "Go home," she suggests. But he wants to talk. She alone in town can soothe him. His tone grows amorous, but she talks of money. As he approaches her on the sofa, he tells of how over money owed he one day cursed and almost beat a peasant—and then out of a sense of sin knelt to ask the man's pardon. He kneels before Kabanicha. She rejects him. "Sit down. Observe good moral precepts" (dobrých mravů). This is the second of four "love scenes"—Tichon and Katya have the first—deliberately contrasting the kind and depth of feeling each of the seven principal characters can sustain. Here in the older generation a crude eroticism arising chiefly out of self-pity is rebuffed by the emotional isolation resulting from overconcentration on money and manners.)

SCENE 2 (18 min.)

That night. A ravine overgrown with bushes; above it, the Kabanov's garden wall. From the ravine a path leads up to a gate in the wall.

song   *Kudriash.* Waiting for Barbara he sings a song (balalaika accompaniment).

Kudriash, Boris and Barbara. Boris arrives. He explains that a strange girl told him to come. Kudriash warns him against his love, a married woman! (vdané). "You're right (Ano)," Boris repeats. He has only seen her a few times, mostly at church, but how much he loves her! Barbara

song   appears singing a jolly song that Kudriash answers. Coming down the path she urges Boris to wait, then strolls off with Kudriash. Boris, moved by the summer night, the songs, and the young lovers, wonders what he will say. Katya appears.

Katya and Boris. She is frightened and urges him to leave. The sin of coming, of her love, lies on her soul like "a heavy stone" (jako kámen). Against his murmurings of love she urges her marriage: he must wish to ruin her. But then, she admits, she has no will; she has come; she cannot resist him. Embracing him passionately she sighs, "My life! (živote můj)." And he answers "Živote můj!" She talks of death as the only solution to her marriage: she cannot go on. He urges her not to talk or think of such things, and they embrace again.

Barbara and Kudriash. Returning, they send Boris and Katya for a stroll. They will call when it is time. Kudriash is unhappy at Katya's assignation and fearful that Kabanicha will awake and discover her absence. While Barbara recites her precautions, in the distance can be heard Katya and Boris: "Živote můj!" (In the summer night the two love scenes proceed simultaneously. The one in the distance rapturous, deeply felt and guilt-ridden; the one in the foreground prosaic, shallower and carefree.)

Barbara asks the hour. "One o'clock (jedna)," says Kudriash, and starts a sing-song of everybody "home" (domů). Boris answers, "I hear you" (slyšim).

Barbara and Kudriash start up the path singing a three-verse **song** with a syllabic refrain, "aj leli, leli, leli." As they reach the gate, Katya and Boris hurry in below. Katya starts up the path alone, Boris gazing after her. (Their feelings are expressed by three highly charged phrases in the orchestra followed by two forlorn arpeggios, bassoon and cello, ending in a sustained chord that wavers into the minor before settling in the major.)

Vocabulary, Act II

Vida! Neštěstí	vee.dah nesh.tesh.tee	Look! My unlucky fate
ne, ne, nikdo	neh . . . nik.doh	no, no, no one
uvidím . . . Borise	oo.vee.deem . . . Bor.ees.eh	I will see Boris
dobrých mravů	doh.bree mrah.voo	good moral precepts
vdané	vdah.nay	a married (woman)
ano	ah.no	yes (you're right)
jako kámen	yah.koh kah.men	a heavy stone
živote můj	shjee.voht.eh mooee	my life
jedna	yed.nah	one o'clock
domů	doh.moo	home
slyšim	slee.shim	I hear you
aj leli, leli	ay lay.lee . . .	(syllabic refrain)

(If the opera is performed in two rather than three acts, the break usually is made here.)

ACT III (28 min.)

(For ten nights Katya joined Boris, then Tichon returned home.)

SCENE 1 (8 min.)

Evening of the day of Tichon's return. An arcade of an abandoned building. Through its arches can be seen the public park and the Volga. The townspeople are promenading. Lowering sky. Rain. *Kudriash and Kuligin, his friend.* They take shelter from the rain, followed by others. Examining the arcade's walls, they see traces of frescoes depicting the hell-fires of Gehenna. Persons of every class are shown burning and about to burn.

Kudriash, Kuligin and Dikoy. The people bow to Dikoy when he enters. Despite his rudeness Kudriash and Kuligin try to explain to him the theory of lightning rods. The storm is electricity (elektřina). Dikoy angrily insists that storms are punishments sent by God. What kind of person would attempt to deflect God's punishment, a Tartar (Tatar)? When Kudriash quotes a scientist on the mind's ability to rule nature, Dikoy turns to the others present, saying wildly, "It's just you scoundrels who tempt a person to sin." Then, suddenly calm, he asks if the rain has stopped. "Seems so (zdá se)," says Kudriash. Imitating him contemptuously, Dikoy goes out followed by the others. For a moment the arcades are empty.

Barbara and Boris. Hiding behind a pillar she signals to Boris. What can they do about Katya? "What happened?" he asks. Tichon has returned, and she is acting strangely. Boris can think only that he will not see her again, but Barbara warns him that Katya seems crazy, wandering about the house, weeping and mumbling. At any moment she may blurt out everything. And Kabanicha suspects. Boris is frightened. Behind the arcade appears the Kabanov family. Boris slips off.

Katya, Barbara and others. Thunder. Katya runs in, seizing Barbara's hand. "It is my death!" she cries. Others, expecting rain, shelter in the arcade; some are drawn by Katya's odd behavior. Barbara and Kudriash try to calm her, but she sees Boris and grows more excited.

Dikoy, Kabanicha and Tichon enter. To keep them away from Katya, Barbara urges her to kneel and say a prayer. Dikoy and Kabanicha point and stare at Katya. Suddenly kneeling, she cries out to Kabanicha and Tichon that she has sinned. Ten nights, while he was away, she left the house to meet a man. While she sobs, Tichon tries to lift and embrace her, Barbara insists that her mind is wandering, and Kabanicha with Dikoy asks, "With whom? With whom? (S kým)." Amid thunder and lightning (over the tympani phrase) she cries out, "With Boris." Kabanicha sneers at Tichon, "This is what you get," and Katya, breaking from his embrace, runs out into the storm.

SCENE 2 (20 min.)

Later the same night. On the bank of the Volga. Very dim light. *Tichon and Glasha.* He searches the area, followed by Glasha with a lantern. His mother, he says, thinks Katya deserves to be burned alive, but he loves her too much to harm her. They hurry off as Glasha calls into the night, "Katerina."

Kudriash and Barbara. They run in, Barbara complaining bitterly of Kabanicha. But what can she do? "Run away (utéci)," says Kudriash. "Utéci?" Yes, to Moscow. With him. She agrees, and both exit quickly. In the distance Tichon and Glasha call "Katerina."

Katya. She enters slowly and alone, her thoughts on Boris. Softly, almost vaguely, she wonders if she will see him again. To take leave and perhaps to die. Her confession has brought her no peace. Offstage a man's voice trails off the end of a song.

She crouches to avoid discovery. Will she remember how he talked to her? No, for her nights are full of terror and darkness. She hears from offstage phrases of a wordless chorale (symbolizing the Volga) and grows frightened: it sounds like a burial. Dawn is always so welcome. A drunken man, passing, stares at her.

Traditionally, she murmurs, they killed women like her. But now they say, "Live, live! (Žij, žij)." Let your sin torment you. "Why? What for? (Nu, nu, nač)." She longs only for death, and whatever she sees or hears only hurts her heart. She points to it.

If only she could see Boris. In ecstasy she calls to the winds to carry her sadness to him. Going to the river bank she cries, "Živote můj!" How much I love you.

Boris and Katya. He enters, at first unaware of her. Then with one voice they cry, "So, I see you again! (přece Tě ještě vidím). They embrace, and she weeps. She meant him no harm by her confession. What will he do now? "Uncle has banished me to Siberia, to the house in Kiakhta." "Take me," she cries, but immediately adds, "No."

"What will you do?" he asks. Everyone scorns me, she says. Tichon is alternately kind and, when drunk, angry. She had something else, though, to say. "Time to go," says Boris.

She remembers. On his journey will he give alms to every beggar. (The wordless chorale of the Volga sounds.) "So, goodbye (Bud' sbohem!)," she says, and he departs sighing, "How difficult to part (jak těžko se loučím)." (The chorale sounds, more insistently.)

Katya goes to the river's bank. "Little birds," she says, "will light on the mound and flowers grow. Such beauty! (tak krásně). And I must die." Crossing her hands, she jumps.

Others. Shouts along the bank. Tichon rushes in, blaming Kabanicha for Katya's suicide. Kabanicha pulls him from the bank: Katya is not worth the danger.

Dikoy carries in the body and lays it down. Tichon drops beside it crying her name. Dikoy, moved, turns away. Kabanicha bows to the crowd, thanking the people for their help.

Vocabulary, Act III

elektřina	el.ek.tree.nah	electricity
Tatar	tah.tahr	a Tartar
zdá se	zhdah.seh	seems so
s kým	skeem	with whom?
utéci	oo.teh.tsee	run away
žij, žij	zjhee . . .	live, live
nu, nu, nač	noo . . . nahtch	why . . . what for?
živote můj	shjee.voht.eh mooee	my life
přece Tě jěstě	pret.seh 'teh yesh.teh	So, I see you again
vidím	vee.deem	
bud' sbohem	budh 'sboh.em	so, goodbye
jak těžko se	yak tesh.koh seh	how difficult to
loučím	low.cheem	part
tak krásně	tahk kras.n'yeh	such beauty

PŘÍHODY LIŠKY BYSTROUŠKY

(The Cunning Little Vixen)

Opera in three acts. World premiere, Brno, Nov. 6, 1924; British prem. (in English), London, March 22, 1961; American prem. (in Eng.), New York, May 7, 1964. Music by Leoš Janáček; also the text, based on a novelette by Rudolf Těsnohlídek, first published in serial form, with pictures, in the Brno newspaper, *Lidové Noviny,* during 1920.

PRINCIPAL CHARACTERS

Bystrouška, "Sharp-Ears," the vixen	soprano
A fox, her mate	soprano
(though sometimes sung by a tenor)	
A badger	bass
A dog	mezzo-soprano
The Forester	baritone
His wife	alto
The Schoolmaster	tenor
The Parson	bass
Harašta, a poacher	bass

No time or place is set for the action, which occurs in both a real and a fantasy world. Janáček presumably meant the setting to be contemporary in a timeless way. But for the literal-minded: in as much as the text is written in Líšeň (Brno) dialect, the setting is the Moravian countryside when life was still predominantly agricultural.

In its original form, a kind of early comic strip, the story of the vixen, "Sharp-Ears," was a series of animal pictures with captions in rather slangy verse. The episodes were short, only loosely connected and not very profound. Through the animals Těsnohlídek and the artist, Stanislav Lolek, poked fun at humans.

Janáček took the principal incidents, gave those involving the vixen a descriptive subtitle (see below) and connected them all with a narrative. But more important, he added a point of view about life, aging and death: roughly, man like the animals is part of nature and should accept his place in nature's cycle of youth, maturity, death and renewal. Though individuals may die, life renews itself in others.

The theme is similar to that of his next opera, *The Makropulos Affair,* but cast in a quite different mold. There it is worked out in an ingenious, complicated story filled with the apparatus of urban life: lawsuits, wills, exotic sex, opera singers and lots of talk, much of it witty. In contrast *The Cunning Little Vixen* is pastoral: simple, full of quiet moments, little talk and much choreographed movement. The music is more melodic, balanced and rhythmic—yet no less original. It is remarkable that Janáček within twenty-five months should have produced on a similar theme two operas so different.

In various ways the vixen's story illustrates Janáček's feelings about man and nature. The vixen clearly is symbolic of femaleness in its broadest sense: that is part of her fascination for the Forester. Because in nature passionate love is right in its season and wrong out of it, the vixen's love affair at her age is right; but the hankering after a young girl by two older men, the Forester and the Schoolmaster, only leads to unhappiness. Similarly with death. The Forester's anger and grief at the vixen's death—just to make a muff—is assuaged by the realization that her life is renewed in her cub.

The opera's staging presents difficulties: chiefly the relative size of the humans and animals. For example, in the first scene when the Forester is asleep in the wood, a frightened frog jumps onto his nose, and later the Forester picks up a baby vixen by the scruff of the neck—and both frog and vixen are singing roles. Few operas depend so much for their success on how such problems are solved.

But there must be nothing coy or sweet in the solutions. Neither dramatically nor musically did Janáček sentimentalize the story. He, not Těsnohlídek, introduced into it the vixen's untimely death, and at the end though the Forester is reconciled to death and nature's renewal in another generation, the music does not revert to its first, happiest state. Despite understanding and reconciliation, there is sadness in individual death, and that, too, is appropriate.

Within the acts there are no divisions between scenes: each flows into the next, connected often by a ballet or interlude. But to reveal better an act's structure, scenes are indicated and also timings for the longer ballets and interludes.

ACT I (29 min.)

SCENE 1 (The vixen is caught—14 min.)

In the forest. A hot summer afternoon. A badger, smoking a pipe, pokes his head from a hole. Gnats and midges, led by a blue dragonfly, **ballet** buzz about him (4 min.). (The insect and small-animal parts are played by children with thin, piping voices.) The Forester enters, perspiring, tired, and talks himself into a nap. He will tell his wife that he was chasing poachers. He sleeps.

The animals dance around him (1 1/2 min.) led by a grasshopper **waltz** with a barrel-organ. A frog tries to catch a mosquito who flies off angrily. A young vixen stares at the frog, asking her mother, who is not so close as she thinks, whether the frog would be good to eat. The frightened frog jumps, landing on the nose of the Forester, who wakes, seizes the vixen and, inspecting her triumphantly, decides to take her home.

After he leaves, the insect movement starts again (4 min.) The blue

ballet dragonfly circles about, searching in vain for the vixen; finally it gives up, settles and folds its wings.

SCENE 2 (The vixen in the yard of the Forester's house—6 min.)

A prelude (2 min.), alternately sad and restless (the vixen in captivity), covers the scene change. Autumn. Afternoon sun. To the right the Forester's house; to the left a kennel with the vixen and the Forester's dog before it.

The Forester and his wife come out with milk for the animals—she is appalled by the vixen's fleas—and reenter the house.

The vixen starts moaning and is scolded by the dog. What of *his* solitary life? *His* pangs in May when lovers court? And when to console himself he howls at the moon—he is beaten for it. What is love anyway? He never had it.

Neither, says the vixen, has she, but she has heard the starlings talk, and she repeats some of what she has heard. The dog, aroused, approaches her with dishonorable intent. She rebuffs him: "Shame on you, dog!" And he crawls onto the rubbish heap.

Pepík, the Forester's son, brings his friend Frantík to show him the vixen. They tease her until she bites Pepík. During the ensuing commotion—Pepík and his mother wailing; Frantík and the Forester chasing the vixen—she almost escapes, but is caught and tied to the kennel. The humans leave, the dog creeps into the kennel, and the vixen is alone in the yard.

INTERLUDE (4 min.)

vision Night falls, and from the vixen, asleep before the kennel, emerges a beautiful girl, the essence of the female. The vixen moans slightly, and with the coming of dawn the girl disappears into the vixen.

SCENE 3 (The vixen indulges in politics—3 min.)

In the Forester's yard the cock and hens mock the vixen. She cannot lay or hatch an egg. The complacent hens cluck; the cock struts. The vixen urges the hens to take command, to build a better world: "Sisters! Do without the cock!" Enraged, the cock warns that the vixen wants only to eat them. The hens scatter.

Announcing that such a male-dominated world is not for her, the vixen proposes to bury herself alive. She makes her preparations and lies as if dead during a tiny interlude.

SCENE 4 (The vixen escapes—2 min.)

The hens, curious, come closer. The vixen, leaping up, strangles the cock and several hens while the head-hen cackles the alarm.

The Forester and his wife rush out, she blaming him for all the trouble the vixen has caused. He starts to beat the vixen, but she bites through the rope, upsets him and escapes.

ACT II (40 min.)

SCENE 1 (The vixen expropriates the badger's hole—3 min.)

A prelude (1 min.) leads to the wood and the badger's hole. Late afternoon. The vixen admires the hole, and the badger tells her to move on. She cleverly turns the animals against him—he's rich, she's poor—and, when they are fully on her side, piddles on his doorstep. The badger angrily departs, and the vixen takes his hole.

SCENE 2 (7 min.)

An interlude (2 min.) covers the scene change to the inn, where in a back room the Forester and the Schoolmaster are playing cards. The **song** Parson enters, slightly drunk, and as a joke the Forester announces that the Schoolmaster is to be married. Then he improvises a song about the Schoolmaster's shyness with a lady, Verunka. The Parson keeps repeating a Latin tag: *Non des mulieri corpus tuum* (Do not give your body to women), and the Schoolmaster changes the subject to the Forester's vixen. The Forester describes with irritation her escape and soon, as first the Schoolmaster and then the Parson leave, is alone. He persuades himself to have another drink but when the innkeeper, making conversation, asks about the vixen, he angrily departs.

SCENE 3 (9 min.)

An interlude (1 min.) covers a scene change to a part of the wood. A path, bordered by a hedge, leads up a hill. Behind the hedge, but in view of the audience, is a tall sunflower in full bloom. Night. Moonlight.

The Schoolmaster, walking slowly and swaying from drink, is angry at himself. He stops and soliloquizes. He sees the sunflower move (the vixen for a joke is making it tremble and bow), and he imagines it to be Terynka, a beautiful and wanton girl he once desired—still desires. Impulsively he runs toward her, trips and falls behind the hedge, where he remains.

The Parson enters, trying to recall the source of another classical tag: Always remember to be a good man. But his thoughts run back to a girl. The vixen's eyes gleam from the bushes, and he remembers the girl's eyes. Though she went off with a butcher's boy, still he could never again look at a girl altogether innocently. But he is old now, and anyway the tag is from Xenophon's *Anabasis*.

Offstage, the Forester shouts at the vixen and shoots twice. The Parson and the Schoolmaster flee, leaving the stage to an angry and disappointed Forester.

SCENE 4 (The vixen is courted—16 min.)

An interlude (2 min.), with an offstage wordless chorus (in broad-**chorus**   ened form used to end the act), leads to the wood before the vixen's hole. It is a warm midsummer night bathed in moonlight. The vixen lies outstretched, her snout on her paws. The bushes rustle and amid their leaves appear the golden-brown eyes of a fox.

"Did I frighten you?" he asks, stepping gracefully forward. "No-o," she says, and soon is telling him about herself, exaggerating a bit here and there. He is tremendously impressed by her human upbringing and indignant at the treatment she received. Politely he takes his leave after requesting permission to call again.

Alone the vixen luxuriates in the feeling of being attractive to someone—and attracted.

The fox soon returns with a rabbit for breakfast. Their talk turns to **love duet**   love, and he embraces her. She pushes him away, but he protests that he loves her, truly, passionately. Doesn't she feel the same for him? He kisses her violently. "Don't you want me?" "Yes!" she sighs, and leads him into the hole.

SCENE 5 (The vixen is wed—5 min.)

A ballet (2 min.), led by the blue dragonfly, joins this to the previous **ballet**   scene. During it the light dims to sunset.

An owl screams into the wood, "Oh, what I've just seen! Our little vixen is as bad as any." Squirrels titter, and behind a tree stump a hedgehog puts out his tongue.

The vixen crawls from the hole, moaning. The fox is most solicitious, **ballet and chorale** and she whispers her condition to him. He proposes to find a parson at once. A woodpecker pronounces them married, and the animals of the wood start a wedding dance while "voices of the wood" resume in broadened, choral-like form the wordless chant with which the courtship began. (Thus, says Janáček musically, mating and children is the end to which passion leads.)

ACT III (34 min.)

SCENE 1 (8 min.)

After a prelude (2 min.) hinting at tragedy, the curtain rises on the edge of the forest. Autumn, midday and a clear sky. Harašta, a poultry dealer and frequent poacher, wanders uphill, his poultry basket empty. From afar he is spied by the Forester.

Harašta and the Forester. Harašta sings a three-verse song in which a **song** boy urges a girl to leave home and wander with him. The Forester hails Harašta and is put out to hear that he is about to marry Terynka, who plainly had attracted the Forester as well as the Schoolmaster. Severely the Forester warns Harašta against poaching. Harašta, pleading innocence, points to a dead hare, killed by a fox, and the Forester, speaking angrily of his escaped vixen, sets a trap. The men go off in different directions with Harašta laughing slyly.

SCENE 2 (The vixen tries to entrap the poacher—The vixen is killed—7 min.)

The vixen's cubs enter at once, singing a children's song (2 min.) and **song and ballet** skipping about until they see the hare. The vixen sniffs at it: "Funny thing"—the cubs echo her—and she quickly discovers the trap. "So obvious," she concludes. "What a fool!" And the cubs repeat, "What a fool!"

The fox, caressing her, asks how many cubs they have, and she doesn't know. Will we have more? he asks. Wait till next May, she says.

Behind the scene Harašta sings, and the foxes hide. The vixen waits to lead him away from her cubs. He sees her, puts down his basket now full of chickens, and takes out a poacher's gun. "A muff for Terynka," he says.

The vixen, pretending an injury, limps down the path. "So that's it," she says. "Beat and kill just because I am a fox." (The phrase "beat and kill," a wide jump down from a high note, underlies the music to the scene's end.) Harašta, trying to assemble his poacher's gun and keep her in sight, falls and scrapes his nose. Meanwhile the vixen has doubled back and with the fox and cubs is tearing at the poultry bag. Harašta fires at random, hits the vixen, and the others scatter. The **Requiem** vixen lies dying. The curtain falls, and Janáček gives her a tiny Requiem (in which, at the end, the wide jumps of "beat and kill" predominate).

INTERLUDE (4 min.)

SCENE 3 (6 min.)

At the inn. The garden near the bowling alley. It is unusually still. The Innkeeper's wife brings out beer.

The Forester, Schoolmaster and Inkeeper's wife. The Forester tells the Schoolmaster that the vixen's den is deserted and jokes him about courting girls among sunflowers. No more use for courting, sighs the Schoolmaster. Terynka is married today. "And with a new muff," interjects the Innkeeper's wife. The Forester is surprised by the tear in the Schoolmaster's eye, and the Schoolmaster, that the Forester doesn't connect the muff with the vixen. Then the Forester, suddenly understanding the pain of both, abruptly says that he must be off. Where to? The wood. He goes alone now. The dog is too old.

SCENE 4 (The vixen's cub, the living image of her mother—10 min.)

An interlude (2 min.) leads to the wood where the opera started. It has rained. The sun shines. The Forester climbs the hill.

The Forester. With affection he thinks of his wife. Years ago they had come here together, so in love that in their passion they had crushed the mushrooms. In the spring, when new life stirs, the woods are lovely.

He sits and falls asleep, smiling. The animals surround him. The Forester, dreaming, mutters that he cannot see the vixen. Her cub (played by a child) runs up to him. In his dream he sees her. How like her mother! He'll take her home and this time bring her up properly. He reaches out and instead of the vixen snares a little frog. Well, he asks, Where did you come from? The frog stammers: "T . . . t . . . t'isn't me. Tha . . . tha . . . that was my grandfather! He used to tell me b . . . b . . . bout you."

The Forester smiles again. His gun slips and falls to the ground. He dreams.

VĚC MAKROPULOS
(The Makropulos Affair)

Opera in three acts. World premiere, Brno, Dec. 18, 1926; British prem. (in English), London, Feb. 12, 1964; American prem. (in Eng.), San Francisco, Nov. 19, 1966. Music by Leoš Janáček; also text, based on Karel Čapek's play, *The Makropulos Affair,* first performed, 1923.

PRINCIPAL CHARACTERS

Emilia Marty, an opera singer	dramatic soprano
Albert Gregor, plaintiff in *Gregor v. Prus*	tenor
Dr. Kolenatý, his lawyer	bass-baritone
Vítek, Dr. Kolenatý's clerk	tenor
Krista, Vítek's daughter	mezzo-soprano
Jaroslav Prus, defendant in *Gregor v. Prus*	baritone
Janek, his son	tenor
Count Hauk-Šendorf, an ex-diplomat	operetta tenor

The action takes place in Prague, 1913

Čapek's play is a philosophic discussion of a person's need to grow old and die. Without death—he gives his leading character a chance at immortality—life becomes intolerable. The play, which he called a comedy, is ingeniously worked out, thoughtful, witty—and wordy. An unlikely subject, some might think, for an opera.

Janáček, however, was stirred by the predicament of the heroine, Emilia Marty, whose eternal youth failed to bring her happiness. And although he changed the play's text little, chiefly cutting some of the philosophic discussion, he changed its focus by concentrating on the heroine. In the play Emilia Marty is a concept; in the opera, because of the music, a human.

In both the play and the opera, the plot is uncovered slowly by hints, but because knowledge of the plot is needed to understand the overture, it is best revealed in advance.

Though the action of the opera takes place in Prague, 1913, many events crucial to it occurred earlier, the first in 1591 at the court of the Habsburg Emperor Rudolf II (1552–1612). The Emperor wished to preserve his youth, and his Greek physician Hieronymous Makropulos offered him a potion. Rudolf, fearing a trick, required Makropulos to test it on the physician's sixteen-year-old daughter Elina. She became ill, almost died, and the enraged Rudolf imprisoned the father. Elina recovered, however, and leaving the court took with her the potion's formula, a prescription written in Greek and guaranteeing 300 additional years of life. (The Czech word "věc" in the opera's title and text refers to this *document,* and the title would be translated better as *The Makropulos Document* or perhaps *Secret,* than *Affair* or *Case,* which have become traditional.)

Elina Makropulos aged normally until mature, and then aging stopped. To avoid suspicion as contemporaries died, she moved from country to country, changing her name but always retaining along with her beauty and exceptional voice the initials E.M. Thus at various times she has been known as Ekaterina Myskina, Elsa Müller, Ellian MacGregor, Eugenia Montez and, finally, Emilia Marty.

As Ellian MacGregor in 1806, however, she did something that dominates her life as Emilia Marty in 1913. In love as Ellian with a Bohemian Baron, Ferdinand Prus, she lent him the prescription, but he died without using or returning it. Now in 1913 her additional 300 years of life are passed, and unless she can recover the prescription from the Baron's heirs and drink another cup of the potion, she will die. The central strand of the opera around which all else twines is her pursuit of the document—to discover its whereabouts, to obtain it.

OVERTURE (5 min.)

Full of vigor, it suggests the color and excitement of Rudolf's court when Elina Makropulos was young and the court a European center of art and science. Frequent offstage fanfares (brass and tympani) represent the Emperor, and these recur in Act III when Emilia Marty insists to the disbelieving that she was born Elina Makropulos in 1575. At its end the overture trails swiftly into a long trill and the curtain rises. The next notes, cast in a short phrase of narrow compass and complaining tone, instantly proclaim that the rich violence of the Renaissance Court has been left for the desiccated atmosphere of a twentieth-century law office. The change is accomplished in a bar, the kind of swift, dramatic touch at which Janáček excels.

ACT I (34 min.)

Prague, 1913. Dr. Kolenatý's law office. His clerk Vítek is filing papers.

Vítek and later Gregor. Vítek looks for the file on *Gregor* v. *Prus,* "Causa Gregor Prus." It stretches back almost a hundred years, "Causa Gregor Prus." But nothing lasts forever, not even the nobility. Sitting on the library ladder, he quotes Danton against the nobility. Gregor, entering, mistakenly ascribes the speech to Marat, and Vítek has the pleasure of giving the correct citation: speaker and date.

Gregor is eager to know the decision in *Gregor* v. *Prus.* Vítek calls the courthouse, but no decision has been announced and Dr. Kolenatý is reported to have left for his office. Vítek regrets the end of such a long, distinguished case, but Gregor is ready either to win millions or to end his debts, if necessary, by suicide.

Krista, Vítek and Gregor. Vítek's daughter Krista enters: "Oh, father, Marty is fantastic!" "Who?" "Marty! Emilia Marty!" Krista, who studies singing, cannot imagine not knowing of Marty, the great opera singer. "Oh, she is so lovely!" How old? Gregor asks. No one knows, says Krista. But when Gregor says kindly that he would prefer to watch Krista than some old diva, Krista is indignant.

Dr. Kolenatý enters with Emilia Marty. (They evidently have just met and at her entrance, according to the score, "odd light flares." These surrealistic touches, discrete at first, increase throughout the opera. Also, here and later Marty is accompanied by a viola d'amore, an old-fashioned viola with a soft and mysterious tone.) Vítek and an excited Krista tiptoe out.

Kolenatý, Marty and Gregor. She has come, she says, to learn about the Gregor case. Gregor asks to be introduced, and she, without much interest, suggests that he stay.

Dr. Kolenatý recounts the case from its start. (During his recitation Marty constantly interrupts him with remarks suggesting personal knowledge of the people and facts, and Kolenatý, irritated, takes refuge in precise legal phraseology. But Gregor, seeing the possibility of new facts in his favor, is delighted with her. Much of the wit of their conversation is lost in the opera, even in translation, and for many persons this part is confusing and dull.)

The case turns on the missing will of Baron Ferdinand Prus—Marty calls him "Pepi"—who died in 1827. While alive he had made oral statements that his most valuable estate, Loukov, should pass to Ferdinand Gregor, a student in the Academy in Vienna. During the Baron's life the boy received all the estate's income and was referred to as its owner. Further, the director of the Academy had agreed to serve as trustee of the estate if Prus died before the boy came of age. All this was to be confirmed by the will.

But the will was not found, and Prus, dying in a fever, kept repeating that the estate was to go to Gregor Mach. No such person was ever discovered, and in the absence of a will the estate passed to a cousin, Baron Emmerich Prus. Ferdinand Gregor sued, and the case has continued through the generations to Ferdinand's great-grandson, Albert Gregor.

"It is nonsense," says Marty. "Pepi meant Ferdinand Gregor."

"*Litera scripta valet,*" intones Kolenatý. "The written word prevails."

To Gregor's delight Marty quickly resolves the problem. Ferdinand Gregor was of course Pepi's illegitimate son and the mother—Marty pretends for a moment to think—was the opera singer Ellian (ell.ee.an) MacGregor. So, says Gregor, Prus was not repeating Gregor Mach, but MacGregor. And the illegitimate son, Marty continues, who never knew his mother or her name—he was called merely Gregor to save her embarrassment—could not explain the confusion to the court.

What do you need to win? Marty asks. A valid will. Who owns the house where Pepi lived? The present Baron Prus. Well then, in the cupboard in the study each drawer has a date. In the drawer for 1806, where Pepi kept Ellian MacGregor's love letters, is the will. How can you know? demands Kolenatý. Never mind that, says Marty. Search the drawer. Kolenatý is about to refuse, but Gregor, threatening to hire another lawyer, forces him to go.

Marty and Gregor. She is a miracle, he says. But why, why should she come to help him? That's my affair, she replies. When he offers her money as payment for her help, if he wins the suit, she is angered.

They talk instead of Ellian MacGregor. Did she love Baron Prus very much? In her way, says Marty. Gregor, not knowing that he is talking to his great-grandmother, grows amorous and is indignantly rebuffed. While he is insisting that she is beautiful, a light flares in which she suddenly appears very old.

There is one thing, she says, he could give her. Can he read Greek? No? Then the document is of no use to him. But Gregor swears he knows nothing of such a document. Idiot, she cries. Look for it. Bring it here. That's what I came for.

Kolenatý, Prus, Marty and Gregor. Kolenatý, full of apologies, hurries in followed by Prus. The will was there. And the love letters and a document in Greek. Gregor, says Marty, is giving me those. But, says Prus, before the property becomes Gregor's there must be written evidence that Ferdinand Gregor was the son of Ferdinand Prus. Very well, says Marty, I will send it to the lawyer in the morning.

Kolenatý gasps. Do you carry these things around with you? Marty cuts him dead and turns her charm on Prus, who at the moment controls the document.

ACT II (34 min.)

(Between acts Marty sends Kolenatý a letter signed by Ellian Mac-Gregor stating that Ferdinand Prus was the father of her son Ferdinand Gregor.) A few days later. Backstage at the theatre where Marty the night before gave a last performance. Rolled-up scenery and a few odd properties, including a throne.

Charwoman and Stagehand. They are gossiping of Marty's success when Prus enters, looking for her. Advised to wait, he wanders off into the shadows and they return to work.

Krista and Janek. Prus's son Janek and Krista are also backstage. Janek, shy and timid, loves Krista, who loves him but at the moment can chatter only of Marty. Just as he succeeds in stealing a kiss, to his consternation his father steps from the shadows.

Marty, Prus and others. She comes from the manager's office, irritated and tired. Sitting on the throne she asks Janek questions about her performance to all of which he answers, "Yes, ma'am." Turning to Prus she declares Janek an idiot.

She is no more polite to Gregor, who gives her a bouquet with a jewel box concealed in it. She throws the flowers on the floor, returns the box unopened and offers him money to pay his debts. Even Vítek, who had entered with Gregor, is scolded for comparing her to the famous singer Strada.

Seeing Krista and Janek holding hands, she asks if they have been to bed yet. Vítek is shocked. In any event, Marty continues, it is not worth it. Is anything worth it? asks Prus. No. Nothing.

Marty and Hauk-Šendorf. He is very old and almost senile. He kneels and with halting voice offers his bouquet. Oh, how she reminds him of his great love fifty years ago, Eugenia Montez! Marty recognizes him. Bending over his shaking head, she cries, "Maxi! Kiss me!" Confused, he begins to weep. With Spanish words of passion she excites him till he breaks down, sobbing, "It is she, it is she"—and wanders off.

Next, says Marty.

(For many persons this scene and its companion in the next act are the most disturbing of the opera. They dramatize best what seems wrong when passions continue out of season and life goes on too long. Though Hauk-Šendorf is onstage only briefly, because of his music he haunts the memory.)

Marty and Prus. Dismissing the others she turns to Prus. You knew, he says, of the will and the letters. Did you know of the old document? Marty, betraying her interest, asks him to describe it. But Prus deliberately shifts the topic to Ellian MacGregor. The letters are extraordinarily passionate, and they could be from someone else, for they are signed only E. M. No, says Marty, only Ellian MacGregor. How about Elina Makropulos? asks Prus, sure that he is onto something but uncertain of what.

Marty swears. Pepi's will, continues Prus, gives the date and place of birth of the illegitimate Ferdinand. And the parish register for that date records the birth of a Ferdinand: father's name, unknown; mother's name, Elina Makropulos. So the estate will remain with the present Baron Prus unless the Gregor family can establish their claim through a Ferdinand Makropulos.

And if they cannot? asks Marty. I keep the document, says Prus. Desperately she asks his price for it, but he, now fully confident, laughs and departs.

Gregor and Marty. He wants to love her and to have her love him. Her mind is elsewhere. He must retrieve the Ellian MacGregor letter that she sent to Kolenatý, and she must write another signed Elina Makropulos. Gregor does not understand. When he continues his protestations of love, in boredom she falls asleep in his face. Kissing her hand, he goes.

Marty, Janek and later Prus. She wakes to find Janek in fascination staring at her. She calls to him, turns on him the full power of her charm and asks him to steal something for her from his father's drawer. Just as he agrees, Prus steps from the shadows, and Janek, thoroughly ashamed, creeps out.

Prus explains that he had thought Janek was waiting for Krista. Marty presses against him. Bring me the document, she urges. Prus hesitates. When? he asks. Tonight! Agreed, he says and goes out quickly.

ACT III (31 min.)

Early the next morning. A hotel room; the bed behind transparent drapes through which figures can be seen, dressing. Marty appears in a negligee; Prus follows, half-dressed in a dinner jacket.

Marty, Prus and a maid. Marty demands the document, and he without a word throws it on the table. She scans it, exclaims "Good!" and puts it in her bosom. You have defrauded me, says Prus. You were cold, as though dead. He is disgusted, chiefly with himself.

A maid hurries in. A servant of Prus is downstairs with a message. Prus finishes dressing and hurries out. The maid, combing Marty's hair, suspects bad news: the servant was crying.

Prus, looking stunned, returns and the maid exits hastily. It is Janek, says Prus. He has killed himself, explaining in a note that he, like his father, was infatuated with Marty. Prus weeps; Marty continues combing her hair. So, she says, lots of people kill themselves. Prus is ready to strike her but Hauk-Šendorf enters.

Hauk-Šendorf and Marty. Hurry, he urges. We will go back to Spain. He has his wife's jewels, and so long as a man can love, life is worth living. Marty agrees to go and hurries to pack but is interrupted by Kolenatý, who leads in others, among them a doctor for Hauk-Šendorf.

Kolenatý, Gregor, Vítek and others. Kolenatý insists on a few questions. The photograph of Emilia Marty that she inscribed for Krista and the letter that she sent to him purportedly from Ellian MacGregor have identical handwriting. What does it matter? says Marty. Neither are forgeries. But she refuses to answer more questions, and when they demand to search her trunks, she tries to hold them off with a pistol.

Gregor disarms her, charging her with responsibility for Janek's death. She runs to her room to finish dressing, and while she is gone, they open the trunks, discovering mementos, letters, seals with all her names, and always the initials E. M.

Kolenatý and others. He puts on his legal robes and, when Marty returns, slightly drunk, questions her with the authority of a court:

What is your name? Elina Makropulos.

Where were you born? Crete.

In what year? 1575.

No one believes her, and Kolenatý and the others continue to question her. Are you related to the Elina Makropulos who was Pepi's mis-**interrogation**   tress? She and I are one. Are you related to Ellian MacGregor? She and I are one. They do not believe her. If you are Ellian MacGregor, why didn't you tell Ferdinand Gregor where the will was hid? He could go to hell, like all my children. Kolenatý scolds her for vulgar language. (But, philosophical point: if a person has immortality, eternal youth, what role can children have in that life?) For a long time now, says Marty, I've been a vulgar person. (Philosophical point: would immortality necessarily lead to boredom, drinking and degradation?)

Yes, she says, I did love Pepi (the music confirms it), and I lent him the document, which he kept to make me return to him. Finally to get it I did come back, and now that I have it, I don't give a damn for any-**confession**   one. She presses it to her bosom, saying that it was written by her father for the Emperor Rudolf (music from the overture) and she describes what happened at his court.

You're lying, Kolenatý insists, as Marty intones the opening of a prayer, "Pater hemon. . . ." Your real name? He demands. Elina Makropulos, she cries, and faints. One after another they conclude, She is not lying!

They carry her into the bedroom, and the hotel doctor is called. But Marty almost immediately reappears, like a ghost or a shadow, and a pale green light overflows the stage. (Two ways to play the scene: Čapek and Janáček imagined her here as tremendously aged. Some directors rejuvenate her so that she dies, in her ecstasy, as the sixteen-year-old Elina Makropulos.)

Marty. Death, she says, has touched her. Why did she ever fear it? They apologize for not believing her and offstage a chorus (tenors and **catharsis**   basses) affirm that dying and living are one. Marty wrings her hands. It is a great mistake to live so long. Death gives life meaning. Without death there is no joy in goodness, no joy in evil, on the earth or in the sky.

She offers the document to Krista, some recompense for Janek. With it Krista can be famous and sing like Emilia Marty. Take it, she says. No, cry the others, and Krista, holding it over a candle, burns it. With a final cry, "Pater hemon . . ." Marty dies.

Z MRTVÉHO DOMU

(From the House of the Dead)

Opera in three acts. World premiere, Brno, April 12, 1930; British prem., Edinburgh (in Czech), Sept 5, 1964; American prem. (in English), on television, Dec. 3, 1969; American stage prem. (in Eng.), New York, Aug. 28, 1990. Music by Leoš Janáček; also the text, based on Dostoyevsky's novel, *The House of the Dead,* 1862.

PRINCIPAL CHARACTERS

Alexandr Petrovič Gorjančikov, called "Petrovič," an aristocrat and political prisoner	baritone	
Luka Kuzmič (whose real name is Filka Morosov), a murderer	tenor	
Skuratov, a murderer	tenor	
Aljeja, a young Tartar, accessory to a murder (though the role has been sung by light tenors)	mezzo-soprano	al.yay.ah
Šapkin, a burglar	tenor	shap.kin
Šiškov, a murderer	baritone	shish. kov
Commandant of the prison	bass-baritone	
other prisoners, though with individual lines, are designated merely "The Big Prisoner," "The Small Prisoner," etc.		

The action takes place in a Russian prison on the river Irtysh in Siberia, in the mid-nineteenth century.

In writing his libretto Janáček made many changes in Dostoyevsky's mixture of fact and fiction about the life and men in a Siberian prison camp. He merged characters, shifted incidents and established new relationships and symbols. Where Dostoyevsky had reported in detail the depravities of which men were capable and offered no hope for the prisoners' human regeneration, Janáček affirmed the dignity of man, even in prisoners, suggesting that its highest expression, arising from the universal longing for freedom, is the ability to rejoice in the freedom of others.

The theme is similar to that of *Fidelio,* but it is better structured. There is no anticlimactic scene following the great moment; the climax, drawing together all the real and symbolic strands developed earlier, comes as a catharsis at the opera's end. Janáček wrote at the top of the score, "In every creature a spark of God," and at the end the audience, if the performance is good, will feel emotionally purged by the depth and intensity of Janáček's compassion. The opera is an exercise in love.

It is not, however, an opera in the usual sense. There are a number of genre scenes of life in the camp, its brutality, its grotesque gaiety and utter wretchedness, but there is no hero, not much plot and not even many events. There is a frame—a prisoner arrives and then departs, each time in a short scene with the commandant—but the opera's core consists of narratives by four prisoners in which each describes the events that brought him to the prison.

These are dramatic monologues; the prisoners must change the timbre and pitch of their voices for the story's characters, and the tension is carefully controlled. The music, fitful, exaggerated, explosive, is attuned to the man. Though the four wear identical prison garb, they are individuals. And one not only tells a story, the first, but under his true name, unknown to the others, is the villain of the last, to which he must listen as he lies dying. Obviously the opera is one that *must* be presented in translation.

Janáček died before the opera was produced and left behind for scholars an argument over whether he had finished it. For the world premiere two of his pupils revised the score, chiefly making the orchestration less harsh and, by a small change at the end (see synopsis below), giving it a more festive, *Fidelio*-like closing. In this version the opera was performed until 1964 when the National Theater of Prague, preparing a new production for the Edinburgh Festival, returned to the score as Janáček left it. This is now the current version and the one described below.

OVERTURE (7 min.)

It is a rondo, ABACADA, with a tiny coda of seven bars. It ends— typically Janáček—simply by breaking off. Silence. Then four successive loud chords, as the curtain parts. The first and second chords make a rising phrase; the third (the first repeated) and fourth, declining, ending in ominous minor.

ACT I (24 min.)

The courtyard of the prison. Early morning. Winter. The prisoners straggle from the barracks, wash at buckets and go to the kitchen. In a corner some tease a crippled eagle.

The Prisoners Assemble. Some mutter excitedly that the day will bring a new prisoner, a gentleman. A big prisoner orders a small one out of his way, and they yell at each other. A third, Luka Kuzmič, mocks them: they are equals; both have been beaten. Some prisoners call: "They bring the gentleman." (Janáček sets off the entrance with a poignant line for violin solo, the first of many flashes of tenderness by which he reveals his point of view.)

Petrovič and the Commandant. Guards lead in Petrovič, who is about thirty-five, still in city clothes and terrified. The Commandant (roll on solo snare drum ending in snarling trombones) enters and begins the interrogation. He sneers at Petrovič's clothes and pulls the gentlemanly moustache. Your offense? Political, says Petrovič. The Commandant, flying into a rage, strikes him and orders a punishment of a hundred lashes. Petrovič is led off and for a time his agonized cries punctuate the scene.

The Eagle. A prisoner holds him by the beak, complaining that he resists. Some say he will die; others, not. They release him, but the bird, his wing broken, can only crawl into a corner. The Commandant, passing through, shouts to the guards to continue the flogging.

Skuratov. Some prisoners leave for outside work; others begin to sew shoes. One of these, Skuratov, starts a comic song, but Luka likens him to a wolf howling. Skuratov's feelings are hurt, and after a bitter but comic exchange with Luka he starts a dance, which he continues till he falls to the ground exhausted.

Luka. He ignores Skuratov and, asking the youngest prisoner, Aljeja, for some thread, starts to recount one of his crimes. In a jail where he **Luka's story** was imprisoned, the Commandant treated everyone roughly. "I am both your Tsar and God," he would say. One day Luka, oh, so politely, challenged him and, sidling closer and closer, suddenly jammed a knife into his belly. The man slowly tipped over.

"More thread," demands Luka, delaying the story. "Were you punished?" ask the prisoners.

"And how!" says Luka. "Hand me the scissors." (Meanwhile Petrovič, half-conscious, is dragged in by the guards and left on the ground.) Luka describes his emotions as they put the noose about his neck. "And did you die?" interrupts an old prisoner. "Idiot!" cries Luka, throwing down his tools.

The guards, returning for Petrovič, half-carry, half-drag him through a gate at the back. (In the revision by Janáček's pupils Petrovič, in dumb show, briefly considers opposing the guards but is too weak and allows himself to be dragged off. As nothing in the music supports this, it is better left out. The point of his presence is that none of the prisoners, with the possible exception of Aljeja, will interrupt the story to aid him.)

ACT II (33 min.)

A year later. Winter (though sometimes staged, apparently for variety, in summer). Sunset and a blue sky on the banks of the Irtysh River. Some prisoners repair a ship; others lay bricks. In the distance, snatches of song.

Petrovič and Aljeja. They have become friends, and Petrovič, to Aljeja's delight, offers to teach him to read and write.

The prisoners at the boat unstep the mast, and the day's work is finished. The cook, a prisoner, excitedly tells Petrovič and Aljeja that there will be a celebration and acting. Bells ring; officials enter and depart; a priest blesses the food and the river; and the prisoners set up tables and sit to eat. They discuss the possibility of a camp inspection by a general.

Skuratov. His crime, he says, was love. "It's a lie," says a drunken prisoner. But the others listen, and Skuratov continues. When he was young and a soldier, he fell in love with a girl named Louise, and whenever he tried to bed her, she would laugh and say, "Marry me." So he decided to do it. "All lies," cries the drunk. But then Louise **Skuratov's story**   ceased to see him, and he demanded an explanation. A rich, elderly relative wanted to marry her, and she was going to do it. The next day Skuratov went to the man's office and peeked through the window. The man was a watchmaker, with a crooked nose, staring eyes and forty-five! "I wept." When the drunk cries "Lies, all lies," Skuratov knocks him to the ground.

A day or two passed, and he went to call on the old man, taking his pistol. Louise was there. They had words and, well, he shot him. He was caught and flogged.

"And Louise?" ask the prisoners. "O, Louise," cries Skuratov in a strained voice. The prisoners laugh at him. (The cry of "Oh, Louise" is important. In the next act Skuratov in delirium will call on Louise. In his youth did he really love her? Does he still? The singer must make it clear.)

The Plays. At the end of Skuratov's story the prisoners set up a few planks for a stage, and the first play begins, acted by prisoners in their fetters with improvised costumes. It is "Kedril and Juan," a half-remembered version of Don Juan's final supper. It is played broadly, mostly by gesture, and the prisoners laugh at the crudest parts. A pantomime, "About the Miller's Beautiful Wife," immediately follows, and it shows Don Juan pulled to hell by devils, but only after the beautiful wife has betrayed the miller three times, the last with Don **waltz** Juan disguised as a Brahmin. It ends with a waltz in which Juan and the wife fall dead and the devils continue dancing.

The prisoners drift off to the barracks. Petrovič and Aljeja linger, sipping tea that they have bought. A young prisoner, striking a bargain with a whore, goes off with her.

The Small Prisoner, Petrovič and Aljeja. The small prisoner, looking for a grievance, is directed to it by Luka, who mocks Petrovič and Aljeja for their tea, the aristocrats' drink. It smacks of distinction, a difference, and in the camp, cries the small prisoner, all are equal. Other prisoners echo him. Petrovič offers the man a drink, but the prisoner picks up the kettle, throws it at them and seriously injures Aljeja. Prisoners, shouting and shoving, gather round, and guards running in push them back.

ACT III (40 min.)

SCENE 1 (33 min.)

Weeks later. Evening. The prison hospital, bunks on either side. To the back, an oven, on which sits an old prisoner.

Aljeja, Petrovič, Luka and others. Aljeja is in bed, feverish. Petrovič sits by the bedside. They have been discussing the Bible. Aljeja likes best God's command to do no harm, but to love.

Another prisoner brings them some tea. "You servant," sneers Luka, who is in a nearby bunk, dying, and he calls to others to look at "the servant." The prisoner urges Luka to hurry and die, and Luka's retort is cut off by his gasps of pain.

The old man on the oven asks God's mercy for Luka, who continues groaning.

Šapkin. Reminded of his own pain by Luka's groaning, Šapkin tells the story of his long ears. One time he and four vagrants broke into a merchant's house, were caught and taken before the district commis-**Šapkin's story** sioner. The Commissioner interrogated them (Šapkin, a tenor, imitates the Commissioner, a bass). But no one would admit to anything. Suddenly the Commissioner ordered Šapkin to sit down and write. Apparently a clerk somewhere had run off with money. Šapkin, illiterate, could only make scratches, but the Commissioner kept pulling his ears to force him to write. And he pulled . . . and pulled . . . and then had Šapkin flogged.

Before the story's end Skuratov, delirious, begins to scream, "Louise, Louise!" and the prisoners knock him into his bunk and hold him down.

The darkness thickens till the only light is a candle held by the old man on the oven. The prisoners begin to sleep (a solo violin suggests their release from pain), and the old man, reminded of his children whom he will never see again, asks God's mercy.

Šiškov. He is telling his story to another prisoner and meets all interruptions with "Wait, wait, don't rush me!" (This is the longest of the **Šiškov's story** four stories and the longest scene in the opera. Šiškov, in fact, is the opera's leading role and must be played by an exceptional singing-actor.)

The story divides in nine parts, each reaching its own, small climax.

1. Šiškov is describing a rich man: he goes to the market and everyone bows, "Good morning, Sir; good morning." He had two sons and a daughter named Akulka. "Your wife?" asks the prisoner. "Wait. Don't rush me. She was defamed by Filka Morosov."

Luka, hearing his true name, tries to rise, gasping "Oh . . . oh!"

2. This Filka, continues Šiškov, was in business with the merchant, but he withdrew, demanded an accounting and refused to marry

Akulka, saying that he had slept with her for a year and no longer wanted her. What's more, he would slander her to the whole town.

"Ah . . . ah!" groans Luka.

3. "Wait. Don't rush me," says Šiškov. Filka led a gang of ruffians to smear her gate with tar, a public symbol of her dishonor, and her parents beat her and the girl wept. (The sleeping prisoners utter a deep sigh.) And from the street Filka cried: "Akulka. You wear white, you whore. Say, who do you love?"

Luka groans.

4. One day when the girl had looked at Šiškov with her big, strange eyes (sleeping prisoners sigh) and her mother had scolded her for being a slut, Šiškov's mother, who was angry at him, told him to marry Akulka: "They'll give her to you now." But Filka, when he heard of the engagement, threatened to sleep with her whenever he wanted (prisoners sigh).

5. "Don't rush me!" The marriage was performed and the couple were left in a room together. Šiškov, who was drunk, had a whip to beat her, and she sat on the bed, pale and frightened. Then—so strange!—she proved to be . . . she was . . . (prisoners sigh) . . . a virgin! Innocent! Oh, why did Filka publicly defame her?

Šiškov knelt before her. Together they laughed and cried (prisoners sigh); her parents, too. And her father said, "Had I known she was pure, I'd have given her to someone better."

6. "Wait. Don't rush me." The next day Šiškov, drunk, ran through the town shouting, "Give me Filka Morosov." But when he found him, Filka said that Šiškov after the wedding was too drunk to know the pure from the defiled. So Šiškov ran home and beat Akulka, beat her and beat her.

The old man on the oven cries, "You scoundrel. You son of a bitch!" And the prisoners, waking, cry "Shut up!"

7. "Wait. Don't rush me." About Filka. On his way to join the army—he was actually sober—he left town with a crowd and stopped at Akulka's gate. She was there. He bowed and asked her forgiveness. She hesitated, then bowed and asked forgiveness of him.

"Ah," sighs Aljeja happily.

8. Šiškov took her upstairs and demanded to know what she had said to Filka. "Ah . . . ah!" sighs Aljeja nervously. And she replied, "I love him, I love him more than the world!" That whole day Šiškov did not speak to her, and in the evening he told her he would kill her.

"Ah . . . ah!" gasps Luka, rising in pain and falling back dead.

(Thus Luka, the bravura storyteller, the loud-mouth troublemaker, on his death bed had to face the consequences of his acts—a torture worse than flogging. And the girl had loved him! He had spoilt his best chance for a decent life.)

9. The next morning Šiškov took Akulka to the fields. (The old man approaches Luka's bunk.) And there he seized her by the hair, pulled out a knife and cut her throat.

Interrupting, the old man calls: "Guards, a man has died!" Šiškov, along with others, gather at Luka's bunk, and suddenly Šiškov cries, "Filka, is that you?"

Softly the old man says, "He, too, was born of woman. . . ." But Šiškov curses the corpse as guards carry it out. "Son of a bitch!"

The guards, returning, call for Petrovič, and everyone is startled.

SCENE 2 (7min.)

Morning. The prison courtyard. (The scene change is covered by a brief orchestral interlude.)

Commandant and Petrovič. Guards bring in Petrovič. The Commandant is drunk. He wants to apologize. He had Petrovič flogged for no reason, and he regrets it. He wants to be reconciled. While the prisoners giggle, he embraces Petrovič.

Then he reveals that Petrovič's mother has obtained her son's freedom. Petrovič is released. The guards knock off his fetters, and Aljeja throws himself on Petrovič: "You are my father!"

The prisoners excitedly decide to release the eagle from his cage. He soars into the sky, and they rejoice in his freedom.

Petrovič and Aljeja embrace, and as Petrovič leaves, Aljeja falls to the ground. The guards enter and order the prisoners back into the barracks. (In the version revised by Janáček's pupils the final few bars with the guards were eliminated and the excitement and musical motifs of freedom continued to the end.)

LA FANCIULLA DEL WEST

(The Girl of the Golden West)

Opera in three acts. World premiere, Metropolitan, New York, Dec. 10, 1910; European prem., Covent Garden, London, May 29, 1911.

Music by Giacomo Puccini; text by Guelfo Civinini and Carlo Zangarini, based on David Belasco's play *The Girl of the Golden West,* first performed, 1905.

PRINCIPAL CHARACTERS

Minnie, owner of "The Polka," a mining-camp bar and dance hall	soprano
Nick, the bartender	tenor
Dick Johnson (Ramerrez), a bandit	tenor
Jack Rance, Sheriff	baritone
Ashby, agent of the Wells Fargo Transport Co.	bass
Jake Wallace, a travelling camp-minstrel	baritone
Sonora, a miner	baritone
Larkens, a homesick miner	bass
Billy, an Indian	bass
Wowkle, his squaw	mezzo-soprano
Castro, one of the Ramerrez gang	bass

The action takes place in a mining camp at the foot of the Cloudy Mountains, California, during the days of the gold fever, 1849–50.

The opera marks a deliberate change in Puccini's style. He had written his publisher in February 1907, "We have had enough now of *Bohème, Butterfly,* and Co.! Even I am sick of them!" He wanted to do something "modern in construction," by which he seems to have meant a tighter drama, a less pathetic heroine and a more subtle use of the orchestra. "Never before have I felt time flow more swiftly and so intense a desire to go on. But *on,* not back!"

His urge was financially risky because much of his income arose from the style he wished to change. The public adored the pathetic heroines with the lush, short arias that fit so neatly on a record or into sheet music. It seemed not to care that in the operas the arias were sometimes ill-prepared or even irrelevant; it seemed almost ready to prefer the excerpts to the opera. Puccini was not, and his desire to go "on" was partly to insure that the impact of the whole was greater than that of its parts.

As he and his librettists turned the Belasco play into *La Fanciulla del West,* they transformed it from a story of individuals in the real West into a kind of morality play set in a mythical arena where everything is outsize: the blizzard, the redwood trees, the miners' homesickness, the poker game, the evils of lust and banditry, and Minnie's simple goodness. American audiences in particular are frequently put off by the lack of realism—miners greeting each other "Hello, ragazzi"—but as in his final opera, *Turandot*, Puccini here was aiming less at realism than fable. He was trying to stir in the audience its deepest feelings of right and wrong. When the opera is well staged—and the final act among the redwoods is particularly difficult and crucial—it has great impact.

Musically it has fewer "hit" tunes than the earlier operas, or at least fewer that can be easily excerpted, but the first-act love scene develops more naturally than in *Bohème*, where the meeting is very contrived, and less crudely than in *Butterfly*, where the tenor repeats "Vieni" (come) twenty times. And throughout the opera the orchestration is more interesting. Puccini had been listening to Debussy and to Richard Strauss, and far more than in his earlier operas the audience should keep an ear on the orchestra.

ACT I (55 min.)

There is a short orchestral introduction intended to suggest the primeval forest of California, the musical counterpart of the scenic lantern-slides with which Belasco had begun his play. Thereafter the curtain rises on the interior of "The Polka" in semidarkness. Outside the miners are heard calling to one another, and Nick, the bartender, lights the lamps in the saloon. Rance, the Sheriff, is smoking by the chimney; across from him a miner, Larkens, sits with his head in his hands.

The Miners. They gather for whiskey, cigars and cards. Outside, Jake Wallace, the camp minstrel, sings of home, "Che faranno i vecchi miei **solo with chorus** là lontano" (What are they doing my old folks there far away). When he enters, still singing, all join in, and soon Larkens, overcome by longing, breaks down. The others, led by Sonora, raise a stake to send him home. (The song's tune is the contemporary "Old Dog Tray," and with varied orchestration Puccini uses it throughout the opera to suggest the loneliness of the miners' lives. The opera's chorus is entirely male, and often, as here, to depict the miners' lack of sophistication Puccini will have them sing in unison and octaves. But to avoid monotony he varies the sound with passages of humming and by breaking the line into interjections for individuals or small groups.)

A miner, Sid, is caught cheating at cards, and Sheriff Rance, "il sceriffo," prevents a lynching by ordering him to wear a card on his chest as the sign of a cheat. (This card scene sometimes is cut.) The Wells Fargo agent, Ashby, steps in to warn that the bandit Ramerrez and his men are in the valley. Nick announces drinks on the house, and when all toast Minnie, Rance goes further, boasting that she soon will be his wife. Sonora challenges the statement, and a quarrel starts. When Rance rushes him, Sonora pulls his pistol and fires; but his friends deflect his aim. Before the two can grapple, Minnie steps between them.

Minnie. She restores calm by threatening to stop her school for the miners. To placate her they offer little gifts, the remorseful Sonora producing a red silk handkerchief and also a small sack of gold to square his bar account.

Minnie gives the men a Bible lesson by reading from the 51st psalm **Bible scene** and explaining that in all the world there is no sinner who cannot find "una via di redenzione" (a path of redemption).

The postman distributes letters, including one to Ashby from Ramerrez's allegedly discarded mistress, Nina Micheltorena. She writes that at midnight Ramerrez will be at "The Palms," another saloon. Rance warns that Nina is untrustworthy, but Ashby is inclined to believe her and leaves.

Rance and Minnie. Soon only they are left at the bar. "Ti voglio bene, Minnie" (I love you), he begins, but she cuts him short: What of his wife? He will leave her. "Basta, basta" (enough, stop it), Minnie says. When he is offended, she asks why: she spoke honestly. "Minnie," he **arioso** says, "dalla mia casa son partito" (when I left home), no one cared. No one ever had loved him, nor he anyone. Gold alone had not deceived him. Yet now for her kiss he would throw away a fortune: "or per un bacio tuo, getto un tesoro!"

Real love, Minnie replies, is very different: "L'amore è un' altra cosa." "Poesia," he sneers. She describes her parents: "Laggiù nel So- **arioso** ledad ero piccina" (down in Soledad when I was a girl). Building to a climax on high C, she cries out twice, "S'amavan tanto!" (how very much they loved). So, too, in marriage she wants love.

A stranger enters whom Minnie once had met and never forgotten. Sensing a rival Rance is rude, but Minnie welcomes the man. His name, he says, is Johnson and he comes from Sacramento While he and Minnie recall their chance meeting on the road to Monterey,

Rance tries to incite the miners to throw the stranger out. But when Minnie vouches for him, they refuse.

The Miners. A waltz starts in the dance hall, and though Minnie claims never to have danced, the miners urge her to accept Johnson's invita-
waltz   tion. (Puccini later uses the waltz as a theme of their love.) While they are offstage dancing, there is an uproar in the saloon. Ashby has captured a bandit, Castro. The miners are for lynching him, "al laccio" (to the noose), but because he offers to lead them to Ramerrez, Ashby spares him. When Johnson enters from the dance hall, Castro whispers to him—for Johnson is . . . Ramerrez!—that the ruse has succeeded. He will lead all the men away from "The Polka." The posse forms and departs, leaving Johnson alone with Minnie.

Johnson and Minnie. (The love duet is built chiefly on variations of the waltz.) "Strana cosa" (strange thing), he muses, "ritrovarvi qui" (to find you again here). Minnie assures him that she can look out for herself. Even, he asks, if a man wanted to steal only a kiss, "un bacio?" That has happened, she admits, "ma il primo bacio debbo darlo an-
love duet   cora" (but my first kiss I have still to give). Closing the bar, she reveals where the gold is hidden but feels, she says, that she can trust him. Life, they agree, is confusing: to know who you are, where you are going. She describes herself as "oscura e buona a nulla" (a nobody and good for nothing); yet she feels a desire to talk more expressively to him, to raise herself up, up, like the stars, "su, su, come le stelle" (B natural). I felt something, too, he says, when we were dancing, a strange joy, a new peace, "una gioia strana, una nuova pace."

Nick interrupts them. He has seen a bandit. Johnson stops Minnie from going out with Nick. They hear a whistle. "Il segnale" (the signal), Johnson murmurs, but he continues to talk with Minnie.

She describes how she would defend the miners' gold with her life, for they have endured loneliness and hardship to help others at home. Johnson rises to leave. "Che peccato" (what a pity), she says, suggesting they continue their talk at her cabin as soon as the miners return. He agrees, and she warns him not to expect too much: she had only a thirty-dollar education. Beginning to cry she repeats that she is "oscura e buona a nulla." "No, Minnie, non piangete" (don't cry), he urges, you don't know your worth; you have the face of an angel, "un viso d'angelo." After he has gone, she repeats with a sigh, "un viso d'angelo."

Vocabulary, Act 1

che faranno i vecchi	kay fah.rah.noh ee	what are they doing
miei là lontano	vek.key m'yay lah	my old folks there
	lohn.TAH.noh	far away
sceriffo	shair.EE.foh	sheriff
una via di redenzione	oo.nah vee.ah dee	a path of redemption
	reh.dehn.tsee.OH.nay	
ti voglio bene	tee vohl.yoh bay.nay	I love you
basta, basta	BAH.stah . . .	enough, stop it
dalla mia casa son	dah.lah mee.ah cah.sah	(when) from my house
partito	sohn pahr.TEE.toh	I left
or per un bacio tuo,	or pair oon bah.cho	now for your kiss, I
getto un tesoro	too.oh jet.toh oon	would throw away a
	tay.zohr.oh	fortune
l'amore è un' altra cosa	lah.MOH.ray eh oon	love is another thing
	AHL.trah COE.sah	
poesia	poh.ez.EE.ah	romantic love
laggiù nel Soledad ero	lah.jew nehl . . .	down there in Soledad
piccina	air.oh pee.CHEE.nah	when I was a girl
s'amavan tanto	sah.mah.van tahn.toe	how much they loved
al laccio	ahl LAH.choe	lynch him (to the noose)
strana cosa	strah.nah COE.sah	strange thing
ritrovarvi qui	ree.troh.VAHR.vee	to find you again here
	kwee	
un bacio	oon BAH.cho	a kiss
ma il primo bacio	mah ell pree.moh	but my first kiss I
debbo darlo ancora	bah.cho deb.boh	still have yet to
	dahr.lo on.coh.rah	give
oscura e buona a nulla	os.kuh.rah eh	a nobody and good
	bwoh.nah ah	for nothing
	NOOL.ah	
su, su, come le stelle	soo soo koh.may lay	up, up, like the
	STELL.ay	stars
una gioia strana	oon.ah joy.ah	a strange joy
	strah.nah	
una nuova pace	oon.ah nwoe.vah	a new peace
	pah.chay	
il segnale	eel seh.n'yall.ay	the signal
che peccato	kay peh.CAH.toh	what a shame
. . . non piangete	nohn p'yahn.JAY.tay	don't cry
un viso d'angelo	oon vee.soh	the face of an angel
	d'ahn.jay.loh	

ACT II (45 min.)

An hour later. Minnie's cabin, a single, large room, simply furnished, with a fireplace. Outside, wind and frost.

Wowkle, a squaw who keeps house for Minnie, sings a prayer for her baby. Her man, Billy, enters and they agree to be married as Minnie has urged. When she arrives and hears of the wedding plan, she is pleased, but her mind is on Johnson.

Minnie and Johnson. On entering he attempts to embrace her, and she is offended. Conversation lags until she relents and (to phrases from the waltz) asks slyly why he came to "The Polka." Had he missed the road to Nina's cabin? Johnson turns the subject to Minnie's life in the camp, and with enthusiasm she describes the mountain riding in summer and in winter the "Accademia," her school for miners. He offers to **love duet**   send her some books, and after she requests love stories, he tries again to embrace her, "un bacio, un bacio solo!" (a kiss, one kiss). She hesitates, then sends Wowkle home, though it has begun to snow. Alone with him, when he repeats "un bacio," she throws herself in his arms: "Eccolo! È tuo . . . Ah!" (here it is, it is yours). The wind opens the door, and snow swirls about them as they embrace.

They confess their love, but a life together, he says, is a vain dream, and with resolution he prepares to go: "Sii benedetta! Addio" (God bless you. Goodbye). But the blizzard: it is destiny, she says; stay!

Outside there are pistol shots. Stay, she urges. Passionately he cries, "io non ti lascio più" (I'll never leave you again). Between kisses they swear to love "eternamente" (eternally).

While the storm howls, Minnie makes up two beds, but before retiring asks "Dimmi il tuo nome" (tell me your name) "Dick," he says. "Per sempre, Dick" (for always). "Per sempre!" he replies.

Outside, voices call and a knock comes on the door. Hiding Johnson, she admits Rance, Ashby, Sonora and Nick. They have news: the stranger, Johnson, is Ramerrez. She hardly hears more. "Che dite? Che dite? Che dite?" (what do you say?) "Non è ver" (it's not true). But Nina Micheltorena has given them a photograph. Nick, meanwhile, has noticed Johnson's cigar stub and quietly offers to remain if Minnie wishes, but she pushes him out with the others.

Then she confronts Johnson: "Un bandito, un bandito! (a bandit), and orders him out, "Va, va, va!" (go). He asks to speak "una parola

aria   sola" (just one word). "Sono un dannato" (I am a bad man), but he did not come to rob her. When first they met, he dreamed of a new, honest life. But it was a dream and is finished. God may forgive you, says Minnie, but I cannot: you have stolen my first kiss, "il primo bacio." Let them kill you outside; what does it matter?

He goes, is shot, falls against the closed door which she opens, dragging him in despite his protests. "Non può morir!" (you shall not die), she insists. With difficulty, she succeeds in pushing him up a ladder, "su, su" (up) into a loft.

Minnie and Rance. A fist pounds on the door: she opens, and Rance enters. Although sure that Johnson is in the cabin, he cannot find him, and he turns to Minnie. The sense of her presence overcomes him, and he tries to embrace her. "Ti voglio . . . ti voglio" (I want you). She fights him off, and he is about to go when he discovers blood on his hand. It is dripping from the loft. Johnson is discovered.

Ordered down, he descends, assisted by Minnie, and collapses unconscious in a chair by the table. Minnie desperately offers Rance a hand of poker: if Rance wins, he wins her as well as Johnson; if he loses, he loses both. Rance is impressed: "Come l'ami!" (how you love him). He agrees. Two hands out of three.

Minnie deals, and wins the first hand; Rance, the second. In the third Rance announces three kings, and Minnie, looking faint, asks for **poker game**   whiskey. While Rance pours it, she improves her cards. You fainted because you have lost, he cries. No, because I have won: "Tre assi e un paio!" (three aces and a pair). Rance, dumbfounded, coldly bids her good night, "buona notte," as Minnie breaks into hysterical laughter, "È mio, è mio, è mio" (he is mine).

(In a letter to his publisher in 1911 Puccini put his finger on a difficulty with the libretto: "At first hearing the drama can get in the way of the music, but at a second or third the action is familiar and the surprises no longer are so intense; then the music can be heard." There is hardly an opera or scene of which this is more true.)

Vocabulary, Act 2

accademia	ah.cah.DAY.m'yah	school
un bacio, un bacio solo	oon bah.cho . . . so.loh	a kiss, one kiss
eccolo! è tuo . . . ah	ek.ko.lo eh too.oh	here it is yours
sii benedetta . . . addio	see beh.nay.DET. tah ad.dee.oh	be blessed . . . goodbye

Vocabulary, Act 2 (continued)

io non ti lascio più	yo nohn tee lah.shoh p'you	I'll never leave you again
eternamente	ee.tair.nah.men.tay	eternally
dimmi il tuo nome	dee.mee.eel too.oh noh.may	tell me your name
per sempre	pair sem.pray	for always
che dite?	keh dee.tay	what do you say?
non è ver	nohn eh vair	it is not true
un bandito	oon bahn.DEE.toh	a bandit
va, va, va	vah . . .	go, go, go
una parola sola	oon.ah pah.rohl.ah sohl.ah	just one word
sono un dannato	soh.no oon dah.NAH.toh	I am a bad man
il primo bacio	eel pree.moh bah.cho	my first kiss
su, su	soo, soo	up, up
ti voglio	tee vohl.yoh	I want you
come l'ami	koh.may l'ah.me	how you love him
non può morir	nohn p'woh mohr.rear	you shall not die
tre assi e un paio	tray ahs.see eh oon pie.yoh	three aces and a pair
buona notte	bwahn.ah NOT.tay	good night
è mio, è mio . . .	eh mee.oh . . .	he is mine . . .

ACT III (26 min.)

A week later. (Rance, as he promised Minnie, did not reveal where Johnson was hidden, but Johnson, on trying to escape, was seen, and the miners are hunting him through the forest.) A clearing on the edge of the redwood forest. Huge tree trunks soar into the sky; in the distance, snow-covered mountains. Early dawn, with mist. Nick and Rance sit by a fire; to one side, lying on the ground, is Ashby, listening for sounds of the chase.

The act divides in three parts: Nick and Rance; the man-hunt, ending with Johnson's near-lynching; and Minnie's rescue of him by an appeal to the miners.

Nick and Rance. Nick wishes that he could turn back the clock to the weeks before Johnson appeared. Rance, his bitterness turned to acid, rages at Minnie: what can she see in the man? Nick smiles. "Amore, amore" (love); "paradiso, inferno" (heaven, hell), but it comes to everyone, and now it has come to Minnie.

The man-hunt. A cry from the forest interrupts them, and then another.

Ashby rises, unties his horse and rides off. As the cries grow louder, Rance waves an arm in the direction of Minnie's cabin and exults: "Or piangi tu" (now you weep). Groups of miners rush in, and out. (Their excited cries, near and far, should sweep across the stage in ever-increasing washes of sound.) Nick, seeing the Indian, Billy, begin to make a noose, gives him a handful of gold and orders him to delay a lynching as long as possible. Then he runs off to bring Minnie.

Shouting "a morte, a morte" (to death), the miners drag Johnson into the clearing. Ashby delivers him to Rance for justice, implying that a lynching would be proper; then he rides off. Rance, lighting a cigar, begins to taunt the prisoner, but the miners are impatient: "Al laccio, al laccio" (to the noose). When they accuse Johnson of every violent death in the valley, he retorts, "No! non è vero" (it's not true) . . . "fui ladro, ma assassino mai!" (I was a robber, but a murderer, never).

He asks to speak "della donna ch'io amo" (of the woman I love). After an outburst from the miners, Rance allows him "un minuto, sii **aria** breve" (one minute, be brief). Johnson sings "Ch'ella mi creda libero e lontano, sovra una nuova via di redenzione" (let her believe me free and far away, on a new path of redemption). As he ends, Rance strikes him.

Minnie's appeal. The lynching is about to proceed when a cry is heard. It is Minnie. The miners hesitate. Rance rushes toward Johnson, shouting "impicatelo" (hang him), but no one moves. "Impicatelo, impicatelo," screams Rance, as Minnie throws herself in front of Johnson. Pull her away, Rance orders, but when two miners move toward her, she threatens to shoot Johnson and herself. Sonora cries out "lasciatela" (let her go), the miners stop in confusion and Rance, defeated, draws apart.

Minnie reminds them that no one ever told her "basta" (stop, enough) when she shared their troubles. And so they should not tell her "basta" now. Johnson is hers, "è mio," the bandit died a week ago in her cabin, and before them is a new man. "Voi non potete acciderlo" (you cannot kill him), "No!"

Softly she appeals to each miner while they mutter that they cannot free the man. But good deeds done are remembered, and sometimes even in strange circumstances goodness can have a reward. The sound builds, the miners' hearts melt—they will do it, for Minnie—and Johnson is released to her. Slowly the two ride off to a new and better life—"addio, addio" (goodbye)—leaving the miners with the ache of loneliness for something lovely that has been lost.

Vocabulary, Act III

amore	ah.MOHR.ay	love
paradiso, inferno	pah.rah.DEE.soh een.FAIR.noh	heaven, hell
or piangi tu	or p'YAHN.jee too	now you weep
a morte	ah MOHR.tay	to death
al laccio	ahl LAH.cho	to the noose (lynch him)
no, non è vero	no, nohn ay VAIR.oh	no, it is not true
fui ladro, ma assassino mai	foo.ee.LAH.droh, mah ah.sahs.SEE.noh, my	I was a robber, but a murderer, never
della donna ch'io amo	del.lah dohn.nah keh.EE.oo ah.mo	of the woman I love
un minuto, sii breve	oon meh.NOO.toh, see breh.veh	one minute, be brief
ch'ella mi creda libero e lontano, sovra una nuova via di redenzione	k'ell.lah me cray.dah lee.bair.oh (eh) lohn.tah.no so.vr(ah) oo.nah nwoh.vah v'yah dee reh.dehn.tsee.OH.nay	let her believe me free and far away, on a new path of redemption
impicatelo	im.pee.CAH.teh.lo	hang him
lasciatela	lah.SHAH.teh.lah	let her go
basta	BAH.stah	stop, enough
è mio	eh MEE.oh	he is mine
voi non potete ucciderlo	voy nohn poh.TAY.teh oo.CHEE.dehr.loh	you cannot kill him
addio	ah.DEE.oh	goodbye

LA RONDINE

(The Swallow)

Lyric comedy in three acts. World premiere, Monte Carlo, March 27, 1917; American prem., Buenos Aires, May 24, 1917; United States prem., Metropolitan, New York, March 10, 1928; British prem., London, Dec. 9, 1966. Music by Giacomo Puccini; text by Giuseppe Adami from a German libretto by Alfred Willner and Heinz Reichert.

PRINCIPAL CHARACTERS

Magda de Civry, Rambaldo's mistress	soprano	
Lisette, her maid	soprano	
Ruggero Lastouc, a young man from Montauban	tenor	roo.shjair.oh
Prunier, a poet	tenor	proon.yay
Rambaldo Fernandez, a rich Parisian	baritone	ram.BAHL.doh

The action takes place in Paris and on the Riviera toward the end of the Second Empire (*c.* 1865).

In 1914, before World War I, Puccini contracted with the directors of the Carltheater in Vienna to write a light opera in the Viennese style. It was to be an opera, however, not an operetta with spoken dialogue, and he would compose to an Italian translation of the German libretto. Because of the war the contract was renegotiated and the opera's premiere shifted from Vienna to Monte Carlo, technically neutral. Further, Adami rewrote rather than translated the libretto. Nevertheless the opera that emerged is comic and sentimental rather than tragic or melodramatic; and its music is light—though its many waltzes, as might have happened in any case, are more Latin than Teutonic in feeling.

The story concerns two women, Magda, a rich man's mistress, and Lisette, her outspoken maid. Each tries for a time to be someone other than her nature has decreed. Lisette, aided by the poet Prunier, ventures onto the stage as a chanteuse and has a disaster; Magda similarly fails with true love; and both women choose to return to their former state. Lisette's adventure is comic, Magda's sentimental; and though Lisette is a role for a leading singer, Magda is "the swallow" who migrates toward love and then home again, and the opera is bittersweet, more sentimental than comic. To succeed it needs singers with charm, and an intimate theatre. The third act is the weakest musically and also the most difficult theatrically to project.

ACT I (40 min.)

Paris. Magda's living room. To the back, a conservatory with a view of the Tuilleries in fading sunlight. Magda and Rambaldo are entertaining.

As the curtain rises, the poet Prunier has just declared that romantic love is again in fashion, and a lady laughs, "Ah, no, no " Prunier insists, "A Parigi si ama" (in Paris one loves). Lisette, passing coffee, contradicts him, and Prunier complains of her to Magda, who urges forgiveness: "in casa mia l'anormale è una regola" (in my house the unusual is a rule). Lisette, with a curtsey to Magda, launches a last word at Prunier and continues with the coffee.

On Magda's request Prunier repeats his news, only to be mocked by several of the ladies: "Amore!" (love). (Though they mock, Puccini scores the underlying theme warmly and uses it throughout the opera to represent true love.) Encouraged by Magda's support, Prunier announces that no woman, "nessuna," is safe from the new plague, not even Doretta, "anche Doretta." When asked, Who is she? he goes to the piano and sings his latest song, "Chi il bel sogno di Doretta potè indovinar?" (Who can explain the sweet dream of Doretta?).

In her dream the King desired her and offered money for her love— Prunier makes a dialogue of it—but she refused, for gold can never purchase happiness. There Prunier ends, saying he cannot imagine **aria** how the tale proceeds. Magda, taking his place at the piano, improvises a second verse. (When sung in concert or recorded the aria usually consists only of this second verse with the guests' admiring interjections omitted.) As Magda continues the story: a student one day kissed Doretta and awakened in both of them true love. Carried away by her own emotion, Magda in a tiny coda (to the theme of true love) ends passionately, "O sogno d'or poter amar così!" (Oh golden dream to be able to love like this!). The guests are moved, and Prunier, taking roses from a vase, scatters them at her feet. Rambaldo draws from his pocket a small box which he says he had forgotten to give her before dinner and presents her with a pearl necklace.

The slight awkwardness of the moment, considering the song's sentiment, is broken by Lisette chattering to Rambaldo that a young man who has been trying to see him is likely to return at any moment. With Magda's consent Rambaldo orders him to be shown in while Prunier complains to Magda that Lisette is too much of a chatterbox to be borne. But Magda defends her as "una brava ragazza" (a good girl) who brightens a dull life.

When the others protest that her life is full, Magda asks if they don't all feel a lack, and while Rambaldo and some of the men smoke in the conservatory, she recounts an experience she has never forgotten. The aria, "ore dolci e divine" (hours sweet and divine), has five short parts and a coda.

aria 1. One night, escaping her aunt's watchful eye, she went to

Bullier, a dance hall favored by students. When she arrived, a distant voice seemed to warn her:

2. (to a barrel-organ waltz) Love is everywhere; "difendi, difendi, difendi il tuo cuore" (defend your heart), for the magic of kisses and smiles is paid with a flood of tears.

3. With a student she sat at a table and he ordered some wine, paying for it with a gold piece and asking no change. The guests laugh and urge Magda to continue.

4. (to a new waltz) The student asked her name, and she wrote it on the table. Beside it he wrote his, and they sat in silence gazing at each other. What then? ask the guests.

5. (the barrel-organ waltz) As if from afar came the warning, "difendi, difendi, difendi il tuo cuore!"

Coda: With the present suddenly mingling with the past Magda rises, crying out, "Potessi revivere . . . la gioia, la gioia d'un ora" (would that I might relive the joy of that hour).

Her guests laugh gently, and soon Prunier has offered to read palms while Rambaldo receives the young man, who presents a letter of introduction. Prunier, making a great to-do over the lines in Magda's hand, announces, "Forse come la rondine" (perhaps like the swallow), you will migrate over the sea to a land of dreams, "verso il sole, verso l'amore" (toward the sun, toward love).

The palm reading is interrupted, however, by Rambaldo asking what place to recommend to the young man, Ruggero Lastouc, for an amusing first evening in Paris, "la prima serata a Parigi." Lisette leads the discussion and settles on Bullier, for there he will find "amore."

The party breaks, and the guests depart. Alone, Magda muses on Prunier's prophecy: "forse come il rondine . . . verso il sole . . ." omitting the final phrase, "Verso l'amore," and after hesitation substituting "Bullier!" Quickly she goes to her bedroom to dress.

For a moment the stage is empty, then through opposite doors ap-
duet pear Prunier and Lisette. They kiss and have a love scene (to a furtive tune which will accompany them throughout the opera). Lisette is in Magda's clothing and on Prunier's advice she replaces the hat and cape for others more becoming.

After they have gone, Magda appears dressed as a grisette (i.e. in a cheap grey material often worn by seamstresses and shop assistants). Regarding herself in the mirror, she murmurs "Chi mi riconoscerebbe?" (Who would ever recognize me?), "Chi il mistero di

Doretta potè indovinar?" (Who the mystery of Doretta can explain?).
Then resolutely, as she starts for Bullier, "Chi mi riconoscerebbe?"

Vocabulary, Act I

a Parigi si ama	ah pah.REE.jee see ah.mah	in Paris one loves
in casa mia l'anormale è una regola	in cah.zah mee.ah l'ah.nor.mah.lay eh oo.nah REG.oh.lah	in my house the unusual is a rule
amore	ah.MOHR.ay	love
nessuna	neh.SOON.ah	no woman
anche Doretta	ang.kay dohr.ET.tah	even Doretta
chi il bel sogno di Doretta potè indovinar	k'eel bell sohn.yo dee . . . poht' ehn.doh.vee.nahr	who can explain the beautiful dream of Doretta
o sogno d'or poter amar così	oh sohn.yo d'or poh.tair ah.mar coh.see	oh dream of gold to be able to love like this
una brava ragazza	oon.ah BRAH.vah rah.GAH.tsah	a good girl
ore dolci e divine	or.ay dohl.chee(e) dee.VEE.nay	hours sweet and divine
Bullier	BOOL.yay	(the dance hall)
difendi . . . il tuo cuore	dee.fen.dee . . . eel t'woh kor.ay	defend . . . your heart
potessi revivere . . . la gioia . . . d'un ora	poh.tess.ee ree.vee.vair lah joy.yah d'oon or.ah	would that I might relive the joy of that hour
forse come la rondine	for.say coh.may lah ROHN.dee.nay	perhaps like the swallow
verso il sole	vair.soh eel soh.lay	toward the sun
verso l'amore	vair.soh l'ah.mohr.ay	toward love
la prima serata a Parigi	lah pree.mah sehr.ah.ta (ah) pah.REE.jee	the first evening in Paris
chi mi riconoscerebbe	key me ree.cohn.osh. ehr.ebb.eh	who would recognize me

ACT II (28 min.)

At Bullier. To one side an elegant staircase; to the back a garden; along the walls, inside and out, tables with flowers and colored lights. A constant bustle of waiters, flower girls and dancers.

chorus While the crowd sings its excitement, Ruggero arrives and, after extricating himself from the flower girls, sits at a table to watch the scene.

Magda appears on the stairway and some students, seeing her alone, approach her. When she rebuffs them, they assume she is joining a man who is waiting and escort her to Ruggero.

"Scusatemi" (excuse me), she murmurs to him; after the students leave, so will she. "No, restate, restate" (stay), he says; she is so different from the others. "Veramente?" (truly?), she asks. "Veramente!" More modest, more like the girls at home. She agrees to a dance, and they slowly disappear into the crowd. (Puccini has them go off to the act's big waltz tune, but these first eight bars, which they sing, he sets in 4/4 rather than 3/4 time. The effect on the ninth bar as the chorus begins the waltz is of a slight acceleration, a gathering excitement, **waltz interlude** which soon will be greatly increased by an orchestral interlude, representing the dancing and played "col massimo slancio" or "with maximum swoop and glide." This sense of acceleration, and later of deceleration, provides an otherwise long waltz scene with an arch of excitement.)

The scene ends with the entrance of Prunier and Lisette, arguing happily over her lack of decorum. As they join the crowd, Magda and Ruggero return to their table. He orders wine, and she asks him to pay for it with a gold piece and without asking for change. When he does, asking why, she says only "fantasie, fantasie." He proposes a toast to their health, to which she replies with one to their love. Be careful, he warns; he would want her for a lifetime, "per tutta la vita."

He asks her name, and she writes on the table "Paulette." Beside it he writes "Ruggero." But when he starts another question, she warns against it. They kiss and fall silent. The crowd quietly sings its approval.

Lisette's cry separates them. "Dio," she exclaims to Prunier, "la mia padrona!" (my mistress). Prunier grasps the situation and confuses Lisette by agreeing that Ruggero is Ruggero but insisting that Magda is not Magda. Taking Lisette to the table, he asks if Ruggero has enjoyed

Bullier. Ruggero, recognizing Lisette and Prunier, introduces Magda as Paulette and invites them to sit. His confidence convinces Lisette who, much to Prunier's amusement, chatters to Magda about borrowing the clothes of "la mia padrona."

Ruggero proposes a toast to love, which Magda seconds and the **quartet and chorus** chorus later joins. (The piece frequently stops the show and, because the opera is so unabashedly light rather than serious, often is repeated.) At its end both couples kiss, and the crowd showers them with flowers.

On the stairway, watching, is Rambaldo. Prunier sees him and warns Lisette and Magda. To Ruggero he lies "I see my wife" and asks him to take Lisette away quickly. Ruggero rises at once and disappears with Lisette. When Rambaldo reaches the table, Magda and Prunier are alone.

Prunier greets Rambaldo gaily, remarking on the size of his emerald ring, but Rambaldo is not to be put off, and Prunier withdraws.

"Would you care to explain?" Rambaldo asks Magda. "I have nothing to add to what you have seen"—"Then it is just an adventure, shall we go?" (andiamo?)—"It is useless, I am staying"—"You're staying?" (restate?)—"I love him" (l'amo, l'amo, l'amo).

Passionately she insists it is her destiny. "Lasciatemi, lasciatemi, è finita!" (leave me, it is finished)—"è più forte il mio amore" (my love is too strong). Rambaldo bows, "Possiate non pentirvene!" (may you not repent it).

She is alone. The hall and garden are deserted, and dawn is breaking. From a distance comes the voice of a young girl on her way to work. Her song ends "nell' amor non fidar" (in love place no trust).

Ruggero returns, and they leave together: "mia vita, mio amor" (my life, my love).

Vocabulary, Act II

Bullier	bool.yay	(the dance hall)
scusatemi	skoo.ZAH.tay.me	excuse me
no, restate, restate	noh reh.stah.tay . . .	no, stay, stay
veramente	vair.ah.men.tay	truly
fantasie	fahn.tah.see	fantasy
per tutta la vita	pair too.tah lah vee.tah	for all of life
dio . . . la mia padrona	DEE.oh . . . lah mee.ah pah.droh.nah	Lord! . . . my mistress

Vocabulary, Act II (continued)

restate?	reh.stah.tay	you are staying?
l'amo, l'amo . . .	L'AH.moh	I love him
lasciatemi . . . è finita	lah.SHAH.tay.me eh fee.NEE.tah	leave me . . . it is finished
è più forte il mio amore	eh p'yoo FOR.tay (ee) l me.oh ah.MOR.eh	my love is too strong
possiate non pentirvene	poh.see.ah.tay nohn pen.TEER.vay.nay	may you not repent it
nell' amor non fidar	nell' ah.MOR nohn fee.DAHR	in love place no trust
mia vita, mio amor	m'yah VEE.tah m'yah.MOR	my life, my love

ACT III (35 min.)

Near Nice. The terrace of a small summer house that Ruggero has rented. Mid-afternoon in spring. Fruit trees and roses are in bloom; in the distance, through a grove of olives, is the sea. Flights of swallows cross the sky. The act is built on three dialogues, two for Magda and Ruggero separated by one for Lisette and Prunier.

Magda and Ruggero. While having tea they recall (to reminiscent waltzes) their meeting at Bullier. From the first, says Magda, it was love, "l'amor, l'amor, l'amor." Remembering how the crowd showered them with flowers, she strews rose petals on Ruggero, and they embrace.

To mark the beauty of the day he will tell her a secret, "un segreto." To the tune of the second-act quartet (the toast to love, but here more lightly orchestrated) he slowly reveals it: he has written to his parents not only for money to pay the bills but for consent "al nostro matrimonio" (to our marriage). At the word Magda draws back. "Ruggero, Ruggero, hai fatto questo" (you have done this). Despite her agitation—"dimmi tutto, dimmi tutto!" (tell me all)—he continues calmly that he wants her love "per sempre" (forever). "Per sempre," she repeats, and he says, "Tu che non sei l'Amante, ma l'Amore!" (you are not just a lover, but Love itself).

He describes his vision of their happiness, inviting her "alla mia casa," to his house in the country, where they will be near his mother, "mia madre," and where perhaps they will have a child, "un bambino." Someday, "e chi sa? e chi sa?" (and who knows?). He kisses her hair, then hurries inside to see if the letter from his parents has come.

Magda, alone, is in turmoil. Should she confess her past or continue to be silent? Can she give him up? "No, no!" But then, can she continue the deception? Undecided, uncertain of what she wants, she enters the house.

Lisette and Prunier. Lisette is in a state close to terror, and Prunier is bored by it. "M'hai rovinata" (you have ruined me), she says . . . "Dio! che disastro!" (Lord, what a disaster). To periodic whistlelike sounds in the orchestra, their dialogue reveals that the previous night in Nice she had made her debut as a chanteuse, accompanied by Prunier, and was whistled off the stage. "Dammi la pace!" (give me peace, the quiet life), she cries. In every whisper now she hears a whistle, and after a loud one in the orchestra she insists "un fischio" (a whistle), but Prunier has not heard it. He promises, however, to lead her back to safety, "ti riconduco alla tua mèta!" (I am leading you back to your purpose—i.e., destiny—life as a maid.)

A butler appears, and Prunier asks for the lady of the house, saying they are friends from Paris. The description upsets Lisette. "Io non sono sua amica" (I am not her friend). "Che cosa sei?" (What are you?), he asks. "Lo vedrai prima di sera" (you will see before evening). Waiting for Magda, they fight over nothing, and Lisette says furiously, "ti sprezzo" (I hate you).

When Magda appears, Lisette greets her, "Mia Signora," (Milady), while Prunier inquires if she is happy. "Interamente" (entirely), she assures him, but her tone says otherwise. Prunier reports that friends in Paris suspect she is bored, but when Magda cuts this short, he shifts to Lisette's disaster. She wants no more of the stage, only again to be a "cameriera" (maid). Lisette asks to be taken back, and Magda agrees, "ma certo" (but certainly). "Finalmente" (finally), sighs Lisette, and as she takes off her hat and resumes her old calling, the love theme associated with her and Prunier in the first act recurs in the orchestra.

Prunier remarks to Magda that someday she, too, will have to give up illusion and return to her true self. Though Magda tries to stop him, he continues: there is in Paris a man ready to help her. Then, having delivered Rambaldo's message, he leaves, asking softly when Lisette will be off in the evening while she bustles in and out of the house, happy to be again in "servizio."

Magda and Ruggero. He has a letter from his mother, "mia madre," and he asks Magda to read it, "leggi." If his wife-to-be is a good woman, writes his mother, then may she be blessed, "sia benedetta," and give her a kiss for me, "donale il bacio mio."

As Ruggero leans to kiss her, Magda pulls away. "Non, non posso" (I cannot). She tries to tell him of her past, but he does not care, he will not listen. Desperately she insists, "nella tua casa non posso entrare!" (in your house I cannot enter). She loves him and for that reason she cannot marry him. "Non voglio rovinarti" (I do not wish to ruin you). "No, non lasciarmi solo" (No, don't leave me alone), he cries . . . "No, rimani!" (stay). But she insists, "non voglio rovinarti."

Lisette comes from the house and, knowing of Rambaldo's offer and having just passed through a similar crisis, she understands what has happened. She goes slowly to Magda, and together they start down the hill for Nice and Paris.

Vocabulary, Act III

l'amor	l'ah.mor	love
un segreto	oon say.gret.oh	a secret
al nostro matrimonio	ahl nohs.troh mah.tree.moh.n'yo	(consent) to our marriage
hai fatto questo	high.ee fah.toh ques.toh	you have done this
dimmi tutto	dee.me too.toh	tell me all
per sempre	pair sem.pray	for always
tu che non sei	too kay nohn say.ee	you are not just
l'Amante ma	l'ah.MAHN.tay mah	a lover, but
l'Amore	l'ah.MOR.ay	Love itself
alla mia casa	ah.lah me.ah kah.zah	to my house
mia madre	me.ah mah.dray	my mother
un bambino	oon bahm.BEE.noh	a child
e chi sa?	ay key sah	and who knows?
m'hai rovinata	my.ee roh.vee.nah.tah	you have ruined me
dio . . . che disastro	dee.oh . . . kay dee.ZAHS.troh	Lord . . . what a disaster
dammi la pace	dah.me lah pah.chay	give me peace
un fischio	oon FEES.k'yo	a whistle
ti riconduco alla tua mèta	tee ree.coh.doo.koh ah.lah too.ah MAY.tah	I am leading you back to your end (destiny)
Io non sono sua amica	yo nohn soh.no soo (ah) ah.mee.cah	I am not her friend
che cosa sei	kay coh.sah say.ee	What are you
lo vedrai prima di sera	loh vay.dry.ee pree.mah dee sair.ah	you will see it before evening

ti sprezzo	tee spreh.tsoh	I hate you
interamente	in.teh.rah.men.tay	entirely
cameriera	k'ah.mehr.ee.ehr.ah	maid
ma certo	mah chair.toh	but certainly
finalmente	fee.nahl.men.tay	finally
servizio	sehr.veets.ee.oh	(in) service
leggi	leh.jee	read
sia benedetta	see.ah ben.eh.det.tah	may she be blessed
donale il bacio mio	dohn.nahl (il) bah.cho me.oh	give her a kiss for me
no, non posso	. . . nohn pohs.so	I cannot
nella tua casa non posso entrare	nell.ah too.ah kah.zah . . . en.trah.ray	in your house I cannot enter
non voglio rovinarti	. . . vohl.yoh roh.veen.ar.tee	I do not wish to ruin you
no, non lasciarmi solo	. . . lah.sharm.ee soh.lo	don't leave me alone
no, rimani	. . . ree.mah.nee	no, stay

IL TRITTICO

(The Triptych)

Three one-act operas, *Il Tabarro, Suor Angelica* and *Gianni Schicchi,* intended as a single evening's entertainment. World premiere, Metropolitan, New York, Dec. 14, 1918; European prem., Rome, Jan. 11, 1919; British prem., Covent Garden, June 18, 1920. Music by Giacomo Puccini; texts described under individual operas below.

The three operas display facets of love and death. In *Il Tabarro,* the love is sensual and ends in a murder caused by jealousy; in *Suor Angelica,* it is maternal and mystic, ending in a suicide pardoned by the Virgin Mary; in the comedy, *Gianni Schicchi,* a death of natural causes precedes and the predominant love, displayed by grieving relatives, is of money, with a subtheme of a young, healthy love that brightens the world.

Puccini wanted the operas kept together. Impresarios, certain they knew better, soon began to separate them, with *Gianni Schicchi* and *Suor Angelica* respectively the most and least frequently performed. In the 1960s the trend reversed. Impresarios and presumably audiences began to find that the operas strengthened each other; their contrasts were effective; they revealed, as Puccini's title implied, a common subject. Or do they? The argument continues.

The *Trittico* is the longest by thirty minutes of Puccini's operas, all relatively short. Exclusive of intermissions it runs roughly 2 hr., 35 min.; followed by *Butterfly* and *Fanciulla del West*, 2 hr., 5 min.; *Manon Lescaut*, 2 hr.; *Turandot*, 1 hr., 55 min.; *Tosca*, 1 hr., 50 min.; *Bohème* and *Rondine*, 1 hr., 45 min.

IL TABARRO

(The Cloak)

Text by Giuseppe Adami based on Didier Gold's play *La Houppelande* (*The Cloak*), first performed in Paris, 1910.

PRINCIPAL CHARACTERS

Michele, skipper of a barge, age 50	baritone	me.KAY.lay
Giorgetta, his wife, 25	soprano	jor.JET.tah
Luigi, a stevedore and Giorgetta's lover, 20	tenor	
Tinca, a stevedore, 35	tenor	
Talpa, a stevedore, 55	bass	
Frugola, Talpa's wife, 50	mezzo-soprano	FROO.go.lah

The action takes place in Paris, 1910, on a barge moored in the Seine.

The story concerns life on a barge and the search for happiness of the various persons connected with it. "How hard it is to be happy," says Giorgetta. Her search leads her into being unfaithful to her husband; his, into strangling her lover. Neither is a wholly sympathetic character: Giorgetta's infidelity is unattractive, yet she is trapped and her small dreams are pathetic; Michele's appeals for love are moving, yet his frank enjoyment of murder is terrifying. Contrary to Puccini's earlier practice, in this opera he favors no one; he simply presents what happens. This may be one reason that the opera is less popular than *Bohème*, but it is also a source of strength. When well performed, the opera delivers a solid punch. Atmosphere is part of that. Note the care Puccini takes with little touches.

A SINGLE ACT (55 min.)

The curtain rises (Puccini's direction) before the music begins. To the front, the barge, filling almost the whole stage; behind, connected by a gangplank, the quai; and in the background Notre Dame looming into a sunset sky.

The orchestra starts softly, a slow theme rising and falling like the river. Giorgetta does her chores, the stevedores carry sacks of cement from the hold to the quai, and Michele stands silently by the wheel, watching the sunset. From afar comes the hoot of a tugboat, the honk of an automobile horn. Throughout the opera the men call Michele "il padrone" (the boss) and Giorgetta "la padrona."

Giorgetta and Michele. She suggests some wine for the men: they have worked hard. Michele consents, but her concern for others wounds him: "E a me, non hai pensato?" (And of me, you have not thought?). "A te?" (Of you?), she says, "Che cosa?" (What do you mean?). When he tries to kiss her, she offers only her cheek. He goes below.

Luigi, Giorgetta, Tinca and Talpa. As she serves the wine, an organ grinder appears on the quai. Luigi hails him, "Professore! Vien qua" (Professor, come here), and Giorgetta requests music for dancing. Tinca offers himself as a partner, but when he steps on her foot, Luigi pushes him aside, and he and Giorgetta dance until Talpa warns, "Ragazzi, c'è il padrone" (kids, it's the boss). The men resume work.

Giorgetta and Michele. She asks about his plans. Will they stay in Paris? How many will he keep on? Tinca? Talpa? When he adds Luigi, she is surprised. "I don't want him to starve," says Michele.

A song-peddler followed by girls comes along the quai. His song is of love and spring, "primavera," but its two verses end in death: "E la storia di Mimì" (and that's the story of Mimì). Nevertheless, the girls buy a copy and go off singing it. (In each verse, before the closing line, Puccini quotes a phrase associated with Mimì in *Bohème*.)

To the background of the song Michele asks Giorgetta, "Have I ever made a scene?" He has not, she admits, but sometimes she would prefer a beating to his silence. What bothers him? "Nulla . . . nulla" (nothing), he replies.

Talpa's wife, Frugola (the frugal woman), comes on board with a sack of odds and ends she has collected from dustbins. Talpa, who at the end of each day wants only to rest, also has a symbolic name—the mole, or the dullard. And Tinca, who drinks too much, is named after a fish.

Giorgetta and Frugola. Waiting for Talpa, Frugola shows Giorgetta the objects she has found. In another bag she has food for her cat, "Caporale." While the orchestra gives two miaows, she starts a song in praise of the cat, which offers love without jealousy. "Ron, ron, ron" (purr). The men come on deck, and Michele asks Luigi to return for work in the morning.

Giorgetta, Frugola, Talpa, Tinca and Luigi. Frugola scolds Tinca for drinking too much, but he says it is better than thinking. Michele goes below, and Luigi in an outburst defends Tinca. "Hai ben ragione; **aria** meglio non pensare" (you have good reasoning; better not to think), for they live without hope. Every joy must be fought for or stolen, even love. "Segui il mio esempio—bevi!" (follow my example—drink), says Tinca. "Basta" (enough), Giorgetta interrupts, but Tinca, unchastened, departs for a bar.

Frugola sings quietly of her dream: a house with a garden, two pine trees, her cat "Caporale" and Talpa stretched out in the sun, all waiting quietly for death, the remedy of all ills.

"My dream is different," Giorgetta says. She wants the city, Paris. She describes the suburb where she was born, "Belleville." Luigi knows it well. She wants the excitement of the shops, the people and **duet** the sidewalks where you can hear your footfall—not like the river. Luigi joins her, and ecstatically they sing of Paris.

"I understand you," Frugola remarks, but as she and Talpa start homeward they murmur to each other of a cottage in the country. Alone and fearful, Luigi and Giorgetta swear to be true to each other: "E sempre uniti" (and always together).

Michele and Luigi. Michele is surprised to find Luigi still aboard, but Luigi has a request: to be taken to Rouen where he may find work. Michele advises him to stay in Paris; there is no work in Rouen. With a "buona notte" (good night), he returns to the cabin to light the lamps.

Luigi and Giorgetta. He was trying to leave; he can't bear to be so near **duet** her: "E la gioia rapita . . ." (it's a joy seized) with fear. They plan to meet that night. "Fai lo stesso signale?" (Do you make the same signal?), he asks. "Si" (yes). She will strike a match.

Luigi sings of his passion. He wants no other man to touch her. For **arioso** her he would kill and from the drops of blood make her a jewel. Overcome, he rushes off.

Giorgetta, alone, says sadly, "Come è difficile esser felice" (how hard it is to be happy).

Michele and Giorgetta. As he lights the lanterns, they talk of the number of men they need. She suggests that he fire Tinca, who is always drunk. His wife is unfaithful, Michele says; he drinks in order not to kill her. Approaching Giorgetta, Michele asks: "Perchè non m'ami più?" (Why don't you love me anymore?). "Perchè?"

I do, she says, but the cabin is stuffy, and I cannot sleep. "Non posso, non posso" (I cannot). He reminds her of their happiness before the baby died, "nostro bimbo."

"Il nostro bimbo," she cries. "Taci, taci" (keep silent). With her love, Michele continues, he was secure and happy. He begs her: "Resta vicino a me" (stay close to me). Return to your old self, he pleads: "Ritorna."

We are older now, she says, and enters the cabin.

Michele. "Sgualdrina!" (whore), he cries. In the distance a couple sing a popular song and at a barracks a bugle sounds.

Michele listens at the cabin. "Nulla" (nothing). He peeks in. She is still dressed, waiting. Who for? "Chi?" Who has changed her? Talpa? **soliloquy** Too old. Tinca? Too drunk. Luigi? But he wanted to leave for Rouen. Anger floods Michele. He wants to crush the unknown, shouting at him "Sei tu! Sei tu!" (it's you). Exhausted, he ends, "la pace è nella morte" (peace is in death). Absently he lights his pipe.

At the light, Luigi starts for the barge. Michele sees the shadow and is puzzled. Then he recognizes Luigi and grabs him.

Luigi and Michele. Luigi denies that he loves Giorgetta. But Michele forces him to admit and repeat, "ripeti," that he does. "L'amo" (I love her), gasps Luigi, as Michele strangles him.

Giorgetta and Michele. She calls. Michele sits, concealing Luigi's body under his cloak. She comes out, saying she is afraid. Wouldn't Michele like her to sit with him? Wrapped in my cloak, "nel mio tabarro?" he asks. She agrees, quoting his maxim that every man's cloak hides a joy and a sorrow.

Rising, he adds savagely, "And sometimes a crime." Luigi's corpse rolls at her feet, and Michele forces her down on it.

Vocabulary

il tabarro	eel tah.BAR.roh	the cloak
il padrone	eel pah.DRO.nay	the boss
la padrona	lah pah.DRO.nah	the mistress

Vocabulary (continued)

e a me, non hai pensato	eh (ah) may, nohn'ay.ee pen.SAH.toh	and of me, you have not thought
a te? che cosa?	ah tay? kay coh.sah?	of you? What do you mean?
professore, vien qua	proh.feh.SOR.ay v'yen qwah	professor, come here
ragazzi, c'è il padrone	rah.gah.tsee ch'l . . .	kids, it's the boss
primavera	pree.mah.VAIR.ah	spring
è la storia di Mimi	eh lah stor.yah dee me.me	that's the story of Mimi
nulla . . . nulla	NOOL.ah . . .	nothing
Caporale	cap.or.AHL.ay	Corporal (the cat's name)
ron, ron	ron	purr
hai ben ragione; meglio non pensare	hi ben ra.JOWN.nay may.l'yo nohn pen. sah.ray	you're right; it's better not to think
segui il mio esempio— bevi	seg.gw' eel m'yo 'semp.yoh—beh.vee	follow my example—drink
basta	BAH.stah	enough
Belleville	Bell.veel	(suburb of Paris)
e sempre uniti	eh sem.pray oon.nee.tee	and always united
buona notte	bwah.nah NOT.tay	good night
è la gioia rapita	eh lah je.OY.ah rah.PEE.tah	its a joy seized (with fear)
fai lo stesso signale	fie loh steh.soh seen.yahl.lay	do you make the same signal
come è difficile esser felici	cohm(e) eh dee.fee.cheel.ay es.say fay.lee.chay	how hard it is to be happy
perchè non m'ami più	pear.kay nohn m'ahm.ee p'yoo	why don't you love me anymore
non posso	nohn ph.soh	I cannot
nostro bimbo	no.stroh beem.boh	our baby
taci	TAH.chee	keep silent
resta vicino a me	res.tah vee. chee.n' ah may	remain near me
ritorna	ree.TOR.nah	return
sgualdrina	sgwahl.DREE.nah	whore
chi	key	who
sei tu	say too	it's you
la pace è nella morte	lah pah.chay nell.ah MOR.tay	peace is in death
ripeti	ree.PEH.tee	repeat
l'amo	l'ah.moe	I love her

SUOR ANGELICA

(Sister Angelica)

An original text by Giovacchino Forzano.

PRINCIPAL CHARACTERS

Suor Angelica		soprano	swor ahn.JELL.ee.cah
La Zia Principessa,		contralto	lah TSEE.ah
her aunt			PRIN.chee.PESS.ah
The Abbess	officers	mezzo-soprano	
The Monitor	of	mezzo-soprano	
The Mistress of	the	contralto	
Novices	convent		
Sister Genevieve		soprano	

The action takes place in a convent in the latter part of the seventeenth century.

Suor Angelica is of noble family, about twenty-five years old, and has been in the convent for seven years, placed there by her family. She had formed a liaison or married (it is not clear) a man whom her family considered unsuitable. By him she had a son whom the family had taken from her and raised without permitting her to see him. The man has disappeared from her life, even in memory, but for the son she yearns without ceasing. She is a woman of strong emotions that can veer toward hysteria and, possibly because of her misfortunes and the influence of the convent, she is ready to think of death as a better state than life.

A SINGLE ACT (55 min.)

The interior of a convent with a small church and cloister. To the back, beyond the arches, are the cemetery and the garden; in the scene's center are some cypress trees, a cross, herbs and flowers; to one side is a fountain. An evening in May.

The Prayer. The curtain rises on an empty stage. Bells toll, and within the church the Sisters sing an "Ave Maria." Two Lay-Sisters, late for the service, stop to listen to a bird (offstage piccolo) before entering the chapel. Suor Angelica, also late, hurries after them, but she remembers to kneel and kiss the threshold, the penance of latecomers.

The Penances. The service ended, the Sisters emerge, bow to the Abbess and gather before the Sister Monitor, who imposes the day's penances. First, the two Lay-Sisters who were late for service and forgot to kiss the threshold: twenty prayers for the oppressed. For Sister Lucilla, who made everyone laugh in chapel: some spinning in silence. For Sister Osmina, who concealed flowers in her sleeve—"Non è vero" (it is not true), says Sister Osmina—her cell. Watched by all she leaves, and a cell door slams. The penances administered, the Sister Monitor declares the hour free for recreation.

Recreation. The sisters scatter. Suor Angelica waters flowers while Sister Genevieve and others chatter about the sunset. Three evenings a year in May the sun strikes the fountain at such an angle that it turns the water to gold. But since that happened last, a sister has died, and for a moment in silence all think on her.

Sister Genevieve suggests that when the water turns to gold, they sprinkle some on Sister Bianca Rosa's grave. "She would like that," the **arioso** others agree. Angelica, however, observes that "likes" or desires are flowers only for the living. They do not bloom for the dead because the Virgin anticipates every wish. Passionately (the first loud music of the opera) she ends, "O sorella, la morte è vita bella" (O my sister, death is life made beautiful).

In life, too, says the Sister Monitor, we should abjure vain or worldly desires. Even if they are innocent? asks Genevieve. She confesses that she, who was a shepherdess, longs to hold a lamb again to her bosom (a flute and oboe trill lamblike bleats). And Sister Dolcina starts to say—but the others confess for her—that she likes good food.

Has Angelica, they ask, any desire? "No," she says, but they whisper that she lies. She waits for news that never comes. She was noble, and banished from her home. No one knows why. Seven years in the convent and never a visitor!

A sister hurries in from the infirmary. (This scene, 2 min., is sometimes cut.) She asks Angelica, who is expert in the use of herbs, to make a potion for Sister Chiara, who has been stung by wasps.

Return from the Collection of Alms. Two sisters who have been collecting alms lead in the convent's donkey (two hee-haws in the orchestra). They give the oil, eggs and cheeses to the housekeeper and some raspberries to Sister Dolcina, who under prodding shares them. Outside the gate, they report, is a magnificent coach; someone rich and noble is with the Abbess. Angelica intently asks about the coach's markings but the sisters become confused. The others, seeing her agitation, hope the visitor will be for her.

The Abbess enters. "Suor Angelica," she calls, and dismisses the others with a gesture.

Excitedly Angelica asks, "Madre, madre, parlate! Chi è? Chi è? (Mother, speak! Who is it?). For seven years she has waited, expiating her sins. The Abbess, interrupting, orders her to calm herself, and while the sisters in the cemetery sing a short requiem for Bianca Rosa, Angelica prays. Soon she says, "Madre, sono serena e sottomessa" (I am serene and submissive), and the Abbess announces, "vostra zia Principessa" (your aunt, the Princess).

La Zia Principessa. She is old, icy and dressed in black. Entering slowly and leaning on a cane, she glances at her niece and extends a hand to be kissed. Angelica, kneeling, searches her face for affection, but her aunt stares straight ahead.

"Your father and mother," she begins, "dying twenty years ago entrusted me with their children and their children's inheritance. The latter I was to divide as I saw need, and this I have done. Here is the instrument. Examine it, discuss it, sign it—"Osservarla, discuterla, firmarla."

"Dopo sett' anni" (after seven years), asks Angelica, does not this "luogo santo" (holy place) move you? This "luogo di clemenza . . . luogo di pietà (place of mercy . . . place of compassion). "Di penitenza" (of penitence), replies the aunt.

The reason for the division of the inheritance, she continues, is the marriage of your sister, Anna Viola. "Sposa?" (married?), exclaims Angelica. Little Anna Viola! But then "Ah, ah, sett' anni" have passed. She asks the husband's name, but her aunt says only, "one who for love can forgive the disgrace with which you stained us."

Angrily Angelica retorts, "Sorella di mia madre, voi siete inesorabile!" (sister of my mother, you are inexorable, i.e., merciless). The word stings the Principessa. "Inesorabile?" How dare you invoke your mother "contro di me" (against me). More calmly, she describes praying in the family's chapel, communing with Angelica's mother, and each time the mystical vision fades, she is left with the same message for Angelica: "Espiare, espiare" (to expiate, i.e., repent). Offer penance to the Virgin, she commands.

"I have offered all to the Virgin, all," says Angelica, "except the memory of my son. That I cannot give up. Tell me of my son." (At the words "mio figlio" Puccini begins a grinding phrase in the orchestra that he repeats sixteen times. Twice he raises it a minor third as Angelica's voice mounts almost to a shout, dropping down again as her emotion exhausts her.) "Parlatemi di lui" (speak to me of him), she begs.

Her aunt, however, is silent, and Angelica asks "Perchè? perchè?" (Why?). Speak up, she demands, the Virgin is listening, and she will judge you.

Two years ago, states her aunt, the child fell ill, everything possible was done for him. "È morto?" (He's dead?), gasps Angelica, and sobbing falls to the ground. Her aunt starts to her side then moves away to pray. After a moment she rings for pen, ink and a writing table. When they are brought, Angelica signs the document. As the aunt starts to go, she turns toward Angelica, who shrinks from her. On the threshold the aunt glances back but says nothing.

The Grace. Angelica, alone in the gathering darkness, thinks of her son. "Senza mamma, o bimbo, tu sei morto!" (without your mother, child, you are dead). Kneeling, she mourns the relationship that never existed, the child who died without knowing a mother's love. In the
aria   aria's second half her mood shifts and the melody broadens. "Ora che sei un angelo del cielo" (now that you are an angel in heaven), when can I join you, when find release in death? In a tiny coda she urges, "Parlami, parlami, amore, amore, amore!" (The aria ends softly on an A. Thus far, Puccini asks for restrained passion.)

The cloister is now dark. The Sisters who have been lighting lanterns in the cemetery pass through, assuring Angelica that the Virgin has heard her prayer. Against a background of their voices Angelica declares "La grazia è discesa dal cielo" (The Virgin's blessing has descended from heaven). In her certainty her excitement mounts to high C, after which she hurries to her cell, whence her voice is heard, "La grazia è discesa dal cielo."

interlude   There is a short interlude, 3 min., based on the melody of "Ora che sei un Angelo" during which Angelica reappears, picks some herbs and flowers, and prepares a potion.

The flowers, she sings, were always her friends. Now they will provide a poison, "veleno." Turning toward the cells, she bids her sisters "addio" (farewell). Her son has called. In heaven she can see his face. To a tremendous outburst in the orchestra she embraces the cross and drinks the poison.

The Miracle. Clouds conceal the moon and stars, and in anguish Angelica cries, "Ah, son dannata!" (I am damned). By taking her life she will die in mortal sin. "Madonna, Madonna," she begs, "salvami, salvami!" (save me). "Per amor di mio figlio!" (for love of my son).

She seems to hear the Angels (including tenors and basses, the only men's voices in the opera) imploring the Virgin on her behalf, and she begs for a sign of grace. A mysterious light begins to radiate from the chapel and in its doorway the Virgin appears, gently urging a small child toward its dying mother. (A usual critical complaint is that the miracle occurs only in the staging, not in the music.)

Vocabulary

non è vero	nohn eh VAIR.oh	it is not true
O sorella	oh sor.ELL.ah	Oh sister
la morte è vita bella	lah mort. (eh) eh vee.tah bell.ah	death is life made beautiful
madre, parlate	MAH.dray, pahr.LAH.tay	mother, speak
chi è?	key eh	who is it?
sono serena e sottomessa	so.no say.ray.nah ay soh.toh.MESS.ah	I am serene and submissive
vostra zia Principessa	voh.strah TSEE.ah preen.chee.PESS.ah	your aunt, the Princess
osservala	oh.SAIR.vah.lah	examine it
discuterla	dis.COOT.ayr.lah	discuss it
firmarla	feer.MAHR.lah	sign it
dopo sett' anni	do.poh set AH.nee	after seven years
luogo santo	l'woh.go SAHN.toh	holy place
luogo di clemenza	. . . dee cleh.MEN.tsah	place of mercy
luogo di pietà	. . . dee p'yay.TAH	place of compassion
di penitenza	dee pen.ee.TENS.ah	of penitence
sposa	SPOH.sah	married
. . . voi siete inesorabile	voy see.YAY.tay een.es.or.AH. bee.lay	you are inexorable, i.e., merciless
contro di me	cohn.tro dee may	against me
espiare	es.pee.AH.ray	to expiate, repent
mio figlio	mee.oh FEEL.yoh	my son
parlatemi di lui	par.LAH.tay.mee dee LOO.ee	speak to me of him
perchè	pair.KAY	why
è morto	ay MOR.toh	he is dead
senza mamma, o bimbo, tu sei morto	sent.sah . . . beem.boh, too say . . .	without a mother, o child, you are dead

Vocabulary (continued)

ora che sei un angelo del cielo	or.ah kay say (ee) oon an.jell.oh del chay.lo	now that you are an angel in heaven
parlami, amore	PAR.lah.mee, ah.MOR.ay	speak to me, love
la grazia è discesa dal cielo	lah grah.ts'yah dee.SHAY.sah dahl chay.loh	the blessing has descended from heaven
veleno	veh.LAY.noh	poison
addio	ah.DEE.oh	farewell
ah, son dannata	. . . sohn dah.NAH.tah	I am damned
Madonna	mah.DOHN.nah	Madonna
salvami	SAHL.vah.mee	save me
per amor di . . .	pair ah.MOR dee . . .	for love of (my son)

GIANNI SCHICCHI

Text by Giovacchino Forzano, an original libretto based on a reference in Dante's *Inferno,* Canto 30.

PRINCIPAL CHARACTERS

Gianni Schicchi	baritone	johnny skee.kee
Lauretta, Schicchi's daughter	soprano	
A Doctor from Bologna	bass	doh.TOR.ray
A Notary	bass	noh.TAH.roh

and relatives of the deceased Buoso Donati,
nine in all, of whom the most important are:

Zita, the old woman	mezzo-soprano	
Rinuccio, her nephew	tenor	ree.NOO.tcho
Simone, the old man and one-time mayor of Fucecchio	bass	see.MOAN.ay

The action takes place in Florence in 1299.

Gianni Schicchi, a historical figure, was best known before the opera because he was mentioned by Dante in the thirtieth canto of the *Inferno.* Together with a lady named Myrrha, he appears on the Eighth Circle of Hell. Dante disapproved of them because each, to gain an end, pretended to be someone else. Myrrha pretended in the dark to be her mother so that she could go to bed with her father. Schicchi pretended to be a rich old man, Buoso Donati, and dictated a will in which he bequeathed Donati's prize mare to himself. Dante's wife was a Donati, and the fact perhaps accounts for some of his anger at Schicchi.

Gianni Schicchi is Puccini's only comic opera and possibly the greatest of its kind in the century. Gianni is short for Giovanni.

A SINGLE ACT (50 min.)

The bedroom of Buoso Donati's house in Florence. French doors lead onto a terrace and through a large window can be seen the domes and towers of the city. Donati, on the bed, has just died.

The Relatives. They sob by the bedside: "I'll cry for days; me for months; me for years . . ." "Povero Buoso" (poor Buoso). Then one whispers that "lo dicono a Signa" (they say at Signa) that Donati left everything to the monks. Mourning ceases while the relatives consider the possibility of being disinherited. Zita asks Simone as the eldest, "il più vecchio," for an opinion. Simone, who had once been mayor of a suburb, advises that if the will is filed in court, nothing can be done. But if it is in the room. . . . All search for it.

The Will. Rinuccio finds it and as its price asks his aunt's permission to marry Lauretta, Schicchi's daughter. It is not the moment for such talk, the relatives insist, and to end it Zita half-assents. Rinuccio sends out the boy to find Schicchi and his daughter.

The relatives read the will, and the rumor proves true: the monks, "i frati," get the bulk of the property. The relatives laugh bitterly. Imagine at Buoso's death, says Zita, being truly heartbroken.

Can they, perhaps, change the will? Again they appeal to Simone, "il più vecchio." But Rincuccio interrupts: only Schicchi can help them. The boy rushes in, saying that Schicchi is on his way. The relatives unite in abusing him: a peasant, a nouveau. It is out of the question for a Donati to marry his daughter.

Rinuccio. He sings in praise of Florence: "Firenze è come un albero **aria** fiorito" (Florence is like a flowering tree), a city to which men of all degree have contributed and which has grown strong and beautiful by the talents of such newcomers as Arnolfo, Giotto and the Medici. Therefore, they should welcome Gianni Schicchi. As the aria ends, Schicchi enters.

(This aria and "O mio babbino caro," below, are the two daubs of sentiment in the opera. Purists object to them as hangovers from Puccini's earlier style and out of place in a swiftly paced *opera buffa.* Others argue that they are dramatically necessary for a change of pace, to give the audience a chance to collect its wits and catch up with the composer.)

The Relatives and Schicchi. Observing their sad faces as he enters, Schicchi remarks that Buoso Donati's health must be improving. But on discovering that Buoso is dead, he urges them to cheer up, since now they have an inheritance. Zita loses her temper and shrieks the truth at him: they've all been disinherited, and now she'll never let Rinuccio marry Lauretta, a peasant's daughter without a dowry.

Schicchi explodes with anger: "Brava, la vecchia . . ." (well done, old hag . . . that's the way to behave). This lets loose a babble through which Rinuccio and Lauretta despair, "Addio, speranza bella . . ." (farewell, lovely hope).

Rinuccio insists that the relatives show Schicchi the will. But Schicchi flatly refuses to help that crowd—"Niente, niente" (never).

Lauretta. She pleads with him. "O mio babbino caro" (oh, my Daddy
aria dear. . . for my sake). She'll throw herself under the Ponte Vecchio if she can't marry Rinuccio. "Babbo, pietà, pietà" (Daddy, have pity).

Schicchi. He hesitates, examines the will and announces that nothing can be done, "niente da fare." The lovers again despair, "Addio, speranza bella." But then Schicchi has an idea. After sending Lauretta out to the terrace to feed the birds, he questions the relatives. Who has been in the room? No one but them. Who else knows that Buoso is dead? No one. He has them put the corpse in a closet and orders the ladies to remake the bed. Before he can explain, there is a knock on the door.

The Doctor. He has come to see his patient. (He talks with a Bolognese accent because during the Middle Ages the University there was famous for its medical school. Similarly, in the *commedia dell' arte* the doctor was always from Bologna.) The relatives keep him a distance from the bed while Schicchi, behind the curtains, imitates the dead man's voice: he is feeling better and wants to sleep; the Doctor should return that evening, "A stasera" (till this evening). Everyone agrees, "a stasera," and the Doctor departs, pleased with the proof of his skill.

The Plan. His masquerade a success, Schicchi outlines for the slow-
aria witted relatives his plan (to catlike tread music). he will put on the nightcap, pull up the sheet, lie in Buoso's bed and redictate the will. His voice swells with pride, and the aria rises to a high G.

The excited relatives, however, haggle over how the property is to be divided. The three best pieces are "la mula" (the mule), "la casa" (the house) and "i mulini di Signa (the mills at Signa).

Schicchi suggests that the division be left to him. Suddenly, amid the ensuing disagreement, the town bell tolls a death. It proves to be that of the mayor's major-domo but, thoroughly frightened, the relatives agree to let Schicchi divide the property.

The Costuming. While the women tidy the room and help Schicchi into Donati's bedclothes, each relative whispers in his ear a bribe for "la mula," "la casa" and "i mulini di Signa"; and to each he replies, "Sta bene" (agreed).

After Schicchi is dressed for his part, the three women surround **trio** him, admiring him extravagantly and calling him "nostro salvatore" (our savior). (Some critics think this trio, accompanied by solo woodwinds and harp, the most perfect music in the opera.) With comic emphasis the women end by calling Schicchi "a letto" (to bed).

The Warning. First, however, he warns them of the penalty for fixing a will or assisting at it: exile and amputation of the right hand. And throughout the deception which follows he reminds them of it by repeating the verse "Addio, Firenze, addio, cielo divino" (goodby, Florence, farewell, heavenly sky).

Dictating the Will. Rinuccio has fetched a notary and two witnesses, a cobbler and a dyer. Schicchi whimpers that because of paralysis he cannot write and must dictate. The notary starts the will in Latin: "In Dei nomini . . ." and Schicchi adds, "Annullans, revocans . . ." (annulling and revoking all wills heretofore made by me). The relatives exclaim delightedly, "Che previdenza" (what foresight). Schicchi directs that his funeral must cost only two florins; the relatives exclaim "Che modestia" (what modesty). He bequeaths to the monks, "ai frati," only "cinque lire" (five lira). "Bravo," cry the relatives. Then he makes, in order, a small bequest to each relative until he has left to dispose only "la mula," "la casa" and "i mulini di Signa."

He leaves "la mula" to—Gianni Schicchi. The relatives are incredulous. He leaves "la casa" to—Gianni Schicchi. They are furious. Through their ill-suppressed growls of rage he reminds them of exile and amputation: "Addio, Firenze, addio, cielo divino." Finally, repeating the warning after each phrase, he bequeaths himself "i mulini di Signa." Then he directs Zita to pay the notary and witnesses out of her own pocket.

Funding young love. As soon as the notary and witnesses have gone, the relatives fall on Schicchi with cries of "ladro" (robber) and revenge themselves by grabbing what silver or candlesticks they can. He chases them out, and as the hubbub fades, the bedroom doors open, revealing the lovers on the terrace and behind them Florence bathed in sunlight. **love duet** To the tune of "Addio, speranza bella," now warmly orchestrated, they sing of their love for each other and for Florence, which seems to them "il Paradiso" (paradise).

Schicchi, returning, watches them embarce. As the curtain falls, he steps before it and, indicating the young lovers behind him, asks the audience what better use could be made of Buoso's money. For his deception Dante condemned him to "the inferno," but with all deference to "gran padre Dante" he hopes that, if the audience has enjoyed the evening, it will acquit him for extenuating circumstances.

Vocabulary

povero Buoso	poh.vair.oh Bwoh.so	poor Buoso
lo dicono a Signa	loh DEEK.oh.noh ah seen.yah	they say it at Signa
il più vecchio	eel pyew vek.yoh	the eldest
i frati	ee FRAH.tee	the brothers (monks)
Firenze è come un albero fiorito	fee.REHNTS(eh) ay cohm (eh) oon ahl.bay.roh fyo.REE.toh	Florence is like a flowering tree
brava, la vecchia	BRAH.vah lah vek.yah	well done, old hag
addio, speranza bella	ah.dee.oh spair.ahn. tsah bell.ah	farewell, lovely hope
niente	nee.EN.tay	nothing, never
o, mio babbino caro	oh me.oh bah.BEE.noh kar.oh	oh, my Daddy dear
babbo, pietà	bah.boh p'yay.tah	Daddy, have pity
niente da fare	. . . dah FAH.ray	(there is) nothing to do
a stasera	ah stah.SAY.rah	till this evening
la mula	lah MOO.lah	the mule
la casa	lah kahs.ah	the house
i mulini di Signa	ee moo.lee.nee dee seen.yah	the mills at Signa
sta bene	stah bay.nay	agreed (it is well)
nostro salvatore	noh.stroh sahl. vah.TOR.ay	our savior
a letto	ah leht.toh	to bed

addio, Firenze, addio,	ah.dee.oh	goodby, Florence,
cielo divino	fee.RENTS.ay	farewell, heavenly
	. . . chell.oh	sky
	dee.VEE.noh	
che previdenza	kay preh.vee.DEN.tsah	what foresight
che modestia	kay moh.dest.yah	what modesty
cinque lire	chink.way lee.ray	five lira
bravo	BRAH.voh	well done
ladro	LAH.droh	robber
gran padre Dante	grahn pah.dray	old man Dante
	dahn.tay	

TURANDOT

Lyric drama in three acts. World premiere, La Scala, Milan, April 25, 1926; American prem., Buenos Aires, June 26, 1926. United States prem., Metropolitan, New York, Nov. 16, 1926; British prem., Covent Garden, June 7, 1927. Music by Giacomo Puccini, the last duet and final scene being completed by Franco Alfano after Puccini's death; text by Giuseppe Adami and Renato Simoni from Carlo Gozzi's fable, *Turandote,* first performed, Venice, Jan. 22, 1762.

PRINCIPAL CHARACTERS

Liù, a young slave girl	soprano	lee.oo
The Prince, whose name is Calaf	tenor	
Timur, his father and a dethroned Tartar king	bass	tee.moor
The Princess Turandot	soprano	toor.an.dot
Ping, the Grand Chancellor	baritone	
Pang, the General Purveyor	tenor	
Pong, the Chief Cook	tenor	
The Emperor Altoum	tenor	

The action takes place in Peking in legendary times.

The opera is based on a Venetian play. But behind the play, and even behind Shakespeare's more gentle *Merchant of Venice,* is a fairy tale, common to most cultures, of the proud princess who slaughters her suitors. She despises men and is the personification of Anatole France's remark that of all sexual aberrations chastity is the strangest. Always, finally, comes a man who wins her, who chooses the casket concealing Portia's portrait, defeats Atalanta in the foot race or correctly answers Turandot's riddles.

True to its fairy-tale origin, the opera preserves a dreamlike unreality. Scenes of great cruelty mix with those of fantastic beauty, and the characters symbolize as much as portray human feelings. Yet scenes and characters have a barbaric validity; the color, sound and simple emotions are effective—especially when the opera is theatrically produced. Puccini sets the first act, for example, "by the walls of the great Violet City: the City of the Celestial Empire. Massive bastions circle the stage. To the right the curve is broken by a high portico covered with sculptured monsters, unicorns, phoenix, and with pillars rising from the backs of huge tortoises.

"Near the portico a heavy bronze gong hangs from two arches.

"From the bastions spears suspend the heads of the unfortunate suitors. To the left three gigantic gates open from the walls. The curtain rises on a glorious sunset. In the distance, bathed in golden light, is Peking."

Obviously, this is easier to enjoy than to create on a stage.

The fairy tale, as Puccini tells it, reveals the liberating effect of love. Turandot, the Princess of ice and death, is released to a fuller, better life when for the first time she responds to a man's love. With a final, double twist, however, the tale proclaims that for love to flower it must be mutual. Under torture a slave girl saves the Prince's life by refusing to reveal his name, but her love for him, unrequited, ends in death. Soon after, by a similar silence Turandot saves the Prince, and her love, requited, ends in life and universal joy. Love, says the poet, can be cruel as well as beautiful.

The opera has two confusions. First, how to pronounce its title: the three syllables should have equal stress and the final "t" be sounded; second, how much of it is pure Puccini. Before his death on Nov. 29, 1924, he had completed its composition and orchestration through the funeral cortege of Liù in Act III and sketched some musical ideas for the rest. Franco Alfano, using these sketches, composed the final duet for Turandot and the Prince (11 min.) and the last scene (4 min.). The break in style is noticeable, chiefly in the harsh brassiness of the duet's introduction.

ACT I (35 min.)

A crowd fills the square of the Violet City. It listens, motionless, while a court official, a mandarin, reads a decree.

The Mandarin. "Popolo di Pekino" (People of Peking) "la legge è questa" (the law is this): Turandot will be the bride of him who correctly answers the three riddles; he who tries and fails must die. The Prince of Persia has just failed and at moonrise will be decapitated.

The Crowd. It rushes to the palace calling for the executioner. In the confusion, an old man falls. His companion, a young girl, calls for help, "pietà, pietà," and a stranger kneels beside her.

Liù, Timur and the Prince. The stranger, who is the Prince, recognizes his father, "padre, mio padre," and Timur rejoices to find his son, "mio figlio." They were parted in the battle that lost the father his kingdom, and since then, Timur says, Liù has cared for him. Who is she? asks the Prince, and she replies, "nulla sono . . . una schiava, mio signore" (I am nothing . . . a slave, my lord). When he asks why she has been so good to Timur, she says that once in the palace the Prince smiled at her. (In Puccini's vocabulary her melodic phrases, ending on a high B-flat, proclaim love.)

The Crowd. The executioner's assistants begin to sharpen the great ax. As the people watch, their excitement rises and they call for blood, which always flows where Turandot reigns, "dove regna Turandot." With its edge honed the ax is returned to the palace, and the people softly invoke "la luna," the moon. Why does it delay? When it rises, they call for the executioner, and a procession for the Prince of Persia, led by children, winds through the square. But on seeing the victim the crowd's mood shifts, and it calls to the Princess, "Principessa," to have mercy, "grazia," and pity, "pietà."

Turandot in all her dazzling beauty appears on her balcony. With a gesture she signals death for the Prince, and the procession, followed by the crowd, disappears through the gates. (Turandot's silence here is an exception to the general rule in opera that a leading character is best introduced in song. Turandot does not reappear or sing until Act II, Scene 2, yet by this single, brief, silent appearance her character and presence are sufficiently established to dominate the action.)

Liù, Timur and the Prince. The Prince is overcome by the sight of Turandot: "o divina bellezza" (oh, heavenly beauty), "o meraviglia" (oh, marvel). He will try the riddles. Timur and Liù beg him to come away, but he insists and, crying "Turandot," is about to hit the gong and present himself when Ping, Pang and Pong, three officers of the court, surround him.

Ping, Pang and Pong. They try to dissuade him: even if he saw Turandot naked—it's just flesh, not good to eat; better to have 200 other legs than her mere two, however fine. "Va' via" (go away). The Prince says only, "lasciatemi passar" (let me pass).

From the balcony Turandot's maids request "silenzio là" (silence there). The Princess is sleeping. Shades of her previous suitors pass across the bastions. Softly they urge the Prince to sound the gong so that they may once more see Turandot, they who loved her. "No, no," cries the Prince, "io solo l'amo" (I alone love her).

Ping, Pang and Pong try again. Turandot, they say, is a phantom. She doesn't exist, "non esiste"; only the executioner is real. At that moment he appears on the wall holding the Prince of Persia's head.

Liù. Timur urges her to stop the Prince. She begs him, "Signore,
aria ascolta. Liù non regge più" (My lord, listen. Liù can bear no more).

The Prince. He is kind but unmoved. "Non piangere, Liù" (don't
aria weep). He asks her to lead his father away and to continue to tend him.

Liù, Timur, the Prince and Ping, Pang and Pong. All try to hold him back. While the crowd offstage sings quietly of death, the Prince sings of Turandot. Freeing himself, he bangs the gong. Liù and Timur sink in despair; Ping, Pang and Pong run off laughing.

Vocabulary, Act I

popolo di Pekino	poh.poh.loh dee peh.KEE.noh	people of Peking
la legge è questa	lah lej'ay kwes.tah	the law is this
pietà	p'yay.tah	have pity
mio padre	mee.oh PAH.dray	my father
mio figlio	mee.oh FEEL.yoh	my son
nulla sono . . . una schiava, mio signore	nul.lah so.no . . . oo.nah sk'yah.vah m'yo seen.YOR.ay	I am nothing . . . a slave, my lord
dove regna Turandot	doh.vay rain.yah Toor.an.dot	where Turandot reigns
la luna	lah loo.nah	the moon
Principessa	prin.chee.PESS.ah	Princess
grazia	grah.ts'yah	mercy
o divina bellezza	oh dee.VEE.nah bel.lets.ah	o heavenly beauty
o meraviglia	oh meh.rah.VEEL.yah	o marvel
va' via	vah' VEE.ah	go away
lasciatemi passar	lah.SHAH.tay.mee pass.ahr	let me pass

silenzio là	see.len.ts'yoh lah	silence there
io solo l'amo	yoh so.lo lah.moh	I alone love her
non esiste	nohn ay.ZEE.stay	she does not exist
signore, ascolta	seen.yor.ay ah.SCOHL.tah	my lord, listen
Liù non regge più	lee.oo nohn reh.jay p'yoo	Liù can bear no more
non piangere, Liù	nohn p'yahn.jehr.ay . . .	don't weep, Liù

ACT II (40 min.)

SCENE 1 (8 min.)

A Pavilion, formed by a huge curtain decorated with fantastic and symbolic figures.

Ping, Pang and Pong. In privacy they discuss the situation. As usual, for the new suitor they will have lanterns ready for either a wedding or a funeral, but sadly they predict the latter. Ping leads a lament, "O China," where for centuries life was beautiful. Each wails in turn, "Poi nacque . . ." (then was born), and they end together, "Turandot." Life has become three bangs on a gong, three riddles and a severed head. They review the count: in the year of the mouse, six; of the dog, eight; and now in the year of the tiger, counting the new suitor, thirteen. They are merely assistants to an executioner.

Nostalgically Ping describes his house in Honan, on a lake of "blù" (blue), surrounded with "bambù" (bamboo). Better there than at court racking his brain over sacred books, "libri sacri." Pong has forests near Chang-Te and Pang a garden close to Kiù. For a moment the three sit motionless, dreaming.

They rise with gestures of despair. Oh world, "O mondo," so full of crazy lovers. They recall the suitors. This one with earrings, that with furs; all killed, "uccisi." From behind the curtain the crowd begins to call softly for blood.

Overcome by the slaughter, they sing farewell to love and future generations, "addio amore, addio razza." China is finished: "È finisce la China"—until the day they can sing like this, "così": of a wedding with colored lanterns, flowers, serenades and of Turandot surrendering to love.

Trumpets interrupt their reverie. The trial is about to begin. The pavilion fades into a square before the palace; to a ceremonial march the crowd gathers.

(This dialogue for three is the opera's most controversial scene. Some persons find it boring: nothing happens. Others find the music, with its constant shifts in color, rhythm and vocal line, extremely expressive and beautiful. Unfortunately, singers without faith in the music often spoil the scene by running about in what they presumably conceive to be an oriental fashion.)

SCENE 2 (32 min.)

The square in front of the Palace. An enormous marble staircase rises to a triple arch before which is the Emperor's ivory throne.

The Crowd. It comments softly on the officials as they arrive. First are
ceremonial march   the eight wise men, tall and pompous: "They have the answers." Then come Ping, Pang and Pong. Incense burns on huge tripods. War flags pass in review. Finally, like a vision, at the top of the stairs appears the Emperor. He is very old, tired and sacred.

The Emperor and the Prince. Only his oath makes the Emperor continue with the slaughter of suitors. Three times he begs the Prince to retire, but each time the Prince replies, "Figlio del cielo, io chiedo d'affrontar la prova!" (Son of Heaven, I ask to confront the test). Sadly the Emperor concedes his right to try.

The Mandarin. As in the first act, he reads the conditions of the trial. The crowd calls quietly for Turandot. She enters and takes her place at the foot of the throne.

Turandot. In a long aria she explains her coldness. "In questa reg-
aria   gia . . ." (in this palace) many years ago her ancestor, the Princess Louling, had been captured, dragged out and killed by a man, a Tartar Prince. Passionately Turandot insists, "Mai nessun m'avrà!" (no man shall ever have me). "Straniero" (stranger), she warns: "Gli enigmi sono tre, la morte è una" (the riddles are three, death is one). "No, no," cries the Prince, "gli enigmi sono tre, la vita è una" (. . . life is one).

The crowd asks for the trial to begin, and Turandot imperiously addresses the Prince, "Straniero, ascolta" (stranger, listen).

First Riddle. What is that to which all the world turns, which each dawn dies but in the human heart each night is reborn?

The Prince responds "La Speranza" (hope). The wise men check their scrolls. He has answered correctly.

Second Riddle. What flares like a flame, burns like a fever, grows sluggish if idle, is cold in death, hot in love and red like a sunset?

The Prince correctly answers "Il Sangue" (blood). The crowd is now wholly for the Prince, and Turandot orders it to be silent. She comes down the staircase, and the Prince kneels before her.

Third Riddle. What is that ice which fires you, yet from your fire grows colder still; that force which in liberating you makes you a slave and in accepting you as a slave makes you a king?

The Prince hesitates. She leans over him malignantly. "Su, straniero" (up, stranger), that ice which gives you fire, what is it?

The Prince rises and cries "Turandot." He has answered correctly, and the crowd rejoices with a hymn of praise.

Turandot. She turns to the Emperor. She asks, she begs not to be given to the Prince. The Emperor replies that he is bound by his sacred oath. She rants that she is sacred. The crowd insists that the oath is binding. She taunts the Prince, saying that she will lie in his arms like ice. Is that what he wants? In her fury her voice twice rises above the chorus to high C. "No, no," cries the Prince. He wants her on fire with love. (His high B-flat is optional and often omitted.)

The Prince. He offers her a riddle. No one knows his name. "Dimmi il mio nome" (give me my name). If she can discover it before dawn, she can kill him at daybreak. Turandot accepts the challenge. The Emperor wishes the Prince good luck, and the crowd bursts out with the Peking national anthem.

Vocabulary, Act II
Scene 1

O China	oh key.nah	Oh, China
poi nacque	poy NAHK.(eh)	then was born
blù	bloo	blue
bambù	bam.boo	bamboo
libri sacri	lee.bree sah.cree	sacred books
O mondo	oh, mohn.doh	Oh, world
uccisi	oo.CHEE.zee	killed
addio amore	ah.dee.oh ah.mohr.ay	farewell love
addio razza	ah.dee.oh raht.tsah	farewell race
è finisce la China	ay fee.NEE.sheh . . .	China is finished
così	coh.see	like this

Vocabulary (continued)

Scene 2

figlio del cielo	feel.yo del chell.oh	Son of Heaven
io chiedo d'affrontar la prova	yo k'yay.doh d'ahf.frohn.tahr lah PROH.vah	I ask to confront the test
in questa reggia	een.ques.tah red.jah	in this palace
Principessa Louling	prin.chee.PESS.ah loo.leeng	Princess Louling
mai nessun m'avrà	my nes.soon m'ah.vrah	no man shall ever have me
straniero	strahn.YAIR.oh	stranger
gli enigmi sono tre, la morte è una	lee eh.NEE.me so.no tray, lah MOR.tay (eh) oo.nah	the riddles are three, death is one
. . . la vita è una	. . . lah VEE.tah (eh) oo.nah	. . . life is one
la speranza	lah speh.RAHN.tsah	hope
il sangue	eel SAHNG.gway	blood
dimmi il mio nome	deem.(ee) eel m'yo no.may	give me my name

ACT III (40 min.)

SCENE 1 (36 min.)

In the Palace garden, "very vast and undulating." Among the bushes bronze statues of the gods reflect the dim light cast by incense burners. Night.

The Heralds. In the distance they repeat Turandot's edict: on pain of death, "nessun dorma" (let no one sleep) until the Prince's name is discovered. All through the city the cry goes out.

The Prince. He repeats it: "Nessun dorma." Not even Turandot shall
aria sleep tonight, he exults, for I shall triumph, "vincerò."

Ping, Pang, Pong and the Crowd. The three creep from the bushes. They despair of learning his name and beg him to save them from torture for failing. They offer him maidens, alluring and seminude. He refuses. They offer riches; he refuses. They offer to help him win glory—somewhere else. The crowd begs him to flee. He refuses. Pathetically they describe what they will suffer if he doesn't go—the knife, the wheel, the pincers. The whole world may die, he replies, but he will have Turandot. Furiously they threaten him: "Parla, parla; il nome, il nome, il nome" (speak, the name).

Soldiers drag in Liù and Timur. The crowd turns on them. They were seen with the Prince. They know his name. The crowd calls for the Princess to begin the torture; she enters and indicates the old man is to be first. But Liù steps forward; she alone knows the name, and she will die before revealing it. The soldiers bind her, twist her arm, but she says nothing. Turandot asks where she gets the strength to resist. From love, "l'amore," Liù answers proudly. "L'amore?" Turandot repeats with surprise.

Liù. "Tanto amore . . ." (so much love) has she for the Prince that **aria** she will happily die for him. The greater the torture the greater the proof of her love. The crowd rages at her, and the tortures are increased until she agrees to speak.

Softly she begins: "Tu che di gel sei cinta" (you who in ice are **aria** bound) will melt before the Prince's passion. Whereas Liù, who also loves him, will never see him again. She snatches a soldier's dagger and kills herself. The crowd, balked of the name, is infuriated. *Timur and the Crowd.* He is aghast at the crime against Liù. And the crowd, as it realizes the extent of her sacrifice, is awed and forms a funeral procession for her. All march slowly offstage, leaving the Prince and Turandot. (Here Puccini ended, and Alfano began.)

The Prince and Turandot. "Principessa di morte" (Princess of death) and "di gelo" (of ice), he starts, look on this girl you have killed. Roughly he tears off her veil. Turandot, startled but imperious, replies that she is different from other mortals; her soul, "anima," is in heaven. Possibly, he says, but your body is here, and he moves closer to embrace her. "Non profanarmi" (don't profane me), she cries. As he forces her head back, she desperately insists "è un sacrilegio!" (it is a **duet** sacrilege). After his kiss she declares "la mia gloria è finita" (my glory is finished) and starts to weep. It only begins, he replies, with the miracle of your first kiss and of your first tears. She confesses she was afraid of him from the start. He is free to go. His name is unknown, and dawn is about to break. But he, trusting in her tears, reveals his name, "Calaf." She is triumphant. He insists he has no life but in her. Offstage, trumpets summon the court to learn the result of Turandot's trial.

SCENE 2 (4 min.)

With no break in music, the scene shifts to the great staircase of the Palace, its cold white marble turning pink with the first streaks of dawn. The Emperor, court and crowd are assembled.

Turandot leads in Calaf. She mounts the stairs, announcing to the Emperor that she has learned the Prince's name. She turns to gaze down at him. "Il suo nome," she begins—and finishes "è Amor" (is love). Everyone rejoices. The opera ends.

Vocabulary, Act III

nessun dorma	nes.soon dor.mah	let no one sleep
vincerò	vin.CHAIR.oh	I shall triumph
parla . . . il nome	par.lah . . . eel NO.may	speak . . . the name
l'amore	l'ah.mor.ay	love
tanto amore	tahn.t'(oh) ah.mor.ay	so much love
tu che di gel sei cinta	too kay dee jell say.ee cheen.tah	You who in ice are bound
Principessa di morte	prin.chee.PESS.ah dee mor.tay	Princess of death
Principessa di gelo	. . . dee jell.oh	. . . of ice
anima	AH.nee.mah	soul
non profanarmi	nohn proh.fah.NAHR.me	do not profane me
è un sacrilegio	'oon sah.cree.leh.joh	it is a sacrilege
la mia gloria è finita	lah m'yah gloh.r'yah (eh) fee.NEE.tah	my glory is finished
del primo pianto	dell pree.moh p'yahn.toh	of the first tears
il suo nome è Amor	eel s'woh no.may ay ah.MOR	his name is Love

ARIADNE AUF NAXOS

(Ariadne on Naxos)

In its original form an opera in one act; with music by Richard Strauss, text by Hugo von Hofmannsthal and intended to cap a production of Molière's *Le Bourgeois Gentilhomme* for which Strauss had also composed incidental music. This, the less frequently performed version, had its premiere with the play at Stuttgart on Oct. 25, 1912; British prem. (in English), London, May 27, 1913. A revised "two-act" version, with the play dropped and a musical Prologue (42 min.) preceding the opera, had its prem. in Vienna, Oct. 4, 1916; British prem. (in

German), Covent Garden, London, May 27, 1924; United States prem., Philadelphia, Nov. 1, 1928. This is the version described.

PRINCIPAL CHARACTERS

In the Prologue

The Major-domo	speaking role	
The Music Master	baritone	
The Composer	soprano	
The Tenor (later Bacchus)	tenor	
The Prima Donna (later Ariadne)	soprano	
Dancing Master	tenor	
Zerbinetta, leader of a troupe of *commedia dell'arte* players	soprano	zair.be.NET.tah
Arlecchino	baritone	ahr.leh.KEY.no
Scaramuccio	tenor	scah.ra.MOO.cho
Truffaldino	bass	troo.fahl.DEE.no
Brighella	tenor	bree.GHEL.lah

In the Opera

Naiad	soprano
Dryad	contralto
Echo	soprano
Ariadne	soprano
Bacchus	tenor
Zerbinetta and her troupe	as above

The action is set in Vienna in the eighteenth century in the palace of a very rich nobleman. The Prologue takes place in the backstage of his private theatre; "the opera" turns that stage to face the audience.

The history of Strauss's incidental music for a production of Molière's *Le Bourgeois Gentilhomme,* a *comédie-ballet,* can be roughly summarized as follows. The original idea was to provide a cut version of the play with music for its songs and ballets, and in place of the Turkish ceremony to end the play with an opera. This plan produced eleven numbers of incidental music and *Ariadne 1.* Double casts for play and opera, however, were too costly for most theatres, and the opera was split off, slightly revised and provided with a Prologue, becoming *Ariadne 2* The play was returned to full length and ten more numbers of incidental music added. Later Strauss took nine of the musical numbers from the play and combined them into his delightful *Le Bourgeois Gentilhomme Suite* (36 min.). He also made a longer *Suite* with vocal soloists and chorus that is seldom presented. The opera's original version, *Ariadne 1,* with the cut play, is still sometimes performed, notably at Glyndebourne, but the revised version with the Prologue is far more common.

The Prologue, which concerns the preparations to present "the opera," has its disparagers. It is full of talk, not always clear and sometimes downright silly. To make it seem less long it is often presented in translation when the opera which follows is not. Even so, for many persons it remains part of the price of admission to the glories of the opera. Yet the Composer, who appears only in the Prologue, is a charming character and has exquisite music. The role at its premiere catapulted Lotte Lehmann to fame, and great singers do not scorn it.

The orchestra, as would befit a private performance in an eighteenth-century house, is small, only thirty-nine instruments. Among them are a piano, harmonium and celesta, and the proportion of woodwinds to strings is unusually high. The opera was one of the first in the twentieth century to reverse the trend of the nineteenth century to ever larger orchestras.

THE PROLOGUE (42 min.)

Major-domo and Music Master. The rich man's major-domo explains to an incredulous Music Master that in the evening's entertainment the Composer's *opera seria, Ariadne,* will be followed by an Italian *opera buffa.* On behalf of his pupil the Music Master protests but is reminded that the rich, who pay, call the tune.

A footman shows an army officer to Zerbinetta's dressing-room door, where the officer dismisses the servant with startling rudeness. Plainly the comedians attract the vulgar.
The Composer. He wishes to rehearse the orchestra once more and asks the footman to summon "the fiddles." Lacking feet, the fiddles cannot walk, says the footman. Naively the composer explains that he meant the players. They are at dinner, says the footman. The Composer is appalled: eating and drinking, with a performance in fifteen minutes! No, says the footman, playing for the dinner guests.

The Composer decides instead to rehearse Ariadne's music with the Prima Donna. He starts mistakenly for Zerbinetta's door and is warned by the footman, who exits laughing, that the lady is occupied and will not see him. The Composer knocks, but the door remains closed.

Alone, his anger turns to meditation. Through his head runs a musical phrase, introduced by a flute. It fades and returns, swelling out of words referring to Bacchus in the opera, "Du almächtiger Gott!" When he has its outline firmly in mind, "O du Knabe! Du Kind! Du almächtiger Gott!" (O thou boy, thou child, thou almighty God), he finds that he has no paper on which to record it and runs to the tenor's dressing room.

The door bursts open as the tenor ejects the wig maker. Neither will listen to the Composer's request. He is distracted, however, by the sudden appearance of Zerbinetta, the Prima Donna, the Music Master and the Dancing Master. Nodding toward Zerbinetta he asks, who is that beautiful girl? So much the better if you like her, says the Music Master, and tells him of the *opera buffa* that is to follow *Ariadne*.

The Composer is furious but softens as the fugitive melody again returns. Quick, paper, he asks the Music Master, who produces a sheet.

Around the scribbling composer confusion spreads. The Prima Donna complains of the vulgar comedians, Zerbinetta of the boring **arietta** opera; the Dancing Master has an arietta on the saving grace for the evening of the *opera buffa,* and the Music Master assures the Prima Donna that the guests will have ears only for *Ariadne*.

Major-domo. He announces a further change in the order of musical events. Instead of the comedy succeeding the opera, they will be performed simultaneously; and together they must not last longer than the opera alone, for fireworks are to follow.

All. The comedians find the idea amusing, but the Composer is ready to quit, until the Music Master reminds him of the fee. The Tenor and the Prima Donna each suggest cuts in the other's music, and the Dancing Master recounts the opera's story to Zerbinetta. A princess, Ariadne, is abandoned on an island by her lover, Theseus. She yearns for death, "den Tod." "Den Tod!" exclaims Zerbinetta. What Ariadne really wants, "natürlich," is another lover. "Natürlich" (naturally), agrees the Dancing Master, adding that one soon comes.

"Nein, Herr, so kommt es nicht!" (No, sir, so comes he not), says the Composer, eager to reveal the opera's deeper meaning. Ariadne is a woman of great soul who gives her heart to one man, Theseus, forever. Therefore when she sees Bacchus, she truly believes him to be the God of Death, for which she yearns, and for that reason only she joins him in his ship, "sein Schiff." When Zerbinetta expresses disbelief, the Composer shouts that Ariadne is not like her. "Ariadne ist die eine unter Millionen" (Ariadne is the one in a million), "sie ist die Frau, die nicht vergisst" (she is the woman who does not forget).

"Kindskopf" (child-head, i.e., nonsense), says Zerbinetta, and begins to relay the plot to her troupe. There is a jilted princess on a beach with no lover in sight. We will be lively travellers who, arriving by chance, try to cheer her up.

The Composer, interrupting, in solemn tones insists that Ariadne goes to her death, where wonderful transformations occur. In the arms of Bacchus she is reborn, and through love he gains his divinity.

Zerbinetta and the Composer. Unable to follow him, she quells him with a sample of what she understands. Looking into his eyes she says, **love duet** "Ein Augenblick ist wenig" (a moment in time is a little thing) but "ein blick ist viel" (a human's glance is much). She fascinates him, then runs off to dress.

Music Master and Prima Donna. He directs everyone to their places: the opera is about to begin. The Prima Donna balks: she will not set foot on a stage with Zerbinetta. Where better, asks the Music Master, to demonstrate the gulf, "Abstand," that separates them. "Abstand," repeats the Prima Donna; rather a world, "Eine Welt!" And she prepares to prove the point.

The Composer. Still under Zerbinetta's spell, he rhapsodizes on music. "Die Dichter" (the poets) can write words for music, and yet, and yet—"jedoch, jedoch!" With jubilant voice he cries that he has the courage, "mut," to face the world. "Was ist denn Musik? (What then is music), he asks. "Musik ist eine heilige Kunst" (Music is a holy art) which unites with the Cherubim all who dare to find beauty in the **aria** world. "Das ist Musik" (that is music), the most holy of the arts. (Unquestionably Strauss had his tongue in cheek, and he directed that the aria be sung "with almost drunken solemnity." But at "Musik ist eine heilige Kunst," a large part of the audience will turn to jelly and dissolve.)

For the Composer, however, reality intrudes. He sees the comedians practicing their gestures and realizes that Zerbinetta's affection was only a ruse. He upbraids the Music Master for allowing him to agree to the comedians. Better to have forfeited the fee. But it is too late—the opera is about to begin.

Vocabulary, Prologue

du allmächtiger Gott	doo ahll.MEHK.tik.er got	thou almighty god
o du Knabe, du Kind	oh doo k'NAH.bch, doo kint	oh thou boy, thou child

den Tod	den toht	death
natürlich	nah.TEUR.lik	naturally
nein, Herr, so kommt es nicht	nine, hairr, so kohmt es nikt	no, sir, so comes he not
sein Schiff	sine shif	his ship
Ariadne ist die eine unter Millionen	ahri.AHD.neh ist dee EYE.neh oon.ter milli.OH.nehn	Ariadne is the one in a million
sie ist die Frau, die nicht vergisst	see ist dee frow, dee nikt fair.GIST	she is the woman who does not forget
Kindskopf	kints.kop'f	child-head, i.e., nonsense
ein Augenblick ist wenig	eye'n OW.gen.blik ist VAIN.ik	a moment in time is a little thing
ein blick ist viel	eye'n blik ist feel	a glance is much
Abstand	AHP.shtahnnt	a distance, fig., a gulf.
eine Welt	eye.neh velt	a world
die Dichter	dee DIK.ter	the poets
jedoch, jedoch	yay.DOHK	and yet
mut	mooht	courage
was ist denn Musik	vahs ist den mooz.EEK	what then is music
Musik ist eine heilige Kunst	. . . HI.lik.eh koonst	music is a holy art
das ist Musik	dahs ist mooz.EEK	that is music

THE OPERA (89 min.)

OVERTURE (4 min.)

The Overture is an orchestral portrait of Ariadne abandoned, one of the great classical scenes of grief and one which has always attracted composers. Reputedly, the first popular aria in the history of opera is Monteverdi's "Lamento d'Arianna," 1608, in which he combined music of love, sadness and fury into a powerful dramatic scene. Less intense but equally effective is Haydn's cantata for soprano and piano, *Arianna a Naxos,* 1789, consisting of two arias each with introductory recitative. Eighteenth-century *opera seria,* which Strauss here is re-creating in modern harmonies, was still less direct, its style more restrained; it sought to express noble emotions by long, stately melodies of great beauty. Strauss's Ariadne, therefore, is the most passive of the three; she has finished with rage, accepted her fate and awaits only death.

———

The curtain rises on a small island, a rock with a grotto and in the background the blue-green sea. Three nymphs of water, wood and air—Naiad, Dryad and Echo—are watching Ariadne, who lies motionless on the grotto's threshold. As was customary in eighteenth-century *opera seria,* all are clothed in eighteenth-century style.

The Nymphs. The Overture's melodies are continued by the nymphs in **trio** a quiet, wordless trio in which their cool, dispassionate voices soon take on the impersonal sounds of their elements, the soft murmurs of water, leaves and air.

Their song awakens Ariadne, who stirs with a sigh—Ah!—repeated by Echo. Looking about she asks, "Wo war ich? Tot?" (Where am I? Dead?) But the scene is only too familiar and, disappointed, she sighs, again answered by Echo.

From the wings the comedians poke in their heads and comment: how pretty she is, how hard to comfort. Ariadne ignores them and, introduced by a horn passage, begins her lament. This vocal counterpart of the overture, some of whose melodies she repeats, has three parts divided by interruptions.

Ariadne's Lament. 1. "Ein Schönes war, heiss Theseus–Ariadne" (how beautiful once were Theseus and Ariadne). She muses on their names, **Ariadne's lament** so closely entwined. As if to recall her to individuality the Nymphs sound her name alone, but she is too engrossed to heed them.

2. She will live in her grotto free of sin and emotion with a mind serene and heart untainted until the day she is released by death. "Und eine Tote sein" (And to be a dead person).

Arlecchino's Interruption. The comedians surge around her, intending to save her with music, and Arlecchino, with Echo assisting, sings a lit- **song** tle street song in three verses: love, hate, hope or despair— "Lieben, Hassen, Hoffen, Zagen"—it is better to live than to die, for joy may come tomorrow. But his efforts are in vain. Ariadne continues lost in thought.

Ariadne's Lament cont. 3. Solemnly she states, "Es gibt ein Reich" **Ariadne's lament cont.** (there is a land) where all is pure. She names it: "Totenreich" (Kingdom of Death). She calls for the God of

Death to claim her. She is ready. "Du nimm es von mir" (you take it—i.e., life—from me). "Bei dir wird Ariadne sein" (by you will Ariadne be).

The Comedians. The nymphs have disappeared during the lament, and **First song and dance**   immediately at its end the four comedians, at first without Zerbinetta, try to cheer Ariadne with a song and dance. "Es gilt, ob Tanzen, ob Singen tauge" (if to dance, to sing is of use). But again they fail, and Zerbinetta dismisses them.

Zerbinetta. She addresses Ariadne directly, woman to woman, and what follows (12 min.) is possibly the most difficult and beautiful coloratura aria in the present operatic repertory. It consists of an introductory recitative and an aria which divides into three parts, of which the last is a rondo.

Recitative: Great and almighty Princess, she begins, of course no common girl can fully understand the sufferings of those so far above her, and yet, does not each have a woman's heart? (During the recitative **Zerbinetta's aria**   Ariadne gradually withdraws into the grotto and Zerbinetta increasingly addresses the audience.) Would it not be better to share your secret sorrow? Even a common girl has been abandoned. Men are faithless, it seems, and women unfortunately not immune to them.

Aria, 1. "Noch glaub' ich dem einen . . . noch mein' ich mir selber . . ." (Just when I think that my constancy will repel every attack, strange yearnings begin to assail me . . .) And so it is: even before an old love is dead, a new is born, and she is scheming to deceive the old while wishing still to be true to it.

2. "So war es mit Pagliazzo" (so was it with Pagliaccio), Mezzetino, Caricchio, and the list grows longer while her voice runs up and down the scale and, after a series of rising trills, soars to a high E.

3. She ends with a rondo in which the recurring theme symbolizes the arrival of each new love. "Als ein Gott kam jeder gegangen" (like a god each one came), and by his kiss she was struck dumb, "stumm."

The Comedians. You preach to deaf ears, says Arlecchino, bounding **Second song and dance**   from the wings. With song and dance he and his colleagues each offers himself as Zerbinetta's new love. She finally chooses Arlecchino, and they secretly depart, leaving the others searching the stage for her. "Psst, wo ist sie" (psst, where is she), and as they realize the truth, they scold Arlecchino, "ai, ai, ai, der Dieb!" (oh, oh, oh, the thief).

The Nymphs. To trumpet calls and violin tremolos, they rush onstage announcing a wonder: a boy, a young god, is approaching—Bacchus! With excited cries they describe his childhood: his mother dead, he was raised by nymphs. Grown, he set forth in the world and met Circe, the enchantress; too powerful for her, he escaped her charms; and—they call eagerly to Ariadne—he is almost here!

trio In the distance Bacchus can be heard mocking Circe, and as Ariadne emerges from the grotto, she confesses herself strangely moved by his voice. Softly, in a trio, the Nymphs urge her to continue to respond, "Töne, töne, süsse Stimme" (sound, sound, sweet voice). The cries to Circe draw nearer, and Ariadne with closed eyes stretches her arms toward them, believing that Death has finally come.

Ariadne and Bacchus. But when Bacchus steps into view, in a moment of terror she cries out "Theseus," then, correcting herself, greets him as the God of Death.

love duet He asks if she is the goddess of the island, and for a time they talk at cross purposes: she, urging him to take her, and he, confused by her ardor and meaning. How will you transform me, she asks, by touch, or wand or wine? She longs for the forgetfulness of death.

Deeply moved, Bacchus states, "Bin ich ein Gott" (since I am a god), then "sooner shall the eternal stars die than you should die in my arms." For a moment she draws back in fear, then fainting gives herself to him. Bacchus, saying that only now does life begin, kisses her.

Slowly she revives and sees the world transformed. What is your magic? she asks, but he replies, "Du! Alles du!" (Thine, all is thine), for "ich bin ein anderer" (I am a different being from what I was). As the Nymphs sing, "Töne, töne, süsse Stimme," Ariadne and Bacchus slowly disappear together.

From the wings Zerbinetta gives her view of what happened, "Kommt der neue Gott gegangen . . . stumm" (So the new god came [and she was] struck dumb). One man or another, it's all the same. But in the distance the voices of Ariadne and Bacchus proclaim something different. "Nun bin ich ein anderer," he sings, and through love promises life: sooner shall the eternal stars die than you should die in my arms.

Vocabulary, The Opera

Ah	ah	ah
Wo war ich? Tot?	woh vahr ik? toht?	Where am I? Dead?
ein Schönes war, heiss	eyo'n shern.es vahr	how beautiful once
Theseus–Ariadne	hice . . .	were . . .

und eine Tote sein	oont eye.neh TOHT.eh sine	and to be a dead person
Lieben, Hassen, Hoffen, Zagen	LEEB.en, HAHS.en, HOF.en, TSAH.gen	to love, to hate, to hope, to despair
es gibt ein Reich	es ghipt eye'n ry'k	there is a land
Totenreich	TOHT.en.rye'k	kingdom of death
du nimm es von mir	doo nim ess fon meer	you take it (life) from me
bei dir wird Ariadne sein	by deer veert . . .	by you will Ariadne be
es gilt, ob Tanzen, ob Singen tauge	es ghilt, op TAHNT.sen, op SING.en TOW.geh	if to dance, to sing is of use
noch glaub' ich dem einen . . . noch mein' ich mir selber . . .	nok glowb' ik dem eye'nen . . . nok mine' ik meer SELB.er . . .	Just when I think my constancy will repel every attack, strange yearnings begin to assail me.
So war es mit Pagliazzo	so vahr ess mit pahl'.YAH.tsoh	so was it with Pagliaccio
als ein Gott kam jeder gegangen	ahls . . . YAID.er geh.GANG.en	like a god each one came
stumm	shtoomm	dumb, mute
psst, wo ist sie	pst, wo ist see	pst, where is she
ai, ai, der Dieb	eye, eye, dehr deep	oh, oh, the thief
Circe	seer.suh	Circe, the enchantress
töne, süsse Stimme	tern.uh seus.suh shtimm.uh	sound, sweet voice
bin ich ein Gott	bin ik eye'n got	(since) I am a god
Du! Alles du!	doo ahll.es . . .	You! All is you!
ich bin ein anderer	. . . AHN.der.er	I am a different (being)
kommt der neue Gott gegangen	komt der NOY.eh . . .	came the new god . . .

DIE FRAU OHNE SCHATTEN

(The Woman Without a Shadow)

Opera in three acts. World premiere, Staatsoper, Vienna, Oct. 10, 1919; American prem., Buenos Aires, Oct. 4, 1949; United States prem., San Francisco, Sept. 18, 1959; British prem., London, May 2, 1966. Music by Richard Strauss; text by Hugo von Hofmannsthal.

PRINCIPAL CHARACTERS

The Nurse	mezzo-soprano
The Emperor	tenor
The Empress	soprano
Barak, the Dyer	bass-baritone
The Dyer's Wife	soprano

The action takes place in a legendary empire in the South Eastern Islands.

Hunting one day with his falcon, the Emperor of the Islands surprised a white gazelle that upon capture dissolved into a woman. She was the daughter of Keikobad, Ruler of the Spirit World, and she and the Emperor, loving one another, married. Her Nurse, who joined her in the palace, disapproved and wished the Empress to return to the Spirit World. Yet she also wished the Empress to be happy, and in her confusion often worked at cross purposes. The marriage was troubled, however, by other, more important reasons that the couple only dimly understood.

The Emperor's falcon had disappeared and with it a talisman belonging to the Empress. The Emperor, in the first intoxication of his love, had struck the falcon because it had attacked the fleeing gazelle. Bloodied and weeping, the falcon had flown off, taking with it the Empress's talisman, a gift from her father and the means by which she transformed herself into other shapes or beings. Having lost the power of transformation she was more human, but she still had a spirit's transparency. Light shone through her; she cast no shadow.

Her condition was no obstacle to the Emperor's love, and their happiness was disturbed only by the strange and somehow ominous loss of the falcon and the talisman. What they did not know was that the Empress as a woman without a shadow could not conceive, and by a law of the Spirit World a man marrying a spirit must transform her within twelve moons into a woman capable of childbearing—i.e., make her wholly human—or be turned to stone. Further, the Nurse, eager for her charge to return to the Spirit World, did not tell the Empress that with each moon Keikobad inquired if his daughter yet cast a shadow. The law would be enforced.

The opera begins at the waning of the twelfth moon and recounts the efforts of the Empress, on learning of her husband's impending fate, to avert it by gaining a shadow. With the Nurse as a guide she leaves the palace for the world of common folk, hoping to find in the three days remaining before judgment a woman who will give up the possibility of motherhood and with it her shadow. She finds one, a dyer's wife, but in the end, though the Emperor has begun to petrify, she refuses to take the other woman's shadow because to do so would be to injure another couple. By her renunciation she demonstrates full humanity, gains a shadow of her own and saves her husband. The opera is the last full bloom of that Romantic strain in German music and literature in which a doomed man—Wagner's Dutchman is the archetype—is saved by a woman's love.

Hofmannsthal's text has been criticized as overly symbolic and pretentious; in performance, however, clarified and reinforced by Strauss's music, its magic and symbolism can be extremely effective. In this, the fourth of their six collaborations—*Elektra, Rosenkavalier, Ariadne, Frau, Ägyptische Helena* and *Arabella*—the two men consciously attempted a profound statement about life: what is the very core of humanity. And the effort drew from Strauss some of his most beautiful melodies and an exceptional grandeur and subtlety in his use of the orchestra.

Any listener will soon hear how Strauss has organized the opera's three levels of existence. At one extreme is the workaday world of the Dyer and his wife, and at the other, the Spirit World of Keikobad, his messengers and the Falcon. Between the two, partaking of each, are the Emperor and the Empress. The tunes sung by the Dyer and his fellows are all simple and solid, based firmly on the musical interval of a third and with narrow skips in pitch. In the Spirit World the melodies are more open and ranging, based on the interval of a fourth and often with large skips in pitch. They also are accompanied by less than full orchestra, in effect by a chamber orchestra. As the Empress in her search for a shadow passes from one world to the other, the accompanying music of the interludes reflects her passage in the change of melody and orchestration.

The opera is long, and the third act is often cut, as described below. Even so, each act runs approximately 67 min. In 1946 Strauss constructed a "Symphonic Fantasy from *Die Frau ohne Schatten*" (22 min.) using the opera's themes, roughly in order.

ACT 1 (66 min.)

SCENE 1 (23 min.)

A flat roof overlooking the palace garden. A door leads to the royal suite. The Nurse crouches in the shadows.

The Nurse and Keikobad's messenger. She sees a flicker of light, a flowing radiance, but an unfamiliar figure materializes. The spirit announces, I am not Keikobad, "Keikobad nicht," but his messenger. The Nurse is suspicious until asked, "wirft sie einen Schatten?" (does she cast a shadow?). "Keinen, keinen" (none), reports the Nurse.

She describes the Emperor's love for the Empress, and the messenger says that the two have only three more days, "drei Tage," together. The Nurse rejoices and asks the Emperor's fate. "Er wird zu Stein!" (He will turn to stone). Solemnly she intones the judgment, and the messenger dissolves, warning "drei Tage!"

The Nurse and the Emperor. Will she tend the Empress while he is away? He plans to hunt in the mountains where he first saw the Empress, a white gazelle, "weissen Gazelle," that cast no shadow, "keinen Schatten." Later, after she had become "mein Weib" (my wife), he had struck and lost his falcon, "Falken," but today perhaps he will find it.

"You will be gone overnight?" asks the Nurse. Perhaps "drei Tage,"

arioso   he replies, and before departing sings warmly of the joys of hunting to provide for his wife.

The Nurse and the Empress. The Empress, regretting the lost talisman, wonders if she could dream herself into a "weissen Gazelle." Noticing a falcon on a tree, she recognizes it as the Emperor's lost favorite. "O Tag der Freude" (O day of joy), she cries out, calling to the bird "Falke! Falke!" and asking why it weeps. Because, it replies, "Die Frau wirft keinen Schatten" and "Der Kaiser muss versteinen!" (The Emperor must turn to stone).

Slowly, imperfectly, the Empress recalls that such a curse was carved on the talisman. The Nurse explains to her the Spirit World's law. "Hilf deinem Kind" (help your child), cries the Empress. Where can I get a shadow?

"Bei den Menschen! Bei den Menschen! (from the world of common men), says the nurse, and they are disgusting. But the Empress is not put off. "Ich will den Schatten" (I will have a shadow), "ich will! ich will!"

"Ein Tag bricht an" (a day is about to break), warns the nurse, a human's day, "ein Menschentag," foul to eye, ear and nose. "Hinab! hinab!" (down), cries the Empress, and she and the Nurse "plunge into the abyss of the human world."

INTERLUDE (Descent to the Common World—2 min.)

SCENE 2 (41 min.)

The Dyer's one-room house, where he lives with his wife and his three maimed, misshapen brothers.

Barak, his brothers and his wife. She stops the brothers fighting by dousing them with water, for which they abuse her. When she orders them from the house, Barak, who has entered, supports her: there is work to be done outside.

Barak and his wife. The brothers, she says, must go—for good. Barak urges that they grew up in the house. "Kinder waren sie einmal" (children were they once), attractive, loving members of a large family. She has heard that before, and how even for thirteen children "there was always food enough." "Gib du mir Kinder" (you give me children), he says, and there will be food enough. "Wann gibst du mir die Kinder dazu?" (When will you give me those children).

Gently he touches her, but she pulls away. "Ei du," he exclaims, " 's ist dein Mann" (eh you, this is your husband). She knows, she says, what that means: she's bought and paid for. He tries to soothe her, but she angrily walks away. The orchestra has a two-minute interlude **interlude: Barak's goodness** (without change of scene) expressing Barak's goodness.

Returning to her discontent, she says that for three and a half years he has tried to make her conceive and failed. Now he must put aside his desires. He replies patiently that he will await the blessings to come. There will be none, she says. Determined not to give way to unhappiness, he shoulders a bundle of skins for market and departs singing.

The Dyer's Wife, the Nurse and the Empress. As soon as Barak has gone, there is a shimmering of air and before his startled wife appear the Nurse and the Empress in servant's clothes. The Nurse immediately begins complimenting the wife on her face, her cheeks, her eyelashes and her slender body. Such beauty! To be spoiled by childbearing! Such waste! The wife, who has been hostile, suddenly weeps.

The Nurse starts to leave, saying the wife already knows the secret, "das Geheimnis." What secret? asks the wife. The way to be rich and beautiful forever, replies the Nurse, and for the price of only a shadow.

From the air she pulls a fillet of pearls and other finery that she hands to the wife even as she transforms the room into a royal boudoir **first tempting** filled with flattering handmaids. With amazement the wife sees herself transfigured in a large mirror. Then suddenly, she is once more in rags in the wretched house.

Supposing I wished it, she asks, how could it be done? The Nurse delays, continuing to lament that motherhood should spoil such beauty. The wife cries out, "Meine Seele ist satt geworden der Mutterschaft" (my soul is sated with motherhood). She will abjure her husband. "So ist es gesprochen" (so it is spoken).

Quickly the Nurse responds. "Abzutun Mutterschaft" (to put aside motherhood) is an act of glorious disdain. For three days she and her friend (the Empress) will act as servants in return for the wife's shadow. Thereafter the wife will savor even greater delights.

But the wife interrupts. Barak is returning, and his supper is not ready. No matter, says the Nurse, and at a wave of her hand five fish "fly through the air and land in the pan, the fire ignites and half of the Dyer's bed breaks away to become a bed for one."

As the Nurse and Empress leave and the Dyer's wife stares in amazement, the voices of unborn children are heard calling from the pan: "Mutter, Mutter . . . O, Weh!" (mother . . . woe).

When Barak enters, his wife tells him that he will hereafter eat and sleep alone. In the morning two of her aunts will enter the house as servants. "So ist es gesprochen." Barak tries to curb his disappointment. Outside, the town's watchmen on their rounds urge all husbands and wives to love one another and to sleep together. Do you hear? Barak calls softly to his wife, but only the voices of the watchmen come back to him. With a sigh he lies down alone.

Vocabulary, Act I

Keikobad nicht	KY.koh.bahd nikt	not Keikobad
wirft sie einen	veerft see eye.nen	does she cast a
Schatten	SHAHT.en	shadow
keinen	KY.nen	none
drei Tage	dry TAH.geh	three days
er wird zu Stein	air veerd tsoo shtine	he will turn to stone
weissen Gazelle	vice.en gah.ZEL.uh	white gazelle

mein Weib	mine vipe	my wife
Falken	FAHL.kuh	falcon
O Tag der Freude	. . . der FROY.duh	O day of joy
die Frau wirft	dee frow . . .	the woman casts
keinen Schatten		no shadow
der Kaiser muss	der KY.zer moos	the Emperor must
versteinen	fair.SHTINE.en	turn to stone
hilf deinem Kind	hilf dine.em kint	help your child
bei den Menschen	by den MENSH.en	from the world of
		common men
ich will den Schatten	ik vill . . .	I will have a
		shadow
ein Tag bricht an	. . . brikt an	a day is about
		to break
hinab	hin.AHPP	down there

Scene 2

Kinder waren sie	KINT.er var.en see	children were
einmal	eyen.mahl	they once
Gib du mir Kinder	gib doo meer . . .	you give me children
Wann gibst du mir	vahnn . . . dah.TSOO	When will you give
die Kinder dazu		me those children
ei du 's ist dein	eye doo (e)s ist	eh you, this is
Mann	dine mahnn	your husband
das Geheimnis	duss geh.HIME.niss	the secret
meine Seele ist satt	mine SAYL.uh ist	my soul is sated
geworden der	saht geh.VOR.den	with motherhood
Mutterschaft	der MOOT.ter.shahft	
so ist es gesprochen	soo . . . geh.SHPROK.	so is it spoken
	en	
abzutun Mutterschaft	ahp.TSOO.tuhn	to put aside
	. . .	Motherhood
Mutter . . . oh weh	. . . oh vay	Mother . . . oh, woe

ACT II (68 min.)

SCENE 1 (13 min.)

The Dyer's house. The Empress, acting as a servant, helps Barak with his bundle, and the scene begins as he leaves for market.
The Nurse, the Dyer's Wife and the Empress. The Nurse offers to materialize the man of whom the Dyer's wife is thinking. The wife protests that she thinks only of Barak; the Nurse, however, insists there is another. Shyly the wife admits that she sometimes thinks of a young man

she saw once, crossing a bridge. He was young, almost a boy, and had not noticed her.

Stealthily the Nurse prepares the magic to materialize him while the **second tempting** Empress grieves at the course they are pursuing. When the Nurse claps her hands, the young man stands before the Dyer's Wife. She is ashamed, however, and though voices in the air urge her to be quick and bold, she will not move toward him. The sound of Barak returning ends the moment, and the Nurse, throwing a cloak over the young man, causes him to vanish.

Barak, his wife, brothers, and street children. Barak has food for a feast and half the neighborhood to eat it. The brothers and children sing excitedly, "O Tag des Glücks, O Abend der Gnade!" (Oh, the happy day; oh, the blessed evening). To the wife, waking from her dream, the noisy turmoil seems unbearably coarse, and she tells Barak sourly that she will have no part in it. He asks the Nurse and the Empress to help with the food, and the scene ends in a raucous celebration.

INTERLUDE (5 min.)

The joyous noise of Barak's common world resolves into falcon cries, which in turn are followed by the Emperor's hunting song played **cello solo** in a minor key by a solo cello.

SCENE 2 (10 min.)

A hunting lodge deep in the woods, in moonlight. The Emperor, led by the Falcon, rides in, dismounts and hides behind a tree.

The Emperor. "Falke, Falke," he softly calls. Why has he been led here, to the lodge where his wife had planned to spend the "drei Tage" while he was hunting? But "das Haus ist leer" (empty). "Still" (quiet), **Emperor's scene** mein Falke," something moves in the air.

To his astonishment he sees the Empress and the Nurse entering the lodge, trailing behind them "Menschendunst . . . Menschenatem," the fumes and scents of common men. "O weh" (woe), "Falke, o weh." She has deceived him and must die.

He aims his arrow, "Pfeil, mein Pfeil," but cannot bear to release it, for it had won him the "weisse Gazelle." He draws his sword, "Schwert, mein Schwert," but it, too, had helped to win her. And his hands, "meine Hände," lack the will. The Falcon must lead him to some rocky cleft where he can lament unheard. "Weh, o weh!"

INTERLUDE (2 min.)

The Emperor's hunting song is overwhelmed by the theme of his fate—to be turned to stone—harshly proclaimed by full brass, while the falcon's terrified cries vanish in the distance.

SCENE 3 (16 min.)

The Dyer's house. Barak is preparing for market, while his wife and the Nurse exchange impatient glances.
Barak, his wife, the Nurse and the Empress. When his wife nags him for being slow, Barak says that nothing this morning has gone easily and requests a drink. The Nurse hands him one which is drugged, and he soon falls asleep on the floor.

His wife is both angry and not angry at the Nurse, resentful of her power yet eager to use it. The Nurse, sure that she understands the **third tempting** wife, in a flash of light materializes the phantom lover. When the wife is again indecisive, the Nurse causes the man to fall as if in a faint. When the wife, alarmed, bends over him, his hand reaches for hers. Frightened, she turns to Barak, "Wach auf!" (wake up), "ein Mann ist im Haus" (a man is in the house). Aided by the Empress, she succeeds in rousing him while the Nurse crossly dissolves the lover.

Barak, still groggy, fails to appreciate his wife's agitation, and she begins to berate him. He is dimly aware, however, that strange powers are operating, and his chief fear is that they will somehow interfere with his livelihood, on which so many depend. His wife is angered that he should think of his work when she is trying to explain something important, and she goes off with the Nurse. The Empress, however, stays to help Barak collect his tools.

INTERLUDE (2 min.)

Barak's goodness has stirred a conscience in the Empress and filled her mind with conflicting ideas.

SCENE 4 (9 min.)

At the hunting lodge. The Empress's bedroom. She is asleep; the Nurse also, at the foot of the bed.

The Empress. Her sleep is haunted by Barak's tormented eyes, and she
Empress's nightmare   cries, "Dir—Barak—bin ich mich schuldig!"
(against you—Barak—I have sinned). She dreams of a great cave with
a bronze door. The Emperor approaches, led by the Falcon; before the
door he pauses. Strange voices call, and the Falcon grieves, "Die Frau
wirft keinen Schatten, der Kaiser muss versteinen!" The Emperor goes
in, and the door closes behind him.

Waking, the Empress cries "Wehe, mein Mann!" (woe, my husband). The door closed like a tomb. "Alles ist meine Schuld" (all is my
fault). Barak, the Emperor—she injures both. Better that she be turned
to stone, "zu stein."

INTERLUDE (2 min.)

In the Empress's mind the conflict of ideas continues.

SCENE 5 (9 min.)

The Dyer's house. Throughout the scene the room grows darker.
Barak, his wife and brothers, the Nurse and the Empress. Barak complains of the increasing darkness, and the brothers as well as the Nurse
all remark that mysterious powers are at work. In a concerted passage
each exclaims his thoughts, ending with Barak's wife protesting that he
Dyer's wife   is impossible; he never understands anything. Well,
she has had enough; she has taken a lover. She will have no children,
by Barak or anyone else, ever. She has sold her shadow and received a
good price for it.

"Das Weib ist irre" (the woman is out of her wits), exclaims Barak.
Stir up the fire so that I can see her face.

As the fire flares, the brothers cry out that she casts no shadow, even
as the Nurse urges the Empress to seize it. Turmoil again breaks out,
during which the Empress refuses to take the shadow because there is
blood on it.

Barak announces that his wife does not deserve to live, and he himself will drown her in a sack weighted with stones (stones, stoniness,
the undeveloped heart, the equivalent of death). When he raises his
hand, a sword leaps into it, and his brothers rush to restrain him.

His wife is impressed. "Barak!" she cries, "ich hab' es nicht getan!"
(I have not done it). She had the thought but without the deed. She had

never imagined her husband as a noble, stern judge. If she must die, then "Barak, so töte mich schnell!" (kill me quickly).

The brothers, however, hold him back, and the sword flies out of his hand. Judgment is not for Barak to deliver. The earth opens, and he and his wife are swallowed up while through the cracked walls a river pours into the room. The Nurse conjures a boat in which she and the Empress float away as trumpets and trombones in the distance call everyone to a judgment.

Vocabulary, Act II

O Tag des Glücks	oh tahg dess glerks	oh happy day
O Abend der Gnade	oh AH.bent der g'NAH.de	oh blessed evening
Falke	FAHL.kuh	falcon
drei Tage	dry TAH.geh	three days
das Haus ist leer	duss howss ist lair	the house is empty
still	shtill	quiet
Menschendunst	MEN.shen.doonst	men's scents
Menschenatem	MEN.shen.ah.tem	men's breathings
O weh	oh vay	oh, woe
Pfeil, mein Pfeil	pfile . . .	arrow, my arrow
weisse Gazelle	vice.eh gah.ZEL.uh	white gazelle
Schwert, mein Schwert	shvairt . . .	sword, my sword
meine Hände	mine.eh hen.de	my hands
Wach auf!	vahk owf	wake up
ein Mann ist im Haus	eyen mahnn ist in howss	a man is in the house
dir—Barak—bin ich mich schuldig	dir . . . bin ik mik shoold.ik	against you— Barak—I have sinned
alles ist miene Schuld	ahl.les . . . shoolt	all is my fault
das Weib ist irre	duss vipe ist eerr.eh	that woman is out of her wits
ich hab' es nicht getan	ik hab ess nikt ge.TAHN	I have not done it
so töte mich schnell	so tert.eh mik shnell	so kill me quickly

ACT III (with usual cuts, 67 min.)

SCENE 1 (12 min.)

In the orchestra solemn chords on the brass proclaim that judgment is at hand for the Dyer, his wife, the Emperor and the Empress. Particularizing, a solo bassoon sounds the discontent of the Dyer's wife, and then flutes, clarinets and celesta present the voices of her unborn children. The curtain rises, revealing an underground vault divided by a thick wall. Separated by it and unaware of each other are:

Barak and his wife. She urges the voices of the children, "Schweigt doch" (do be still). "Ich hab' es nicht getan!" (I did not do it). Humbly she calls to her husband, wherever he may be. She had wanted to leave him, had planned to leave him, but at the crucial moment instead had waked him. "Barak," she cries. "Barak, Barak."

He, on his side of the wall, then sings (in one of Strauss's most moving arias) of his duty to protect his wife, "mir anvertraut" (entrusted to me). For a time their voices join, but soon his continues alone. "Mir **aria, duet** anvertraut"—and he had threatened to harm her. "Weh mir" (woe is me). If only he might see her once more to tell her, "Fürchte dich nicht! Fürchte dich nicht!" (don't be afraid).

From above a voice summons him to mount the stairs that miraculously appear. In her cell, after she once again passionately calls to him, similar stairs appear and a voice advises her, too, to go up.

INTERLUDE (3 min.)

The scene changes to a rocky terrace outside the cave of which the Empress had dreamt and into which she had seen the Emperor pass, its great bronze door closing on him like a tomb. On the steps leading to the door, awaiting her and the Nurse, is Keikobad's messenger. As soon as he has seen them, approaching in the boat that the Nurse had summoned at the close of Act II, he leaves to report their arrival to Keikobad.

SCENE 2 (17 min.)

The Nurse and the Empress. The Nurse is anxious to get away, "Fort von hier" (away from here). But when a trumpet sounds, the Empress recognizes it as a call to judgment: "Mein Vater, ja? Keikobad?" (it is my father, yes?). The Emperor is within. "Ich will zu ihm" (I will go to him).

"Fort" (away), the Nurse urges. She will find a shadow somehow, but now, "Fort."

A wrangle begins (large cuts often made) in which the Empress, relying on her love for the Emperor, is determined to face judgment—"Hell ist in mir" (light is in me), "ich muss zu ihm"—while the Nurse continues to advise evasion. The Empress ultimately rejects the Nurse and enters the cave alone.

The Nurse, the Dyer and his wife. (Sometimes entirely cut.) As Barak and his wife, yearning for each other, make their ways up to the seat of judgment, the Nurse keeps them apart by misdirecting them.

The Nurse and the messenger. (Usually partially cut.) She determines to follow the Empress, whom she loves. To open the door she calls "Keikobad." The messenger appears and orders the boat to bear her away. She has no part in the future of the Empress. In the distance the voices of the Dyer and his wife are heard calling for each other.

INTERLUDE (1 min.)

Tremendous, crashing chords while the scene changes to the cave's interior. (In some productions the change is very slight.)

SCENE 3 (22 min.)

The Empress. She is met by spirits who urge her to have courage in her test. Outside can still be heard the voices of Barak and his wife. Before the Empress a fountain of golden water springs up, and a spirit urges her to drink. Then the shadow of the Dyer's wife will be hers. The Empress refuses. "Blut ist in dem Wasser, ich trinke nicht!" (Blood is in the water, I will not drink). The fountain subsides.

To her invisible father she says that she will take her place as a human beside her husband. The Emperor is revealed to her, and except for his eyes he is stone. (Cuts throughout here). Again the fountain rises; again she is urged to drink; and again, on hearing the voices of Barak and his wife, she refuses: "ich—will—nicht!"

The fountain vanishes. From the Empress a shadow falls on the ground. The Emperor, restored to life, rises. Separately and together they rejoice and with them their unborn children.

INTERLUDE (2 min.)

While the Emperor and Empress embrace, the scene changes to a landscape with a golden waterfall. Above it, together, appear the Emperor and the Empress; on its banks, separated by it, the Dyer and his wife.

SCENE 4 (10 min.)

The Dyer, his wife, the Emperor and the Empress. Barak calls to his wife and her shadow, falling across the water, turns into a bridge on which they meet. All rejoice, together with a choir of unborn children.

Vocabulary, Act III

Schweigt doch	shvy dok	do be still
ich hab' es nicht getan	ik hab ess nikt ge.TAHN	I did not do it
mir anvertraut	meer AHN.fair.trowt	to me entrusted
Weh mir	vay meer	woe is me
fürchte dich nicht	ferk.teh dik nikt	do not be afraid
fort von hier	fort fon heer	away from here
mein Vater, ja	mine FAH.ter ya	my father, yes?
ich will zu ihm	ik vill tsoo eem	I will go to him
Hell ist in mir	hel ist in meer	light is in me (I understand)
Blut ist in dem Wasser	bloot . . . dem vahss.er	blood is in the water
ich trinke nicht	ik trink.eh nikt	I will not drink

INTERMEZZO

A middle-class comedy in two acts, with orchestral interludes between the scenes. World premiere, Dresden, Nov. 4, 1924; United States concert prem., New York, Feb. 11, 1963; stage prem., Philadelphia, Feb. 25, 1977; British prem., Edinburgh, Sept. 9, 1965. Music and text by Richard Strauss.

PRINCIPAL CHARACTERS

Christine Storch, wife of	soprano
Robert Storch, a composer	baritone
Franz, their eight-year-old son	(speaking role)
Anna, the chambermaid	soprano
Baron Lummer	tenor

The action takes place in the 1920s at Grundlsee, near Salzburg, and Vienna.

The opera, which Strauss once described as "this harmless little slice of life," is a character study of a composer's wife: her tantrums, her foolish acceptance of a young man's flattery and her groundless suspicion of her husband's fidelity. Christine Storch is silly, snobbish, sentimental, selfish, yet also vibrant and stimulating. In her way, which includes a strong sexual response, she loves her husband Robert.

The portrait is based on Strauss's wife Pauline and is a good likeness. Not quite so accurate was the picture he gave of himself: easygoing, sympathetic, wise. Yet it was recognizable, and in the premiere production the parallel between the real and the operatic couple was stressed. The sets for the Storch home reproduced the furnishings of the Strauss home, and the singer playing Storch wore a mask to make him resemble Strauss.

Many persons found this display of private life distasteful, and the confusion resulting as some producers played up and others down the autobiographical elements may have hurt the opera's chance to establish itself in the repertory. After the initial round of productions it seldom was played, except in Munich and Vienna, until the 1960s when interest in it revived. Meanwhile Strauss, before dying in 1949, had come to believe that the work was best staged without reference to himself or his wife, and this has been the steady trend.

Of Strauss's fifteen operas *Intermezzo,* the eighth, is unique in its musical form and its contemporary subject. It is also, except for his first opera, *Guntram,* the only one for which he wrote his own libretto. Following *Die Frau ohne Schatten* and preceding *Die Ägyptische Helena,* it is the result of his determination to compose something besides myths and costume dramas, something with real people and daily life. He was sixty at the time, and using his married life of twenty-five years earlier, he composed a contemporary drama with ski pants, sleds, telephones and card games. These were not typical operatic fare at the time, and to present them he deliberately changed his style.

The opera consists of thirteen scenes connected, within the acts, by symphonic interludes, which are a major part of the score. All but four of the scenes are short, seven minutes or less, and the impression they leave is of a series of conversational snapshots which the orchestra then develops in the interludes. Within the scenes the conversation is presented sometimes in spoken dialogue, most often in a declamatory line, and only seldom in long, lyrical passages. To insure that the words are heard Strauss frequently has the conversational phrases spoken or sung without any orchestral accompaniment. (In his preface to the vocal score he discusses in detail the difficulties of combining words and music.) The precision necessary, however, for the orchestra to enter instantly into the conversational pauses and as instantly to fall silent as the voices reenter makes this possibly the most difficult to play of all Strauss operatic scores. For the singers, however, with few high notes or coloratura passages, the problems are in the acting, particularly for the leading soprano. Christine Storch is a complicated character and, if not carefully presented, is simply irritating.

The orchestra required is not large—roughly, fifty players: double woodwind, brass, three horns, modest percussion, piano, harp, harmonium, eleven first and nine second violins, five violas, five cellos and three double-bass—and the opera does best in small houses. It also needs translation for non-Germans.

In *Capriccio,* his final opera, Strauss and his librettist created a story that deals directly with the great problem of operatic form: the uniting of words and music in a happy marriage. In *Intermezzo* it is possible—and because of the preface to the vocal score perhaps justified—to interpret the story as an allegory on the subject.

The opera (150 min.) is often presented with slight cuts, no more than ten minutes in all, with the largest, of several minutes each, made in the final scenes of the two acts.

Strauss later drew from the opera an orchestral suite, *Four Symphonic Interludes,* that is not so clear-cut as its title implies. The first, entitled "Fever of Departure and Waltz Scene," includes the opera's opening bars, the interlude following Act I, Scene 1, and the waltzes of the interludes surrounding Scene 3 as well as of the scene itself. The second, "Reverie at the Hearth," is the final bars without voice of Act I, Scene 5, and its subsequent interlude. The third, "At the Card Table," is the music introducing and closing Act II, Scene 1. And the fourth, "Happy Ending," is the interlude before the final scene.

Other excerpts also occasionally appear on concert programs or records, and these are indicated in the synopsis.

ACT I (86 min.)

Scene 1 (24 min.). Early morning, Storch's dressing room at his house in Grundlsee. Christine, helping him to pack for a trip to Vienna, abuses him, the maid and the cook. Then as he is about to leave, her mood changes, and she expresses her love. After his departure she accepts a neighbor's invitation to go sledding.

Interlude (1 min.). leads into orchestral *glissandi* for the "swosh" of the sleds.

Scene 2 (3 min.). Christine, coming down the hill, collides with a young man on skis. She is furious at him until she discovers that he is Baron Lummer and therefore well connected. She invites him to call.

Interlude (2 min.). waltzes.

Scene 3 (4 min.). Christine and the Baron, who claims to suffer from ill health, dance at an inn at Grundlsee.

Interlude (3 min.). waltzes. (The sequence of waltzes in these two interludes and scene sometimes appear in concerts or on records as *Waltzes* **waltzes** *from Intermezzo*.)

Scene 4 (3 min.). Christine rents a furnished room in the local Notary's house for Baron Lummer, whose needs and ailments she describes at length to the Notary's wife. Her interest in the Baron is motherly and managing.

Interlude (2 min.)

Scene 5 (21 min.). In the dining room of the Storch house Christine writes her husband about the new escort she has found. The Baron enters hoping to borrow money, but she neatly avoids the subject while assuring him that her husband doubtless will help him with the cost of his studies. When the Baron leaves, Christine in a reverie by the fire muses on her newfound young man and then thinks lovingly of her husband, so good and true.

Interlude (3 min.). (The music following the Baron's exit in the previous scene, including the soprano's reverie, and this Interlude are **Fireside Interlude** sometimes performed in concerts or on records as *Interlude from Intermezzo* or *Traumerei am Kamin* [*Dream by the Fireside*].)

Scene 6 (4 min.). The Baron's room in the Notary's house. His girlfriend, in ski pants, looks in but is hustled away before the Notary's wife can see her. The Baron, promising to join her later, writes to Frau Storch asking for money.

Interlude (2 min.). Cheerful music suggests the Baron's hopes.

Scene 7 (5 min.). Christine reads the letter in her dining room. A thousand marks! The man is mad. The Baron arrives, and she scolds him for the letter. The maid enters with another. Though it is addressed to

Kapellmeister Storch, Christine opens it and reads aloud in horror: "My beloved. Send me two tickets again for the opera tomorrow. Afterwards in the bar as usual. Thine, Mieze Maier" (pron. Mitzi My.er). "Das ist das Ende!" Christine proclaims. She dismisses the Baron, writes a telegram to Storch in Vienna—"You know Mieze Maier. Your infidelity is proven. This is goodbye forever!"—and sinks into a chair, unhappy and exhausted.

Interlude (2 min.). Passionate commentary on her feelings.

Scene 8 (7 min. or, with cuts, 4). Christine sits by her child's bed, crying. She complains to the boy of his father, but he insists, "Papa ist gut." It is she who makes the scenes. (Frequently some of Christine's self-pity and the child's defense of his father are cut.) She kneels by the bedside in prayer.

ACT II (64 min.)

Scene 1 (13 min.). In Vienna Storch joins four friends for Skat, a Ger-**Skat party** man cardgame. (The cardplay is in spoken dialogue; the men's gossip, chiefly about Storch and his wife, in music.) Christine's telegram arrives. One friend, Stroh, is surprised that Storch should know Mieze Maier, whom he describes as "so-so, la-la." But Storch does not know her and can make nothing of the telegram. Upset, he excuses himself, leaving his friends to comment and continue their game.

Interlude (2 min.)

Scene 2 (4 min.). At the Notary's house in Grundlsee, Christine asks the Notary to represent her in an action for divorce. He irritates her by assuming at first that the Baron is involved and then by refusing to proceed without consulting Storch, whom he respects. Christine leaves in anger.

Interlude (1 min.)

Scene 3 (5 min.). In the Prater (a park in Vienna). Storm. Storch, in the rain, paces back and forth in agitation. Christine will not answer his letters or telegrams. Stroh runs in and with embarrassment declares that the original note was intended for him. He has checked with Mieze Maier, who in looking up the address in the phone book became confused—Stroh-Storch—and copied the wrong one. Storch, much relieved, insists that Stroh go to Grundlsee and explain it all to Christine

Interlude (4 min.). Storch's agitation ends in tranquility, followed by the emotion still raging in Christine.

Scene 4 (7 min.). Christine's bedroom at Grundlsee. Chaos as she packs to leave. She has sent the Baron to see Mieze Maier in Vienna but forgot to give him Storch's photograph for identification. She blames the maids for all her own mistakes. A telegram arrives from Storch, and the maid Anna persuades her to read it: Herr Stroh, who is on his way, will explain the mixup. Almost immediately he is announced, and Christine allows Anna to persuade her to see him.

Interlude (3 min.). Christine's excitement at Storch's imminent arrival.

Scene 5 (25 min. or, with cuts, 20). The dining room at Grundlsee. The anticipation has exhausted Christine's emotions and in a sudden reversal she greets Storch coldly. When he asks amiably, "What's the trouble?" she replies that he doesn't appreciate how much she has suffered. When she persists in self-pity, he loses his temper, scolds her for her behavior and leaves the room. She is astonished.

The Baron enters to report that he has seen Fräulein Maier, who claims to know Storch well. But Christine, knowing the truth of the mixup, dismisses the Baron as a bungler.

Storch reenters, asking who the man was. Then to Christine's delight he confesses—or pretends—that the Baron was the cause of his return. He had heard from the Notary and feared for Christine's affections. The young man, she declares, is unimportant, and tells of his request for money. Storch thinks it a great joke. The two are reconciled and sing of their happiness in marriage.

(The ending has been admired as lovely and criticized as overly sentimental. It is both, without being false. For Strauss marriage and the pleasures of home were very rewarding, and he celebrated them not only here but in his *Symphonia Domestica,* in *Die Frau ohne Schatten,* and in the *Four Last Songs.*)

DIE ÄGYPTISCHE HELENA

(The Egyptian Helen)

Opera in two acts. World premiere, Dresden, June 6, 1928; American prem., Metropolitan, New York, Nov. 6, 1928. Music by Richard Strauss; libretto by Hugo von Hofmannsthal, using part of the story of Helen of Troy but based less on Homer's epic than on Euripides' play *Helen* and on several legendary, lost poems.

The opera generally is considered the weakest, musically and textually, of the six by Strauss and Hofmannsthal, *Elektra, Rosenkavalier, Ariadne, Frau, Helena,* and *Arabella.* Yet it has continued in the repertory at Munich and is revived occasionally in German houses. It has several gorgeous arias, which Strauss-lovers treasure in rare recordings, and its libretto, though unusually confusing, is interesting as an early effort in opera to present psychiatry and marriage counseling, two very twentieth-century topics.

During World War I Hofmannsthal became interested in the victims of war neuroses of various forms and in the treatment to prepare them for a return to civilian life. He took the problem and grafted it onto the story of Menelaus and Helen. How can Menelaus return to a happy married life with Helen after ten years of war caused by her rejection of him in favor of Paris? In the synopsis an interpretation of Hofmannsthal's allegory is offered in parentheses.

The Trojan War is over and Menelaus, with Helen retaken, is on his way home. He plans to kill her as a sacrifice to those who because of her died in the war.

ACT I (68 min.)

The opera opens at the palace of a sorceress (psychiatrist) Aithra (ah.ee.tra) on a small island near Egypt. Her dinner table is set for two, and she awaits Poseidon. From her large, magic Seashell (aquatic television) she learns that Poseidon is detained in Ethiopia and by chance "pans in" on Menelaus aboard his ship, about to execute the sleeping Helena. Aithra creates a storm, smashes the ship and brings Helena (hay.lay.nah) and Menelaus (men.nay.lahs) to her palace. She hides behind a screen as they enter, a good-looking but middle-aged and presently bedraggled couple. (A difficulty of the opera is that, despite its serious themes, it veers often toward Offenbach.)

In a duet Helena invites Menelaus to enjoy the dinner spread before them and later, by implication, her charms; Menelaus remains grumpy and slowly works his temper up to her execution. Aithra intervenes and by means of elves creates the illusion of Helena and Paris running out of the palace together (as they must have done years before in Sparta). Menelaus rushes off in pursuit (reliving his experience).

Aithra comforts Helena, gives her some lotus juice (a tranquilizer), and revives all her youthful beauty. Then she conceals her.

Menelaus returns announcing that he has killed Paris and Helena;

their blood is on his sword. In fact, it is spotless. Aithra tells him that Helena was never at Troy; that was a delusion. She was at a castle on Mount Atlas in a deep sleep for ten years awaiting Menelaus. Now she is here, and after Menelaus, too, has drunk some lotus juice, Aithra with a gesture reveals a young and radiant Helena. He takes her for a phantom—for he's just killed Helena—but falls in love with her (i.e., he is in love with his memory of how Helena was, not as she is). The couple embrace lovingly, and in a trio Aithra proposes now to waft them home. Helena, however, asks to be sent for a short time to some place where she and Troy are unknown, and Aithra agrees to transport them to the Atlas mountains.

ACT II (72 min.)

Mid-morning. A tent opening wide onto a palm grove, behind which loom the Atlas Mountains. Seated before a mirror, Helena binds pearls into her hair and, in the opera's most famous aria, exclaims on the joys of the night: "Zweite Brautnacht!" (Second bridal night). Menelaus **Helena's awakening** comes out, and at first all goes well. But when Helena, rummaging in their trunk for more lotus juice, upsets his sword, he snatches it up, and from his eye and speech she realizes that beneath the effects of the tranquilizing juice his neurosis—the desire to execute Helena—is still virulent. (With her execution, fixing guilt for the war on her, he will free himself of any guilt—a common psychological ruse among humans.) The only hope for a cure, she decides, is to face the problem directly and resolve it without deceptions.

A local sheik, Altair, rides up with his son, Da-ud, and retainers. In the mind of Menelaus the clatter of arms and hooves recalls the Trojan War. First Altair and then Da-ud proclaim themselves smitten by Helena's beauty, and Menelaus cries out that Da-ud is Paris come again. Leaving Helena, whom he is beginning to believe is not the real Helena but a substituted nymph, he goes hunting with Da-ud whom he kills, just as he killed Paris at Troy and the phantom Paris at Aithra's palace.

Aithra, who has flown in, suggests more lotus juice for Menelaus, but Helena proposes instead to give him a potion of full remembrance. She wants her husband back, fully aware, without illusions about her. Menelaus, preceded by Da-ud's body carried on a carpet, enters in a daze. He bids Helena farewell as a nymph who came for a night to comfort him after his real wife's death. He realizes now that it is the real and (he thinks) dead Helena whom he loves, the woman to whom he was bound by shared guilt and long years of suffering. Helena offers him a drink, knowing that if he fully regains his memory, he once again may want to execute her; Menelaus takes it, thinking that it will kill him, purify him of guilt, and unite him with the real, dead Helena. But on drinking it he recognizes in the nymph before him the bride of his youth, his middle-aged wife, and the mother of his child Hermione, whom Aithra materializes before them. He accepts Helena for what she is and was and, with Da-ud's body before him, himself, too (as a man of violence he had enjoyed the Trojan War and fought it as much for fun and glory as for Helena's sake). The opera ends with a duet of joyful reunion (in a psychological sense Menelaus and Helena have come home from the war).

The interpretation, based on Hofmannsthal's Preface to the opera, leaves some loose ends; but no other seems to do better. Though Strauss tried by some revisions in Act II to clarify the story, with its real and imagined Helenas it is still confusing. And not altogether attractive: why should the audience rejoice in Menelaus's cure when the treatment required the killing of the innocent Da-ud?

The question points to the opera's most deep-seated difficulty: the imposition on Helen of Troy and Menelaus of twentieth-century concepts of guilt. In the culture of Homer or even of Euripides, neither felt any guilt for the Trojan War; and as long as Da-ud died in a fair fight, Menelaus would incur no guilt. But once modern concepts of guilt are imposed on an ancient story, they must be imposed all the way. Hofmannsthal believed that myths made the most powerful dramas, but this opera might have been clearer and more powerful if the protagonists had been kept a post–World War I couple and played in modern dress.

ARABELLA

Lyric comedy in three acts. World premiere, Dresden, July 1, 1933; British prem., Covent Garden, London, May 17, 1934; American prem., Buenos Aires, Aug. 16, 1934; United States prem., Metropolitan, New York, Feb. 10, 1955. Music by Richard Strauss; text by Hugo von Hofmannsthal, based distantly on his novel *Lucidor*, published 1910.

PRINCIPAL CHARACTERS

Count Theodore Waldner	bass	
Adelaide, his wife	mezzo-soprano	
Arabella ⎱ their daughters	soprano	
Zdenka ⎰	soprano	
Mandryka	baritone	man.dree.kah
Matteo	tenor	mah.TAY.oh
Elemer ⎫	tenor	ell.eh.meer
Dominik ⎬ Arabella's suitors	baritone	
Lamoral ⎭	bass	LA.mor.ahl
Fiakermilli	coloratura soprano	
Fortune-teller	soprano	

The action takes place in Vienna, 1860, on the morning and evening of Shrove Tuesday, the last day of Carnival. (In Catholic countries the connotation of Shrove Tuesday, from "shriving"—i.e., confession and absolution—is of the acknowledgment of one's true self.)

The opera was the sixth and last collaboration of Strauss and Hofmannsthal—*Elektra, Der Rosenkavalier, Ariadne auf Naxos, Die Frau ohne Schatten, Die Ägyptische Helena, Arabella*—and during its composition Hofmannsthal died. Out of respect for him Strauss set the libretto as it was, without reworking one or two scenes. He had no doubt of his artistic loss: "Hofmannsthal was the only poet who, besides his strength as a poet and gifts for the stage, had the sympathetic ability to present a composer with dramatic material in a form ready for music—in short the ability to write a libretto that was at once stageworthy, rewarding as literature, and composable."

In earlier operas, such as *Ariadne, Frau* and *Helena,* the two men had presented, sometimes ironically, sometimes seriously, profound ideas about humanity. In *Arabella* they attempted less: the opera is a simple love story with the usual misunderstanding that threatens but does not displace the happy ending. Its particular charm lies perhaps in the heroine's combination of sensitivity and common sense set off against the extravagances of the characters surrounding her.

The exotic minor characters, however, can be a danger. Whereas the serious operas sometimes fail because a singer, stage designer or director has muddled the symbolism, *Arabella* can fail if the minor characters are pushed into caricature—as often happens when the roles are taken by old, fading singers who think they can act. With the heroine, on the other hand, the danger is that the singer may be too placid, appearing from the start so certain of the happy ending that she seems too self-assured, even prim, and perhaps a trifle smug. Yet generally the final scene can rescue any failures. Though the sight of a girl coming downstairs while holding a glass of water may seem prosaic, in the theatre, in the circumstances, with music—it is magic.

ACT I (56 min.)

The drawing room of a hotel suite. Vienna, 1860. The Countess, Adelaide, is at a card table with a fortune-teller. Nearby, her daughter Zdenka is sorting bills. The curtain rises immediately.

The Fortune-teller and Adelaide. While Zdenka receives bills at the door, the Fortune-teller gives the audience the necessary background. She sees the Count gambling, and losing. Adelaide declares the only hope to be a rich marriage for her beautiful daughter. But to her alarm the Fortune-teller sees an Officer, "Offizier," a type likely to be poor. "Matteo," gasps Zdenka. Then the Fortune-teller sees the bridegroom, a stranger from afar, who has been summoned by letter. "Graf Elemer," sighs Adelaide happily. And there is a forest, a large forest, and then a difficulty, a delay. "Heil'ge Mutter Gottes" (Holy Mother of God), exclaims Adelaide. The difficulty seems to lie in a second daughter, "eine zweite Tochter." Who is she? Adelaide explains that the family, unable to afford debuts for two girls, has always encouraged Zdenka to dress as a boy. But as Zdenka adores her elder sister . . . "Die Karten lügen nicht" (the cards never lie), says the Fortune-teller. Adelaide takes her into the next room to try the cards again.

Zdenka. Alone, she despairs over the bills and then, listening at her mother's door, over Matteo, the Officer. Her mother has forbidden him to call, and for love of Arabella he soon will kill himself. "Mein Gott," she begs, don't let that happen. She will do anything to prevent it, even continue in boy's clothes.

Zdenka and Matteo. He slips in hoping to find Arabella. "Kein Wort? Kein Brief?" (no word? no letter?), he asks. Zdenka shakes her head, but she insists that Arabella loves him. Consider her letters (in fact forged by Zdenka without Arabella's knowledge). There'll be another today for sure. If not, Matteo declares, he will request a transfer to Galicia and probably shoot himself: "den Revolver." After he has gone, Zdenka concludes that her forged letters are not enough. She must persuade Arabella to love Matteo.

Arabella and Zdenka. Returning from a walk, Arabella dismisses the chaperone. Then, noticing some roses, she asks if a Hussar brought them or perhaps the valet of a foreign gentleman. "Nein," says Zdenka, "sie sind von Matteo" (they are from Matteo). Arabella quickly puts them aside and shows equally little interest in the gifts of her other suitors, Elemer, Dominik and Lamoral. When Zdenka insists that Matteo loves Arabella, she is interrupted with the question "Are you in love with him?" "Sein Freund bin ich!" (his friend am I), cries Zdenka passionately. Perhaps it is time, Arabella suggests, for Zdenka to put off boy's clothes. Better a boy, says Zdenka, than a proud, cold-hearted flirt.

Arabella answers the charge seriously: "Er ist der Richtige nicht für **aria** mich!" (he is not the right man for me). Attraction comes quickly and as quickly goes. She cannot explain it. "Aber der Richtige" (but the right man) someday will stand before her, and there will be no doubt and no question, "und keine Fragen." She will be happy and docile as a child, "wie ein Kind."

Zdenka promises to help her to happiness, and a duet develops as **duet** Zdenka expresses her affection and Arabella repeats her belief in "der Richtige." (This is one of those Straussian passages in which the sopranos' voices should blend so perfectly that it becomes difficult to distinguish who has the top line: Zdenka.)

Sleigh bells tinkle in the street. It is Elemer calling to take Arabella for a drive. He is not "der Richtige," says Zdenka. Perhaps not, Arabella agrees, but still Carnival's fun must have an end, and "heut abend" (this evening) she must make a choice. "O Gott," gasps Zdenka, thinking of Matteo.

At the window Arabella muses on a stranger she had noticed in the street. She had half-expected he would send her flowers. Zdenka offers her Matteo's roses, then leaves as Elemer enters.

Arabella and Elemer. "Heut ist mein Tag!" (today is my day), he begins triumphantly. The suitors drew lots, and he won. Then "ich bin die Sklavin" (I am the slave), she says. Girls prefer not to be given entirely to one man, but then perhaps, "vielleicht," soon that will change. Elemer hopes that he will be the one to change it. Meanwhile, the horses are ready. She promises to be down in a half-hour, with Zdenka as her chaperone. He leaves to await them downstairs.

Arabella and Zdenka. From the window Arabella calls excitedly to Zdenka, "Er! das ist er! mein Fremder! da!" (him, it is him, my stranger, there). She is sure he is searching for her, but he passes by. They leave to dress for the sleighride.

Count Waldner and Adelaide. He shuffles the bills. Not one friend has responded to his letters, not even the rich, eccentric Mandryka. For him he enclosed a picture of Arabella in the half-hope that the old man might want to marry the girl. Adelaide suggests that they join Aunt Jadwiga in the country, and when no solution seems in sight, she leaves, wringing her hands. To ease despair Waldner orders a cognac, but the waiter reports the hotel has cut off all credit. A moment later he brings a visiting card: Mandryka.

Count Waldner and Mandryka. Waldner, stepping forward to greet his friend, discovers a stranger. The man pulls out a letter smeared with blood—the result, he says, of a bear's embrace (growls in the orchestra)—and asks if Waldner wrote it. To my regimental friend, says Waldner. "Das war mein Onkel. Er ist tot" (that was my uncle; he is dead). The stranger is now Mandryka. Producing the photograph of Arabella, he asks if she is "unvermählt?" (unmarried). "Unvermählt," says Waldner. Betrothed? Not yet. Then why, Mandryka asks, did you send the picture? "Mein Gott," says Waldner, to amuse the old man.

Mandryka, beginning an aria, asks: suppose my uncle, a real man, in
aria   the prime of life, had seen the picture and had rushed here, as any man would, to say "so gib das Mädel mir zur Frau" (so give the girl to me for a wife), what then?

Well, Waldner stammers.

With increasing emotion Mandryka continues: the uncle is dead. "Mein sind die Wälder" (mine are the forests), mine all the villages,
aria   fields and peasants. Give me your daughter "zur Frau." Waldner hesitates but nods permission for Mandryka to court Arabella. Rushing ahead, Mandryka describes his excitement over the picture and the sale of a forest to raise money for the journey (from Slavonia) to Vienna. Taking out his billfold he shows Waldner the small fortune the sale has produced.

Waldner's eyes bulge, and he joyfully repeats Mandryka's description of the forest as Mandryka tells him of the many more that he has.
aria   Thrusting the billfold at Waldner he urges, "Teschek, bedien'dich" (take one, it's all yours).

Waldner takes one bill, then another, and offers to introduce Mandryka to Arabella at once. But Mandryka refuses. In a hushed voice he explains that for him the meeting will be like something holy. He will call at the Countess's command. Meanwhile he will put up at the hotel.

And abruptly he leaves. (The entire scene from his entrance has superb vitality; if the audience is not swept along by it, the performance is poor.)

Count Waldner, Zdenka and Matteo. Zdenka can make no sense of her father, who keeps repeating "Teschek, bedien'dich." When he goes out waving the bank notes, Matteo enters, looking for Arabella or at least a letter, "den Brief." Zdenka hurries him away with the promise of a letter later at the ball.

Arabella. She is ready for the sleighride, and Zdenka is not. But the horses are restive, Arabella says. The horses "und dein Elemer" (and your Elemer), says Zdenka, as she runs off to dress.

"Mein Elemer," muses Arabella. (The aria is introduced and highlighted by a solo viola.) "Er mein—ich sein" (He mine—me his). It **aria** sounds so strange. Who is it that she longs for? Matteo? No. Perhaps if she could hear that stranger's voice, she could forget him. Should she marry Elemer? The thought makes her shudder. "Ist das der Fremde Mann" (is it the strange man) who most attracts her? "Herr Gott," probably he is married. "Und heut" (and today), she remarks, her thoughts brightening, is the day of my ball, "mein Ball," when I will be Queen, "Königen." "Und dann" (and then). . . . But Zdenka comes out, and they leave for the sleighride.

Vocabulary, Act I

Offizier	oh.fee.SEER	officer
Heil'ge Mutter Gottes	HILE.guh moot.ter got.tes	Holy Mother of God
eine zweite Tochter	eye.nuh TSVY.tuh tohk.ter	a second daughter
die Karten lügen nicht	dee KART.en leur.gen nikt	the cards do not lie
kein Wort	kine vort	no word
kein Brief	kine breef	no letter
den Revolver	den reh.vohl.ver	the revolver
sie sind von Matteo	see sinnt fon . . .	they are from Matteo
sein Freund bin ich	zine Froyn't bin ish	his friend am I
er ist der Richtige nicht für mich	er ist der RISH.tee.guh nikt feer mik	he is not the right man for me
aber der Richtige	ah.ber . . .	but the Right man
und keine Fragen	oont kine.uh FRAH.gen	and no questions

Vocabulary, Act I (continued)

German	Pronunciation	English
wie ein Kind	vee eye'n kint	like a child
heut abend	hoyt AH.bent	this evening
heut ist mein Tag	. . . mine tahg	today is my day
ich bin die Sklavin	. . . dee SKLAF.in	I am the slave
vielleicht	fee.LY'sht	perhaps
er! das ist er!	. . . FREM.der	him, that is him,
mein Fremder! da!		my stranger, there
das war mein Onkel.	. . . ONG.kel	that was my uncle.
Er ist tot	. . . toht	He is dead.
unvermählt	oon.fair.MAYL't	unmarried
so gib das Mädel	. . . MAYD'l	so give that
mir zur Frau		girl to me
		for a wife
mein sind die Wälder	. . . VAYL.der	mine are the
		forests
teschek, bedien'dich	TEH.shek beh.DEEN dish	take one, its all yours
und heut	oont HOYT	and today
mein Ball	. . . bahll	my ball
Königen	KERN.ig.in	queen
und dann . . .	oont dahnn . . .	and then . . .

ACT II (44 min.)

The anteroom to a ballroom. A staircase leads to a balcony that overlooks the dancing. Arabella and her mother slowly descend to Mandryka and Waldner, who await them.

The Introduction. She is an angel, sighs Mandryka. Waldner grumbles that his wife and daughter are always late. On the stair Adelaide comments on Mandryka's elegance, and Arabella, murmuring that this is "the final choice," hesitates. Her mother continues down to be introduced to Mandryka. Then Arabella comes forward—"Meine Tochter Arabella," says Waldner, and he and Adelaide withdraw.

Arabella and Mandryka. Their conversation begins awkwardly, interrupted by Dominik and Elemer asking Arabella for "diesen Walzer" (this waltz). She promises each, "später" (later).

Mandryka describes himself for her: "ich habe eine Frau gehabt . . ." (I had a wife) who died after two years. He was then too young and immature for such an angel. When Arabella expresses surprise, he exclaims that he is half a peasant, moving slowly but, once moved, feeling deeply. With Arabella her picture, "einem Bild," set his heart on fire.

She asks how he came to have her picture, and he, growing more passionate, declares it hardly matters. In his fields and woods her image impressed itself on him. She is startled by his vehemence, and he apologizes for a country nature that speaks directly.

Her third suitor, Lamoral, interrupts, asking for "einen Walzer," and again she promises, "später." Softly, she tells Mandryka that she knows of his desire to marry her. Does he realize that her family is not very grand, in fact almost disreputable? But he cares nothing about her social position. Her face proclaims her character, and he invites her, "so kommen Sie mit mir" (so come you with me).

Half-aloud Arabella muses: when "der Richtige" appears, there will be no doubt, no questions, "keine Fragen," and all will be sparkling clear, like a river in the sun.

Like the Danube before my house, he says; and if you were a maid **the custom** in one of my villages, this very evening, "und heute abend noch," you would go to the well behind your father's house, draw a glass of clear water, "klares Wasser," and present it to me on the threshold as a token that I am your betrothed.

You bring your countryside with you, she exclaims, and what does not relate to you, does not exist for you. Therefore, he responds, I can live only with a person to exalt above me, and in this hour I choose you for my wife, "zu meiner Frau." Where I am master, you shall be mistress.

Softly she replies: "Dein Haus wird mein Haus sein" (thy house will **Betrothal song and duet** be my house), and in your grave will I lie beside you. Thus do I give myself to you for always. In duet they repeat their pledge. Then they agree that she will stay at the ball to bid farewell to her girlhood and fulfill her role as Queen, and he will stay to watch though not to speak to her.

Fiakermilli et al. A crowd of dancers swirl up to them, and Fiakermilli, the cabdrivers' mascot, "a pretty little person in a gaudy dress," presents Arabella with a bouquet and, with much coloratura and yodeling, invites her to be Queen of the Ball. With Dominik as her partner, Arabella leads them all into the ballroom.

In one corner of the anteroom, Mandryka excitedly tells Adelaide and Waldner of his success, ordering a supper for the family, champagne (Moët-Chandon) for everyone, and carriages filled with roses and camellias to take Arabella home. In another corner Matteo complains bitterly to Zdenka that Arabella has no glance or word for him. *Arabella and the suitors.* Returning with Dominik, she bids him "adieu." When he protests, she says, "Aber der Richtige für Sie, die war nicht ich . . ." (but the right one for you, that was not I). "Adieu."

With Elemer, who protests more strongly, she is less nostalgic, more forceful, and leaves him still protesting. With Lamoral she is tender, kissing him on the forehead before returning to the ballroom to finish the waltz. (From here to the act's end the quality of this almost perfect opera slightly declines. The plot intrudes, and the words and music become perfunctory. Almost certainly, if Hofmannsthal had lived, he and Strauss would have reworked this section.)

Zdenka and Matteo (overheard by Mandryka). Zdenka, finding no solution to Matteo's unrequited love for Arabella, in desperation follows her own emotions. Instead of another forged letter she gives him the key, "der Schlüssel," to her bedroom, saying that it is the key to Arabella's room. In a quarter-hour Arabella will receive him in the dark and make him happy. Matteo in disbelief keeps repeating, "Der Schlüssel zu Arabellas Zimmer"; then both he and Zdenka rush off to keep the appointment.

Mandryka et al. He has overheard Matteo and sends his footman to stop him, but too late. He argues with himself that a second Arabella may be at the ball. Fiakermilli and Elemer ask him to restore to the ball its Queen: he will know where she is. A footman delivers a note to him from Arabella: "I say good night for tonight. I'm going home and from tomorrow am yours.

Convinced now that Arabella is playing him for a country bumpkin, Mandryka orders wine for everyone, flirts bitterly with Fiakermilli and, as the wine befuddles him, speaks more and more sarcastically of Arabella. When Waldner protests, Mandryka says that he has ceased to be a churl from the provinces and has learned the manners of Viennese counts. Offended, Waldner announces that he and his wife will go with Mandryka to the hotel and find Arabella.

Mandryka orders drinks for everyone, and as he with Waldner and Adelaide leave the party, the guests cheer him. (In Munich and Vienna this final chorus generally is cut and Act III follows immediately with its Prelude serving as an intermezzo while the scene is changed.)

Vocabulary, Act II

meine Tochter Arabella	my.nuh TOHK.ter . . .	my daughter Arabella
diesen Walzer	deez.en VAHLT.ser	this waltz
später	shpayt.er	later
ich habe eine Frau gehabt	ish hah.buh eye.nuh frow geh.hapt	I had a wife
einem Bild	eye.nem bilt	a picture
so kommen Sie mit mir	so kom.men see mit meer	so come you with me
der Richtige	der RISH.tee.guh	the right man
keine Fragen	kine.uh FRAH.gen	no questions
und heute abend noch	oont HOY.tuh ah.bent nok	and this very evening
klares Wasser	klar.es VAHS.er	clear water
zu meiner Frau	tsoo mine.er . . .	for my wife
dein Haus wird mein Haus sein	dine howss veert . . . sine	thy house will my house be
adieu	ah.d'yuh	farewell
aber der Richtige für Sie, die war nicht ich	. . . dee vahr nik ish	but the right one for you, that was not I
der Schlüssel	. . . SHLEURSS.el	the key
der Schlüssel zu Arabellas Zimmer	. . . TSIM.er	the key to Arabella's room

ACT III (46 min.)

PRELUDE (4 min.)

Depicting the passage of love between Matteo and Zdenka, whom in the darkness he believes is Arabella.

As their passion ends, the curtain opens on the main hall of the hotel. Stairs rise to a landing from which several doors lead off. Matteo, straightening his clothes, emerges from one and is about to descend when the hotel's doorbell rings. The porter admits Arabella.

Arabella and Matteo. She enters with themes of the ball and the right man swirling in her head. Pausing at the stair (traditionally sitting in a **aria** rocking chair), she sings of how Mandryka will take her to his country estate and introduce her to his peasants.

Matteo, coming down, recognizes her and mutters that it is impossible: he has just left her in her room. She greets him, "Sie hier? So spät?'" (you here? so late?). And he, thinking she is once again mocking him, asks her, "Sie hier?" She replies that she has come from the ball, "vom Ball," and is going to her room, "Zimmer." She bids him "Gute Nacht!" (good night). Incredulous, he repeats, "vom Ball . . . Zimmer." "Gute Nacht," she says, and asks why he laughs. He wishes, he says, to thank her. "Danken—wofür?" (to thank—what for?), she asks. Almost in anger he echoes, "Danken—wofür?" Her acting is too good. Not understanding, she says coldly, "Gute Nacht." Passionately he protests: only a quarter-hour past, "vor einer Viertelstunde," she loved him; at least now give him a loving look. She tries to pass; he stops her. The doorbell rings, and they are caught on the stairs arguing loudly. *Mandryka, Arabella et al.* What are you doing? her mother asks. "Aber nichts, Mama, garnichts" (but nothing, absolutely nothing). Mandryka aloud identifies Matteo as the man "mit dem Schlüssel" (with the key) and, pointedly asking Adelaide's permission to withdraw, orders his footman to start packing. When Arabella offers to explain who Matteo is, Mandryka cuts her short. Waldner thereupon asks her if Matteo brought her from the ball. When she denies it, he insists to Mandryka that nothing has happened. It is time to say "Gute Nacht."

Mandryka, however, attacks Arabella directly. "Ich müsste blind sein" (I must be blind) not to see the game afoot. Arabella, growing angry, repeats that nothing has happened, and Matteo offers on her behalf to challenge Mandryka. But Mandryka is her betrothed, she says, and Matteo has no right to defend her, no standing. She asks him to say so. Matteo stammers, "Nein . . . keines . . ." (no . . . none), and Arabella turns to Mandryka, "Sie hören!" (you hear). But Mandryka accuses her of cutting off Matteo before he could say "Nein, keines—ausser" (except).

Arabella, now thoroughly angry, charges Matteo with trying to wreck her marriage out of spite, and Mandryka presses him: "Ausser" (except what?) "Kein Wort!" (not one word), says Matteo. Anything else? asks Arabella. "Nein," he replies. Mandryka congratulates him on his discretion after a conquest, and Waldner now challenges Mandryka to a duel, though his pistols, he adds, are pawned.

While the men discuss weapons, Arabella grieves that Mandryka is acting without reason; he is so weak, "so schwach ist," that he lacks the strength to believe in her. (In this passage, which Strauss slights a bit musically, Hofmannsthal has Arabella face reality: her "Richtige" is after all an ordinary man, and her passage from girl to woman—the heart of the opera—is not in the farewell waltzes of Act II but in this and the subsequent passages in which she accepts Mandryka as he is.)

The quarrel has drawn the guests from their rooms, and they hang over the banister, listening. Matteo insists that any blame is his. Mandryka, losing all control, bluntly asks Arabella to admit that Matteo is her lover. She replies, "die Wahrheit ist bei mir!" (the truth is by me). I saw the boy, Mandryka says, give Matteo the key to your room, "Schlüssel . . . Zimmer." Arabella realizes that he must mean Zdenka but, unable to state what actually happened, repeats "die Wahrheit ist bei mir." Mandryka asks if she wants to marry Matteo, with whom she had an assignation only ten minutes after her betrothal to another. When she turns from him, he orders (spoken lines) his footman to bring swords for the duel and asks the guests to retire.

Zdenka et al. In negligée, revealing her true sex, she runs down the stairs, kneels before her father and laments her shame. She will kill herself in the morning. Arabella promises to stand by her, and Zdenka, pointing at Matteo, says that he is innocent. Swiftly her story is told. Mandryka, going directly to Arabella, apologizes, but she, paying no attention, thanks Zdenka for a good lesson: a heart in love should withhold nothing but continue always to give of its love. Zdenka, for her part, gives thanks for Arabella's strength and asks not to be forsaken "was jetzt noch kommt!" (whatever now may come). Both Mandryka and Waldner repeat the phrase, Mandryka looking dejectedly at Arabella, and Waldner, at the pistols and swords. And Mandryka, preparing to leave, echoes it, "was jetzt noch kommt—"

But Arabella takes his hand. He is not worthy, he says, of such forgiveness! "Still" (hush), she replies. We won't talk of it now. We have all forgotten what has happened here and in good spirit will accept "was jetzt noch kommt!"

Why then, he says, it must be matchmaking, and taking Matteo by the hand he leads him to Waldner and presents him as Zdenka's future husband. Waldner accepts him. "Oh, Theodor," sighs Adelaide, "what a change." "Kolossal!" agrees Waldner, before leaving to rejoin his card game. The others also retire, and before going upstairs Arabella asks Mandryka to have her footman bring her a glass of fresh water from the hotel's well, to clear her head after so much conversation.

Arabella and Mandryka. He watches the footman deliver the water, wishing that she had looked back just once, though doubtless he did not deserve a glance. Did she request the water only to mock him? If so, it was a kind of notice, an unearned grace.

Then, as he is looking up, she appears at the top of the stair holding

the glass of water out to him as he had described the custom to her. Slowly she descends and on the bottom stair begins, "Das war sehr gut,
aria   Mandryka" (it is so good) that you have not gone. She had intended to drink the water but instead, already refreshed by his love, offers the untouched draught to him on "den Abend, wo die Mädchenzeit zu Ende ist für mich" (the evening when girlhood ends for me).

He drinks and smashes the glass. And so, she says, we are betrothed. Will you, he asks, stay as you are? I can do no other, she replies; take me, as I am!

Vocabulary, Act III

sie hier	see heer	you here
so spät	so shpayt	so late
vom Ball	fom Bahll	from the ball
Zimmer	TSIM.er	room
gute Nacht	GOOT.uh nahkt	good night
danken—wofür	DAHNGK.en—wo. FEUR	to thank—what for
vor einer Viertelstunde	for EYE.ner FEERT.el.shtoon.de	for a quarter-hour
aber nichts, Mama, garnichts	AH.ber nikts . . . gahr.nikts	but nothing . . . absolutely nothing
mit dem Schlüssel	mit dem SCHLEURSS.el	with the key
ich müsste blind sein	ish MEURS.teh blinnt sine	I must be blind
nein . . . keines	nine . . . kine.es	no . . . none
Sie hören	see HEUR.en	you hear
nein . . . keines . . . ausser	. . . OWS.ser	no . . . none . . . except
kein Wort	kine vort	no word
so schwach ist	so shvahk ist	so weak is
die Wahrheit ist bei mir	dee VAHR.hite . . . by meer	the truth is by me
was jetzt noch kommt	vahss yetst nok kommt	whatever now may come
still	shtill	hush
kolossal	kol.os.AHL	colossal
das war sehr gut, Mandryka	dahs vahr sair goot . . .	it is so good . . .
den Abend, wo die Mädchenzeit zu Ende	den AH.bent . . . MAIT.ken.tsite	the evening when girlhood ends
ist für mich	. . . EN.de . . .	for me

DIE SCHWEIGSAME FRAU

(The Silent Woman)

Comic opera in three acts. World premiere, Dresden, June 24, 1935; American prem. (in English), New York, Oct. 7, 1958; British prem. (in Eng.), Covent Garden, London, Nov. 20, 1961. Music by Richard Strauss; text by Stefan Zweig, based distantly on Ben Jonson's play, *Epicoene, or The Silent Woman,* first performed in 1609.

The opera's premiere production led to a battle between Strauss and German (Nazi) officials over the librettist. Because Zweig was a Jew, the officials planned to leave his name off the handbills, and Strauss forced them to print it. But after the opera's first four performances, the government banned it throughout Germany. A few foreign productions followed, but the opera was effectively silenced until after World War II.

Its structure is conventional, and much of it is in set numbers, arias, duets, sextets, connected by spoken dialogue. The orchestra is relatively small, only six double-basses, and the orchestration is light and clear. Unlike most Strauss operas, men's voices predominate and the tenor has a major role. Because of its length the opera is almost always cut, and the timings below are of a typical cut performance. Thus far the opera has had only a fitful success. The key seems to lie in its production. Not only must the singers be good actors but they must be well directed, or their antics become tiresome.

Zweig moved the time of Jonson's play to 1780 and made the chief character, Sir Morosus, a retired Admiral. The opera's single set shows the living room of his London house, with models of ships, flags and other naval memorabilia. Because he is exceptionally sensitive to noise, the doors are soundproofed with blankets and sacking.

OVERTURE (4 min.)

Strauss entitled it "Potpourri," understating its careful construction. It is gay, light, brilliantly scored, and presents most of the opera's chief themes.

ACT I (with cuts, 47 min.)

The housekeeper (contralto) tells the barber (baritone) that what the house needs, what Morosus needs, is a good wife, suggesting herself.

The barber disagrees, and their rising voices draw Morosus (bass). While the barber shaves him, Morosus complains about the talkative housekeeper, the noisy neighborhood and the clanging clocks and church bells. The barber describes the companionship that a young, silent wife might offer, and the old man, musing on the idea, reveals his loneliness.

They are interrupted by the arrival of Morosus's nephew Henry (tenor), long believed dead. Morosus is overjoyed. Here is a son, an heir—no need now of a wife. But Henry has brought with him from Italy a troupe of singers booked for the Haymarket Theatre. Worse, he is one of them, singing in public, for money! And worse yet, he has married the troupe's chief ear-splitter, Aminta (coloratura soprano). Having insulted the singers, Morosus disinherits Henry and storms from the room, swearing in the morning to marry a silent woman.

The troupe—Aminta, Isotta (coloratura soprano), Carlotta (mezzo), Morbio (baritone), Vanuzzi and Farfallo (basses)—are indignant. The barber urges them not to judge the Admiral too harshly: he is hypersensitive to noise because a shipboard explosion damaged his eardrums. Aminta is sympathetic but the others want redress. The barber urges Henry to regain his uncle's favor, as the old man is rich. He suggests that perhaps Isotta or Carlotta might marry him, but Isotta claims to be too happy not to joke and laugh about the house and Carlotta, too fond of music not to sing. Suddenly the barber has an inspiration: a mock marriage to a silent woman who turns out to be a shrew. Then when freed of his wife, Morosus will turn to Henry in relief. Meanwhile the singers can have their revenge by playing the roles of parson, lawyers and witnesses. With delight the troupe adopts the idea.

ACT II (with cuts, 57 min.)

To a courtly minuet and disapproving comments from the housekeeper, Morosus dons his dress uniform for the wedding. The barber arrives with three candidates for the position of wife: Carlotta, acting the country bumpkin, and Isotta, the intellectual, are rejected; Aminta, as Timida, a poor but well-bred gentlewoman, is chosen. Morosus is overwhelmed by her charm and sends the barber to fetch a parson and lawyer at once.

Alone with Aminta, Morosus pours out his heart, revealing his gentleness, and her conscience begins to nag her. They are married, with

Vanuzzi and Morbio as the parson and the notary. All are invited by Morosus to remain for the small wedding breakfast. Suddenly a gang of sailors (Farfallo and others of the troupe) burst in, claiming to be old shipmates come to celebrate the wedding. They call in the neighbors and create such a racket that when Morosus finally succeeds in ousting them, he is near collapse. Now it is Aminta's turn, and she acts the shrew, kicking, yelling, throwing the furniture about. Henry appears, throttles her with a neck-hold and sends her wailing to her room. Morosus begs to be free of Timida, and Henry promises to procure an annulment the next day. He sends his uncle to bed and joins with Aminta in a lovers' duet punctuated offstage by feeble cries of thanks from Morosus.

ACT III (with cuts, 37 min.)

The next morning Aminta, still acting Timida, directs workmen (the troupe) in redecorating the room. Despite the housekeeper's pleas for less noise, they make as much as possible, and in the midst of the uproar Henry, disguised as a singing teacher, arrives with a harpsichord to give Timida her lesson. Morosus is in despair, but his hopes rise when the barber announces the arrival of the Chancellor of the Diocese (Vanuzzi) and the Assessors (Morbio and Farfallo) to consider the petition for annulment. The barber proposes to produce witnesses that Aminta has cohabited with a man other than her husband. She denies it, and after much testimony and play with latin words the petition is dismissed.

Morosus is crushed and amid a noisy ensemble throws himself by a sofa to cover his ears with pillows. The barber stops the charade, and Henry and Aminta, kneeling by the old man, invite him to forget a bad dream. After explanations Morosus is ready to laugh at himself, and at the curtain he sits companionably with Henry and Aminta while musing: how beautiful is music, when it is ended; how wonderful a silent woman, married to someone else.

The opera invites comparison to Donizetti's *Don Pasquale,* and to the latter's advantage. Aside from preferences in length, melody and orchestration, there seems to be an area of sensibility in which Donizetti triumphs. The story of the old man tricked by the young couple has a strong potential for sadism, and Strauss seems often to press the joke too far. It may be that his eight—instead of Donizetti's three—

against one is too many. Or that Morosus with his physical disability is made too individual and sympathetic too early in the drama. Donizetti keeps Pasquale almost a stereotype until the climactic scene in which he is slapped. But whatever the cause, in Strauss the balance between humor and sadism falters. It is an area in which the cuts and stage direction can make a great difference.

FRIEDENSTAG

(Peace Day)

Opera in one act. World premiere, Munich, July 24, 1938; American prem., Los Angeles, April 2, 1967; British prem., a radio (BBC) performance, May 29, 1971. Music by Richard Strauss, text by Josef Gregor based on a libretto by Stefan Zweig.

Thus far *Friedenstag* (80 min.) is one of the least performed of Strauss's later operas. Its message—that in peace, not war, humanity best reveals itself—was not popular with Nazi leaders, and after ninety-eight performances in Germany and Austria the opera was unofficially banned. After World War II, partly perhaps because of its grim setting, it had few revivals.

The subject is unique for Strauss, and it drew from him some uncharacteristic and interesting music: a grief-stricken march in which starving people cry for bread, a poetic passage in which the bells of peace begin to ring, and a deliberately over-assertive, banal military march based on *Ein' feste Burg*. But for many persons the opera seems to fail just where it needs most to succeed, in the final chorus celebrating peace. The sentiment is right, but its musical realization too often seems merely long and noisy.

The story takes place on October 24, 1648, the last day of the Thirty Years' War. The setting is the large, circular assembly hall of a citadel in a Catholic town besieged by Lutheran troops. The war has continued so long that among the townspeople and soldiers an entire generation has never known peace.

As morning breaks, the soldiers on duty gaze at the ravaged countryside and comment that the night's sally captured nothing, not even a little food. An Italian civilian (tenor) who has brought a message through the lines and whose country is not at war sings snatches of a happy song. Outside the townspeople complain of hunger and cry for bread.

A deputation led by the Burgomaster (tenor) asks the citadel's Commandant (baritone), a dour personality devoted to duty, to surrender. He refuses, reading aloud a message from the Emperor requiring him to hold out at all costs. But the cries outside grow louder, and the people's leaders refuse to be put off. Finally the Commandant agrees, but only at midday and only on his signal, which will be unmistakable. After the deputation leaves, it becomes clear that he intends to blow up the citadel with himself and as many of his soldiers who may wish to stay with him.

For a moment the stage is empty, and then his wife Maria (soprano) enters, musing on the town's plight. Her husband, whom she loves, is dedicated to war. Yet she hopes that, as the sun triumphs over darkness, someday in him joy and optimism will rise to banish grimness. He enters and explains his plan. In a duet she chooses to stay with him in life and death.

Some soldiers enter, one with a fuse to blow up the citadel. But before it can be taken to the powder room, three cannon shots are heard, and then mysteriously bells begin to ring, bells which have not been heard since the war began.

The Burgomaster rushes in. It is the signal. It is peace. The Lutherans are coming in peace. But the Commandant's mind by now is so used to war he cannot imagine peace. He tries to bar the Lutherans from the citadel but is too late. Led by their commander, they march in to a quick-step. The Lutheran leader is eager to shake hands with his noble foe, but the Commandant refuses and draws his sword. Maria begs her husband to acknowledge that brotherhood and love can oust strife and hate. He hesitates, looks at her and, throwing his sword away, embraces the Lutheran. The opera ends with an extended hymn to peace.

DAPHNE

Bucolic tragedy in one act. World premiere, Dresden, Oct. 15, 1938; American prem., Buenos Aires, Sept. 17, 1948; United States concert prem., New York, Oct. 10, 1960; stage prem., Santa Fe, July 29, 1969. Music by Richard Strauss; text by Joseph Gregor.

PRINCIPAL CHARACTERS

Peneios, Daphne's father	bass
Gaea, her mother	contralto
Daphne, a young girl	soprano
Leukippos, her unwanted suitor	tenor
Apollo	tenor

The action takes place in Thessaly within sight of Mount Olympus and near the hut of Peneios, close by the river bearing his name.

The opera, based loosely on a Greek myth, is the third for which Strauss used the one-act form to present the moment of crisis in a young woman's life and her subsequent death. And like *Salome* and *Elektra, Daphne* requires a large orchestra, lasts roughly a hundred minutes, and examines an episode that is primarily sexual, or at least is most often interpreted in sexual terms. In *Daphne* the episode concerns a girl who does not wish to be, or perhaps is incapable of being, sexually aroused. She does not wish to become a woman; she would prefer to become a tree.

In the ancient Greek world, at least of this opera, such a wish was unusual perhaps, but not perverted. In those early days mythology still merged with daily life, and humanity was not yet the decisive state it later seemed always to have been. Daphne's father, for example, had been the god of the river Peneios, and he can remember that time though now he is merely a fisherman, Peneios, living beside the river. Apollo, still wholly a god, mingles with humans and can share all their feelings; and gods and humans alike live so close to nature that either easily can become an animal, a tree or flower, or a constellation of stars.

Daphne, therefore, is not violating some immutable human law by her desire; rather she is searching for her true identity, for from birth she has felt closer to the trees than to the humans surrounding her. The opera recounts the pain of her self-discovery and, ultimately, the joy. Some persons even interpret the opera, despite lack of evidence from the poet or composer, to be a gentle plea for the right of women to choose a role other than mating and motherhood.

The opera is in every way less powerful than either *Salome* or *Elektra;* the libretto lacks the others' dramatic confrontations, and the music is less interesting structurally and melodically. That said, many virtues remain. Strauss successfully created a pastoral atmosphere, and much of the orchestration, with emphasis on the woodwinds, is beautiful. The leading roles, for soprano and two tenors, require large, healthy voices and in return display them magnificently. And the final transformation scene, when well staged, is entrancing, as a laurel tree gradually obscures Daphne and her voice, ceasing to articulate words, becomes a happy sigh sounding through the branches.

A SINGLE ACT (104 min.)

The prelude (2 min.) sets the pastoral tone as solo woodwinds—in order, oboe, basset horn, clarinet, flute and English horn—weave a succession of melodic fragments ending in a summons, on alpine horn, for the shepherds to gather for the feast of Dionysius. The curtain rises to the sound of sheep and cattle being herded to corrals along the river bank. Evening. Shepherds cross the stage calling to one another, and in a brief chorus they bid the day farewell. Then Daphne enters, alone.

Daphne. (First of three long soliloquies, 8 min.) She begs the sun not to set: "O bleib, geliebter Tag" (O stay, beloved day). Night is dark and cold, and she can no longer see the trees, which she prefers to men. When Apollo enters his dwelling on Olympus (i.e., sets behind the mountain), she would remain with the trees. As she encircles one with her arms, Leukippos steps from behind it.

Leukippos and Daphne. He offers himself in place of the tree, and is rejected. He reminds her of her pleasure in his flute. Only because, she retorts, its sound is like the wind. He breaks his flute: enough of pretending. "Daphne, Daphne—ich liebe dich!" (I love you), he cries. But she evades his embrace, and he leaves as Gaea enters.

Gaea and Daphne. (Gaea's range is very low, *contralto profondo,* sinking frequently to E♭.) She reproves Daphne for rejecting Leukippos. The time will come when Daphne's body and spirit will awaken: she should prepare for it. Two girls offer Daphne a robe, headdress and jewelry for the feast, but she refuses to wear them, and runs off. Gaea follows, disapproving.

The Maids and Leukippos. The girls remark on Daphne's beauty and then, seeing the grieving Leukippos, suggest that he don her clothes and join the girls' chorus for the feast. Thus he can be close to Daphne. Laughing, they lead him off.

Peneios, Gaea, Shepherds and Apollo. Led by Peneios, who predicts that a god will join them, all gather for the feast. Offstage there is a sound of cattle crashing through the underbrush, laughter echoes in the distance, lightning flashes and suddenly Apollo appears before them dressed as a cattleman. He describes the stampede of his herd along the river bank (imitative orchestration), and the others, accepting him as a cattleman, drift away.

Apollo and Daphne. The full moon has risen, casting a misty light over the scene. Daphne appears, and Apollo is captivated by her. A duet develops in which he refers to himself as her "Bruder" (brother) and, quoting her soliloquy "O bleib, geliebter Tag," promises her eternal daylight. Believing him to be the sun or its emissary, she sinks into his embrace. But his kiss is a lover's kiss, and she struggles free.

She accuses him of misleading her: "Bruder!" He replies forcefully, "Ich liebe dich, Daphne." An end to dreaming, he cries. "Wahrheit bring ich!" (the truth I bring). But she protests that he has brought fear.

Shepherds et al. The community gathers, and some shepherds in masks start a wild dance (5 min.) in honor of Dionysius. At its end Leukippos, disguised as a maid, offers Daphne a drink and invites her to dance.

Apollo, Leukippos and Daphne. Apollo angrily proclaims that the feast is a mockery, a deception. When the others protest, he swings his bow through the air, and in response thunder claps. Terrified, all rush out except Apollo, Leukippos and Daphne.

Accused by Apollo of deception, Leukippos throws off his girl's clothes, and then demands the same honesty of Apollo. Daphne, too, demands the cattleman, who spoke so movingly of the sun and warmth, to reveal his true identity. Apollo "spreads out his arms with great rhapsodic power" and describes how every morning he drives his chariot across the heavens. "Die Sonne Seht in mir!" (Behold the sun in me).

Daphne, overcome, kneels before him, but Leukippos calls him "Lügner" (liar), for the feast is in honor of Dionysius, not Apollo. And Daphne, remembering the ardor of Apollo's kiss, also rejects him. Leukippos thanks her and, turning, curses the god. Apollo kills him instantly.

Daphne. (Second soliloquy, 8 min.) She grieves over Leukippos. Once again she hears his flute, and now it reveals to her his heart and all he suffered. For her he died, and she will bring to him blossoms, boughs, all that she holds dearest. She will guard his grave until the gods bring death to her.

Apollo. (6 min.) The fault is his. Let the gods hear him now. He put on

Dionysius's garments and stole his place at the feast. (Allegory: for Leukippos, a human, failure to be true to his identity ended in death; for Apollo, a god, dishonor. Moral: be yourself.) Let the gods take Leukippos to Olympus where he may play his flute always, and (kneeling) may Daphne's wish be granted her. Let her become the glorious laurel.

Then, rising, he sings an incantation: her spirit will serve at the altar of Phoebus Apollo who loved her; and the leaf from the laurel forever will serve as the symbol of valor and worth acknowledged.

Daphnes Verwandlung (*Transformation Scene*). (Third soliloquy, followed by a long orchestral passage, 10 min.) "Ich komme. Ich komme" (I come), she calls to the trees. With blossoms and branches now she will greet Apollo, life-giving light and truly "Bruder!" May humans make of her leaves a symbol of love never-ending.

In the full moonlight stands the tree, and through its branches comes her voice in wordless echo of the orchestra.

Vocabulary

O bleib, geliebter Tag	oh bly.b' geh.LEEP.ter Tahg	O stay, beloved day
ich liebe dich	ik (or ish) LEEB.eh dik	I love you
bruder	BROOD.er	brother
Wahrheit bring ich	VAHR.hite bring ik (or ish)	the truth I bring
die Sonne Seht in mir	dee SON.eh sayt in meer	behold the sun in me
Lügner	LERG.ner	liar
ich komme	ik (or ish) kom	I come

CAPRICCIO

A Conversation Piece for Music in one act. World premiere, Munich, Oct. 28, 1942; British prem., London, Sept. 22, 1953; United States prem., New York, April 2, 1954. Music by Richard Strauss; text by Strauss and Clemens Krauss, based distantly on a short opera by Antonio Salieri and Giovanni Battista Casti, *Prima la musica e poi le parole,* first performed in conjunction with the premiere of Mozart's *Der Schauspieldirektor,* Feb. 7, 1786.

PRINCIPAL CHARACTERS

The Countess, Madeleine	soprano	ma.dell.EYE'N
The Count, her brother	baritone	
Flamand, a musician	tenor	flah.mahn(n)
Olivier, a poet	baritone	oh.lee.v'yay
La Roche, a theatrical producer	bass	la rosh
Clairon, an actress	contralto	clair.on(n)

The action takes place in a chateau near Paris at the time when Gluck was introducing his reforms into opera (*c.* 1775).

Strauss wrote in all fifteen operas, and in this, his last, he dramatized his feelings about the form. His subtitle, "A Conversation Piece for Music," is apt, for his subject is the form's perennial question, the balance between words and music: which is the more important? *Prima la musica . . .* or *prima le parole?* The opera's characters put the question directly in their conversation and indirectly in their relationships: chiefly, will the Countess choose as her lover the poet or the musician?

The period of the opera's action being elegant, the personal question is not so bluntly stated, or answered. Rather the characters at the end of their conversation, with the questions still unresolved, decide to present the Countess with an opera to be composed by the poet and the musician. In it they will all play themselves, and the subject will be their afternoon's conversation: which first, words or music? Since they reached no conclusion, however, the opera's ending is uncertain, and it is left to the Countess to determine the ending in the morning by choosing between the arts—and the artists. Thus is an opera started within an opera, and what the audience sees is the opera that the characters within *Capriccio* have decided to write.

The cleverness is typical of the opera's sophistication, and there are many moments when Strauss, with music of great beauty, projects all the layers of meaning. Yet for many persons there are moments, too, when the conversation drags wearily on. Though the opera runs two and a quarter hours, Strauss intended it to be played without intermission; but unlike Wagner in *Das Rheingold,* of similar length, he offers no change of scene and only one instead of three orchestral interludes in which the characters are removed from the stage and the audience can rest its eyes. Some producers, therefore, have introduced a break after the first fifty-two minutes, and some, though fewer, make cuts.

Such an authority as Lord Harewood, the editor of *Kobbé,* thinks the opera will "gain ground in the repertory as the years go by." Meanwhile it is more often a festival specialty, or its finale, a sixteen-minute solo for the Countess, is sung at concerts. The whole, however, can be an enchanting experience.

Though Strauss requires a large orchestra, the instruments are more for color than for volume, and much of the time the sound is of a chamber ensemble.

In the synopsis the scenes are of music, not locale, and all start with the arrival onstage of a character who gives the conversation and music a new twist. They are indicated here along with the subdivisions of Scene 9 as a way of revealing the opera's structure.

A SINGLE ACT (132 min.)

As part of the opera's cleverness, its action begins with the Overture. The characters, it will later be revealed, have gathered to rehearse the entertainment for the Countess's birthday, a few days hence. The program is to include a string sextet by the musician, a play by the poet, and a production with singers and dancers from the producer's company; rehearsals are held in the chateau's private theatre, just offstage. When the curtain rises on the Countess's salon, the opera's only set, the rehearsal of the string sextet—in fact the opera's Overture (8 min.)—is drawing to an end.

The salon, a rococo room with french doors opening on a terrace and a park, is furnished with comfortable chairs, a spinet, a harp with music stand and candelabra. The producer, an older man, is asleep in a chair; the poet and the musician stand by the door to the private theatre where they can see the Countess, who is offstage at the rehearsal.

SCENE 1 (9 min.)

Flamand and Olivier, musician and poet, each discovers that the other also loves the Countess; but each is confident that she prefers his art. "Wort oder Ton?" (words or music), poses Olivier. "She will decide," answers Flamand. "Prima le parole—dopo la musica!" says the poet. "Prima la musica—dopo le parole!" counters the musician. (Such pairing runs through the opera, not only in words and attitudes but in characters and scenes.)

The sextet in the theatre offstage finishes its rehearsal, and the pro-

ducer, La Roche, awakes saying: "Soft music is the best soporific."
Both artists attack him as a Philistine. He defends himself vigorously:
Gluck's reforms have ruined opera with too much recitative. The public wants arias and high notes as in Lully, Rameau and Piccini (musical
references—for those who can catch them). And beautiful leading
ladies such as Clairon, who is coming to rehearse the play. With the
stage now free he suggests that they start to work, and they exit.

SCENE 2 (5 min.)

The Countess, still hearing the sextet, enters with her brother. He
slyly suggests that she loves the composer, not the music. She counters
that she also loves the works of Couperin and Rameau (musical references); but with Flamand, she confesses, she cannot altogether separate man and music. The Count declares a preference for Olivier's
play. His enthusiasm, she teases, is for the actress Clairon. Between the
poet and the musician, he asks, which will she choose? Neither, for in
choosing one she will lose the other. Together brother and sister sing
their points of view: he, brisk and carefree; she, more serious and
introspective.

SCENE 3 (2 min.)

La Roche, Flamand and Olivier reenter, declaring that the program
for the birthday celebration is settled: the sextet, the play and a selection by the producer. From the window the Count announces the arrival of Clairon.

SCENE 4 (7 min.)

She enters, and after the compliments to her and her art she regrets
that the poet had not sent her the play's love scene. Olivier protests that
until this very morning (with a glance at the Countess) he had lacked
inspiration, but now he has a sonnet.

Clairon and the Count recite their lines in the love scene, ending
with his passionate declamation of the sonnet. (It is a translation of one
by Ronsard, and since three other characters will later recite or sing it,
it follows entire.)

Kein Andres, das mir so im Herzen loht,
Nein, Schöne, nichts auf dieser ganzen Erde,
Kein Andres, das ich so wie dich begehrte,
Und käm' von Venus mir ein Angebot.
    No other burns so in my heart,
    No, fairest, nowhere on this earth.
    No other could I yearn for so,
    Though Venus came herself to me.
Dein Auge beut mir himmlisch-süsse Not,
Und wenn ein Aufschlag alle Qual vermehrte,
Ein andrer Wonne mir und Lust gewährte—
Zwei Schläge sind dann Leben oder Tod.
    Thine eyes fill me with pain and joy;
    One glance my sorrows multiply,
    Another sends me ecstasy—
    Two blows encompass Life and Death.
Und trüg ich's fünfmalhunderttausand Jahre,
Erhielte ausser dir, du Wunderbare,
Kein andres Wesen über mich Gewalt.
Durch neue Adern müsst' mein Blut ich giessen,
In meinen, voll von dir zum Uberfliessen,
Fänd' neue Liebe weder Raum noch Halt.
    Could I live five hundred thousand years,
    Except for thee, thou Wunderbare,
    No other person could hold me.
    In new veins my blood would have to course
    For mine with thee are overflowing,
    So new love lacks the room to enter.

Complimenting the Count on his talent, Clairon passes the sonnet to the producer, who hurries them into the theatre for rehearsal.

Olivier, giving a copy to the Countess, starts to recite the verses as a slightly veiled declaration of his love. Flamand at the spinet improvises to them. Suddenly, excited, he takes from the Countess the copy she had been following and runs from the room.

SCENE 5 (5 min.)

Olivier is indignant: his poetry will be spoiled by music. But alone with the Countess he now presses his suit openly. His art, he says, will win her. There is another art and artist, she replies. You prefer music? he asks. She is refusing to say as much when Flamand reenters with the sonnet composed.

SCENE 6 (6 min.)

At the spinnet he sings the verses. Thereafter a trio develops: the **sonnet and aria** Countess wonders if the words always implied the melody, Olivier regrets the spoiling of his verse, and Flamand, repeating lines, makes corrections on his manuscript.

To whom does the sonnet now belong? asks Olivier. To the poet or to the musician? To me, replies the Countess, taking it from Flamand. La Roche enters, requesting the poet's presence at the rehearsal of his play, and Flamand is left alone with the Countess.

SCENE 7 (10 min.)

Flamand declares his love, describing softly how he watched her one day in the library. Till dusk he sat hidden in his corner. Music flooded his mind, he closed his eyes, and she was gone. He quotes her a *pensée* of Pascal, and she parries with another. He begs for an answer, if only a sign or a word. Not now, she insists, not here. When? Where? In the library tomorrow morning at eleven.

He impetuously kisses her arm and rushes out. She is left musing. In **reverie** an orchestral passage (3 min.), music associated with him fills her mind, but gradually shouts and laughter from the theatre rouse her. She rings, and tells the butler, "We will have our chocolate here in the salon."

(When the opera is given in two acts, the break is here. Her order is followed by five bars from Flamand's love scene and the last bars of the sonnet, which after the intermission are repeated to raise the curtain.)

SCENE 8 (3 min.)

The Count enters quickly from the theatre, extolling Clairon, who has complimented his acting. For a little flattery, mocks the Countess, he will surrender his freedom. Her choice, on the other hand, has become more difficult. The sonnet has united poet and musician. The

Count, faced with "Wort oder Ton?" has no doubt: "Word," and
Clairon.

SCENE 9 (48 min.)

Everyone gathers for the chocolate, and La Roche summons from
the theatre a dancer and a trio of musicians (violin, cello and harpsichord). Throughout much of the first dance, a Passepied (3 min.), La
Roche chatters to the Count about the ballerina's background and,
three dances   under his direction, her great future. In the second
dance, a Gigue (2 min.), Olivier, the poet, compliments Clairon on her
recitation, but she declares that the curtain has fallen on their previous
relationship and moves to sit beside the Countess. In the final dance, a
Gavotte (1 min.), all watch without talking. At its end the Count congratulates the dancer, and as she and the musicians return to the theatre, he remarks to Flamand that in ballet certainly music is the
subservient art. "A charming mistake," says Flamand. "Without music
no one would lift a leg."

A discussion starts, in the form of a fugue on the theme, "Wort oder
fugue   Ton." Olivier extols the clarity and precision of words; Flamand, the ability of music to express the inexpressible. La Roche observes that in the theatre all arts are servants. Flamand replies that
music only reluctantly supports the theatre's trickery, and the Countess
reproves him: not trickery, "Nicht Trug!" The theatre reveals the
meaning of life. (Beneath her words for the first time and very briefly
the orchestra introduces the theme that Strauss associates with opera as
the most sublime art):

(It will recur, most often sounding in the French horn.)

Everyone expresses a point of view, until finally the Count cries "Halt!" Another step and they are face to face with opera. "A beautiful sight," says the Countess. "A hybrid art," says Clairon. "Und Rezitativen! Und Rezitativen!" (and recitatives), groans the Count, and he states flatly (to a more extended snatch of the opera theme, this time on the horn), "Eine oper ist ein absurdes Ding" (an opera is an absurd thing). And the argument continues. To end it, the Countess asks La Roche to bring in his two Neapolitan singers to demonstrate the vitality of Italian vocal art.

The Neapolitans sing a duet (4 min.) of parting, "Addio," with a **duet** cheerful tune and many word repetitions. The Count and La Roche are delighted, the others less so, and the Countess invites the singers to remain for chocolate and liqueurs. (Throughout the rest of the scene their gauche manners are a source of comedy.) Meanwhile, the Count and Clairon confirm their interest in each other in an exchange of affectionate barbs.

At the Countess's request La Roche describes his part of the birthday entertainment. The first act of his homage will be an allegory: The Birth of Pallas Athene, who sprang full grown from Zeus's forehead after he had devoured her mother. The legend strikes most of the **laughing octet** guests as ludicrous and an octet entitled "Laughing-Ensemble" (2 min.) develops. La Roche is angry, and the Countess soothes him by inquiring his plans for the second act.

It is to be "The Fall of Carthage," and La Roche enthusiastically **dispute octet** describes the scenic effects. Again an octet develops, "Dispute-Ensemble" (3 min.), in which Olivier and Flamand attack him for debasing art. The Count and Countess defend him. Clairon says that he will defend himself, and the Italian tenor worries about his advance while the soprano, fuddled by the liqueurs, warbles "Addio."

Suddenly La Roche explodes and by force of personality holds the others silent (10 min.) while he describes himself and his art as the true **La Roche's monologue** conservator and inspiration of all that is best in the theatre. Let the poets and musicians cease to bicker over precedence and compose great works. He, La Roche, will give them glory on the stage, and he ends by reciting the admiring epitaph that will be inscribed on his tomb. (Curiously, and then again perhaps not, Strauss seems to have identified himself more with La Roche, the man of the theatre, than with Flamand, the musician.)

As La Roche ends with a heartfelt "Amen" at his own epitaph,

Clairon runs to kiss him, and the Countess comes to the stage's center, urges all three arts to cease dispute and, uniting (to the opera theme), to create Beauty.

Clairon hails her as the Goddess of Harmony and leads the representatives of the arts, Flamand, Olivier and La Roche, in a "Homage-**quartet**   Quartet" (2 min.). At its end the Count laments that uniting the arts will lead to opera, and immediately the subject for one is debated. Should it be *Ariadne auf Naxos*? Or perhaps *Dafne*? (musical references to operas by—ahem!) The Count suggests instead an opera on real, live people. Why not on themselves and their dispute?

At first all are rather taken aback, and then enthusiastic. La Roche fears that "the whole thing will be one great indiscretion," but agrees. The chocolate hour is over. The Countess withdraws, and the guests prepare to depart.

SCENE 10 (2 min.)

The opera theme sounds briefly. La Roche summons his singers; the Count accompanies Clairon to the door; and Flamand and Olivier leave, muttering "Prima la musica" and "Prima le parole." La Roche is last out, comparing himself to a Field Marshal of the stage.

SCENE 11 (4 min.)

Eight servants enter and discuss Master, Mistress and guests. The Count is off on a tender adventure, and the Countess is in love but does not know with whom. She will certainly not learn from opera. The Major-domo orders them to set the dining-room table for supper and then to take the evening off. Ah, "Gloria," they exclaim.

SCENE 12 (4 min.)

A mouse of a man with a large book hurries in from the theatre. He is Monsieur Taupe, the prompter, who fell asleep in his box and has been forgotten by the producer. He and the Major-domo sing softly (almost speaking) of theatre and the nature of reality. The Major-domo leads him to the kitchen, promising to send him in a coach to Paris. (The scene is sometimes cut, as often to save the cost of two more singers as to save the minutes. In the opera's structure it apparently was intended to balance the extended and spoken love scene recited by the Count and Clairon.)

SCENE 13 (20 min.)

The stage remains empty, the salon in semidarkness. To the back the moon's soft light whitens the terrace and seeps through the glass doors. **symphonic interlude**   The orchestra has an interlude, a horn serenade (4 min.), built entirely on the theme of opera as the sublime unification of all the arts. The Countess, the personification of the ideal, enters in evening dress for dinner. Moving slowly to the back she opens a door, steps out to the terrace and stands in moonlight. (For opera lovers this can be one of those moments of breathtaking beauty that makes up for all of the form's many failures.)

Servants enter with candles, and the Major-domo reports two messages. The Count will not be home for dinner. He has accompanied Mlle Clairon to Paris. And Monsieur Olivier will pay his respects in the morning to learn how the opera will end. "Den Schluss der Oper?" (the conclusion of the opera), asks the Countess. When will he come? He will wait in the library. But when? "Morgen mittag um elf" (tomorrow morning about eleven). The Major-domo leaves, and the Countess begins her final monologue (16 min.). Strauss had a special gift for composing for the soprano voice, and this is one of his happiest efforts, not only as music but as the dramatic summation of the opera. It has a good claim to be one of the most successful finales in twentieth-century opera.

"Morgen mittag um elf!" The time, and place, that she promised to give her answer to Flamand. He will be astonished to find the poet in **Countess's monologue**   the library. Yet since the sonnet they are inseparable. How can she decide the opera's end, "Den Schluss der Oper," and choose between "die Worte" and "die Töne"?

Going to her harp, she puts Flamand's manuscript on the music stand and begins to sing the sonnet. After its first eight verses she stops to exclaim over the impossibility of any choice. Resuming, she finishes and, rising, crosses the stage impetuously. Nor can she choose between the artists: Flamand with his great soul and beautiful eyes, and Olivier, the man of strong spirit and passion.

Catching sight of her reflection in the mirror, she asks it to choose. But it looks back ironically and is silent. "Oh, Madeleine," she cries to it. What shall be the opera's end? Is there any that isn't trivial, "der nicht trivial ist?"

The Major-domo enters to announce supper. She smiles at her reflection, shakes her fan at it coquettishly and leaves it with a deep curtsey. Then, humming the sonnet, she goes to dinner in the best of humors. The Major-domo, before following her, glances in puzzlement at the mirror.

Vocabulary

Wort oder Ton	vort OH.der tohn	word or tone (music)
prima le parole	PREE.mah lay pah.ROH.lay	first the words
dopo la musica	DOH.poh lah MOO.zee.cah	after (second) the music
Nicht Trug!	nikt troohk	not trickery
Halt!	hahllt	stop
und Rezitativen	oont ray.tsee. tah.TEE.ven	and recitatives
eine Oper ist ein absurdes Ding	eye.nuh OH.per ist eye'n ahp.SOOR.des ding	an opera is an absurd thing
addio	ah.DEE.oh	farewell
Den Schluss der Oper	dain shloos der OH.per	the ending of the opera
Morgen mittag um elf	MORG.en MIT.tahg oomm elf	tomorrow morning about eleven
der nicht trivial ist	der nikt tree.v'yahl ist	that is not trivial

DIE LIEBE DER DANAE

(The Love of Danae)

Cheerful mythology in three acts. World premiere, Salzburg, Aug. 14, 1952 (though on Aug. 16, 1944, a Salzburg production completed a final dress rehearsal before being cancelled because of the war). British premiere, London, Sept. 16, 1953; American prem. (in English), Los Angeles, April 10, 1964. Music by Richard Strauss; text by Joseph Gregor.

Of all of Strauss's later operas, *Die Liebe der Danae* thus far has had the fewest performances. Critical opinion on it is divided, but probably productions have been too few for any judgment to be certain. Some of the opera's difficulties are: the last act is long (81 min.); the chief character, Danae, is less interesting than the subsidiary Jupiter; and the mixture of frothy mythology and the serious themes, of aging and married love, is awkward. On the other hand: Jupiter, the older suitor who loses the girl, is well portrayed; the opera's finale, his long duet with Danae (31 min.), is moving, as is also the orchestral Interlude, "Jupiter's Resignation," that leads into the final scene; and Strauss's handling of themes and his orchestration throughout are excellent. It is still possible that with the right cast, conductor and producer the opera will come gloriously alive.

The "Symphonic Fragment" for orchestra of extracts from the opera was prepared by Clemens Krauss in 1952, after Strauss's death.

ACT I (50 min.)

SCENE 1 (6 min.)

On the Greek island of Ios King Pollux, father of Danae (dan.ah.ay), faces his creditors. He is nearly bankrupt; even his throne has been seized for its gold; and his last asset is his beautiful daughter, Danae. He promises his creditors that she will marry Midas (mee.dahs), the richest man in the world; skeptical, they strip the throne of what gold is left.

INTERLUDE (The Shower of Gold—3 min.)

Jupiter, disguised as a shower of gold, visits Danae in a dream.

SCENE 2 (10 min.)

Danae (soprano) describes her dream, in which gold caressed her lips and breasts. Her maid Xanthe interprets it as a bankrupt's wishful thinking, but Danae considers it a marriage portent: she must marry the man who can give her the gold that aroused her.

SCENE 3 (12 min.)

Pollux and the creditors are heartened by a golden bough that Midas has sent before him. The king's four nephews and their wives, Semele, Europa, Alcmene and Leda (all former loves of Jupiter), describe in an octet Midas's extraordinary golden touch. Outside, the people cheer the arrival of a golden ship, and everyone rushes to the harbor except Danae.

Midas (tenor), disguised as his friend Chrysopher, enters to prepare Danae to meet Midas (in fact, Jupiter) who is still on shipboard. Midas-Chrysopher is young and handsome, and the two fall in love. (This entrance and duet unfortunately is one of the opera's weaker moments.)

SCENE 4 (19 min.)

At the harbor the crowd welcomes Jupiter-Midas (baritone), who is dressed all in gold. Danae recognizes him as the man of her dream but no longer is sure that he is the man she loves. She faints, and the curtain falls.

ACT II (49 min.)

The bridal chamber. Semele, Europa, Alcmene and Leda are decorating the bed. Jupiter-Midas enters dressed in gold but the ladies as former lovers instantly penetrate his disguise. He explains his plot. The real Midas is merely a donkey-driver. Jupiter gave him the golden touch so that Midas might prepare the way into Danae's bed. Jupiter wants to experience human sexual response and can do so only if Danae believes him a mortal: Midas. Besides, the disguise is a way of evading Juno's jealous eye.

Midas-Chrysopher enters, and the ladies leave. Jupiter, already a little jealous, warns Midas to stick to their bargain, merely to prepare the way, or the golden touch will be withdrawn. Jupiter leaves, and Midas dons the golden clothes.

The four ladies, singing a wedding march that delightfully parodies the one in *Lohengrin,* lead in Danae, but when they see Midas, not Jupiter, they flee. Danae is confused by Chrysopher in Midas's clothes, and Midas explains as much as he dares. He turns the room into gold, so he is Midas; equally he is Chrysopher whom she loves. She falls into his arms. There is a thunderclap followed by darkness (Interlude, 1 min.), and Danae has been changed into a golden statue.

Midas curses himself and his gift. Jupiter enters, claiming Danae, but Midas now insists on the rights of true love. Each offers the immobilized Danae what he has to give, and her voice chooses Midas, poverty and love, over Jupiter, riches and power. In a flash of lightning she resumes her humanity, and runs off with Midas, leaving Jupiter alone to lament his loss.

ACT III (81 min.)

PRELUDE (2 min.)

A thematic recapitulation in gentle 3/4 time of the opera thus far.

SCENE 1 (14 min.)

Danae and Midas awake beside a road somewhere in Asiatic Greece. Midas is again a donkey-driver, and he explains to Danae his bargain with Jupiter. She realizes he has given up wealth for her, and she assures him that it was not his gold that attracted her but his kindly glance. Singing in unison, they start together down the road.

INTERLUDE (2 min.)

Depicting the lovers in spiritual union.

SCENE 2 (22 min.)

Deep in a mountain forest Jupiter silently broods, to Wagnerian orchestration, on his godhead and passion. Mercury (tenor) descends to describe how the gods are laughing at him and to urge him to move on quickly before the creditors find him.

First to arrive, however, are his four former loves, Semele, Europa, Alcmene and Leda. He tries to frighten them away with talk of a thunderbolt, but they just laugh. As they prattle, he bids each farewell. They are happily married, but he is not, and with this last misadventure he is retiring from the field of love.

The autumnal mood is shattered by the arrival of the creditors demanding compensation. On Mercury's suggestion Jupiter produces a shower of gold that falls offstage, and the creditors rush after it.

Jupiter, however, has no joy in the trick. He has been hurt by Danae's rejection, and Mercury therefore suggests that he try once more. Perhaps Danae will have tired of poverty and will welcome a god with money. Jupiter smiles sadly.

INTERLUDE (Jupiter's Resignation—5 min.)

He will visit Danae again but as an acknowledged older man bringing serenity, not love, and warming his heart, if he can, from her love for another.

SCENE 3 (36 min.)

In Midas's hut Danae sings of her happiness (5 min.). Jupiter enters disguised in a burnoose. Danae, inviting him to rest awhile, remarks that another old man similarly dressed had once appeared to her husband. "Old man," sighs Jupiter. "Das Ende!"

He tests her contentment by reminding her of her golden dreams, but the memory no longer stirs her. She loves Midas. Jupiter, with still a wisp of hope, tells her the story of Maia, from whose union with Jupiter sprang flowers. But Danae ignores the suggestion of physical union and interprets the story as an allegory of Spring. Recognizing defeat, Jupiter turns to go, but Danae restrains him in order to make a parting gift, the gold clasp from her hair. He embraces her and leaves. She sets about her household chores, and the orchestra on six horns sounds Midas's theme. Happily calling his name, she runs out to meet him.

RIDERS TO THE SEA

In one act, form unspecified, merely "set to music." World premiere, London, Dec. 1, 1937; American prem., Cleveland, Feb. 26, 1950. Music by Ralph Vaughan Williams; the text is a slightly cut version of J. M. Synge's play, first performed, Dublin, Feb. 25, 1904.

The opera is short (35 min.) but musically and emotionally it is on a large scale. At the turn of the century a family in the Aran Islands, off Ireland's west coast, lives by the sea and is destroyed by the sea. Against wind and water human skill and endurance do not prevail, and with the drowning of her last son Maurya is both defeated and released from fear.

The play's structure, poetic language and intensity of feeling make it one of the finest short plays of this century, and Vaughan Williams successfully transferred it from the spoken to the musical stage. Though some poetry of language was lost, by music the sea's presence and role as adversary were enhanced.

Both play and opera, because of their power, have had difficulty finding suitable companion pieces to fill an evening. It may be that the opera, at least, would be best set off *not* joined to another stage work but presented as the climax of a concert or recital. The orchestra required is not large, and the cast needs only five solo voices and a small chorus of women. The leading role, Maurya, is for contralto.

The opera begins with a Prelude (1 min.), in which the sea moans below the cliffs not far from the family's cottage. Cathleen is spinning in the kitchen; her mother Maurya, resting in the next room. Nora, Cathleen's sister, enters from outside—the wind howls through the door—with a shirt and sock taken from a man found drowned, miles down the coast. They are to decide from the clothing if the man is their missing brother Michael. But they hear Maurya stirring and hide the clothes in the loft.

Maurya cannot sleep. She worries that Bartley, the last of her six sons, will take the two horses by boat to Galway Fair. He enters, looking for rope for a halter. He will ride the mare and lead the grey pony. And he will not be dissuaded by his mother. At the door he asks God's blessing on the family, and though he waits, Maurya refuses her blessing in return. He goes.

The sisters reproach their mother and, noting that Bartley left without his bread, send her to give him it and her blessing where the path crosses the road. Maurya, with a stick, starts out. At the door she sings mournfully, "In the big world, the old people do be leaving things after them for their sons and children, but in this place it is the young men do be leaving things behind for them that do be old."

In her absence the sisters hastily examine the clothing, and Nora recognizes the stitching in the sock. They start to cry but, hearing Maurya outside, again hide the clothes.

Maurya sits by the fire keening to herself. In answer to Cathleen's questions she says that she saw Michael riding the pony behind Bartley, and the blessing stuck in her throat. It wasn't Michael, says Cathleen, because now we know he drowned. But Maurya takes the vision to portend Bartley's death.

Offstage a chorus of women begin to wail. Over their voices Maurya describes the successive deaths of her husband and six sons. The door opens, and the keening women file in. "Is it Patch or Michael or what?" asks Maurya. "It's Michael," says Cathleen. But the drowned man laid on the table is Bartley. The grey pony bumped the mare and knocked Bartley into the sea.

Maurya stands by his corpse. Above the keening women she sings, "They are all gone now, and there isn't anything more the sea can do to me. . . . I'll have no call now to be going down and getting Holy Water on dark nights." She blesses her dead, one by one, and also those "left living in the world." Michael has had a clean burial and Bartley will have a good coffin and deep grave. "What more can we want than that? No man at all can be living forever, and we must be satisfied."

She kneels. The wind blows open the door. In the distance the sea moans and roars. The stage grows darker. Offstage a keening soprano voice grows fainter, till the stage finally is quite dark and the only sound is of the wind and the sea.

MOSES UND ARON
(Moses and Aaron)

Opera in three acts (the first two completed 1930–32, third uncompleted and seldom performed). World concert and radio premiere, Hamburg, March 12, 1954; stage prem., Zurich, June 6, 1957; British stage prem. (in English), Covent Garden, London, June 28, 1965; American prem., Boston, Nov. 2, 1966. Music and text by Arnold Schoenberg; text based on the Bible, Book of Exodus, particularly Chapters 3, 4 and 32.

PRINCIPAL CHARACTERS

Moses	speaking role	
Aaron, his brother	tenor	AH.ron
Voice from the Burning Bush	six solo singers (three male and three female voices) and speaking chorus	
Young Girl ⎫	soprano	
Young Man ⎬ supporters	tenor	
Another Man ⎭ of Moses	baritone	
Priest, doubtful of Moses	bass	
People of Israel	chorus	

The action takes place in Biblical times in Egypt and in the Sinai Desert.

The opera is wholly of its time. Its music is in a style inconceivable before 1925, and its theme, the preservation of spiritual values in a society preferring charisma to content, is particularly apt to a century that has produced so many totalitarian leaders. Yet, somewhat like Rossini's *Guillaume Tell* (1829), which so perfectly exhibited the romantic and nationalistic strains of the nineteenth century, *Moses und Aron* is thus far a musician's opera, more often analyzed than performed. It may prove to be one of those indigestible masterpieces whose power and originality the public concedes while preferring to listen to something else.

Schoenberg, thinking first in terms of an oratorio, took certain aspects of the Biblical story of Moses and Aaron and fashioned a kind of Platonic dialogue on the question: can spirituality be made plain? Moses in the desert has an experience of God, whom he conceives to be without body or form of any kind, a Deity so infinite, so omnipresent, so powerful that it cannot be described. This God orders Moses to take word of it to the Israelites, captive in Egypt, and when Moses protests that he cannot translate such a God into terms the people will understand, it promises that Aaron, who is more articulate than Moses, will help him. But under pressure from the people Aaron creates a Calf of Gold, a very different God from the one Moses experienced.

In the opera's two most static scenes, the brothers debate the conflict between idea and form and the need when dealing with the people to speak, as Aaron says, "more simply than I understand." Much of the text reads like a scholastic wrangle: "Your image faded at my word!" "But your word was denied image. . . ." Even at the German-speaking Vienna Staatsoper the libretto is peddled with the double-edged cry: "Textbuch! Textbuch! Sehr notwendig. Man versteht kein Wort!" (Libretto! Libretto! Very much needed. One does not understand a word!).

Nevertheless, one can understand much because elsewhere Schoenberg created scenes in which action or emotion supports the intellectual message: Moses' humility before his God, the degeneration of the Israelites as they worship the Calf of Gold and, at the end, Moses' sense of failure.

The music throughout is in the twelve-tone idiom and based on a single note-row:

The opera opens with a wordless six-measure introduction by the Voice from the Burning Bush. To give God's voice a unique sound,

Schoenberg placed six solo singers in the orchestra pit, each seated next to an instrument. Whenever a singer sings, his or her instrument accompanies him or her in unison. The pairs are: soprano–flute, mezzo–clarinet, alto–English horn (alto oboe), tenor–bassoon, baritone–bass clarinet, and bass–cello. To these six pairs, when the Burning Bush begins to articulate words, Schoenberg adds a speaking chorus. But for the opening measures, the twelve voices and instruments simply hover in tensionless chords that, according to some critics, represent God's eternity and infinity. The notes of the first two chords are the first and last three notes of the row gathered into chords.

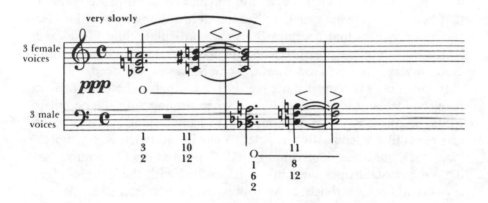

When the Voice from the Burning Bush, in response to Moses' opening sentence, starts to intone actual words, an underlying theme swells in the orchestra, starting on a double bass and a cello, repeating on a viola, and ending on a solo violin. In the bass clef the notes are 4 through 9 of the row.

Some critics associate this theme with the concept of God as an articulate Will and Thought. The opera lends itself endlessly to this sort of musical and textual analysis.

Throughout, with a short exception, Moses does not sing but speaks, though in strict musical rhythm. This style, *Sprechstimme,* was largely created by Schoenberg and first used extensively in his *Pierrot Lunaire,* 1912. In contrast to Moses, Aaron sings; symbolically, speech represents pure thought, and song, compromise with the needs of emotions. Though in some of Schoenberg's works the *Sprechstimme* may seem arbitrary, its clarity of purpose here gives it dramatic force.

ACT I (48 min.)

Moses is in the desert and not in Egypt because as a young man, in a period before the opera begins, he had slain an Egyptian taskmaster who had beaten an Israelite. Forced to flee, Moses had gone to Midian, married a priest's daughter and started a family. One day, in taking the sheep to graze, he went "to the backside of the desert and came to the mountain of God," where he saw a burning bush which "was not consumed." Stopping to examine it, he heard the voice of God.

SCENE 1 (The Calling of Moses—9 min.)

Moses addresses the Burning Bush: "Einziger, ewiger, allgegenwärtiger, unsichtbarer und unvorstellbarer Gott!" (sole, eternal, omnipresent, invisible and inconceivable God). The Voice from the Bush—six solo voices and a speaking chorus—orders him to be God's prophet and lead the Israelites to freedom. Moses is doubtful. "Ich bin alt" (I am old). The people will not trust him. The Voice assures him that he will be heard. But "meine Zunge ist ungelenk" (my tongue is not articulate). In its longest speech, which closes the scene, the Voice tells Moses that Aaron will be his mouth, relaying Moses' thoughts to the people as Moses relays God's to Aaron. For "dieses Volk ist anserwählt" (this folk is chosen). Aaron even now is on his way. Softly the Voice fades. "Verkünde" (speak out, prophesy).

SCENE 2 (Moses meets Aaron in the Desert—7 min.)

Aaron approaches, to a light, dancing tune for flute solo and accompaniment. On his arrival a duet starts for speaking and singing voice. Aaron questions Moses about the new God and is distressed by its abstraction. He is pleased that the Israelites are chosen, "Auserwähltes Volk," but doubts that the people can worship what cannot be seen or even described. Moses repeats the God's qualities: "Unvorstellbar" (unconceived) . . . "unsichtbar" (unseen), but the brothers talk past each other. When Aaron speaks of offerings to the God, gold and food, Moses angrily issues a command (the only lines he sings, and Schoenberg's most direct message to the audience): "Reinige dein Denken, lös es von Wertlosem, weihe es Wahrem" (purify your thinking, free it from the worthless, turn it to the true). But as the scene ends, there is still no understanding.

SCENE 3 (In Egypt. The People waiting for Moses and Aaron—6 min.)

In order, a young girl, a young man and another man, all of whom will become fanatic supporters of Moses, describe Aaron going into the desert on a god's command to find Moses. "Moses?" asks a Priest, "who killed the taskmaster?" "Moses!" cries the chorus, "who fled, leaving us to suffer Pharaoh's anger." Argument flares. The three fanatics talk excitedly of the new God, "der neue Gott," and win over some of the people. The Priest leads the doubtful. The two groups oppose each other to a point where, in the effort to dominate, each shouts its lines: "Lasst uns in Frieden!" (leave us in peace) and "Er wird uns befrein!" (He shall make us free). The scene ends as the young girl in a frenzy of excitement sings on a soaring line, "er wird uns befrein."

SCENE 4 (Moses and Aaron present God's message to the People—26 min.)

The brothers approach in the manner described by the chorus: Moses, rod in hand, moving slowly; Aaron, though not young, with lighter step, sometimes before, sometimes behind Moses. They arrive, and the people clamor to give offerings to the new God.

Moses begins, "Einzige, Ewige . . . unsichtbare, unvorstellbarer. . . ." But Aaron bursts in: "He has chosen this folk before all . . . on your knees to worship him." The people, however, are puzzled. "Wo ist er?" (where is he). He can only be seen, Aaron replies, with an inward eye and by the righteous. The fanatics exclaim with delight, but the Priest wonders why a murderer should fear a God who does not reveal himself. The people, singing and speaking, reject such a God. Moses grieves, "Allmächtiger, meine Kraft ist zu Ende" (Almighty, my strength is at an end).

the rod Aaron seizes the rod, "Stab," from Moses' hand and throws it to the ground where it turns into a serpent, "Schlange." Then, reversing the magic, he returns the rod to Moses. The people are impressed, but can the rod overcome Pharaoh?

the plague Aaron accuses them of being sick at heart. He holds up Moses' hand, strong and healthy. Then he sickens it. "Aussatz" (leprosy), gasp the people. Then he places it over Moses' heart, "Herz," from which he removes it once again healthy. Their courage can be similarly strengthened. The people are convinced. They are ready to kill the Egyptians and march into the desert, "Auf in die Wüste."

the blood and water The Priest, however, calls them madmen. How will they nourish themselves in the desert? Moses starts to say that purity of thought will sustain them when Aaron interrupts with a third marvel, changing water into blood, "Blut," and back again. The God who has chosen them will lead them to a land of milk and honey, "Milch und Honig."

march The people are ecstatic. They have been chosen. They will be led to "Milch und Honig." They will leave Egypt; they will be free, "frei . . . frei."

Vocabulary, Act I

einziger	EYE'N.tsik.er	the only
ewiger	AYV.ik.er	the eternal
allgegenwärtiger	ahll.geg.en.VAIR. tik.er	the omnipresent
unsichtbarer	OON.sikt.bar.er	the invisible
und unvorstellbarer Gott	oont OON.for.shtell bar.er got	and the inconceivable God
ich bin alt	ik bin ahlt	I am old
meine Zunge ist ungelenk	mine.eh TSOONG.eh ist OON.geh.laynk	my tongue is inarticulate
dieses Volk ist auserwählt	deez.ehs follk ist OWSS.air.vailt	this folk is chosen

Vocabulary, Act 1 (continued)

German	Pronunciation	English
verkünde	fair.KEUN.deh	speak out
reinige dein Denken	RY.nig.eh dine deng.ken	purify your thinking
lös es von Wertlosem	lersh ess fon VAIRT.lohs.em	free it from the worthless
weihe es Wahrem	VY.eh ess VAHR.em	turn it to the true
der neue Gott	der noy.eh got	the new God
lasst uns in Frieden	lahsst oons in freed.en	leave us in peace
er wird uns befrein	air veert oons be.FRY.en	he will free us
wo ist er?	voh ist er	where is he?
Allmächtiger, meine Kraft ist zu Ende	ahl.MEK.tik.er my.neh krahfft ist tsoo EN.deh	Almighty, my strength is ended
Stab	shtahp	staff
Schlange	SHLAHNG.eh	serpent
Aussatz	OWSS.zahts	leprosy
Herz	hairts	heart
auf in die Wüste	ouf in deh VOEST.eh	on into the desert
Blut	bloot	blood
Milch und Honig	milk und HOHN.ik	milk and honey
frei	fry	free

ACT II (53 min.)

Before this act begins, Moses with miracles and plagues has appealed to the Pharaoh to let the Israelite people go, but the Pharaoh would not. So the Israelites, led by Moses, marched off, following the signs of his God who by day was "a pillar of cloud" and by night "a pillar of fire." They passed through the Red Sea dryshod, and the Pharaoh's army pursuing them was drowned. In the desert they were sustained by manna from heaven. After a time Moses went up into a mountain to confer with his God. The mountaintop was covered by a cloud, and Moses was gone forty days and forty nights. Before he returned, the people had begun to lose heart and to question.

INTERLUDE (3 min.)

The people whisper: "Wo ist Moses? Wo ist der Führer? Wo ist er?" (where is Moses, the leader; where is he); "Wo ist sein Gott? Wo ist der Ewige?" (where is his God, the infinite). "Wo ist Moses?"

SCENE 1 (Aaron and the Seventy Elders before the Mountain of Revelation—4 min.)

Throughout the scene Aaron is silent while the elders complain. "Vierzig Tage!" (forty days); when will it end? The people are dissatisfied. The revelation is a pretext. Moses' silence means flight. "Hört! Hört! Zu spät!" (hear, hear, too late), they cry to Aaron, as the furious people burst onto the stage from all sides.

SCENE 2 (The People and Aaron—8 min.)

"Wo ist Moses?" the people cry. They will kill him. They will have back their old gods, and they threaten the Seventy Elders, who appeal to Aaron, "Aron, hilf uns!" (help us).

"Volk Israels," Aaron begins, urging the people to have faith but revealing also that even he does not know what Moses and God are doing. The people again threaten the Elders, who cry "Aron, hilf uns."

"Volk Israels," Aaron cries, "I return your gods to you." If the people will provide the gold he will make the image. Then they will be happy. In a long chorus the people rejoice, "Juble Israel" (joyous Israel).

SCENE 3 (The Golden Calf and the Altar—26 min.)

(The scene is almost entirely Schoenberg's invention, the Biblical orgy being very sparse on details.)

After Aaron presents the Golden Calf to the people, herds of animals are driven before it in preparation for the sacrifice. (The orchestration, which has an oriental quality, requires the violins and violas to be struck on open strings with the wooden, backside of the bow and **The Golden Calf** the lower stringed instruments to play harmonics in chords. Meanwhile two mandolins, a harp, piano, celesta and xylophone start a melody which is later taken up by trombone and piccolo.)

A Dance for Butchers follows (four-part *glissando* on three trombones and tuba).

An Invalid Woman thanks the God for her recovery. Male and Female Beggars offer it their tatters and morsels, while several Elderly Persons offer it their last moments and slay themselves before it.

Twelve Tribal Leaders gallop in. Dismounting, they kneel before the statue. The fanatic young man bursts through them and urges the people to abandon idol worship. The Leader of Ephraim kills him.

An Orgy of Drunkenness and Dancing begins. The Seventy Elders sing their approval. Four Naked Virgins, one of them the fanatic young girl, step before the Calf. They sing to it, are embraced by four priests, and then slaughtered.

The sacrifice starts an Orgy of Destruction and Suicide. Stone jars are smashed and, Schoenberg directs, "everything possible is flung about. . . . In a frenzy some throw themselves . . . upon swords. Still others leap into the fire and run flaming across the stage . . . wild dancing with all this."

An Erotic Orgy begins. "A naked youth runs to a girl, rips off her clothes and, holding her high, runs with her to the altar. . . . A whole succession of naked people, screaming and yelling, run past the altar and disappear in the background." Gradually the fires die, exhaustion overcomes the people, and all motion onstage ceases.

SCENE 4 (The Return of Moses—1 min.)

From backstage a man suddenly cries: "Moses steigt vom Berg herab!" (Moses comes down from the mountain). The sleeping wake, and the people pour onstage to hear Moses condemn the Calf, which vanishes on his gesture. Complaining that Moses has once again replaced joy with gloom, the people exit.

SCENE 5 (Moses and Aaron—11 min.)

Moses sternly asks, "Aron, was hast du getan?" (what have you done), and Aaron replies (with an ill-fated line, apt to cause laughter in the audience), "Nichte Neues!" (nothing new).

They argue how best to present Moses' God to the people. "No folk is faithful unless it feels," says Aaron. "They must comprehend the idea," insists Moses. Aaron pleads to be permitted to describe the God, at least in vague terms. There must be some description. Even the tablets of commandments that Moses has brought down from the mountain are a compromise with the pure idea. Moses smashes the tablets.

Behind them the people, led by a pillar of fire, move out into the desert. They sing of a land of "Milch und Honig." Aaron leaves to join them.

"Unvorstellbarer Gott!" (inconceivable God), cries Moses. "Is this what you want?" "So war alles Wahnsinn" (so was all madness) that I believed before! Sinking to the ground he utters in despair (to a longheld, soft F sharp in unison on the strings), "O Wort, du Wort, das mir fehlt!" (O word, thou word, that I lack!")

Vocabulary, Act II

wo ist Moses	woh ist . . .	where is Moses
wo ist sein Gott	. . . sine got	where is his God
wo ist der Ewige	. . . der AYV.ik.eh	where is the eternal one
vierzig Tage	FEER.tsik tah.geh	forty days
hört, zu spät	hert, tsoo shpayt	hear, too late
Aron, hilf uns	hilf oonns	Aaron, help us
Volk Israels	follk is.ry.ells	people of Israel
juble Israel	YOOB.el . . .	joyous Israel
Moses steigt vom Berg herab	. . . shtykt fom bairk hair.AHP	Moses comes down the mountain
Aron, was hast du getan	. . . vahss hast doo geh.tahn	Aaron, what have you done
nichte neues	nik.teh noy.es	nothing new
Milch und Honig	milk oont HOHN.ik	milk and honey
unvorstellbarer Gott	OON.for.shtell.bar.er got	inconceivable God
so war alles Wahnsinn	so vahr ahl.les VAHN.zin	so was all madness
O Wort, du Wort, das mir fehlt	Oh vort, doo vort, dahs mir failt	O word, thou word, that I lack

ACT III (4 min.)

Schoenberg completed the text for the third act, more truly an epilogue, at the time he composed the music for the other two, 1930–32. But thereafter, though he lived until 1951, he composed only eight additional bars for the opera. He seems always to have expected to complete it, but in his last year, on the chance that he might not, he approved a spoken presentation of it. However, the act's single scene, between Moses and Aaron, adds little if anything to those preceding it, and in most productions the act is cut.

Moses enters. Aaron, in chains, is dragged in by soldiers and followed by the Seventy Elders. Moses and Aaron continue their debate over idea and form, thought versus action, the abstract versus the concrete. Moses accuses Aaron of corrupting the idea to his own ends, winning the people to himself rather than to God. Aaron says he acted to make the people free. The soldiers ask if they should kill Aaron, but Moses orders him to be freed. Whereupon Aaron falls dead, while Moses tells the Elders (and the audience) that only after renunciation of all materiality can unity with God be achieved.

L'HEURE ESPAGNOLE

(The Spanish Hour)

Comédie Musicale in one act. World premiere, Opéra-Comique, Paris, May 19, 1911. British prem., Covent Garden, London, July 24, 1919; American prem., Chicago, Jan. 5, 1920. Music by Maurice Ravel; text by Franc-Nohain (Maurice Legrand), from his comedy of the same title, 1904.

THE CHARACTERS

Torquemada, the clockmaker	tenor	
Ramiro, a muleteer	baritone	
Concepcion, the clockmaker's wife	soprano	
Gonzalve, a poet	tenor	gon.ZAHL.ve
Don Inigo Gomez, a banker	bass	

The action takes place in Toledo in the eighteenth century. Ravel sets the scene "in the shop of a Spanish clockmaker. To the left, an entrance from the street; to the right, a door leading to the clockmaker's apartment; and to the rear, a large window with a view of the street. On either side of the window stands a tall Catalan—or Normandy—clock [a grandfather clock]. Here and there automatons: a bird, a little cock, some musical marionettes. As the curtain rises, Torquemada, his back to the audience, is seated at his workbench. The pendulums tick, and the clocks strike different hours."

Writing to the critic, Jean Marnold, on Feb. 7, 1906, Ravel said:

L'Heure Espagnole is a musical comedy. There are no changes in the play of Franc-Nohain apart from a few cuts. Only in the final quintet, by reason of its form and florid vocal writing, is there a suggestion of the normal operatic ensembles. Apart from this quintet, I have written simple, straightforward declamation rather than florid song. The French language has its stresses and musical inflections like any other. And I don't see why one shouldn't use these correctly in musical prosody.

The spirit of the work is boldly humorous. The irony in it I have sought to express by means of harmony, rhythm and orchestration and not, as in the operetta, by letting the humor of the words pierce the texture.

Ravel's description fits except that "boldly" humorous should read "slyly," for the opera in every aspect is understated. More clocks strike in the orchestra than are heard at first hearing; the muleteer, the strong man of the piece, carries clocks in and out to a march rhythm at first only suggested; and the opera's comic and emotional center, Concepcion's lament, "Ah, la pitoyable aventure" (What a pathetic adventure), is a typical grand scene for soprano, but in miniature. Also "slyly" humorous because, until the final quintet when the five characters turn to the audience with the comedy's moral, Ravel keeps them at a distance: no winking at the audience. The laughter is at, not with them.

The opera has some lovely sounds, delightful rhythms and, when played by sophisticated, droll singers, great charm. It needs a small auditorium.

A SINGLE ACT (47 min.)

Torquemada and Ramiro. Ramiro, who with his mule delivers the city's parcel post, needs his watch repaired so that he will know when to start his rounds. While Torquemada examines it, Ramiro explains that the watch belonged to his uncle, the toreador, and in the arena in Barcelona one time it saved his uncle's life by deflecting a bull's horn. (For a moment Ravel has bullfight rhythms.)

Concepcion, Torquemada and Ramiro. She scolds Torquemada for being late to wind the city's clocks and also for failing to move one of the grandfather clocks into her bedroom. Hurrying to leave, he remarks that a grandfather clock is not easy to lift and suggests Ramiro await his return—which is not what Concepcion had in mind.

Concepcion and Ramiro. "Il reste" (He stays), she murmurs. "Voilà bien ma chance" (Just my luck). It is the one day, the one hour of the week in which she can safely entertain her admirer. Now, all is spoiled. Ramiro too is disconcerted, reflecting that he ought to make conversation but with women can never think of anything to say. Their silence ends when she asks if a grandfather clock truly requires three men to move it. He at once offers to carry one to her room, and after she demurs and he insists, he departs with a clock, observing that he is well employed: "Les muletiers n'ont pas de conversation" (Muleteers have no conversation).

Gonzalve and Concepcion. Her admirer, a poet, enters, rhapsodizing on the clockshop as a garden of joy filled with hours about to blossom into flower. She urges haste for, as she mutters, "Le muletier va revenir" (The muleteer will return). But Gonzalve is enthralled by the riches of his simile. He imagines "Le Jardin des Heures"—"sonnet"; or "Le Cour de l'Horloge"—"poème." After each effusion Concepcion adds "Oui, mon ami" (Yes, my friend), and aside, "le muletier va revenir." And after the last, a possible "sérénade"—"Le Carillon des Amours"—"Et puis, voici le muletier" (And now, here is the muleteer). She pushes Gonzalve behind the remaining clock.

Ramiro, Concepcion and Gonzalve (hidden). The bedroom clock is in place, reports Ramiro, but Concepcion pretends to have changed her mind, "mon caprice" (my caprice). After all, she prefers the other; perhaps he could bring back the first and take up the second? Behind the clock Gonzalve warbles another title: "Caprice de Femme"—"chanson" (song). Ramiro is delighted to be freed from conversation, and as he goes out, Gonzalve observes, "Les muletiers n'ont pas de conversation."

Concepcion and Gonzalve. She puts him inside the clock to be carried to her bedroom. He, noting the clock's resemblance to a coffin, proclaims it a symbol that their love is stronger than death. "Oui, mon ami," she murmurs, but adds "il exagère" (he exaggerates).

Don Inigo, Concepcion and Gonzalve (in the clock). Before Ramiro reappears, the rich, fat banker Don Inigo Gomez enters, intending love. Concepcion pretends not to understand, even when he says he had Torquemada appointed keeper of the city clocks in order to give him a periodic occupation away from home. Flustered, Concepcion announces, as Ramiro returns with the first clock, "J'ai les déménageurs" (I have the moving men).

Ramiro, Concepcion, Don Inigo and Gonzalve (in the clock). "Voilà," says Ramiro, replacing the first clock and starting for the second. It will be heavier, Concepcion warns. "Pooh," he exclaims, shifting it from shoulder to shoulder. Don Inigo urges Concepcion to remain, but she goes off, insisting that she must attend to the clock's works, particularly its pendulum.

Don Inigo. Though rejected, he decides to prefer love to dignity. He will remain, be less severe, more playful: he will hide in the clock, and he squeezes in with difficulty. Hearing footsteps, he calls "Coo-coo." But it is Ramiro. "C'est le déménageur" (it is the moving man), Don Inigo laments and, closing the clock door, conceals himself.

Ramiro and Don Inigo (in the clock). "Voilà ce que j'appelle une femme charmante" (now that is what I call a charming woman), says Ramiro. She does not ask him to talk but, sensible, practical, asks him to carry clocks, which he can do well. Now she has asked him to watch the shop. He looks about and muses: how delicate are the mechanisms of clocks, but how much more intricate and hard to comprehend (soulful, solo violin) is a woman.

Concepcion, Ramiro and Don Inigo (in the clock). "Monsieur, monsieur." It is Concepcion. The clock in her bedroom refuses to work. She cannot bear it. Ramiro leaves happily to bring it back. From within his clock Don Inigo calls "Coo-coo." But Concepcion has forgotten him and assumes it was a clock, remarking to herself that its comment is apt for her situation. When she discovers it is Don Inigo, she tells him not to be ridiculous. He insists, however, that he has something to offer: younger men sometimes are inexperienced. "En vérité, en vérité!" (it's true), she observes. After all, urges portly Don Inigo, there is more to a lover like me.

Ramiro, Concepcion and Don Inigo (in the clock). (As Ramiro enters with the clock containing Gonzalve, Ravel extends a phrase which he has associated with Ramiro into a tiny march.) Ramiro replaces the clock and offers to carry the one containing Don Inigo to the bedroom. Concepcion hesitates, but gives in to Don Inigo's whispered urgings.

Concepcion and Gonzalve. Staying behind for a moment, she tells Gonzalve to get out of the clock and be gone. He is all talk, and she has had enough of it. In irritation she starts for her bedroom and Don Inigo.

Gonzalve. Alone, he decides to stay in the clock until he can compose a song on nymphs who, like him, are imprisoned in wood. It will be titled "Impressions d'Hamadryade" (Impressions of a Wood-nymph).

To savor his sensations further, he encloses himself in the clock as Ramiro returns.

Ramiro and Concepcion. "Voilà ce que j'appelle une femme charmante!" Ramiro is enchanted: "tantôt emménager, tantôt déménager" (a little moving in and a little moving out). "Voilà ce que j'appelle une femme charmante!" No need to talk. The rhythm of the clocks is pleasant, their chimes are merry. What better than to be a clockmaker, with this charming lady as clockmaker's wife. "Monsieur!" It is Concepcion, plainly upset. "The clock bothers you?" asks Ramiro. "There, there. I will fetch it back at once."

Concepcion and Gonzalve (in the clock). (Concepcion's "mad scene" is the longest and most formal of the opera's soliloquies. Ravel begins it **mad scene** with a drum roll.) "Oh, la pitoyable aventure!" (Oh, what a pathetic adventure!) Of two lovers, one lacks temperament and the other is ridiculous. "Oh, la pitoyable aventure!" And they call themselves Spaniards; here in the land of Doña Sol, only two steps from the Estramadure. "Le temps me dure, dure, dure" (the times treat me cruelly, cruelly, cruelly). "Oh, la pitoyable aventure!" One puts all his efforts into silly poems, and the other, with his stomach entangled in the works, could not step out of the clock. My chance is passed, my husband soon will return, and "je reste fidele et pure" (I remain faithful and pure)—only two steps from the Estramadure, in the land of Guadalquivir! "Le temps me dure, dure, dure." Oh, for an object to smash.

She beats with her fists on the clock containing Gonzalve, who opens the door and sighs, "Impressions d'Hamadryade."

Ramiro and Concepcion. He brings in the clock containing Don Inigo—"Voilà"—and offers to return the other to her room. Concepcion muses on his strength and sunny nature. "Do you wish to return to my room?" she asks. "But which clock shall I carry?" "Sans horloge" (without a clock), she says, and Ramiro precedes her upstairs.

Don Inigo and Gonzalve, each in his clock. Don Inigo, poking out his head, wishes he were at home in his easy chair, but he cannot get out of the clock. He calls for help. But when Gonzalve opens his clock door, Don Inigo in alarm closes his own.

Gonzalve, preparing to leave, sings an "Adieu" (Goodbye) to his **song** clock and for once is moved beyond a title to an actual song. Then, seeing Torquemada returning, he rushes to conceal himself, choosing Don Inigo's clock. "Il y a quelqu' un" (occupied), says Don

Inigo, as Torquemada enters and discovers them both.

Torquemada, Gonzalve and Don Inigo. Concepcion's admirers pretend they have been examining the clocks, and Torquemada makes it plain that to avoid a scene each must purchase one.

Ensemble. Concepcion and Ramiro enter, and Torquemada begins to suspect that he has mistaken the situation. And he is further impressed when the others fail to pull Don Inigo from the clock, but Ramiro lifts him out with ease.

"You still have need of a clock?" Torquemada asks Concepcion. "No," she replies, "every morning the muleteer will pass under my window. . . ." "Then let him call up the time from the street," says Torquemada.

All the actors (Ravel's word) then come to the front of the stage and **quintet** address the audience. Take a banker, a poet, a silly husband and a flirtatious wife, mix them together "avec un peu d'Espagne autour" (with a bit of Spain around), and—Concepcion states the result—there will come a moment in the pursuit of love when the muleteer has his turn! "Où le muletier a son tour!"

Vocabulary

le muletier	luh.mool.t'eeay	the muleteer
il reste	eel rest.uh	he stays
voilà bien ma chance	vwah.lah b'yah(nasal) shaw(n).suh	just my luck
les muletiers n'ont pas de conversation	lay . . . naw(n) pah duh con.vair.SASS.'ee. on(n)	the muleteers have no conversation
le muletier va revenir	. . . vah rev.uh.neer	the muleteer is going to return
oui, mon ami	wee, maw(n).n'amee	yes, my friend
et puis voici le muletier	ay pwee vwah.cee . . .	and now here is the muleteer
mon caprice	maw(n) cah.prees.uh	my caprice
il exagère	eel x.ah.shjair	he exaggerates
j'ai les déménageurs	shj.ay lay day.may.nah.shjeur	I have the moving men
voilà	vwah.lah	there
c'est le déménageur	say luh day.may.nah.shjeur	it is the moving man
voilà ce que j'appelle une femme charmante	. . . suh kuh shja.pell.uh oon fahm.uh	there is what I call a charming woman

Vocabulary (continued)

	shar.maw(n).tuh	
monsieur	ms.syuh	sir
en vérité	aw(n) vay.ree.tay	in truth
oh, la pitoyable aventure	oh, lah pee.t'why.ah.bluh ah.vaw(n).ture.uh	oh, the pathetic adventure
le temps me dure, dure, dure	uh taw(n) muh dur.uh . . .	the times treat me hard, hard, hard
je reste fidele et pure	shje rest.uh fee.dell.uh ay poor.uh	I remain faithful and pure
sans horloge	saw(n) or.low.juh	without a clock
adieu	ah.d'yuh	farewell
il y a quelqu'un	eel.yah kel.kuh(n)	here is someone
avec un peu d'Espagne autour	ah.vek un(n) puh d'es pahn.yuh oh.toor	with a little of Spain around
où le muletier a son tour	oo . . . ah saw(n) toor	when the muleteer has his turn

L'ENFANT ET LES SORTILÈGES

(The Child and The Visions)

Fantaisie Lyrique in two parts. World premiere, Monte Carlo, March 21, 1925; American prem., San Francisco, Sept. 19, 1930; British prem., Oxford, Dec. 3, 1958. Music by Maurice Ravel; text by Colette from a poem, subtitled "Ballet pour ma fille," which during World War I she had submitted to the Paris Opéra in search of a composer.

PRINCIPAL CHARACTERS

The Child	mezzo-soprano
The Fire	coloratura soprano
The Princess	soprano

The time is the present, i.e., 1920s; the setting, "a room in the country (with a very low ceiling) opening on a garden." To emphasize the child's perspective, all objects are oversized and his mother appears only as a large skirt and apron disappearing into the low ceiling. The room's furnishings are "in Norman style, old or rather old-fashioned;

large armchairs covered in heavy cloth, a tall wooden clock with decorated dial, and a wallpaper with pastoral scenes. A round cage with a
squirrel hangs near the window. In the large fireplace a small fire burns
peacefully. A teakettle purrs, also the cat. It is afternoon."

The child, "six or seven years old," misbehaves. Punished, he be-
haves still worse, smashing teacups and tormenting pets. When lo! the
inanimate objects, coming to life, begin to taunt him, and subsequently
in the garden the animals he has mistreated attack him. Dimly aware
that evil deeds have isolated him from all he loves, he is miserable—
until a spontaneous act of kindness redeems him.

Some persons see in the opera merely an afternoon's fantasy in
childhood; others, a parable of growing up or, on yet a grander scale,
of the choices facing the human race: destruction or love. Colette
doubtless intended all three.

The word *sortilège* connotes magic for a purpose: to cast horoscopes,
to peer into the future—a connotation largely lost in the title's usual
translation, *The Bewitched Child*. That translation also tends to contract the opera's meaning to a single episode in the life of a particular
child, whereas Colette and Ravel kept expanding it into something
more: the child's room becomes a garden, and the garden, the universe;
the inanimate objects—teapot, chair and clock—are first animated and
then succeeded by living creatures; and the child's petulant outburst,
an afternoon's distemper, becomes the determining crisis of its life.
The sense of expansion, of the presence of ever-larger issues, is part of
the magic of the opera which, in fact, is very little about children.

Three notes about production. Some producers cast a child in the
role—always a mistake. No child's voice is sufficiently strong or well
focused to carry it, as Ravel recognized in asking for a mezzo-soprano,
an adult woman. Others make a ballet of the opera by putting dancers
on the stage and singers in the pits or wings. Also a mistake. The separation of the voice from its body greatly weakens its effect, particularly
in the dialogues between the child and the fire and the child and the
princess. Finally, some producers, in the style of Walt Disney, sentimentalize the child and the animals, most often in the finale where
they are apt to have the animals lay their heads on the child's arm or
snuggle into his lap. But the music remains cool. The animals do not
accompany the child into the human world. They and Ravel keep a
distance between the two.

A SINGLE ACT (43 min.)

The Child and his Mother. The child is bored with his lessons. He would rather go for a walk, pull the cat's tail, cut off the squirrel's, or somehow punish his mother. At that moment "Maman," visible only from the waist down, enters with lunch and asks "Bébé" if he has been good and finished his lessons. The child sulks in silence and soon sticks out his tongue at his mother. His punishment is a lunch of dry bread, sugarless tea and the afternoon alone in his room. After Maman leaves, he cries out that he does not care, he is not hungry, he prefers to be alone. "Je suis très méchant, méchant, méchant!" (I am very wicked). Rushing about the room crying "Hurrah," he smashes the teapot, jabs the squirrel, tweaks the cat, pokes the fire, tears the wallpaper and pulls the pendulum from the clock—all the time insisting "Je suis libre, libre, méchant et libre! (I am free, free, wicked and free).

Exhausted with devastation, he is about to fall into an armchair when—oh, surprise!—it moves from under him.

The Armchairs. With heavy foot they sing and dance a sarabande. Soon life will be better, and they will be free of the Child. All the furniture in the room joins in the concluding phrase, "Plus de l'Enfant!" (No more of the Child).

Motionless and in a stupor, with his back to the wall, he listens and looks on.

The Clock. "Ding, ding, ding!" It advances to the center of the room. Without its pendulum it cannot control its strike. "Ding, ding, ding!" It is too old to be so afflicted. Mournfully it crosses the room, turns its face to the wall and falls silent.

The Teapot (*black Wedgwood*) *and the Cup* (*Chinese*). They join in a foxtrot, mixing a few English phrases with others that might pass for Chinese. With their broken pieces they gesture threateningly at the Child, and then disappear.

Stricken, he sighs "Oh! ma belle tasse chinoise!" (Oh! my beautiful Chinese teacup). Lonely and afraid, he turns to the fire for comfort.

The Fire. It bounds from the hearth, thin, pale and flaring: "Arriè . . . re!" (Away). Fire warms the good, burns the bad, and the Child is bad. "Gare!" (Take care). With coloratura it menaces the Child, but behind the Fire comes the Ash, which slowly envelopes it and leads it back to the hearth.

As the Fire dies, the room grows darker. Twilight enters, and the Child murmurs, "J'ai peur, j'ai peur! (I am afraid).

The Wallpaper. From the torn paper come shepherds and shepherdesses who sing and dance a pastoral. Because of the Child, no longer will they meet in the pattern on the wall. "Adieu" (farewell).

The Child weeps on the floor, his head on the torn leaves of a book. From one of its pages emerges a languid hand, then a head of golden hair and finally a Princess from a fairy story. "Ah, c'est Elle, c'est Elle!" (It is she), cries the Child.

The Princess and the Child. "Oui, c'est elle, ta Princesse enchantée" (your enchanted Princess), whose story only yesterday you were reading, who for long kept sleep from your eyes and for whom you cried out in your dreams. But now, with the pages torn, who can know if the Prince will come before the evil magician turns her into a cloud?

The Prince will come, the Child insists. He himself, if he had a sword ("une épée"), would defend her. "Viens, viens!" (come), he calls to her. (This exchange is the emotional center of the opera's first part, and its direct, open warmth is unusual for Ravel.) "Hélas!" the Princess sighs, you are too weak. "A l'aide! A l'aide!" (help), she calls as the floor opens beneath her. "Mon épée, mon épée," cries the Child as she sinks from sight.

Desolate, the Child seeks the end of the tale among the paper scraps, but can find only lesson books. He pushes them with his foot, and from them numbers emerge, led by a humpbacked, crooked old man with a π for a hat, a tape measure for a belt and a ruler for a sword.

Arithmetic. Led by the old man the numbers do a rapid song and dance, rearranging themselves with giddying speed and leaving the Child on the floor, dizzy and exhausted. "Oh, ma tête, ma tête!" (my head).

The Cats. A white cat from the garden joins the black cat in the room and, pointedly ignoring the Child, they play with each other. (Similar cat numbers in ballet and song are Tchaikovsky's Puss-in-Boots *pas de deux* in *The Sleeping Beauty,* Act III, and Rossini's *Duetto Buffo di Due Gatti.*) During the cats' duet, the walls of the room part, and the Child is in:

The Garden. The moon is up and full, "its light softened by the pink after-glow of sunset. Trees, flowers, a little green pool, a great tree trunk covered with ivy. The music of insects, frogs, toads; the cries of screech-owls, the murmur of a breeze, and of nightingales." (Ravel's evocation of night noises is as remarkable as Verdi's in the Nile scene of *Aida*, Act III, or of Wagner's of Nuremberg in *Die Meistersinger*, Act II.)

The Trees. The Child opens his arms to the garden, "Oh, what a joy to find you!" But a tree groans, "Ma blessure, ma blessure" (my wound), made by the Child with his knife. The other trees, groaning and swaying, take up the cry, "Nos blessures" and "O méchant" (wicked Child).

Dragonflies et al. To what Ravel describes as a "Valse Americaine," the garden's creatures dance in search of their mates. In response to their despairing calls, the Child confesses his cruelty: the dragonfly he pierced with a pin and the bat he killed with a stick. The frogs join the general dance and begin to play, Ravel directs, "in the way that frogs do."

The Frog, The Squirrel and The Child. A frog, tired from playing, props himself against the Child's knee. The Squirrel warns that he will be caught, put in a cage and tormented. It was only the better to see the Squirrel's eyes, says the Child, but the Squirrel replies that since being caged his eyes have only tears. The Child sees the animals happy among themselves. "Ils s'aiment" (they love), he says; "ils m'oublient" (they forget me); "Je suis seul (I am alone); and he calls, "Maman."

Finale. At his cry the animals pause and then in anguish run in circles: it is the Child with the knife, the stick, the net. He must be made to suffer. In their frenzy they injure a squirrel, and the Child binds its paw with a ribbon. The animals stand in amazement. "See," one cries, "he has dressed the wound." In a crescendo of confusion and excitement they decide to help him, and one after another they begin to cry "Maman."

A light goes on in the house. Quietly the animals sing "il est bon, il est sage" (he is good, he is wise), and in friendly procession they start him toward the house. By the tree they stop, while he continues alone, holding out his arms and calling "Maman."

Vocabulary

Maman	mah.maw(nasal)	mother
Bébé	bay.bay	baby
je suis très méchant	shje swee tray may.shawnt	I am very wicked
je suis libre, libre, méchant et libre	. . . lee.bruh,	I am free, free, wicked and free
plus de l'Enfant	ploo duh	no more of the

Vocabulary (continued)

	lah(n).fah(n)	Child
oh, ma belle tasse	oh, mah belle.uh	oh, my beautiful
chinoise	tah.suh	Chinese cup
	sheen.wah.suh	
arrière	ahr.rhee.air.ruh	away
gare	gahr.uh	take care
j'ai peur, j'ai peur	shjay purr	I am afraid
adieu	ah d'yuh	farewell
ah, c'est Elle, c'est	ah, say t'ell . . .	it is she, it is
Elle		she
. . . ta Princesse	. . . tah Prah(n).sess	. . . your enchanted
enchantée	aw(n).shaw(n).tay	Princess
une épée	oon ay.pay	a sword
viens, viens	vee.yah(n) . . .	come, come
hélas	ay.lahs	alas
a l'aide, a l'aide	ah lay.duh . . .	help, help
oh, ma tête, ma tête	oh, mah teh.tuh . . .	oh, my head, my
		head
ma blessure	mah bleh.soor.ruh	my wound
ils s'aiment	eel zaym	they love
ils m'oublient	eel moo.blee	they forget me
je suis seul	shje swee suhl	I am alone
il est bon	eel ay boh(n)	he is good
il est sage	eel ay sah.shjuh	he is wise

A KÉKSZAKÁLLÚ HERCEG VÁRA

(Duke Bluebeard's Castle)

Opera in one act. World premiere, Budapest, May 24, 1918. United States concert prem. (in English), Dallas, Jan. 8, 1946; stage prem. (in Eng.), New York, Oct. 2, 1952. Music by Béla Bartók; text by Béla Balázs, distantly based on the fairy tale *La Barbe-bleue* in the collection *Contes de ma mère l'Oye* published in 1697 by Charles Perrault.

THE CHARACTERS

Bluebeard	bass
Judith	mezzo-soprano

The action takes place in Bluebeard's castle in a legendary time and country.

The opera has an unusual history. Completed in 1911, it was not produced because of alleged musical difficulties until 1918. Though successful, it soon became embroiled in politics. The postwar regime in Hungary demanded that the librettist's name be suppressed, and Bartók refused. After a season the opera was withdrawn and not performed again in Budapest until 1937. Again it was a success, but before it could establish itself in the international repertory, World War II closed most opera houses. In all, between the two wars the opera had less than twelve productions, most of them in small German houses. But in its second quarter-century, roughly 1948–73, it had almost 500 productions, was frequently recorded, and for many persons expressed with remarkable precision—especially considering it was composed 1905–11—the nature and illness of twentieth-century man.

In Perrault's fairy tale, of medieval, Breton origin, Bluebeard, a rich lord who has had six wives, marries again. Shortly thereafter he goes on a journey, leaving with his wife the keys to his castle, including one to a locked room that she is not to enter on pain of death. Overcome by curiosity, she unlocks the door and discovers the bodies of Bluebeard's six previous wives. In her agitation she drops the key, which falls in a pool of blood. Retrieving it, she attempts to wipe off the stains, but the more she rubs the larger they grow. Bluebeard, returning, sees them and orders her to her room to prepare for death. She has already notified her brothers of her predicament, however, and she now prays at such length that they arrive in time to save her and to kill Bluebeard.

In the opera Bluebeard becomes a sympathetic character and the story a psychic adventure in whose unhappy ending both he and Judith share. After their wedding Bluebeard brings her, his fourth wife, to his castle. It is dark and dank, and she, seeing seven locked doors, proposes to open them to let in sun and air. Ignoring his hesitation, she unlocks the first and discovers a torture chamber. Through the open door a beam of red light enters the hall, and she sees that the castle and everything in it is permeated with blood. Despite his warnings she opens the other doors, discovering behind each a different aspect of his character and behind the seventh his three former wives, alive but excluded from his life. Bluebeard orders Judith to join them, and as the door closes behind her, he is again alone in his dark castle.

What does it mean? The librettist in a 1918 interview said, "At our worst we are all Bluebeards because we build our own 'better world' only by the usurpation of other men's souls, whereas redemption can truly be achieved only through self-sacrificing love. The castle of Blue-beard is a symbol for the closed soul. When Judith recognizes the se-cret of Bluebeard's soul and his greatness, it is too late: the magic circle closes, and she too becomes a prisoner of the castle."

Presumably the tragedy of our time is that the number of closed souls is unusually large, and for most the way of redemption has been lost.

The opera, like many in which the props and people are symbols rather than facts or characters, has other interpretations. There is Bluebeard the artist: the sources of an artist's creativity, the good with the bad, must remain secret; they cannot be shared. Or, Bluebeard the private person: all individuality depends on privacy; there are limits beyond which even love must not press, or it will lose its object. Or, simply, the opera concerns loneliness.

But whatever the interpretation—and at any performance perhaps there are as many interpretations as persons in the audience—the excitement of the opera is in the sense of progression that the music conveys. In Judith's determination to let light into Bluebeard's soul she presses on, opening doors, until, between the fifth and sixth doors, events slip from her control and Bluebeard ends where he started, alone and in the dark. Their adventure is a journey, and though the path proves circular, at its outer rim something of importance was in sight and almost grasped. Their failure, suggests the opera, is also ours.

Inevitably the opera's structure is dominated by the opening of the doors, and for the revelation of each Bartók has provided a unique or-chestral sound. After an opening scene to bring the characters onstage the orchestra has, in effect, seven arias, expressed primarily in mood and tone color. Above these Judith and Bluebeard exchange their thoughts in short melodic phrases, but what they have to say is seldom more than a gloss on the aria or a stage direction leading to the next. The possibility of orchestral variety in these seven scenes was plain, the greater artistic problem lay in giving them some unity.

To provide it, Bartók emphasized throughout the opera the interval of a half-tone. It appears at several pitches but most often as G#-A. It also appears in several forms: as a chord, successive chords, a trill, or the top notes of an arpeggio.

The opening and closing of the opera are dominated by the half-tone in successive chords.

When Judith first feels moisture on the castle's walls and assumes it is water, the half-tone is a chord sounded softly on horns and answered by oboes.

Later, when she realizes that the moisture is blood, the half-tone becomes an extended, agonized trill on the flute over muted trombones.

SPOKEN PROLOGUE (often cut; 2 min.)

A Minstrel, as if addressing a medieval court, states that his story is a riddle, and the lords and ladies of the audience should look for the answer as much in themselves as on the stage. While he speaks, the curtain rises and the orchestra begins.

A SINGLE ACT (59 min.)

A round Gothic hall. At one side a narrow staircase leads up to a small iron door. In the hall are seven large black doors, all closed. There are no windows or ornaments; the hall is like an empty stone tomb. At the curtain, the stage is in darkness. Then the small door at the top of the stairs opens, and a beam of dazzling white light shoots down the staircase into the hall. Bluebeard appears leading Judith. *The Arrival.* Does she wish to turn back? His castle is not so cheery as her family's. Descending the stairs, she assures him of her love. "Let the door close," he cries happily, and above them it slowly shuts. But enough light remains in the hall to outline the two human shapes and the seven doors.

Holding Bluebeard's hand, Judith feels her way along the wall. "Your castle is crying," she says, discovering the walls are wet. "You would rather be elsewhere," he replies. No, no, she assures him, it is just so dark. Tearfully she kneels, kisses his hands and then, springing up, promises through her love to introduce sunshine. Noticing the doors, she asks why they are locked. "So that no one may look in." Open them, open them, she cries. Bluebeard warns, "Remember the rumors!" But she insists, banging on the door beside her. The castle sighs (clarinets and wind machine). Startled, she hesitates, then turns the key in the lock. Again comes the sigh.

First Door. Accompanied by a jagged violin trill (B-A#), it opens like a wound, spilling a shaft of blood-red light across the floor. Judith sees a **torture chamber** torture chamber and realizes, as the trill passes into the flute and later into the viola, that the moisture everywhere is blood. "Are you afraid?" asks Bluebeard. She is not and asks for all the keys. He gives her another, warning that the castle's foundations are beginning to tremble.

Second Door. The lock snaps, the door opens, and by the first red beam **armory** of light falls another, yellow-red. It flows from the armory, and the weapons, Judith sees, are stained with blood. Yet there is light. She asks for the other keys; in the name of love she demands them, and Bluebeard gives her three more.

Third Door. It opens with a deep, warm metallic sound, and a golden **treasury** beam of light falls beside the other two. It is the treasury, and from Bluebeard's riches Judith selects a crown and mantle that she places on the threshold. Suddenly, to successive chords of half-tones, she sees bloodstains on them. Puzzled, she turns to Bluebeard, who urges her to open the fourth door.

Fourth Door. The garden. Through the doorway flowery branches **garden** push inward, and a blue-green light crosses the floor. The flowers are beautiful, but soon Judith sees that the stems and petals are bloody. She is frightened. "Who watered your garden?" she asks.

"Love me and ask no questions," he replies. She runs to the next door. *Fifth Door*. The full orchestra with organ peals out solemn chords of pomp and grandeur. Through the door, as if from a high balcony, can **domain** be seen all of Bluebeard's dukedom. Light floods the room, and Judith shields her eyes. The distant clouds cast a bloody shadow.

"Come to me," Bluebeard urges, holding out his arms. But she does not move. Two doors remain, she says. "Leave them," he calls, "come to me." First the doors, she replies, and slowly his arms drop.

No doors, she insists, can be closed to me. Why not? he asks. But she demands the keys, and he gives her one. As she turns the lock, a deep moaning is heard, and he begs her to leave the door closed. *Sixth Door*. As she opens it, the hall becomes darker. An A-minor arpeggio shivers up to G-G# and retreats (double bass, cello, harp, clari- **lake** net and flute). Judith sees a lake, motionless, white, and it chills her heart. "What is this water?" "Tears," replies Bluebeard, and again holds out his arms.

They embrace, but soon she asks about his former wives. Retreating from him, she demands that he open the last door. It conceals the bodies of his wives. The tears are their tears, she states with increasing agitation, and the blood, their blood. The rumors are true. She demands to see the proof, to know for sure; and he gives her the last key. As she fits it to the lock, the fifth and sixth doors close with a sigh and the hall grows darker.

Seventh Door. Moonlight slips through the door, and three women in royal robes emerge. "My wives," says Bluebeard. "But they are alive," **wives** exclaims Judith, "alive!" Bluebeard kneels before them and, as if in a dream, says that they gathered the treasure, watered the garden and increased his lands. All of it is theirs. Rising, he explains that he met the first at red dawn, the second at burning, golden noon and the third at pale, dark evening. The fourth—"Stop!" cries Judith—on a starry, black night. "Stop!" Taking the crown that she had selected, he places it on her head—"No, Bluebeard, take it off"—and the mantle on her shoulders. For a long time they gaze at each other and then, stooping under the weight of her finery, she follows the other wives along the silvery beam of light and through the seventh door, which closes after her.

"Now," says Bluebeard, "it will be night forever . . . always . . . forever." Onstage the darkness has once again become complete, and into it Bluebeard disappears.

LE ROSSIGNOL

(The Nightingale)

A musical fairy tale in three acts (but short, 46 min., and usually presented without break). World premiere (in Russian), Paris, May 26, 1914; British prem. (in Russian), London, June 18, 1914; American prem. (in French), Metropolitan, New York, March 6, 1926. Music by Igor Stravinsky; text (composed in Russian) by Stravinsky and Stepan Mitusov, after a story by Hans Andersen.

PRINCIPAL CHARACTERS

The Fisherman	tenor
The Nightingale	soprano
The Cook	soprano
The Chamberlain	bass
The Bonze, a Buddhist official	bass
The Emperor of China	baritone
Death	contralto

The action is set in legendary China.

The opera, Stravinsky's first, was commissioned in 1909 by a theatre in Moscow which promptly went bankrupt, and Stravinsky, who had finished only the first act, put the piece aside. Four years later, after the theatre's reorganization, he completed it, only to have the theatre collapse once again. After which the ballet impresario, Diaghilev, produced it in Paris and London as part of his 1914 Russian Ballet Season.

The opera's troubled start and first production bequeathed it two unfortunate traditions, one of criticism, the other of production. Because of the long break in composition, during which Stravinsky composed his ballets *The Firebird, Petrushka* and *The Rite of Spring,* there is a change in musical style between Acts I and II. Critics harp on it (such a chance to display a little learning!), but it is relatively unimportant. Most persons won't notice it in performance and won't care if they do.

The production tradition, started by Diaghilev, is to put the singers in the wings or orchestra pit and to have dancers mime the roles. This clears the stage for the ceremonial processions, but it also dehumanizes the action. When the Nightingale bargains with Death for the Emperor, the scene's impact is stronger if each character's voice and presence are united. Yet stage directors often continue to divorce them.

The mistake is serious, for it reinforces the opera's chief weakness, its dramaturgy. Stravinsky was either unwilling or fearful of giving the opera to its chief characters. In the second act he uses roughly half of the sixteen minutes for marching about, leaving only half to present the contest between the real and the mechanical nightingales. By contrast, in the riddle scene of *Turandot,* which makes a strong impact, Puccini gives roughly six of the thirty-two minutes to the processions and the balance to the contest between Turandot and Calaf.

Similarly Stravinsky, after giving the Emperor a magnificent entrance, allows almost no time to develop his character. His illness in the third act is well presented and moving, but his cure and healthy "bon jour" to his startled court is too swift: the character, which had been growing human, returns to pasteboard.

Conversely, the opera's chief strength lies in its extrahuman elements: the atmospheric first act, the ceremonial processions, the court's etiquette and the stylization of Death. The spectacle, supported by some lovely music, is intriguing and colorful. But, more than in most operas, the costume designer can be the cause of success.

Though the opera was composed and first produced in Russian, it has often been given in French, and that, too, is a bad tradition, for there are moments where the difference in sound is great. When the Emperor in his illness calls for music, the Russian "MOO.zi.ki," with its strong accent and consonants, has greater force than the more diluted French, "mes musiciens." Happily, in recent years the trend has been toward productions in Russian. In the synopsis, however, the French is given (with regret) as more meaningful to most.

In 1917 Stravinsky completed a symphonic suite (20 min.), *Chant du Rossignol—The Song of the Nightingale,* using music only from Acts II and III of the opera. Diaghilev presented it as a ballet in 1920. The ballet's scenario is similar to the opera's, starting at Act II.

PRESENTED AS A SINGLE ACT (46 min.)

ACT I (17 min.)

After a murmuring introduction, the curtain rises on a seashore at night, bordered by a forest, with a Fisherman in his boat.

The Fisherman's song serves as a refrain throughout the opera. He **Fisherman's song** sings quietly of the mystery of the night, of the wind, and of fish miraculously freed to become birds. He longs for the Nightingale, "le rossignol," whose song can lighten care.

In the distance the Nightingale, accompanied by flute and later piccolo, describes the evening dew, its drops like crystals from a shattered star encrusting the Emperor's roses. (The song's ornamentation is easy and its pitch not very high, so the voice ought to sound ravishingly beautiful.)

The Cook leads in the Chamberlain, the Bonze and other courtiers. This is the place, she says, where the Nightingale sings; at any moment it will begin. In the orchestra there are two er-rumphs on the cellos and double bass, and the courtiers cry with delight, "C'est lui, c'est lui!" (it is he). No, no, says the Cook, that is the Fisherman's cow. Then there is a kek-kek on the woodwinds, and again the courtiers start to exclaim. But no, it was only a frog. By now it is clear that the Bonze, when excited, begins almost every sentence with "Tsing-Pé," a sort of musical throat-clearing lightly accompanied by cymbals followed by the bass drum.

Suddenly the flute sounds, representing the Nightingale. Tsing-Pé! Tsing-Pé! All are enraptured. The Cook invites the Nightingale to sing for the Emperor, and it agrees to accompany them back to the court. As they depart, the Fisherman resumes his song.

ACT II (15 min.)

Behind a transparent curtain, gently stirring in the wind, the scene is **entr'acte** set during a choral entr'acte (2 min.). Bring lanterns and bells, sing the courtiers, music and light, the lanterns shining like gold in the night and the bells gleaming of silver. As the Emperor's march is heard, the curtains rise, revealing the porcelain palace of the Emperor of China.

During the march (4 min.), the courtiers enter in procession, fol- **march** lowed by the Emperor carried in a chair. After he is placed on a podium and all have made their obeisance, the Chamberlain announces that the Nightingale is present and ready to sing.

On the Emperor's nod the Nightingale starts with an extended cadenza which leads into his song. A second cadenza ends it.

The Emperor declares it beautiful (others in the audience, however, seem generally to prefer the Nightingale's song in the first scene), and offers the Nightingale the Order of the Golden Slipper. But it declines any reward other than the tears, "des larmes," in the Emperor's eyes. Meanwhile the ladies of the court, in an effort to imitate the Nightingale, are gargling with water from china cups.

Three ambassadors from Japan approach, offering the Emperor a gift, a large mechanical nightingale. Its voice is represented by the oboe. During the demonstration, the real nightingale slips away. The Emperor soon tires of the mechanical bird and asks for the other to sing again. The courtiers are too embarrassed to speak, but the Chamberlain announces that the Nightingale has flown away. The Emperor, indignant at such rudeness, proclaims it banished from the empire forever and names the mechanical bird to the position of First Singer. Then on signal to his servants his chair is lifted, and the court in process follows him out.

In the far, far distance the Fisherman sings of the spirit in the Nightingale's voice which can conquer even death.

ACT III (14 min.)

A room in the palace. Night. Moonlight. A gigantic curtained bed on which the Emperor lies, ailing. Death sits at the bedside, wearing the Imperial Crown and holding the Imperial Sword and Standard. After an orchestral introduction (2 min.), from behind the bed emerge a chorus of spectres.

spectres' chorus   You must remember us, they sing. We are your past deeds. Remember us and "tremble" (be afraid). The Emperor is frightened and calls for his musicians, "mes musiciens."

The real Nightingale returns and starts to sing of the Emperor's gardens. Death is entranced and to hear more singing agrees to restore the Emperor's health. The Nightingale sings of Death's garden, where the moon shines sadly and the stars fade, where wreaths of white fog float among the tombstones and the dead sleep in peace. During the song Death rises and slowly disappears.

The Emperor, feeling his health returning, begs the Nightingale not to fly away and offers it first place at court. No, replies the Nightingale, the tears, "larmes," in your eyes are reward enough, and it promises to return each night and sing till dawn.

The courtiers, thinking the Emperor dead, approach the bed in a sol-**solemn march** emn march. Two of them pull aside the curtains, and there is the Emperor in full regalia, good health and brilliant light. "Bon jour à tous!" (Good day to all!) he calls. Then as the curtain falls, from afar comes the Fisherman's voice: the bird now is singing. "Écoutez-bien, et dans sa voix reconnaissez la voix du ceil" (listen well, and in its voice recognize the voice of heaven).

Vocabulary

le rossignol	luh ross.een.y'ohl	the nightingale
c'est lui	say l'we	it is he
tsing-pé	tsing-pay	tsing-pé
des larmes	day lahr.muh	the tears
tremble	trawm.bluh	tremble, be afraid
mes musiciens	may moo.zee.syah(n) (nasal)	my musicians
bon jour à tous	bon(n) shjure ah two	good day to all
écoutez-bien	ay.coo.tay b'yan(n)	listen well
et dans sa voix	ay daw(n) sah v'wah	and in its voice
reconnaissez la voix du ciel	reh.cohn.nay.say lah v'wah due see.ell	recognize the voice of heaven

L'HISTOIRE DU SOLDAT

(The Soldier's Tale)

A work with music by Igor Stravinsky that, according to its title page, is "To be Read, Played and Danced." Not a syllable of text is sung; the story is advanced by the characters and a narrator talking. The work qualifies as an opera only in the general sense that its drama is intended to be conveyed through and heightened by its music. Though in two parts and six scenes, it is short (35 min.) and often presented without a break. The music consists of eleven individual numbers, parts of which are repeated; the orchestra is very small: one violin, double-bass, clarinet, bassoon, cornet, trombone and various types of percussion; the original French text is by C. F. Ramuz. World premiere, Lausanne, September 28, 1918; British (concert) premiere, London, July 20, 1920; United States (concert) premiere, March 23, 1924.

The work most often appears as a Concert Suite, which Stravinsky always intended to draw from it. This suite includes eight of the original eleven numbers (order in the original is indicated in parentheses): "The Soldier's March (1), "The Soldier's Violin" (2), "Royal March" (4), "The Little Concert" (5), "Three Dances": *Tango, Waltz, Ragtime* (6), "The Devil's Dance" (7), "Chorale" (10), and "The Devil's Triumphal March" (11). Omitted are "Pastorale" (3), "The Little Chorale" (8), and "The Devil's Song" (9).

The story, loosely based on Russian folklore, concerns a soldier on leave who sells his soul to the devil. For a time in return he enjoys wealth, and later the love of a princess. By various tricks he prevents the devil from collecting, but in the end he has to pay and loses his soul.

MAVRA

Opera in one act (25 min.). World premiere (in French), Opéra, Paris, June 2, 1922; British radio prem. (in English), April 27, 1934; stage prem., Edinburgh, Aug. 21, 1956; American prem. (in English), Philadelphia, Dec. 28, 1934. Music by Igor Stravinsky; original Russian text by Boris Kochno after Pushkin's poem, "The Little House at Kolomna."

The action takes place in a small Russian town during the reign of Charles X of Sweden (1654–60). A young woman, Parasha (soprano), loves a Hussar cavalry officer, Vasili (tenor). Her mother (contralto) has just lost her cook and laments with a neighbor (mezzo-soprano) on the difficulty of finding another. As a replacement Parasha offers Vasili disguised as "Mavra," and he is hired. But the mother soon discovers "Mavra" shaving, and amid the general consternation he leaps out the window, leaving behind a disappointed Parasha.

The music consists of an overture and thirteen numbers—Parasha's Aria, etc.—connected by dialogue set over full orchestra. Its sound, because of a high ratio of wind instruments, often has a "band" rather than an "orchestral" quality.

OEDIPUS REX

Opera-oratorio in two acts (but short, 52 min., and often presented without break). World premiere as an oratorio, Paris, May 30, 1927; as an opera, Vienna, Feb. 23, 1928. American premiere, oratorio, Boston,

Feb. 24, 1928; opera, New York, April 21, 1931. British premiere, oratorio, London, Feb. 12, 1936; opera, Edinburgh, Aug. 21, 1956. Music by Igor Stravinsky; text in Latin, being a translation by Jean Danielou of a text in French by Stravinsky and Jean Cocteau based on *Oedipus Tyrannus* by Sophocles. Stravinsky composed to the Latin text, which is always used.

PRINCIPAL CHARACTERS

Oedipus,	tenor	eh.dee.puss
King of Thebes		
Creon,	bass-baritone	cray.oh(n)
his brother-in-law		
Tiresias,	bass	tee.ray.see.ahs
a blind seer		
Jocasta,	mezzo-soprano	yo.cah.stah
Queen of Thebes		
A Messenger	bass-baritone	
A Shepherd	tenor	

The action takes place in ancient Thebes, and some of what has occurred before is important.

Laius, Oedipus's predecessor, had also been married to Jocasta and, grieved by their failure to have a child, went secretly to Delphi to consult the oracle. Presumably he asked whose was the fault, but the oracle in its fashion answered another question, telling him that his misfortune was a blessing, for any child by Jocasta would become his murderer. He therefore left Jocasta's bed, though without telling her the reason, which so irritated her that, making him drunk one night, she inveigled him into it. The result was a son, whom Laius snatched from the nurse and, piercing his feet with a nail, left on Mount Citharon to die. In Sophocles, Jocasta abandons the child.

A Shepherd found the baby, named him Oedipus (swollen foot) and took him to Corinth where the King and Queen, Polybus and Periboea (also known as Merope), raised him as their son.

Taunted one day on his lack of resemblance to his supposed parents, Oedipus started for Delphi, presumably to ask about his lineage. But before the question was put, he was ordered from the shrine because he was an impure suppliant: "You will murder your father and marry your mother."

Loving Polybus and Periboea, Oedipus turned his back on Corinth and started eastward. In the mountains between Delphi and Daulis, in a gorge where the road from Delphi meets those from Athens and Thebes, he encountered a man in a chariot. Though Oedipus did not know it, the man was Laius, on his way once again to consult the oracle. "Make way for your betters," cried Laius to the pedestrian, but Oedipus, standing fixed, retorted that he knew no betters except the gods and his parents. "So much the worse for you," said Laius, urging his horses forward. But Oedipus, when the chariot wheel bruised his foot, became enraged, knocked Laius to the ground and, while the king's hands were entangled in the reins, lashed the horses so that they dragged Laius to his death. Later, when the body was found, the king of Plataea gave it a royal burial.

Oedipus, meanwhile, at the juncture of the three roads turned left to Thebes and at Mount Phicium met the Sphinx, who was decimating the countryside by asking wayfarers a riddle: what being, with but one voice, has sometimes two feet, sometimes three, sometimes four, and is weakest with the most? When her victims answered wrongly or in their terror stayed silent, she devoured them. To end this scourge Laius had started for Delphi to ask the riddle's answer.

Oedipus, however, solved it instantly: man, he said, because he crawls on all fours as an infant, stands firmly on two feet in youth and leans on a staff in old age. The Sphinx, mortified by defeat, threw herself from the mountain into the valley and died. The grateful Thebans thereupon made Oedipus king in place of Laius, reported slain by highway robbers, and married him to Jocasta, whom he did not know was his mother.

Some ten or twelve years later a plague descended on Thebes, and Oedipus sent Jocasta's brother, Creon, to Delphi to ask the cause. At this point both the play and the opera begin, and the story's sequel is more familiar: how Oedipus gradually learns that he has indeed killed his father and married his mother, and that he, the great king, is the cause of the plague; how in despair he blinds himself, but with the loss of physical sight gains spiritual understanding; and how in leaving the city, in accepting his fate wholly and without prevarication, he reaches what Sophocles suggests is the truest greatness attainable by man: acceptance of the inevitability of suffering and the necessity of destiny.

The play achieves a monumental grandeur in which its chief characters are human yet heroic, a man and woman of immediate passion yet ennobled by a remote dignity. The remoteness intrigued Stravinsky and was a reason he wanted a Latin text. Latin also seemed to him

more rough-hewn and monumental than any of its vernacular deriva-
tives. To join the six scenes, Cocteau suggested a Speaker using the
language of the audience, and the device further emphasized the play's
remoteness, without preventing the music from underlining the imme-
diacy of the passions. Though the form is a curious hybrid of opera
and oratorio, for the particular text it worked well.

The piece is opera, however, not oratorio, and Stravinsky put in the
score directions for its staging. He wanted as little movement as possible. Onstage the chief characters were to remain fixed in position, like
figures in a frieze, moving only their arms and heads: "They should
give the impression of living statues." Most productions allow more
movement, if only in exits and entrances, and probably gain thereby.
Certainly in the final chorus, "Behold King Oedipus," it is more dramatic to have him, blinded, led onstage by his daughter, than merely in
position to change his mask.

The work is more often presented as an opera than an oratorio and
more often in one act than two. It is constructed of six scenes, each introduced by the Speaker, each designed to show a new side of Oedipus,
and each building to a more powerful musical climax than the last.

PRESENTED AS A SINGLE ACT (52 min.)

The Speaker. He proposes to recall the story for the audience "as we go
along." Thebes is ravaged by plague, and its people implore Oedipus,
who vanquished the Sphinx, to save them. He promises.

The curtain rises on a shallow stage with Thebes and its people
presented as if in a frieze. The chorus (tenors and basses) calls on Oedi-
the plague   pus "e peste serva nos" (from the plague preserve us),
"serva urbem morientem" (save the dying city). He replies, "vos li-
berabo" (I will save you), "eg(o) Oedipus" (I, Oedipus). When the chorus continues its plea, he adds that he has already sent Creon (often
shortened to Creo) to Delphi to consult the oracle. Creon enters and is
greeted by the chorus.

The Speaker. The oracle demands the punishment of Laius's murderer,
who is in Thebes. He must be discovered. Oedipus prides himself on
solving mysteries; he will uncover the murderer and drive him out.
Creon. "Respondit deus" (the god replies), "Thebis peremptor latet"
Creon   (in Thebes the murderer is concealed). Because of him the

city suffers plague. He must be expelled. "Apollo dixit deus" (so spake the God Apollo).

Oedipus assures the chorus, which continually repeats "deus dixit," that he will solve the riddle of Laius's death. "Solve, solve!" (solve it), cries the chorus.

The Speaker. Oedipus calls in the seer, Tiresias, who refuses to speak, for he knows the truth. His silence angers Oedipus, who accuses him of being the murderer. Forced to speak, Tiresias reveals "the king's murderer is a king."

The chorus invokes the aid of the gods and when Tiresias enters, greets him "Salve Tiresia," urging him to speak quickly, "dic, dic" (speak).

Tiresias   Tiresias replies, "dicere non possum" (I cannot speak), and warns Oedipus not to compel him. Cunningly Oedipus says, your silence accuses you; "tu peremptor" (you are the murderer). Miserable man, answers Tiresias, "dico" (I speak): "Inter vos peremptor est" (among you is the murder); "regis est rex peremptor" (the murderer of the king is a king).

Oedipus   Angered by the implication Oedipus, with soft insinuating tones, tells the chorus that jealousy hates good fortune, "invidia fortunam odit." Whose job was it to solve riddles? Tiresias! And who vanquished the Sphinx? Oedipus! But "invidia fortunam odit." Another mystery now is solved and again by Oedipus: Creon seeks the throne and Tiresias is his accomplice. "Invidia fortunam odit."

Alarmed by the angry voices, Jocasta appears and is greeted by the chorus, "Gloria, gloria, gloria!" (When the opera is presented in two acts, the break follows this brief chorus, which is repeated to open Act II.)

The Speaker. The noise of the quarrel draws Jocasta, who attempts to soothe the men and shame them for wrangling in the midst of a stricken city. She does not believe in oracles. She can prove they lie. For instance, one foretold that Laius would die by a son of hers but in fact he was murdered by robbers where three roads meet on the road to Delphi. "Trivium"—a place where three roads meet. The word startles Oedipus, and he recalls the old man he killed.

Jocasta   *Jocasta* (her aria is roughly in ABA form). Are you not ashamed to raise your voices, "clamare, ululare," in a quarrel? To faster tempo (B), she warns them to put no trust in oracles, "oracula." They lie, and she gives her example, "Laius in trivio mortuus" (Laius died at the place where three roads meet). Returning to her original, slower tempo, she repeats her warning against "oracula" and that Laius died "in trivio." In an ominous tatoo the chorus repeats "trivium, trivium."

Oedipus is intrigued and says to Jocasta, "Ego senem cecidi" (I
duet   killed an old man) at just such a place. Jocasta, now thoroughly agitated, urges him to come into the palace and stop seeking advice. "Cave, cave oracula" (beware of oracles). But Oedipus, though increasingly upset, insists on learning the truth. "Sciam" (I shall know).

The Speaker. A Messenger reveals that Polybus is dead and that Oedipus was his son only by adoption. Jocasta, seeing the whole truth before Oedipus, rushes into the palace. This Oedipus, so proud of his skill in riddles! He is in a trap, and soon only he fails to see it. Truth comes to him like a blow on the head. When he falls, he falls headlong.

A Messenger and a Shepherd enter. The Messenger announces,
Messenger and Shepherd   "Mortuus est Polybus" (Polybus is dead) who was only a "falsus pater" (not true, i.e., adopting, father) to Oedipus. Further, the Messenger reports that he first saw Oedipus when the Shepherd brought him as a baby down from the mountain. The chorus still believes in Oedipus and expects to hear of some divine birth, but as the Shepherd begins to speak, Jocasta grasps the full truth and turns hastily into the palace.

The Shepherd describes finding the abandoned baby, his feet pierced. Oedipus, seeing Jocasta leave, assumes she is ashamed, "pudet," of an upstart husband without home or ancestry, but he will press on and learn his descent. "Sciam." "Ego exul exsulto" (I exult in my exile, i.e., abandonment).

The Messenger and the Shepherd briefly repeat their statements, and the chorus understands: Oedipus is "natus," born of Laius and Jocasta; is "peremptor," the murderer of his father Laius; and "coniux," the spouse of his mother Jocasta. The Messenger and the Shepherd withdraw.

Oedipus now sees the truth. "Natus sum quo nefastum est" (I was born of whom it is forbidden); "concubui cui nefastum est" (I lay with whom it is forbidden); and "cecidi quem nefastum est" (I killed whom it is forbidden). Quietly he says, "Lux facta est" (light is wrought, i.e., Truth has dawned), and enters the palace.

The Speaker. Now you will hear the famous monologue, "The sacred head of Jocasta," in which the Messenger tells of Jocasta's death. She has hanged herself, and with her golden brooch Oedipus puts out his eyes. Then follows the epilogue. The king is fallen, and for a portent he shows himself to all. Gently, very gently, the chorus urges him to leave the city, and he goes.

Messenger and Chorus. "Divum Jocastae caput mortuum!" (the sacred
choral finale head of Jocasta is dead). She entered her chamber, tearing her hair, wailing, and bolted the door. "Divum Jocastae caput mortuum!" When Oedipus burst open the door, she was there, hanging before him. He took her down, laid her on the floor and with her brooch ground out his eyes. "Divum Jocastae caput mortuum!" The black blood from the sockets runs down his chest and he curses himself. See now the doors open, and he shows himself. "Divum Jocastae caput mortuum!"

Oedipus appears. "Ecce regem Oedipoda" (Behold King Oedipus), the chorus sings. "Vale!" (farewell). "Tibi valedico" (farewell to you).

Vocabulary

e peste serva nos	ay pes.tay sair. vah no.s	from the plague preserve us
serva urbem morientem	. . . oor.bem mohr.ee.en. tehm	save the dying city
vos liberabo	voh.s lee.bair. ah.boh	I will save you
eg(o) Oedipus	egg(o) Eh.dee. puss	I, Oedipus
respondit deus	reh.spohn.dit day.oohs	the god replies
Thebis peremptor latet	Thay.bis pair.emp.tore lah.tet	in Thebes the murderer hides
Apollo dixit deus	. . . dee.ksit day.oohs	so spake the god Apollo
solve	sohl.vay	solve it
salve Tiresia	sahl.vay Tee.ray.see.ah	hail Tiresias
dic	deek	speak
dicere non possum	deek.ehr.ray known poh.soom	I cannot speak
tu peremptor	too	you are the murderer

Vocabulary (continued)

	pair.emp.tore	
dico	deek.oh	I speak
inter vos peremptor est	in.tair vohs . . . es't	among you is the murderer
regis est rex peremptor	reh.gheese es't . . .	the murderer of the king is a king
invidia fortunam odit	in.vee.dee.ah for.too.nahm oh.dit	jealousy hates good fortune
clamare, ululare	klah.mah.ray ool.ool.lah.ray	to make noise
oracula	or.ah.koo.lah	oracles
Laius in trivio mortuus	Lah.oohs in tree.vee.oh mohr.too.uhs	Laius at the three-way cross road died
trivium	tree.vee.uhm	three-way crossroads
ego senem cecidi	egg.oh seh.nem kek.ee.dee	I killed an old man
cave, cave oracula	cah.vay . . .	beware of oracles
sciam	skee.ahm	I shall know
mortuus est Polybus	mohr.too.us es't Pol.ee.boos	Polybus is dead
falsus pater	fahl.suhs pah.tair	adopting father
pudet	poo.det	she is ashamed
ego exul exsulto	. . . eks.uhl eks.uhl.toe	I exult in my exile
natus	nah.toos	born
coniux	cohn.yuks	spouse (husband)
natus sum quo nefastum est	. . . neh.fah. stoom es't	. . . it is forbidden
lux facta est	looks fact.tah es't	light is wrought
divum Jocastae caput mortuum	dee.voom Yo.cahst.ay kah.poot more too.uhm	the sacred head of Jocasta is dead
ecce regem Oedipoda	ek.kay reh.ghem . . .	behold king Oedipus
vale	vah.lay	farewell
tibi valedico	t'bee vah.lay deek.oh	farewell to you

THE RAKE'S PROGRESS

Opera in three acts and an epilogue. World premiere, Venice, Sept. 11, 1951; American prem., Metropolitan, New York, Feb. 14, 1953; British prem., Edinburgh, Aug. 25, 1953. Music by Igor Stravinsky; text in English, "a fable," by W. H. Auden and Chester Kallman.

PRINCIPAL CHARACTERS

Anne Trulove	soprano
Tom Rakewell	tenor
Trulove, Anne's father	bass
Nick Shadow	baritone
Mother Goose, the Madam of a brothel	mezzo-soprano
Baba the Turk, a bearded lady	mezzo-soprano
Sellem, an auctioneer	tenor
Keeper of the madhouse	bass

The action, covering a year from spring to spring, takes place in eighteenth-century England.

The opera, like Menotti's *Amahl and the Night Visitors,* is one of the few to have a visual source. Early in 1947 in Chicago, Stravinsky saw an exhibition of English art in which was the series of eight scenes by William Hogarth, *A Rake's Progress.* The last scene in particular stirred Stravinsky's imagination: in the madhouse at Bedlam along with the Rake was a blind beggar playing a one-stringed fiddle.

From this seed grew the opera. Stravinsky asked Auden, who collaborated with Kallman, to prepare a libretto based on Hogarth's scenes. But as Auden later described in his *Secondary Worlds,* this posed certain problems.

Because the series' primary purpose is not to present the Rake's biography but to satirize aspects of eighteenth-century London life, he is present in each picture chiefly as a means of giving some unity to an otherwise unconnected series. He is a passive figure, succumbing to whatever temptation is offered, without personality and, because the other figures in each picture change, without a continuing relationship to anyone. Except for the general statement that he is a young man with money, who lives unwisely and ends in a madhouse, he is a man without a history. The librettists' first problem, therefore, was to particularize him, to give him a name, a background, friends and feelings; to turn him from the pictures' "A Rake's Progress" into the opera's "The Rake's Progress."

They might have done this in a realistic style or through a psychological study but chose instead, aiming at "mythical resonance," to create a mixture of medieval morality play and fairy tale. Tom Rakewell, a callow, country youth, is tempted by the Devil appearing in the form of a servant, Nick Shadow. The action turns on the structural device common to many fairy tales of three wishes. At the start of the opera Tom idly cries, "I wish I had money," and lo!—at the garden gate is a stranger, by name Nick Shadow, with news of the death of Tom's uncle and of an inheritance for Tom. He suggests a visit to London to tend the legacy, and off he and Tom go, leaving behind Tom's anxious fiancée, Anne Trulove, and her disapproving father. The subsequent wishes are: "I wish I were happy," and "I wish it were true" (power). To each Nick offers an astonishing fulfillment. Finally, when thanks to Anne's semi-divine intervention, Tom defeats Nick at cards and so saves his soul, though not his sanity, he cries, "I wish for nothing else."

With the Devil and Anne, who comes to London in search of Tom, the librettists created two characters who can accompany Tom through most of the opera and in the end have a duel of sorts for his soul. But the relationship of the three, as Auden laments, is static. Anne is always loyal and good; the Devil, diabolic; and Tom, weak. To offset this in part they gave Tom a tendency toward manic depression so that musically he can vary frequently between high and low spirits. The story's pre-determined straight line to perdition, however, precluded any real struggle on his part to avoid his fate, and the opera's success in performance often depends on how well two of the minor roles along the way are played.

The lesser of these is the Madam of a brothel, who appears in one picture of Hogarth's series. The librettists have named her Mother Goose, and though they have not given her many solo lines, she must dominate the brothel scene. The right mixture of age, presence, vulgarity and wisdom, however, seems difficult for singers to calculate.

The other character, Baba the Turk, is an original creation of the librettists. In Hogarth the Rake marries an old and ugly heiress for her money. In her place, in as much as Tom has already succumbed to the temptations of wealth, Auden and Kallman substituted the temptation of an *acte gratuit,* a demonstration against order of the kind that some twentieth-century intellectuals have praised as liberating. Tom, to demonstrate his freedom from the compulsions of Passion and Reason, marries Baba the Turk, a lady from the circus with a magnificent Assyrian beard. Auden warns that the role must "on no account be played for laughs. In her own eyes, Baba is as much a grande dame as the Marschallin in *Rosenkavalier*." In performance, however, the right touch has often proved elusive; bravura, not camp, is needed.

The opera is sometimes presented in two rather than three acts; the single break then follows Act II, Scene 2.

ACT I (43 min.)

SCENE 1 (21 min.)

The garden of Trulove's country cottage. Spring afternoon.

Tom and Anne exchange vows, "how sweet . . . to walk, to love," while Trulove frets over his daughter's choice. His doubts increase when Tom rejects a job in London.

Tom, alone, reveals that he believes in Fortune, not merit, and in life **aria and first wish** will "trust to my luck . . . this beggar shall ride." He ends with his first wish (spoken): "I wish I had money."

Immediately at the garden gate is Nick Shadow inquiring for Tom Rakewell, and he tells Tom, and subsequently the Truloves, of Tom's inheritance. An unknown uncle has died and "You are a rich man." In a brief quartet the four with various feelings sing "be thanked O God."

Tom and Anne renew their vows, "O clement love"; then Shadow says that Tom must go to London to mind his money. Urged by all Tom, at first reluctant, soon agrees and grows excited, "let's fly, let's fly to husbandry and make it grow, and make it grow."

The lovers sing their farewells, after which Tom hires Nick Shadow as servant on the latter's terms: "a year and a day hence we will settle our account." Tom, now eager to be off, sings excitedly of London, while Anne regretfully and Trulove fearfully join him. As Tom hurries out the gate and the Truloves enter the cottage, Nick Shadow turns to the audience: "The Progress of a Rake begins."

SCENE 2 (14 min.)

Mother Goose's brothel. London. Summer night.

The scene opens with an introduction and chorus for Whores and

Roaring Boys. The Boys with delight proclaim that their only purpose is to roam the streets and "make a commotion" or "provoke a fight."
chorus The Whores, for their part, assault all men with suggestive glances and by arousing desire hope to separate their victims from their money.

They end with a toast "To Venus and Mars."

To demonstrate Tom's right to join them, Shadow and Mother **catechism** Goose question him on Nature, Beauty and Pleasure: "One aim in all things to pursue: My duty to myself to do." When asked to define Love, however, Tom remembers Anne: "That precious word like a fiery coal, it burns my lips." He cries out, "Let me go; before it is too late." With a gesture Shadow turns back the clock: "You may repent at leisure." Tom stays.

Shadow introduces him to the group which, according to its custom, **cavatina** awaits a song. To a rippling clarinet accompaniment, Tom sings of "Love, too frequently betrayed. . . ." "How sad a song," comment the Whores, "but sadness charms."

Mother Goose as oldest, however, claims Tom for the night, and while the chorus sings a courting song, "Lanterloo," she leads Tom away. The menace beneath the fun becomes clear as Shadow, raising his glass, bids the retiring Tom, "Sweet dreams"—then quietly adds, "for when you wake, you die."

SCENE 3 (8 min.)

The Trueloves' cottage. Autumn night, full moon.

Anne is alone in travelling clothes: "No word from Tom. Has Love no voice?" But from accusing him she quickly shifts to herself. "Love hears, Love knows, Love answers him across the silent miles, and goes."

Softly she asks the night to find and caress him, the moon to guide **aria and cabaletta** her to him. From the cottage her father calls, and for a moment she falters. She kneels to pray. "O God, protect dear Tom, support my father, and strengthen my resolve (in the next act Tom will use the same music for a similar short prayer). Then rising, in true operatic fashion she strides resolutely forward to the footlights and delivers what should be a show-stopping cabaletta—"I go to him"—ending on a long-held high C.

ACT II (41 min.)

SCENE 1 (15 min.)

Tom's house in London. Autumn morning. Tom is at the breakfast table. Nearby is a wig-stand and wigs. Sun pours through the open window, also noises from the street. After one, particularly loud, Tom slams the window shut.

He is bored with loose living, and in a long aria ending in a reprise **aria and second wish** (roughly ABA form) he expresses his dissatisfaction. "Vary the song, O London, change!" For "all your music cannot fill the gap that in my heart—is still." He is tired of being "A gentleman to the clock of fashion," and with a cry of disgust, "City! City!" begins to tick off the evils of London. "Who's honest, chaste or kind? One, only one, and of her I dare not think." Rising excitedly from his chair, he determines to continue a life of pleasure. But then, melancholy again descends: despite the brilliance of London and society he finds "in my heart the dark." He exclaims (spoken): "I wish I were happy."

Shadow enters with a circus broadsheet advertising the bearded lady, Baba the Turk. He suggests that Tom "marry her." Insisting that "I was never saner," he argues that most men act because of pressure; Tom, to demonstrate his freedom, should "take Baba the Turk to **aria** wife." For "that man, that man alone, that man alone his fate fulfills . . . whom neither Passion may compel nor Reason can restrain."

Tom agrees. "My tale shall be told. Both by young and by old." **duet** Shadow urges him on, and they end together: "To Hymen's Altar. Ye Powers, inspire Tom Rakewell Esquire."

SCENE 2 (14 min.)

Street in front of Tom's house. London. Autumn. Dusk.

Anne enters and, on seeing the bustle of servants in and out of Tom's house, loses her nerve. "How strange! Although the heart for love dare **arioso** everything, the hand draws back. . . . London! Alone!" She encourages herself: "No step, no step in fear shall wander nor in weakness delay . . . a love that is sworn before Thee can plunder Hell of its prey." Yet she hesitates, and a procession enters: servants followed by Tom, on foot, leading home Baba the Turk, who is carried in a curtained sedan chair.

While Baba sits concealed in the chair Tom violently begs Anne to denounce him, accuse him—whatever she wishes—but go. And she **duet** refuses. Regaining self-control, he warns her against London: " 'tis wisdom here to be afraid." "How should I fear," she asks, "who have your aid and all my love for you beside?" "Go back, go back," he cries.

Baba, leaning through the curtains, asks: "My love, am I to remain here forever?" Anne, astonished at the heavily veiled face, inquires about the lady. "Your wife!" she exclaims to Tom, adding with slight bitterness, "I see then, it is I who was unworthy." A trio develops: Anne urging her heart "never, never, never" to feel again, "lest you, **trio** alone, your promise keep"; Tom, regretful, "O bury the heart," that "never, never, never" can be revived; and Baba, poking in and out of the curtains, "who is it, pray . . . a family friend? An ancient flame?"

Anne exits hurriedly, and Tom reassures Baba that it was "only a milk-maid, pet, to whom I was in debt." Servants come with lights, and people in the street recognize Baba. As she mounts the steps to enter the house, she turns to face the crowd, unveils, and shows her beard. She blows the crowd a kiss and with arms outstretched milks its applause in the practiced manner of a great artist. (When the opera is performed in two acts, the single break is here.)

SCENE 3 (12 min.)

Tom's house, London. A winter morning. The breakfast room, now cluttered with every conceivable kind of object.

Baba chatters about her souvenirs and circus triumphs while Tom sits silent. When she attempts to humor him, he snarls: "Sit down!" In tears she strides about the room, smashing objects. "Scorned. Abused. Neglected. Baited!" She accuses him of loving the milk-maid. Sitting down, she is in the midst of saying that her rival will never be his wife, when he plumps a wig over her face, silencing her; and for the rest of the scene she sits silent and motionless in place. "My heart is cold," says Tom, "I cannot weep," and stretches on the sofa to have a nap.

While he sleeps, a pantomime takes place. Shadow rolls in a ma-
pantomime and third wish   chine which he demonstrates to the audience. By means of a false bottom, it appears to make a loaf of bread
from bits and pieces of Baba's smashed crockery. From the sofa Tom
cries in his sleep, "O I wish it were true."

Waking, he describes to Shadow his dream. He had devised "an en-
gine that converted stones to bread" and would make the world again
an Eden of goodwill. Shadow shows him the machine; Tom tastes the
bread, and believes: "O miracle!" On his knees, to Anne's five-bar
prayer from the previous act, he asks: "O may I not, forgiven all my
past, for one good deed deserve dear Anne at last?"

Rising, Tom sings excitedly of the good the machine will accomplish
and Shadow, cynically, of the money it will make. In order to sell
shares to the public, Shadow suggests they need backers. As the two
start for the City and its men of business, Shadow asks, "Should you
not tell the good news to your wife?" Tom replies, "I have no wife. I've
buried her."

ACT III (61 min.)

SCENE 1 (18 min.)

The breakfast room in Tom's house, London. Spring afternoon.
Everything as before except covered with cobwebs and dust. Baba is
still seated motionless, the wig over her head, also covered with cobwebs and dust. From behind the curtain there is a cry of "Ruin, Disaster, Shame." When it rises, groups of Respectable Citizens are
examining the room's objects and furniture, which will be auctioned
that afternoon to pay Tom's debts.

As the crowd moves from table to chair, from offstage comes another
chorus   cry of "Ruin, Disaster, Shame." The crowd confidentially
and complacently addresses the audience: "Blasted! Blasted! so many
hopes of gain. . . . Rakewell, Rakewell. Ruin. Disaster. Shame."

Anne enters, asking for Tom, but the crowd only repeats rumors:
he's gone to America, he's dead. She runs out to search the house.

Sellem, the Auctioneer, sets up a dais and, announcing the auction,
auctioneer's waltz   begins to puff the items: a stuffed auk, a
mounted fish, a marble bust. On each the bidding starts to a waltz: "La!
come bid!" Offering the auk, he urges, "Poof! go high!"

He offers Baba, still covered by the wig, as an item "for the truly adventurous," an "unknown object," an "it." The crowd bids excitedly, and "it" is knocked down for a hundred. Sellem snatches off the wig, and Baba finishes singing the very word, "never," which in the previous scene the wig had cut off. Seeing the staring crowd, she orders it out of her house (to her rage aria of the previous scene). But through the window, distracting her and everyone else, come the voices of Tom and Shadow in a street cry, "old wives for sale."

Anne hurries to the window as Baba remarks, "the milk-maid haunts me." But accepting her position, she calls Anne to her. Sellem suggests the two ladies leave, but the crowd insists "a scene like this is better than a sale."

Baba tells Anne, as the crowd comments, "You love him, seek to set **solo with chorus** him right. . . . I know he still loves you . . . so find him, and his man beware! . . . I can tell who in that pair is poisoned victim and who snake!" When Anne asks, "But where shall you . . . ?" Baba interrupts gently. "A gifted lady never need have fear. I shall go back and grace the stage." The crowd murmurs its approval as Sellem despondently declares, "the auction ends."

Through the window in a street song come the voices of Tom and **street song and stretto** Shadow: "If boys had wings and girls had stings. . . ." All urge Anne to hurry, and she runs out. Baba has the last word. To Sellem and the crowd, cowed by her aplomb, she orders: "You! Summon my carriage! Out of my way! The next time you see Baba, you shall pay!"

SCENE 2 (19 min.)

A churchyard on a starless night. Tombs and a newly dug, open grave. Behind it, leaning against a stone, the sexton's spade.

After a solemn prelude (2 min.) Tom and Shadow enter, the former out of breath and the latter carrying a small black bag.

Tom shivers: "how dark," and "there's something, Shadow, in your face that fills my soul with fear!" Shadow, however, feels jolly and to the street song reminds Tom that "a year and a day have passed away . . . and (I) now my wages claim." When Tom pleads poverty, Shadow announces harshly " 'tis not your money but your soul which I this night require." He urges Tom to recognize "Whom, Fool! you chose to hire!" He points to the grave and from his bag takes weapons of suicide for Tom to choose. "Tom Rakewell's race is run." Tom despairs while Shadow chortles. A clock begins to strike midnight, Tom cries out "Have mercy on me, Heaven," and Shadow with a gesture stops the clock three strokes short of midnight.

Sure of his prey and eager to add an extra twist of torment, Shadow offers to cut cards for Tom's soul. "If you can name them [three cards], you are free. If not . . ." he points to the instruments of death, and Tom agrees.

(The card game is set entirely to harpsichord solo. For this Stravinsky has been both praised and criticized. Certainly he succeeded in giving the scene an atmosphere entirely of its own. Did he, by his austerity, sacrifice too much in color and volume? In an opera house is the sound too dry, monotonous and thin?)

Shadow shuffles, cuts and, when Tom hesitates, mockingly suggests that he think of Anne. Tom names "the Queen of Hearts," and wins. The clock sounds the tenth stroke of midnight.

Shadow shuffles, cuts again and, when Tom hesitates, suggests that he rely on Fortune. The sexton's spade falls with a clatter causing Tom to curse, "the deuce!" He names "the two of spades," and wins. The clock sounds the eleventh stroke of midnight.

Shadow now in anger shuffles, picks up the discarded Queen of Hearts from the ground, and cuts to it. This time Shadow gives no hint, and Tom in agony cries out "Return O love—" From offstage Anne's voice answers, repeating a line of her aria when she was about to enter Tom's house to save him (Act II, Scene 2): "A love that is sworn before Thee can plunder hell of its prey."

"I wish for nothing else," speaks Tom (meaning Anne's love, which he always had), and names "the Queen of Hearts, again." As the clock sounds the final stroke of midnight, Tom is saved and sinks senseless to the ground.

In fury and to full orchestra Shadow curses himself, for "my own delay lost me my prey." He has the right, however, to some wages from Tom's sins and with a gesture, before sinking into the ground, declares "Henceforth be thou insane!"

Blackout, followed by dawn. It is spring. The open grave is now a green mound upon which Tom sits smiling, putting grass on his head and singing to himself in a childlike voice. The tune is the street song now orchestrated to suggest madness.

SCENE 3 (21 min.)

The madhouse at Bedlam. Tom stands facing a chorus of the mad, who include a blind man with a broken fiddle, a crippled soldier, a man with a telescope and three old hags.

Tom urges the mad to prepare, for "Venus, queen of Love, will visit her unworthy Adonis." But they are scornful: "Madmen's words are all untrue; she will never come to you. Madness cancels every vow; she will never keep it now." Tom cries, "Come quickly, Venus, or I die," and sits with his face in his hands while the mad mock him with a grotesque minuet.

At the sound of the keeper's key they scatter, and the keeper leads in Anne. She will do better, he explains, to humor the madman's fancy and, left alone with Tom, she addresses him as Adonis.

Kneeling before her he begs forgiveness, which granted, they sing of their love. Soon exhausted by the excitement, he requests a lullaby, **lullaby** and she begins a simple song in three verses which gradually draws all the mad from their cells.

At its end her father enters to take her home. To the sleeping Tom she promises, "my vow holds forever" and bids him "goodbye." (Some persons feel that Stravinsky and his librettists should have ended here; what follows is already implicit.)

Before leaving, Anne and Trulove have a short duet: she promises Tom never to forget and Trulove confesses he is moved. Tom wakes, finds himself alone, and raves that the mad have stolen his Venus. They say "no one has been here." Tom feels "the chill of death's approaching wing," asks his fellows to "weep for Adonis whom Venus loved," and dies. In a final chorus the mad suspect his illusion and "mourn for Adonis."

EPILOGUE (3 min.)

The curtain descends and before it step Anne, Baba, Tom, Shadow and Trulove to sing the ancient moral: For idle hands and minds, the Devil will find work to do—for you and you.

WOZZECK

Opera in three acts, each with five scenes. World premiere, Berlin, Dec. 14, 1925; American prem., Philadelphia, March 19, 1931; British concert prem., London, March 14, 1934; stage prem., Covent Garden, London, Jan. 22, 1952. Music by Alban Berg with a text derived by him from the fragments of an unfinished play by Georg Büchner, 1813–37.

PRINCIPAL CHARACTERS

Franz Wozzeck, a soldier	baritone
Marie, his common-law wife	soprano
Andres, a soldier	tenor
The Captain	tenor buffo
The Doctor	bass buffo
The Drum-Major	heldentenor

Berg did not specify in the score a time and place for the action. Büchner, however, based his drama on a murder done in Leipzig in 1821, and stage designers often follow that lead.

For most persons the best approach to *Wozzeck* in performance is through its drama, taking it as a play with incidental music. Berg himself so advised: "However thorough one's knowledge of the opera's musical forms . . . from the curtain's rise until its final fall no one in the audience should think of the various Fugues, Inventions, Suite and Sonata movements, Variations and Passacaglias. Everyone should be filled only by the idea of the opera, an idea that far transcends the individual fate of Wozzeck."

That idea emerges from the story. Wozzeck, a common soldier, is driven by poverty. Unable to afford the fees to marry, he can support his common-law wife and their child only by constant work in off-duty hours. He gathers firewood, shaves the Captain and sells his body for experiments to a crazy doctor. Always on the run, he is exhausted; superstitious and ignorant, he has terrifying hallucinations.

His one pleasure and firmest grip on sanity is his love for Marie and their child. When she, as much from despair as lust, responds to a Drum-Major's sexual advances, Wozzeck is taunted by the Captain and the Doctor and later physically beaten by the Drum-Major. He turns to violence, kills Marie and soon after, in a state of semiconsciousness, drowns himself. The Captain and the Doctor hear him drowning but do nothing to save him.

The child survives. His playmates tell him that his mother is dead and then run off to look at her corpse. Left alone, the child follows them.

The religiously minded may see in the story a man, with a divine spark in him, whom we—society—crucify; the politically minded, an example of class exploitation; the psychologically minded, evidence that sexual jealousy when aggravated ends in violence. But whatever the point of view the focus is that we—society—are accountable for each other and are judged in Wozzeck's case to be responsible for his fate.

The story is told in fifteen short scenes written in the style of German Expressionist theatre. Expressionism, which flourished in the first quarter of the century and which Büchner anticipated by almost a hundred years, attempted to present truth about man's inner life by emphasizing the unseen or subconscious and by stressing the evocative or symbolic detail. It originated partly in reaction to Naturalism, which approached truth by piling up details of external reality and environment. In Expressionist theatre very little is natural or real. The characters are constantly pushed toward caricature as their costumes, voices or words are exaggerated in order to express some inner reality.

In *Wozzeck* the most natural character is Marie, though even she, in her religiosity in the Bible scene, is overdrawn. The child with only the words, "Hop, Hop," is incredibly wide-eyed, white-faced and silent, and Wozzeck, a passive antihero, verges on insanity. The other chief characters are caricatures: the Captain, fussy, neurotic, easily confused and terrified of dying; the Doctor, obsessed with his plan to achieve fame by his experiments with Wozzeck's diet; and the Drum-Major, male sexuality at its most complacent.

The music is atonal, a style characterized by large and seemingly random skips in pitch. It is the extreme opposite of Italian nineteenth-century operatic style, which favored stepwise progressions of pitch as the best means of achieving a singable vocal line.

Berg, however, was not interested in singing in the usual sense and approaches it rarely, chiefly in set pieces such as a soldier's song or Marie's lullaby or Bible scene. Elsewhere he uses four gradations of speaking as it approaches singing: speaking to little or no musical accompaniment, or *parlando;* speaking above a definite musical commentary, or *melodramma;* singing in strict rhythm and at an indicated pitch but in a speaking tone, or *Sprechstimme;* and a style of his own invention halfway between *Sprechstimme* and normal singing. The distinction between the last two is very subtle and generally lost in performance. The effect overall is of an opera declaimed rather than sung.

The musical style seems perfectly adapted to the story and its expressionistic presentation, and the opera succeeds with many people who in the concert hall find atonal music boring. Much of that success lies in Berg's skillful adaptation of Büchner's play, particularly in his decision to keep the opera short, only eighty-nine minutes.

The orchestra is large, with extra woodwinds and percussion, but except for the interludes connecting the scenes, is used sparingly. Berg wants the words understood.

Composing in an atonal style and without the traditional sense of harmonic cadence, he has given the opera musical coherence by setting each scene in a different musical form. The Doctor with his obsession, for example, is presented to a Passacaglia, the outstanding feature of which is a fixed, constantly recurring theme. These musical forms are often difficult to follow even with a score in hand, and at a performance, as Berg suggested, can be ignored. But they do exist, and in their beginnings and endings help to give the scenes a sense of start and finish.

To interest people in his opera, Berg drew a concert suite from it, the *Drei Bruchstücke* or *Three Fragments from Wozzeck* (19 min., premiere at Frankfurt, June 15, 1924). It concentrates on the most accessible character, Marie, and the fragments follow their sequence in the opera: (1) musical interlude following Act I, Scene 2, and all of Scene 3, containing Marie's lullaby; (2) Act III, Scene 1, Marie's Bible scene; (3)

Act III, Scene 4, after Wozzeck has drowned himself, continuing through the interlude, and all of Scene 5. Except for very minor alterations the music is just as in the opera.

ACT I (33.5 min.)

(This act in its first four scenes shows Wozzeck in relation to the characters most important to him, the Captain, Marie and the Doctor, and also exhibits his incipient insanity. The fifth scene, Marie and the Drum-Major, sparks the action.)

SCENE 1 (8 min.)

The Captain's room. Early morning. Wozzeck is shaving the Captain.

The Captain and Wozzeck. "Langsam, Wozzeck, langsam!" (slowly), begs the Captain. What can either do with the time saved by hurrying? Wozzeck, he estimates, will live another thirty years, "dreisig Jahre." What will he do with the time? "Jawohl, Herr Hauptmann!" (Yes, indeed, Herr Captain), says Wozzeck.

The Captain considers the relation of an instant, "Augenblick," to eternity, but confesses that the problem makes him "melancholisch" (melancholic). "Jawohl, Herr Hauptmann!" says Wozzeck.

Remarking that a worthy man, "ein guter Mensch," takes his time, the Captain shifts to the weather and soon is excitedly comparing the wind to a mouse. Shifting again, he observes that although Wozzeck is "ein guter Mensch," he lacks any moral sense, "Moral," for he has fathered an illegitimate child.

The Lord will not spurn the boy, Wozzeck replies, for the Lord said, "Suffer the children to come to me." Furious, the Captain interrupts but then, confused about what was meant, falls silent.

"Wir arme Leut!" (We poor workers), Wozzeck explains, always need "Geld" (money). Morality is for the rich. Even in heaven, no doubt, the poor will work as thunder-makers.

The discussion has disturbed the Captain, and he hastens to assure Wozzeck that despite the unblessed child he is "ein guter Mensch." Dismissing Wozzeck, the Captain closes the scene, as he began it, by urging Wozzeck to go slowly, "langsam."

MUSICAL LINK (1 min.)

SCENE 2 (5 min.)

An open field outside the town. Late afternoon. Andres and Wozzeck are cutting firewood. (In this scene most of Wozzeck's lines are in *Sprechstimme,* in contrast to the previous scene, which had none.)
Andres and Wozzeck. The strange colors of sunset have unsettled Wozzeck. "Du" (you), he calls to Andres, "der Platz ist verflucht!" (the place is cursed). Andres counters with a hunting song.

"Der Platz is verflucht!" Wozzeck insists. When Andres continues singing, Wozzeck asks him to be "Still" (quiet). Hearing something, he warns, "Das waren die Freimaurer!" (that was the Freemasons). Andres nervously urges him, "Sing lieber mit" (Sing it with me).

Wozzeck, however, stamps the ground. It is hollow. "Es schwankt" (it quakes). As he starts to run, Andres holds him. "He, bist Du toll?" (hey, are you mad). The sun sets, and Wozzeck sees a fire, "ein Feuer," leaping from the earth toward heaven. Andres, feigning calmness, decides it is time to go.

MUSICAL LINK (1 min.)

SCENE 3 (8 min.)

Marie's room. Evening. Marie and the child are at the window watching the military band, led by the Drum-Major.
Marie and her neighbor Margret. Marie admires the Drum-Major, who nods to her. Marie's pleasure excites Margret to criticism, and Marie slams the window in her face, cutting off the band.
Marie and the child. She rocks him while singing, "Eia popeia" **lullaby** (hushabye). Then asks herself, "Mädel, was fangst Du jetzt an?" (Maiden, what can be done now), before returning to "Eia popeia." When the child is asleep, she puts him to bed.
Marie and Wozzeck. He cannot stay. He must report to the barracks. She is upset by his talk of strange shapes in the heaven. Trying to calm him, she shows him "Dein Bub" (your boy), but his mind is elsewhere, and he runs off.
Marie. Alone, with darkness falling, she gives way to Wozzeck's fears.

In a sudden burst of anguish she cries, "Ach! Wir arme Leut" (Ah, we poor workers), and rushes out the door.

MUSICAL LINK (30 sec.)

——

SCENE 4 (6.5 min.)

The Doctor's Study. A sunny afternoon.
The Doctor and Wozzeck. The Doctor complains that Wozzeck is not following the prescribed routine, and when Wozzeck talks of Nature's needs, "Die Natur," the Doctor explodes in anger. He rhapsodizes on the revolution, "Revolution," his experiments will effect in medicine.

Wozzeck tries to calm him by telling of the strange shapes he sees. Recalling them, however, also causes Wozzeck to think of Marie. "Ach, ach, Marie!" he sighs, "wenn Alles dunkel is" (when all is dark). The Doctor concludes that Wozzeck has an aberration, "aberatio," and is increasingly excited about its medical possibilities even as Wozzeck grows more despondent, "Ach, Marie!"

The Doctor urges Wozzeck to follow the diet and to cultivate his hallucinations, "Oh, my fame," the Doctor cries in ecstasy. "I will be immortal"—"unsterblich." Suddenly quite calm, he says, "Wozzeck, show me your tongue." (To emphasize the scene's absurdity Berg asks that the curtain be dropped quickly and, half-down, slowly.)

MUSICAL LINK (1 min.)

——

SCENE 5 (2.5 min.)

Street before Marie's house. Dusk.
Marie and the Drum-Major. He struts; she admires. He proposes that they bed, and she at first refuses, then agrees. "Have your way! It is all the same!" (Berg wants the stage to stand empty for several bars before the curtain slowly falls.)

Vocabulary, Act I

langsam, Wozzeck . . .	LAHNG.zahm voht.zek	slowly, Wozzeck
dreisig Jahre	DRY.sik YAHR.eh	thirty years
Jawohl, Herr Hauptmann	yah.vohl hairr . . .	Yes, Sir, Herr Captain

Vocabulary, Act I (continued)

Augenblick	OW.gen.blick	instant
melancholisch	may.lahn.col.ish	melancholic
ein guter Mensch	ine goot.er Mensh	a good man
Moral	mor.ahl	moral sense
wir arme Leut	veer ahrm.eh LOYT	we poor working people
Geld	gelt	money

Scene 2

Du, der Platz ist verflucht	doo, der plahtts ist fair.FLOOKT	you, this place is cursed
still	shtill	quiet
Das waren die Freimaurer	dass vahr.en dee FRY.mow.er	that was the Freemasons
sing lieber mit	sing LEEB.er mit	sing, friend, with me
es schwankt	ess shvahnkt	it quakes
He, bist Du toll	hey, bist doo tol	hey, are you mad
ein Feuer	ine FOY.er	a fire

Scene 3

eia popeia	eye.yah pop.EE.yah	hushabye
Mädel, was fangst Du jetzt an	MAID.el, vahss fahngst doo yetst ahn	Maiden, what can be done now
dein Bub	dine boob	your boy
Ach, wir arme Leut	veer ahrm.eh LOYT.eh	ah, we poor workers

Scene 4

die Natur	dee nah.TOOR	the Nature
revolution	reh.voh.LOO.shon	revolution
wenn Alles dunkel is	ven AHL.es DOON.kel is	when all is dark
aberatio	ah.ber.ah.t'yo	aberration
unsterblich	OON.shtairp.lik	immortal

ACT II (32.5 min.)
———

SCENE 1 (5 min.)

Marie's room. Sunny morning. She sits with the child half-asleep in her lap. In a piece of broken mirror she admires two earrings given her by the Drum-Major.

Marie and the child. When the child stirs, she urges him to sleep (as if quelling her conscience). When he stirs again, she frightens him with a song. "Mädel" (maiden), shut the window tight lest you be stolen to "Zigeunerland" (gypsyland). When the child continues restless, she grows angry and flashes the mirror in his eyes, saying the glare will blind him if he does not shut his eyes and sleep.

Marie and Wozzeck. He has entered behind her. "Was hast da?" (What's that there), he asks, pointing at the earrings. "Nix" (nothing), she replies. Something glitters under your fingers, he insists. She claims to have found the earrings, but he remarks that he has never found such things—two together.

When she grows angry, he soothes her and turns to the child. Noticing perspiration on the boy's brow, he sighs "Wir arme Leut!" (We poor working people). In a quiet voice, before leaving, he gives her the money he received from the Captain and the Doctor.

After he has gone, Marie says, "Ich bin doch ein schlect Mensch" (I am just a bad lot). In the world, she concludes, everything goes to the devil, man, woman and child. (Quick curtain)

MUSICAL LINK (1 min.)

SCENE 2 (9 min.)

A street. Daytime. The Captain, the Doctor, later Wozzeck. (This scene, at least until the entrance of Wozzeck, is generally played in the broadest caricature.)

The Captain and the Doctor. The Captain tries to stop the Doctor: whither so hasty, "wohin so eilig," old Gravedigger? To which the Doctor replies, whither so slowly, "wohin so langsam," old Spit-and-Polish? A worthy man, "ein guter Mensch," urges the Captain, takes his time. Time presses, "pressiert," snaps the Doctor repeatedly. But with the Captain plucking his sleeve he is forced to stop.

The Doctor's revenge is to describe a girl who sickened of "cancer uteri" and in four weeks was dead. "Oh, oh, oh," gasps the Captain. The Doctor, citing aloud the Captain's thick neck and bloated features, predicts for him "apoplexia cerebri" with paralysis. It will provide an opportunity for experimenting, "Experimente."

The Captain can hardly stand for fear. He sees his own funeral and hears the mourners saying that he was "ein guter Mensch."

The Captain, Doctor and Wozzeck. Wozzeck hurries past, and the

Doctor stops him. The Captain complains that Wozzeck runs as if all the university professors were awaiting a shave. The Doctor turns the reference to soldiers, and the Captain slyly asks if Wozzeck has found a soldier's hair in his porridge. The Doctor asks if Wozzeck's wife is faithful.

"Was wollen Sie damit sagen, Herr Doktor?" (Why do you ask that question), says Wozzeck.

While the Captain and the Doctor snicker over their insinuations, Wozzeck grows increasingly upset. Suddenly he runs off, muttering that the man who hangs himself at least knows where he is, "Dann wüsste man, woran man ist!"

"Er ist ein Phänomen, dieser Wozzeck" (he is a phenomenon, this Wozzeck), comments the Doctor. The Captain debates with himself over who needs "Courage" (courage), "ein guter Mensch" or, referring to Wozzeck, "nur ein Hundsfott" (only a scoundrel).

MUSICAL LINK (30 sec.)

SCENE 3 (1.5 min.)

The street before Marie's house. A grey day. Marie stands by her door. Wozzeck rushes up to her.

Marie and Wozzeck. He starts quietly but soon asks, while strutting like the Drum-Major, was it here in the street that you saw him? The street is public, she replies. Many people pass: "Einer nach dem andern" (one after the other). Losing his control he shrieks at her, You, with him! Angrily she retorts, what of it?

Wozzeck raises his hand to strike her but she cries: "Lieber ein Messer in dein Leib, als eine Hand auf mich" (better a knife in my heart, than a hand on me). My father, "mein Vater," never dared to strike me when I was little.

She enters the house, leaving Wozzeck staring after her. "Lieber ein Messer." he repeats, adding in a frightened whisper, "Der Mensch ist ein Abgrund" (Man is an abyss), and I am falling, falling.

MUSICAL LINK (1.5 min.)

SCENE 4 (8 min.)

Garden of an inn. Late evening. A crowd of young men, soldiers and servant girls. Marie, the Drum-Major, Wozzeck, Andres and an Idiot.

Two Apprentices. Both are drunk, and the efforts of one to give a speech amuses the crowd for a time. The gist of his remarks is "und meine Seele stinkt nach Branntewein" (and my soul stinks of brandywine).
The Dancing. The band strikes up, and among the dancers are Marie and the Drum-Major. As she turns, she happily cries "Immerzu" (on we go). Wozzeck, watching, imitates her. Everything, he cries, twists and turns in lechery. Unable to control himself, he is about to rush onto the floor when the dance ends and the people disperse. Wozzeck sits on a bench by himself.
The Chorus and Andres. The apprentices and soldiers start a hunting song with a refrain "halli, hallo." Andres interjects a verse of a folk song with the chorus responding "halli, hallo," and then he joins Wozzeck, sitting morosely alone. But Andres is quickly bored by Wozzeck's glum responses.
The Sermon. The apprentice who earlier attempted a speech now starts a sermon on God, Man and Vanity. But he soon grows confused and ends with his old refrain "und meine Seele stinkt nach Branntewein." He faints and is carried out as the chorus and Andres resume singing.
Idiot and Wozzeck. The Idiot approaches, saying "ich riech Blut" (I smell blood). "Blut?" asks Wozzeck, then repeats it firmly, "Blut! Blut!" All seems red before me, he cries; they all seem twisting . . . and then . . . rolling on top of each other.

MUSICAL LINK (1.5 min.)

———

SCENE 5 (4.5 min.)

The barracks. Night. A chorus of snoring soldiers as the curtain rises.
Wozzeck, Andres and the Drum-Major. Wozzeck, sleepless, sees Marie dancing and hears her cry of "immerzu." Andres urges him to sleep, and Wozzeck repeats parts of the Lord's Prayer—And lead us not into temptation—ending with "Amen."
The Drum-Major enters, drunk and boasting, "Ich bin ein Mann" (I am a man). He has had a woman. When Andres asks who, the Drum-Major refers the question to Wozzeck. Thrusting a bottle under Wozzeck's face, he demands that Wozzeck drink. Wozzeck refuses and whistles the phrase "und meine Seele stinkt nach Branntewein." The Drum-Major beats him to the floor, crying out, "Black and blue let

him whistle"—and leaves triumphantly. Andres sees that Wozzeck is bleeding but does nothing. Wozzeck sits on his bunk staring before him. Quoting Marie (Act II, Scene 3), he says quietly, "Einer nach dem Andern!" (one after the other).

Vocabulary, Act II

Scene 1

Mädel	MAID.el	maiden
Zigeunerland	tsee.GOYN.er.lahnt	gypsyland
was hast da	vahss hast dah	what's that there
nix	nix	nothing
wir arme Leut	veer ahrm.eh LOYT.eh	we poor working people
ich bin doch ein schlect Mensch	ik bin dok ine shlekt mensh	I am just a bad lot

Scene 2

wohin so eilig	voh.HIN so EYE.lik	whither so hasty
wohin so langsam	. . . LAHNG.zahm	whither so slowly
pressiert (said very fast)	press.EERT	(Time) presses
cancer uteri	cahn.ser oot.er.ee	cancer of the uterus
apoplexia cerebri	ah.poh.PLEX.yah SER.eh.bree	a stroke
Experimente	eck.pair.ee.men.teh	experimenting
was wollen Sie damit sagen, Herr Doktor	vahss VOLL.en see dah.MIT SAHG.en	why do you ask that question, Herr Doctor
Dann wüsste man, woran man ist	dahn vers.te mahn, voh.RAHN mahn ist.	then knows a man, where he is
er ist ein Phänomen, dieser Wozzeck	air ist ine fay.no. MEN deez.er . . .	he is a phenomenon, this Wozzeck
Courage	coo.rahj	courage
nur ein Hundsfott	noor ine hoonds.fott	only a scoundrel

Scene 3

einer nach dem andern	ine.er nach dem ahn.dern	one after the other
lieber ein Messer in dein Leib, als eine Hand auf mich	LEE.ber ine MESS.er in dine lipe, ahls ine hahnt owf mik	better a knife in the body than a hand on me
mein Vater	mine FAHT.er	my father
der Mensch ist ein Abgrund	der mensh ist ine AHP.groont	Man is an abyss

Vocabulary, Act II (continued)

Scene 4

und meine Seele stinkt nach Branntewein	oont my.nuh SAYL.eh shtinkt nahk BRAHN.teh.vine	and my soul stinks of brandywine
immerzu	IM.mer.tsoo	on we go
ich riech Blut	ik reek bloot	I smell blood

Scene 5

ich bin ein Mann	ik bin ine mahn	I am a man

ACT III (22 min.)

SCENE 1 (4 min.)

Marie's room. Night. Candlelight. Marie, alone with the child, is reading the Bible.

Marie. "And out of His mouth there came forth neither deceit nor falsehood." Overcome, she cries out, "Herr Gott, Herr Gott" (Lord **bible scene** God), look not on me. In the next passage the Lord forgives an adulterous woman. "Herr Gott," she cries.

When the child runs to embrace her, she pushes him away but quickly calls him back. She reads of a poor child without "Vater" or "Mutter" and recalls that "Der Franz ist nit kommen" (Franz has not yet come) today or yesterday.

She reads the story of Mary Magdalene, and the Lord's mercy to her namesake increases her sense of unworthiness. "Heiland" (Savior), she cries, have mercy on me. (Slow curtain)

MUSICAL LINK (1 min.)

SCENE 2 (4 min.)

Forest path by a pond. Dusk.

Marie and Wozzeck. She is eager to be home, but he dawdles. They sit on a bench. "Es ist still hier!" (it is quiet here), he says, "und so dunkel" (and so dark). How many years have they known each other? She replies, "Zu Pfingsten drei Jahre" (on Whitsuntide three years).

He taunts her on her beauty. Is she also "gut" (good) "und treu" (and faithful)? He leans toward her and feels her shiver. "Der Nachttau fällt" (the nightdew falls), she says. Whispering to himself, he promises that she will not feel the morning's cold. "Was sagst Du da?" (What are you saying), she asks. "Nix" (nothing).

There is a long pause, ended by Marie: "Wie der Mond rot aufgeht!" (how the moon rises red). Like a bloodred iron, observes Wozzeck, taking out his knife. He kills her, "todt" (dead), and throws the knife into the pond.

MUSICAL LINK (1 min.)

(This link consists only of two orchestral crescendi separated by drum beats. Though both are on the note B, they sound different because the swelling is differently scored. In the first the instruments, besides slowly increasing their volume, enter one after another and all on the same note, the B below middle C. In the second all start at the same time with a tremolo on B in four octaves and slowly increase their volume. To many ears, the first crescendo sounds more intense, perhaps because the constant entry of new instruments with new color gives it a noticeable pulse.)

SCENE 3 (2.5 min.)

A tavern, dimly lit. Night.
Wozzeck, Margret and others. Wozzeck attempts to forget his crime by dancing. But "Margret, du bist so heiss" (you are so hot!). He suggests that she sing instead, but her song does not please him. Suddenly she asks, "Aber was hast Du an der Hand?" (but what have you on your hand). "Ich? Ich? (me, me), asks Wozzeck. "Rot! Blut!" (red blood), she insists and, as Wozzeck rushes out, everyone takes up her cry.

MUSICAL LINK (30 sec.)

SCENE 4 (4 min.)

The forest path by the pond. Moonlight. Wozzeck, later the Captain and the Doctor.
Wozzeck. Upset by Margret, he has returned to find the knife and dispose of it. "Das Messer? Wo ist das Messer?" (the knife, where is the knife). But the place and darkness unbalance him further. "Still! Alles

still und tot" (quiet, all is quiet and dead). Suddenly he shouts "Mörder" (murderer); then realizes that it was he who called.

Still searching, he stumbles on Marie's body and remarks that the crimson cord around her neck was well earned, like her earrings. Again he involuntarily cries "Mörder! Mörder!"

Finding the knife in shallow water, he throws it farther out. But now he thinks the moon betrays him: "Der Mond is blutig" (the moon is bloody). The knife ("das Messer") is still too close to shore. Wading deeper to recover it, he sees blood on himself: "Ich bin blutig" (I am bloody). "Da ein Fleck" (there is a spot), "und noch einer" (and yet another). "Weh" (woe). He cannot clean himself, for even "das Wasser ist Blut . . . Blut" (the water is blood). Walking in farther, he drowns.

The Captain and the Doctor. Passing by, they hear Wozzeck drowning. The Captain is unnerved by the sound; the Doctor, intrigued. The Captain wants to hurry away; the Doctor, to listen: "Stiller" (it grows quieter), "jetzt ganz still" (and now is entirely quiet). The Captain hurries the Doctor away.

MUSICAL LINK (3 min.)

(This is the longest of the opera's twelve links, or interludes, and the only one in which Berg introduces music not heard elsewhere. For that reason it is often said to be his personal song of compassion for Wozzeck.)

SCENE 5 (2 min.)

Before Marie's house. Bright morning. Sunshine. Children at play. Marie's child has a hobbyhorse.

The children sing "Ringel, Ringel, Rosencrantz" and "all fall down!" They are interrupted by others. After some whispering one calls to Marie's child, "Du! Dein Mutter ist tot!" (You, your mother is dead). The boy continues with his hobbyhorse, "Hop, Hop!" The others run off to the pond to see the corpse. Left alone, the child follows them.

Vocabulary, Act III

Scene 1

Herr Gott	hairr got	Lord God
Vater . . . Mutter	FAHT.er . . .	father . . . mother
	MOOT.er	

Vocabulary, Act III (continued)

der Franz ist nit kommen	der . . . ist nit KOM.en	Franz has not yet come
Heiland	HY.lahnt	Savior

Scene 2

's ist still hier	's ist shtill heer	it is quiet here
und so dunkel	oont so DOONG.kel	and so dark
zu Pfingsten drei Jahre	tsoo PFING.sten dry YAHR.eh	on Whitsuntide three years
gut . . . und treu	goot . . . oont troy	good . . . and faithful
der Nachtau fällt	der NACHT.tow felt	the nightdew falls
was sagst Du da	vahs sahgst doo dah	what are you saying
nix	nix	nothing
wie der Mond rot aufgeht	vee der mohnt roht OWF.gayt	how the moon rises red
todt	toht	dead

Scene 3

du bist so heiss	doo bist so hice	you are so hot
aber was hast Du an der Hand	AH.ber vahs hast doo ahn der hahnt	but what have you on the hand
ich . . . ich	ik . . . ik	me . . . me
rot . . . blut	roht . . . bloot	red . . . blood

Scene 4

wo ist das Messer	woh ist duss MESS.er	where is the knife
alles still und tot	AHL.es shtill oont toht	all is quiet and dead
Mörder	MER.der	murderer
der Mond is blutig	der mohnt ist BLOOT.ik	the moon is bloody
ich bin blutig	ik bin BLOOT.ik	I am bloody
da ein Fleck	dah ine flek	there is a spot
und noch einer	oont nok INE.er	and yet another
weh	vay	woe
das Wasser is Blut	dahs VAHSS.er . . .	the water is blood
stiller	SHTILL.er	(it grows) quieter
jetzt ganz still	yetst gahnts shtill	now entirely quiet

Scene 5

Du, dein Mutter ist tot	doo, dine MOOT.er ist toht	You, your mother is dead

LULU

Opera in three acts (the last incomplete). World premiere, Zurich, June 2, 1937; American prem., Santa Fe, Aug. 7, 1963. Music by Alban Berg; text by Berg based on two tragedies by Frank Wedekind, *Erdgeist* (*Earth Spirit*), first published in 1895, and *Die Büchse der Pandora* (*Pandora's Box*), 1904.*

PRINCIPAL CHARACTERS

Animal Trainer (the Prologue)	bass
Lulu	soprano
Walter, the Painter	tenor
Dr. Ludwig Schön, newspaper editor	baritone
Alwa, his son, playwright	tenor
Schigolch, an old man	bass
Countess Geschwitz	mezzo-soprano

Berg does not specify the time and place of the opera's action, nor did Wedekind in his plays. The details of the latter, however, set the action in Vienna, Paris and London at the turn of the century.

Wedekind originally conceived the two plays as a single five-act drama. Dividing it, he created the four-act *Erdgeist* and the three-act *Büchse der Pandora,* so that the former at least might be publicly performed. The latter at the time was considered offensive because its most sympathetic character was a lesbian and another, Jack the Ripper, murdered for sexual pleasure. Not until after World War I was *Die Büchse der Pandora* publicly performed. Berg, however, saw a private production in 1905.

The plays were very much in the avant-garde of Viennese thought at the turn of the century. It was a time when the nineteenth-century romantic view of life, with its belief in an individual's dignity, worth and power, was crumbling. For many it would soon dissolve altogether in the realities of World War I. Hastening its end were the theoretical teachings of the new sciences, particularly chemistry, and also the theories of Freud, who had delivered the third great blow to man's pride. First Copernicus had displaced him from the center of the universe; then Darwin had undermined his claim to a unique position in

---

*Opera completed by Friedrich Cerha and presented as a world premiere at the Opéra, Paris, on Feb. 24, 1979; American prem. of this "complete" version, Santa Fe, July 28, 1979.

the animal world; and finally Freud had shown that he was not master of his mind, that he possessed a subconscious over which he had no control, and which thought a great deal of the time about sex. Small wonder some writers portrayed man as a soulless, will-less animal driven by instincts he could neither understand nor control.

Such a character is Wedekind's Lulu. She passes through the plays like an atom of some unstable chemical element: L^uL^u. She personifies female sex, and her particular chemical property is the ability to attract other atoms, oppositely charged, to fuse with her. It is all impersonal, uncontrolled and without responsibility.

This is a point of view, a thesis about life, and not everyone accepts it. A great humanist of the period, E. M. Forster, emphatically denied it when he wrote in his novel *Howards End,* "Far more mysterious than the call of sex to sex is the tenderness we throw into that call; far wider is the gulf between us and the farmyard than between the farmyard and the garbage that nourishes it." There is none of Forster's tenderness in Lulu; her call is all chemical.

But to announce a thesis from the stage is to give a sermon; a play should demonstrate it through action, through a conflict in which the thesis triumphs. To do this, Wedekind created Dr. Ludwig Schön, who tries to resist Lulu's call, to continue a normal life in the world of business, and even to marry someone other than Lulu. At first he seems likely to succeed. As the play and opera open, he has saved himself by marrying Lulu to a medical specialist, Dr. Goll. But in the first scene Dr. Goll dies of a heart attack when he discovers Lulu in the arms of Walter, a portrait painter. Again Dr. Schön saves himself, by marrying Lulu to Walter. But in the second scene Walter kills himself when he realizes the extent of Lulu's couplings. This time Lulu triumphs over Dr. Schön. She humiliates him, marries him and finally murders him. Just before the end, with a touch of Forster's vision, he looks at his soiled house and life and mutters, "the filth, the filth." But she sees none of that. Even as Dr. Schön dies, she turns her call to his son, Alwa.

This saga of Dr. Schön forms Wedekind's first play, *Erdgeist,* which Berg used for the first four of the five scenes that, together with a prologue and epilogue, make up the unfinished opera. Wedekind's second play, *Die Büchse der Pandora,* in its first act carries Lulu to triumph over Alwa, in its second to a lengthy scene of high life in Paris, and in its last to her death as a whore in London, where she mistakenly tries to fuse with Jack the Ripper, an atom with the wrong chemical properties.

Of this second play Berg completed only the first act, Lulu's conquest of Alwa, her final triumph over Dr. Schön. For a concert suite, however, Berg had orchestrated her death scene, and most stage productions pantomime Lulu's death to this music as an epilogue or third act.

Just why Berg failed to complete the opera is not known. He seems to have had time before his death, and he had done most of the work. The missing scenes, however, may be no artistic loss. For many persons, the existing opera makes its point clearly, and more might be too much. And, most important, with the death of Dr. Schön the conflict has been taken out of the drama. The potentially tragic figure has been removed.

Therein lies a crucial difference between *Lulu* and Berg's other opera, *Wozzeck*. In *Wozzeck* the hero suffers, and the audience is made to feel in part responsible for his suffering. The opera's ending is cathartic. Lulu, on the other hand, never suffers, and the opera's thesis presupposes that she cannot. The bond between her and the audience is more of interest than sympathy. Many may be curious to see how she dies, but few weep for her.

The music is in serial, twelve-tone style, with the basic series freely treated. Berg did not confine himself to it but derived from it other series, even changing the sequence of notes, so that he recognized almost no limitation on how he could develop the music.

The opera's sound is unique and appropriate. To a standard small orchestra, Berg added three instruments associated with the period of the opera's thesis—alto saxophone, vibraphone and piano—all instruments used in jazz bands and here given prominence. For example, early in the opera, when Lulu insists she is only "an animal," the vibraphone with its unearthly rattle punctuates her remark. Later it rattles again after Dr. Schön stutters, "the filth, the filth." And the saxophone throbs horribly as Lulu asks Alwa if they are not lying on the sofa where his father died. The instruments spread their color and timbre throughout the opera. The overall sound frequently is harsh and jagged; often with the vibraphone, it seems strangely hollow and ominous, and with the saxophone deliberately vulgar.

Of melody in the usual sense, there is none. Yet Lulu has a little song with a recognizable beginning and end; so does the Painter; and Lulu has a love duet with both the Painter and with Alwa. The usual forms of opera are present, helping to define the action.

In addition, Berg uses themes that recur. The most important appears first when Lulu is still married to the Painter. She is talking with Dr. Schön, who angrily states that they must never meet except in the presence of her husband. At the word "husband" Lulu insists that Dr. Schön is her true husband—and the theme sounds. Berg brings it back at the opera's most crucial moments: at the close of Act I, as Dr. Schön capitulates to Lulu, saying "Now comes the execution"; toward the close of the next scene, as Dr. Schön dies; and finally at the end of the opera, when Lulu dies. Aurally, it resembles Wagner's theme opening the Prelude to *Tristan and Isolde* and might be called the Love-Death motif.

The concert suite, or *Lulu Symphony* (34 min.), composed to stir interest in the opera, consists of five movements, with two requiring a soprano.

1. Rondo: Andante and Hymn (drawn from duet Lulu-Alwa, II, 1, and end of II, 2—15 min.)
2. Ostinato: Allegro (interlude, II, 1-2—3.5 min.)
3. Lied der Lulu: Comodo (II, 1, to be sung—3 min.)
4. Variations: Andante (interlude, III, 1-2—3.5 min.)
5. Adagio: Sostenato-Lento-Grave (interlude I, 2-3, and end of opera including arietta of Geschwitz—9 min.)

PROLOGUE (4 min.)

The dramatist, dressed as an Animal Trainer, summons the public to his Circus to see the animals perform—not the well-mannered, domesticated animals, but the wild animals. He produces one, the Serpent (it is Lulu in costume for the following scene), and implies that in the jungle of life it can defeat even the predatory tiger (music associated with Dr. Schön). He invites the audience into the tent.

ACT I (56 min.)

SCENE 1 (11 min.)

A large, poorly furnished studio. Walter is painting a portrait of Lulu dressed as Pierrot. Dr. Schön watches and, as the curtain rises, his son Alwa enters.

Alwa, Dr. Schön and others. After greetings, Alwa takes his father off to see a rehearsal of his new play.

Lulu and the Painter. He is attracted to her and stops working. She urges him to continue: her husband will arrive at any moment. When the Painter persists, she throws her shepherd's crook in his face and runs about the room. He pursues, and when she sinks to the ottoman, **love duet** he locks the door. (The music is a canon in three verses. She sings a tune that in the first verse he repeats, starting one measure behind her; in the second, a half-measure; in the third, a third—and they end together.) He is embracing her when in the midst of their cooing (vibraphone), her husband, a medical specialist, knocks furiously on the door.

The Medizinalrat. "Machen Sie auf!" (Open it up). Lulu and the Painter leap apart. "Machen Sie auf!" As the Painter starts for the door, the doctor breaks it open. "Ihr Hunde! Ihr . . ." (You, bastards! You . . .). Cut off by a stroke, he falls gasping to the floor.

Lulu shrinks away, but the Painter rushes to him. "Herr Me . . . , Herr Medizi . . . nalrat." He leaves momentarily to call a doctor.

Lulu. (Saxophone.) Alone, fearful, she approaches her husband. **song** "Pussi," she calls. He looks at my feet, she sings; his eyes follow me everywhere. She pokes him—"Pussi"—and concludes that he is dead: "He has abandoned me."

The Painter and Lulu. Returning, he feels for the doctor's pulse. "Now I am rich," says Lulu. The Painter is flustered by her indelicacy. Taking her hand he asks, can she speak the truth? Does she believe in a Creator? Has she a soul? Has she ever loved? To each she replies, "ich weiss es nicht" (I do not know). He tells her to dress.

The Painter. Alone, he speaks to the dead man. He would change
arioso   places. He was not meant for Lulu. "Wach auf!" (wake up)
I did not touch her. "Wach auf!" Kneeling beside the corpse, he prays
for the strength to bring happiness to Lulu.
She enters, half-dressed, asking to be buttoned up.

INTERLUDE (2 min.)

SCENE 2 (21 min.)

An elegant room in the house of the Painter, now married to Lulu
(whom he calls Eva). Her portrait as Pierrot hangs above the mantel.
Lulu and the Painter. He reads aloud (spoken) the morning's mail.
From Paris his agent reports that his picture of Lulu as "The Dancer"
has sold for 50,000 Marks. And an announcement: Counsellor
Heinrich Ritter von Zarnikow announces the engagement of his
daughter, Charlotte, to Dr. Ludwig Schön. We must congratulate the
doctor, he adds, but Lulu shows no interest.
They start a duet, in two verses divided by a ring on the doorbell. In
duet   the first the Painter confesses happily that Lulu has absorbed
his whole being. In the second, as he goes to the door, she sighs
"Du . . . Du" (you), but referring to the man at the door. The Painter
returns, reporting that it was only a beggar, and goes off to the studio
to work. She admits the beggar.
Lulu and Schigolch. (He is a frail, asthmatic old man. Like several
other characters still to appear, just what he represents is arguable.
Once he was Lulu's lover; now he is almost a father to her.) She gives
him money, and he surveys the room with approval. But when he
comments on her good fortune, she is apathetic. Gently he strokes her
knee, calling her "meine kleine Lulu" (my little Lulu). The name stirs
her. She has not been Lulu for years, not since she was a dancer. "Was
bist du?" (What are you), he asks. With a shudder (vibraphone) she
replies, "ein Tier" (an animal).
The doorbell rings, and as Schigolch departs, Lulu admits Dr.
Schön.
Lulu and Dr. Schön. If he were her husband, says Dr. Schön, he would
not allow her father in the house. But that is not what he came to say.
She must stop visiting him. If the Painter was not so innocent. . . . She interrupts. "Er sieht nichts" (he sees noth-

ing). . . . "Er ist blind, blind, blind" (he is blind). Dr. Schön points out: he has settled Lulu with a second husband and created a market for the man's paintings. Now he is to marry a respectable girl. He will not see Lulu again except in the presence of her husband. "Meines Mannes" (of my husband), Lulu says (as the orchestra swells with the Love-Death theme). If I belong to anyone on earth, I belong to you. Leave me out of it, he insists. Their voices draw the Painter from the studio, and Lulu leaves the men together.

Dr. Schön and the Painter. Dr. Schön suggests, at first indirectly, that the Painter should control Lulu more strictly. "Du hast eine halbe Million geheiratet . . ." (you have married half a million), he repeats. Gradually the Painter realizes that Lulu has had many lovers, that she married him only on Dr. Schön's command, that Dr. Schön is still her lover and is supporting him by creating a market for his pictures through newspaper publicity. "O Gott! O Gott! O Gott!" gasps the Painter and goes off—he says—to speak to Lulu. Almost immediately, however, "appalling groans" come from his room.

Dr. Schön, Lulu and Alwa. Dr. Schön bangs on the locked door, "Mach auf! Mach auf!" (open up). Lulu runs in. The doorbell rings: it is Alwa. "In Paris ist Revolution ausgebrochen" (in Paris revolution has broken out), he reports. At the paper no one knows what to write.

They burst open the door and find the Painter dead, his throat cut. "Ich kann nicht hier bleiben" (I cannot stay here), Lulu shrieks, and runs to her bedroom. As father and son discuss what can be done, she returns in an overcoat. Dr. Schön calls the police. While waiting for them he decides to publish an "Extrablatt" (special edition) on the revolution: it will obscure the scandal of the suicide. The doorbell rings. Wait, cries Lulu, and with her handkerchief wipes some blood off Dr. Schön's hand. "Es ist Deines Gatten Blut" (it is your husband's blood), he observes. It has left no trace, she says. "Ungeheuer!" (monster), he moans and admits the police.

INTERLUDE (3 min.)

SCENE 3 (15 min.)

A theatre dressing room; on the back wall, a poster with the picture of Lulu as Pierrot. Dr. Schön has arranged for her to dance in a panto-mime so that someone rich will see her and propose marriage. Behind a screen she is changing into her costume.

Lulu and Alwa. Will his father be in the theatre? Alwa doubts it and asks if the Prince, who loves her, will come backstage. Of course, replies Lulu, he is going to take me "nach Afrika!" (to Africa). "Nach Afrika . . ." Alwa repeats, breaking off as Lulu steps from behind the screen. "Wissen Sie noch" (do you still remember), she asks, the first time I came into your room? He remembers perfectly. A bell calls her to the stage.

Her essence (in the sound of the vibraphone) remains with him, and he muses (over the opening chords of Berg's *Wozzeck*) that one could write an interesting opera about her, "eine interessante Oper schreiben."

The Prince, Alwa, Lulu and later Dr. Schön. The Prince, an African explorer, enters and talks excitedly of marrying Lulu. Suddenly there is a commotion in the hall, and Lulu totters in, followed by an attendant and the theatre manager. She suffered "eine Ohnmacht" (a fainting fit) onstage. It was caused, she tells Alwa, by seeing Dr. Schön in the audience with his fiancée.

Dr. Schön enters, insisting to Lulu "Du wirst tanzen!" (You must dance). Lulu refuses: not before his fiancée. Then she relents; in five minutes, perhaps. Alwa and the manager leave to put on a substitute number, and Dr. Schön indicates to the others that he wants to be alone with Lulu.

He accuses her of using the play to revenge herself on him. She denies it. "Wirst Du jetzt tanzen?" (will you dance now), he asks. She agrees, and then in a childlike voice asks for one more minute. To make conversation he asks, "Was wollte der Prinz hier?" (what was the Prince doing here). He is taking me with him, "nach Afrika." "Nach Afrika?" exclaims Dr. Schön. You hoped, she reminds him, that someone would take me away. "Doch nicht nach Afrika!" (But not to Africa).

Slowly she dominates him, taunting him about his fiancée, urging him to leave. Soon he is helpless, so that when she orders him to leave, both know he cannot. She hands him writing paper. He pleads, "ich kann nicht schreiben" (I cannot write), but she dictates a letter to his fiancée: "Take back your promise. I cannot reconcile it with my conscience to make you share my terrible fate. . . ." "Du hast recht" (you are right), says Dr. Schön. She continues: "I am unworthy of your love. . . . I am writing to you in the presence of the woman who dominates me entirely. Forget me!—Doctor Ludwig Schön."

"O Gott!" he sobs.

"Postskriptum," she continues: "Do not try to save me."
"Jetzt—kommt—die Hinrichtung" (now comes the execution), he gasps and collapses.

Vocabulary, Act I

Scene 1

machen Sie auf	MAHK.en see owf	open it up
ihr Hunde	eer HOONT.eh	you bastards
Herr Medizinalrat	hair may.de.tseen. AHL.rat	Herr doctor
Pussi	poo.see	pussy
ich weiss es nicht	ik vice ess nikt	I don't know
Wach auf	vahk owf	wake up

Scene 2

du	doo	you
meine kleine Lulu	my.neh kly.nuh . . .	my little Lulu
was bist du	vahs bist doo	what are you
ein Tier	eyen teer	an animal
er sieht nichts	air seet nix	he sees nothing
er ist blind	air ist blinnt	he is blind
meines Mannes	my.nes MAHN.nes	my husband
du hast eine halbe Million geheiratet	doo hast eye.nuh hahlp.eh mill.YOWN ge.heye.rah.tet	you have married half a million
O Gott	oh got	oh God
mach auf	mahk owf	open up
in Paris ist Revolution ausgebrochen	een pah.REES ist reh.voh.loo.S'YOWN ows.geh.BROK.en	in Paris revolution has broken out
ich kann nicht hier bleiben	ik kahn nikt heer BLY.ben	I cannot remain here
Extrablatt	ECKS.trah.blahtt	special edition
es ist Deines Gatten Blut	ess ist dine.es GAHT.ten bloot	it is your husband's blood
Ungeheuer	OON.ge.hoy.er	monster

Scene 3

nach Afrika	nahk AH.free.kah	to Africa
wissen Sie noch	VISS.en see nok	do you still remember
eine interessante Oper schreiben	eye.neh in.ter.ess. AHNT.eh OH.per SHRY.ben	an interesting opera to write

Vocabulary, Act I (continued)

eine Ohnmacht	eye.neh OHN.mahkt	a fainting fit
du wirst tanzen	doo veerst TAHNT.sen	you must dance
wirst Du jetzt tanzen	veerst doo yetst . . .	will you now dance
was wollte der Prinz hier	vahs voll.teh der prints heer	what was the Prince doing here
doch nicht nach Afrika	dok nikt nahk . . .	still not to Africa
ich kann nicht schreiben	ik kan nikt SHRY.ben	I cannot write
du hast recht	doo hahst rekt	you are right
jetzt—kommt—die Hinrichtung	yetst—komt—dee HIN.rik.toong	now comes the execution

ACT II (52 min.)

SCENE 1 (25 min.)

A room in Dr. Schön's home, lavishly furnished in German Renaissance style. Lulu is at the peak of her career; on an easel her portrait as Pierrot stands triumphantly.

Lulu, Countess Geschwitz and Dr. Schön. Geschwitz talks of a ball to which only women will be admitted. She urges Lulu, who shows little interest, to come dressed as a man. Lulu accompanies her to the door.

Dr. Schön. Alone, he muses: "Das mein Lebensabend" (*this*—the evening of my life). "Die Pest im Haus" (plague in the house), "Dreissig Jahre Arbeit" (thirty years' work)—and *this* my family circle, my home. Nervously he wonders who is listening, lurking in the curtains, behind the shutters. Pulling out a revolver, he investigates. Madness, he says, has seized him and he mutters, "Der Schmutz . . . der Schmutz" (the filth). Hearing Lulu's step, he hides the gun.

Dr. Schön and Lulu. She suggests that he stay home from work and wheedles him into the bedroom. Geschwitz, sneaking in, hides behind the fire screen. (The mixture of farce and tragedy in what follows and in the subsequent scene requires extraordinary acting, particularly as from here to the opera's end the number of loose ends and ambiguities steadily increase. It is generally true that about here Berg begins to lose part of his audience.)

Schigolch, Rodrigo (the Athlete) and a Schoolboy. They enter, making themselves at home. Like Geschwitz, each in his way loves Lulu. The Schoolboy is all devotion and has a poem to read to her. The Athlete is mindless body, and alternately a bully or a coward. Schigolch is passion remembered. Lulu enters. Dr. Schön, she says, has gone to the stock exchange. She basks in their adulation until the butler announces Dr. Alwa Schön and they all rush to hide—behind the curtain, under the table and up the stair.

Lulu and Alwa. He starts talking of the theatre, but she diverts him to her dress. As the butler prepares to serve dinner, Lulu tries to seduce Alwa, who resists. Spying from the gallery, Dr. Schön gasps, "mein eigener Sohn?" (my own son). The butler, overcome by lust for Lulu, has difficulty serving, and Dr. Schön remarks, "Der also auch" (that one as well). Alwa, weakening, takes Lulu's hand and calls her Mignon. "Liebst Du mich denn?" (do you love me, then), she asks. "Liebst Du mich, Mignon?" he counters. "Ich weiss es nicht" (I don't know), she replies. He, however, declares "Mignon, ich liebe Dich," and buries his head in her lap. "Ich habe deine Mutter vergiftet . . ." (I poisoned your mother), she remarks.

The Athlete, intending to point out Alwa, catches Dr. Schön's eye. But Dr. Schön aims his gun at the Athlete, who frantically tries to divert his aim to Alwa.

Lulu gets up, and Dr. Schön comes downstairs, grasps Alwa by the shoulders and states: "In Paris ist Revolution ausgebrochen."

Dr. Schön, Lulu and others. The Athlete, trying to escape, hides behind a curtain. Lulu says that he has jumped out the window. Furiously, Dr. Schön turns on her as she asks how he likes her dress. Handing her the gun, he urges her to shoot herself before he loses his mind "und mein Sohn schwimmt in seinem Blute!" (and my son swims in his own blood).

Lulu, taking the revolver, fires a shot into the ceiling. The terrified Athlete scurries up the stairs. Startled, Dr. Schön looks behind the curtains and screen, finds Geschwitz and locks her in the bedroom. Returning to Lulu he again urges her to shoot herself: "Komm zu Ende!" (Come, make an end of it). Lulu suggests divorce. It is too late, he says. While she lives, life for him is "von Abgrund zu Abgrund" (from abyss to abyss). If she cannot pull the trigger, he will. He reaches for the gun.

She breaks away from him and sings: "If men have killed themselves **Lulu's Lied** for my sake that does not lower my value. . . . I have never pretended to be anything other than what I seemed. And no one ever took me for anything other than what I am."

"Nieder . . . nieder" (down), he cries, forcing her to her knees. From under the table the Schoolboy shrieks and Dr. Schön turns. Lulu fires five shots in his back, and he falls, gasping: "Und—da—ist—noch—einer!" (and there is yet another).

Everyone rushes from concealment, protesting Lulu's innocence, while Dr. Schön calls desperately for Alwa. The son tries to aid his father, leaving his side only to unlock the bedroom door. As Geschwitz steps out, Dr. Schön collapses. "Der Teufel" (the devil), he murmurs, and dies. Over everyone's protests Alwa rejects Lulu's pleas and prepares to turn her over to the police. "I shall be hounded out of school," says the Schoolboy.

INTERLUDE ("Ostinato"—4min.)

(Berg originally intended the interlude to be accompanied by a film showing Lulu being tried for Dr. Schön's murder, convicted, imprisoned and transferred to a hospital with cholera. The film usually is omitted. The interlude, called "Ostinato" because of a repeated bass figure, divides in two fairly equal parts, the first suggesting Lulu's trial and imprisonment, the second anticipating her escape. Berg runs the material forward, through a climax, to a point of rest [vibraphone over solo violin], and then—for those who can hear it—runs it backwards.)

SCENE 2 (23 min.)

As before, a year later. The curtains are drawn, dust covers the furniture, and Lulu's Pierrot portrait is faced to the wall.

Alwa, Geschwitz and the Athlete. They await Lulu's arrival so that each may play his part in her escape. The Athlete, disguised as a servant, is to take her and Schigolch across the border, but he protests bitterly that his acrobatic costume is not ready and that Lulu will be too emaciated to make a suitable partner. Alwa pointedly admires Geschwitz's courage and self-sacrifice.

Schigolch and the others. He has come to pick up Geschwitz, who evidently is ill. Alwa suggests she will need money and offers her some, but her attention is entirely on Lulu and the projected escape.

Alwa and the Athlete. In a long section of spoken prose, the Athlete grumbles about his role in the escape and is rebuked by Alwa. (The large number of such seemingly undigested blobs of spoken prose in this scene suggests that Berg was either losing interest in or control of the material.)

Alwa, the Athlete and the Schoolboy. The Schoolboy, who was not expected, arrives with a plan for Lulu's escape, "ich habe einen Plan." The others try to get rid of him. They show him the newspaper account of "Die Mörderin des Dr. Schön an der Cholera" (the murderess of Dr. Schön and the cholera) and insist that she died of the disease. The Schoolboy at first is doubtful, then convinced—"Ich Dummkopf" (what a fool I am)—and is hustled out.

Schigolch, Lulu, Alwa and the Athlete. Schigolch enters with Lulu, who looks like death. The Athlete immediately announces that she cannot possibly be an acrobat and leaves, threatening to call the police. But he is too compromised to dare. Schigolch leaves to pick up the railroad tickets.

As soon as both are gone, Lulu ceases to totter and exclaims with strength, "O Freiheit! Herrgott im Himmel!" (O freedom, dear God in Heaven!). In a long section of spoken prose, she reveals that Geschwitz had deliberately contracted cholera in order to change places with her in the hospital. With amusement Lulu concludes, "And now she lies there as the murderess of Dr. Schön."

Alwa and Lulu. She calls to him, "Komm!" He says that he will write a poem about her. "Komm," she calls, and then "Stop! I shot your father." But he is too excited to care. "Komm," he responds, "Einen **Alwa's Hymn** Kuss! Einen Kuss!" (a kiss). Once across the frontier they can see each other "so oft wir wollen" (as often as we wish). Alwa sings a Hymn to her flesh, her bones, her knees, her legs that close and draw apart. As he buries his head in her lap, she says: "Ist das noch der Diwan—auf dem sich—Dein Vater—verblutet hat?" (is that not the divan on which your father bled to death?) "Schweig. Schweig" (Sh,h,h), says Alwa.

Vocabulary, Act II

Scene 1

das mein Lebensabend	DAHS mine lay.bens.ah.bent	that is my life's evening
die Pest im Haus	dee PEST im hows	the plague in the house
dreissig Jahre Arbeit	DRY.sik yahr.eh AHR.bite	thirty years' work

Vocabulary, Act II (continued)

der Schmutz	der shmoots	the filth
mein eigener Sohn	mine EYE.gen.er sohn	my own son
der also auch	der AHL.zo owk	that one as well
liebst du mich denn	leebst doo mik den	do you love me, then
ich weiss es nicht	ik vice es nikt	I do not know
ich liebe dich	ik leeb.eh dik	I love you
ich habe deine Mutter vergiftet	ik hah.beh dine.eh moot.ter fair.GIFT.et	I had your mother poisoned
in Paris ist Revolution ausgebrochen	een pah.REES ist reh.voh.loo.S'YOWN ows.geh.BROK.en	in Paris revolution has broken out
und mein Sohn schwimmt in seinem Blute	oont mine sohn schvimt in sine.em BLOOT.eh	and my son swims in his own blood
komm zu Ende	kom tsoo EN.de	come, make an end
von Abgrund zu Abgrund	fon AHP.groont . . .	from abyss to abyss
nieder	NEED.er	down
und—da—ist—noch— einer	oont dah ist nok eye.ner	and there is yet another
der Teufel	der TOYF.el	the devil

Scene 2

ich habe einen Plan	ik hah.be eye.nen plahn	I have a plan
die Mörderin des Dr. Schön an der Cholera	dee MER.der.in dess . . . ahn der KOH.ler.ah	the murderess of Dr. Schön and the cholera
ich Dummkopf	ik DOOM.kop'f	what a fool I am
o Freiheit	oh FRY.hite	o freedom
Herrgott im Himmel	hair.got im HIM.el	dear God in heaven
komm	kom	come
einen Kuss	eye.nen kooss	a kiss
so oft wir wollen	so oft veer voll.en	as often as we wish
ist das noch der Diwan—auf dem sich—Dein Vater —verblutet hat	ist dahs nok der dee.vahn owf dem sik dine fah.ter fair.bloot.et hat	is that not the divan on which your father bled to death
schweig	shvyg	sh,h,h

ACT III (completed by F. Cerha—55 min.)
SCENE 1 (26 min.): A Paris casino. Casti Piani, an elegant pimp, suggests Lulu enter a brothel, threatening to expose her to the police if she refuses. She escapes, dressed as a boy, and leaves for London.
INTERLUDE (3 min.): Completed by Berg and used as fourth movement of the *Lulu Symphony.*
SCENE 2 (26 min.): Attic in a London slum. Lulu is now a streetwalker, supporting Alwa and Schigolch. Geschwitz comes from Paris, with Lulu's portrait, from which the paint is peeling. Lulu brings in three customers. The first, a professor, while engaged with Lulu, is robbed by Alwa and Schigolch. The second, an African Prince, kills Alwa; and the third, Jack the Ripper, kills Lulu. As he leaves, he stabs Geschwitz, who, dying, ends the opera singing "Lulu, mein Engel. . ." (Lulu, my angel) to music Berg had used as the fifth movement of the *Lulu Symphony.*

Berg wanted the final scene be staged so that Lulu's three customers are played by the singers who portrayed her three husbands: the professor by Dr. Gol, the African Prince by Walter the Painter, and Jack the Ripper by Dr. Schön. And the music of each husband returns with his alter ego.

But how is an audience to respond to this identity of character and musical return? Is the opera a Gothic thriller? Dr. Schön's revenge? A sermon: Those who live by sex will die by sex? The interpretation offered by Berg's biographer, Mosco Carner, quotes a statement by Karl Kraus, who first produced Wedekind's *Pandora:* The play presents "the tragedy of the hounded grace of woman, eternally misunderstood;" and in its last act "the great retribution has begun, the revenge of the world of men which makes bold to avenge itself for its own guilt." But to many persons Lulu, self-centered, homicidal, childless, has so little "grace of woman" that her death seems quite untragic and the opera in its final act, at least, too long.

L'AMOUR DES TROIS ORANGES

(The Love for Three Oranges)

Opera in four acts and a prologue. World premiere (in Fr.), Chicago, Dec. 30, 1921; European prem. (in Ger.), Cologne, March 14, 1925; Russian prem. (in Russ.), Leningrad, Feb. 18, 1926; British prem. (in Serbo-Croat), Edinburgh, Aug. 23, 1962. Music and text (in Fr.) by Prokofiev, after C. Gozzi's comedy, *Fiaba dell' amore delle tre melarance,* Venice, Jan. 25, 1761. Gozzi based his fable on a story from Giambattista Basile's *Pentameron* (1600), a book of fairy tales in Neapolitan dialect.

PRINCIPAL CHARACTERS

The King of Clubs, ruler of an imaginary kingdom in which everyone wears costumes derived from the pack of cards	bass	
The Prince, his son, sick with melancholy	tenor	
Princess Clarissa, the king's niece	contralto	
Leandro, the King's Prime Minister and chief enemy, dressed as the King of Spades	baritone	
Truffaldino, the Court Jester	tenor	tyuh.fahl.DEE.no
Pantalone, the King's friend	baritone	
Celio, a magician and the King's protector	bass	TCHAY.l'yoh
Fata Morgana, a sorceress in league with Leandro	soprano	
A cook in the employ of Creonta, a sorceress	hoarse bass	
Farfarello, a demon	bass	far.far.ELL.oh
Smeraldina, Fata Morgana's servant	mezzo-soprano	smeh.rahl.DEE.nah

Prokofiev followed closely the text and spirit of Gozzi's play, and the opera is a theatrical extravaganza rather than a drama or even a comedy. The most famous music, which Prokofiev later arranged in an orchestral suite, occurs in the dances, processions and pantomimes; while most of what is sung, generally in a declamatory style, is too closely tied to stage action, visual images of parody or humor, to survive outside the theatre. In performance, however, it is witty.

Some knowledge of Gozzi and his fables will clarify the opera. In Venice in the 1760s there raged a war of theatrical style, with Gozzi representing the old and Carlo Goldoni, the new. In the old, the *commedia dell'arte*, the actors wore colorful masks and costumes to designate their roles—servant, rich old man, etc.—and then played a basic scenario while improvising many of their lines. The style favored extravagance and spontaneity: set speeches could be interspersed with topical improvisations; new pantomime could be introduced at any performance; and if an actor felt in the vein, he could go on and on in a bravura exhibition all the more exciting because no one knew when or how it would end. But in Venice by 1760, with the exception of a single company led by the actor Antonio Sacchi, the form had degenerated into bad jokes and obscenities.

The new style of comedy, largely created by Goldoni, substituted premeditation or plot for improvisation, character development for the relatively fixed personalities of the "masks," and natural speech for inflated language. The Venetians flocked to the new, "realistic" comedies in such numbers that Gozzi, who abhorred "those vulgar scenes from life," announced irritably that, given Sacchi's troupe, he could make the public laugh louder with a child's fairy story—and to prove it he wrote a scenario based on the popular fable, *L'amore delle tre melarance*. A Prince (the Venetian Public) is sick with melancholy and can be cured only by being made to laugh. To effect the cure, Gozzi used all the extravagance, fantasy and theatrical tricks that Goldoni was eliminating.

In the wars of theatrical style realism seems always to defeat fancy; yet somehow fancy is never eliminated, and in every generation returns to do battle. In Gozzi's time the Venetians, and through them much of Europe, ultimately decided in Goldoni's favor, but not before Gozzi and Sacchi had kept the issue in doubt for fifteen years and created a corpus of successful fables. Many of these have become operas. In this century, besides the *L'amore delle tre melarance,* composers have used *Turandote* (Puccini and Busoni), *Il Re Cervo* (Henze) and *La donna serpente* (Casella).

According to Prokofiev, what drew him to Gozzi's play was "the mixture of fairy tale, humor and satire . . . and especially its theatrical qualities." Later, when critics in their fashion began to expound on the opera's hidden meanings, Prokofiev said: "All I tried to do was to write an amusing opera."

Some notes on production: the opera succeeds best—perhaps only succeeds—if translated into the language of the audience and played by a young cast capable of running all over the stage. Truffaldino, in particular, must be agile and always, even when silent, physically in charge of the action. He is the role or "mask" played by Sacchi in the fables and is Sacchi's version, famous throughout Europe, of Arlecchino the busybody, sometimes bumbling servant of the *commedia dell'arte.*

Because the acts are short, the opera is often played with a single intermission, between Acts II and III.

The orchestral suite (14 min.) drawn from the opera has six parts: the Ridiculous Ones, Infernal Scene, March, Scherzo, the Prince and Princess, and Flight. The sources are indicated in the synopsis.

PROLOGUE (4 min.)

The curtain rises at once to reveal an interior curtain framed by two towers, each with several theatre boxes. A group, the Tragedians, rush onstage brandishing umbrellas and demanding a tragedy. They are opposed by others with riding crops who want a comedy. Blows are prevented only by the arrival of a new group carrying green twigs and requesting a romance with moonlight and moments of ecstasy. These are promptly threatened by others with walking sticks, who call for a farce. Finally arrive the Ridiculous Ones, armed with slapsticks (associated with Arlecchino), who demand silence, push the others into the boxes and announce that the entertainment will be a spectacle, *The Love of Three Oranges,* presented in the one true style.

A herald appears. He raises his trumpet, and from the orchestra sounds a one-note fanfare on the bass trombone. The King of Clubs, the herald cries, is desolate because the Prince suffers from incurable hypochondria. The Ridiculous Ones exclaim excitedly, and the interor curtain rises.

ACT I (27 min.)

SCENE 1 (11 min.)

The King's palace. On the throne, the King; near him, Pantalone; and before them, with a collection of weird instruments, the court doctors.

The King grieves for his son as the doctors report the Prince's many ailments, ending with hypochondria "incurable." The diagnosis produces an explosion of grief from the King so severe that the Ridiculous Ones from their boxes warn him that such excess before an audience may cost him his royal prestige. Throughout the opera the different groups comment on the action, often unfavorably.

Pantalone soothes the King, who recalls that the doctors suggested the Prince might be cured if he could be made to laugh. Impossible in this gloomy court, says Pantalone, and calls for Truffaldino.

He enters at full tilt (Truffaldino-Arlecchino should always move fast and appear to be everywhere at once). In measured tones the King asks for games to amuse the Prince, and in barely a second Truffaldino repeats the command and runs out to fulfill it.

The King summons his Prime Minister, Leandro, to inform him of the games, and Pantalone in a loud aside whispers to the audience that Leandro works for the death of the Prince. In addition to the games, the Ridiculous Ones demand a bacchanal, which the King adds to the agenda. As all retire, Pantalone and Leandro snarl epithets at each other.

Orchestral Suite. The first part, "The Ridiculous Ones," opens with the
The Ridiculous Ones prologue's fanfare, develops phrases associated with the group (chiefly a phrase sung by them in Act I, Scene 3),
and closes with Truffaldino's nimble, birdlike theme played on the
flute.

SCENE 2 (4 min.)

The magicians' world. Celio, who protects the King, arrives through
the floor with masses of fire and smoke. Leandro's protectress, Fata
Infernal Scene Morgana, materializes amid thunder and lightning. Hundreds of little devils surround them in a dance while they
play three hands of cards—all of which Celio loses. The scene dissolves
back to the palace.
Orchestral Suite. The second part is this scene entire, the heavy,
punching chords being the cards slapped on the table and a trumpet
substituting for Fata Morgana's triumphant laughter.

SCENE 3 (11 min.)

In the palace Leandro and the Princess Clarissa converse. She will
marry Leandro and ascend to the throne as soon as the Prince is dead.
Does Leandro understand? He urges patience, but she recommends for
the Prince either an overdose of opium or a bullet.

Truffaldino, with preparations for the games, skips through the
background. The games, Leandro explains, are to make the Prince
laugh. Opium or a bullet, says Clarissa.

A vase falls from a table, leading to the discovery of Smeraldina,
Fata Morgana's servant. Aiding Truffaldino, she warns, is Celio, who
just then crosses the stage in an eerie light. Opium or a bullet, cries
Clarissa. Impressed by the strength of their opponents, the three conspirators invoke the aid of Fata Morgana.

ACT II (24 min.)

SCENE 1 (6 min.)

The Prince's chamber. He is dressed in a hospital smock, has com-
presses on his head, and is surrounded by medicines. Truffaldino is
finishing what has evidently been a long comic dance. Funny? he asks.

No, no, no, the Prince replies. While Truffaldino confesses he is almost out of ideas, the Prince groans, coughs and groans, spits and groans, groans. Nevertheless, Truffaldino assures him, you will laugh at the games. Offstage sounds a march, and Truffaldino, after throwing all the medicine out the window, pulls the Prince from the room to attend the games.

ENTR' ACTE (1 min.)

The march in full orchestra. It is possibly the best known of any march composed in the twentieth century. In the United States from 1944 to 1958 it was the musical theme of a popular radio program, *Your FBI in Peace and War,* and elsewhere millions who know nothing **march** of the opera are familiar with it from the suite and piano arrangements.

Orchestral Suite. Part three, the march.

SCENE 2 (17 min.)

The palace courtyard. Truffaldino announces Entertainment Number One, and at his signal doors open, monsters with enormous heads appear, and a mock battle is staged. The courtiers are delighted, but the Prince merely groans. Meanwhile Fata Morgana has entered disguised as an old woman.

Truffaldino announces Entertainment Number Two. With a gesture he raises two large fountains, one of olive oil, one of wine. The kingdom's gluttons and drunkards are invited to help themselves, and though the scramble is comic, the Prince groans.

Dismayed and suspicious, Truffaldino orders the strange old woman to leave the court. Fata Morgana refuses, but in stepping backward slips and falls. The Prince laughs, in fact has a laughing fit, and soon all the court but Clarissa and Leandro are laughing and dancing. Suddenly the light darkens, and Fata Morgana, surrounded by little devils, lays a curse on the Prince: he will fall in love with three oranges. At once he begins to sigh for the fruit and determines to find them even if he has to search the castle of the sorceress, Creonta. The King tries to dissuade him, but the Prince, taking only a reluctant Truffaldino, departs at once. A demon, Farfarello, materializes and with a large hand bellows creates a wind at their backs, driving them on. (If the opera is played in two acts, the single break is here.)

ACT III (43 min.)

SCENE 1 (8 min.)

A desert. Celio is drawing circles in the sand to force Farfarello to appear. When he succeeds, Farfarello proves unexpectedly cheeky. He laughs at Celio, remarks on certain card games lost, and before departing will reveal only that he left the Prince and Truffaldino somewhere near Creonta's castle.

The two enter, visibly deep in search. While the Prince sighs of his great love for three oranges, Celio gives Truffaldino a ribbon to protect them from Cretona's ferocious cook. Farfarello reappears and with his bellows blows them on their way.

ENTR' ACTE (1 min.)

scherzo   A scherzo in tarentella rhythm as they proceed on their way. The scherzo is almost as famous as the march, and snatches of both reappear in the balance of the opera.
Orchestral Suite. Part four, the scherzo.

SCENE 2 (8 min.)

Courtyard of Creonta's castle. Truffaldino is terrified, but the Prince thinks only of the oranges. With a crash the kitchen door opens, and the cook (hoarse bass accompanied by a tuba) emerges armed with an enormous ladle. She soon discovers Truffaldino and is threatening to thrust him in the furance when she sees the ribbon: "Ah, but it is adorable!" While she plays with it—in her hair, on her wrist, against her cheek—the Prince and Truffaldino escape with three oranges.

ENTR' ACTE (1 min.)

The scherzo.

SCENE 3 (25 min.)

Evening on the desert. The two are exhausted with lugging the oranges, which have grown extremely large. Truffaldino is overcome by thirst, but the happy Prince falls quickly asleep.

Desperate for liquid, Truffaldino cuts into an orange. A Princess steps out. Sweetly she sings that she is dying of thirst, and to save her he cuts another orange. A second Princess emerges, also dying of thirst. They do die, and in panic Truffaldino runs off as the Prince awakes. He is puzzled by the litter of dead, but fortunately four soldiers, marching with exaggerated precision, clear the stage of bodies.

Sweet orange, sings the Prince to the one remaining. He cuts it open, revealing a Princess dying of thirst. It is too much for the Ridiculous Ones, who present her with a bucket of water.

love duet The Prince and Princess sing of love, though the duet ends with his leaving, at her request, to find something suitable for her to wear.

Alone, the Princess sits on a rock. Night falls, and Smeraldina and Fata Morgana creep in. Beware, cry the Ridiculous Ones to the Princess, but, too late! Smeraldina sticks her with a pin. The Princess turns into a rat, and Smeraldina takes her place on the rock.

The court enters in procession (the march). The Prince denies that Smeraldina is the Princess, but the King insists that the marriage take place: the royal word has been given.

The Prince and Princess *Orchestral Suite.* Part five, "The Prince and Princess," the suite's chief lyric section. It is composed of a few repeated phrases from the love duet in which the vocal lines have been scored for violin and flute (the Princess) and cello and basoon (the Prince).

ACT IV (12 min.)

SCENE 1 (3min.)

The magicians' world. Celio berates Fata Morgana for cheap tricks, like pin-sticking, while she mocks his feeble rings in sand. Both invoke a good deal of thunder and lightning, but when once again Fata Morgana seems to be winning the contest, the Ridiculous Ones force her into their tower, leaving Celio free to save the court.

SCENE 2 (9 min.)

The palace throne room, which Leandro has decorated for the marriage. The court enters (the march), and suddenly on the throne for the

Princess is discovered a rat. On Celio's command it turns into the Princess, making the Prince deliriously happy. Truffaldino, appearing "from no one knows where," identifies Smeraldina, and the King in an uncharacteristic burst of vision recognizes her, Leandro and Clarissa as conspirators against the throne. In a fury he orders them hanged.

They flee with all but the royal family in hot pursuit, and the chase **flight** goes back and forth across the stage. Fata Morgana breaks out of the tower and, extending her protection over the conspirators, saves them by a sudden exit through the stage floor. The pursuers, left in confusion, cheer the Prince and Princess.

Orchestral Suite. The sixth and final part, "Flight," is the chase in full through the exit of the Conspirators.

THE GAMBLER

Opera in four acts, six scenes. World premiere (in French), Brussels, April 29, 1929; American prem. (in English), New York, April 4, 1957; British prem. (in Serbo-Croat), Edinburgh, Aug. 30, 1962; Russian prem. (in Russian), radio performance, March, 1963. Music by Sergei Prokofiev; also the text, based on Dostoyevsky's novel, *The Gambler,* 1866. Composed to a Russian text in 1915–16 and not performed; revised for the Brussels premiere, 1929.

The opera has problems. It is middling long (124 min.), without attractive characters and very conversational; its first two acts are constructed entirely out of short scenes in which the characters often seem to come and go without reason and talk without purpose. Yet, if it is performed in translation and if the libretto is read in advance, *The Gambler* can be very exciting. Its music is interesting, often exhilarating, and builds steadily to a stunning last act.

The plot is best summarized if divided in two. First, in 1865 in a hotel in Roulettenburg (Wiesbaden), a German spa famous for its casino, lives a retired, impoverished Russian general, aged fifty-five. He is surrounded by: the Marquis, who lends him money at a high rate of interest; Mlle Blanche of the demimonde, whom he is eager to marry; his step-daughter Pauline, a neurotic who because of the general's borrowings has been forced into an affair with the Marquis; and a tutor,

Alexis, for his young children. Alexis, poor but of good family, loves Pauline.

The general waits for a telegram from Moscow announcing the death of his rich aunt, called "Babulenka" or Grandmother. With his inheritance he will pay off the Marquis, overcome Mlle Blanche's reluctance to have a poor husband, and by creating a dowry improve Pauline's chances to marry. But instead of a telegram announcing Babulenka's death, she herself arrives at the spa (Act II finale). And the consternation among her would-be heirs increases when she loses a fortune at roulette. The Marquis departs for St. Petersburg to sell what remains of Pauline's property, which the general has used as collateral for his loans; Mlle Blanche abandons the general for another guest of the hotel, Prince Nilsky; and the general is barred from Babulenka's apartment by her servants.

Intertwined with this collapse of the general's world is the love story of Alexis and Pauline. The opera opens with Alexis reporting to her that the money she gave him to play roulette has been lost. He suspects that she was trying in some way to free herself from the Marquis, but she parries his questions. Later, when he protests his love, she orders him as proof of it to insult a German couple in the garden, which he does (Act I finale).

After Babulenka has left the spa to return to Moscow, Pauline comes to Alexis's room (Act IV, Scene 1). She has a letter from the Marquis explaining that he is selling her property but that she will have a good claim against the general for its value. Pauline, in a highly emotional state, seems about to confess that she loves Alexis.

But he, suddenly sure that he can win, tells her to wait and rushes to the casino. He gambles and breaks the bank. (This scene can be extraordinarily effective. Instead of treating the gamblers and croupiers as a chorus, Prokofiev has given twenty of them individual lines and characters. And although they sing their short lines one right after another or even sometimes together, the effect is quite different from a chorus: more varied, intense and feverish.)

Running back to Pauline, Alexis offers her the money to throw in the Marquis's face. She reacts with hysterical laughter. Alexis tries to calm her, and they excitedly agree that they will return to Moscow together and join Babulenka. But when Alexis embraces Pauline, she pushes him away, demanding the money. He hands it to her, and she, with fury, throws it in his face and runs out. Alexis, stunned, mumbles her name, and then his mind returns to the casino. Laughing madly he shrieks: "Red! On the red, twenty times in a row." And he grips the hotel's table as though it were in the casino with the roulette wheel on it, and the wheel spinning . . . spinning . . . spinning.

Using music from the opera but composing much that was new, Prokofiev made a symphonic suite, Op. 49, 1932, usually entitled "Four Portraits from *The Gambler.*" The portraits are Alexis (5 min.), The Grandmother (6 min.), The General (3 min.) and Pauline (6 min.). To these he added a fifth movement, based on the gambling and final love scenes, The Denouement (5 min.).

BETROTHAL IN A MONASTERY

or

THE DUENNA

Lyric-comic opera in four acts, nine scenes. Though completed in 1940, because of the war: world premiere, Leningrad, Nov. 3, 1946; American prem. (as *The Duenna,* in English), New York, June 1, 1948; British radio prem. (in Russian), London, May 5, 1963. Music by Sergei Prokofiev; also text, based on Richard Sheridan's comic opera, *The Duenna* or *The Double Elopement,* with music by Thomas Linley, Sr., and other composers, first performed, Covent Garden, Nov. 21, 1775.

PRINCIPAL CHARACTERS

Don Jerome, a rich noble of Seville	tenor
Ferdinand, his son	baritone
Louisa, his daughter	soprano
The Duenna, Louisa's chaperone	contralto
Antonio d'Ercilla, who loves Louisa	tenor
Clara d'Almanza, friend of Louisa and loved by Ferdinand	mezzo-soprano
Mendoza, a rich fish merchant	bass
Don Carlos, an impoverished noble and friend of Mendoza	baritone

The action takes place in Seville during the eighteenth century.

Of Prokofiev's seven operas, five are based on novels and two on plays. The latter, both comedies, this and *The Love of Three Oranges,* have the best structures: little or nothing need be added or explained for an audience to enjoy them. The comedy in *Betrothal in a Monastery* is less grotesque than in *The Love of Three Oranges,* the characters more human and the lyricism more pronounced—though Prokofiev's bent for wit and sarcasm is seldom long absent. The opera has been steadily popular in Russia and started about 1956 to enter Western repertories: e.g., Czechoslovakia, 1956; Germany, 1958; Italy, 1959; Rumania, 1964; Poland, 1966; France, 1973; and Switzerland, 1976. Slow but solid success.

ACT I (29 min.)

Following a prelude (1.5 min.), based on the wedding chorus from the opera's finale, the curtain rises on a square in Seville. To one side is Don Jerome's house.

Don Jerome and Mendoza. Mendoza has proposed a partnership to corner the fish market. By combining their capital they can buy up all the boats and then—Mendoza imitates with his hands—"Swim, swim, little fish, into the nets, into the boats and onto the market." The thought excites Jerome: "And there's nowhere else to buy!"

They shake hands, and Mendoza mentions Jerome's daughter Louisa, who has been promised to him in marriage to seal the venture. Jerome confirms it, and while Mendoza in delight walks about, Jerome observes him critically: Mendoza is middle-aged, ugly and with a ridiculous beard; but no doubt he is a better husband for Louisa than a young man without money.

Mendoza, who has never met Louisa, requests a description, and while Jerome recites her beauty, talent and virtue, Mendoza continually exclaims "Oh, what a girl!" "And all," says Jerome, "in return for your fish."

Thinking again of fish, Mendoza has his servant hand him a trout and a lobster, and as he recites their beauties, Jerome mockingly exclaims, "Oh, what a girl!"—until the lobster nips him. The men part, satisfied with their deal, and Jerome enters his house.

Ferdinand and a servant. "Who was that insect?" asks Ferdinand. **arioso** "Mendoza," says the servant. "He sells rotten fish." Ferdinand's mind, however, has already turned to Clara. Oh, if he cannot

win her, he will die. His rapture, however, is broken by the arrival of
Antonio with a guitar and the obvious intent, as darkness falls, of
serenading Louisa. Ferdinand at first is indignant, but then encouraging: better Antonio should serenade Louisa than, perhaps, Clara. Ferdinand leaves.

Antonio. He starts his serenade (it is used throughout the opera as a
aria   love motif), and after the first verse is interrupted by masqueraders who, passing through the square, joke at his lack of success.
Antonio's second verse, however, draws Louisa to the balcony, and
their voices join. It also draws Don Jerome, in dressing gown and
nightcap, to the doorway, and the lovers hastily wave goodbye.

The Masqueraders and Jerome. Returning and finding Jerome standing
pensively in the square, they whirl him about. When he peevishly
scolds them, they reply gaily that it is Carnival and run out.

Jerome, with the serenade in mind, muses on the difficulty of having
arioso   a daughter with a mind of her own. Again the Masqueraders dance about him and out. Where, continues Jerome, did she
learn her tricks: love letters, deceptions, reproaches. There is no mis-
oriental dance   fortune greater, he laments, than a stubborn daughter. Masqueraders in oriental costumes dance about him. So the
answer, he concludes, is to marry her off quickly. To Mendoza. Before
the young man with the guitar steals her. More Masqueraders. Ignoring them, clucking over the prospective profit from the fish, Jerome
enters the house.

The masqueraders disperse. Three cellos sound softly in the wings
and are joined by other strings backstage. New Masqueraders seen
shadow dance   only as silhouettes appear and dance noiselessly.
The night air seems to breathe of love. (In all, the Masqueraders and
their dancing fill about a third of the act. Now and again the music has
the sound of the ballet *Romeo and Juliet,* composed the same decade.)

ACT II (49 min.)

SCENE 1 (At Don Jerome's house—15 min.)

Louisa and the Duenna. They scheme how Louisa can marry Antonio
rather than Mendoza. Louisa is determined, and the Duenna equally
so: she herself will marry Mendoza, allowing his money to overcome
his personal defects. Louisa is sighing over the gentle, handsome Anto-

nio when they hear Don Jerome coming. The Duenna takes one of Antonio's love letters to Louisa so that, as the first step in their plan, Don Jerome can discover it on the Duenna and dismiss her as a go-between. *Don Jerome, Ferdinand and Louisa.* Don Jerome announces that Louisa will soon marry Mendoza, and Ferdinand protests: the match is ludicrous. And Louisa, to her father's exasperation, refuses outright. He threatens to lock her in the house and sends her to her room. Going, she stops in the doorway to repeat: she will never marry Mendoza. Not in a hundred years.

Instead of Mendoza, says Ferdinand, why not Antonio? He is of good family and loves Louisa. Don Jerome dismisses him as an impoverished noble who sings at night. As Ferdinand continues to argue, **arioso**   Don Jerome goes out. Ferdinand, alone, thinks of Clara; without her he cannot imagine happiness. He runs off.

Don Jerome and the Duenna. Their argument starts offstage. He demands Antonio's letter, which the Duenna at first refuses. After reading it, he scolds the Duenna for acting as a go-between, and she cries shame on him to read another's letter. He dismisses her, and she retorts that she is glad to go.

While she gets her cloak, he moans that a daughter, truly, is the **arioso**   plague: sighs, laments, trysts! A father's misfortune grows.

Louisa enters dressed in the Duenna's clothes, with hood and veil. Don Jerome with delight, talking the whole time, hurries her out of the house. The Duenna, watching from Louisa's room, comments that the plan is well started.

SCENE 2 (A fishmarket on the quay—21 min.)

Venders, Mendoza and Don Carlos. The venders cry: "Fish from Mendoza's boats!" The people buy; Mendoza is pleased, but the elderly Carlos, ever the romantic, wishes the fish were weapons, jewels or rings. Anything but fish.

Clara and Louisa. Clara enters and, talking to her maid, reveals that she has run away from home. Her stepmother locked her in her room, and Ferdinand, who somehow had procured a key, entered. He freed her, it is true, but he also by his conduct offended her honor.

Louisa, in the Duenna's clothes, enters. Where will she go? To her friend Clara? While each looks nervously about the square, they back into each other and, turning, exclaim over their costumes and situa-

tions. Clara sings of Ferdinand, who entered her bedroom and by his
aria   embraces dishonored her. She drove him away, as honor demanded; though she had wished he would stay, as love suggested.

Louisa is inclined to take a less lofty view of honor, but is soon distracted by the sight of Mendoza. She conceives a plan based on using
Clara's name for a day. Clara agrees and starts for St. Catherine's
Convent where she will hide, but first describing exactly where it is and
how to enter through a secret door. Louisa, of course, is not to tell Ferdinand. Of course not, says Lousia.

Louisa, Mendoza and Don Carlos. Louisa, announcing that she is Clara
d'Almanza, requests Mendoza's aid. He assumes at first that she is
smitten with him, but she explains that she loves Antonio d'Ercilla.
Will Mendoza help her?

Indeed he will, for, as he explains to Don Carlos, if he joins Antonio
to this Clara d'Almanza, then Antonio will no longer pursue Don
Jerome's Lousia. Enormously pleased with himself, he hastens off to
find Antonio, leaving Clara-Louise to the care of Don Carlos. As the
courtly old gentleman escorts her to Mendoza's house, the venders resume their cry: "Fish! Fish from Mendoza's boats!"

SCENE 3 (At Don Jerome's house—13 min.)

Don Jerome and Mendoza. Don Jerome is laughing at Mendoza's account of Clara d'Almanza's escape from her father's house. "He's a
nincompoop," says Don Jerome.

They await Louisa but she does not appear. A maid whispers to Don
Jerome that her mistress will come only if her father leaves the room.
Don Jerome is astonished, but he leaves.

Mendoza and the Duenna. Veiled and in Louisa's clothes, the Duenna
enters. Conversation at first is slow. Then Mendoza asks to see her
dimple and, on seeing her face, momentarily loses his power of speech.
"Who are you?" he asks. "Donna Louisa," insists the Duenna. "Then
your father must be blind," says Mendoza. "I always dreamt of a
bearded husband," says the Duenna, and Mendoza, touched on his
vanity, warms to her. After all, if not pretty, she is rich.

He asks her to sing, and she chooses a courting song: how quickly
courting song   the maiden learns to simulate the modesty she is
eager to cast aside.

Mendoza, excited, urges her to speak to her father at once. But she
requests to be abducted. It is more romantic. Let him come with a

coach at night and steal her from the garden. Imagining himself as a cavalier, Mendoza agrees.

Don Jerome and Mendoza. As the Duenna withdraws, Don Jerome enters with two bottles of champagne. "Was Louisa charming?" he asks. Mendoza is cautious in his praise, and for a moment Don Jerome **drinking song** is irritated. But then, the bottles opened, they drink to their friendship and profits in fish.

ACT III (37 min.)

SCENE 1 (At Mendoza's house—14 min.)

Louisa, Don Carlos; later, Mendoza and Antonio. Louisa (still using Clara's name) waits with Don Carlos for Mendoza to bring Antonio, and time for her stands still. Don Carlos is moved by her impatience. Then they hear Mendoza coming, and Louisa goes into an adjacent room.

Antonio and Mendoza enter, with Antonio protesting that Clara d'Almanza does not love him and cannot have asked for him. But Mendoza insists that she does and did. She is in the adjacent room: go to her.

Antonio enters the room and from behind its closed door (instruments offstage) softly sounds the lover's motif, Antonio's serenade in Act I. Mendoza, much to the indignation of Carlos, peeps through the keyhole. "Ooo . . . Ooo," he gasps. Carlos insists that he will not be a witness to such ungentlemanly conduct, but—"Ooo . . . Ooo"—he remains. "They are laughing," reports Mendoza, "and he takes her by the hands, and: Ooo . . . Ooo!"

The door opens and Antonio, leading out Clara-Louisa, thanks Mendoza and promises that they no longer are rivals for Don Jerome's daughter. "Good," says Mendoza, for he is going to abduct Louisa that very night. And in answer to their startled questions, he reveals his **quartet** plan. A quartet develops: Antonio and Louisa in love; Mendoza excited about his romantic plot, and Don Carlos softly telling himself not to be bitter because he is too old for love.

SCENE 2 (11 min.)

The next day at Don Jerome's house, where he (clarinet), a friend (cornet) and his servant Sancho (bass drum) are playing a trio, *Lover's*

Minuet, composed by Don Jerome. (The combination of instruments is comic, and Prokofiev has worked into the scene the disasters that frequently overtake amateur music-making.)

Don Jerome and others. "You are not playing in tune," he cries, and angrily attacks the passage on the clarinet. Then, ceasing to play while the others continue, he muses: "Imagine! Louisa eloping with the man she was to marry. It's humorous!" He resumes playing. A servant **trio, Lover's Minuet** enters, and Don Jerome and his friend stop while Sancho continues on the bass drum, until Don Jerome yells at him. The servant announces a visitor.

Don Carlos enters with a letter from Mendoza asking Don Jerome's blessing and consent to the marriage. (The friend and Sancho start, stop and practice.) Don Jerome gives his consent, Don Carlos leaves, and the trio resumes.

Soon a dirty urchin enters with another letter, this one from Louisa asking for her father's blessing and consent to her marriage to the man she loves. "Ridiculous," mutters Don Jerome, "to use two messengers." Nevertheless, as Louisa requests, he hastily scratches his consent, also inviting the couple to a reception at home that evening, and sends it off by the dirty urchin.

Then he orders the servants to prepare the reception for the evening and, returning to the trio, plays the music with gusto.

SCENE 3 (A garden in St. Catherine's Convent—12 min.)

Clara, Louisa and Antonio. Clara, in nun's habit, walks in the garden. Louisa, entering, is astonished at her friend's dress. "Why?" she asks. "Because Ferdinand has dishonored me." "But only out of impetuous love," says Louisa.

Antonio enters, asking if Louisa has heard from her father, and almost immediately the dirty urchin appears with the letter: consent is given (wisps of Don Jerome's trio) and the couple invited to the wedding reception. Louisa suggests they go directly to her father, but An- **duet** tonio insists on the marriage first. They drift off, singing of their love (the love motif), leaving Clara alone with her grief.

Clara and Ferdinand. She has an old-fashioned scene: a slow aria, an interruption (Ferdinand) and a fast aria or cabaletta. She never **Clara's scene** thought she would end her days in a convent, but in this tomb for love (i.e., the nuns with their love of God) she will bury forever her love for Ferdinand.

He enters, fails to recognize her and with quick questions indicates he is in hot pursuit of Antonio, who reportedly is about to marry Clara d'Almanza. He rushes out.

Clara excitedly cries: "He is jealous! Of me! He truly loves me! I will follow and marry him." She rushes out.

Nuns cross the back of the empty stage chanting, "Ah . . . Ah . . . Ah . . . Ah. . . ."

ACT IV (30 min.)

SCENE 1 (A monastery—15 min.)

Monks. They are—all too plainly—carousing, toasting the nuns at the convent and endlessly repeating an inane refrain. (Much of the comedy in this scene is visual. The stage director's problem, however, is to keep it short of becoming slapstick.)

A novice brings word that two gentlemen are outside. With difficulty the more sober of the monks shift the more drunken to intoning a decorous, ascetic chant. Mendoza and Antonio are shown in and ask to be married to the ladies waiting outside. The monks seem not to understand until Mendoza has dropped not one but two purses on the floor.

Suddenly Louisa runs in, covering her face with a veil. Ferdinand follows in a towering rage. Mendoza assumes that he, with his abduction, is the cause of it and exits hastily. But Ferdinand accuses Antonio of stealing Clara and refuses to hear any explanation. He forces Antonio to fight, Louisa faints and then Clara, still dressed as a nun but without her veil, rushes between the men. The monks are goggle-eyed.

Slowly the confusion is cleared and finally, after Ferdinand has dropped a purse, the monks agree to marry the couples. (And before the next scene Mendoza has married the Duenna-Louisa in a church).

SCENE 2 (The wedding reception
at Don Jerome's house—15 min.)

Don Jerome and others. The guests have arrived but as yet not Louisa and Mendoza. Don Jerome cannot understand it. He orders the refreshments to be served, however, and suggests that the musicians (offstage) start with his trio, *Lover's Minuet.*

Mendoza arrives with the Duenna still heavily veiled and hanging back. Don Jerome calls to her to come and embrace her father, and Mendoza pushes her into Don Jerome's arms. Her embrace is overpowering, however, and before Don Jerome can do more than say "oof," the true Louisa and Antonio kneel before him. And also suddenly Ferdinand and a nun, who turns out to be Clara d'Almenza. When the confusions are cleared, Mendoza is furious and curses them all, calling the Duenna "a frog!" "I will be faithful to you forever," she cries, following him out.

Don Jerome looks at the two couples imploring his blessing and decides to give it. If he loses money on one couple, he gains it on the other.

Guests swarm around the family, and a wedding chorus develops which Don Jerome accompanies by striking the wine glasses.

THE FIERY ANGEL

(L'Ange de feu)

Opera in five acts, seven scenes. Though composed to a Russian text, 1919–27, world premiere, concert perf. (in French), Paris, Nov. 25, 1954; radio performance (in French), Paris, Jan. 13, 1955; stage perf. (in Italian), Venice, Sept. 29, 1955; British prem., stage perf. (in English), London, July 27, 1965; American prem. (in Eng.), New York, Sept. 22, 1965. Music by Sergei Prokofiev; also the text, based on the novel *The Fiery Angel* by Valery Bryussov, published 1907.

PRINCIPAL CHARACTERS

Ruprecht, a soldier-of-fortune	bass-baritone
Renata	soprano
Agrippa de Nettesheim, a magician	tenor
Mephistopheles	tenor
Faust	bass-baritone
Count Heinrich von Otterheim, Renata's former lover	mute

The action takes place in Germany in the sixteenth century.

Though in five acts, the acts are short—31 min., 25, 25, 16 and 18— and often two or more are played without break.

The story in brief: Ruprecht, a soldier-of-fortune just returned from America, is attracted to the strange and beautiful Renata, a girl apparently possessed by evil spirits. She enlists his help in her search for her former lover, Count Heinrich—the human incarnation, she believes, of an angel who has appeared to her since childhood. In order to find Heinrich, urged on by Renata, Ruprecht studies the black arts. He even succeeds in consulting Agrippa de Nettesheim, the greatest magician of the day. Heinrich finally is found and on Renata's insistence Ruprecht challenges Heinrich to a duel. Heinrich wins, leaving Ruprecht badly wounded. For a time Renata nurses Ruprecht, and they live happily together. Then Renata, overcome with remorse at yielding to Ruprecht's embrace, abandons him and enters a convent. There her evil spirits return to her, and soon the convent is in an uproar, with half the nuns possessed. The Mother Superior calls in an Inquisitor who concludes that Renata is guilty of carnal intercourse with the devil and must burn at the stake. Ruprecht is unable to save her.

What does it all mean? No one seems to know for sure. Those trying to explain in opera programs or books or synopses rush to big words—Good, Evil, Flesh, Spirit, Mysticism—and, in my opinion, compound the confusion. I will try to be more explicit, but be warned: what follows is a highly personal view.

First, the opera is not about Germany, magic and the sixteenth century, but about a victim of split personality (Renata) examined with twentieth-century eyes. Bryussov, in writing the novel, based much of it on personal experience, with himself as Ruprecht, his mistress as Renata and his friend the Russian symbolist writer Andrey Bely as Count Heinrich. Though he wrote before Freud's theories had become well known, with a poet's imagination he anticipated many of them, and there were always medical descriptions of neurotics on which to draw.

Since Freud—and the opera is post-Freud—the concept of a split personality has become more familiar. In pre-Freudian terms the illness was stated: there was a little girl / Who had a little curl / Right in the middle of her forehead / And when she was good / She was very, very good / And when she was bad she was horrid.

In Renata's case, though she often talks in terms of God, the devil and her salvation, the root of the problem is sexual. She is a person with strong sexual drive and fantasies; but after intercourse, or sometimes merely the desire for it, she has an equally strong sense of revulsion. Many persons share her feelings, but, with less of a swing from anticipation to revulsion, can strike a balance and retain their emotional footing. With Renata the swing is too great for balance; she becomes hysterical. And as she grows older, she has less and less control over her emotions and actions.

Then why Germany, magic and the sixteenth century? For Bryussov, an expert in medieval spiritualism, it was a way of anchoring the
story in strong symbolic terms: God, the flesh and the devil. For Prokofiev, who loved theatrical tricks, the magic offered a chance for
knocks on the wall, skeletons that talk, and a convent full of hysterical
nuns. And the earlier century gave a chance for the kind of satiric
humor he liked: equating the magicians of yesteryear with the psy-
chiatrists of today. For both men, therefore, the medievalism was
merely a frame within which to portray the tragedy of a modern
woman torn apart by an illness for which neither her doctors nor the
man who loved her could find a remedy.

The opera's structure follows the increasingly wide swings of Renata's illness and their increasingly devastating effects. In Acts I and II
she rejects Ruprecht but injures only his feelings. In Act III she accepts
him as her salvation but only after having sent him almost to his death.
In Act IV she moves beyond Ruprecht, an individual, to a community
of nuns; and in Act V, having upset the entire community, is finally
condemned to death, the only solution to her illness.

The music throughout is extraordinarily vital, and the orchestra has
a major role. The vocal line is declamatory but expanding often into
lyrical phrases, particularly when Renata sings of Madiel as she calls
her angel. The opera is best done in translation and needs a strong
singing-actress. The role of Ruprecht, however, is no less important,
for through him, his puzzlement and suffering, humanity enters an
otherwise bizarre case history.

When Prokofiev realized the opera would not be produced, he used
materials from it to compose his Symphony No. 3, Op. 44, first performed, Paris, May 17, 1929. The first movement's principal theme is
Renata's description of Madiel, Act I; the second's, the opening music
chanted by the nuns, Act V; the third's, Renata's hysteria, Act II, Scene
1; and the fourth's, Act II, Interlude and Scene 2.

ACT I (31 min.)

In a wretched inn of sixteenth-century Germany the landlady shows
Ruprecht a room. Taking it, he lies down to sleep. Suddenly in the next
room a woman starts screaming, "Go away. Leave me alone. Foul
beast!" Ruprecht, calling through the boarded door between them,
offers to defend her. When she continues screaming, he breaks down
the door. "There . . . there," she cries, pointing, but Ruprecht can see

only moonlight. To quiet her he recites a Latin prayer, and when she is calmer, carries her into his room and, laying her on his bed, covers her with his coat.

Renata. "I must tell you everything," she begins. (The aria, though musically interesting, continues 10 min., which for many persons is too long. As exposition it is clumsy, but thereafter the opera moves swiftly.) Her name is Renata, and when she was eight the angel (i.e., her sexual desires and fantasies) first appeared to her. She called him Madiel, the fiery angel, and she came soon to love him more than she loved her parents. By day he was often a butterfly; by night, catlike, he shared her bed. On his urging she did good, tending the sick, praying and fasting. People said she was almost a saint.

At seventeen she asked him to have intercourse with her (i.e., she lost her childhood innocence and understood her desires and how they might be satisfied). The angel was furious, scorched and abandoned her. Alone, she yearned for him. Suddenly he reappeared and told her that he would come to her as Count Heinrich von Otterheim (i.e., her fantasies fixed on that man), and for a year she lived in bliss with Heinrich. Then he left her.

Ruprecht. The landlady, aroused by the noise, comes with a waiter. They have a lantern and a pitchfork. Ruprecht questions them about Renata, but they can say only that she is some kind of witch. Ruprecht decides to keep her for the night. She is attractive, and what does he care what goes through her mind. After the others go, Renata excitedly asks Ruprecht to help her find Heinrich. Ignoring her plea, he tries to embrace her and is violently rebuffed. Then, moved by her grief and lack of friends, he apologizes. "Help me to find Heinrich," she begs.

The Sorceress. The landlady brings in a sorceress who has a cat, a toad in a cage, herbs, a pail of water and other magical tools. At the insistence of Renata, who hopes for a sign leading to Heinrich, Ruprecht lets the sorceress stay and pays her fee. She begins her abracadabra: "pista, rista, sista, xista!" "My word," says the waiter, "It's Russian!" "No, English," says the landlady, and they argue. (In this opera about illness there are many jokes about doctors: such as this, about the medieval Latin terminology with which today's doctors keep the laymen confused.) But the sorceress, instead of seeing Heinrich in her pail of water, into which she has ostentatiously dropped the white of an egg, sees blood on Renata's dress and begins to pull at the dress. Ruprecht throws her out, and the waiter remarks cynically that the sorceress (doctor) put on a good show for her fee.

ACT II (25 min.)

SCENE 1 (18 min.)

Renata and Ruprecht are in Cologne, searching for Heinrich. In a furnished room she reads aloud to him: "The three magic circles are divided into nine equal parts. . . ." Ruprecht remarks that it has been an exhausting week: in and out of every church, searching every public place, staring in every face. "But I cannot live without Heinrich," says Renata.

A friend of Ruprecht, Jacob Glock, delivers several books on magic and also a warning against agents for the Inquisition.

After Glock departs, Ruprecht confesses to Renata that he has come to love her. He understands she loves Heinrich, but still he hopes . . . "Don't hope," says Renata. Heinrich is blond and beautiful; you are dark and coarse. But surely, suggests Ruprecht, you feel something for me. If you saw me dead in the street . . . ? "I'd tell them," says Renata, "to sweep up the droppings."

Crushed, Ruprecht collapses in a chair and watches silently (2 min.) as Renata burns herbs, consults her book, adds other herbs—and suddenly there is a knock on the wall. Ruprecht is astonished. "Only a small demon," says Renata. "It happens all the time in magicians' houses." More knocks, and finally when the demon, knocking three times quickly, indicates that he is a friend, Renata becomes very excited. It is Heinrich, she decides, coming up the stairs, and she quickly works herself into hysterics (with scoring for divided strings, Prokofiev creates a unique sound). But no one is outside the door, and Renata falls sobbing to the floor.

Almost immediately Glock enters with more books and a plan for Ruprecht to see Agrippa de Nettesheim, the greatest of all magicians. Ruprecht goes off with Glock, leaving Renata in the room.

INTERLUDE (2 min.)

SCENE 2 (5 min.)

The consulting office of Agrippa. He sits on a dais in flowing cloak and crimson skullcap. Three shaggy black dogs surround him. Books line the walls; retorts and test tubes stand on tables; and from the ceiling hang three skeletons. Ruprecht stands below Agrippa.

(The scene is a verbal duel in which Ruprecht, hoping to find a cure for Renata, tries to force Agrippa to admit that he practices magic and might help her. Agrippa, fearing the Inquisition, denies that he is a magician. Ruprecht thrusts and Agrippa parries above music that seethes with tension and energy.)

R. I have come, most great Magician . . .
A. I am only a philosopher.
R: But you wrote on magic.
A: For reasons too long to recite.
R: Your book tells how to evoke spirits.
A: You read it only superficially.
R: Those dogs . . .
A: I like pedigreed dogs.
R: . . . are domesticated demons.
A: That is your illusion.

Three skeletons rattle their bones and cry: You lie, Agrippa.

With his final question Ruprecht traps Agrippa by touching his vanity: tell me then what magic is? An illusion or the truth? Is it or is it not a science?

A: It is the highest of all sciences, my son, the revelation to wise men of the great mystery of life.

(The curtain falls before Prokofiev has to reveal the secret to the audience, but between the acts Ruprecht receives from Agrippa an opinion on Renata's illness. In his commonsense way, however, he decides that the prescription is only more magical nonsense. The novel throughout keeps ambiguous whether or not there is truth in magic, and Ruprecht in his visit to Agrippa is less impressed by him than by a young doctor who gives rational explanations of magical events.)

ACT III (25 min.)

SCENE 1 (15 min.)

Renata has found Heinrich and been rejected by him. She stands in the street outside his door.

Ruprecht enters and tells her gaily that he has talked with Agrippa. The knocks on the wall are just cheap tricks. "He's in there," whispers Renata, and she describes how Heinrich thrust her aside in disgust, saying that she was an instrument of the devil. Angrily she concludes that he was always an imposter, never the angel Madiel.

Ruprecht offers to take her away from Cologne. She must put the past behind her. "Yes, kill him," says Renata, and to Ruprecht's astonishment she insists that he challenge Heinrich. When Ruprecht demurs, she describes how Heinrich misused her. "Enough," says Ruprecht. He knocks on Heinrich's door and is admitted.

Renata. Softly she asks Madiel to pardon her mistake. She can see now that Heinrich was never Madiel's human incarnation, but always an imposter. Oh, Madiel, Madiel, she cries. Come back as in my childhood.

A window of the house opens, and there is Ruprecht charging Heinrich with the seduction and abandonment of Renata. He throws down his glove.

At the sight of Heinrich, Renata has gone into ecstasy. She begs Madiel to forgive her. She had almost forsworn him. He truly is incarnated in Heinrich.

On Ruprecht's return to the street Renata deliriously warns him against injuring Heinrich. She loves him. "But Renata," asks Ruprecht, "why didn't you tell me that before?" Even Heinrich's insults, raves Renata, are magnificent. In despair Ruprecht runs off, and Renata calls after him, "I'd rather you would die, Ruprecht, than you should injure Madiel."

INTERLUDE (3 min.)
———
SCENE 2 (7 min.)

On the banks of the Rhine. The duel is over. Heinrich moves off, while Ruprecht lies as if dead. His second, Matthew, examines him, pronounces the wound serious and hurries off to find a doctor.

Renata approaches Ruprecht. The duel, she says, has revealed her fate. She loves Ruprecht. His goodness and devotion have triumphed. Passionately she embraces him while he babbles deliriously of America. Offstage voices (chorus of women) sigh ironically, "Love, love, love."

Matthew enters with a doctor. "If you can, Doctor, save his life." "We're not in the tenth century," snaps the doctor. "Nothing is impossible for Medical Science." Matthew shrugs hopelessly.

ACT IV (16 min.)

A quiet square in Cologne. To the right a tavern; to the left the house in which Renata has been living with Ruprecht. She runs out, followed by him, limping and with a cane.

Renata and Ruprecht. Nothing lasts forever, she cries. All is over between us. He hinders her soul's salvation; she will leave him for a convent. He begs her to remain, to marry him. They have been happy together. God cannot intend for them to separate. "Ah, hypocrite!" she cries. "There speaks the devil." (At the word "devil" Mephistopheles and Faust enter and sit at a table before the tavern.) She was crazy to say she loved him, continues Renata. She was disgusted by his embrace. Snatching up a knife she begins to lacerate her shoulder, crying, "This will tame the flesh." Ruprecht tries to hold her. She hurls the knife at him, runs away, and he hobbles after.

Mephistopheles, Faust and later Ruprecht. (This is the opera's most enigmatic scene, and I do not see why Prokofiev included it—except perhaps for fun. He saw Gounod's *Faust* at age nine, adored it, and here perhaps saw a chance both to honor and—split personality—to mock Gounod. Note that, reversing Gounod, he makes Mephistopheles a tenor and Faust a bass.) Mephistopheles calls for wine and food, and when the tavern boy is slow in bringing the food, Mephistopheles swallows him alive. Faust is bored by such tricks. The tavernmaster begs for his boy: tomorrow is market day, and I cannot manage alone. Mephistopheles waves at a pile of garbage and lo! the boy. (In the novel Mephistopheles is presented as Agrippa writ larger and more disreputable, for there is a suggestion that he does his tricks for money. But the ambiguity of what actually happened is preserved.)

Mephistopheles then draws Faust's attention to Ruprecht, and the two ask Ruprecht to show them Cologne. Ruprecht declines, but they refuse to be put off. They will meet him at their hotel tomorrow.

ACT V (18 min.)

In the crypt at the convent. Renata, in the habit of a novice, is prostrate on the stone floor, her arms outstretched to make a cross. Nuns chant offstage.

The Mother Superior asks Renata what she knows of the devil, and Renata denies any knowledge. But since Renata's arrival, says the

Mother Superior, the convent has been upset: knocks on the wall, strange visions before the nuns and some taken with fits. The Inquisitor is coming, and he will judge.

The nuns enter, and then the Inquisitor with attendants carrying candelabra. He begins to question Renata, and violent knocks sound on the wall. Two young nuns scream that they are being pinched. The Inquisitor and other nuns recite an exorcism. More nuns are seized by devils, and through the knocks the devils laugh, "Ha! Ha! Ha!" The Inquisitor pronounces a more powerful exorcism, but the possessed nuns urge their sisters to glorify the devil.

During the pandemonium Mephistopheles and Faust lead in Ruprecht. He starts to go to Renata but is held back by Mephistopheles.

A bell startles Renata. She and six sisters attack the Inquisitor. Others roll on the floor, have fits and praise the devil. Guards rush in and push them back. The Inquisitor, pinning Renata to the floor with his crozier, shouts: "This woman is guilty of carnal intercourse with the devil! To the stake!"

WAR AND PEACE

Opera in two acts of thirteen scenes and an epigraph. World premiere of "final" version in Moscow, Dec. 15, 1959. United States premiere (in English, on television), Jan. 13, 1957. British stage premiere, London, Oct. 11, 1972. United States stage premiere, Boston, May 8, 1974. Music by Sergei Prokofiev, text by him and his second wife, Mira Mendelssohn, after the novel by Tolstoy published in two parts, 1865 and 1869.

PRINCIPAL CHARACTERS

Prince Andrew Bolkónski	baritone
Princess Mary, his sister	mezzo-soprano
Prince Nicholas Bolkónski, his father	bass
Natasha Rostóva	soprano
Count Ilya Rostóv, her father	bass
Sonya, her first cousin	mezzo-soprano
Maria Akrohsímova, a friend of the Rostovs	mezzo-soprano
Count Pierre Bezúkhov	tenor
Countess Helene, his wife	contralto
Prince Anatole Kurágin, her brother	tenor
Dólokhov, Kurágin's friend	bass

Principal Characters (continued)

Kutúzov, Russian Field Marshal   bass
Napoleon   baritone

The action takes place in Russia in the years 1809 through 1812. The text follows Tolstoy almost exactly; in many scenes, word for word.

The date of the opera's premiere is a tangled question. Prokofiev worked on it from 1941 until his death in 1953 and during that period the complete opera as it then existed had a number of isolated performances. Part I, the Peace part, had a run of 105 performances at the Maly Theatre in Leningrad during the 1946–47 season. Then in 1955 a short "final" version was produced in Leningrad and two years later was followed by another, slightly different, at the smaller opera house in Moscow. Finally in December 1959 the big house in Moscow, the Bolshoi, presented the most complete "final" version, which it recorded, and in subsequent years performed outside the U.S.S.R. in Vienna, Milan, Montreal, New York and Washington. For the time being at least, this is the version from which others now vary, mostly by omitting scenes or substituting an overture for the opening choral epigraph. The synopsis follows this Bolshoi "edition," indicating where others are apt to differ.

Over the years, as Prokofiev worked on the opera, he made it more melodic and more martial. Initially it was mostly declamation and to many who heard it, including apparently Prokofiev, often boring. It also at first was chiefly confined to the story of Natasha and Prince Andrew. During World War II, however, on the advice of friends and Communist Party officials, Prokofiev began to expand the character of Kutúzov and the scenes of war with Russia victorious. Some critics have made much of this as an example of government pressure on an artist. Perhaps. But Kutúzov and the war scenes are in Tolstoy, Prokofiev was a patriotic Russian, and such scenes have a long tradition in Russian opera.

Because the opera, like *Boris Godunov* or *Eugene Onegin,* is episodic, a series of scenes taken from a famous story with much of importance left out, several of the scenes can be dropped without destroying the flow of the music. The cuts most often made shift the opera's emphasis to Natasha and Prince Andrew. Depending on taste, this may be an improvement. In Moscow since 1960, in different theatres a short and long version of the opera have played, often simultaneously.

ACT I (Peace—100 min.)

————

OVERTURE (5 min.)

Based on military themes from the opera, ending with one associated with Kutúzov and the Russian people. Not used in most versions where it is replaced by a

CHORAL EPIGRAPH (4 min.)

Intended to balance with the final chorus of the opera. Here the Russian people denounce Napoleon's invasion and predict his defeat. At the opera's end they proclaim it.

SCENE 1 (13 min.)

May 1809. Garden and house of Count Ilya Rostóv at Otradnoe. Prince Andrew, thirty-one and a widower, is stopping overnight with the Count on business. Reading in his bedroom on the ground floor, he sees the moonlight, puts out the candle and opens the window. Spring, love, happiness, he sings, are all illusion.

On the floor above, unaware of Andrew, Natasha also has been drawn to the window by the moonlight. But to her at sixteen the world **duet** is wonderful, the garden a fairyland. Her cousin Sonya urges her to bed, but before prevailing joins in a duet on the beauties of nature.

Their enthusiasm has touched Andrew's soul. If a man is to be **arioso** happy, he decides, he must believe in spring and love and the possibility of happiness.

SCENE 2 (21 min.)

New Year's Eve, 1809–10. A ball in St. Petersburg. The scene is constructed on a polonaise (4 min.), two chorales (6 min.), a mazurka (2 min.), a waltz (5 min.) and, as a coda, an écossaise (1 min.).

The polonaise sets the scene. During the first chorale Count Rostóv enters with Natasha and Sonya. Awed by their first ball, they huddle **polonaise chorales** with Natasha's godmother, Maria Akrohsímova. Count Pierre Bezúkhov and his wife, Helene, enter. He is good-hearted and she beautiful, though her bare shoulders and allegedly loose ways arouse disapproval in Akrohsímova. Tsar Alexander I is announced, and the choir greets him with the second chorale.

The Tsar leads a mazurka in which others join. Prince Andrew **mazurka** enters, and Sonya reminds Natasha that he has spent a night at the Rostóvs.

A waltz is announced, and Pierre introduces Prince Andrew to Natasha. Across the ballroom Anatole Kurágin, Helene Bezúkhov's **Andrew's waltz** brother, admires Natasha, and Helene offers to help him to seduce her. During the waltz Prince Andrew falls in love with Natasha (the waltz returns in scenes 7 and 10 as his memory of a lost love), but she is too excited by the ball to notice.

As the waltz ends, Count Rostóv invites the Prince to visit the family. As Natasha leaves Andrew, he tells himself that if she speaks first to her cousin, then she will be his wife. Natasha speaks first to Sonya. The guests dance an écossaise.

Before the next scene Prince Andrew has proposed to Natasha and been accepted. According to the customs of the day he spoke first to his father, who opposed the marriage: the girl's family was neither rich nor distinguished. Andrew, however, had insisted on his choice, though agreeing to postpone the wedding for a year while he went abroad. Then he had spoken to Natasha's parents, explaining the condition and suggesting another, which the parents accepted: that the engagement not be formally announced, so that Natasha would be free to withdraw from it. Only then did he speak to Natasha. In Tolstoy, Andrew by now has emerged as a complicated, somewhat rigid, proud man capable of great love and self-discipline. Natasha has the charm of youth and the foundation of some great qualities, but she evidently also is self-centered, willful and spoiled by her father.

SCENE 3 (12 min.)

February 1812. The Bolkónski mansion in Moscow. In the year of waiting the Rostóvs have come to Moscow to complete Natasha's trousseau and to pay their respects to Andrew's father, Prince Nicholas Bolkónski.

The Prince refuses to see them, and the butler calls Andrew's sister, Princess Mary, who is mortified by her father's rudeness. Count

Rostóv, pleading an errand (always his solution to a difficult situation), leaves Natasha and Mary to talk. They are not sympathetic; Mary is older, dowdy and interested in religion, and because of the engagement's difficulties avoids talking of Andrew. The old Prince, in a dressing gown and nightcap, bursts in, disparages Natasha's family and in leaving threatens to marry a governess.

Count Rostóv returns, and while he talks to Mary, Natasha in a so- **arioso** liloquy longs for Andrew to return, at once: "I am afraid, for him and for myself."

SCENE 4 (12 min.)

May 1812. At a party given by Helene Bezúkhov. To the back, in the ballroom, couples are dancing to a waltz associated in the opera with **Anatole's waltz** Helene's brother, Anatole Kurágin. To the front, in a drawing room, Helene tells Natasha that Anatole is in love with her.

Count Rostóv enters to take Natasha home, but Helene distracts him into another room and sends in Anatole. He passionately declares his love, and though Natasha protests, before leaving he kisses her and hands her a letter.

Alone, Natasha reads: you must decide my fate—to be loved by you **arioso** or die. He proposes that they elope. A memory of the spring night when she first saw Andrew (Scene 1) comes back to her, and the yearning she has felt in the months apart (Scene 3). But in her mind, as in the orchestra, Andrew's music gives way to Anatole's informal, careless waltz.

Sonya, who has come in, asks sharply: what of Bolkónski? You cannot understand, says Natasha, as the Count appears to take them home.

Before the next scene Akrohsímova, who can be as forthright as Prince Nicholas Bolkónski, calls on him. She reports to the Rostóvs that though the old man will not approve the marriage, it will take place because Andrew wishes it. She delivers a letter to Natasha from Princess Mary begging pardon for her father's behavior and requesting permission to call. But Natasha, without telling her family, replies to Mary that all misunderstandings are over. Availing herself of Andrew's magnanimity, she is ending their engagement. She also writes Anatole that she is ready to elope with him.

SCENE 5 (9 min.)

June 1812. The study of Anatole's friend Dólokhov. (This scene, or part of it, is sometimes cut.)

While Anatole dreamily rehearses the plan for elopement, Dólokhov warns against it. Though he procured the money, the passport, the defrocked priest and even wrote the love letters (echo of Anatole's waltz), what Anatole plans is bigamy: he is already married. But Anatole dismisses that: he adores virgins.

Dólokhov summons the coachman, Balagá, and the three have a parting drink. Then he calls for a sable coat for Anatole to wrap around Natasha, and Dólokhov's mistress, a gypsy, brings one in, though plainly eager not to part with it. But they take it and with shouts to the horses start off for Akrohsímova's house, where Natasha is staying.

Before the next scene Akrohsímova has found Sonya weeping in the hall and uncovered Natasha's plan to elope. She has ordered her servants to lock the gates behind Anatole and to bring him straight to her.

SCENE 6 (20 min.)

Night. Akrohsímova's house. A large glass door leads to the verandah. Natasha is alone, waiting.

A maid runs in to warn that the plan is discovered, but Natasha is too single-minded in her purpose to listen and hurries out to get a shawl.

Anatole enters through the verandah. From behind a curtain steps Akrohsímova's butler, who requests Anatole to follow him. There is a struggle, during which Natasha returns in time to see Anatole escape. In despair she collapses on the sofa.

Akrohsímova enters and unburdens her mind: what a way to return hospitality; behavior typical of Helene and her circle! Had Natasha thought of the duel which her father, brother or Prince Andrew would have to fight? Why did Anatole have to steal her like a gypsy? Natasha replies that no one understands her, that she has broken the engagement to Prince Andrew, that Anatole is a fine man. But unable to answer why he could not approach her honestly, she runs from the room.

The butler announces Pierre Bezúkhov, and Akrohsímova decides to receive him. He is the person to reach Natasha. After explaining to him all that has happened and learning that Anatole is already secretly married, she goes to send Natasha to him.

While waiting, Pierre soliloquizes: he himself is a bit in love with Natasha; but how could she exchange Andrew for Anatole? When Natasha enters and learns that Anatole is married, the tawdriness of her betrayal of Andrew sweeps over her and, broken, she requests Pierre on her behalf to ask Andrew to forgive her.

When Pierre urges her to look forward, not back, she despairs: her life is ruined. No, cries Pierre, if I were free, even at this moment I would ask for your hand and love. Overcome by emotion, he leaves.

Alone, Natasha repeats phrases of their conversation and runs off to attempt suicide. She takes arsenic but loses her nerve, calls to Sonya for help and is saved.

SCENE 7 (9 min.)

Later that night. Pierre Bezúkhov's study. (Sometimes cut.)

Helene, Anatole and two Frenchmen are chatting when Pierre enters, indicating he wants to speak alone with Anatole.

He demands the truth and is prepared to use violence to get it. He forces Anatole to hand over Natasha's letter and then more calmly discusses arrangements for removing Anatole from Moscow. Left alone, he muses on the uselessness of his life, ending with an acknowledgment to himself that he loves Natasha.

A friend enters with news that Napoleon is on the frontier. It looks like war.

ACT II (War—90 min.)

SCENE 8 (26 min.)

August 25, 1812. Before the Battle of Borodino. At the Rajevsky Redoubt in the Russian lines. (Parts, particularly of the military choruses, are often cut.)

While peasant militia build a bastion, Prince Andrew and Lieutenant Denísov converse. With 500 men, says Denísov, he could cut the French lines of communication. The militia sing of Napoleon's certain defeat by the Russian people, led by Father Kutúzov.

Prince Andrew thinks bitterly of Natasha, of how much he had **arioso** loved her (themes from his arioso, Scene 1, and his waltz,

Scene 2) and how little had Anatole Kurágin. He wonders how he could ever have believed in romantic, idealized love. The reality was so much simpler and disgusting.

He sees Pierre, who has come to survey the battlefield, and while two allied German generals discuss the terrain, Andrew assures Pierre that the Russians will win not because of German tactics but because they are fighting for their homeland. The militia and some soldiers join in a chorus to greet Kutúzov, who is inspecting the lines.

Kutúzov greets the men with praise for the unique, wonderful and **the Russian people**   invincible Russian people. (This theme of the invincibility of the Russian people constantly returns.)

Soldiers pass in review, followed by a chorus of Cossacks. Kutúzov asks Andrew to join the staff, but Andrew prefers to remain with his regiment. The militia and all the soldiers have a chorus on the invincibility of the Russian people, and then a cannon fires. There is silence, and then a second cannon. (With a marvelous bit of orchestration, Prokofiev suggests the tension of waiting.) The battle begins.

SCENE 9 (9 min.)

Later the same day. On the Shevardino Redoubt. Napoleon and his Marshals. (Sometimes cut.)

Napoleon at first is sanguine, but as reports come in, he realizes that the Russians are not defeated. His generals ask for reinforcements, which he at first refuses and then orders a division to the front, only to recall it. His touch no longer is sure.

His steward offers breakfast, but Napoleon waves it away. Why is this battle not like the others? An unexploded cannonball lands at his foot. He kicks it aside. (Notice the use of trumpets to suggest the battle's tension and excitement.)

SCENE 10 (15 min.)

Two days later. Napoleon holds the battlefield, but the Russian army, though retreating, is intact. Evening. A peasant's hut at Fili. The closing moments of Kutúzov's council of war with his generals.

At question is whether to risk the army in defense of Moscow or insure its survival by abandoning the city. The generals disagree, and Kutúzov decides to retreat. While the generals depart for their posts, a soldiers' chorus starts in the distance.

Alone, Kutúzov sings a hymn to Moscow. At its end the soldiers'
Moscow aria   chorus grows louder. (The Moscow hymn appears
repeatedly in the remaining scenes and ends the opera.)

SCENE 11 (15 min.)

September-October 1812. A street in Moscow, occupied by the
French. (All or parts frequently cut.)

Confusion and danger lurk in the streets, with the French anxious
that their victory is so incomplete and the Russians of all ranks hostile.
In a sudden swirl of people Pierre meets a servant of the Rostóvs and
learns that they have left the city, taking with them a number of
wounded—among whom, unknown to Natasha, is Andrew.

The French arrest Russians suspected of arson, among them Pierre
and a soldier, Karatájev, whose good-natured philosophy impresses
Pierre. Some freed lunatics run in, followed later by actors from the
Comédie Française, whose building is on fire. Soon the entire city is in
flames. Napoleon, though depressed, admires the people's resolution,
while they promise him defeat for the destruction of their city.

SCENE 12 (13 min.)

A dark hut outside Moscow. On a cot, Prince Andrew, dying, often
in delirium.

His pain is suffocating, like a tower of needles over his face, and in
his head an exhausting, endless "piti, piti, piti . . ." (the words, sound
without meaning, are in Tolstoy). He thinks of Moscow, which he will
not see again, and of Natasha, whom he loved and hated so very much.
If only he could see her once again.

She comes, having just learned of his presence, and asks forgiveness.
He loves her, he replies, and she responds that she will never leave him
again. Will I live? he asks. She is sure of it. But in his head the pain
returns, "piti, piti, piti, boom!" Murmuring "That's enough, please
stop . . . please . . ." he dies.

SCENE 13 (12 min.)

November 1812. On the road to Smolensk as the French retreat
during a blizzard. (Parts of the scene generally cut.)

Two French soldiers discuss the hopelessness of their situation. At the end of the column among the prisoners are Pierre and Karatájev, who can't keep up and is shot. Partisans led by Denísov and Dólokhov harass the French and free Pierre. Denísov tells him that Moscow is reviving. Kutúzov is announced, but there enters first a detachment of female partisans (necessary for the chorus). Kutúzov proclaims that Russia is saved, and all join in a final chorus built on Kutúzov's hymn to Moscow.

In Tolstoy, the following year Pierre and Natasha marry, and Natasha on becoming a wife and mother also becomes less interesting. "In her face there burned none of her former, ever-glowing animation which had been her charm." Her mother remarked of her that "all Natasha's outbursts had been due to her need of children and a husband" and that she was allowing her love for her family to "overflow all bounds so that it even becomes absurd."

THE DEVIL AND DANIEL WEBSTER

Folk opera in one act. World premiere, New York, May 18, 1939. European radio premiere, London, BBC. June 5, 1955. Music by Douglas Moore; text by Stephen Vincent Benét, based on his short story first published in the *Saturday Evening Post,* 1936, and collected in *Thirteen O'Clock,* 1937.

Benét's story is a literary "tall tale" of the kind that flourished orally in the nineteenth century in areas of the United States where the frontier was still fresh in memory. Typically the tales—grotesque, humorous or romantic—were full of realistic details of local custom and celebrated a regional hero, often by wild exaggeration: Paul Bunyan logging on the Big Onion River in the winter of the blue snow, when it was so cold that the cuss words froze in the air; or Bunyan greasing his giant hotcake griddle by skating on it with sides of bacon strapped to his feet. In Benét's story New England's greatest lawyer, Dan'l Webster, to save a neighbor's soul opposes the devil before a court of the damned.

Jabez Stone, a New Hampshire farmer, has sold his soul to the devil in return for ten years of prosperity. And how he prospers! He clears his farm of rocks and mortgages, is elected a State Senator, becomes engaged to Mary, a fine New Hampshire woman, and has the great

Dan'l Webster as a wedding guest. Another guest, however, a stranger to all but Stone, is Mr. Scratch, a Boston attorney, shabby in dress and carrying a black tin box.

To celebrate the wedding, Webster calls for a tune, and when the fiddler can't keep his fiddle on pitch, Scratch takes it and, playing beautifully—though with gloves on—sings a very unpleasant song. Angrily Webster orders him to leave.

Meanwhile the aggrieved fiddler has opened Scratch's black box, from which flutters a white moth. More astonishing still, the moth, in a voice that all recognize as that of Miser Stevens, calls for help: he has sold his soul to the devil. As the moth flies about, the church bell tolls the death of Stevens, and the guests realize that Stone is next. They denounce him for trafficking with the devil and leave.

Alone with his wife, Stone confesses the bargain and urges her like the others to flee him. When she refuses, insisting that she will get the county judge to help him, Stone despairs: "Who'll face the devil and face him down. . . . There isn't a lawyer known to man!"

Webster, however, has returned to take the case. Demanding a jury trial he argues procedure with Scratch, finally agreeing to a jury of the dead so long as it is an American judge and an American jury. Scratch summons them: Simon Girly, who joined the Indians to raid his neighbors; Walter Butler, Loyalist in 1776; King Philip, whose war on the frontier drove settlements back more than a hundred miles; Blackbeard Teach, the pirate; eight more like them, and Justice Hathorne, who sat at the Salem witch trials and did not repent.

The case is argued, and the facts and motions go against Webster. Abandoning the law, he appeals to the jury's memory of what it is to be a man: "Now here is a man, with good and evil in his heart. . . . He is your brother. Will you take the law of the oppressor and bind him down? . . . There is sadness in being a man, but it is a proud thing, too. There is failure and despair on the journey, the endless journey of mankind." That journey he sees as a quest for liberty. "I see you, mighty, shining liberty, liberty! I see free men walking and talking under a free star! God save the United States and men who have made her free!"

Moved by his eloquence and contrary to the evidence, the jury acquits Stone. Then, to a trumpet call like the sound of a cock's crow, judge and jury vanish.

At Webster's call the New Hampshire neighbors return and they start Scratch on the road to Massachusetts—where he'll be more at home.

The opera is short (58 min.) and melodic, though Moore was careful not to allow any lyrical effusion to delay the story. Music and verse are used for moments of heightened emotion, but these frequently are connected by unaccompanied prose dialogue of casual, everyday speech. Much of the trial and Webster's appeal to the jury is set as melodrama, spoken words over music, and here both poet and the composer matched the eloquence they sought to convey. Intoned by a resonant voice, Webster's vision of the United States is moving. The opera does best in relatively small theatres and has a vigorous life in touring and university groups.

THE BALLAD OF BABY DOE

Opera in two acts, eleven scenes. World premiere, Central City, Colorado, July 7, 1956. European premiere (by Santa Fe Opera), Berlin, Sept. 26, 1961. Music by Douglas Moore; text by Moore and John Latouche, based on the life of Baby Doe Tabor, 1854–1935.

PRINCIPAL CHARACTERS

Horace Tabor, Mayor of Leadville	baritone
Augusta, his wife	mezzo-soprano
Mrs. Elizabeth (Baby) Doe, a miner's wife	soprano
Mrs. (Mama) McCourt, her mother	contralto
William Jennings Bryan, a candidate for president	bass-baritone

The action takes place in Colorado and in Washington, D.C., 1880–99.

Moore conceived the opera in 1935 when he read in *The New York Times* an obituary article with the headline: "Widow of Tabor freezes in shack; famed belle dies at 73 alone and penniless, guarding the Leadville bonanza mine." The article told the story of Baby Doe, whose marriage to Horace Tabor, a Colorado silver baron, had delighted and scandalized the nation. A picture showed Baby Doe "at the height of her famed beauty and career." The story's poignancy and American background appealed to Moore, but twenty years and four operas intervened before *The Ballad of Baby Doe* was realized.

The delay was caused chiefly by Moore's difficulty in finding a congenial librettist. The first, Pearson Underwood, was poetic enough but insufficiently dramatic—though the story would seem to tell itself. (The newspaper headline, for example, is a summary of the opera's final scene.) The second, the dramatist Paul Green, who had done the libretto for Kurt Weill's *Johnny Johnson,* wanted to make a play with musical accompaniment, not an opera. Finally Moore went to John Latouche, a Broadway lyricist. This time, with Moore in unquestioned command, the collaboration succeeded.

The opera's subject is loyalty: Baby Doe gave her heart to Horace Tabor. That was that: for all time. When his silver mine failed and he died, for thirty-six years thereafter she waited at the mouth of his Matchless Mine for death to rejoin them.

Moore, a modest man, was modest in his opera: the story is simply told and the music is very direct. Consider how the same theme was treated by two sophisticated Europeans, Hugo von Hofmannsthal and Richard Strauss. In *Ariadne auf Naxos,* Ariadne out of loyalty to Theseus awaits death at the mouth of a grotto on Naxos—and there are layers of culture to be peeled and enjoyed: Greek legends, *commedia dell'arte,* eighteenth-century *opera seria* and, ultimately, a touch of cynicism wholly absent in *Baby Doe.* Moore's simplicity and directness is an enduring facet of American culture.

The work has proved one of the most successful of American operas in the last quarter-century. Beside the quality of its music a reason seems to be that, like *Bohème* or *Traviata,* it can accommodate itself to large or small voices, large or small theatres, even to tents or theatres in-the-round.

ACT I (70 min.)

SCENE 1 (12 min.)

Leadville, Colorado. 1880. Outside the Tabor Opera House, a small building but straining toward grandeur. To one side, a saloon; to the other, the entrance to the Clarendon Hotel.

The curtain rises on boisterous music, a pistol shot rings out, and a miner is ejected from the saloon. He is followed by the bouncer. The miner claims a right to celebrate: he has found a peerless, matchless silver mine. The bouncer tells him to calm down. There's a concert in the new opera house, and "decent folks don't want no noise." The saloon girls whirl the miner around, start him for home, and reenter the saloon.

Tabor. With four cronies he emerges from the concert to smoke a cigar during the string quartet. Stimulated by the beauties of his opera house, he sings of himself (four verses with chorus): "I came this way **Panhandlin' man** from Massachusetts through the Kansas Territory, Pick and shovel in my hand, Belly full of gin and glory." With the girls, who had come out of a saloon, he and his cronies are doing a turn when they are discovered by

Augusta. She and the men's wives have come looking for their husbands, and Augusta is indignant to find them dancing with "these Jezebels." Tabor is willing for himself and the men to be lectured, but sees no reason for Augusta to snub the girls. "Remember," she says, "who you are." The intermission bell rings and the men, chastened, follow their wives in. Tabor lingers.

Baby Doe. She enters (to a waltz associated with her), asking the way **Baby Doe's waltz** to the Clarendon. Tabor points it out, introducing himself and, before reentering the opera house, hoping that "we'll meet again." Though the meeting was accidental, Baby Doe knows who he is and promises herself, "Indeed we'll meet again."

MUSICAL LINK (The waltz—1 min.)

―――

SCENE 2 (12 min.)

Later the same evening. Outside the Clarendon Hotel.

The concert is over, and the men and their wives parade home. Augusta enters the hotel, where she and Tabor have an apartment, while he sits on the step to have a cigar. Two girls from the saloon pass by, angry at Baby Doe for flirting with Tabor. Her husband in Central City, they surmise, cannot afford her, and she is looking for someone rich. "Baby Doe," muses Tabor. "So that's her name."

Baby Doe. At the hotel piano, close by a large window, she sings a **willow song** "Willow" song of loneliness (e.g. in *Otello* by either Verdi or Rossini, or in *The Mikado* by Gilbert and Sullivan): "Willow, where we met together. Willow, when our love was new. . . . Pray tell him I am weeping, too." At its end Tabor, deeply moved, applauds, and she comes to the window.

Tabor. Warmly he talks of memories she has stirred, of youthful won-

arioso   der, of longing and pain, of the beginning of love. He kisses
her hand.

Upstairs a light goes on and Augusta calls, not unkindly. Obediently
he goes up to her.

SCENE 3 (11 min.)

Several months later. In the living room of the Tabor's apartment at
the Clarendon Hotel.

Augusta. While waiting for Tabor and instructing the maid, she sorts
the papers on his desk. Among them is a check for Jake Sands, dated
only yesterday. She is aghast. He wants to buy another mine!

She finds a pair of white lace gloves and is moved that after twenty-
seven years of marriage he should think of her. Putting on her spectacles she reads the card, ". . . Pray wear them that I know, Thy hand
and heart are mine, dear, My dearest"—turning over the card—"Baby
Doe!" So, what her friends have insinuated is true!

Upset, she moves to the window. Is Mrs. Doe pretty? she asks the
maid. Does she have slender hands? The maid nods. Augusta looks at
her own, red and wrinkled, rough with working, cooking, scrubbing,
and mending. They are not pretty hands. "Not like hers!"

Tabor and Augusta. He enters, going straight to the desk and searching
for the check. She questions the wisdom of the Sands investment, and
in the argument that follows she confronts him with the gloves. For a
man of his age it is disgusting. "Can't you realize your position, if you
won't give heed to mine?" Angrily he taunts her: Baby Doe is warm
and tender, where she is cold. "Cold, am I cold?" Augusta cries. "We'll
see about that!" As she storms from the room, he, fearing he has gone
too far, calls anxiously after her.

SCENE 4 (14 min.)

Shortly thereafter in the hotel lobby.

Baby Doe. She comes down with her bags packed, and the clerk quietly
letter aria   orders the bellboy to find Tabor. Writing a letter to
"Dearest Mama," she describes the breakup of her marriage to Harvey
Doe, her mother's promise that her beauty someday would win her a
rich man, her excitement at finding him, and her distress that he is
married. "I know he needs me and that I love him, but I have to give
him up, and we must part forever." After reading it over, she signs it.

(Like a "willow" song, a "letter" aria is part of conventional operatic structure. Though the emotions here, and in the confrontation scene that follows, are relatively shallow, Moore nevertheless makes them seem genuine. For deeper emotions consider the comparable scenes in *La Traviata*.)

Augusta and Baby Doe. Augusta enters, introduces herself and threatens trouble if there is not an end to the affair. Baby Doe assures her it is over, with nothing shameful in it. Tabor, she says earnestly, is a great man, an unusual man, above conventions. Augusta, she adds patronizingly, must try harder to understand him and give him greater freedom to follow his destiny.

"The man is a child," Augusta snaps, "a weakling." The Matchless Mine was pure luck. Without her to manage his affairs Tabor would hold on to nothing. He will never leave her. "Without me he'd be lost!" With a firm "goodbye" she goes.

Tearing up her letter, Baby Doe decides to stay.

Baby Doe and Horace. He rushes in and embraces her. She promises to remain with him always. Trying to disengage, she warns that people **duet** will "see us." Let them, cries Tabor. "What will they see? Only two people in love." Together they start up the stairs.

SCENE 5 (5 min.)

A year later. Augusta's parlor in Denver. She sits in a high-back chair, flanked by four friends.

"What," they ask, "do you intend to do?" "I intend to do," she replies, "nothing at all." But, say the friends, he keeps Baby Doe "like a fluffy kitten on a satin cushion." "What is there to do?" Augusta intones. "Nothing at all."

The friends whisper: "Divorce!" Tabor, says one, has already done it, using a corrupt judge in a different county. Alarmed, Augusta weakens. Prodded again, she rises majestically. "If he ever tries to divorce me, I'll make him rue the day that he was ever born." Eagerly her friends urge, "Shout it from the housetops. Shout it from the housetops."

SCENE 6 (ACT I, Finale—15 min.)

Two years later, in Washington, D.C. 1883. Tabor, appointed a "thirty-day" Senator to fill out another's term, is giving Baby Doe a

Washington wedding. She has divorced Harvey Doe, and Tabor, Augusta; but neither has mentioned either divorce to the officiating priest. The wedding reception takes place in a suite at the old Willard Hotel. Mama McCourt, Baby Doe's mother, is fussing at the decorations while waiting for the bride and groom to appear. Mr. McCourt, his sons, daughters and their spouses sit uncomfortably on gilt chairs; and "a group of four Dandies (doubtless from the State Department) stand apart and aloof."

While the McCourts sigh with pleasure over the beauty and cost of the decorations, the Dandies discuss politics and gossip about the couple's reputation for scandal. Soon Tabor enters with Baby Doe. She is ravishingly dressed, and the Dandies exclaim, "None but the rich can afford the fair."

Tabor joins the men, and a political discussion starts with the Dandies asserting, "The silver standard is out of date. Silver has got to go . . . silver is doomed." Tabor grows angry, and Baby Doe intervenes.

Baby Doe. "Gold," she says, "is fine for those who admire it. Gold is **silver aria** like the sun, but I am a child of the moon, and silver is the metal of the moon." Charmed, the Dandies gather round her. When she finishes, Tabor with a grand flourish presents her with Queen Isabella's jewels, hooking them around her neck. The guests gasp in admiration.

Mama McCourt and the Priest. Sighing, she wishes Harvey Doe were present. "Who is he, m'am?" asks the priest, and hears for the first time of the two divorces. "I was not told the truth!" he declares loudly. (In fact, the historical priest learned of them only after the wedding, from the newspapers.) His angry departure stirs the suspicion of scandal, and the guests are edging toward the door when

President Chester A. Arthur arrives and saves the situation for the Tabors. (In fact, Arthur not only attended the reception but stayed late and soon after included the Tabors in a party at the White House.)

ACT II (64 min.)

SCENE 1 (16 min.)

Ten years later, 1893. The Governor's Ball in the Windsor Hotel, Denver. On a balcony off the ballroom.

After a short prelude based on Baby Doe's waltz, the curtain rises on the women of Denver talking about her. They disapprove of her effrontery, her clothes and manners, and lament for "poor, poor Augusta." Their husbands come to take them back to the ball, and on their way they have a chance to snub Baby Doe, who with her mother is taking a rest from dancing. Mama McCourt is indignant, but Baby Doe is unperturbed: "I have a love that will keep me aglow as the world grows gray and cold, and that is more than they ever will know." *Augusta, Baby Doe, Tabor.* Augusta has come to warn Baby Doe that new legislation in Washington makes it plain that silver is finished. While there is time, Tabor, who has mortgaged all his assets, should sell the Matchless Mine.

Tabor enters and, despite Baby Doe's protests that Augusta came in friendship, scorns the advice and attacks Augusta personally. "I want nothing from her. Kindness least of all. She has none to give."
Tabor and Baby Doe. "Silver will rise," he insists, and she, handing him her jewels, says, "Place my bet on silver." On his urging she agrees to hold on to the Matchless Mine—"always."

SCENE 2 (7 min.)

A club room in Denver, two years later, 1895.

Over a poker game Tabor's cronies discuss his declining fortunes. "Got to look sharp. It's dog eat dog." Tabor joins the game. He tries to persuade them to abandon McKinley and the Republican Party, to back the Democrats and William Jennings Bryan, who speaks for the common people and for "free silver." The cronies indignantly refuse and leave, followed by Tabor's jeers. Just wait, he predicts, the people will back Bryan.

SCENE 3 (12 min.)

A sunny afternoon in 1896. A political rally for Bryan at the mouth of the Matchless Mine in Leadville.

The miners' wives are decorating the speaker's stand when Baby Doe enters with her two daughters. She is more simply dressed than in past years. The youngest daughter has a bouquet to present to Bryan.
Bryan   While the crowd waits, Tabor harangues it. Then he brings in Bryan, who starts a speech for free silver: "Never, never shall we bow down in worship before the calf of gold." Interrupting him,

Tabor's daughter presents her bouquet, and Bryan receiving it christens her "Silver Dollar." (In fact, he gave her the name but in Tabor's home, not at a rally.) Continuing, he soon has the crowd frantically cheering, "Bryan! Bryan! Bryan!"

SCENE 4 (9 min.)

Augusta's parlor in Denver, November 1896.
Augusta and Mama McCourt. Augusta at the window listens to the newsboys—"McKinley wins. Bryan defeated"—and Mrs. McCourt is announced. She has come secretly to ask help for Tabor, who is ruined. Augusta replies that Tabor told her "to leave him in peace." She quotes him: "I want nothing from her. Kindness least of all. She has none to give."

He is humbled, says Mrs. McCourt. Then let him come here himself, suggests Augusta. But that, says Mrs. McCourt would cost him the last thing that keeps him going—"my Lizzie's respect." Augusta concludes, "I can do nothing." In leaving, Mrs. McCourt angrily accuses her of miserliness.

Augusta. Alone, she asks herself "how can you turn away? . . . Go to **Augusta's lament** him now. . . . Forget your pride. . . . Alas, the years have twisted you. . . . This is your failure, too. . . . Now at last, now that Tabor needs Augusta, I should go but I am afraid . . . I cannot go."

SCENE 5 (20 min.)

The stage of the Tabor Grand Theatre in Denver, 1899.
Tabor. Old, dressed in working clothes, he walks slowly onto the stage. The doorman protests, but Tabor, asking who has a better right to take a bow on this stage, looks slowly about, remembering when he built it.

Suddenly a spotlight reveals a politician, a figure in Tabor's memory. The man, repeating a scene of the past, on behalf of the citizens of Denver presents Tabor with a gold watch fob. "Not gold," murmurs Tabor. "It should have been silver." The stage doorman is confused.

The politician recites the history of Tabor's westward journey. It began in Vermont—and in Tabor's memory a woman's voice calls "Horace!" "Yes, maw!" says Tabor aloud. The doorman leaves to get help.

Tabor's mother, severe, critical, fades into Augusta as a young girl. Tabor, who works as a stonecutter in her father's quarry, courts her with his dreams of being "someone, someday." Her schoolgirl friends comment archly: to get ahead, "marry the boss's daughter."

Then comes the westward trek, "Pick and shovel in my hand in a search for fame and glory," with Augusta always urging him to drink less and save more. The riches when they come are overwhelming, but also fleeting, and Augusta warns that he'll die a failure. "How can a man measure himself?" he cries. The excitement was real, and there is the love of Baby Doe and their two daughters. The elder, says the visionary Augusta, will change her name and abandon the family. (In fact, she did.) There's Silver Dollar, Tabor insists, but across the years he sees her as she will be, in garish clothes, half-naked, staggering drunkenly between a racetrack tout and a sailor.

"Oh God," cries Tabor. "Ain't there never no one, nothing, nohow, nowhere, no time, not dust in the hands?" "Look at me," calls Augusta. "You see me through your eyes. You do not see me truly." But rejecting her he mutters, "Nothing, nohow, no time, no where." And Augusta's image fades.

From offstage Baby Doe calls to him and is brought in by the doorman. She is dressed in a black cloak with a mantle over her head. "Have you come to tell me I have failed you?" he asks. "Dearest, I have come to take you home." He touches her face, feels her tears, and cries, "Then you are real!" He calls into the shadows, to Augusta and all the others: "What have you to say of her? You cannot divide us."

"No one can divide us," Baby Doe says. "I will always walk beside you."

He slumps to the stage, and kneeling beside him she covers him with her cloak. Softly she starts the closing aria. Its essence is: Loyalty. Through love she will be with him always. (The aria's form is ABA, particularly suitable here for the return of the first section, more familiar on second hearing, can be charged with a sense of finality. A more extended example of this form used to close an act is Mozart's "Non più andrai," ABACA, with which Figaro closes Act I of Le Nozze di Figaro.)

As Baby Doe softly proclaims her love, the light fades on Tabor, and she is alone onstage. She rises (section B) and lifting the mantle from her head reveals hair that has turned white. Behind her now looms the shaft of the Matchless Mine, and she takes a position before it. Calmly, with certainty (as the first section of the aria returns), she sings that despite time "I shall change along with him, so that both are ever young."

A light snow falls as she starts her long wait for death and reunion.

DIE KLUGE

(The Wise Woman)

Unspecified form in twelve scenes (76 min.). World premiere, Frankfurt, Feb. 20, 1943; American prem. (in English), Cleveland, Dec. 7, 1949; British prem. (in Eng.), London, July 27, 1959. Music by Carl Orff and also text, based on a fairy tale, "Die Kluge Bauerntochter" (The Story of the King and the Wise Woman) first published in *Die Kinder-und Hausmärchen der Brüder Grimm,* 1812 and 1814.

A peasant finds a golden mortar while ploughing and takes it to the King, hoping for a reward. He is thrown in prison for not producing the pestle, too—just as his daughter had warned him. The King, hearing of her wisdom, summons her to court, and three thieving vagabonds, who throughout the opera comment on events, as well as acting in them, watch her go. The King offers to free the father and daughter if she can answer three riddles (answers at end of synopsis):

1. A guest enters a house not by walking, riding or flying. After he is in, the house falls out its windows. Who is the guest?

2. An ivory bird hops from house to house consuming everyone and everything. What is the bird?

3. A millstone floated on the water, supporting a blind man, a lame man and a naked man. The blind man saw a rabbit, the lame man ran and caught it, and the naked man put it in his pocket. What is it?

The daughter solves the riddles, and the King, delighted, marries her.

Some peasants bring a dispute to the King. While a muledriver and a donkeyman slept at an inn, the donkey bore her foal. But the muledriver claims it because it lay nearer to his mule, and with the aid of the three vagabonds he illustrates his story with a dumbshow. The King, ignoring the fact that mules cannot reproduce, awards the foal to the muledriver.

That evening the Queen, heavily veiled, tells the donkeyman that she will send word how to recover his foal. Meanwhile the vagabonds get drunk and sing of virtue cast down and vice triumphant. The King, passing through the marketplace, sees the donkeyman casting a fishnet in the dust and demands an explanation. If mules can give birth, the man says, then fish will swim in the ground. The King recognizes his wife's cleverness and, jailing the donkeyman, banishes her. She may take with her only her trunk and whatever one thing her heart most desires. She chooses wisely and lives happily ever after.

Orff wanted to simplify opera, even to the extent of avoiding its name, and to reestablish for it the popular base that he felt it had lost in the early twentieth century. To his mind rhythm—rather than harmony, counterpoint or tone rows—was the key, and his music is extremely rhythmic and percussive. Melodically it is simple and repetitive. The story in 1943 was consciously anti-Nazi and is still politically symbolic: the King from whose land virtue has departed is a totalitarian bully until he is redeemed by a combination of wisdom and love. Also, as part of Orff's drive for simplification, the opera presents life at its most basic: eating, drinking, loving, stealing, praying. The sexual imagery throughout is strong, mortal and pestle, and the characters express their feelings without any of the doubt or guilt so common in twentieth-century man. (Answers to the riddles: a fish in a fishnet; dice and gambling; a lie. And what she put in her trunk as dearest to her heart was the King.)

FOUR SAINTS IN THREE ACTS

"An Opera to be sung," in a prologue and four acts. World premiere, Hartford, Conn., Feb. 8, 1934; British prem., London, May 27, 1983. Music by Virgil Thomson; libretto by Gertrude Stein.

Thomson and Stein, in Paris 1927, agreed to make an opera together. He proposed that it should be something from the lives of the saints, and she, that it should take place in Spain and concern Teresa of Avila and Ignatius Loyola. As Thomson later wrote: "The fact that these two, historically, never knew each other did not seem to either of us an inconvenience."

Stein once described her purpose in writing a play "to tell what could be told if one did not tell anything." She wished not to present the events of what had happened but the essence, and she proposed to do it by ignoring the particularities of time, place and person.

Her theories challenged not only the realistic drama fashionable at the turn of the century but even the premise of most drama, that it concern recognizable humans: their problems and emotions. Though the ancient Greeks might play Oedipus in a mask, the drama still focused on Oedipus the man, a particular individual. And the social and moral assumptions of the time and place in which he (or the playwright) lived were crucial to the drama.

In *Four Saints in Three Acts* Stein followed her theories closely. The subject was religious life, and the chief characters were St. Ignatius and St. Teresa, the latter divided between a soprano and alto into St. Teresa I and St. Teresa II. The opera was plotless, and its characters by their ritualized gestures and incantations of words and nonsense verse attempted to convey something without actually saying anything—just by sound.

Thomson provided an amusing, joyful score of simple melody and harmony, based in part on American nineteenth century hymns and marches. He also advised listeners: "Please do not try to construe the words of this opera literally or to seek in it any abstruse symbolism. If, by means of the poet's liberties with logic and the composer's constant use of the simplest elements in our musical vernacular, something is here evoked of the childlike gaiety and mystical strength of lives devoted in common to a nonmaterialistic end, the authors will consider their message to have been communicated."

The opera initially had a great success, perhaps mostly for extrinsic reasons: the exoticism of its cellophane scenery and all-Negro cast, its exquisite staging by the choreographer Frederick Ashton; and the instant celebrity of its most famous line: "Pigeons on the grass, alas."

It soon became clear, however, that though most critics adored *Four Saints,* if only for the chance it gave to expound on its meaning, techniques, and symbolism, the public was a lot less enthusiastic; and the frequency of performance plummeted. A chief reason seems to be that a sizeable portion of any audience finds the opera incomprehensible and, with its lack of plot and individual characterization, boring. For these people opera, with its emphasis on the human voice, seems by nature averse to the kind of abstract drama that Stein and Thomson proposed. Critics, on the other hand, continue to be excited by it, in part because they find in it seeds that flowered later into the sort of non-narrative opera that dominated the century's final quarter. They hear in Thomson's simple harmonies and melodies techniques later employed by Philip Glass and John Adams, and see in its abstractions and repetitive gestures the origins of further developments in staging, notably those of the American director-designer Robert Wilson. Perhaps someday audiences will join the critics in their praise of *Four Saints,* but until then, it seems likely to remain an opera more talked about than performed.

THE MOTHER OF US ALL

Opera in two (originally three) acts, eight scenes. World premiere, New York, May 7, 1947; British prem., London, June 26, 1979. Music by Virgil Thomson; text by Gertrude Stein.

For the second of their two operas together, Thomson and Stein, took as their subject Susan B. Anthony (1820-1906), who from the mid-1850s until her death campaigned for Woman's Rights. One of her famous acts was an attempt to vote in the 1872 presidential election, claiming she had the right under the Constitution's 14th amendment. She was arrested, fined $100, refused to pay, and never paid. Eventually in 1920, "the Anthony amendment" to the Constitution, the 19th, gave women the right to vote.

For this opera, set in the United States "in the 19th century without too much precision as to decade" (but c. 1870), with an epilogue "some years later" in the halls of Congress, Washington, D.C., Stein applied her theories of language less rigidly than in *Four Saints and Three Acts,* allowing the opera a more specific story and structure. Anthony's lifelong campaign for women's suffrage provides a narrative thread that allows her to strive, to suffer, to triumph, and then to muse on the worth and meaning of her achievement. Meanwhile around the central strand of "Susan B." Stein and Thomson wove a pageant of American nineteenth-century life.

The cast of thirty characters ranges over a hundred years, 1820-1920; some are historical, such as John Adams and Daniel Webster; and others fictional, Jo the Loiterer, Chris the Citizen, and Jo's fiancee, Indiana Elliot. Without regard to time or place, Stein mixes them in scenes that are essentially impassioned declarations by clashing individuals. Susan B. and Webster, for example, have a debate in which they are plainly opposed though they speak on different subjects, and the scene begins and ends with Jo Loiterer teasing Angel More, who is dead, about a mouse.

The disjointed dialogue resembles snatches of overheard conversation, and the juxtapositions can be comic, poignant, confusing, or clarifying. Some loose ends are eventually tied, others left dangling. One subordinate but continuous theme is the marriage of Jo Loiterer to Indiana Elliot and the question of whose name, if any, should be changed. She proposes an exchange: Indiana Loiterer and Jo Elliot. "All right, says Jo, "I never fight." And the chorus sings soothingly, "She is quite right, Indiana Loiterer is so harmonious, so harmonious."

At the end, Susan B., now a marble statue in the Congressional hall, wonders, "But do we want what we have got, has it not gone, what made it live, has it not gone because now it is had, in my long life in my long life. Life is strife, I was a martyr all my life not to what I won but to what was done. Do you know because I tell you so, or do you know, do you know. My long life, my long life."

Thomson once described his score as "a musical memory book," for he recreates the sound of nineteenth-century America: its sentimental ballads, gospel hymns, bugle calls, marches, waltzes and patriotic songs. For United States audiences, the opera reviews a part of the national heritage. And because Thomson kept his orchestration light, the words as well can be heard.

The opera has no overture, runs 100 minutes, and from it Thomson drew an orchestral suite of four short movements, one of which sometimes is used as an overture or as an interlude between scenes. One way his work has proved its worth is by its ability to retain its impact even with poor staging or with cast and orchestra reduced. In the United Sates alone, before its British premiere, it had more than a thousand performances in two hundred productions, and the pace continues.

PORGY AND BESS

Opera in three acts. World premiere, Boston, Sept. 30, 1935; European prem., Royal Opera House, Copenhagen, March 27, 1943; British prem., London, Oct. 9, 1952. Music by George Gershwin; text by Du Bose Heyward and Ira Gershwin, based on the play *Porgy* by Du Bose and Dorothy Heyward, first performed in 1927. The play was based on Du Bose Heyward's novel *Porgy,* 1925.

PRINCIPAL CHARACTERS

Porgy, a crippled beggar, who loves	bass-baritone
Bess, of easy virtue and the woman of	soprano
Crown, a stevedore	baritone
Sporting Life, who peddles a dope, "happy dust"	tenor
Serena, wife of Robbins, a fisherman killed by Crown	soprano
Clara, a young mother and wife of	soprano
Jake, a fisherman	baritone

The action takes place in the couryard of Catfish Row, "a former mansion of the aristocracy but now a Negro tenement on the waterfront of Charlestown, South Carolina"; in Serena's room overlooking the courtyard; and on Kittiwah Island. Time: the "recent past," i.e., c. 1930.

Gershwin conceived the work as a "folk opera," and much of it is given to showing life in Catfish Row, in the morning and evening, on Saturday night and Sunday, in fair weather and foul, in fun and in sorrow. Further, of the nineteen Negro roles for singers and four white speaking parts, many are *genre* roles: Strawberry Woman, Honey Man (Peter), Crab Man, the Undertaker, the Coroner. These *genre* scenes and roles, though often well realized musically, pose a theatrical problem, for finding the right balance between them and the development of the story is not easy. But that is only part of a larger problem.

With each new production of *Porgy and Bess,* debate resumes as to whether it should be presented as a musical comedy or an opera, whether its scenes and songs should be joined by spoken dialogue or by Gershwin's music, and how much if any should be cut from a work that, uncut, runs three hours, not including intermissions. The original production, with Gershwin's blessing, substituted dialogue for recitative and made sizable cuts; and in the United States at least this "musical comedy" tradition continued unbroken until 1976, when a successful production presented "the opera" as Gershwin wrote it. In Europe, on the other hand, the work generally has been cast and produced as an opera. But neither solution has proved entirely satisfactory, and the debate continues.

This much, however, is generally conceded: Gershwin's gift was for song, and the work's songs are its strongest asset. He also could compose a good chorus. But a song or chorus does not necessarily make a scene, and often the scenes based on them seem short-winded. They appear suddenly, like "the buzzard" song and scene, and as suddenly end, as if coming out of and leading nowhere.

This is partly the result of the *genre* roles, so many characters, each with a scene, and partly because of Gershwin's particular talents. Predominantly a songwriter, he excelled at portraying an individual's feelings, but in this, his first opera, he had not yet developed the ability to bring two or more characters together and to keep them individual while merging their voices in a duet, trio or quartet. For example, Porgy's duet with Bess, "You is my woman now," is a melody with three verses: he has the first, she has the second, and they share the third. Aside from the melody's beauty, the duet succeeds because between the two characters there is only one mood and thought. By contrast Bess's duet with Crown, "What you want wid Bess?," in which mood and thought are opposed, is not so effective. And the musical confrontation of Porgy, Bess and Crown that should be inevitable— consider how Verdi in *Il Trovatore* or *Aida* brings his characters face to face—is evaded.

Gershwin also is weak in the purely orchestral moments: the fugue to which Porgy kills Crown is unexciting, and too many short scenes are joined merely by a rush of sound up and down the chromatic scale. At such moments dramatic tension drains away. Finally, lacking dramatic and orchestral skills, Gershwin works the songs too hard: "Summertime" is sung twice by Clara and once by Bess; many others are sung or played twice or more, and much of the final scene consists of orchestral reprises.

Still, to cut or not? To use Gershwin's recitative or faster-paced dialogue? The question is: how best to set off the extraordinary songs?

A typical cut performance omits about forty-five minutes of music and substitutes considerable dialogue in the singing roles (the four roles of white men were conceived entirely in dialogue, in contrast to the Negroes, who sing). In the synopsis those parts sometimes cut are enclosed in parenthesis, and an empty parenthesis, ( ), indicates a passage in which individual lines are often cut.

ACT I (58 min.; with cuts, 43 min.)

SCENE 1 (37 min.; with cuts, 27 min.)

Catfish Row. Summer. Saturday night. After a few introductory chords, the curtain rises (Jasbo Brown is at the piano, playing a blues while couples dance). Lights slowly illuminate the set.
Clara. She sings her baby a lullaby: "Summertime and the livin' is
Summertime   easy, Fish are jumpin', and the cotton is high."
The Crapgame begins. ( ) The chief players are Jake and Sporting Life. Robbins enters the game over the protests of his wife, Serena. On Saturday night "A man's got a right to play." Jake takes the baby from
A woman is a sometime thing   Clara and sings his lullaby to it: "A woman is a sometime thing." The baby wails, the men laugh and Jake returns to the game. Peter, the Honey Man, enters calling his wares.
Porgy. He drives in, kneeling in his cart pulled by a goat, and eager to play. The men accuse him of loving Crown's Bess, but he passes it off: "When Gawd make cripple, He mean him to be lonely. Night time, day time, he got to trabble dat lonesome road."

The Crapgame continues. Crown enters, drunk and with Bess. He joins the game ( ) in a quarrelsome mood, and when he loses ( ), buys some "happy dust" from Sporting Life. Continuing to lose, Crown picks a fight with Robbins and kills him with a cotton hook.

While Serena wails over the corpse, the crowd scatters. Crown warns Bess that he will be back for her, and runs. Sporting Life, giving her some "happy dust," suggests that they team up and go to New York. She refuses, and he slides away. Left alone, she knocks at several doors, but no one will take her in. Except Porgy.

SCENE 2 (21 min.; with cuts, 16 min.)

Serena's room. The following night. Robbins's body on the bed, a saucer on his chest. Mourners entering drop coins in the saucer.
Saucer Burial. The mourners sing: "He's gone, gone, gone, gone, gone." Bess helps Porgy into the room, but when she starts toward the saucer, Serena refuses her money until assured that it comes from Porgy, not Crown. All sing "Overflow, overflow, oh fill up de saucer till it overflow."

A white detective and policeman enter. The detective orders that Robbins be buried within twenty-four hours, or the corpse will be given to medical students. Then, hoping to break the silence about Crown's whereabouts, he arrests Peter, the Honey Man, as a witness of the murder and takes him to jail.

Serena laments over Robbins, "My man's gone now," and the Undertaker enters. The saucer contains only fifteen dollars and twenty-five are needed, but on Serena's promise to pay he agrees to bury Robbins. Bess leads all in ( ) "Headin' for the Promise Lan'."

ACT II (83 min.; with cuts, 62 min.)

SCENE 1 (31 min.; with cuts, 27 min.)

Catfish Row. A month later. Early morning.
Jake and the fishermen. While they repair their nets, they sing, "It take a long pull to get there, huh! . . . But I'll anchor in de Promise' Lan'" (verse cut).
Porgy. Overhearing Jake and Clara arguing amicably about the need
I got plenty o' nuttin   to make money, he sings, "I got plenty o' nuttin', an nuttin's plenty fo' me." Between verses others comment on his happiness since Bess began to live with him.

(*Sporting Life and Maria*. He saunters over to her, and she deliberately spills the dope in his hand. When he protests his friendship, she threatens him with a knife while singing, "Oh, I hates yo' guts." He slips away when the arrival of Lawyer Frazier distracts her.)

Lawyer Frazier, Mister Archdale and Porgy. Frazier, in a long scene (in which dialogue often is substituted for recitative), persuades Porgy to buy a divorce for Bess from Crown. As he signs and seals the impressive-looking document, a white man, Mister Archdale, enters. He has come to tell Porgy that because in the old days his family had owned Peter's family as slaves, he will post bond for Peter at the jail. Peter's family can expect him soon. Archdale looks at Frazier's document and begins to scold him for fraud when all are distracted by the **Buzzard song** shadow of a low-flying buzzard. (Porgy sings, "Boss, dat bird mean trouble. . . . Buzzard, on yo' way!" The others join him and then begin to disperse to their rooms.) Sporting Life sidles up to Bess and offers her some "happy dust," which she refuses. Porgy grabs Sporting Life's wrist and almost breaks it. Sporting Life pulls away and scuttles off with Porgy calling after him, "Get out, you rat, you louse, you buzzard!"

Porgy and Bess. Alone with Bess, he starts, "Bess, you is my woman **Bess, you is my woman now** now, you is, you is! An' you mus' laugh an' sing an' dance for two instead of one." In the second verse she replies, "Porgy, I's you' woman now"; and the third they sing together. (The scene, musically and theatrically, as she kneels beside him, is one of the opera's most effective.)

The Crowd and Porgy. Everyone appears in lodge regalia for the picnic on Kittiwah Island. The Charleston Orphans' Band marches onstage, is joined by all, singing, "Oh, I can't sit down," and leads the picnickers off to the boat. Maria urges Bess to come. At first she declines but then on Porgy's urging she goes. Alone, he sings happily, "Oh, I got plenty o' nuttin'."

SCENE 2 (16 min.; with cuts, 10 min.)

Kittiwah Island. Evening, the same day.

The picnic is ending amid general gaiety (and all sing, "I ain' got no shame doin' what I like to do!").

It ain't necessarily so *Sporting Life*. He draws everyone's attention with a mock sermon, "It ain't necessarily so. . . . De t'ings dat yo' li'able to read in de Bible, it ain't necessarily so." The song has a non-

sense refrain in which all join: "Wadoo—Zim bam boodle-oo, Hoodle ah da wa da—Scatty wah."
(*Serena.* She breaks into the circle, accuses Sporting Life of working for the Devil, and orders them all to pack up and get back to the boat.)
Bess and Crown. As she starts to leave, Crown calls to her from a thicket. He assumes that she will stay with him, but she tells him ( ) that she is Porgy's woman now and "livin' decent." When Crown laughs and threatens to hold her by force, she sings, "What you want wid Bess? She's gettin' ole now." He insists, however, that she is his, rubs his hands on her and kisses her passionately. As she weakens, he triumphantly orders, "Git in dat thicket."

SCENE 3 (19 min.; with cuts, 15 min.)

Catfish Row. Before dawn. A week later. Bells herald the day while fishermen loll about sleepily.
Jake and the fishermen. They start off after a reprise of "It take a long pull to get there."
Porgy, Serena and others. (From Porgy's room Bess can be heard moaning deliriously about Kittiwah Island.) Peter, the Honey Man, returns from jail and hears from the others that Bess came home from the picnic two days late, alone and sick. When he suggests a hospital, Serena insists indignantly that she can do more with prayer. Kneeling, she begins, "Oh, doctor Jesus." At five o'clock, she predicts, Bess will be well.

The Strawberry Woman, the Honey Man and the Crab Man offer their wares. A clock strikes five, and Bess appears in Porgy's doorway, her fever passed. "How long I been sick?" she asks and starts to explain **I loves you Porgy** what happened on the Island. Porgy stops her: "I know you been with Crown." ( ) The choice is hers. "I loves you, Porgy," she declares, and he joins her happily, "You got Porgy, you got a man."

(The wind rises; the people hurry to close their shutters; the hurricane bell rings and Clara, thinking of Jake at sea, faints.)

SCENE 4 (17 min.; with cuts, 10 min.)

The storm. Serena's room. Dawn of the following day.
The Crowd. (Huddling in fear, they try to drown the storm with a cho-

chorale   rale led by six soloists.) Their appeal becomes more collo-
quial with "Oh, de Lawd shake de Heavens an de Lawd rock de
grown'." In the midst of it Clara sings a verse of "Summertime" (while
Bess and Porgy conjecture that the high water will sweep across Kittiwah Island and Crown will be drowned).

The storm worsens, and there is a furious banging on the door. All
sing, "Oh, dere's somebody knockin' at de do'." (The implication is,
Death.) It is Crown.

Crown and the Crowd. He grabs Bess, scornfully knocking Porgy to the
floor. He laughs at the others for their prayers and taunts them with the
red-headed woman   ribald, "A red-headed woman . . . she's got
somethin' dat drives men wild." To drown out his blasphemy, everyone sings louder.

At the window Clara screams. She has seen Jake's boat in the river,
upside down. Handing her baby to Bess, she rushes out. Bess asks for
some man to accompany Clara. With a laugh Crown suggests Porgy,
then he goes himself, promising to return for Bess. As he plunges into
the storm, the others resume the opening chorale.

ACT III (40 min.; with cuts, 30 min.)

SCENE 1 (9 min.)

Catfish Row. The next night. After the storm.

The crowd prays for those who are missing, Clara, Jake and Crown,
to have faith in Jesus: "Rise up and follow Him home." Sporting Life
suggests to Maria that if Crown is alive that means trouble for Bess.
She is still tending the baby and at Clara's window sings a verse of
"Summertime"; then disappears.

The courtyard is empty. Crown enters furtively. Dropping to his
hands and knees, he crawls toward Porgy's door. Above his head the
shutter slowly opens. A hand emerges with a knife that is struck into
Crown's back. As Crown staggers upright, Porgy leans from the window, grasps Crown's throat and strangles him.

SCENE 2 (13 min.; with cuts, 9 min.)

Catfish Row. The next afternoon.

The Detective and the Coroner have come to investigate Crown's death. Serena pretends to have been sick and seen nothing. ( ) Her friends also saw nothing. The Coroner suggests ( ) that Porgy could identify the body. Porgy refuses: he won't look on Crown's face. But he is led off to the morgue.

Sporting Life and Bess. He insinuates that Porgy will be gone for a long time, "maybe one year, maybe two year, maybe—" And he offers her **There's a boat** "happy dust" to "scare away dem lonesome blues." She refuses: "Take dat stuff away, Buzzard!" But he forces it on her, and she suddenly yields. "There's a boat," he urges, "dat's leavin' soon for New York. Come wid me." He offers more dope and she flees into Porgy's room. Confident that she will come, he leaves the dope on the doorstep.

SCENE 3 (18 min.; with cuts, 12 min.)

Catfish Row. A week later.

(There is a four-minute prelude, during which the courtyard gradually awakens and the people begin to go about their business.)

The Crowd. "Good mornin'. Tell me how are you dis mornin'?"

Porgy. He returns, brought back by the police. He refused to look on Crown's face, was jailed for contempt and while in prison won at craps. He has presents ( ) for all and distributes them (underlying music of "I got plenty o' nuttin' " and "Bess, you is my woman now"). Gradually he notices the crowd's embarrassment and asks, "Where's Bess?"

Their confusion and assurances that all is for the best at first lead him to assume that she is dead. When he learns, however, that she has gone to New York with Sporting Life, he calls for his goat cart. "Where you goin' Porgy?" they ask. "Ain't you say Bess gone to Noo York? Dat's where I goin'. I got to be wid Bess. Gawd help me to fin' her." He holds up his arms, the men lift him into his cart, and he leaves: "I'm on my way. Oh Lawd, I'm on my way."

LES MAMELLES DE TIRÉSIAS

(The Breasts of Tiresias)

Opéra-Bouffe in two acts and a prologue (but short, 53 min., and intended to be presented without break). World premiere, Opéra-

Comique, Paris, June 3, 1947; American prem. (in English), Waltham, Mass., June 13, 1953; British prem., Aldeburgh, June 16, 1958. Music by Francis Poulenc; text by Guillaume Apollinaire (Wilhelm-Apollinaris de Kostrowitski) from his "drame surréaliste" of the same title, first presented in 1917.

PRINCIPAL CHARACTERS

Thérèse-Tirésias	soprano	Tee.ray.see.uhs
Le Mari (the Husband)	baritone	
Le Gendarme (the Policeman)	baritone	

Poulenc changed the time of the action from 1917 to 1910–14, "an epoch that is for me typically Apollinairian" (Apollinaire died in 1918); he also changed the setting: "I think that exoticism has nothing to do with the story, so I have preferred to locate Apollinaire's Zanzibar somewhere between Nice and Monte Carlo, where the poet grew up."

Apollinaire called his play a "surrealist" drama (said to be the first use of the word) because it proceeded on a principle of "a reasonable use of improbabilities." As Poulenc later observed, it "has no consistent plot. It is made up of sketches . . . buffoonery, with no other logic than caprice. . . . If my music succeeds in producing laughter, while still allowing to be felt through it moments of tenderness and true lyricism, my aim will have been fully attained, since then I shall not have been false to Apollinaire's poem, in which the most violent buffoonery alternates at times with melancholy." In fact, by adding a lyrical beauty and musical structure not present in the text, Poulenc transformed a series of farcical improvisations into a more profound and moving statement.

The crux of the opera is Thérèse who, bored with making meals and children, determines to change sex. Releasing her breasts—balloons—she grows a beard, leaves home and husband, and adopts a man's name, Tirésias. (The original Tiresias, the Greek seer, in an extraordinary alteration lived for seven years as a woman, thus establishing a claim to wider experience than anyone else. When asked—because of course the Greeks did ask—whether man or woman had the greater enjoyment from intercourse, he replied, woman, nine times more.) Later Thérèse, having resumed her sex, returns to her husband. Lacking her balloons she is, as he remarks, "flat as a tack." Still, without hesitation they agree to love, for "love the white or love the black, it's merrier with a change. You only need to see it right."

For Apollinaire's mixture of simplicity and sophistication, lightness and gravity, Poulenc's gifts of melody and sharp pointed rhythms were ideally suited. No matter how swift the text's change of mood, Poulenc smoothly matched it. Despite eighteen short, excited scenes the opera flows, leaving behind an impression of unity.

PRESENTED AS A SINGLE ACT (53 min.)

PROLOGUE (6 min.)

The house curtain rises, revealing a painted curtain before which steps the manager to explain the opera's significance, aesthetic and human. Its purpose is "to reform manners," and as it concerns children, "a domestic subject," it is treated "in a familiar tone." It will appeal to common sense, aiming to amuse rather than to preach the audience into observing its moral: "faites des enfants (make some children), "vous qui n'en faisiez guère (you who have been making very few). (In the years immediately after World War I and again after World War II, when lovers often were parted by distance or death, this seemingly silly sentiment—get on with life—was both poignant and profound.)

The manager then talks with great excitement—the Prologue is in three parts: slow, quick, slow—of the dramatist's right to use tricks to reinforce his message: crowds can speak with one voice, time be telescoped and space imagined. On the stage the play is the universe and the dramatist, god-the-creator.

Excusing himself for taking so long, he again urges the moral, "faites des enfants, vous qui n'en faisiez guère," and disappears slowly downward through a trapdoor.

ACT I (24 min.)

The square of Zanzibar, a Riviera town. A café, a newspaper kiosk, a bar-tabac shop with above it an apartment, and in the distance the Mediterranean.

Thérèse and the Voice of the Husband. Broom in hand, she steps from the apartment house announcing that she has had enough. She will no longer recognize the authority of man. Though her husband wooed her "dans le Connecticut" (in Connecticut), she need not cook for him in Zanzibar.

From the apartment window comes his voice, "Donnez moi du lard" (Give me some bacon).

Thérèse throws down the broom. She will be a congressman, a lawyer. "Faire des enfants, faire la cuisine" (to make children and to cook), "non, c'est trop" (no, it is too much). His voice floats down, "Donnez moi du lard."

She half-opens her blouse, revealing her breasts, red and blue balloons. As she releases them, they float skyward but are held in check by strings. To a rhythmic waltz she sings: "Envolez-vous" (fly away), "oiseaux de ma faiblesse" (birds of my frailty). "Comme c'est joli" (how pretty they are). Then with her cigarette lighter she pops them and runs to examine her new-grown beard in the bar's mirror. Turning to the audience she expresses her virility in strong Spanish rhythms.

Thérèse and the Husband. He emerges with a bouquet for Thérèse but singing, "Donnez moi du lard." She brusquely interrupts and befuddles him with her transformation. "Oh, ma p'tit' Thérèse, où es tu?" (Oh, my little Thérèse, where are you?) Deciding that she has been killed and the assassin assumed her clothes, he is about to kill her, when she stops him with a gesture and to musical phrases slow and majestic announces that she is no longer his wife, or even Thérèse; she is now a man, Tirésias. Leaving him stunned, she enters the apartment, calling from upstairs, "I'm moving out."

The Husband. From the window, preceded by a long drum roll, comes a chamberpot—"Le piano," gasps the Husband (i.e., it must be played seated)—and a urinal—"Le violin" (i.e., it can be played standing). "La situation devient grave" (the situation becomes serious). He enters the building, shoulders sagging.

Presto and Lacouf. A fat and a thin man, both drunk, bounce from the café dancing a polka and discussing their card game. The conversation, as is not unknown with drunks, is disjointed. Presto claims to have lost everything playing Zanzibar. Lacouf insists he has won nothing and anyway they are not "à Zanzibar" (in Zanzibar) but "à Paris" (in Paris). They argue courteously and decide on a duel; "il le faut" (it is necessary). As Tirésias and the Husband reappear, Presto and Lacouf shoot each other dead—though later they revive.

The Dead, Tirésias, the Husband and sixteen People of Zanzibar. Tirésias, very chic in new clothes, leads out the Husband, now dressed in her castoffs and with his hands tied. She rejoices in her freedom and for her first act decides to buy a newspaper. Slowly turning the pages of *Le Petit Zanzibar* she begins to read from it, very poetically. The story, as newspaper stories often do, makes no sense but is taken up and repeated by everyone. "As he was losing a game of Zanzibar, Monsieur Presto has lost his bet on the pari-mutuel (shortened to pah.ree); since we are in Paris (pah.ree), Monsieur Lacouf has won nothing, since the scene (sen.uh) is placed in Zanzibar, just as much as the place of the Seine (sen.uh) is in Paris." (The text is strewn with such puns, difficult to realize musically. For the most part Poulenc leaves them to be caught in passing—by those who can.)

The bodies of Presto and Lacouf are carried off, and Tirésias, despite her proclaimed boldness, on hearing a horse's hoof exits rapidly.

The Husband and the Gendarme. The representative of Authority in Zanzibar enters on a toy horse and begins to inspect the premises. The Husband calls to him and, dressed in woman's clothing and with his hands tied, is taken for a damsel in distress. "Ah, la belle fille" (the pretty girl), exclaims the Gendarme, his hand on his heart. "Dites ma belle enfant" (tell me my pretty child) who has treated you so meanly? "Il me prend pour une demoiselle" (he takes me for a girl), says the Husband and for a time plays at cross-purposes with the gallant Gendarme, who soon proposes marriage. Exasperated, the Husband reveals his sex just as offstage the People of Zanzibar hail Tirésias with cries of "Plus d'enfants" (no more children).

The Husband. In a tirade which leaves the Gendarme speechless, the Husband says: you hear the cry "plus d'enfants." Zanzibar, however, must have children. If the women fail in this regard, then I, I will make them.

Finale. The paper-seller, a woman, announces through a megaphone: "Vous qui pleurez" (you who weep) "en voyant la pièce" (in seeing the play), pray for prize-winning children. The people of Zanzibar urge the prayer on each other as the Husband tells the Gendarme to return that night if he wants to see children born of man. Suddenly onto the stage on roller skates come Presto and Lacouf, swinging to the left and right and demanding the names of these extraordinary children. The act ends in general confusion with the curtain scored to fall a line too soon.

ENTR' ACTE (3 min.)

After a monent's pause the orchestra sounds the "Vous qui pleurez" melody, but now in a strikingly different orchestration. Couples enter and dance a gavotte before the drop curtain. Facing the audience they repeat "Vous qui pleurez en voyant la pièce," pray for prize-winning children. And lo! from the orchestra pit, growing ever stronger, a cry of "Papa."

ACT II (20 min.)

As before, but the square now is filled with cradles. Sunset.

The Husband and the Newborn. With the aid of an incubator he has produced in one day 40,049 children, and he is happy. The babies sing "Tra la, la la," and he responds "silence, silence."

The Husband and the Reporter for a Paris paper. A knock at the door, "Entrez," and enter the Reporter. "Hands up," he cries in English, and a whiff of crime hangs over the scene. He begins his interview with the assumption that because of the number of children the Husband must be rich. Not at all, says the Husband, he expects in old age to be supported by his children. One son, "Arthur," has already made a fortune as a hoarder of skimmed milk while another, "Joseph," has written a famous novel, *Quelle Chance!* (What Luck!) He gives the Reporter a copy to read but grows irritated when the Reporter begins to snicker over double meanings. With exaggerated politeness the Reporter leads up to a request to borrow money, and with equal politeness he is thrown out.

The Husband. Alone, he ruminates. (His soliloquy is spoken.) The more children he has, the richer he will be. Economists who advise against large families are simply mistaken. Consider the cod, who spawn thousands, and who ever heard of a cod dying in poverty. He will have more children, and with enthusiasm he creates a reporter who leaps from the cradle full-grown.

The Husband and the Son. But the son is a disappointment to his dear old dad, for he begins their relationship with an attempt at blackmail. He is rebuffed and after reciting a few news items, including one that Picasso has made a picture that rocks like a cradle, is gently sent away. (The two scenes with reporters are the opera's weakest: seemingly, no matter how skillful the singers in performance the scenes do not project. The difficulty may be that Apollinaire's view of the public world is too harsh and unrelieved by sufficient buffoonery. Or perhaps Poulenc's inspiration for a moment flagged. He reached the heart of Presto and Lacouf with the first bars of their polka; both reporter scenes lack such clear melodic and rhythmic definition.)

The Husband. "That child did not turn out well. I have a mind to disinherit him." He considers creating a tailor child. To be well dressed is important.

The Husband and the Gendarme. The Gendarme asks where Zanzibar is to find the food to feed everyone. The Husband suggests ration cards, available at the fortune-teller; sufficient food is a problem of foresight.

The Fortune-Teller (Thérèse in disguise), the Husband and the Gendarme. She comes down the center aisle, throwing cadenzas right and left and refusing to be put off by either the Gendarme, who reminds her that her trade is illegal, or the Husband, who hopes she is the barber. When the Gendarme attempts to arrest her, she scratches him and he falls dead on the café chair. She reveals herself to the Husband who, bursting with joy, exclaims "Thérèse." At the woman's name the Gendarme revives. "Mais te voilà" (But look at you), continues the Husband, "plate comme une punaise" (flat as a tack). The Gendarme, indifferent, enters the bar.

"Qu' importe?" (What does it matter), says Thérèse. "Il faut s'aimer" (we must love) "ou je succombe" (or I succumb). And the Husband agrees.

Finale. Starting with a waltz built on "il faut s'aimer," Poulenc reviews the play's moral. When the Husband offers Thérèse a bouquet of balloons, so that she will no longer be "plate comme une punaise," she releases them, "envolez-vous," as an unnecessary complication. "Aimez le blanc" (love the white), "ou bien le noir" (or love the black . . . "suffit de s'en apercevoir" (it's enough to see it right). In the end, a sentiment in which all agree, "faites des enfants."

Vocabulary

faites des enfants	fay.tuh day zaw(nasal). faw(n)	make children
vous qui n'en faisiez guère	voo key naw(n) fuzz.ee.yay gware.uh	You who have been making few
dans le Connecticut	daw(n) luh . . .	in Connecticut
donnez moi du lard	dun.nay mwah doo lahr	give me some bacon
non, c'est trop	naw(n), say trow	no, it is too much
envolez-vous	aw(n).vohl.lay voo	fly away
oiseaux de ma faiblesse	wah.so duh mah fay.bless.uh	birds of my frailty
comme c'est joli	kum say shjow.lee	how pretty it is

Vocabulary (continued)

oh, ma p'tit' Thérèse	oh, mah p'teet . . .	oh, my little Thérèse
où es tu	oo ay too	where are you
la situation devient grave	lah sit.twah.see.aw(n) duh.vee.ah(n) grah.vuh	the situation becomes serious
à Zanzibar	ah tsahn.tsee.bar	in Zanzibar
à Paris	ah pah.ree	in Paris
il le faut	eel luh foh	it is necessary
ah, la belle fille	ah, lah bell fee	ah, the pretty girl
dites ma belle enfant	deet mah bell . . .	tell me, my pretty child
il me prend pour une demoiselle	eel muh prah(n)d poor oon dem.wah.sell	he takes me for a young woman
plus d'enfants	ploo d'aw(n).faw(n)	no more children
vous qui pleurez	voo key pl'her.ay	you who weep
en voyant la pièce	aw(n) v'why.aw(n) lah p'yes.suh	while watching this piece
silence	see.lawh(n).suh	silence
quelle chance	kell shaw(n).suh	what luck
mais te voilà	may tuh vwah.lah	but look at you
plate comme une punaise	pla.tuh kum oon poo.nay.zuh	flat as a tack
qu'importe	k'am por.tuh	what does it matter
il faut s'aimer	eel foh say.may	we must love
ou je succombe	oo shje suk.kawn.buh	or I succumb
aimez le blanc	ay.may luh blaw (n).kuh	love the white
ou bien le noir	oo b'yan(n) luh n'wahr	or love the black
suffit de s'en apercevoir	soo.fee duh soh(n) ah.pair.suh.v'wahr	it's enough to see it right

DIALOGUES DES CARMÉLITES

Opera in three acts. World premiere (in Italian), La Scala, Milan, Jan. 26, 1957; French prem. (in French), Opéra, Paris, June 21, 1957; American prem. (in English), San Francisco, Sept. 20, 1957; British prem. (in Eng.), Covent Garden, London, Jan. 18, 1958. Music, composed to a French text, by Francis Poulenc; text from the play by

Georges Bernanos (1948) adapted from Gertrud von Le Fort's novel *Die Letzte am Schafott* (1931) and an unused film scenario by Philippe Agostini and Reverend V. Bruckberger.

PRINCIPAL CHARACTERS

Le Marquis de la Force	baritone
Le Chevalier, his son	tenor
Blanche, his daughter (Sister Blanche of the Agony of Christ)	soprano
La Prieure, the Prioress of the Carmelite Convent (dies at the close of Act I)	contralto
Mère Marie, Assistant Prioress (Mother Marie of the Incarnation)	mezzo-soprano
Soeur Constance, a very young nun (Sister Constance of St. Denis)	light soprano
Madame Lidoine, the new Prioress	soprano

The action, starting in April 1789 and ending in July 1794, takes place in Paris and at the Carmelite Convent in Compiègne, France.

The opera, play and novel make use of an incident of the French Revolution. On July 17, 1794, only ten days before the fall of Robespierre and the end of the Reign of Terror, sixteen Carmelite nuns of Compiègne were guillotined for defying the secularization order of the Revolutionary Tribunal. In 1906, by order of Pope Pius X, they were beatified. (During the Terror, which began with the fall of the Girondin party in June 1793, approximately 20,000 persons in France were executed, many of them without trial. At the height of the period, the forty-nine days from June 10 to July 27, 1794, there were 1,376 executions in Paris alone.) Except for the fact of the nuns' deaths, however, their personalities and actions in the opera are fictitious.

Poulenc (1899–1963) was known in his youth chiefly as a clown. Drawing on the sounds and sentiments of the music hall and circus, he composed much light-hearted music that was clever, elegant and, thus far, lasting. His opera *Les Mamelles de Tirésias* (1947) is the climax of this strain.

By the late 1930s, however, it was evident that he also had a religious side, which he expressed in much the same sophisticated style. In 1936 he composed the *Litanies à la Vierge Noire de Rocamadour,* the following year a *Mass,* and in 1938, when Europe was threatened by war, an exquisite setting of some lines of a seventeenth-century poem by Charles d'Orléans, "Priez pour Paix" (Pray for Peace). "I have tried in this mélodie," wrote Poulenc, "to give an impression of fervour and above all, of humility, which for me is the first quality of prayer."

The war came, and with it death for many and for many more the fear of death. For almost five years the northern half of France was occupied by the Germans and the southern half dominated by them. From both parts Frenchmen were sent to work in forced labor camps and, if Jewish, to gas chambers. It was a time when to help a fugitive, to deliver or receive a letter or even to be seen talking to someone suspected, might lead to arrest, torture and death. Fear, and each person's response to it, was a part of daily life.

While this atmosphere was still raw in memory, Bernanos produced his play *Dialogues des Carmélites,* which offers a religious response to the fear of death, and in 1953 Poulenc began to compose the opera. The story, opening at the start of the Revolution, shows a girl almost paralyzed by fear overcoming it through participation in a community of Carmelite nuns. The "dialogues," however, are plural, and the responses of several nuns to terror and death are examined.

Poulenc dedicated the score, his largest work, to four composers. To Debussy, "who gave me the taste for writing music"—and in some respects the opera follows the example of *Pelléas et Mélisande:* an almost word-for-word setting of the text, a refusal to repeat words to gain emphasis or fluency, and a great care that every word should be audible. But the other three composers, "who have served one here as models," are Monteverdi, Verdi and Moussorgsky. Poulenc, far more of a humanist than Debussy, has nothing ethereal or symbolic about his nuns: they are solid, individual and wholly human in their fears. And far from eschewing the "big scene," Poulenc plots several through the acts and uses the Revolution to create a Terror that can end only at the guillotine.

Musically, the opera exhibits many of Poulenc's virtues. Though without tunes, it is lyric throughout in its setting of the words and phrasing; and though the orchestra is large, the voices always predominate. The scoring is sensuous and graceful, and if the conductor is careful, Poulenc's indicated silences, the long and short pause, will be effective. Some themes or phrases recur, chiefly in the orchestra, but Poulenc uses them less as motifs for characters than as rhythmic devices to propel the vocal line. Overall the opera has an air of serious charm shattered frequently by violence.

Each act has four scenes connected by a musical link, by an interlude in which a short scene is played before a drop curtain, or sometimes by both. The opening curtain rises on the eighth bar of music.

ACT I (56 min.)

———

SCENE 1 (16 min.)

Paris. April 1789. Late afternoon. The library of the Marquis de la Force, who dozes in a chair.

The Chevalier. He bursts in, demanding, "Où est Blanche?" (where is Blanche). The Marquis, startled, scolds him but soon asks affectionately, "Mais que voulez-vous à Blanche?" (But what do you want with Blanche). The Chevalier fears for her. The people are rioting, and she is in the family coach somewhere in the city.

The Marquis. The words "le carrosse" (the coach) and "la foule" (the crowd) recall an image that haunts his sleep. With mounting excitement he describes the night (May 30, 1770) when Paris celebrated the Dauphin's marriage (to Marie Antoinette). While the crowd watched the fireworks, he and the Marquise, who was pregnant, started for **Narrative** home. Suddenly some boxes of rockets exploded, causing the people to panic. Faces of furies appeared at the carriage window, the glass was shattered and—he pauses with hands pressed to his forehead—the soldiers arrived in the nick of time. That night the Marquise died giving life to Blanche.

Yet, he assures his son, no harm will come to Blanche. The Chevalier, however, is worried about psychological harm: "mais pour son imagination malade" (but for her sick imagination). His father urges "patience" (patience): a good marriage and children will steady her nerves. The Chevalier disagrees: fear is destroying Blanche.

Blanche. In haste she enters. Despite the familiar carriage she had been terrified, for between the crowd and her had been only a fragile window. Pleading fatigue, she starts for her room. The Chevalier urges her to take a candle, for as a child she used to say that every night she died only to be reborn each morning. There has been only one resurrection, she states firmly, Christ's, at Easter; though for her every night is like Christ's Agony.

Her remark leaves the men confused. The Chevalier goes off to see the coachman, and the Marquis settles back in his chair. Suddenly, offstage Blanche screams, and a servant enters, explaining that his shadow had terrified her. She follows immediately, with an air of desperate resolution.

The Marquis and Blanche. He makes light of the incident, but she sees in it a portent, concluding "Avec votre permission, j'ai décidé d'entrer au Carmel" (with your permission, I have decided to enter the Carmelite Order, i.e., to become a nun). "Au Carmel!" the Marquis exclaims: one doesn't become a nun out of a moment's fervor or spite at the world. She pleads that she neither hates nor despises the world, rather, it is an element alien to her, one in which she cannot live. "Oui, mon père." Physically she cannot bear its noise and agitation. Though moved, he questions whether she has truly tried to live in it.

Blanche. Kneeling, she begs, "Oh par pitié" (out of pity), let me hope that I shall find some cure for my torment. God, I believe, is guiding my life. If I have not tried hard enough, He will forgive me. I give Him all. "J'abondonne tout" (I abandon all). "Je renonce à tout" (I renounce it all). "So that he may restore me to Grace."

The Marquis, lost in thought, strokes her head at his knee.

MUSICAL LINK (3 min.)
———

SCENE 2 (8 min.)

Several weeks later. The parlor at the Carmelite Convent at Compiègne. The Prioress and Blanche, separated by a double grill, are conversing. The Prioress is old and ill. As the curtain rises, she is attempting to move her chair closer to the grill.

The Prioress and Blanche. The Prioress apologizes for her clumsiness. The nuns insist that she use the chair, and she finds it hard to resume luxuries long abandoned. Blanche compliments her on her "détachement" (detachment) from comfort. Habit gives "détachment," observes the Prioress, and a nun is not free of pride until she is free of her "détachement."

After a long pause the Prioress says, I see that the "sévérités de notre Règle" (formidable rules of our Order) do not frighten you. They attract me, Blanche replies.

Another pause, and the Prioress asks, what has drawn you "au Carmel" (to the Carmelite Order)? Urged to speak openly Blanche replies, the quest for "une vie héroïque" (an heroic life). "Une vie héroïque?" snaps the Prioress That is not the purpose of the Order. "La prière" (prayer) is its sole purpose and justification.

Blanche weeps, but says that she still feels drawn to the Prioress and the Order. There is no other refuge.

"Notre Règle n'est pas un refuge" (our Order is not a refuge), says the Prioress. It is not the Order which guards us, my daughter, but we who guard the Order. More gently she asks: if admitted as a novice, by what name do you wish to be known?

Blanche replies, "Je voudrais m'appeler Soeur Blanche de l'Agonie du Christ" (I would like to call myself Sister Blanche of the Agony of Christ). The Prioress is startled and closes the interview: "Allez en paix, ma fille" (go in peace, my daughter).

MUSICAL LINK (3 min.)

SCENE 3 (7 min.)

The Convent's workroom. Blanche and a young nun, Sister Constance, take in provisions passed to them by a third nun at the door. *Sister Constance and Blanche.* Constance chatters happily, and Blanche chides her for such gaiety when the Prioress is dying. But to Constance the Prioress's death at fifty-nine is natural. For herself she decided long ago that since life is so "amusante" (amusing), death must be also. Blanche asks, "Et maintenant?" (And you think that now). "Oh, maintenant," Constance says, she hardly thinks of death, since so much of life "m'amuse" (amuses me). Tartly Blanche remarks that God may tire of so much good humor.

Startled, Constance asks if Blanche wants to hurt her, and Blanche without stating the reason confesses that she has envied Constance. The idea is incredible to Constance, who suggests that they pray together, offering their lives in place of that of the Prioress. Blanche refuses: the suggestion is infantile. Constance declares, however, that she has always known that she would die young. And when she first saw Blanche, she knew that the two of them somewhere, someday would die together. Blanche declares the notion ridiculous, and then suddenly afraid cries, "Stop it! Stop it at once!"

Constance murmurs that she meant no offense.

MUSICAL LINK (2 min.)

SCENE 4 (Death of the Prioress—17 min.)

A cell in the Convent's infirmary; the Prioress, in bed; at her bedside, her Assistant, Mother Marie. (The musical scene divides roughly in three parts.)

The Prioress and Mother Marie. The Prioress hopes to sit in a chair while receiving the nuns for the last time. It will help to simulate a composure she does not feel. Interrupting Mother Marie she murmurs, "se voir mourir" (to see yourself die). The common phrase describes her position exactly. "Je suis seule, ma Mère, absolument seule" (I am alone, Mother Marie, absolutely alone). After a pause she asks how long the doctor gives her to live.

Mother Marie puts a crucifix to the Prioress's lips: The doctor fears the struggle will be hard. God . . .

God is a shadow, cries the Prioress. Thirty years a nun, thinking of death every hour and now none of it a help!

She asks after Blanche. Does the novice hold to her choice of name? "Oui," says Mother Marie, "Soeur Blanche de l'Agonie du Christ"; adding, "You seem moved by this choice."

It was the name, the Prioress reveals, that she chose for herself many years ago, and now of all her daughters Blanche is the greatest cause for worry. As Prioress, "je vous remets Blanche de la Force" (I entrust you with Blanche de la Force). You will answer for her to me before God. "Oui, ma Mère" (yes, my Mother), swears Mother Marie.

There is a knock, and Blanche enters while Mother Marie goes off to call the doctor.

The Prioress and Blanche. Because you are the newest, the Prioress states, of all my daughters you are the dearest, but also the one most threatened. To avert the danger I would give my life—Blanche weeps—but all I can offer is my death, "une très pauvre mort" (one very humble death). After a pause she talks of the saints and of others who, though poor and needy, also glorified God. Misunderstanding, Blanche murmurs that she has no fear of being poor. Not money but spirit, says the Prioress. Blanche must have courage and "surtout ne vous méprisez jamais" (especially, never despise yourself). With a blessing, she dismisses Blanche, "adieu" (farewell), as Mother Marie reenters with the doctor and Sister Anne.

The Prioress and Mother Marie. The Prioress asks for medicine before facing the nuns, and the doctor refuses it. The Prioress appeals to Mother Marie, who urges her to forget the nuns and think on God. Violently the Prioress cries, "Let him first think on me." Shocked, Mother Marie exclaims, "Votre Reverence delire" (Your Reverence is delirious), and she orders the window closed as the Prioress begins to groan. When Sister Anne seems about to faint, Mother Marie scolds her gently.

Suddenly the Prioress calls hoarsely, "Mère Marie . . . Mère Marie. . . . Je viens de voir notre chapelle vide et profanée" (I just saw our chapel empty and desecrated). "The altar split in two; straw and blood on the gound. . . . God has forsaken us. God has renounced us."

Soothingly Mother Marie urges her to say nothing that . . . "Ne rien dire!" (say nothing), exclaims the Prioress. "Ne rien dire . . ." when despair clings to the skin like a mask. "Oh, if I could only tear away this mask with my nails."

Mother Marie orders Sister Anne to inform the others that they will not have their daily interview with the Prioress. Through the opened door appears Blanche, as if walking in her sleep. The Prioress, sinking rapidly, beckons her to the bed. But before dying she is able only to breathe a few incoherent words on the fear of death—"peur de la mort!" Blanche, sobbing, buries her face in the sheets.

Vocabulary, Act I

Où est Blanche?	oo ay Blaw(n).shuh	Where is Blanche?
mais, que voulez-vous à Blanche?	may, kuh voo.lay-voo ah . . .	but what do you want with Blanche?
le carrosse	luh kah.ROSS.uh	the coach
la foule	lah foo.luh	the crowd
mais pour son imagination malade	may poor saw(n) ee.mah.jeen.ah. see.aw(n) mah.lah.duh	but for her sick imagination
patience	pah.see.o(n)suh	have patience
avec votre permission, j'ai décidé d'entrer au Carmel	ah.vek vo.truh pair.miss.yon(n) shjay day.cee.day den(n).tray oh kar.mell	with your permission I have decided to enter the Carmelite Order (i.e., to become a nun)
au Carmel	oh kar.mell	join the Carmelites
oui, mon père	whee maw(n) pair.uh	yes, my father
oh, par pitié	oh par peet.yay	oh, for pity's sake
j'abondonne tout	shjah.bon(n).don(n) too	I abandon all
je renonce à tout	shjuh re.naw(n).suh ah too	I renounce it all

Vocabulary, Act 1 (continued)
Scene 2

détachement	day.tash.uh.maw(n)	detachment
sévérités de notre Règle	say.vair.ee.tay duh no.truh reg.luh	formidable rules of our Order
au Carmel	oh kar.mell	to the Carmelite Order
une vie héroïque	oo.nuh vee air.oh.eek	an heroic life
prière	pree.air.uh	prayer
notre Règle n'est pas un refuge	no.truh reg.luh nay pah uh(n) ref.ooshjuh	our Order is not a refuge
je voudrais m'appeler Soeur Blanche de l'Agonie du Christ	shjuh voo.dray mah.pell.ay suhr . . . duh l'ag.own.ee duh Creest	I wish to be called Sister Blanche of the Agony of Christ
allez en paix, ma fille	ah.lay on(n) pay, mah fee.uh	go in peace, my daughter

Scene 3

amusante	ah.moo.zah(n).tuh	amusing
et maintenant	ay mah(n).teh.naw(n)	and now
m'amuse	m'ah.moo.zuh	it amuses me

Scene 4

se voir mourir	se v'wah moo.rear	to see yourself die
je suis seule . . . absolument seule	shjuh swee ser.luh . . . ahb.so.loh. me (n) t ser.luh	I am alone . . . absolutely alone
je vous remets Blanche de la Force	shjuh voo ruh.meh . . .	I entrust you with Blanche de la Force
une très pauvre mort	oo.nuh tray paw.vruh mohr	a very humble death
surtout ne vous méprisez jamais	suhr.too nuh voo may.pree.say shjam.may	especially never despise yourself
adieu	ah.d'yuh	farewell
je viens de voir notre chapelle vide et profanée	shjuh v'yen duh v'wah noh.truh sha.pell vee.duh ay pro.fah.nay	I have just seen our chapel empty and dese- crated
ne rien dire	nuh ree.y'an deer	say nothing
peur de la mort	purr duh lah mohr	fear of death

ACT II (45 min.)

SCENE 1 (5 min.)

The Convent's chapel. The dead Prioress lies in state, attended by Blanche and Constance. It is night, and the chapel is lit only by six tall candles around the casket.

Blanche and Sister Constance. Singing alternately they ask the Lord "dona requiem" (give rest) to the Prioress. "Amen." The clock strikes, and Constance goes to fetch their replacements. Left alone with the corpse Blanche grows frightened and starts for the door.

Blanche and Mother Marie. "Que faites-vous?" (what are you doing), Mother Marie demands. Then, sensing Blanche's terror, she speaks more kindly. "Une tâche manqué est une tâche manqué" (a task left undone is a task left undone). Do not brood on it. For now, "couchez-vous" (go to bed); and tomorrow ask God's pardon, "demander pardon à Dieu."

INTERLUDE 1 (5 min.)

Before the drop curtain Blanche and Sister Constance enter with flowers for the grave of the Prioress.

Blanche and Sister Constance. They discuss the Prioress's death. Constance, wondering why she died with such difficulty, decides that the Lord gave her another's death, "la mort d'une autre." Blanche asks, "la mort d'une autre?" What do you mean?

That someone else whose death would have been hard, explains Constance, will now find it easy. We do not die for ourselves alone, but for each other. Or sometimes even instead of each other. "Qui sait?" (who knows), she asks, implying that perhaps the Prioress received Blanche's death.

SCENE 2 (9 min.)

The Convent's chapter room. The nuns are gathered to meet their new Prioress, Madame Lidoine, sent to them from another convent. As the curtain rises, the ceremony of obedience is ending, and each nun kisses the hand of the new Prioress.

The Prioress. She regrets the death of her predecessor and suggests that because of the Revolution the nuns face a difficult future. Still, their purpose remains: they are joined to pray to God, "reassemblées pour prier Dieu." She urges them, "méfions-nous" (let us distrust) anything that turns us from prayer, "la prière," especially thoughts of martyr-dom, "du martyre." For "la prière est un devoir" (prayer is a duty) and "le martyr est un récompense" (martyrdom is a reward). With an apol-ogy for her lack of eloquence, she asks Mother Marie to find a proper end for the talk.

Mother Marie, to emphasize that "notre première devoir est la **Ave Maria** prière" (our first duty is prayer), leads the nuns in an Ave Maria.

INTERLUDE 2 (4 min.)

Before the drop curtain. The doorbell rings violently, and the Prior-ess and Mother Marie enter from one side and Sister Constance from the other.

Constance reports a man asking for the Prioress at the side gate in the alley. Impressed by his apparent care not to be seen, the Prioress sends Mother Marie. In a moment she returns: he is Blanche's brother and wishes to talk with Blanche before leaving the country. Because of the troubled times the Prioress permits the interview but requires Mother Marie to be present.

SCENE 3 (9 min.)

The Convent's parlor; Blanche and her brother, separated by a grill; Mother Marie at the back.

Blanche and Le Chevalier. Distressed by the coolness of her welcome, he goes quickly to the point: her father thinks the convent no longer safe. However that may be, Blanche says, here at least I am "heureuse et déliverée" (happy and free). "Heureuse, peut-être" (happy, per-haps), he replies, "mais non pas déliveréc" (but not free), meaning free from fear. He suggests that she should face her fear and return home to care for their aged father.

You think I am kept here "par la peur?" (by fear), she exclaims. "Ou la peur de la peur" (or by the fear of fear), he says. With increasing heat she accuses him of trying to sow doubt in her mind, to poison her peace. He asks, "You are no longer afraid?" And she replies ambiguously, "Where I am nothing can harm me." "Hé bien," he says, "adieu, ma chérie" (well then, goodbye, my dear).

Before he can leave, however, she angrily protests that he is still treating her as a child, refusing her the mutual respect of adults who each in his own way faces the dangers of life. He gives her a long look of affection and departs.

Blanche and Mother Marie. Emotionally exhausted, Blanche supports herself by the grill. "Remettez-vous, Soeur Blanche" (compose yourself), Mother Marie says sharply. Blanche confesses that she lied. She could not bear her brother's pity and she responded to it with vanity and pride. "There is but one way to conquer pride," says Mother Marie, "to rise above it." "Tenez-vous fière" (you must have courage).

SCENE 4 (13 min.)

The Convent's sacristy. The Chaplain, surrounded by the nuns, is replacing religious ornaments in a cupboard.

The Chaplain. Under the new laws he can no longer perform his duties. The Mass they have celebrated is the last. He bids them "adieu" and **Ave Verum** leads them in an Ave Verum. At its close Blanche excitedly asks what will become of him. Urging her to be more calm, he assures her that he will be close by.

The Nuns. Sister Constance is outraged that the French government should persecute priests. Another Sister says of its officials, "ils ont peur" (they are afraid), and each passes his fear to his neighbor. Blanche wonders if "La peur peut-être, an effet, une maladie" (fear perhaps, in fact, is a sickness).

The Prioress remarks calmly that when there are not priests enough, the number of martyrs increases and so the balance of grace is preserved. Mother Marie turns the observation around: so that France can have more priests, the daughters of Carmel have only their lives to give (i.e., become martyrs). Quickly the Prioress reproves her: it is not for the nuns to decide if someday they shall become martyrs (i.e., seeking martyrdom is a form of pride and therefore sinful). She goes off, followed by Mother Jeanne, while the others, dumbfounded, look at Mother Marie.

The Revolution. The doorbell rings. It is the Chaplain, caught between a troop of soldiers and a hostile crowd whose voices grow louder. Soon it is at the door, and the nuns, except for Mother Marie, huddle in terror.

Mother Marie orders the door opened and four Commissioners enter. Soldiers hold back the crowd. A Commissioner reads a decree of August 17, 1792: the nuns are expelled from their house, and the convent will be sold. Mother Marie asks for clothing, since the nuns will no longer be allowed to wear their usual habits. The Commissioner mocks her but is impressed by her courage. In an aside he tells her that he once was a sacristan and will lead the crowd away.

When the nuns are again alone, some pray, others stare before them, and Blanche in obvious terror cringes on a stool. Mother Jeanne enters, saying that the Prioress must leave immediately for Paris. Seeing Blanche, Mother Jeanne goes to the cupboard, takes out a small statue of Jesus, and gives it to Blanche. "He will give you courage," she says. But when the crowd outside cheers, Blanche drops the statue, which shatters on the floor.

Vocabulary, Act II

que faites-vous?	kuh fet-voo	what are you doing?
une tâche manqué est . . .	oo.nuh tah.shuh maw(n).kay ay . . .	a task left undone is . . .
couchez-vous	koo.shay-voo	go to bed
demander pardon à Dieu	day.maw(n).day pahr.daw(n) ah D'yuh	to ask pardon of God

Interlude 1

la mort d'une autre	lah mohr d'oon oh.truh	the death of another
qui sait?	key say	who knows?

Scene 2

rassemblées pour prier Dieu	rahs.aw(n)m.blay poor pree.ay d'yuh	gathered in order to pray to God
méfions-nous	may.f'yaw(n)-noo	let us distrust
la prière	lah pree.air	the prayer
du martyre	doo mah.tee.ruh	of martyrdom
la prière est un devoir	. . . ay uh(n) deh.vwah	prayer is a duty
le martyr est un	. . . ay uh(n)	martyrdom is

Vocabulary, Act II (continued)

récompense	ray.kohm.pah(n). suh	a reward
notre première devoir est la prière	noh.truh prehm.y'air deh.vwah . . .	our first duty is prayer

Scene 3

heureuse et déliverée	err.erse ay day.lee.vray.uh	happy and free
heureuse, peut-être	. . . puh.tet.ruh	happy, perhaps
mais non pas déliverée	may naw(n) pah . . .	but not free
par la peur	pahr lah purr	by fear
ou la peur de la peur	oo lah purr duh . . .	or by the fear of fear
hé bien, adieu, ma chérie	ay b'yah(n), ah.d'yuh, mah shair.ee	well, then, good-bye, my dear
remettez-vous	ruh.meh.tay-voo	compose yourself
tenez-vous fière	ten.ay-voo f'yair.uh	you must have courage

Scene 4

ils ont peur	eels aw(n) purr	they are afraid
la peur peut-être, en effet, une maladie	. . . aw(n) eh.fay, oon mah.lah.dee.uh	fear perhaps is, in effect, a sickness

ACT III (47 min.)

SCENE 1 (7 min.)

The Convent's chapel. The prophecy of the dead Prioress has been fulfilled: the chapel has been invaded and profaned; foul straw and plaster litter the floor. The Chaplain is present in torn and soiled civilian clothing. A nun watches at the door while the others surround Mother Marie.

The Vow of Martyrdom. Mother Marie asks the Chaplain to address the nuns on the pledge they are going to make. He declines: in the absence of the Prioress, Mother Marie should raise the question. (Throughout her speech Blanche, who appears exhausted, is watched by Constance.)

Mother Marie proposes that they take "le voeu du martyre" (the vow of martyrdom) in order to be worthy of "Carmel" and to contribute to the health of the country. The nuns show little enthusiasm, and one of the more elderly questions the appropriateness of it. Mother Marie then adds that if even one nun votes against it, the idea will be dropped. The decision, she suggests, should be "par un vote secret" (by a secret vote) given to the chaplain. At that Blanche brightens and Sister Mathilde, noticing her, remarks that there will be at least one vote against.

The Chaplain stands behind the altar, and each nun whispers her vote to him. On his report Mother Marie announces calmly: "il y a une seule opposition. Çela suffit." (There is only one against. That is enough.) Sister Mathilde, glancing at Blanche, exclaims, "on sait laquelle . . ." (one knows which).

"Il s'agit de moi" (it was I) cries Constance, as Blanche begins to weep. The Chaplain knows I speak the truth, Constance continues, but now I wish "prononcer ce voeu" (to take this vow). The Chaplain rules that she may and proposes to administer the vow to the nuns, two by two, starting with the youngest, Blanche and Constance. They kneel before him and make their pledge; but then as the others mill about, finding their places according to age, Blanche flees.

INTERLUDE 1 (4 min.)

Before the drop curtain three Revolutionary Officers advancing from the left confront the Carmelites on the right. The nuns—without Blanche—are led by the Prioress, returned from Paris, and all are in civilian clothes with meager bundles in hand.

The First Officer. Citizens, he begins, we congratulate you on your behavior thus far. There is, however, to be no more living in communities. The nuns must appear in court, one by one, to receive identity cards that will restore to them the blessings of liberty. He and his officers depart as the Prioress with a gesture detains the nuns.

The Prioress and Mother Marie. The Prioress orders a Sister to warn the Chaplain that they cannot now hold Mass: it would be too dangerous for all. Do you not think so? she asks Mother Marie.

Mother Marie replies that she must be guided by the Prioress and possibly she did wrong to propose the vow of martyrdom. What has been done, however, cannot be undone, and "Comment accorder l'esprit de notre voeu avec cette prudence?" (how can we reconcile the spirit of our vow with this caution). She goes out (presumably to start her search for Blanche in accordance with her promise to the former Prioress, though the libretto is not specific).

The Prioress, watching her go, says quietly to the others that each would have to answer to God for her vow and conscience, but she, as Prioress, must answer for them all.

MUSICAL LINK (2 min.)

———

SCENE 2 (6 min.)

Paris. The library of the Marquis de la Force, pillaged and half-destroyed. In the center, a folding bed; on the hearth, a simple stove with an earthen pot that Blanche, ill-dressed and haggard, is tending. Mother Marie, in civilian clothes, enters quickly, startling Blanche. *Blanche and Mother Marie.* "C'est vous!" (it is you), cries Blanche. "Oui" (yes), I have come to take you back; "il est temps" (it is time). Later, perhaps, says Blanche. "Non" (no), says Mother Marie, in a few days "il sera trop tard" (it will be too late). "Trop tard pour quoi" (too late for what), asks Blanche. "Pour votre salut" (for your safety).

Blanche protests that she is safer in her father's house. No one will look for her there. Then, when her pot of stew boils over, she turns angrily on Mother Marie: "C'est votre faute" (it is your fault). But when Mother Marie helps her to save the stew, Blanche weeps. The kindness, she says, has upset her. With sudden violence she asks why everyone reproaches her. "La peur n'offense pas le bon Dieu" (fear does not offend the good Lord). She was born in fear and lived always in fear. Since the world despises fear, it is right that she should be despised. Only her father could soothe her, and he has been guillotined. Now she is a servant to others who strike her. With a kind of defiance she repeats "Oui, ils m'ont frappée" (yes, they have struck me).

The real, the only misfortune, says Mother Marie, is to despise oneself. As if issuing a command she calls, "Soeur Blanche de l'Agonie du Christ!" and Blanche rises, with dry eyes. Memorize this address, orders Mother Marie. You will be safe there.

Blanche insists, "I will not go." "You will go," says Mother Marie. But when from offstage a woman's rasping voice cries, "Blanche! The errands!" Blanche runs to it, abandoning Mother Marie.

MUSICAL LINK (2 min.)

INTERLUDE 2 (3 min.)

Paris. A street near the Bastille. Blanche, overhearing a conversation, learns that the nuns in Compiègne have been arrested and denies that she has ever been there. (This Interlude, entirely spoken dialogue punctuated by drums, wood block and tam tam, is sometimes cut.)

SCENE 3 (10 min.)

Paris. A prison cell in the Concièrgerie. All the nuns except Blanche and Mother Marie are present. The Prioress sits on a broken chair, the others on benches. A barred window overlooks a dark courtyard where day breaks.

The Prioress. She congratulates the others on their behavior: the first night in prison is the most difficult. About "ce voeu du martyre" (this vow of martyrdom): whether it was wise or not, she will now join the others in it. "Hé bien, j'assume ce voeu" (very well, I assume this vow). They will be together in whatever may come. "Soyez tranquilles" (be tranquil).

Sister Constance. She asks, where is Blanche? But the Prioress does not know. "Elle reviendra" (she will return), says Constance. A Sister asks how she can be so sure. "Parce que . . . parce que" (because) of a dream, she says. The others laugh.

The Jailer. He enters brusquely to read a proclamation: "Le tribunal révolutionaire . . ." (the Revolutionary Tribunal) declares that the following nuns—he reads their names—for crimes against the state "sont condamnées à mort" (are condemned to death).

The Prioress. She comforts the others and closes "avec ma maternelle bénédiction" (with my maternal blessing).

INTERLUDE 3 (2 min.)

Paris. A street near the Bastille.

The Chaplain and Mother Marie. They meet stealthily, and he reports that the nuns have been condemned to death. She instantly plans to join them: "J'ai fait le voeu du martyre . . ." (I have taken the vow of martyrdom). To God, not to her companions, he replies. If God chooses not to claim her, she is released. "Je suis déshonorée!" (I am dishonored), she says, for at the last they will look for me in vain. But the Chaplain says firmly, you must think on God and His will.

MUSICAL LINK (3 min.)

SCENE 4 (8 min.)

Paris. Place de la Revolution (later de la Concorde) with the guillotine. On the right the Carmelites are descending from the tumbrels. In the front row of the dense, restless crowd is the Chaplain, dressed like a revolutionary. As the first nun ascends the scaffold, he murmurs the absolution, makes a furtive sign of the cross and quickly disappears. *The Execution.* The crowd sings only syllables, "oh" and "ah." The nuns sing the "Salve Regina," a prayer to the Virgin Mary prescribed at this church season to be sung at the end of the day. Led by the Prioress they one at a time mount the scaffold. As each is executed, their chorus grows weaker. Finally only Constance, the youngest, is left. As she starts up the steps, she gazes over the crowd. Coming through it is Blanche, her face free of fear. At the sight of her Constance stops for an instant, radiant with happiness. Then, continuing with the "Salve Regina" she goes to her death. Blanche, stepping free of the crowd, begins the last four lines of the "Veni Creator." She mounts to the scaffold and is executed. The crowd, without comment, begins to disperse. After which, Curtain.

Is the final scene too theatrical? Some admirers of opera think so. To them it overwhelms rather than caps what has gone before. The sensitivity of the dialogues is abandoned, even trivialized, in violence extended for its own sake. Others reply that the violence, as in life, has been there right along: in the origins of Blanche's fear, in the death of the first Prioress, and in the animosity of the revolutionaries toward the nuns.

Another question: why does Blanche sing the "Veni Creator" rather than the "Salve Regina"? Would not the latter, which the nuns have been singing, indicate better her intention to be one of them in life and death? An answer: the sudden shift is theatrically effective and, though Poulenc does not say so, may have religious significance. The "Veni Creator" was frequently used at the ordination of priests and at the consecration of bishops and churches. As such it may more appropriately signify Blanche's final and complete commitment to the Carmelite Order.

And last: the scene's construction is interesting. No words, except those of the two Latin hymns, are sung. The crowd has only its syllables: no cries or interjections. And at the end before the curtain—Poulenc is quite specific—the crowd begins to disperse. It has no comment on what it has seen. It does not comprehend the miracle of God's grace upon an individual. That final observation is part of the opera.

Vocabulary, Act III

Scene 1

le voeu du martyre	luh vuh doo mahr.tear.uh	the vow of martyrdom
par un vote secret	pahr uh(n) voh.tuh seh.kreh	by a secret vote
il y a une seule opposition	eel y'ah oon ser.luh oh.poh.zee s'yawh(n)	there is one in opposition
çela suffit	suh.lah soo.fee	that suffices
on sait laquelle	oh(n) say lah.kell	one knows which
il s'agit de moi	eel s'ah.jee duh mwa	it was I
prononcer ce voeu	proh.noh(n).say suh vuh	to take this vow

Interlude 1

Comment accorder l'esprit de notre voeu avec cette prudence?	kow(n).maw(n) ah.cor.day l'es.pree duh noh.truh vuh ah.vek set pru.daw(n).suh	How can we reconcile the spirit of our vow with this caution?

Scene 2

c'est vous	say voo	it is you
oui . . . il est temps	whee . . . eel ay taw(n)	yes, it is time
il sera trop tard	eel seh.rah troh tar	it will be too late
trop tard pour quoi	. . . poor kwah	too late for what
pour votre salut	. . . voh.truh sah.loo	for your safety

Vocabulary, Act III (continued)

c'est votre faute	say voh.truh foh.tuh	it is your fault
la peur n'offense pas le bon Dieu	lah purr n'aw(n).faw(n).suh pah luh baw(n) d'yuh	fear does not offend the good Lord
oui, ils m'ont frappée	whee, eel maw(n) frah.pay	yes, they have struck me

Scene 3

ce voeu du martyre	suh vuh doo mahr.tear.uh	this vow of martyrdom
hé bien, j'assume ce voeu	ay b'yah(n), j'ah.soom . . .	very well, I assume this vow
soyez tranquilles	s'why.ay trah(n).keel.uh	be tranquil
elle reviendra	ell ruh.v'yah(n). drah	she will return
parce que	pahr.suh kuh	because
le tribunal révolutionaire	luh treeb.yu.nahl ray.voh.loo tsy'aw(n).air.uh	The Revolution- ary Tribunal
sont condamnées à mort	saw(n) kaw(n).dahm. nay ah more	are condemned to death
avec ma maternelle bénédiction	ah.vek ma mah.tary. nell.uh bay.nay.dik tsy'aw(n)	with my maternal blessing

Interlude 3

j'ai fait le voeu du martyre	shj.ay fay . . .	I have taken the vow of martyrdom
je suis déshonorée	shj.uh swhee days.ohn.or.ay	I am dishonored

Scene 4

Salve Regina	sahl.vay reh.jee.nah	hail queen

The four lines of the "Veni Creator" sung by Blanche are:

Deo Patri sit gloria	Glory be to God the Father,
Et Filio qui a mortuis	And to the Son who from the dead

Vocabulary, Act III (continued)

Surrexit ac Paraclito	Rose, and to the Holy Ghost,
In saeculorum saecula . . .	Into the centuries of centuries . . .
	(i.e. world without end)

LA VOIX HUMAINE

(The Human Voice)

Lyric Tragedy in one act (41 min.). World premiere, Opérá-Comique, Paris, Feb. 6, 1959; American prem., New York, Feb. 23, 1960; British prem., Edinburgh, Aug. 30, 1960. Music by Francis Poulenc; text by Jean Cocteau, based on his one-act play *La Voix Humaine,* first performed on Feb. 17, 1930. The opera, like the play, has only a single character, Elle (She), and was composed for Denise Duval, who introduced it to France, Italy, Britain and America.

In his play Cocteau, presenting a woman in the final moments of losing the man she loves, restricted himself to her side of a telephone call. Yet the play's success throughout the 1930s in the repertory of the Comédie-Française and in broadcasts in Britain proved that it offered more than a mere theatrical trick or avant-garde chic. It had also an excellent structure designed to display what was then called "feminine sensibility," meaning a particular approach to life thought to be endemic to women. Today, if the same term is used, it is applied as often to men as to women and thought not to be a product of a person's sex. Poulenc, setting a trimmed version of the play, reinforced both the structure and the sensibility by adding the sensuousness and sometimes harshness of the orchestra as well as pointing up and coloring many of the words and phrases.

In its broadest units the opera's structure turns on the lies told by both parties and on her realization of their implications. In the first unit, 1, below: she tells a series of "white" lies, some of which the audience—though not her lover—can see are untrue. Then, in 2, he starts a guessing game in which he misleads her as to where he is and what he is doing. Essentially, her lies are to cover her desolation; his, merely to be free of her the easiest way. Their connection is broken, 3, and by calling his home, where he is not though he said he was, she discovers his lies. In 4 she conceals her knowledge but now tells the truth about herself. She has attempted suicide. Suddenly, 5, she hears music played on a gramophone and is faced with the thought that he is calling from the other woman's apartment. Angered, she talks directly of her situation: she is alone in life. He changes the subject to her dog. There is interference on the line, 6, followed by her assurance that she will not attempt suicide again. She insists she is not lying but implies ever so gently that he may be, hoping that he will be truthful with her. But he is merely furious, and, 7, they are cut off. Overwhelmed at the possibility that they may part with him thinking ill of her, she begs God to have him call her back. When he does, she is almost abject in explaining that she was not accusing him of lying. And the conversation, through her courage, is brought to an end.

The opera's text is far richer in detail than a synopsis can suggest, and it should be read, even if the performance is to be in translation. Casting all shade and subtlety aside, however: his callousness constantly results in her humiliation.

To avoid any possible misinterpretation, Poulenc put a Note on the score that the role should be taken "by a young and elegant woman. This is not a play about an aging woman abandoned by her lover."

The opera takes place in her bedroom. As it opens, she is angry at a neighbor who has cut in on the party line (a telephone line shared by several householders), and she hangs up, asking the operator to reconnect her call.

1. She continues: she had just walked in. It is not so late. Is he at home? Then he can see the clock in the hall. No, last night she did not sleep well. She took one pill, only one. Tonight she dined at Martha's and wore her red dress and black hat. Yes, she still has it on. (The audience can see she is bareheaded, wearing a nightgown beneath her housecoat, and from the mess in the room has probably not been out all evening.) And he? He stayed home? What lawsuit?

Her voice drops. Their letters? He can have them whenever he wishes. No need to apologize. Of course it is difficult. He should not blame himself. The fault is hers. Does he remember that Sunday in Versailles? She was the one who led him on. And on a Tuesday, the 27th of the month, she was the first to telephone. Ah, well; she has the dates by heart.

No. At the moment she has no plans. And he? Tomorrow! She had no idea he would leave so soon. Well then, she will leave the bag with his clothes and letters with the concierge, and he can send Joseph to pick them up. Perhaps she will stay in town, or visit Martha in the country.

2. Suddenly their connection threatens to break. She cannot hear him. At his end there is a buzz. His phone is not like its usual self.

He asks her to guess what he has on. His red foulard, with his sleeves rolled back a little. In his left hand? The receiver, and with his right he is drawing hearts and stars on the pad. Ah, well: she has eyes in her ears. Oh, no! He must not describe her. She can no longer look in the mirror: she sees an old woman with white hair and small wrinkles. A face that everyone envies? That is for actors. She preferred to be called "Funny Face!" Does he remember? She is lucky that he is not good at pretending and that he loves her, or the phone could become a weapon, one that leaves no trace.

3. They are cut off. She gives his number to the operator and reaches his butler, Joseph. "No, Monsieur is not at home." She apologizes. Of course, he was calling from a restaurant, but when they were cut off, she did not stop to think. "Bon soir, Joseph" (Good night). She waits in agony. It rings.

4. No, she did not try to call him. He is good to call back (she begins to cry). No, nothing is wrong, except all this talk, talk. . . . Listen; she lied to him before. She did not dine with Martha; she stayed home all evening, waiting for his call. And pacing about the room she nearly went crazy (high C, the highest note of the score). She even thought of taking a taxi to his house just to look at the windows. And last night. She took not one but twelve pills, in a lump. Death was slow, however, and she felt so ill that she called Martha, who brought a doctor. Yes, she is all right now. He has only to talk to her, and she feels well again.

5. What music is that? So Loud? Then he should knock on his neighbor's wall. Yes (pacing about), the doctor will return. He must forgive her for this scene; for five years she has lived only through him, and now her only link is the phone. She has even taken it to bed with her. Martha, after all, has her life organized; she is alone: "seule."

No, the dog has suffered, too. He won't leave the hall, won't be petted, won't eat. He loves you, too.

6. A neighbor cuts in on the line to discover if they have finished. There are harsh words, and the neighbor hangs up. She urges him not to be upset by it. People will never understand. Oh (a stifled gasp of sorrow), for a moment she thought they were talking as always, and then she remembered. Don't worry, no one ever tries to kill herself twice. She wouldn't know where to buy a "révolver" (revolver).

No, she is not lying. She couldn't—though there are times when lying helps. If, to make their separation less painful, he lied to her. . . . No, she did not say he was lying. No, no, she meant. . . .

7. They are cut off. She murmurs over and over: "Mon Dieu, faites qu'il me redemande" (Dear God, make him call me back). . . . It rings.

She meant only that she would love him more. Now she can feel his voice, for she has wound the cord around her neck. To Marseille?! Please, would he not go to that small hotel where they had always stayed. Because what she does not have to imagine does not exist. Thank you. He is good.

Lying across the bed with the telephone in her arms, she urges him, "Coup, coup vite!" (hang up, hang up quickly). When he does, she gasps, "Je t'aime. Je t'aime. Je t'aime" (I love you), and the phone falls to the ground.

(Some stage directors, by having the woman earlier gulp down a handful of sleeping pills, indicate that she dies a suicide as the curtain falls. The text of neither the play nor the opera suggests this, and as death for her would be a release from pain, it seems contrary to the play's point.)

DIE DREIGROSCHENOPER

(The Threepenny Opera)

Opera in a prologue, three acts, eight scenes. World premiere, Berlin, Aug. 31, 1928; American prem. (in English), New York, April 13, 1933; British prem., London, Feb. 9, 1956. Marc Blitzstein version in English, world prem., Waltham, Mass., June 14, 1952. Music by Kurt Weill; text by Elisabeth Hauptmann with lyrics by Bertolt Brecht. The text is a version of John Gay's *The Beggar's Opera* with ballads arranged and composed by J. C. Pepusch, first performed, London, Jan. 29, 1728.

PRINCIPAL CHARACTERS

A Streetsinger
Jonathan J. Peachum, entrepreneur in misery
Mrs. Peachum, his wife
Polly, their daughter
Macheath, alias "Mac the Knife," a highwayman
Tiger Brown, Chief of Police
Lucy, his daughter and Mistress of Old Bailey Prison
Jenny, a whore

The action takes place in London in the days immediately before and including the coronation of Queen Victoria, June 28, 1838. (Programs sometimes mistakenly give the date of her accession, June 20, 1837.)

In Gay's *The Beggar's Opera* Peachum, a receiver of stolen goods who improves his living by informing on his clients, is outraged by the marriage of his daughter Polly to a highwayman, Captain Macheath. He decides to place her in "the comfortable estate of widowhood" by informing on his son-in-law, and Macheath is arrested and sent to Newgate Prison to await execution. There Macheath captures the heart of Lucy, the warder's daughter, and while she and Polly quarrel over his affections, he laments, "How happy could I be with either, Were t'other dear charmer away." Ultimately, despite her jealousy, Lucy helps him to escape, and with none of the plot's complications resolved everyone rejoices in a sudden happy ending.

Gay's purpose was satiric, and though the work has an overture and sixty-nine ballads it is more of a play than an opera, its strength in its racy language and constant inverse logic. Gay's targets were the politicians of the day and the conventions of Italian opera. Audiences took Macheath to be Robert Walpole, the favorite minister of George I; the irrelevant happy ending, a mockery of Handel's librettos; and the coarse verbal duel between Lucy and Polly, a reference to the feud between London's reigning sopranos, Francesca Cuzzoni and Faustina Bordoni.

Brecht's purpose in reworking the material was chiefly political. By advancing the period to the start of the Victorian Age, and by rewriting most of the dialogue and lyrics to reflect conditions in Germany in 1928, he was able to blame the troubles of the Weimar Republic and even the existence of an underworld on bourgeois, capitalist society at the start of its proverbially smuggest period. He, and perhaps Weill, intended the middle class at any given performance to be shamed by the exposure of its hypocrisy and to feel threatened by the vigor, number and desperation of its creations, the poor and criminal.

The message, however, is obscured for many by the happy ending, the pleasures of the music and the wit of the play. Mrs. Peachum says to her daughter: "Ah, Polly, so here you are. Change your dress. Your husband's going to be hanged. I've brought your widow's weeds. You'll look lovely as a widow! Now give us a little smile!" And the audience, outdoing Polly, laughs.

Brecht's problem—and every new production must resolve it or fail—was how to keep the audience sufficiently amused so that it would remain in the theatre to be insulted. He feared that Weill's music was too attractive, and so it has proved. For since the opera has become a twentieth-century classic, the text's abrasiveness is in danger of being lost: "Pirate Jenny" today, instead of a barmaid's explosion of hatred against all who can afford a hotel room or a meal in a restaurant, is often an art song with traditions of performance most appreciated by those who eat constantly in restaurants.

The opera initially was very successful in Germany, where it perfectly expressed the despair of many during the last years of the Weimar Republic. But as soon as the Nazis came to power in 1933, they banned it. Thereafter, it had a fitful existence abroad until March 10, 1954, when in an English version by the composer Marc Blitzstein it began a run in New York that continued for six years. Since then there have been many revivals in the original, the Blitzstein or newer versions, and the opera has a solid claim to be the most frequently performed of any composed after World War I.

The opera's ballad form lends itself to rearrangements. Though the songs are frequent, twenty-one in all, they are not connected, and their pitch can be raised or lowered to suit a voice. Several, such as the moralizing finale to Act II, can be sung by any character and often are assigned to the best voices regardless of role. Because the work is as much play as opera, Weill kept the vocal lines simple, and the roles can be taken—often are best taken—by actors rather than singers. In that respect the work is quite different from *Aufstieg und Fall der Stadt Mahagonny,* which requires trained voices.

Weill's orchestra calls for eleven musicians and twenty-three instruments. The sound and style is cabaret-1920s: strident, jazzy, nostalgic, sardonic and, at the same time, sentimental. The concert suite for wind orchestra, *Kleine Dreigroschenmusik* (20 min.), is not merely excerpts strung together but a reworking and orchestration of: the Overture, Ballad of Mac the Knife, "Instead of" Song, Ballad of the Good Life, Polly's Song, Tango Ballad, Army or Cannon Song, and Threepenny finale. (In the synopsis timings, except for the Overture and Prologue, are not given as the length of acts and scenes vary greatly depending on the amount of dialogue included.)

OVERTURE AND PROLOGUE

The opera opens with an Overture (2.5 min.) leading into a Prologue (3.5 min.) set in the market square of London's Soho district. While the crowd parades behind him, a street-singer describes Macheath in the **Mac the Knife** ballad "Mac the Knife," comparing him to a shark and ascribing to him all the recent revolting crimes. He is the opera's hero.

ACT I

SCENE 1 (Peachum's Shop)

Peachum is an advocate of free enterprise, and his various undertakings, which he organizes with the ruthlessness of Rockefeller, include outfitting beggars with filthy clothes, scrofulous sores or false amputations gruesome enough to win pennies from the stoniest heart. **"Instead of" song** Mrs. Peachum informs him that their daughter Polly has been seeing Macheath, and they fear an elopement.

SCENE 2 (A Stable in Soho)

Macheath marries Polly—or she pretends to believe it—and they celebrate the ceremony in a deserted stable that his gang furnishes with stolen goods. To entertain the men Polly sings the ballad "Pirate **Pirate Jenny** Jenny," in which a barmaid imagines her fortunes reversed and herself in a position to order everyone richer to be executed. (Sometimes this ballad is saved for Jenny, the whore, in which case instead of mocking the usual wedding toast of a happy life, etc., it serves to explain Jenny's anger at the world and willingness to betray Macheath.) A wedding guest enters, terrifying the gang. It is Tiger Brown, the Chief of Police and Mac's friend from army days. Together **Army song** they sing the "Army" or "Cannon Song," after which Macheath explains to the gang that he regularly pays off Brown and in return has advance notice of any police raid. The scene closes with Mac and Polly alone, singing a "Love Song."

SCENE 3 (Peachum's Shop)

Barbara song   Polly explains to her parents in the "Barbara Song" that with Macheath she could only take off her clothes: she couldn't say no. While Peachum fits a mutilated arm to one beggar and a stump on another, he suggests that Polly divorce Macheath at once. She refuses. So he decides to have Macheath hanged. Mrs. Peachum will arrange with Chief of Police Brown for the hanging. Polly explains that Brown and Macheath are friends, but Peachum insists that life is dog-eat-dog and every man has his price.

ACT II

SCENE 1 (The Stable in Soho)

Polly warns Macheath of his danger, and he plans to leave town. He shows her the account books of his business, directs her to reduce personnel by turning over one employee to Brown for hanging, and calls in some men from the other room to introduce them to the gang's captain in his absence: Polly. One of the men worries aloud about having a woman in the post, but Polly tells him off in such gutter language that he is cowed and Macheath pleased.

SCENE 2 (A Brothel in Wapping)

Mrs. Peachum offers Jenny, the whore, ten shillings to turn in Macheath. She assures Jenny in the "Ballad of Sexual Obsession" that he won't be able to stay away from the whores.

tango   Later, same scene. Thursday. The whores are washing, sewing and ironing: a middle-class idyll of womanhood. Macheath enters—Thursday is his regular day—and he and Jenny sing a love duet describing their life together as pimp and whore. They dance a tango, and before it ends police arrive with Mrs. Peachum and arrest Macheath.

SCENE 3 (Old Bailey Prison)

The Good Life   Brown feigns grief to see Macheath in prison but is ignored. Alone, Macheath sings his philosophy of life: "One must live well to know what living is." Lucy enters, accuses him of marrying

Polly, which he denies, and when Polly comes in, the two women have **Jealousy duet** a "Jealousy Duet." Polly, however, is soon dragged off by her mother, and Lucy effects Macheath's escape—much to Brown's relief.

The Act's finale brings Macheath and Mrs. Peachum before the curtain to answer the question: "What keeps a man alive?" The answer is "Food," and as only the rich can be assured of it, only they can be moral about obtaining it. The rest must cheat, steal and kill to get it. Moral: the rich should stop preaching and start feeding the poor.

ACT III

SCENE 1 (Peachum's Shop)

He is organizing the beggars for the Coronation and also to put pressure on Brown to rearrest Macheath. From Jenny he learns that Macheath is with the whore Suky Tawdry. He threatens Brown with a beggars' riot in which the police on the Coronation route will have to club 600 cripples to the ground: "It will look bad. It will be disgusting. Enough to make one sick. I feel ill, Brown, to think of it. A small chair, please." Brown gives in.

INTERLUDE

Jenny, the whore, appears in front of the curtain with a hurdy-**Solomon song** gurdy. In the "Solomon Song" she concludes, with Macheath as her example: if you can't control your lust, you are better off without it.

SCENE 2 (Old Bailey Prison)

Polly attempts by guile to discover from Lucy where Macheath is hid. The ladies spar until to their consternation Macheath is brought in under arrest.

Later, at the death cell. Macheath, waiting to be hanged, sings a ballad of appeal to his friends, not one of whom responds. Because of the occasion he begs all men to forgive him, though confessing that he wants to smash them with a crowbar. Just as he is about to be hanged, a messenger arrives from the Queen with a pardon for him, a patent of nobility, a deed to a castle and a pension for life.

Everyone exclaims, and Peachum draws the moral: in real life messengers seldom come, and if you kick a man, he's likely to kick you back. Therefore never be too eager to oppose injustice.

AUFSTIEG UND FALL DER STADT MAHAGONNY

(Rise and Fall of the City Mahagonny)

Opera in three acts, twenty scenes. World premiere, Leipzig, March 9, 1930; American prem., excerpts in concert form, New York, Feb. 23, 1952; stage prem., Stratford, Canada, July 2, 1965; British prem., Stratford-on-Avon, Jan. 9, 1963. Music by Kurt Weill; text by Bertolt Brecht.

This opera (135 min.) of total despair is probably Weill's masterpiece; its text, both prose and songs, ranks high in Brecht's work; and its history from its first performance has been extraordinary.

Three crooks on the run, Ladybird Begbick, Trinity Moses and Henry Wilson, alias Fatty the Bookie,* create the get-rich-quick city of Mahagonny (ma.ha.GO.nee), or Suckerville, and lure into it the discontented of the world. First to arrive are six whores led by Jenny, who sings with them "Oh! Moon of Alabama." Soon after come four men—Jimmy, Jake, Bill and Joe—who have spent seven years working in Alaska and have selected Mahagonny for their fun. The city, however, proves disappointing until on the night of its threatened destruction by a hurricane Jimmy proposes a ban on any prohibition. All should do as they like: theft, rape, murder—whatever. The hurricane spares the city, which prospers—except that Jake dies of gluttony, "Alaskawolf" Joe is killed in a prizefight, Bill puts money before friendship, and Jimmy commits the only crime the town recognizes: he becomes penniless and fails to pay his bills. He is executed. Inflation undermines the economy and the city burns, while the inhabitants sing of their love of money. Even God, who appears in a parody playlet,

---

* These are the names used in the Auden-Kallman translation of the opera libretto, which varies from the play as published in the collected works of Brecht.

cannot save the city or its people, for man has corrupted it, and himself, beyond salvation. The moral sung at the end is: No one can help a dead man, or even a live one, including you and me.

In short, no hope at all for mankind, which onstage is shown in all cases to be vile—if the stage director has had the courage to follow the script. The message is delivered with greater force than in *Die Dreigroschenoper* because there is no *deus ex machina* at the end. Unlike Macheath, Jimmy is executed, and the sentimental in the audience, or onstage, cannot retreat into a belief that it was all a fairy tale of what might have been. Weill and Brecht hold a picture before the audience and scream: look at yourself!

But it is a picture, not a mirror, for there is some good in mankind. And such complete negativism ultimately seems childish, for it has nothing constructive to offer. The opera is a tantrum, a hugely theatrical tantrum thrown by two brilliant children furious with the world; and it perfectly caught the mood of certain German intellectuals in the last days of the Weimar Republic. It is, and was meant to be, offensive, and Nazis, communists and many mere humanists disliked it. The premiere ended in a riot. Subsequent productions fared better, but not always, and as soon as the Nazis came to power, they banned it. After they took over Austria in 1938, they confiscated from Weill's publisher in Vienna all copies of the full score and orchestral parts. Thereafter the opera survived only in vocal scores and was seldom performed except in excerpts to piano accompaniment. It seemed dead.

In the mid-1950s interest in it revived, no doubt because of the continuing success of *Die Dreigroschenoper*. A project to record the opera under the artistic direction of Weill's widow, Lotte Lenya, led to the discovery of an orchestral score, and a stage performance followed at Darmstadt in November 1957. In the last fifteen years it has been given all over the world, generally with great success. It is superb theatre, with all the Brechtian paraphernalia of placards and projections, and apparently once again reflects a prevalent mood. Some productions treat it as a period piece; others update it with placards and projections of current political problems and personalities.

The opera requires an orchestra of only thirty players but some unusual instruments: zither, accordion, saxophone, banjo, bass guitar. The general sound and style is of jazzbands of the 1920s—strident, yet often sentimental.

STREET SCENE

Opera, in two acts. World premiere, New York, Jan. 9, 1947; European prem. (in Ger.), Dusseldorf, Nov. 26, 1955; British prem., June 6, 1983. Music by Kurt Weill, lyrics by Langston Hughes, based on the play by Elmer Rice.

PRINCIPAL CHARACTERS

Anna Maurrant, wife and mother	dramatic soprano
Frank Maurrant, her husband	bass-baritone
Rose, her grown daughter	lyric soprano
Willie, her young son	child's voice
Sam Kaplan, in love with Rose	tenor
Harry Easter, an admirer of Rose	light baritone
Henry Davis, handyman	high baritone
Steve Sankey, in love with Anna Maurrant	speaking role

And all the inhabitants of a New York City tenement house, Jews, Italians, Swedes, Germans, Americans, together with the many others who pass along the street before it.

The action takes place on a sidewalk in the city during two days in June 1929.

The opera began its stage life with a seeming failure, caused in part by a problem of identity. Weill had written what he called "an American opera," but for its premiere on Broadway in 1947 its producers, convinced the word "opera" spelt death at the box office, advertised it as "a dramatic musical"—which, with operatic voices, 100-member cast, and 35-piece orchestra led by former Metropolitan Opera conductor Maurice Abravanel, it plainly was not. To Weill's disappointment it ran only 148 performances, few for a musical—it was competing against *Finian's Rainbow* and *Brigadoon*—and, as it happened that year, few for an opera, for Menotti's more honestly titled Broadway double bill of *The Telephone* and *The Medium* achieved 212. Weill published the vocal score, however, with the subtitle, "An American Opera," believing, as he once said, "in seventy-five years *Street Scene* will be considered my most important opera."

Unfortunately for the work's early history the claim rankled further many classical musicians and operagoers already irritated by Weill's insistence that "if there will ever be anything like an American opera, it is bound to come out of Broadway. . . [which] represents the living theater in this country." Opera at the Metropolitan, he felt, had "lost contact with the theater and leads the existence of a museum piece toilsomely preserved by its devotees."

For these sentiments many of the critics, musicians, and operalovers who might have been expected to rally to the work often talked it down. And when Weill died in 1950, the leading theoretical critic of the day, the German T. W. Adorno (See Compendium), in an obituary dismissed him as a musician, stating he owed any success primarily to collaboration with Bertolt Brecht and his music lacked "real craftsmanship, from the simplest harmonization to the construction of large forms." At most Adorno sneered: "Perhaps he had something of the genius of those who lead the great fashion houses. He had the ability to find melodies appropriate to the annual shows; and this supremely ephemeral thing in him may last."

In the world only one opera company, the New York City Opera, took *Street Scene* into its repertory and remained faithful to it. Three times in the years 1959-1979 the City Opera gave it strong productions, all to enthusiastic audiences, with the last, broadcast on television, seen and heard by thousands. Gradually critical opinion changed, influenced in part by the astounding success of Marc Blitzstein's translation (1952) for *The Threepenny Opera,* a production that ran in New York for 2,611 performances.

But the advance of *Street Scene* still was slow. The British premiere in 1983 was only the opera's second staging in Europe, but by 1989 it was in the repertory of both the Scottish Opera and English National Opera; in 1987 there was a production in Cologne, and in 1990 another by the New York City Opera; with premieres in Australia in 1988, and in Portugal and Italy in 1995 and 1996. Yet Weill's "seventy-five years" would not be reached until 2022.

The skeleton of the opera's story is simple. A middle-aged woman, disappointed in marriage, finds some happiness with a lover, and the husband shoots the man and her. A subplot of almost equal importance concerns her grown daughter, loved by a young and sensitive man who feels trapped by poverty and the tenement; but she decides against marriage, and leaves the city without him. Surrounding both stories is the despair of life in a rundown tenement, leavened by hope, the American dream.

In its plot the opera observes the classic unities of time, place, and action, its three scenes all taking place on the sidewalk before the tenement on an evening, next morning, and afternoon. But in its musical structure— a point that seemed not to bother audiences—some critics think it badly balanced, the first of the two acts being mostly "Broadway" solo numbers, without much sequential relation, and the second, mostly "operatic" ensembles. Further there is an ambiguity of tone. The two stories are serious, ending in death and separation, but several numbers, like the "Ice Cream Sextet" and "Lullaby" for two nursemaids, are satiric to the point of caricature. To which audiences might reply: street theatre and mordant humor is usual in urban life, where newspapers daily hurl tragedy in the public's face. Lastly, there is the problem of the opera's diction. Many operagoers expect serious sentiments to be expressed in elevated, poetic language, and in *Street Scene* much of the language is ordinary, even banal. Yet Elmer Rice the playwright, and Langston Hughes, the lyricist, both had exceptional ears for accent and rhythm, and their words, however ordinary, once heard stick in mind, whole phrases such as "wrapped in a ribbon and tied in a bow." The fact is, as critics slowly realized: If opera is defined as an apt merger of text and music, *Street Scene* is masterful.

Weill, with his belief in the vitality of the Broadway style, connected his songs and ensembles by passages of dialogue, though many of these, as in *Fidelio* or *Carmen,* are spoken over orchestral accompaniment. In the synopsis the musical titles of the numbers are those of the vocal score, while some of the characters' physical descriptions, not mentioned in the score, are taken form the play, which the opera closely follows. With regard to the orchestra, Weill as always did his own orchestration, and asked for a flute, oboe, bass clarinet, basoon, two each of clarinets, horns trumpets, trombones, a harp, piano, percussion, and strings.

ACT I (1 hr. 25 min.)

The sidewalk before a brownstone, "walk-up" tenement, with stoop steps, in a "mean quarter of New York."

1. *Introduction and Opening Ensemble.* The opening four bars sound the theme, "Lonely House," of Sam Kaplan who loves Rose Maurrant; and then follow twenty-six bars of the syncopated rhythms of New York. The curtain rises, revealing Mr. Kaplan at one window of the house, reading newspapers, and on the opposite side of the front door Mrs. Fiorentino leaning out of hers. While Mr. Kaplan complains about the bourgeois papers, the woman of the house gather on the stoop, complaining of the weather: "Ain't it awful the heat! Ain't it awful?" They soon are joined by Mr. Kaplan, Mr. Olsen, and two Salvation Army girls passing by and the ensemble ends as a septet.

2. *Blues.* The house handyman, introduced by a brief guitar solo, emerges from the areaway under the stoop: "I got a marble and a star."

3. *Scene and Trio.* Willie Maurrant, a disorderly boy of twelve, from the street calls to his mother, at a second-storey window, for a dime for ice cream. Mrs. Fiorentino, blowzy and good-natured, Mrs. Olsen, somewhat slow, and Mrs. Jones, apt to be censorious, discuss Mrs. Maurrant's apparent involvement with the milk collector, Steve Sankey: "Get a load of that!"

Dialogue: Mrs. Maurrant, a woman of forty, reveals a kind nature and liking for music and books, as does also young Sam Kaplan, who is disappointed Rose is not yet home. Mr. Buchanan, whose wife upstairs is expecting a baby, stops on the stoop.

4. *Arietta.* Buchanan (tenor buffo) complains, "When a woman has a baby. . . it's awful hard on a man." The women sympathize, but laugh.

5. *Scene and Aria.* Frank Maurrant, a tall, powerfully-built man of forty-five, with a rugged, grim face, comes home from his job as a stagehand, and is upset that Rose is not yet home. He is rude to his wife—she should know where Rose is and at Mrs. Fiorentino's mild reproof, "Things are diff'rent nowadays," becomes almost aggressive. Storming into the house, he leaves the women alone, and Mrs. Maurrant tells the others how different her life has been from what she had hoped. "Somehow I never could believe, that life was meant to be all dull and grey. . . I always will believe there'll be a brighter day."

6. *Scene and Quartet.* Sankey walks by, sees the group, and after a few remarks says he is off to the drugstore to buy ginger ale for his wife. Soon Mrs. Maurrant says she'll walk a block or two to look for Willie: Mr. Maurrant doesn't like him out late. But as she goes off, the three housewives and Mr. Olsen exclaim: "Get a load of that. . . She must think we're dumb."

Dialogue: Over ominous tympani the neighbors discuss the possibility of Maurrant, a violent man, someday shooting Sankey. Mrs. Olsen reports that she just now saw Sankey and Mrs. Maurrant talking, and he had his hands on her shoulders. Maurrant comes out on the stoop, and the neighbors hush. Then Mr. Fiorentino, "Lippo," enters carrying a handful of ice cream cones, which he distributes.

7. *Ice-Cream Sextet.* Two women, four men, led by the fat, happy Lippo, a musician, praise ice cream. Is the sextet too much of a caricature? It certainly is comic, and as one critic remarked, almost with regret, constructed with the skill of Mozart. But there may be more to it. It may be Langston Hughes's ironic comment on Wallace Stevens's well-known poem on the mutability of life, "The Emperor of Ice Cream," in which Death is "the only Emperor." The sextet then would be comic, joyous, and a fore-shadow of the deaths to come. Certainly Hughes, a poet who adored ice

cream, knew the Stevens poem.

Dialogue. Mrs. Maurrant returns without Willie, and Maurrant promises to give the boy "a fannin'". She begs him not to beat the child, and Mr. Kaplan starts an argument with Maurrant about imposing morality by force, which soon leads him, as everything does, to his ideas about the class struggle. Maurrant loses his temper at all the "Red talk," and moves to hit Kaplan but is prevented by the others.

8. *Aria,* ("dark, menacing"). Maurrant: "Let things be like they always was. . . That's good enough for me."

9. *Scene and Ensemble.* Offstage children's voices sing a school song. Jenny Hildebrand, whose family faces eviction from the tenement the next morning for nonpayment of rent, has graduated from high school, with honors, and she tells everyone about it: "We sat in our snowy white dresses. . . Your diploma, they said, and I took it, wrapped in a ribbon and tied in a bow." "Good for you!" the elders sing; but then at the thought of eviction Mrs. Hildebrand weeps, and is comforted by Mrs. Maurrant.

Dialogue. Sam Kaplan brings in Willie who is in tears. When the street bully told him his mother was a whore, Willie fought, and lost. As the old people tut-tut over Mrs. Maurrant, Sam yells: "Stop it! Can't you let her alone?" and rushes out, while they slowly enter the house.

10. *Arioso.* Sam returns and sings "Lonely house," the phrase that opened the opera. "Lonely, me!. . . Unhook the stars and take them down. I'm lonely. . . in this lonely town."

Dialogue. Rose Maurrant walks in with Harry Easter, She's pretty, twenty, and cheaply but rather tastefully dressed; he's thirty-five, good-looking, obviously prosperous, and works in the same real esate office. They greet Mrs. Fiorentino who is at her window, and she pulls down the shade.

11. *Scene and Song.* Easter is fascinated by Rose and in a tempting, insinuating rhythm offers her the easy life in return for love: "Wouldn't you like to be on Broadway. . . I'll show you the way."

12. *Cavatina and Scene.* Calmly Rose rejects him: "What good would the moon be, unless the right one shared its beams?" As the song ends, from inside the house comes a scream as Mrs. Buchanan's labor begins. Easter departs, but not before he is seen by Maurrant who, over repetitive chords, questions Rose about him. She quietly defends her behavior and sends her father into the house, saying she wants another moment of fresh air. Alone, she muses on Easter and what he could do for her; but then returns to "What good would the moon be. . ."

Dialogue: Buchanan rushes out of the house, and sends Rose for the doctor; rushing back as his wife screams again.

13. *Song, Scene and Dance.* Mae Jones, who lives in the house, comes by with her boyfriend Dick, who wants a kiss and perhaps more. He sings, "Moon-faced, starry-eyed," and after drinking some gin they do an exciting jitterbug dance; and she agrees to go with him to a friend's vacant apartment.

Dialogue. Much ado about the coming baby. Mrs. Jones's son Vincent, a bully, tries to paw Rose, knocking down Sam who leaps to her defense. On a call from his mother, and with a final sneer at Sam, Vincent goes in, leaving Rose and Sam together.

14. *Duet and Finaletto.* Sam is discouraged and wants to talk of his love for Rose, but she stops him by asking for the truth about her mother. His silence confirms her fear. As Mrs. Buchanan screams again, Sam sings of pain, and of death: "What else has life got to give?" She reminds him of a poem he once recited to her ["When Lilacs Last In The Dooryard Bloomed," by Walt Whitman] and of which she remembers best the line: "the sprig with its flower I break" [suggesting rebirth of life and hope and reconciliation after a death]. They sing together, "And when you see the lilac bush. . . Remember that I care."

The doctor for Mrs. Buchanan arrives. From the upstairs window Maurrant calls to Rose. She goes in, leaving Sam with a kiss. Henry, the handyman comes up from the cellar, "I got a marble and a star." Rose, at a window, calls "Goodnight" to Sam, on the stoop. Slow curtain.

ACT II (64 min.)

SCENE 1 (40 min.). Early morning.

15. *Introduction and Children's Game.* The children imitate Park Avenue manners, debutantes, and drunks.

Dialogue. The tenants discuss the Buchanan's baby. Rose tries to talk to her father about her mother, urging him to be a little nicer and to drink a little less.

16. *Scene and Trio.* Maurrant replies angrily, and when Mrs. Maurrant appears, the three join voices, Rose appealing to her father, Maurrant threatening, Mrs. Maurrant defensive and, after he leaves, despairing. Rose ends the scene: "If there was only something I could do!"

17. *Song.* Mrs. Maurrant straightens Willie's necktie and collar for school.

Dialogue. Shirley Kaplan, Sam's older sister, asks Rose to leave Sam alone. He needs time for law school, and anyway, "it's better to marry with your own kind." Sam comes out, and a discouraged Rose consults him about Harry Easter's proposal, saying, "If you don't pay for things in one way, you do in another." Sam is horrified, and suggests they leave the house and city together. But she's unsure.

18. *Duet and Scene.* They sing of "When we go away together." Easter comes by, but Rose declines to go with him to a fellow worker's funeral; and they leave separately. Sankey appears and Mrs. Maurrant asks him to come up: they must talk. Mr. Maurrant, she assures him, has gone to New Haven and Rose won't be back for an hour. Sankey goes in. Sam sees, and deeply perturbed sits on the stoop. A girl goes to the Fiorentino apartment for a violin lesson.

Dialogue. The girl on the violin practices Dvorak's "Humoresque." The City-Marshal comes to evict the Hildebrands, and soon after, Maurrant unexpectedly returns. Sam tries to stop him from entering and calls to Mrs. Maurrant. From her apartment comes a scream of terror, the violin stops, two shots are fired, then a third; and Maurrant, gun in hand, runs from the house. He escapes, and police, entering the house, pronounce Mrs. Maurrant and Sankey dead. Rose returns, and Sam tries to warn her away.

19. *Choral Scene and Lament.* Sam leads the lament: "Now love and death have linked their arms together."

INTERLUDE (3 min.)

———

SCENE 2 (21 min.) Mid-afternoon.

20. *Lullaby.* Two nursemaids, titilated by the double murder, have wheeled their babies to view the house.

21. *Scene.* Rose enters, in black. Sam reports he has taken Willie to the boy's aunt. Rose is grateful and goes up to the family apartment, asking Shirley to accompany her.

Dialogue. Shots offstage. Police bring in Maurrant, covered with blood and grime. Rose runs to him.

22. *Finale.* Rose: "Why?" He replies: "It might not have looked like it to you, but I loved her, too." A general lament swells: "He loved her too." The police lead him off.

Sam is left with Rose, who plans to leave. He wants to go with her, but she won't let him, not now. "Oh, Rose, this is the end of my world." But she reminds him of the lilac bush: "Remember that I care." Sam breaks away and enters the house. Rose watches him, and then goes off. The tenants begin to complain of the weather: "Ain't it awful the heat. Ain't it awful?"

DOWN IN THE VALLEY

Folk opera in one act (45 min.). World premiere, Bloomington, Indiana July 14, 1948; European prem., Bristol, Oct. 23, 1957. Music by Kurt Weill; text by Arnold Sundgaard.

The opera, parts of which are based on American folk songs, was conceived primarily for nonprofessional groups, and with these it has had a great success. In 1975–76, for example, it ranked fifth among the contemporary operas most frequently performed in the United States (after four operas by Menotti), and most of the performances were by students in colleges or universities. For many Americans, onstage or in the audience, *Down in the Valley* is the first or early intense experience of opera.

It stirs in many persons, however, only a great sadness. Weill's career, these feel, falls in three parts, and only in the second did he compose music of any significance. The divisions are roughly: 1922–27, when with Hindemith and others he was a leader in Germany of the neo-classic movement; 1927–33, when with Bertolt Brecht as his librettist he produced among other works *Die Dreigroschenoper* (*Threepenny Opera*) and *Aufstieg und Fall der Stadt Mahagonny* (*Rise and Fall of the City of Mahagonny*); and 1933 until his death in 1950, when as a refugee from Nazi Germany he settled in the United States and wrote musical comedies and this opera.

Those whom it saddens feel that Weill's creative roots in some mysterious manner were so deeply embedded in German soil and culture that when the Nazis forced him from Germany, because his music supposedly was "degenerate" and represented "cultural bolshevism," they achieved their aim of destroying his ability to compose good music. And within Germany they not only banned performances of his existing music but literally destroyed it in whatever form they found it: manuscripts, published scores, films or phonograph records.

Certainly the best music of Weill's second period is more vigorous, imaginative and individual than any of the third. Yet are his American works so bad? Is it, perhaps, just the comparison to what went before? And how remarkable that a German should be able to compose an American folk opera more popular than those by such native composers as Douglas Moore, Carlisle Floyd, Aaron Copland or Virgil

Thomson! It would seem as though creative roots can be transplanted or, at least, regrown. But whatever the conclusions, Weill's career—for the questions it raises about the sources of creativity—is one of the most fascinating of the twentieth century.

The opera opens with a Chorus onstage in a large semicircle singing the Kentucky mountain folk song "Down in the Valley." Its leader promises the story of Brack Weaver, who loved Jennie Parsons and died on the gallows for the slaying of Thomas Bouché. As the opera proceeds, the Chorus, except for a few who take part in the action, remains in place, and to music most often derived from the folk song it introduces or comments on the scenes, which are played in the semicircle before it.

Brack Weaver (tenor or high baritone) is in prison awaiting execution in the morning. He sings of his love for Jennie and decides he must see her before dying to be sure of her love. He breaks out, counting on the few hours of darkness to find her before he is caught.

Jennie (soprano) waits for him on her porch, and her father (speaking role), who forbade her to write or visit Brack, urges her to forget him. Alone, she sings of her love for Brack.

He comes, and they sit in a field as men looking for him pass by the house. They sing of their love (folk song: "The Lonesome Dove"). Again the pursuers pass by. But despite Jennie's urging Brack refuses to flee. He wants only his hour with Jennie.

In a series of flashback scenes they reenact a meeting at church (folk song: "The Little Black Train") and their walk home together during which he asked her to the Saturday night dance and she accepted (folk song: "Hop Up, My Ladies").

At home Jennie finds her father and Thomas Bouché (bass) on the porch. Bouché, an older man, asks her to the dance, and she refuses. After he goes, her father points out that Bouché is helping the family financially. Jennie still rejects him, and her father tells her that she need not go to the dance with Bouché, also she must not go with anyone else.

Jennie and Brack go to the dance (folk song: "Sourwood Mountain"). Bouché, who is drunk, attacks Brack with a knife, and Brack kills him.

The Chorus, ending the flashback, returns the scene to Jennie and Brack in the field. Dawn is breaking. Their hour together is passed and with a last goodbye Brack walks off into the dark. Jennie stands looking after him. The Chorus ends the opera with a reprise of "Down in the Valley" in which the voices of Brack and Jennie are heard.

The words of the folk song that constantly recur in the opera are:

> Down in the valley, the valley so low,
> Hang your head over, hear the wind blow.
> Roses love sunshine, violets love dew,
> Angels in heaven, know I love you.

THE MIDSUMMER MARRIAGE

Opera, in three acts. World premiere, Covent Garden, London, Jan. 27, 1955; Australian prem., Adelaide, Feb. 25, 1978: American prem., San Francisco, Oct. 15, 1983. Music and libretto by Michael Tippett.

PRINCIPAL CHARACTERS

Mark, a young man of unknown parentage	tenor
Jenifer, his betrothed	soprano
King Fisher, Jenifer's father, a businessman	baritone
Bella, King Fisher's secretary	soprano
Jack, Bella's boyfriend, a mechanic	tenor
Sosostris, a clairvoyant	contralto
The Ancients, priest and priestess of the temple	bass and mezzo soprano

Few contemporary operas have been so angrily criticized as this, the first of Tippett's five full-length operas, followed by *King Priam* (1962), *The Knot Garden* (1970), *The Ice Break* (1977), and *New Year* (1989). The music, however, was not the irritant; the anger focused on the libretto, often said to be obscure, even incomprehensible, with a jumble of symbols torn arbitrarily from the world's mythologies. It was also said to be unreasonable in its scenic demands, in the number of principals and choristers needed, and in assigning a crucial role to ballet. In an age of limited finances, why such a grand opera?

Conversely, few operas have been so loyally supported—and in a way that counts most. Though eighteen years passed before a house other than Covent Garden would mount it, in that period Covent Garden revived it three times while also producing Tippett's later operas. Today those who believed in it seem vindicated. The audience for it has grown, other houses have taken it up, and critics increasingly write of it as a masterpiece.

Tippett has called the opera a comedy and explained it as follows: "There is only one comic plot: the unexpected hindrances to an eventual marriage . . . [and] the mechanism of hindrance to successful marriage, or to any relationship, is our ignorance or illusion about ourselves." The kernel from which the opera grew was a vision "of a wooded hill-top with a temple, where a warm, soft young man was being rebuffed by a cold, hard young woman (to my mind a very common present situation) to such a degree that the collective magical archetypes take charge—Jung's *anima* and *animus.*"

The initial goal is to be a whole person: a successful joining of both sides of the personality, body and mind, the unconscious and the conscious. A Tippett theme, often repeated, occurs in his oratorio *A Child of Our Time:* "I would know my shadow and my light, so shall I at last be whole. Then courage, brother, dare the grave passage." The opera for Mark, Jenifer, and the audience is "the grave passage," the psychoanalysis leading to the birth of a newly balanced personality. Then a successful marriage of persons is possible.

The opera's action takes place in a clearing on the wooded hilltop of Tippett's vision. To the back on high ground is a sanctuary with a temple in Greek style. To the right a stone stairway rises and breaks off in mid-air; to the left it descends through gates into the earth. Time is the present, and the characters wear modern dress except for the Ancients of the temple, guardians of "the collective magical archetypes," who wear Greek tunics.

ACT I (Morning—62 min.)

A chorus of men and women, friends of Mark and Jenifer, gather in
chorus   the clearing for the couple's outdoor, midsummer marriage. From the temple, dancers emerge followed by a He-Ancient and a
stick dance   She-Ancient. The dancers do a stick dance and are about to repeat it when Mark enters and stops them. He wants a new dance on his wedding day. Against the protests of the Ancients, he insists on it. The dancers begin the old dance again. The He-Ancient trips one, and he falls. (The idea seems to be that tradition cannot be changed without risk of harm.) Mark is indignant, and the Ancients and dancers retire within the temple.

Mark sings of his love for Jenifer. She arrives and rebuffs him. Mar-
aria   riage, after all, is not for her; she will pursue "the light" (ap-

parently chastity, independence and the intellect) and leave for Mark "the shadow" (body and instinct). They part quarreling. She mounts the stairway and vanishes into the light; he in pique passes through the gates into the earth.

King Fisher, Jenifer's father, arrives in time to see Mark disappear. With him is his secretary Bella. He is determined to prevent the marriage: Mark is unworthy of his daughter. He orders Bella to ask the Ancients to open the gates. They refuse, and Fisher sends Bella to find Jack, her boyfriend, who is a mechanic. Fisher will force the gates.

aria While Bella is gone, Fisher hires the men of the chorus to act as lookouts. The women of the chorus, however, refuse to work for him: "No truck with a bribe."

chorus As soon as Jack starts to work on the gates, a voice calls, "Beware." When it calls a second time, Bella grows nervous and Fisher indignant. The men of the chorus urge Jack to continue, but the women, to stop.

Suddenly Jenifer appears at the top of the stairs, "in white, partially transfigured." At the same moment Mark appears at the gates, "in red, partially transfigured." (According to Tippett her prototype is Athena; his, Dionysus.) The Ancients, coming out, say to the two: "Prepare to justify your strife."

aria Jenifer describes "the light" where, free of the world's pressures, she felt her soul begin to flower. "How can I such lovely visions of the mind deny?"

aria With much sexual imagery, Mark describes the shadow "where stallions stamp, young men dance, and man's animal nature is recognized as the source of creation."

The men of the chorus ask to be shown "another birth," but Jenifer protests at the price exacted by births. Taking a mirror, she holds it before Mark so that he can see the animal in his face. He, however, counters with a golden branch, and the mirror falls from her hand.

chorus Shocked, Jenifer now goes through the gates "to find the beast" even as Mark mounts the stairs to find the light. Fisher protests, "Now is this nonsense at its noon," but the chorus senses that the two are engaged in a quest for self-knowledge from which all may gain. (The hindrance to successful marriage is "ignorance or illusion about ourselves." Mark and Jenifer must bring body and mind, instinct and rationality, masculine aggressiveness and feminine receptivity into a better balance.)

ACT II (Afternoon—33 min.)

chorus A dancer stands motionless, listening. Soon he begins to dance. But when he hears the chorus offstage singing of midsummer, he runs behind the temple.

duet Bella, Jack and a few choristers enter. Bella draws Jack away from the others, who go off; she wants to talk. It is time they married. He is agreeable, and they sing of marriage as they understand it: "a little house," for which Bella does the housework while Jack earns the money, and someday "a little Jack or little Bella." Kissing, they walk into the wood's shadow.

three ritual dances Then follow the first three (12 min.) of the opera's four Ritual Dances. In the first, "The Earth in Autumn," a hound (female dancer) hunts a hare (male). Twice the hare is almost caught but in the end escapes. In the second dance, "The Waters in Winter," an otter (female dancer) hunts a fish (male). The hunt is more violent, and the fish escapes only with a final wrench that plainly leaves him injured. The third dance, "The Air in Spring," portrays a hawk (female dancer) striking a bird (male) with a crippled wing. This dance would end in the bird's death except that Bella, who has been watching, screams.

(The critics agree universally—so they must be right—that these dances depict the sexual chase or unconscious conflict between the sexes. But, as some in any audience will have thought, hounds don't mate with hares, otters with fish, or hawks with other birds. What is shown is a chase for food. The symbols don't "work out." Or even granted that the chase is sexual, is the female always the hunter! If Tippett's message here is "the devouring female," it fits oddly with the rest of the opera. Finally, why must the chase end in death and not, as in nature, merely in a coupling? Such questions nag this opera throughout, just as similar questions for some persons nag Wagner's *Ring*.)

cosmetics aria Jack comforts Bella. "I wasn't born for these mysteries," she says. As she straightens her hair and makes up her face, her good humor returns. "Then we paint it. Some on this cheek. Some on that. . . . I'm quite myself again."

She tells Jack that King Fisher has another job for him. Jack recoils. "Our love has spoken," she says. "Our home is sure." But for the moment they need King Fisher. Running into the wood she calls, "Catch me."

    The chorus closes the act with its song of midsummer: "She must **chorus** leap and he must fall when the bright sun shines on midsummer day."

ACT III (Evening and Night—58 min.)

    The chorus is ending a picnic. Some are drinking, others dance, one **chorus** is half-tipsy. They all await King Fisher.

    Carrying a belt and a holster with pistol, he enters with Bella. The Ancients, he tells her, aren't the only ones with access to the subconscious; he has brought his private clairvoyant, Madame Sosostris, and he sends the chorus to greet her with song and lead her up the hill.

    The chorus carries in a litter on which is a figure dressed in a green cloak, conical hat and holding before its face a crystal bowl. It reveals itself as Jack. But while attention is on him, the real Sosostris takes her position in center stage, "a huge contraption of black veils of roughly human shape, though much more than life size."

    Fisher calls on Sosostris to reveal Jenifer's whereabouts. In a deep, **Sosostris's aria** slow voice she starts her incantation (the longest unbroken aria in the score). At its end gazing into the crystal bowl, she sees Jenifer and Mark in a meadow engaged in the act of love.

    Furious, Fisher smashes the crystal bowl and demands the truth. Sosostris remains silent. He orders Jack to unveil her, and on Bella's urging Jack refuses, choosing "to strip the veils not from Sosostris but myself." Declaring himself "a builder" (a creative, not destructive person), he goes off with Bella.

    Though warned by the Ancients that it is sacrilege, Fisher begins to strip the veils from Sosostris. The stage darkens and with the fall of the last veil is revealed "an incandescent bud." It slowly opens, like a huge lotus, and in its center are Mark and Jenifer transfigured and posed in mutual contemplation. (Tippett: in Indian mythology, Mark and Jenifer would be transfigured as Shiva-Shakti, Shiva and Parvati.) Fisher aims his pistol at Mark, but "Mark and Jenifer turn their faces towards him in a gesture of power," and he falls dead.

    The chorus with a dirge carry his body into the temple: "Mourn not **dirge** the fall of a man that goes down leaving the room for someone beautiful."

A male and female dancer begin the fourth Ritual Dance, "Fire in Summer" (6 min.). The dancers create fire by twirling a stick on a **fourth ritual dance** block. When the stick is aflame, the male dancer holds it high, and Mark and Jenifer, relaxing their "compassionate pose," assume one of "increasing vigour and ecstasy." The chorus sings: "Fire! Fire! St. John's Fire in the desert in the night. Fire! Fire!" The dancers meanwhile begin to close the incandescent bud, and the flaming stick is held above Mark and Jenifer, who seem slowly to recede into the bud's interior. The chorus sings of "carnal love through which the race of men is everlastingly renewed becomes transfigured as divine consuming love whose fires shine from God's perpetually revealed face." The stage grows very dark, and only the burning stick is visible. It finally is drawn down within the bud, which breaks into flame as the chorus sings, "Fire! Fire!"

When the smoke clears, the stage is dark except for moonlight on the white stone of the temple. "Was it a vision? Was it a dream?" asks the chorus.

The moonlight fades, the stage is totally dark. Then birds begin to sing. Dawn breaks, and from opposite sides Mark and Jenifer appear, dressed for their wedding. As the sun rises, they sing with the chorus: "All things fall and are built again and those that build them are gay." The stage fills with light and, adds Tippett, "Were the mists to lift again it would be seen that the temple and the sanctuary of buildings were only ruins and stones silhouetted against the clear sky."

THE KNOT GARDEN

Opera in three acts. World premiere, Covent Garden, London, Dec. 2, 1970; American prem., Evanston, Illinois, Feb. 22, 1974. Music and libretto by Michael Tippett.

THE CHARACTERS

Faber, a civil engineer, aged about 35	baritone
Thea, his wife, a gardener	mezzo-soprano
Flora, their ward, an adolescent girl	soprano
Denise, Thea's sister, a dedicated Freedom-fighter	soprano
Mel, a Negro writer in his late twenties	baritone
Dov, his white friend, a musician	tenor
Mangus, a psychiatrist	baritone

The action takes place in a high-walled house-garden in an industrial city of today. No particular city or country is specified, so the characters, though initially English, by costume and accent can be rooted elsewhere.

A knot garden, like a chalk, rose or heather garden, is usually only a part of a larger garden. Developed in Elizabethan England, it consisted of clipped dwarf evergreens, often box, arranged in geometrical patterns with sand or pebble walks between. Sometimes flowers or rose trees are planted within the patterns. To the imaginative, depending on the height of the hedges and whether flowers are in bloom, the garden can seem bright and happy or, perhaps in its restricting patterns, a maze and threatening.

The opera tells of the loves, hates and indifferences of six persons, all of whom are or soon will be in a state of emotional confusion. A seventh, the psychiatrist, attempts to help them by bringing them together in a series of confrontations or charades, during which each is forced to recognize some truth about himself or some other. The garden changes with the inner situations, growing more roselike when love is on the increase and more mazelike when anger or confusion rises.

The confrontations and later the charades, in which the characters act bits of Shakespeare's *The Tempest*, are very brief. Sometimes, as Tippett explains, "the dramatic action is discontinuous, more like the cutting of a film. The term used for these cuts is Dissolve, implying some deliberate break-up and re-formation of the stage picture." In all there are eight "dissolves," five of them in the final act where the charades take place; for the first six their music is unvaried, ten bars of loud, rather jangly music followed by five of *dimunendo* timpani roll and a soft note on a horn or cellos.

Recognizing "dissolves" is fun but not vital. It is important, however, to realize from the start that because of its structure the opera is paced very fast. It is short (81 min.) and yet has thirty-two scenes. The longest are the finales of the three acts, and to make up for their many minutes, other scenes are reduced to one or even less. The opening scene, for example, introduces the psychiatrist Mangus, who appears "to be lying on a couch as a still point in a whirling storm." Rising he says, "So, if I dream, it's clear I'm Prospero: man of power. He puts them all to rights." He holds for a moment "a pose of self-satisfaction," and the scene, ending in a dissolve, cuts directly to the garden. Those in the audience slow to raise eye and ear to the stage may miss it all:

Mangus as "the still point" in the characters' emotional storm; the suggestion of the opera as a dream; the start of the Shakespearean analogue; and the nuance of Mangus's personality.

ACT I (Confrontation—30 min., including prologue)

Thea and Faber are unhappily married, he more than she because less skillful in manufacturing an emotional refuge. She has her garden; he has his work at the factory, but he is more bothered than she by an unreleased sexual urge.

Their ward, Flora, senses that urge and feels threatened by it. Left alone with Faber she is apt to scream and rush for protection to Thea, who then reproves Faber for something that, whatever his thoughts, he has not done. To help with what seems to be Flora's problem Thea has asked Mangus, the psychiatrist, to the house, and after a typical exhibition by Flora he concludes that the root of the trouble is in the unhappy marriage.

Thea also has invited to the house Dov and Mel, a musician and a writer, and when Flora first meets them they are dressed as Ariel and Caliban for the charades Mangus is planning. Startled, Flora retreats into her little girl's voice. Plainly her personality is not yet fully formed.

Though Dov and Mel are lovers, when Thea perhaps inadvertently indicates a sexual interest in Mel, he abandons Dov to follow Thea into her garden. Dov, dropping to all fours, howls in distress, like Ariel's dog. Faber, entering, is astonished, and even more so at Dov's relatively open explanation of his love for Mel. Faber says suggestively to Dov, "Come closer: to me: Faber." At that moment Thea and Mel **finale** emerge from the garden, but before any of the four can speak, the finale begins: Flora, followed by Mangus, runs in screaming that Thea's sister Denise has arrived: "She looks . . . she looks. . . ."

Denise the Freedom-fighter enters. She has been disfigured by torture. Her aria is the opera's longest: "I want no pity. This distortion is **aria** my pride." She ends asking herself and them, "How can I turn home again to you, the beautiful and damned?"

Her presence and question unsettle the others, and in an ensemble they sing their fears, the four most emotionally insecure in Mel's Negro **ensemble** "blues" style: Mel, who is bisexual, let Denise, a woman, not torment me; Dov, who is homosexual, let Mel not desert me; Flora, let no one assault me; and Faber, let Thea not castrate me. Thea, strong enough to sing in her own style, wonders if Mel is the man for her. Denise continues her narcissistic aria, and Mangus comments to the audience that without some change all will end in despair.

ACT II (Labyrinth—21 min.)

The garden as a threatening maze in which the characters, as if puppets at the command of Mangus-Prospero, suddenly are brought face to face and equally suddenly torn apart. In the nightmare their loves and hates appear "more naked and more violent." Finally, "the two characters most lost and most alone are thrown clear of the maze onto the forestage, and the maze recedes." (Ideally Tippett would like the maze on a turntable, which literally could whirl the characters in and out of their confrontations.)

Thea and Denise. Though sisters, as in a dream they talk past each other.

Denise and Faber. Desperate for affection, Faber suggests, "let us explore." Denise rejects him. "I have no need of you."

Faber and Flora. On seeing him, Flora, who is sorting some flowers, screams. "Grow up," he insists. "You're a woman." Then suggestively, "Give me those flowers." He reaches for her, but she is whirled away.

Thea and Faber. She horsewhips him for his attack on Flora, forcing him to the ground like a dog.

Dov and Faber. "Bow-wow," says Dov ironically. "Has some woman put you down?" Dov should know, counters Faber. Then, realizing that he and Dov are both free because rejected, he says: "Come, I never kissed a man before." But the maze whirls him away.

Dov and Mel. Against a fast, bitter blues background Mel bids Dov farewell: "Between black and white" there is "no family." "The heart's my family," Dov says. Mel admits his love for Dov was real, but it is finished. When Dov begins to howl, Mel merely says: "Become yourself: Go turn your howls to music."

Mel and Denise. For her he is the symbol of what she fought to free. In his mind he hears phrases of "We Shall Overcome" and is drawn to her.

Single Sentences. (Here the characters have only phrases or less. Ideally Tippett would like the maze to whirl in reverse, seeming to bring back in order the characters whisked off.) As Mel starts to follow Denise, Dov returns to mock: "There's no family between black and white!" When Thea appears and looks over at Mel, he tells her, "Go water your roses!" Rejected, she sighs, "Briars and thorns!" Flora runs on, followed by Faber. For a moment Thea and Faber face each other. Dissolve.

Dov and Flora. The two characters "most lost and most alone" comfort
finale each other. To stop her crying he suggests that she sing a song, and she sings three lines from Schubert's *Die liebe Farbe* (exqui- sitely orchestrated). Dov responds with an account of his life in south-
aria ern California. Under the influence of his music, of their shared kindness, the garden begins to be a rose garden. But as the song ends, a shadow enters: Mel. "I taught you that," he says to Dov. The garden fades while Flora and Dov look on in dismay.

ACT III (Charade—30 min.)

Five of the opera's characters have roles in the Charade: Mangus-Prospero, Dov-Ariel, Mel-Caliban, Flora-Miranda, Faber-Ferdinand. These roles are never absolute; they are dropped at need. Thea and Denise remain themselves. Anyone may be a spectator when not in the Charade.

Mangus sets the scene: the garden is an island. As the creating artist he says, "The power is in the play." Denise, politically oriented, insists, "Power is in the will." Thea, more of a humanist, puts it in "Forgive-ness . . . I know no god but love." Dissolve.

Charade #1. Mangus-Prospero shows the island to Flora-Miranda. They discover Mel-Caliban grunting about the ground and Dov-Ariel imprisoned by Caliban's mother, Sycorax, locked in a tree. Prospero frees Ariel, who rushes to kick Caliban—far harder than the script re-quires. Prospero dissolves (music varied) the scene.

Comment. Thea remarks that Prospero's power is limited: Dov's real emotions overpower his acting. Denise cannot see why: in freedom-fighting "the mind was clear; to kill, even, or be killed." Mel will teach you, says Thea, that "in love the purities are mixed." "Never," says Denise. Dissolve.

Charade #2. Flora-Miranda is asleep and Mel-Caliban leaps on her, attempting rape. Denise suddenly intervenes and pulls him off.

Comment. Denise reproves Mel, who says he only plays his part. You do more, she says; and when he admits as much, she bursts into tears and runs off. Dov sadly urges Mel to follow her. Mel goes, wondering if he is anything more than "black earth for white roses." Thea accuses Mangus of being no more than a pimp or voyeur.

Charade #3. Its opening draws an involuntary "Ah, no!" from Thea. Faber-Ferdinand and Flora-Miranda are playing chess. Each talks in a false voice. "Sweet Lord you play me false!" and "I would not for the world." "Oh, yes, you would," cries Flora, upsetting the board and fleeing.

Comment. "That scene went wrong," says Faber. "That scene went right," says Mangus, and he asks Thea to help to collect the chess pieces. "Here's the king," says Faber. "And here's the queen," says Thea. "Catch." (The moment is the opera's climax, and in Tippett's words "a burst of bright music greets the action." The libretto by itself does not sustain or explain the climax; it is in the music. Presumably Thea has realized that by withholding her love she is partly responsible for Faber's erratic behavior.) Mangus hurries Faber off, and Thea left alone sings, "I am no more afraid . . . now I know nature is us." Dissolve.

Charade #4. Mangus-Prospero prepares to leave the island with Flora-Miranda. Before going he frees Dov-Ariel, who exclaims, "Now free. Music is my muse." Mel-Caliban is brought, but Mangus-Prospero hesitates. "All, all are free," cries Flora-Miranda. But Dov-Ariel shows that he for one is not, for he dances provocatively around Mel-Caliban. With a gesture Mangus-Prospero ends the Charade.

Finale. Speaking directly to the audience, Mangus acknowledges limits on his power. He cannot resolve all problems, not Dov's, not Mel's.

All but Thea and Faber sing: "If for a timid moment we submit to love [and] exit from the inner cage [to] turn each to each to all," then, so runs the implication, most problems can be resolved. But before the implication can be fully stated, Dov has started a farewell ensemble based on Ariel's song, "Come unto these yellow sands."

The characters begin to go: Mel with Denise, Flora alone and dancing, and Dov—though he might wish to follow Flora, he is drawn by a backward look from Mel to follow Mel and Denise. "Ah, Dov, I pity you," says Mangus before himself departing. Dissolve (in a modified version).

Epilogue. Thea and Faber remain. "Our enmity," they say, "is transcended in desire." As they begin to move toward each other, they exclaim together, "the curtain rises."

Tippett's success in making his seven characters come alive is quite extraordinary. Even without music, in the brief libretto, their personalities are clearly differentiated. Musically his success seems to rest, at least in part, on an eclecticism that has divided the critics. Besides the normal Tippett style, much sparer here than in *The Midsummer Marriage,* he uses such diverse styles as Negro "blues," nursery rhyme, and an artificial coloratura, particularly for Denise. There are also the lines of the Schubert song, the reminiscence of "We Shall Overcome" and Elizabethan flourishes recalling Shakespeare. Is it too much? Because of it does the opera lack an organic unity making the parts and whole one? Or is it an artisitc reflection of contemporary life in which, because of radio, records, tape and television, we far more than previous generations are immersed day and night in just such a mixture of styles?

REGINA

Opera in a Prologue and three acts. World premiere, New York, Oct. 31, 1949; Euopean prem. (in revised version), Glasgow, May 16, 1991. Music and libretto by Mark Blitzstein, based on Lillian Hellman's play *The Little Foxes* (1939).

PRINCIPAL CHARACTERS

Regina Hubbard Giddens,	soprano (or mezzo-soprano)
Alexandra (Zan), her daughter	soprano
Horace Giddens, her husband	bass
Benjamin Hubbard, her brother	baritone
Oscar Hubbard, her brother	baritone
Birdie Hubbard, Oscar's wife	soprano
Leo Hubbard, son of Oscar and Birdie	tenor
Addie, Regina's Negro maid	contralto
Cal, a Negro servant	baritone
William Marshall, visitor from Chicago	tenor

Chorus of townspeople, field workers, and others.

Place: the Giddens house in Bowden, Alabama; Time, spring 1900.

The opera exists in versions, which may be grouped as long (153 min.), standard (130), and shortened, depending on the amount of music used. Before and early in its opening run on Broadway (56 perfs.), at playwright Hellman's demand, Blitzstein made cuts, chiefly of jazz and ragtime music and minor characters who struck Hellman and the producers as irrelevant. The cuts changed the balance between music and spoken dialogue, emphasizing the strong underlying play but leaving the opera "talky." For forty years this version was "standard," though shorter ones, usually tightening Act II, from time to time were staged. Then, in 1991, the Scottish Opera, led by the American conductor John Mauceri, produced the long version, returning the title role to mezzo-soprano, and restoring all cuts. But because its reception was somewhat cool, the medium-length standard seems likely to remain the version most often performed, and is the one described here.

The story is of greed. The Hubbards, two brothers and a sister, have a chance to make a deal with a Chicago banker to build a cotton factory in their town. In the course of negotiations, Regina's brothers steal from her husband, she blackmails them, kills her husband by a deliberate inaction, but alienates her daughter. And there are more horrors.

Blitzstein based the opera on dance rhythms, ragtime, blues, and jazz to represent the decent people, the Negroes, Alexandra, her father and Aunt Birdie, and waltzes and galops to represent the grasping, newly-rich Hubbards. In addition there were to be offstage spirituals for the Negro field hands and an operatic aria of nostalgia for Aunt Birdie, who represents the best of the Old South, taste, kindness, honor, but who, married by Oscar Hubbard for her cotton fields, has been crushed and abused by him.

In his opera, however, Blitzstein was plagued by two disabilities, one primarily musical, the other, literary and political. Musically, his ragtime, jazz, and blues don't match the excellence of several of his more operatic numbers, such as in Act III "the Rain quartet" and Birdie's aria of nostalgia—and restoring more of the less than best may not be helpful.

His other weakness strengthened flaws minor in the play. Both playwright and composer, but especially Blitzstein, hated rich capitalists, and saw the Hubbards as typical of their class, a blight on the land. In addition, and again especially Blitzstein, both sympathized with the poor and downtrodden. He, however, was quite simplistic in his political ideas, and to suggest that just as in the opera the Negro-influenced forms of jazz, ragtime, blues, and spirituals ultimately triumph over waltzes and galops of the white upper class, so too, in the real world, in the great day a coming, a more equalitarian, diversified economic structure would topple white capitalism, was a political fantasy, an anachronism causing him to sentimentalize the role and position of the Negroes. An audience can see the problem displayed onstage in several small ways. For one, in Act III Blitzstein, wanting the Negro servant Addie's contralto voice for "the Rain quartet," has her sitting, drinking wine, and eating cookies with her white employer, his daughter, and sister-in-law. In 1900? No. Not in the North or the South, no matter whether the servant was white or black.

And in a larger way Blitzstein's sentimentality misleads him in the opera's best and longest aria, Aunt Birdie's self-reflection. She longs for life as it was on her family's plantation, the parties, the kindness, the "singing on the river;" now, in middle-age, she admits, "I drink." But was the past so good? Addie might not say so. Blitzstein comes close to turning into an ideal good the unfettered capitalist structure he deplores.

But in performance such confusions fade. Profundity aside, the story offers a gripping melodrama about greed, with a superb role for a singing-actress. Regina Giddens is one of opera's great monsters, and her story, taken purely as melodrama, makes excellent entertainment.

PROLOGUE (6 min.)

Late morning in the spring, 1900; on the veranda of the Giddens house. Alexandra (Zan) is at breakfast, served by Cal, with Addie working close by. Addie is singing a spiritual, "Want to join the Angel Band." Cal and Alexandra join in, and the tempo shifts into ragtime. Regina interrupts, sending them to their chores. (In the long version this prologue doubles in length, and the "Angel Band" becomes a Dixieland band, led by Jazz, a character cut from the standard version.)

ACT I (36 min.)

That evening; in the living room of the Giddens house. Offstage Regina's dinner party for the Chicago banker, Mr. Marshall, is just ending, and Birdie enters excited by her talk with him about music. But her husband, Oscar Hubbard, reproves her for drinking too much. The others enter, and while pleasantries are exchanged, Blitzstein creates [perhaps awkwardly] "an abstract choral ensemble" of family members that advances action by comment: "The company have the table quit. . . The honored guest is distressed by the questionable jest." It becomes clear that the Hubbards have negotiated a business deal with Marshall, and Regina promises a party to celebrate its signing when he returns the next week. After he departs, to be driven to his hotel by Zan and Leo, Regina and her brothers exult: now they will be "Big Rich!" Birdie wistfuly speaks of restoring her family's plantation, Lionnet, but is silenced by Oscar.

Regina's brother Ben asks about her third of the Hubbards' investment. Does she have her $75,000? She points out her husband Horace, whose bonds she will use, is in a Baltimore hospital with heart trouble; but she will send Zan to bring him home. For his money, however, so necessary to close the deal, she wants more than a third of the Hubbard share in the new partnership. Ben offers forty percent, the additional seven to be taken from Oscar. When Oscar protests, Ben soothingly suggests that Zan someday may marry Oscar's son Leo.

Zan and Leo return. Regina in an aria asking Zan to go to Baltimore starts quietly but on meeting resistance from her **aria** daughter grows savage. In life, "The best thing of all, is to want something with all of your heart. To aim, with no shame. . ." At its end, having cowed Zan, she makes a grand exit up the stairs.

As the others go to the hall for their coats, Birdie warns Zan of the plan for her to marry Leo. Zan, in a dreamy, short aria wonders about life and love: "What will it be for me?" [her opening phrase is similar to her mother's, "The best thing of all. . ." suggesting that Zan, for all her gentleness, has reserves of strength.] She assures Birdie that she will never marry the feckless Leo: "I'm grown now. No one can make me do anything." Oscar overhears Birdie's warning, and after Zan starts upstairs, he slaps Birdie hard. Zan, hearing a cry, calls down, but Birdie replies she twisted her ankle.

ACT II (43 min.)

SCENE 1 (25 min.)

The living room, a week later. Evening. Everyone is preparing for the party.

Regina, in a wrapper, darts in and out, giving orders to Addie and Cal. (She delivers her lines at express-train speed, which while hardly musical can be exciting.)

Leo enters, and sings a characteristic song: "Deedle doodle, **Leo's song** deedle deedle doodle, Love a party, I love a party." He searches the room for his Uncle Horace's cigar box, and is caught by his father.

Oscar asks if Zan and Uncle Horace have arrived. There has been no word, and if Horace doesn't come tonight, how will Regina get the $75,000? Leo, who works in Horace's bank, reports that his uncle has a safe deposit box with $88,000 in bearer bonds, revealing he has seen them and knows where the key to the box is kept. Oscar hints Leo should steal the bonds, to put the deal through, and to cut out Regina. But Leo doesn't understand, and Oscar laments, "I've begot me a fool."

Zan and her father, very ill, arrive, and Zan is upset to hear of the party. Explaining to Addie that her father's medicine is important, she leaves one bottle in the room and, going upstairs to dress, carries the other with her to put in his bedroom. Alone with Addie, Horace hears of the plan to have Zan marry Leo [ominous music]. The Hubbards enter, and after greetings Regina and Horace are left together [drums pounding]. Their talk veers toward quarrel, avoided by an arietta for Regina, "Look at me. . .", comparing the two of them to old dry-bones. But she wants to talk about the money, and he does not, so she enlists her brother Ben to aid her. Marshall will be arriving soon, and they must know if they have Regina and Horace's third in hand. But Horace refuses to join the scheme.

Leo tells Oscar he now understands his father's hints, and the three Hubbard men retire to discuss plans. Regina, alone in the room and watching Zan help her father upstairs, announces "I'll have my party. Of course I'll have my party." And without the curtain descending, the scene slowly changes to the veranda, with the party in the room behind.

SCENE 2 (18 min.)

The Party. On the veranda the guests, townspeople, have a long chorus (sometimes shortened) in which they comment on the hated Hubbards, "There's none they have not double-crossed," while excluding from that judgement Horace, "Can't believe Regina would command sick Horace to be present." They go indoors to begin the party.

On the veranda Horace asks his loyal assistant at the bank to come in the morning with paper and the safe deposit box; he wants to draft a new will. Regina comes out briefly, flirting with Marshall. They all go in, with Zan pushing Horace in his wheelchair.

Ben, Oscar, and Leo come out, and the brothers, believing Leo's report that Horace never looks in his box, send Leo to the bank to steal the bonds.

Oscar scolds Birdie for drinking too much, and when she begins to weep, leaves her. Addie consoles her with a blues-like number, "Night could be time to sleep."

Next, Regina and Horace come out and on hearing that he will not invest in the scheme, she flirts with an old beau, John Bagtry, recalling how they had talked once of marriage, and now he has a thousand rivals for she is "in love with things." Horace, meanwhile, has gone in, and Regina and Bagtry follow, as he tries to kiss her. (This flirtation is sometimes shortened and, to reduce the number of roles, the old beau transformed from Bagtry into Marshall.)

Leo has the bonds, and gives them to Ben, who reports to Marshall that the Hubbards are ready, "the deal may be considered settled." In saying goodnight to Regina, Marshall remarks that he is glad all is "settled at last, leaving her confused, for she knows that Horace has not put up the money. Somehow her brothers have cut her out. The party heats up, the dancers do a galop, with the chorus in full cry, and Regina confronts Horace: "I hope you die. I'll be waiting for you to die." The dance stops as Regina's voice rings out, "I'll be waiting." Curtain.

ACT III (45 min.)

The living room. The next afternoon. Horace has drawn his new will, and the safe deposit box, into which Leo reported his uncle never looked, is on the table. Outside, a rainy day. The good people, Horace, Birdie, Alexandra, and Addie are in the room.

A quartet develops. "Make it a quiet day." [The secne, dramatically dubious, is musically delightful. In its central section, where **Rain quartet** Horace with his bass voice, sings "Consider the rain," Blitzstein fits words and music into an unforgettable phrase as surely as did Verdi with Aida's "Numi, pieta"—though the success here highlights the mediocrity elsewhere.]

Offstage field hands sing a rousing song, "Have you been baptized? Certainly, Lord."

Birdie now has her great aria, recalling the plantation, "Lionnet," her unhappy marriage, her worthless son, and her drinking. She predicts Zan will end up like her, lashed to the Hubbards. **Birdie's aria** "Oh, Lionnet, Lionnet." [Though wordy and melodically less sure than the quartet, the aria dramatically conveys the humiliation and despair of a woman broken by the men in her life.]

From here to the opera's end, there is much talk and declamation, with only a few breaks of lyricism. Horace asks Addie to take Zan away and reveals where cash is hidden to do it. He confronts Regina with the empty deposit box, telling her that Leo stole the bonds, which was why Ben was so sure and happy. Then in an arietta he tells Regina he has drawn a new will and left the missing bonds to her, "that's all;" adding, "I'm sick of you." Whereupon she goads him into a heart attack, and when he spills the medicine, won't fetch the upstairs bottle. He crawls to the stairs, starts up, and collapses. She calls in Cal and Addie, who carry him to his bedroom.

The Hubbards enter, and she confronts Ben with her knowledge of Leo's theft. For them to avoid exposure and jail, she suggests they give her a seventy-five percent share of the Hubbard investment with Marshall. Ben, in another fine match of words and music responds, "Greedy girl, what a greedy girl." They hear Addie weeping. Horace has died, and Zan, coming downstairs, asks her mother, "What was Papa doing on the staircase?" She suspects what happened. Regina, ignoring her, continues to threaten Ben: "Tomorrow I shall go straight to court." And Ben, for all the Hubbard men, agrees to her demands. After all, he observes, there is plenty of money to be made, and he predicts, "Hundreds of Hubbards, just like us, will own this land!" But he also warns Regina, by repeating Zan's question, "What's a sick man doing on a staircase?" that he, too, has guessed how Horace died. The Hubbards exit, leaving Regina facing Zan.

Off stage the field hands begin to sing, "Certainly Lord." Zan tells her mother that she now understands what her father had been trying to tell her about the Hubbards and other capitalists who "eat all the earth." She's leaving. Regina is astonished: "You do have spirit after all!" Off stage a field hand asks in song, "Is a new day a-coming?" And comes the reply, "Certainly, certainly, certainly, Lord."

AMELIA AL BALLO

(Amelia Goes to the Ball)

Opera buffa in one act. World premiere (in English) at Philadelphia, April 1, 1937. European prem. (in Italian), San Remo, April 4, 1938. British prem., Liverpool, Nov. 19, 1956. Music and text by Gian Carlo Menotti, who composed to the Italian text.

This was Menotti's first opera, composed when he was twenty-three and produced three years later. It had an immediate success, played briefly on Broadway in 1937, for two seasons at the Metropolitan before World War II, at La Scala after the war, and since then has continued to be one of Menotti's more popular operas, particularly in those cities of Europe and South America where Italian is a first or second language. Though composed in the United States, where Menotti studied, it is wholly an Italian *opera buffa.*

Unlike *The Telephone,* which followed ten years later, it is not a chamber opera but requires three principal singers, two good comprimarii, a full chorus and full orchestra. The orchestra, besides a four-minute overture, has two other extended solo passages. The music throughout is light, melodic and attractively scored.

The action (60 min.) takes place about 1910 in Milan (or any other large European city) in the bedroom of a rich bourgeoisie. Amelia is dressing to go to the ball, and her lady friend waits impatiently. Finally, after every bauble is perfectly placed, they are about to leave when her husband enters in a fury: Amelia will not go to the ball.

The friend hastily departs, and the husband accuses Amelia of having a lover. He has found a suggestive letter addressed to her and signed "Bubi." She promises to tell all, if he will take her to the ball. He agrees; but when she reveals that "Bubi" is the mustachioed man in the apartment above, the husband runs off with a pistol to avenge his honor.

Fearing that a row will keep her from the ball, Amelia goes to the balcony and calls her lover down. She intends for him to escape, but he dawdles. And when she hears her husband returning, she has to hide the lover.

Her disappointed husband is now ready for the ball, but she takes too long primping and he discovers the lover. He draws his pistol, aims and—it fails to fire. The lover advances menacingly on the husband. Let us not be hasty, cries the husband; let us talk the situation over. Amelia, growing frustrated as the men talk, and talk, smashes a vase on her husband's head, and he falls as if dead. Frightened, she runs out on the balcony, calling to the world for help.

Neighbors and the police arrive. She has the lover arrested as a robber, has her husband taken to the hospital, and with the Chief of Police as her escort—hence her reputation absolutely secure—Amelia goes to the ball.

THE OLD MAID AND THE THIEF

A Grotesque Opera in fourteen scenes. Originally conceived as an opera for radio, world premiere broadcast by the National Broadcasting Company, New York City, April 22, 1939. World prem. stage performance, Philadelphia, Feb. 11, 1941; German and probably European prem., Mannheim, Feb. 22, 1947; British prem., London, July 14, 1960. Music and text by Gian Carlo Menotti.

THE CHARACTERS

Miss Todd, a respectable woman	contralto
Laetitia, her housemaid	soprano
Miss Pinkerton, her neighbor	soprano
Bob, a young tramp	baritone

The action takes place in "the present" in a small town somewhere in the United States.

Though perhaps not so musically attractive as either *Amelia al Ballo* or *The Telephone,* the opera (58 min.) had a great success and in the United States is still frequently performed. The overture (4 min.) was added for the first stage performance.

On radio there was scarcely a break between scenes, time only for an announcer to set the next with a sentence. To insure the same swiftness in stage performances, Menotti states in the score, "the opera must be staged in such a way that no curtain or pause is required." And he gives another clue to successful production in his subtitle, "A Grotesque Opera."

Its gist is how a virtuous woman can make a thief of an honest man. This reversal of usual morality, which runs throughout, would leave a sour taste unless the opera, in costumes, gestures and singing, is played as grotesque exaggeration. Not for a moment, not even at the end, must the audience feel any sympathy for Miss Todd.

The curtain rises on Miss Todd and Miss Pinkerton at tea, gossiping. A tramp looking for food stops at the back door. Reported by the maid Laetitia to be young and good-looking, he causes a flutter of interest in the ladies. Later, after he has been fed, because Miss Todd and Laetitia would like a man to care for, Miss Todd invites him to spend the night. In the morning, urged on by Laetitia, she invites him to spend the week. Soon afterward she hears from Miss Pinkerton of a convict who has escaped from prison. His description seems to fit Bob. But Miss Todd and Laetitia, both by now a little in love, decide the safest plan is to keep him in the house.

Miss Todd steals from her friends' pocketbooks, leaving the money around the house for Bob to pick up. When he requests liquor, because she as a leader of the Prohibition Committee cannot be seen purchasing a bottle, she and Laetitia after midnight raid the store. But when Bob prepares to move on, she feels betrayed and threatens to report him to the police. In the confusion of identities it becomes clear that he is not the escaped convict. What's more, he is not the least bit in love with Miss Todd or about to run away with her. Scorned, she departs for the police station to turn him in for all the crimes she has committed. Laetitia warns Bob that Miss Todd, a pillar of society, will be believed. In desperation Bob agrees to run away with Laetitia in Miss Todd's car, and they take with them all Miss Todd's jewels, money and silver. She returns to find the house ransacked. As she screams for help, Miss Pinkerton enters, takes in the scene with a glance and smiles triumphantly at the story she will have to tell.

THE MEDIUM

Tragedy in two acts. World premiere, New York, May 8, 1946. European prem., London, April 29, 1948. Music and text by Gian Carlo Menotti.

THE CHARACTERS

Madame Flora (Baba), a medium	contralto
Monica, her daughter	soprano
Toby, a mute	—
Mrs. Gobineau ⎱	soprano
Mr. Gobineau ⎬ her clients	baratone
Mrs. Nolan ⎰	mezzo-soprano

The action takes place "on the outskirts of a great city" and "in our time."

The opera is possibly the century's most successful supernatural thriller; in the theatre, in any language, its melodrama works. Whether it offers more is questionable. Menotti entitled it a tragedy and once wrote of it: "Despite its eerie setting and gruesome conclusions, *The Medium* is actually a play of ideas. It describes the tragedy of a woman caught between two worlds, a world of reality which she cannot wholly comprehend, and a supernatural world in which she cannot believe."

A personal experience gave Menotti the idea. In 1936, when visiting friends near Salzburg, he was invited to a seance. "Although I was unaware of anything unusual, it gradually became clear to me that my hosts, in their pathetic desire to believe, actually saw and heard their daughter. . . ." The question was posed: if thinking can create reality, then for the imaginative where does safety lie? But at any performance, for most of the audience the play of ideas with its implicit tragedy is wholly absorbed by the melodrama.

In that tendency lies much of the critical argument over Menotti. He is superbly theatrical, but does he push the virtue to a fault? Does the scene in which Madame Flora whips the mute, Toby, exhibit in her character any trait necessary for the opera? Certainly it makes the average person cringe; probably it also distracts him from the opera's subject, the play of ideas about reality. Similarly, in the final scene, why at its start should Madame Flora lock Monica in the bedroom or at its end let her out? Monica's pounding on the door and moaning as she later crosses the stage doubtless raises the level of one kind of excitement; but her screams for help also divert attention from the medium's final question to the mute, now dead boy, "Was it you?"

Such artistic problems become important, however, only on repetition. At first hearing the opera is gripping. Its success lies chiefly in its concision—it runs only fifty-six minutes—and in its almost unique vocal sound. There are not many leading roles for contraltos, and fewer still with the equivalent of a "mad" scene. A good singing-actress can make the blowzy, superstitious, sometimes drunken Madame Flora unforgettable. For her "Am I afraid? Madame Flora afraid!" the low, hooty, sometimes mushy contralto timbre is just right. A soprano voice, however well used, cannot match it.

Menotti conceived the opera for small theatres and scored it for thirteen instruments and fourteen players: piano (four hands), flute, oboe, clarinet, basoon, horn, trumpet, percussion and a string quintet (two violins, viola, cello and double bass). In larger houses the strings usually are increased.

ACT 1 (27 min.)

A squalid, interior room of a rundown apartment. To one side, the door to a bedroom; opposite, a door leading to the stairs and street. The furnishings include a puppet theatre, a large astrological chart on the wall, a small statue of the Virgin with a candle burning before it, and in the room's center an old-fashioned three-legged table lit by a hanging lamp. Because of the lack of windows the time of day is always ambiguous.

There is a brief prelude built on a harsh, descending phrase of five chords that serves as a theme for the medium's dabbling in the spirit world. It also introduces Act II and dominates the opera's closing moments.

Monica, Toby and Mme Flora. In Mme Flora's absence the children, instead of preparing for the seance, have begun to play. Monica sings and combs her hair while Toby rummages in a trunk to find a costume. Admiring his choice, Monica proclaims him the King of Babylon; she will be his bride from the north. But suddenly Mme Flora has returned: "How many times I've told you not to touch my things! . . . Is anything ready? Of course not!" When she threatens to strike Toby, Monica, who calls her mother "Baba," restrains her.

Quickly all the deceptions are tested and made ready. From the control box concealed in the puppet theatre Toby lowers the lamp and levitates the table, while Monica dons a white dress and covers her head with a white veil. The doorbell rings, the children disappear to their posts, and Mme Flora, after pushing the buzzer to admit the guests downstairs, sits at the table, pretending to be absorbed in solitaire.

Mr. and Mrs. Gobineau, Mrs. Nolan and Mme Flora. With sparse civility, Mme Flora asks her clients to enter. The Gobineaus have been coming every week for almost two years, but Mrs. Nolan, a middle-aged widow, is new. She hopes to contact her sixteen-year-old daughter, Doodly, who died the previous year, and she is uncertain and nervous. The Gobineaus reassure her. Their son, Mrs. Gobineau explains, cannot talk to them, since he drowned in a fountain while still a baby. As she recalls the episode, she begins to weep.

The Seance. Their hands on the table, touching, they sit in darkness except for the candle before the Virgin. Mme Flora, simulating a trance, moans and groans, ending in a shriek, and soon in a dim blue light behind the astrological chart Monica in white veils begins to materialize. Three times, to a phrase built on four descending half-tones, D^b–C–B–B^b, she calls, "Mother, mother, are you there?" After Monica has answered a few simple questions, Mrs. Nolan is convinced that the apparition is Doodly.

When Monica appears to have made a mistake, however, in mentioning a gold locket that Mrs. Nolan cannot recall, the apparition quickly fades—much to Mrs. Nolan's distress. It is then the Gobineaus' turn, and Monica without appearing imitates a baby's laughter. The Gobineaus recognize their son, Mickey, and talk to him until the laughter vanishes into the darkness.

The Incident. Suddenly Mme Flora gasps, clutches her throat and cries, "What is it? Who touched me?" None of her clients can understand her agitation, and when she orders them out, they ask, "But why be afraid of our dead?"

As soon as they have gone, Monica rushes in, still in her veils. "Baba, what has happened?" Mme Flora pours a drink, considers and then states, "We must never do this again." At her throat she felt "a cold, cold hand" and "it wasn't the hand of a man." "You're imagining things," Monica suggests. "You've been drinking again."

"No, no," says Mme Flora. "I'm afraid." Going to the puppet theatre she thrusts its curtain aside, uncovering Toby, motionless, as if in a trance. "He! He's the one!" she cries, pulling him to the floor and threatening to beat him.

Monica draws her away and starts a gypsy song, "Black Swan." **Black Swan** Gradually she calms her mother, who finally joins in the song. Then offstage a thin, childish voice calls, "Mother, mother, are you there?" Though Monica hears nothing, Mme Flora is convinced that someone is in the room or on the stairs. She sends Toby to look, but he can find no one. Terrified, she begins to pray while Monica resumes the song. Offstage there is a sound of childish laughter, but only Mme Flora hears it. Burying her head in Monica's lap, she covers her ears.

ACT II (29 min.)

Mme Flora's apartment, evening, a few days later.
Monica and Toby. He finishes a puppet show and steps from behind the little theatre to acknowledge Monica's applause. "And after the theatre," she cries, "music." She starts a waltz to which he improvises a **Monica's Waltz** dance, and a kind of love duet develops in which she sings for both while he mimes his part. The reality of his love, however, breaks through her representation of it and, overcome, he suddenly hides his face in his hands. Monica, not altogether understanding, tells him that he has "the most beautiful voice in the world."

A door slams, and they hear Mme Flora on the stairs. Monica runs into the bedroom; Toby crouches in the corner.
Mme Flora and Toby. The incident of a few days before is still on her mind, and with calculated kindness she begins to question Toby, reminding him of how she found him in the street, took him in and gave him a home. Now she will give him a red silk shirt if he will say whether he touched her throat. "I won't punish you. I just want to know. That's all." When he does not respond, she grows angry; when he runs from her, she clutches his shirt, which tears. She takes a whip from the cupboard—"So you won't answer, eh!"—and whips him until the doorbell rings and Monica rushes in from the bedroom.
Mr. and Mrs. Gobineau, Mrs. Nolan, Mme Flora and Monica. "There

will be no more seances," says Mme Flora. Brusquely she throws money on the table, explaining to her clients that she has cheated them. They deny it. Through her they have talked with their dead. To demonstrate the fraud, Mme Flora manipulates the table, lowers the lamp and orders Monica to sing "Mother, mother are you there?" and to laugh like a child. But her clients' faith remains unshaken. "You may have thought you were cheating," says Mr. Gobineau, "but you were not." They plead for another seance. Unnerved by their conviction, she angrily dismisses them.

Then, no longer sure herself that the seances were entirely fraudulent, she orders Toby to go—for good. Despite Monica's pleadings, she drives him out and orders Monica into the bedroom. After Monica goes, slamming the door, a child's voice calls "Mother, mother, are you there?"

Mme Flora. She runs to the door. "Is it you, Monica?" She locks the door, starts back to the table and again hears the voice. "Stop it!" she screams. A long silence follows. Relieved, she pours a drink, sits and ponders. "Afraid, am I afraid?" In her life she has seen many horrors, but "the dead never come back." Drowsily and a little drunkenly she begins "Black Swan." Suddenly (the audience hears nothing), she whirls in her chair, shouting "Who's there?" When no one answers, she resumes singing and again hears something but can discover nothing. Better to laugh at it, she decides, and then in the midst of laughter growing increasingly hysterical begins to pray. Gradually she falls asleep.

Toby enters, hoping to speak to Monica and to retrieve his tambourine. While searching for it in the trunk, he allows the lid to fall. The sound wakes Mme Flora, and he darts behind the puppet theatre. The movement of its curtain terrifies Mme Flora. "Who is it?" she gasps. Taking a revolver from the drawer, she cries, "Speak out, or I'll shoot! I'll shoot!"

She fires. Toby's hand briefly appears above the curtain, blood spatters the cloth from behind and a great red stain runs its length. "I've killed the ghost!" she exults. Under Toby's weight the rod breaks, and tangled in the curtain he falls into the room. Monica pounds on the bedroom door, and Mme Flora unlocks it. As Monica runs screaming for help, Mme Flora returns to the dead boy. Caught between the reality of two worlds, she is still unsure. Kneeling beside him, in a hoarse whisper she asks, "Was it you?"

THE TELEPHONE
or
L'amour à trois

Opera buffa in one act. World premiere, New York City, Feb. 18, 1947. European prem., London, April 29, 1948. Music and text by Gian Carlo Menotti.

This curtain raiser (22 min.) is one of the most successful of its kind in the second half of the twentieth century, succeding Ermanno Wolf-Ferrari's *Il Segreto di Susanna,* 1909. In the latter a jealous husband (baritone), smelling tobacco in the house, suspects his pretty wife Susanna (soprano) of secretly entertaining a lover. Her secret, however, is that she herself smokes. In Menotti the triangle is formed with another symbol of modern woman, the telephone. The orchestration is simple—flute, clarinet, oboe, bassoon, horn, trumpet, percussion, piano and strings—with the piano as much as the strings providing the basic texture of sound.

prelude After a skittish, lyrical prelude (2 min.), the curtain rises on Lucy's apartment which could be in any large city of today. Lucy (soprano) is opening a present brought by Ben (baritone). She unwraps a piece of abstract sculpture: "Oh, just what I wanted!" Ben tells her that his train leaves in an hour and as he is so fond of her, he would like to ask. . . .

aria But the phone rings, and Lucy—"Hello! Hello? Oh, Margaret, it's you"—gossips about her friends. Toward the end, in her enthusiasm she abandons words for coloratura scales, and to Ben's dismay seems to resume the conversation at its beginning when, perhaps by mistake, it suddenly ends. "That was Margaret!" says Lucy. (The aria is sometimes sung in concerts.)

Ben again leads up to his question, and the phone rings: to Lucy's indignation, a wrong number. When he warns her that their time together is "getting shorter," she stops him to dial for the exact time: "four-fifteen and three and a half seconds."

Again when he starts, the phone rings. This time, however, Lucy is immediately on the defense as her friend George accuses her of loose talk and in anger hangs up on her. Bursting into tears, Lucy refuses to be comforted by Ben and disappears into her bedroom to find a handkerchief.

Ben, left alone, notices a pair of scissors on a table. Arming himself with them, he approaches the telephone. It rings in alarm, and Lucy runs in, taking it protectively in her arms.

Ben begs for a moment of "quiet talk," and Lucy consents—but only after she has called Pamela. It is absolutely necessary that she get her side of the George-story to Pamela before Pamela hears of it from **duet**   someone else. While she chatters on, and on, Ben complains of the phone that always comes between him and Lucy. He loves her and wants to marry her, but "now I have to go, and she will never know." Somberly he mutters, "There is only one thing left."

Lucy, ending her conversation, is surprised to find him gone, and a bit depressed. "I have a feeling he had something on his mind."

At one side of the stage Ben can be seen dialing at a public phone. Lucy's phone rings. She quickly powders her nose, fixes her hair and lifts the receiver. It is Ben. He proposes marriage, and she accepts, ask- **waltz duet**   ing him only not to forget one thing while he is gone. "Your eyes?" he suggests. "Your lips? Your hands?" No, her telephone number, which she insists he write down. And while he struggles with pencil and paper, she dictates it to him: Stevedore two . . . three . . . four . . . nine."

THE CONSUL

Musical drama in three acts. World premiere, Philadelphia, March 1, 1950. European prem., London, Feb. 7, 1951. Music and text by Gian Carlo Menotti.

THE CHARACTERS

John Sorel	baritone
Magda Sorel, his wife	soprano
The Mother (of John)	contralto
Secret Police Agent	bass
Assan, the glasscutter	baritone

At the Consul's Office

The Secretary	mezzo-soprano
Mr. Kofner	bass-baritone
The Foreign Woman	soprano
Anna Gomez	soprano
Vera Boronel	contralto
The Magician (Nicholas Magadoff)	tenor

The action takes place in the present, the years immediately after World War II, and in an unnamed European city.

With few exceptions, chiefly *The Medium* and *Amahl and The Night Visitors,* Menotti's serious operas deal with contemporary problems: *The Consul* (1950), political refugees; *The Saint of Bleecker Street* (1954), religious faith and skepticism; *Maria Golovin* (1958), prisoners of society; *The Most Important Man* (1971), racial prejudice; and *Tamu-Tamu* (1974), modern morality. Of these *The Consul* still seems the most satisfactory, perhaps because its story, music and production seem the most evenly matched.

The story concerns the destruction of a family unable to emigrate to escape persecution. Its enemy is twofold: its own repressive government and that of the neighboring "free" society that will not practice the humanity it preaches. In the years before and after World War II, when refugees were fleeing fascist and later communist governments, the twofold problem was much in people's minds. Typically the "free" societies rescued the artistically distinguished or scientifically useful but doomed the ordinary by entangling them at the consulate or border in red tape. The problem was never solved, and many families of the ordinary were simply destroyed. Among audiences in the Western, "free" countries, Menotti's story pressed on a nerve of despair and guilt.

Musically the part of the opera most interesting to him were "those nervous little passages" of recitative in which he tried to match the quick-paced dialogue of the current theatre. These give the opera its pace and tension, though in performance—for much of the audience—they will pass unnoticed. The more obvious impact lies in those moments of expansion in which Menotti extends a mood into a trio or quintet, and in the extraordinary theatricality with which he develops the story. Few operas make such use of violent contrast and surprise. Audiences apparently have found the technique acceptable, however, because they know that political persecution teems with theatrical violence.

The opera had an enormous success throughout the 1950s, including a run on Broadway of 269 performances. Thereafter its pace slowed, but for a quarter-century it has held a place in the international repertory.

Note: The recorded song heard twice in the opera is "Tu Reviendras" (You will come back), sung by Mabel Mercer, a nightclub favorite of the period.

ACT I (35 min.)

SCENE 1 (18 min.)

The Sorel's small, shabby apartment. By the window to the back and center is an old gas stove; by the door to the hall, at the extreme left, a workbench with tools; and opposite, an alcove leading to the bedroom. Furnishings are sparse: a table, a few chairs, a telephone and a cradle. As the curtain rises, the room is empty and dark. It is early morning. Through the open window from the café in the street comes the music of a record, "Tu reviendras. . . ."

John Sorel, his wife Magda and his Mother. The door from the hall is flung open and Sorel staggers into the room. He clutches at the workbench, upsets it and drags himself to a chair. His Mother and Magda rush in. As Magda dresses the wound in his leg, she asks, "It was the police, wasn't it?" "Yes, of course." "Oh, John," his mother exclaims, "What have you done? Think of your child!"

After he has described the political meeting, the surprise by the police and the death of his friend Marcus, his Mother bursts out bitterly, "Damn you and all your friends! Why don't you bring home some bread and not only fear and blood?" Magda quiets her, but soon herself is lamenting this "bitter love, this love of freedom that locks the very air we breathe." Anxiously John begs her not to fail him. At the window his Mother gasps, "the Police!"

For a second they all freeze. Then the women hurry him through the alcove to the roof, rush about the room tidying it, and then—just in time—sit. The Police enter.

The Interrogation. Ignoring the women, the police search the apartment while the Mother quietly sings, "Shall we ever see the end of all this!" Like others who are old, she has seen too many tears, too much blood. "Even death seems too slow in granting us our rest."

The Police Agent approaches Magda: "What is your name?" "Magda Sorel." When he fails to learn anything, he grows menacing. "Courage is often lack of imagination." The police can quicken the beat of a person's heart, and no one can withstand "the beat of your own heart!" Then, suddenly, polite, he departs.

From the window the Mother watches the police in the street. "They're taking Michael, the shoemaker, away!" A woman's screams are heard.

John, his Mother and Magda. Despite Magda's protests he plans to leave for the frontier at once, and his Mother supports him. He tells Magda to go to the Consul's office tomorrow and arrange for the family to emigrate. Meanwhile she must not see his friends. When a child throws a stone through the window, she must call Assan, the glasscutter, who will bring news. Bending over the cradle, he kisses his son.

  Magda begins a trio, "Now, O lips, say goodbye. The word must be
trio said, but the heart must not heed." (The music is some of the opera's most attractive, and its opening phrase returns in the last act at a crucial moment.) After embracing Magda and his Mother, John leaves.

INTERLUDE (1 min.)

(There are three of these, one in each act to cover a change of scene. Possibly in order not to diminish the impact of the vocal scenes, Menotti has kept these musical links extremely short and simple. A more symphonically minded composer—say, Richard Strauss—might have treated them very differently.)

SCENE 2 (16 min.)

  Later the same day. The Consul's waiting room, cold and cheerless. A few benches and wall desks and at a desk behind a heavy wooden railing the Consul's Secretary. Behind her the door to the Consul's office. As the curtain rises, the Secretary is typing and, seated on a bench, Mr. Kofner and the Foreign Woman are waiting.

The Secretary and Mr. Kofner. "Next," she calls. Mr. Kofner, an elderly gentleman with a slightly professorial air, hurries to the railing. "I believe we have seen you before," she says. "Oh, yes—yesterday and the day before yesterday, and the day before and every day for oh, so long!" As they have often done, they go through his papers. All are in order except that one lacks a seal and the photographs are the wrong size. "For God's sake!" he cries. "When will it be right?" "Well, well, Mister Kofner," she says, "after all, it isn't our fault. . . . Next!"

The Secretary, the Foreign Woman and Mr. Kofner. The Foreign Woman, an old peasant, speaks only Italian, and Mr. Kofner translates for her. Three years ago her daughter ran away with a soldier from the Secretary's country. Now he has abandoned her and their child, and she is sick. She has written to her mother, who wishes to leave at once to nurse her daughter and care for her grandson. The Secretary produces a visa application form, saying that it will require several months at least to process the papers. The news, translated, stuns the mother, and Mr. Kofner leads her gently to a wall desk to begin with the first form.

The Secretary and Magda. Struggling to control her agitation, Magda asks, "May I speak to the Consul?" "No one is allowed to speak to the consul; the Consul is away." Despite Magda's story, which she blurts out in broken phrases, the Secretary will only repeat: "I give you these papers. This is how to begin: Your name is a number. Your story's a case. Your need a request. Your hopes will be filed. Come back next week." In a daze Magda takes a seat among the others on the bench.

The Magician, Vera Boronel, Anna Gomez, Mr. Kofner and Magda. The Magician, bored with waiting, offers to do a trick: now you see it; now you don't. A quintet develops with each inwardly expressing the same

quintet thought, "In endless waiting rooms the hour stands still . . . the answer comes too late or death too soon . . . Oh, give us back the earth, and make us free." As they sing, the daylight fades, leaving visible at the end only their despairing faces.

ACT II (44 min.)

———

SCENE 1 (21 Min.)

A month later, at the Sorel's apartment. Late afternoon, and from the café, "Tu reviendras. . . . "

Magda and the Mother. Magda is discouraged. She has made no progress at the Consul's office. Always another paper is needed, another questionnaire: what is your name? Magda Sorel. Age? Thirty-three. John has sent no word, and the baby is sick, dying. She goes to the bedroom to hide her tears.

The Mother, alone with the child, tries to amuse him but, unable to stir a response, sits wearily and sings a lullaby, "I shall find for you

lullaby shells and stars." Before its end Magda has returned, sat at the table and, putting her head on her arms, fallen asleep. The Mother leaves quietly.

Magda's Nightmare. An eerie glow fills the room. John appears, bloodstained and bandaged. Behind him is the Secretary, her face sub-

nightmare tly changed to seem evil. Throughout the dream she hovers around him like an oppressive shadow.

Magda sets the table for John's supper. In reply to her questions he says the Secretary is his sister, but Magda thinks she is Death come for the baby. When John asks to see their child, Magda pulls aside the curtain to the alcove, revealing a monstrous fetus. Her scream awakes her, and the Mother rushes in.

Magda, the Mother, the Secret Police Agent and Assan. While Magda tells the Mother of her dream, a stone shatters the window. The signal! Magda immediately telephones Assan, but the Secret Police Agent arrives first. He reviews her situation and suggests how she could join her husband: lead the police to his friends. Magda orders him out. As he goes, Assan arrives and is distressed to be seen by the police.

Assan reports that John is still in the mountains, refusing to cross the border until Magda can join him. "Tell him we'll join him soon," says Magda. "Is it the truth?" "Oh, no! He mustn't know the truth." While she goes to the bedroom for a package to send John, the Mother reveals to Assan that the child has died. He is not to tell John. Assan departs.

Magda and the Mother. Noticing the Mother's stillness, Magda guesses what has happened. While she fetches a candle, places it by the cradle and weeps, the Mother sings a lament less for the child than for John and for herself who now will die soon: "Old people live for simple **lament** things: to see a birth, to bury the dead . . . now let me fold my things . . . I believe that God receives with kindness the empty-handed traveler."

INTERLUDE (1 min.)

SCENE 2 (22 min.)

A few days later, at the Consul's office.

The Secretary and Anna Gomez. The Secretary, reading from Anna Gomez's papers—three years in concentration camp. Husband, prisoner. Whereabouts, unknown—concludes, "No documents. I don't see what we can do for you." When Mrs. Gomez points out that her permit to remain will soon expire and to return to her country of origin is certain death, the Secretary hands her a questionnaire.

Magda hurries in and, brushing past the Magician, who is next, asks to speak to the Consul. The Magician protests, then relents, but the Secretary will take no one out of order.

The Secretary and the Magician. To impress the Secretary and to reassure himself, he does several tricks before explaining that he needs "a visa, a simple little visa." After all, he is a great artist. She asks for his documents, and he does more tricks. The other applicants are impressed, but the Secretary is not. In desperation he hypnotizes the others and sets them waltzing about the room. His documents, demands the Secretary. "All right," he cries. "Hold this!" and hands her a rabbit from his pocket. Angrily she asks that he wake up the dancers. "Don't you know how to behave in a consulate?" Unable to prove his identity and start his visa application, he leaves, dismissed.

The Secretary and Magda. She reports that she can do nothing with Magda's application until more documents are produced. Magda replies that the police will not allow them to be issued. She will never have them. Meanwhile her child has died and her mother-in-law is dying. The Consul must allow an exception. "There are thousands of cases like yours," retorts the Secretary.

The exchange leads to Magda's aria "To this we've come," the emotional center of the opera, in which she denounces the bureaucracy that so arbitrarily condemns people to endless waiting, despair and even death. (In performance the Secretary and others in the waiting room interject comments, but in a concert version or recording these are often cut. In form the aria is declamatory rather than lyric, and made up of contrasting melodic phrases rather than a continuous line. It needs power and passion.) "To this we've come: that men withold the world from men . . . tell me, secretary, tell me! Who are these dark archangels? . . . Have you ever seen the Consul? . . . Papers! Papers! **aria**   . . . What is your name? Magda Sorel. Age? Thirty-three. . . . Occupation? Waiting, waiting. . . . Oh, the day will come I know. . . . Warn the Consul, Secretary, warn him! That day neither ink nor seal shall cage our souls."

The Secretary is deeply disturbed and after a quick consultation with the Consul reports that he will see Mrs. Sorel as soon as his present visitor leaves. Nervously Magda waits. The door to the Consul's office opens. The Secret Police Agent emerges, and Magda faints.

ACT III (23 min.)

SCENE 1 (11 min.)

Several days later, at the consulate. The scene begins with a short prelude, the music to which the Secret Police Agent had emerged from the Consul's office now softly played as if driven in cold steel into Magda's soul. As the curtain rises, she waits on a bench while the Secretary talks with Vera Boronel.

The Secretary and Vera Boronel. All Mrs. Boronel's papers are in order. As she signs each, she and the Secretary sing happily, "All the documents must be signed. . . . One must have one's papers."

Assan and Magda. He enters hurriedly and with bad news. John refuses to cross the frontier. He has heard of the death of his child and of his mother and insists on returning to Magda. "Oh, no," she exclaims, **quartet** "we must stop him." A quartet develops among the Secretary, Vera Boronel, Assan and Magda. It ends with Assan pleading, "You must find a way to stop him."

While the music from Act I, Scene 1, "Now, O lips say goodbye," swells in the orchestra, Magda goes to a wall desk and writes a note. In it (later events make the contents plain) she tells John not to return, for by the time he reads the note she will be dead. She gives it to Assan, and they leave as the Secretary and Vera Boronel sing, "It is all over. . . . Goodbye."

The Secretary. Alone, preparing to close the office, she recalls, "All those faces! . . . One must try not to remember."

The Secretary, John and the Secret Police. John runs into the room, asking for Magda. As the Secretary realizes his situation, she is very upset. The police enter and take him away. "I'll speak to the Consul first thing tomorrow morning," she calls after him. "Don't lose heart Mr. Sorel. I'll call your wife myself."

INTERLUDE (2 min.)

From a long series of soft, descending chords a slow, limping (5/4 time) march emerges.

SCENE 2 (10 min.)

The Sorel's apartment, immediately following the preceding scene. The phone rings and then is still.

Magda. She enters, repeating in a dazed fashion, "I never meant to do this." Using her coat and John's she stuffs the cracks under the door and window. She puts a chair before the stove and, draping the Mother's shawl over her head and the burners, turns on the gas.

Slowly light fades from the room. Figures from the Consul's waiting room appear to her. Also John and the Mother, each dressed in wedding clothes. "All aboard!" the chorus sings to the dead March, "Death's frontiers are open . . . Horizons!" Magda's figure rises to join them. Suddenly, from nowhere, booms the voice of the Police Agent: **hallucination**   what is your name? Magda Sorel. Age? Thirty-three. Soon the Magician sets the figures dancing, and then they begin slowly to fade. John comes forward: why did she let their child die? It was the hunger and cold, she insists. The Magician guides her figure back to the stove. "Breathe deeply. Breathe deeply." Offstage the others quietly call, "Horizons! Horizons!"

The phone rings. At the stove Magda weakly reaches a hand for it, but the effort exhausts her body. The orchestra thunders out the close of her second-act aria: "That day will come, I know, when our hearts aflame will burn your paper chains. . . . That day will come!"

AMAHL AND THE NIGHT VISITORS

Opera in one act. World premiere (on television), New York, Dec. 24, 1951; American stage prem., Bloomington, Indiana, Feb. 21, 1952; European prem., possibly in Wiesbaden, Dec., 1952; British prem., London, Dec. 6, 1964. Music and text by Gian Carlo Menotti.

PRINCIPAL CHARACTERS

Amahl, a crippled boy, about 12	boy soprano
his Mother, a widow	soprano
The Three Kings:	
Kaspar, who is slightly deaf, carries a chalice of myrrh (symbol of death)	tenor
Melchior, carrying a coffer of gold (symbol of power)	baritone
Balthazar, a Nubian, carrying an urn of incense (symbol of prayer)	bass
their Page, a Nubian	bass

The action takes place in the Holy Land shortly after Christ's birth. Like Stravinsky's *The Rake's Progress,* the opera has a visual rather than a literary source. The idea for it came to Menotti as he looked at the *Adoration of the Magi* by Hieronymus Bosch (*c.* 1450–1516), which hangs in the Metropolitan Museum in New York. The painting depicts the Three Kings presenting their gifts to the Virgin and her Child. She sits, with him on her lap, on a pillow in the ruined court of a stone building. Behind her, over a low, broken wall, is the winter countryside with sheep, shepherds, a road between distant towns and travellers upon it. Overhead, in place of a roof, angels support a green carpet, and above them shines a large gold star.

Before her, making the base of a triangle of which her face forms the top, are Joseph at the left, kneeling and leaning on his cane, and at the right Kaspar, the eldest king, kneeling to present his chalice of myrrh. He has removed his crown and, bald and white-bearded, looks earnestly upward to the Virgin and the Child. Further to the right are Melchior, appearing more like a merchant than a king, and black Balthazar, the most elegant of the three. Outside this central area are a dove, a dog, a cow, a shepherd warming his hand at a fire and two others who gaze at the scene with astonishment. Even to those who may not believe in Christ's divinity, the picture is charming.

For the opera Menotti invented a story preceding the moment of the picture. The Three Kings on their way to Bethlehem stop for rest at a shepherd's hut, where Amahl, a crippled boy, lives with his mother. Because of events there a miracle occurs, and Amahl's weak leg is made strong. At the opera's end he is leaving for Bethlehem with the Three Kings to make a gift of his crutch to the Child. For the imaginative, therefore, the Bosch picture becomes the opera's final, silent scene with Amahl, perhaps, replacing Joseph kneeling and leaning on his cane.

The kings, despite their fame as the first Gentiles to believe in Christ, do not appear in the New Testament. In the Gospel according to St. Matthew, 2:1–12, those who follow a star to Bethlehem with gifts of gold, frankincense and myrrh are Magi or wise men, and their number is undetermined. The idea that they were kings and three in number (probably because of the number of gifts) did not appear till the third century, and in the Latin West their names did not become fixed until the seventh century and differ from those in the Syrian and Armenian traditions. In the Middle Ages they were venerated as saints, and the Milanesi claimed to possess their relics, brought previously from Constantinople. In 1162 these were taken to Germany by Frederick Barbarossa and are now in the Cologne Cathedral.

In its structure and sound, the opera is traditional. Amahl has a tune for his shepherd's pipe, the kings have an entrance march, and the shepherds an *a cappella* carol as well as a dance that ends in a tarentella. The orchestration is simple, clear and with emphasis on the woodwinds: flute, two oboes, clarinet, bassoon, horn, trumpet, harp, piano, percussion and strings.

Though the opera was the first to be composed for television, Menotti made little use of the medium's special techniques, and it can be performed equally well in an opera house—except that casting the leading role becomes more difficult. A boy's voice compared to an adult's is weak. In a television or recording studio the fact is unimportant, for the engineer can control the relative volumes; but in an opera house of more than, say, 1,200 seats, the imbalance becomes crucial.

Menotti has done what he can by keeping the orchestration light, but beyond that, perhaps with the frequent fate of *Hänsel und Gretel* in mind, he has taken a firm stand, stating in the published score: "It is the express wish of the composer that the role of Amahl should always be performed by a boy. Neither the musical nor the dramatic concept of the opera permits the substitution of a woman, costumed as a child." He is right, just as Ravel is right to insist on the reverse in *L'Enfant et les sortilèges.*

A SINGLE ACT (47 min.)

The stage is divided in two areas, indoors and out, each of which by lighting can be brought into focus separately and so serve as a change of scene. The interior is of a shepherd's hut, simple, clean and bare; outside is the countryside of the Bosch painting. A road winds through the distant hills, disappears offstage, then reappears to pass before the hut. Snow lies on the ground. Above, stars shine with one, the Star of the East, irradiating the sky.

There is a short prelude whose music reappears twice: as an interlude while those in the hut sleep and outside the Star of the East shines brightly; and at the opera's focal point when Melchior explains to Amahl's mother that the child they seek will build his kingdom on love. The curtain rises on Amahl outside the hut playing his pipe (in orch., oboe).

Amahl and his Mother. She calls him to bed, but he dawdles, overcome by the beauty of the night. Inside he irritates her further by talking of an extraordinary star that hangs over the hut. She treats it as a fairy tale, scolds him for lying and then reveals the true cause of her emotion: they are at the end of their resources. In the morning they will have to go begging. She weeps.

He hobbles to her side, comforts and chaffs her. He will play his pipes; she can sing. "The King will ride by and hear your loud voice and throw us some gold to stop all the noise. At noon we shall eat roast goose and sweet almonds, at night we shall sleep with the sheep and the stars." They kiss good night, and the scene shifts to the outside.

Arrival of the Kings. They appear first as tiny figures (Menotti suggests puppets or children) on the road in the hills. They sing as they come, and by the end of their second verse they have arrived, full size, at the hut's door. Melchior knocks.

Amahl hobbles to the door, cracks it open, then hurries in astonishment to his Mother. There is a king outside. She scolds him for fibbing. There is another knock; Amahl hobbles over, then returns—two kings! Another knock. Three kings! The Mother wearily goes to the door herself. Balthazar asks her if they may rest a while. Apologizing for her poverty, she asks them in.

Entrance of the Kings. In a dumb show (1 min.) they march in, preceded by a Page. Kaspar, the eldest, a bit fussy and deaf, is first: then **march** Balthazar and finally Melchior. They are magnificently dressed. After they are seated, the Page spreads a rug before them and puts on it their gifts for the Child. Melchior explains that they are following a star and cannot stay long. Amahl's mother goes outside to search for firewood.

Amahl alone with the Kings. He goes to Balthazar. "Are you a real king? Yes. Have you regal blood? Yes. Can I see it? It is just like yours. What's the use of it then? No use." He shifts to Kaspar but with less success, for Kaspar's deafness is a hindrance. Nevertheless Kaspar shows him a travelling box with magic stones to cure disease, beads to play with and licorice to eat—and he gives Amahl a piece. When the Mother enters with the firewood, she sends Amahl to ask the shepherds to bring whatever food they can.

Mother alone with the Kings. She is fascinated by the gifts on the rug, and Melchior explains that they are for a Child. "Which child?" she asks. "We don't know. But the Star will guide us to Him." Melchior, **quartet** followed later by the other kings, begins a description of the Child while the Mother, absorbed in her own thoughts, thinks of Amahl.

The Shepherds. Coming down from the hills to the hut, they sing an *a* **carol** *cappella* carol made up mostly of names: "Carolyn, Carolyn, Matthew, Veronica, give me your hand, come along with me." Once inside, before the kings, the names change to food: "Olives and quinces, apples and raisins . . . this is all we shepherds can offer you."

To entertain the kings the shepherds dance, beginning slowly but end-**dance** ing in a joyous frenzy. Then they sing good night and depart, leaving those in the hut to sleep.

INTERLUDE (1 min.)

The lights in the hut dim to suggest a passage of time and then revive slightly pink to indicate the approach of dawn.

The Mother's theft. She eyes the gold on the rug and thinks what a bit of it could do for her child. "Why should it all go to a child they don't even know?" As she takes some of it, she is seized by the Page crying "Thief, thief!"

The kings and Amahl awake. Amid the commotion the kings ask her to give back what she has taken, the Page threatens to beat it out of her, and Amahl tries to defend her. "Don't you dare, ugly man, hurt my mother!" Hobbling to Kaspar, he begs her freedom. "She cannot do anything wrong. I'm the one who lies; I'm the one who steals." Returning to the Page, he attacks him feebly. Kaspar signals to the Page, and as the Mother is released, Amahl staggers toward her and collapses sobbing in her arms.

Melchior tells her quietly to keep the gold. "The Child we seek doesn't need our gold. On love, on love alone He will build his Kingdom." Turning to the others he suggests they go.

"No, wait," cries the Mother, kneeling before them and spilling all she had taken onto the rug. "For such a King I have waited all my life." If not so poor, she would send him a gift herself.

Amahl's Gift. "But, Mother, let me send him my crutch. Who knows, he may need one, and this I made myself." Without thinking, he holds it out to the kings and steps toward them. "I walk," he gasps. Another step, and another. "This is a sign from God," the kings conclude. As Amahl jumps excitedly about, they ask permission to touch him, for he is blessed. "Oh, Mother," Amahl cries, "let me go with the Kings! I want to take the crutch to the Child myself." The kings urge her to agree, and soon they and Amahl, followed by the Page, start on the road to Bethlehem, the Virgin and the Child.

THE SAINT OF BLEECKER STREET

Musical drama in three acts, five scenes. World premiere, New York, Dec. 27, 1954; European prem., Milan, May 8, 1955; British television prem., London, BBC, Oct. 4, 1956; British stage prem., London, July 27, 1962. Music and text by Gian Carlo Menotti.

As with *The Consul,* Menotti entitled this opera a "musical drama" and constructed it on a series of highly theatrical scenes based often on violence. Because of the addition of a chorus, however, it is on a larger scale, and several of its finales in style and color approach grand opera. Yet despite good choral writing and effective scenes, it has not matched the success of *The Consul,* and the reason may lie more in the libretto than in the music. In *The Consul* it is perfectly clear with whom the audience should sympathize and why, but here it is not. The story is plagued by ambiguities—perhaps reflecting ambivalent feelings in Menotti—and the opera is prevented from making a clear statement.

ACT I (51 min.)

SCENE 1 (25 min.)

In an Italian immigrant section of New York known as "Little Italy," on Good Friday in the early 1950s, neighbors have gathered in the apartment of Anina (soprano) a sickly girl who has frequent vi-
chorus sions. In other years on Good Friday she has received the stigmata and reputedly she can effect cures. The priest (baritone)
aria brings her from her bedroom. She has a vision of the Cruci-fixion, and as she describes the nails piercing Christ's hands, the stigmata appear on her own. She faints, and though the priest has forbidden the neighbors to touch her, they are soon with frenzy pulling and pawing at her. (Ambiguity: a moving demonstration of faith or

superstition? And the priest? Don't touch, he says, but he brings the girl out where she *will* be touched. God's servant or Anina's exploiter?)

Anina's brother Michele (tenor) enters. Furious, he drives the neighbors out, carries Anina to her room, and returns to berate the priest. "I only came when I was called," says the priest. Asked if the **dialogue** visions are God's work or the delusions of a sick mind, he hedges: "A priest is not a judge but only a guide." Michele has no doubt. His sister needs a doctor, and her brother, not the priest, will be her guide. The priest leaves, saying that it is not he but God who is Michele's rival. (Ambiguity: to be taken seriously or, in view of the priest's role thus far, as priestly cant? The music does not make clear and, as often in this opera, the stage director's point of view is crucial.)

INTERLUDE (2 min.)

SCENE 2 (22 min.)

In a vacant lot facing Mulberry Street. A wire fence with its gate open borders the sidewalk.

A neighbor sings a lullaby while Anina and her friend Carmela (so-**lullaby** prano) sew a child's costume for the San Gennaro festival that evening. Carmela shyly tells Anina that instead of taking the veil she will marry Salvatore. Anina is delighted. The neighbor and Carmela ask about heaven, and Anina describes how in a dream St. Mi-**trio** chael showed her the gates of Paradise. The others exclaim in wonder.

A neighbor runs in to warn Anina that "the Sons of San Gennaro" want her, their local saint, to lead their procession, and they talk of beating up Michele to seize her. Michele enters, and the neighbors scatter.

Anina fears for Michele because he makes people hate him. He argues that he wants to save her from exploitation. Why should God choose her, a sickly "numbskull"? "Perhaps," she answers calmly, **duet** "because I love him." He cannot understand her faith and grows angry. He will never let her take the veil. "I could never live without you by my side."

The procession begins at the end of the street. Men stealthily enter the lot, beat and tie Michele to the wire fence and carry off a frightened

chorus and spectacle   Anina. The procession passes, and after its last stragglers, blowing paper trumpets and eating candy, have gone, Desideria (mezzo-soprano) appears and releases Michele. He bursts into tears, and she embraces him passionately.

ACT II (32 min.)

Months later, in an Italian restaurant in the basement of a house on Bleecker Street. The wedding reception of Carmela and Salvatore. The curtain rises as the photographer snaps the wedding picture, and the group breaks up. Dancing starts, a young man toasts the bride with a song, and the guests slowly go off into the adjoining banquet room for **arietta**   the cutting of the cake. Anina gently urges Salvatore, "Be good to her, be kind," and then a guest calls them into the banquet room.

Desideria enters and has the bartender fetch Michele. She points out that since she has begun to sleep with him, she is not invited to weddings. Let him take her into the banquet room. He protests: he did not **dialogue**   ask for her love and no price for it was set. When she continues, he says that their appearance in the other room would upset Anina. "Always Anina," cries Desideria in rage. "Why don't you leave her alone?" They argue bitterly and finally, reluctantly, Michele agrees to take her in.

The priest coming out blocks their way: Desideria will not be welcome. Instantly Michele is on her side, and his angry words draw Anina and the guests. "It is always you," says Salvatore, "who causes **aria**   trouble." Michele sings, "I know that you all hate me. . . . I was always the rebel. . . . Look at yourselves. . . . You live in this land like strangers. . . . You are ashamed to say: 'I was Italian.'" And he ends by throwing wine in their faces. (Though without ambiguity, the aria has an equivocal effect. It is apt to lessen rather than increase the audience's sympathy for Michele. Why castigate the victims rather than the perpetrators of prejudice? Far from a great rebel, Michele seems merely a self-pitying neurotic.)

The guests leave, and Anina urges Michele, "Let's go home." "Yes," says Desideria, "go!" and she accuses Michele of being in love with Anina. She taunts him with it, and he stabs her. Then he runs out, leaving Desideria to die in Anina's arms.

ACT III (39 min.)

SCENE 1 (13 min.)

In a subway station Anina, now visibly ill, waits by the newspaper stand to meet Michele. "Stop worrying," urges her neighbor (soprano) the newsdealer. The priest won't betray him, not after Michele asked for help at the confessional. She chatters on (sometimes cut) about always hoping to see her picture in the papers but the only way, it seems, is to murder someone. Anina dozes fitfully beside her.

The priest enters, looks around and beckons Michele. "Remember," he warns, "she is very sick." He goes, and brother and sister sit on a bench outside the newsstand. Anina urges Michele to give himself up, but he insists, "I'll fight to the end." She tells him that she will die **aria** soon. Her voices have told her. "Forget them," he cries. "Tell me goodbye," she says. "I am going to take the veil." He protests. He needs her. But her mind is made up, and firmly she tells him goodbye. In a frenzy he replies, "You will carry with you my guilt and be followed forever by my curse." He rushes out, leaving her collapsed and sobbing, to be comforted by the newsdealer.

INTERLUDE (3 min.)

SCENE 2 (Anina's apartment—23 min.)

She is dying, and her neighbors have come. They pray that permission for her to take the veil will arrive in time for her to die a nun. The permission comes, and the ceremony begins, led by the priest, assisted by a nun. Dressed in Carmela's wedding dress, her hair covered by a **chorus and spectacle** white veil, Anina presents herself. The neighbors intone, "Gloria tibi Domine . . . Kyrie eleison . . ." and finally "Veni, sposa Christi. . . ." Anina prostrates herself, her extended arms forming a cross. The nun covers her with a black cloth.

"You are now dead unto the world," recites the priest. "Arise and be reborn in Christ." As the neighbors chant, Michele bursts into the room. He is seized by two men and held motionless. Everyone turns toward him except Anina who, even when he calls her name, keeps staring at the improvised altar before her. The ceremony resumes. The nun removes Anina's white veil, the priest cuts her hair and says, "Receive now the ring of faith." All kneel except Michele, and Anina starts toward the priest. The effort exhausts her, and she sinks to the floor. Carmela catches her, and the priest, lifting her lifeless arm, places the gold ring on her finger.

(The scene, like others in the opera, is theatrically effective. But ultimately is the opera about Anina or Michele? If about Anina and her desire to be a nun—compare, for example, Schubert's song "The Young Nun"—then what relevance has the storm and stress of Michele? How does it reveal something about Anina? And vice versa, if the opera is about Michele. But a good performance will obliterate these questions, at least for a time.)

PAUL BUNYAN

Operetta in a prologue and two acts. World premiere, New York, May 5, 1941. European radio prem., London, BBC, Feb. 1, 1976; stage prem., Aldeburgh, June 4, 1976. Music by Benjamin Britten; libretto by W. H. Auden.

This operetta, often considered to be Britten's first opera, has an unusual history. After it played for a week at Columbia University, Britten withdrew it, forbade further performances, did not assign it an opus number and, in effect, struck it from his career. Then in the last year of his life he allowed it to be revived, after thirty-five years.

Though some of the New York critics in 1941 had dismissed the work with sarcasm, the reason for its live burial seems to have been less a matter of hurt feelings than an inability of Britten and Auden to agree on revisions. Britten went on to compose *Peter Grimes* with Montagu Slater, and Auden to write the libretto for Stravinsky's *The Rake's Progress*. The two never again worked together, and Britten did not permit the revival until after Auden's death—perhaps to avoid argument, or perhaps as a way of honoring the deceased poet.

The opera is a curiosity in that its hero never appears onstage. Paul Bunyan, the mythical lumberman, who supposedly stood forty-two ax handles tall, is only a speaking voice, thus avoiding the problem of physical representation and also distinguishing him from the sung roles. Onstage the leading character is Johnny Inkslinger, an introverted intellectual who acts as Bunyan's bookkeeper. The opera uses

the Bunyan legends to reflect, in Auden's words, "the cultural problems that occur during the first stage of colonization of the land and the
conquest of nature." It ends with the frontier tamed and Bunyan bidding his men farewell because now he is no longer needed.

The music is eclectic. The opera opens and closes with choral set-
pieces and between has many short numbers in a variety of styles: folk
ballad, blues quartet, lyrical love duet, sentimental cowboy song and
advertising jingle. For years opinion believed the work too arty, too
clever, with tricks such as a dog and two cats sung by women to bring
female voices into the all-male lumber camp. Then after a recording in
1988 and a surge of productions following, opinion changed: The opera now was a brilliant lark, profound in its view of humanity's attack
on nature.

PETER GRIMES

An opera in three acts and a prologue. World premiere, Sadler's Wells,
London, June 7, 1945; American prem., Tanglewood, Mass., Aug. 6,
1946. Music by Benjamin Britten; libretto by Montagu Slater, derived
from "The Borough," a poem by George Crabbe, published in 1810.

PRINCIPAL CHARACTERS

Peter Grimes, a fisherman	tenor
Boy (John), his apprentice	(silent)
Ellen Orford, a widow, schoolmistress of the Borough	soprano
Captain Balstrode, a retired merchant skipper	baritone
Auntie, landlady of "The Boar"	contralto
Niece 1 ⎱ main attractions of "The Boar" Niece 2 ⎰	sopranos
Bob Boles, fisherman and Methodist	tenor
Swallow, a lawyer	bass
Mrs. (Nabob) Sedley, a widow of an East India Company's factor	mezzo-soprano
Rev. Horace Adams, the rector	tenor
Ned Keene, apothecary and quack	baritone
Hobson, carrier	bass

The action takes place "towards 1830" in The Borough, a small fishing town on the East Coast of England.

Crabbe's poem, "The Borough," is a series of twenty four letters in
heroic couplets describing the town and inhabitants of Aldeburgh,

where Crabbe was born in 1754. His point of view is realistic, even harsh, but so was life in the small, poor town. In Letter XXII he describes a fisherman, Peter Grimes, whose original counterpart was a man named Tom Brown. Grimes lives alone, fights everyone and hires orphan boys as apprentices rather than men to help him. He treats the boys sadistically and after three have died in his employ, the town through its Mayor forbids him to hire another and ostracizes him. Thereafter he works alone, and in his solitude his mind gradually fails. Shortly before death in a moment of delirium he imagines his dead father and the three boys returned to torment him.

> Still did they force me on the Oar to rest,
> And when they saw me fainting and opprest,
> He, with his Hand, the old Man, scoop'd the Flood,
> And there came Flame about him mix'd with Blood,
> He bade me stoop and look upon the place,
> Then flung the hot-red Liquor in my Face;
> Burning it blaz'd, and then I roar'd for Pain,
> I thought the Daemons would have turned my Brain.

In transforming Crabbe's Grimes into the protagonist of a twentieth-century opera, Slater made several important changes. He lessened Grimes's culpability by reducing his sadism to roughness and the number of dead apprentices from three to two. He also moved the period of the story from the eighteenth century "towards 1830," a time when because of the example of Byron, 1788–1824, the rebellious hero was coming into vogue. Yet the townsfolk in a small, provincial town like The Borough would still be much as Crabbe described them.

The result is a character study quite different from Crabbe's. In place of the religious background and imagery is a conflict between an individual and society. Whereas Crabbe's Grimes is "untouched by pity, unstung by remorse, and uncorrected by shame," Slater's Grimes has feelings of poetry and tenderness but cannot bring them into balance with his resentments against the townfolk. He is at war not only with society but with himself.

Because of the changes, Slater's Grimes is now hero as well as villain, and the opera is tense with an ambiguity never wholly resolved. Who is responsible for Grimes's suicide? Himself, who rejects all advice and aid, or society? Some German productions in the early 1960s presented the opera as a clinical study of a sensitive individual driven mad by the demands of mass mediocrity. At the other extreme, some have stressed the town and folk wisdom: society, threatened by an individual's erratic behavior, preserves itself by ejecting him. Most take the middle ground that Britten and Slater intended: the pity of it, that the only solution should be suicide.

At its premiere the opera was hailed as a masterwork, and by February 1950 it had received 50 performances in England and 142 elsewhere, a record of international success matched in the postwar years only by Menotti's *The Consul* (1950) and Stravinsky's *The Rake's Progress* (1951). Curiously, though the fact may have no significance, all three were composed to English texts. With *Grimes* and the operas that quickly followed, Britten established himself as probably the world's most important operatic composer, a position he held for thirty years, until his death.

The opera's structure is traditional: arias, choruses, a mad scene, a storm, dance background, offstage church music and six orchestral interludes to connect scenes or introduce acts. Four of these—I, III, V, and II in that order—have had an independent life in the concert hall as *The Four Sea Interludes from Peter Grimes* (13 min.). Sometimes the fourth interlude, "The Passacaglia," is added to them.

PROLOGUE and ACT I (54 min.)

PROLOGUE (The Inquest—9 min.)

At The Borough's Moot Hall, an inquest is in session to fix the cause of death of Grimes's apprentice. The town's lawyer, Swallow, sits as coroner, and as the opera opens, to the excitement of the townfolk, Hobson the carter, who is serving as crier, calls Peter Grimes to the stand.

In response to Swallow's questions, Grimes describes how he and the boy made a large catch, too large to sell locally, and so set sail direct for London. But the wind changed, they were blown off course, drinking water gave out, and after three days at sea the boy died. Grimes thereupon threw the catch overboard and sailed for home.

So much no one can deny, and throughout the account the townfolk remain quiet. But when Grimes describes his arrival at The Borough, they begin to murmur, revealing their dislike of him and eagerness to believe him responsible for the boy's death. A few had been helpful and sympathetic—Ned Keene, the apothecary, Ellen Orford, the widowed schoolmistress, and "Auntie," who runs the town pub. But Bob Boles, a fisherman, had begun to shout, and Mrs. Sedley, a widow, had tried to interfere—at least, according to Grimes—and had earned the harsh words he'd given her.

Swallow, voicing the majority's opinion, wonders how a woman such as Ellen Orford could have helped a man so "callous, brutal and coarse." Gratuitously he advises Grimes not to seek another apprentice but in future to hire a man. Then he concludes on the evidence that the apprentice "died in accidental circumstances," adding prejudicially, "but that's the kind of thing people are apt to remember."

Grimes protests: like any fisherman he must have an apprentice, and if he is to be judged in this manner, "let me speak, let me stand trial. Bring the accusers into the hall." The townfolk's murmurs swell into a hubbub, and Swallow ends the hearing by closing his books and leaving. Hobson calls for the court to be cleared, and only Ellen Orford remains with Grimes.

As he broods on the ineffectiveness of truth against rumor, she tries to comfort him, promising new shoals to catch, a new life to come. Though he is doubtful, he is swayed by her kindness, and they finish together, in unison: "Here is a friend."

INTERLUDE 1 (The Sea at Dawn—3 min.)

The sea has an equivocal role at The Borough: it supports life, yet with its tides and storms that erode the coast it destroys life. Though at the moment it is calm, the waves lap restlessly on the beach, pulling the shingle back into the sea. This ambiguous motif of peace and menace dominates the first scene, and returns in the opera's final chorus.

SCENE 1 (22 min.)

The Borough's beach and High Street, with the Moot Hall, Boar Inn, Keene's shop and Church porch. A cold, grey morning.

The people sing quietly as they start about their work: "Oh, hang at open doors the net, the cork." Between phrases they make characteristic remarks: Auntie invites the men into her pub, Bob Boles condemns

chorus   drinking, Captain Balstrode notes the possibility of a storm, and Auntie's nieces greet the world from a window of the Boar while Mrs. Sedley and the Rector exchange greetings in the street. Ned Keene promises a visit that night to the nieces, which Boles deplores, and then from offstage Grimes calls for a hand to help him haul his boat.

At his voice everyone stops, and Boles calls, "Haul it yourself, **chantey** Grimes." But Balstrode, Keene and Auntie move to the capstan, and after several turns the boat is beached and Grimes enters.

Keene tells him that he has found a new apprentice for him and asks **arioso** Hobson to pick up the boy on his carting rounds. Hobson refuses: his cart is full, and a round late at night, going "from pub to pub," is no place for a boy. But Ellen Orford offers to accompany him to fetch the boy. When some of the town disapproves of her helping Grimes, she admonishes them, "Let her among you without fault cast **arietta** the first stone," and tries to explain "how a poor teacher widow'd and lonely finds delight in should'ring care." (Her long, slow, descending phrases suggest a simple person determined to do good and in their lack of passion a feeling for Grimes that is as much maternal as romantic.)

As Ellen and Hobson depart, Mrs. Sedley asks Keene for her laudanum (an opium extract), but he has none in stock and won't until Hobson's return. If she wants some that night, she must come to the pub to get it. Suddenly Balstrode announces that the wind has shifted and "veers in from the sea at gale force!"

The townfolk are aghast. "Now the flood tide and sea horses . . . will gallop over the eroded coast." The chorus builds in a fugal ensemble, **chorus** ending with a mighty appeal, thrice repeated: "O tide that waits for no man, spare our coasts!" The people scatter, leaving Grimes, who has been silent, with Balstrode.

Balstrode and Grimes. Their dialogue, against the mounting storm, falls in three parts with a coda for Grimes.

1. Balstrode suggests that Grimes, as "a lonely soul," leave The Borough and ship on as a merchantman. But Grimes insists he is "rooted here . . . by familiar fields, marsh and sand, ordinary streets, prevailing wind." Balstrode warns that the town's dislike is too strong to be overcome: however unfairly, it holds Grimes responsible for the boy's death.

2. Grimes recalls the fatal expedition. (Each phrase begins with an upward leap of a minor ninth which, being a half-tone more than the usual octave, suggests his inner tension.)

3. "This storm is useful," says Balstrode. "You can speak your mind." Grimes does so, but in Balstrode's opinion conceives falsely how to win The Borough's approval. "They listen to money," says Grimes. "I'll win them over." "With the new apprentice?" asks Balstrode. "I'll fish the sea dry," says Grimes, and when rich, he cries, "I'll marry Ellen."

"Man, go and ask her," Balstrode urges, "without your booty, she'll have you now." "No, not for pity," Grimes insists. "Then," says Balstrode, "the old tragedy is in store." As the wind rises, they argue till Balstrode angrily strides off to the Boar.

Coda. Grimes gazes intently into the approaching storm and wonders (this time with an upward leap of a *major* ninth), "What harbor shelters peace?" Thinking of Ellen, he is sure, "With her there'll be no quarrels. With her the mood will stay. Her breast is harbor, too, where night is turned to day."

INTERLUDE 2 (The Storm—4 min.)

Musically, in three sections: the first and last, built on the figure, much accelerated, with which Balstrode announced the storm; the middle, on Grimes's cry "What harbor shelters peace?" In part, therefore, the physical storm symbolizes the emotional storm in Grimes.

SCENE 2 (Inside "The Boar"—16 min.)

The storm outside is ever present and bursts in each time someone opens the door to enter.

The first to arrive is Mrs. Sedley, come to meet Ned Keene and pick up her laudanum; then Balstrode and a fisherman, and Bob Boles and more fishermen. The wind howls through the door, and the shutters on a window break, shattering the glass. Auntie's nieces, scantily clad, hurry down from upstairs rooms. "Oo, Oo!" they cry, clutching each other for protection.

Balstrode mocks them, "Oo, Oo!" and Auntie takes it ill. "Loud **arietta** man," she says, "a joke's a joke and fun is fun . . . but be polite for all that we have done."

Two fishermen, entering, struggle to close the door. They report a landslide up the coast. Boles, drunk and leering, approaches the nieces. "I want her," he coos. "Turn that man out," cries Auntie, and Balstrode steps before the girl. Boles tries to push past, but Boles is easily overpowered and settled in a chair. Balstrode, supported by the others, **aria, chorus** declares the pub's rule: "We live and let live, and look—We keep our hands to ourselves."

Keene enters, much to Mrs. Sedley's relief, and reports that the earth cliff by Grimes's hut is down. While Mrs. Sedley protests to him about the drunken females and brawling, everyone suddenly calls out, "Mind that door!"—and Grimes enters, wet, without oilskins, his hair wild. Mrs. Sedley faints, and the others gasp: "A devil he is . . . awaiting his apprentice."

Stirred by the storm, oblivious of the others, Grimes declaims on life's meaning (melody in orchestra, in canon, starting with double basses, followed by cellos, violas, violins): "Now the Great Bear and **aria** Pleiades, where earth moves, are drawing up the clouds of human grief. . . . Who . . . who . . . who can decipher in storm or starlight . . . a friendly fate."

The others murmur nervously, and the drunken Boles cries out, "His exercise is not with men but killing boys." He lifts a bottle to hit Grimes, but Balstrode knocks it from his hand. "For peace sake," Balstrode cries, "someone start a song." Keene begins a round (with three **round** tunes to it): "Old Joe has gone fishing," and the others join in. Suddenly Grimes takes it up, momentarily breaking the course of the round, but the others after a moment's hesitation finish with determination.

The door opens, and Hobson, Ellen and the apprentice enter, sopped, muddy and bedraggled. Though Auntie urges Grimes to let the travelers dry out, Grimes wants to leave at once with the apprentice. "Goodbye," Ellen says to the boy, "Peter will take you home." "Home?" cry all the others. "Do you call that home?"

ACT II (48 min.)

INTERLUDE 3 (The Sea on Sunday Morning—2 min.)

A calm day. Above a steady sea swell (horns in unison slowly rising and falling), and sun dances on the water's surface (woodwinds) in a light, staccato figure related to that of the storm, but here spread out and drained of tension.

SCENE 1 (29 min.)

Sunday, several weeks later. On The Borough's High Street, as in Act I, Scene 1. The church bell rings, a few latecomers hurry into Morning Prayer. The first half of the scene is played against the offstage congregation singing a hymn, canticle, and responses and reciting the General Confession and the Apostles' Creed. Ellen, coming down the street with the apprentice, sits on a breakwater and takes out her knitting. The boy plays quietly beside her.

Ellen. As he shows no inclination to talk, she describes her life as a schoolteacher, intending a cheering example. At first she found it bleak and empty, but soon she had come to know the children and understand their problems. Perhaps he has heard stories of the other apprentice. (The boy says nothing but stops playing.) "But when you came," Ellen continues, "I said, Now this is where we make a new start. Every day I pray it may be so."

Then, seeing a tear in his coat and examining it, she declares with agitation, "That was done recently." (Mrs. Sedley, late for church, pauses at the door to listen.) Ellen unbuttons the boy's collar. "A bruise," she cries, "Well. . . . It's begun." He, too, must know already the roots of sorrow, "how near life is to torture." The only peace to soothe the heart's despair is "a sleep like oceans deep."

Ellen and Grimes. He hurries in, searching for the boy. He has sighted a shoal. Ellen protests: it is the boy's day of rest. That was their bargain. "He works for me," cries Grimes. "He's mine." Ellen is shocked and asks what peace such hard-earned profits can buy. "Buy us a home, buy us respect," cries Grimes. She asks about the bruise. Merely "the hurly-burly" of fishing, says Grimes. "Were we right," she asks in worry, to try for a new start. When he begins to shout at her, she concludes, "We've failed."

Striking her, he cries out in agony, "So be it!—And God have mercy upon me!" The boy runs off, followed by Grimes, and Ellen in her agitation hastens up the street without her knitting.

The Townfolk. Several have watched the argument, and Keene, Auntie **trio** and Boles now emerge. "Grimes," says Keene, "is at his exercise." The others repeat it.

The service over, the congregation comes out, eager to learn more of the quarrel they only half-heard. Boles, despite Keene's efforts to stop him, talks loudly of evil and, egged on by Mrs. Sedley, tries to excite the people to action: "Grimes is at his exercise." Ellen, returning for her knitting, is forced to explain her relation to Grimes. "She helped him," Boles insists, and others agree, "in his cruel games."

"As a friend," says Ellen, she tried to help Grimes "to a new start." She would mend the apprentice's clothes, see that he had regular meals and bring comfort to lives that were stark. Though some of the town-folk accept her motives, others talk of Grimes as a likely murderer, and Boles persuades a majority to march out to Grimes's hut to confront him. Hobson gets his drum and, with the Rector and Swallow leading, the men march off, many of them inflamed with self-righteousness: "Now is gossip put on trial. . . . Bring the branding iron and knife: What's done now is done for life."

Four women are left on stage: Ellen, Auntie, and the two nieces. **quartet**   They close the scene with a lament on the lot of women and their disappointment in men, in life.

INTERLUDE 4 (The Passacaglia—5 min.)

As used here, Passacaglia means a short piece of bass music, a figure, repeated over and over with changing upper parts; in this case, a theme introduced by a solo viola and then followed by nine short variations. The bass figure is taken from Grimes's cry of pain after striking Ellen, "God have mercy upon me," and it sounds alone twice in the first six measures. In the sixth measure the solo viola starts and continues through the thirteenth where the first variation, on woodwinds, begins. The ninth variation, in fugal form, leads directly into the next scene, which opens with a series of disjointed cries by Grimes, suggesting that, like the storm, the obsessive bass figure and repeated theme reflect the gathering tension in Grimes's mind. (A tenth and final variation over the bass figure will close the scene. See below.)

SCENE 2 (In Grimes's hut—12 min.)

Grimes and the apprentice. The boy staggers in, pushed, and Grimes follows. Excitedly he throws the boy's sea gear at him. The boy sobs silently, and Grimes shakes him. "Look. Now's our chance." The sea "is boiling" with fish. The Borough listens to money. With a good catch "I will set up . . . house and home and shop. I'll marry Ellen."

The boy continues weeping, and Grimes helps him off with his jacket. In a softer tone Grimes tells of his dream: a kindlier home, a woman's care—then he stops. Sometimes he dreams of the dead apprentice, sees him right here in the hut. The boy stares at Grimes in horror as he describes the apprentice at sea dying of thirst.

Outside in the distance, but coming nearer, sounds Hobson's drum and the townfolk singing.

Furiously Grimes turns on the boy. "You've been talking. . . . You're the cause of everything. . . . Will you move, or must I make you dance?" Driving him out the back door, he orders him down the eroded cliff and throws the gear over. The townfolk knock at the hut's front door, and Grimes turns back. The boy on the cliff loses his hold and with a scream falls to his death. Grimes, snatching up some gear, swings over the cliff and disappears.

The townfolk enter at the front door and, finding nothing amiss, feel sheepish. Lawyer Swallow draws a moral: "Gentlemen, take this to your wives: Less interference in our private lives." They depart.

Balstrode, who has followed them reluctantly, remains. To the tenth and final variation of the Passacaglia (solo viola, with the theme inverted, and celesta) he examines the hut, opens the cliffside door and, after looking about, hurriedly climbs down the way Grimes and the boy went.

ACT III (39 min.)

INTERLUDE 5 (The Sea at Night—4 min.)

A brooding sea with gentle swell and glints of moonlight (flutes and harp).

SCENE I (20 min.)

A summer evening a few days later. A subscription dance at the Moot Hall with constant traffic between it and "The Boar." Much of the scene's first half is played against the dance music.

Swallow and the two nieces. He is attracted to one and suggests in his legal style, "Assign your prettiness to me. . . ." But he cannot lure her from her sister. The girls with much giggling stick together. "Bah!" he exclaims, and enters the pub alone.

Keene and Mrs. Sedley. Keene, too, is attracted by a niece, but pursu-

ing her is waylayed by Mrs. Sedley. She is sure that Grimes has murdered the apprentice. Neither has been seen for two days, and she has
arioso   thought of little else: "Murder most foul it is. Eerie I find
it. . . ." But Keene, thirsty and bored, breaks away and enters the pub.
The old men and Mrs. Sedley. Several old men, including the Rector,
leave the party, bidding each other warmly, "good night." Mrs. Sedley,
avoiding them, hides in the shadow of a boat and broods: "Crime,
which my hobby is, sweetens my thinking. . . ." She remains hidden as
Ellen and Balstrode come up from the beach.
Ellen and Balstrode. "Is the boat in?" she asks. "Yes," he says, "for
more than an hour," but he has been unable to find Grimes.

Ellen shows him the boy's jersey that she had embroidered. She
Embroidery aria   found it by the tide-mark. "Embroidery in childhood," she recalls, "was a luxury of idleness. Now my broidery affords
the clue whose meaning we avoid."

The jersey is wet, and Balstrode wrings it out. "We'll find him;
maybe give him a hand," he says. "We have no power to help him
now," says Ellen. Balstrode disagrees: "We have the power . . .
[though] Nothing to do but wait since the solution is beyond life—beyond dissolution." They go out.
Mrs. Sedley, Swallow and the townfolk. She calls Swallow from the
pub: the boat is in, Grimes's boat. Swallow summons Hobson, who
forms a posse to search for Grimes. The dancing stops, the people pour
chorus   into the street, voicing their feelings: "Who holds himself
apart, Lets his pride rise, Him who despises us, We'll destroy." The
chorus steadily mounts, built on the two themes in this scene in which
Mrs. Sedley with Keene and Swallow (and brooding by herself) has
launched the rumor of murder. Thus rumor in the community's venge-
ful mind musically becomes established as fact; and finally with three
tremendous cries, "Peter Grimes! Peter Grimes! Grimes!" the manhunt
begins.

INTERLUDE 6 (3 min.)

Over muted horns holding a single chord echoing out of the shouts
for Grimes, other instruments sound fragmentary phrases that drift by
like fog blowing in from the sea. And the first sound on the curtain's
rise for the next scene is the posse's faraway cry of "Grimes!" still on
the same chord.

SCENE 2 (12 min.)

Same as before, a few hours later. Thick fog. Empty stage. In the distance a foghorn (tuba offstage), and faint cries of "Grimes! Peter Grimes!"

Grimes. He enters alone, weary and demented. "Steady! Nearly home! The first one died, just died. The other slipped, and died . . . and the third will. . . ." Hearing the voices calling, he shouts bitterly, "Here I **mad scene** am! Hurry, hurry, hurry! Now is gossip put on trial. Bring the branding iron and knife for what's done now is done for life!" He remembers Ellen and his hopes. The voices come closer, grow more distinct, and he shouts back at them, "Peter Grimes! Peter Grimes!"

Ellen, Balstrode and Grimes. The two enter, and Ellen says softly to Grimes, "We've come to take you home." But he does not notice her. Sweetly he sings: "What harbor shelters peace. . . . Her breast is harbor, too, Where night is turned to day."

Balstrode goes up to Grimes and speaks intently. "Come on, I'll help **spoken** you with the boat." "No!" Ellen gasps. "Sail out," continues Balstrode, "till you lose sight of land. Then sink the boat. D'you hear? Sink her. Good-bye Peter." He takes Grimes to the boat, helps him to launch it and returns to lead Ellen away.

The Borough. Dawn penetrates the night sky, the fog lifts, and the Borough comes to life. Lawyer Swallow reports that the Coast Guard has sighted a boat sinking, too far out to help. As the townfolk go about their business, they sing softly of the tide that "in ceaseless motion" creeps shoreward, filling the broad channel to the sea, and then "with strong majestic sweep" rolls back into the eternal deep.

THE RAPE OF LUCRETIA

Opera in two acts. World premiere, Glyndebourne, July 12, 1946; American prem., Chicago, June 1, 1947. Music by Benjamin Britten; libretto by Ronald Duncan, after the play *Le Viol de Lucrèce* (1931) by André Obey and based on the works of Livy, Shakespeare, Nathaniel Lee, Thomas Heywood and François Ponsard.

THE CHARACTERS

Male Chorus	tenor
Female Chorus	soprano
Collatinus, a Roman general	bass
Junius, a Roman general	baritone
Prince Tarquinius, son of the Etruscan tyrant, Tarquinius Superbus	baritone
Lucretia, wife of Collatinus	contralto
Bianca, Lucretia's nurse	mezzo-soprano
Lucia, Lucretia's maid	soprano

Throughout the opera the Male and Female Chorus sit at either side of the stage. Though clothed in togas, they are contemporary figures, presenting the drama to the audience as a didactic fable: man's nature is violent; until he learns to control it, his fate will be tragic; the only hope for such control is in following Christ. They initiate the story, comment upon it throughout, and at its end state the moral.

The story takes place in Rome circa 500 B.C. and, according to legend, the rape led to the insurrection in which the Romans expelled the Etruscans from the city.

The opera requires no chorus (in the usual sense) and is scored for only thirteen players and seventeen instruments: flute (doubling piccolo and alto flute), oboe (doubling English horn), clarinet (doubling bass clarinet), bassoon, horn, two violins, viola, cello, double bass, harp, percussion, and a piano played by the conductor for recitatives. It was Britten's first chamber opera, and its success, like that of Menotti's *The Medium,* was not limited to small houses. Even in medium-sized houses the small orchestra could project its sound satisfactorily.

ACT I (49 min.)

SCENE 1 (26 min.)

The curtain rises at once. At either side of the stage are the Male and Female Chorus, seated, usually on thrones half-set in niches, and holding books. Behind them a drop curtain, usually portraying Lucretia's tomb, conceals the rest of the stage.

Prologue. The Male Chorus, looking up, sets the story's time and place: "Rome is now ruled by the Etruscans." He describes the Tarquins' rise to power: bloody, violent, and they "govern by sheer terror." To distract the people, adds the Female Chorus, they have warred against the

Greeks, and a Roman army is encamped outside the city. Joining their voices (in music that will reappear to close the Prologue to Act II and to end the opera) they state their position: They will stand as observers between the audience and the action, interpreting it from a Christian point of view.

The Roman Camp. The drop curtain rises, revealing the camp with the generals' tent in the foreground. The Male Chorus sets the scene. The night is hot, and a storm threatens. Crickets (harp) scratch the dry air; bullfrogs (double bass glissandi) "brag on their persistent note."

The tent flap opens. Collatinus, Junius and Prince Tarquinius are drinking. Discussing the previous night's joke they begin to fall out. The Male Chorus explains: the generals rode to Rome to see whose wives were faithful. Only Collatinus's Lucretia had proved so. Tarquinius mocks Junius for "a cuckold," and Junius angrily retorts that Tarquinius, unmarried, knows only "the constancy of whores." Tarquinius stands on rank: "You forget I am the Prince of Rome!" (The four accented notes underlying "Prince of Rome," C-B-A-G♯, serve throughout the opera as a motif for Tarquinius.)

Collatinus parts them, suggesting they drink a toast. Tarquinius proposes "the chaste Lucretia!" (The twisting phrase of notes underlying her name, G-C-E♭-D-B-C-G, forms the other major motif of the opera.)

The toast drunk, Junius rushes from the tent, closing its flap behind him. "Lucretia!" he cries. "I'm sick of that name!" His wife's infidelity has wounded him, but more he fears that Collatinus will gain politically because of Lucretia's good name. The Male Chorus comments on how quickly jealousy can fill a small heart. (This jealousy motif will return twice.)

Collatinus, coming out of the tent, reproves Junius for raging at Lucretia because of disappointment in his own wife, and Junius with a show of good fellowship apologizes. But after Collatinus has left for bed, Junius incites Tarquinius to test Lucretia's chastity. Tarquinius at first does not respond, remarking that Junius's aim in life is not sexual enjoyment but political power. Yet as Junius continues to dwell on Lucretia's charms, suggesting that the Prince "will not dare" to try them, the idea takes hold in Tarquinius's mind. They part, and after Junius has gone, the Male Chorus says for Tarquinius: "But I am the Prince of Rome" (motif), and above the murmur of the bullfrogs and the crickets sighs, "Lucretia! Lucretia!"

"My horse!" cries Tarquinius.

VOCAL INTERLUDE (3 min.)

The drop curtain falls, and the Male Chorus describes the ride to Rome: Tarquinius leaping on the horse's bare back, the horse trotting, cantering, galloping, until stallion and rider are one. At the Tiber's **Ride to Rome**   bank they stop and trot up and down searching for a ford. Finding none, they enter the river and swim across (slow crescendo from flute solo to full orchestra). (The crossing is described to the motif of Junius's jealousy, which caused the ride.) It ends with a long, wailing cry: "Lucretia!"

SCENE 2 (20 min.)

The hall of Lucretia's house. The drop curtain rises. Lucretia is sewing; **spinning song**   Bianca and Lucia, spinning. The Female Chorus starts a song (harp figuration) in which to the first three verses Lucretia, Bianca and Lucia individually respond while in the fourth all four sing together. Lucretia breaks it off: she hears a knock and hopes it is a letter from Collatinus. But Lucia reports that no one is at the door.

Lucretia comments: "How cruel men are to teach us to love!" and then to "ride away while we still yearn."

With Bianca and Lucia she folds the household's linen. In a kind of **trio**   lullaby the two maids vocalize on the vowel "Ah" while the Female Chorus sings of domestic work: "Home is what man leaves to seek. What is home but women?" Lucretia, thoughtful, remains silent.

The women are about to go to bed when the Male Chorus sings Tarquinius to Lucretia's door. The Prince's sudden loud knock rings through the hall. The women, startled, stand motionless. "It is too late for a messenger," says the Female Chorus, and "the knock was too loud for a friend." The two Choruses describe the Prince's entry (his motif), his glances at Lucretia, and his request for hospitality, claiming that his horse is lame. The women are dismayed, but, observes the Female Chorus, "etiquette compels what discretion would refuse," so Lucretia leads Tarquinius to his chamber. The three women bid the **quartet**   Prince good night. He kisses Lucretia's hand and then all, with due formality, wish each other a final good night.

The characters leave the stage. The Male and Female Choruses pick up their books and resume reading. The house curtain falls.

ACT II (60 min.)

SCENE 1 (23 min.)

The curtain rises, revealing the two Choruses before the drop curtain, reading their books.

Prologue. The Female Chorus recalls the historical background: "The prosperity of the Etruscans was due to the richness of the soil. . . . Through all their art there runs this paradox: passion for creation and lust to kill. . . ." Offstage voices cry, "Down with the Etruscans" and "Rome for the Romans." The Male Chorus, closing his book, comments: "All tyrants fall, tho' tyranny persists . . . for violence is the fear within us all, and tragedy the measurement of man, and hope his brief view of God." Joining, they sing in solemn tones the quatrain with which they closed the Act I Prologue.

Lucretia's bedroom. The drop curtain rises. Lucretia is asleep with a **lullaby** candle burning at the bedside. The Female Chorus sings a lullaby: "She sleeps as a rose upon the night. . . ."

At its end the Male Chorus, in hushed tones over sinister drums and cymbal, brings Tarquinius into the room. The Prince, admiring Lucretia's beauty, softly urges her to wake, while the Female Chorus, to the lullaby, urges her to sleep on. Tarquinius kisses Lucretia and, to the crack of a whip—an unusual sound in opera but here highly effective—she wakes.

Tarquinius declares his desire, and she rejects him. (The scene may seem unnaturally slow unless the audience has been led by the stage director to expect, despite the naturalistic bullfrogs, crickets and linen folding, a highly stylized rape.) Tarquinius and Lucretia wrangle— "Though I am in your arms, I am beyond your reach"—and the Choruses join the argument with Christian comments.

Finally Tarquinius, pulling the coverlet from the bed, threatens Lucretia with his sword and mounts the bed. At that moment he, Lucretia **quartet** and the Choruses begin a short *a cappella* quartet (starting on the motif of Junius's jealousy that has led to the rape and ending with the Lucretia and Tarquinius motifs). On its last note Tarquinius beats out the candle with his sword, and the drop curtain instantly falls.

VOCAL INTERLUDE (4 min.)

Above music representing the struggle of the rape, dwindling into exhaustion as Tarquinius, his passion spent, leaves Lucretia, the Choruses comment: Here is virtue assailed and overwhelmed by sin, a frequent scene causing endless sorrow and pain for Christ. To Mary, Mother of God, they pray: "help us to lift this sin which is our nature and to find your love which is His Spirit flowing to us from Him."

SCENE 2 (33 min.)

duet *The hall of Lucretia's house.* The drop curtain rises. The hall is bright with early morning sun. Bianca and Lucia arrange flowers for the house, leaving the orchids, Collatinus's favorite flower, for Lucretia to arrange. Bianca thinks Prince Tarquinius already has departed, for she heard a horse go out.

Lucretia enters, somber, unresponsive and then, when handed the orchids, hysterical: "How hideous! Take them away!" She orders Lucia to send for Collatinus. "Tell the messenger to take my love. Yes! give my love to the messenger . . . to the stable boy . . . the coachman, too. . . . For all men love the chaste Lucretia!" Lucia runs out.

aria Lucretia takes the orchids from Bianca and, singing a mournful aria, "Flowers alone are chaste . . ." binds them into a wreath. When Bianca remarks on it, Lucretia replies: "That is how you taught me as a child . . . do you remember?" She leaves, and Bianca, who now suspects what has happened, recalls Lucretia in the first flush of her beauty and love for Collatinus. When Lucia returns, Bianca sends her out again to stop the messenger: Collatinus "must not come; words can do more harm than good; only time can heal. . . ." But the messenger has gone.

Almost at once Collatinus and Junius enter. From Bianca's evasive answers and Junius's account of Tarquinius's morning arrival at the camp, Collatinus can guess the truth.

dirge Lucretia enters, dressed in purple mourning, and walks slowly toward Collatinus. (The orchestra in a brief dirge, with the grieving tune carried by the English horn, suggests the essence of the tragedy.) Collatinus attempts to reassure her of his love and, after she has told him of the rape, insists, "If spirit's not given, there is no need of shame; Lust is all taking, in that there is shame." He kneels before her. But she feels too defiled to live. Seizing a sword (poetically most apt if from Junius), she stabs herself—"See, how my wanton blood washes my shame away!"—and dies.

The orchestra starts a funereal passacaglia that continues beneath **passacaglia** the vocal lines to the end of the Roman story. (The recurring figure is a rising phrase of six eighth-notes, G#-A-B-C#-D#-E, followed by two quick phrases in punctuation to the rhythm of "it is all.") Collatinus, Bianca and Lucia mourn over Lucretia, but Junius, seeing a political opportunity, goes to a window and harangues the crowd that is gathering: "Romans arise! See what the Etruscans have done!" The Choruses join the lament and reinforce the question that the mourners, including Junius, ask: "So brief is beauty. Is this it all? It is all! It is all!" The Romans, falling silent, remain kneeling by Lucretia.

Epilogue. The Female Chorus repeats the question: "Is it all? . . . Are we lost . . . in our wilderness?" The Male Chorus responds: "It is not all. Though our nature's still as frail. . . . He bears our sin. . . . In His Passion is our hope. Jesus Christ, Saviour. He is all!"

Together, as the stage lights fade on the Roman mourners, the Choruses sing to the music that closed each act's Prologue: Here, in words and music, is the human tragedy, that since time and life began, love has been defiled by fate or man.

The opera has suffered some very bad performances, caused often by the belief that a chamber opera, needing only a few singers and players, will be easy to produce. But, to the contrary, because the vocal and instrumental lines are so exposed—no orchestral mush to cover mistakes—every artist involved must be first rate, in technique and understanding.

ALBERT HERRING

Comic opera in three acts, five scenes. World premiere, Glyndebourne, June 20, 1947; American prem., Tanglewood, Mass., Aug. 8, 1949. Music by Benjamin Britten; libretto by Eric Crozier, freely adapted from a short story by Guy de Maupassant, *Le Rosier de Madame Hus son,* published in 1888.

This was Britten's first comic opera and an immediate success, particularly with German and Slavic audiences who, more than their Latin cousins, seemed to enjoy the social satire in the comedy. Though a chamber opera intended for small theatres—without chorus and scored for only fifteen instruments and percussion—its sound is not muted. The percussionist has thirteen instruments to crack, bang and tap; the opera's thirteen characters sing vigorously, constantly gathering for ensembles of six or more; and the impression left by a good performance is of a boisterous romp spilling off the stage. The timings are: Act I, 55 minutes (Scene 1, 30; Interlude, 2; Scene 2, 23); Act II, 55 minutes (Scene 1, 28; Interlude, 6; Scene 2, 21); and Act III, 30 minutes.

For a comic opera the source is remarkably grim. De Maupassant's *Le Rosier de Madame Husson* tells of a self-appointed guardian of virtue in a small French town who destroys what she wants most to preserve.

Mme Husson, eager to do good, proposes to the Mayor of Gisors, in Normandy, that they honor virtue. She suggests a banquet and proclamation of some girl, selected for virtuous conduct, as the *rosière* (rose-queen) of Gisors; and she offers as a purse, 500 francs. The Mayor agrees, and Mme Husson begins to survey the likely candidates.

It soon becomes apparent, however, that no girl in Gisors is of a purity sufficiently unquestioned to satisfy Mme Husson, and after a conference with the Abbé, she selects as virtue personified: Isidore, a shy, stupid young man who helps his mother run a grocery. Gisors, instead of a *rosiére,* will have a *rosier,* and its girls thereby will be reproved.

Before his selection Isidore had been the town joke, but at the prospect of his receiving 500 francs without exerting himself in the slightest, the citizens are startled into a grudging respect. Isidore enjoys his new position, and at the banquet he tastes wines sweeter and dryer than he has ever had before. A few days later he disappears, and after a week is found "not merely drunk but so filthy a dustman would not touch him." At once *"le rosier de Mme Husson"* becomes the town's expression for a drunk, while Isidore, continuing his dissipation, abandons his mother and the grocery, and soon dies of *delirium tremens.* So much for Mme Husson's good intentions.

Crozier and Britten transferred the story to East Suffolk, England, advanced its period fifty years to 1900, and changed the direction of its thrust. The good intentions now lead not to degradation but to emancipation. Isidore's counterpart, Albert Herring (tenor), goes to a midday banquet, has the first drink of his life when his lemonade is spiked with rum, and that night starts on a pub-crawl. The next afternoon, presumably after some hard thought, he asserts himself against his domineering mother and the town's do-gooders. Though a bit late, he takes command of his life.

De Maupassant in his story, careful perhaps not to diffuse its point, kept details to a minimum. The minor characters—Isidore's mother, the Mayor, the Abbé, and Mme Husson's housekeeper—are mentioned barely. Crozier and Britten, with a different point to make, develop these and add more to create a world of social comedy.

Mme Husson in East Suffolk is Lady Billows (soprano), the social leader of the small market town of Loxford. She is Church of England and has a constant ally, though not quite social equal, in the Vicar (baritone). They are the town's landed gentry. Loxford's Mayer (tenor) and Superintendent of Police (bass) are townspeople and middle class. When Lady Billows, meeting with the three men, exclaims, "Tobacco stink! Nasty masculine smell!" she means not the Vicar but the Mayor and the Superintendent.

Besides the men Lady Billows has two women on her committee to select a virtuous Queen of the May for Loxford: Florence Pike (contralto), her housekeeper, and Miss Wordsworth (soprano), head teacher of the Church School. Both are of uncertain position socially, somewhat unsettled by the fact but responding to it differently. Miss Wordsworth has become nervous and self-effacing, whereas Florence (for so Britten calls her in the score) has become sharp-eyed and a bit cynical. When Lady Billows, rejecting all the town girls as tainted, suggests the possibility of a pure farm girl, Florence states succinctly, "Country virgins, if there be such, think too little and see too much." In desperation the committee selects Albert to be King of the May.

Albert and his "Mum" are lower middle class, in trade. Mrs. Herring (mezzo-soprano) is a widow with nothing in life but the grocery and her boy. Though she sent Albert to the Church School, she is "teetotal" and doubtless the family at one time was Methodist. Mrs. Herring has worked hard and by her lights done everything she could to bring up Albert straight and pure. That her program has worked to her benefit rather than to his no doubt would strike her, if she could grasp it at all, as God's plan for the world. When she thinks Albert dead, she clutches his photograph, remembers it was taken on an outing to the beach, and recalls exactly what she paid for the frame and the glass.

Two other characters, discounting some children, complete Albert's world: Sid (baritone), the butcher's assistant, and Nancy (mezzo-soprano), the baker's daughter. They are Albert's contemporaries and as close as he has to friends. It is their relationship and their attitude to life that spurs Albert to grow up, and it is Sid who in exasperation with Albert and mockery of him spikes his lemonade at the banquet and thereby sparks Albert's revolt.

Though Britten in the Act II interlude associates a tune of molelike docility with Albert, for the most part he does not give the characters particular themes or instrumental colors; rather he reflects their interests and personalities in their musical lines. When the committee gathers in the first scene, Miss Wordsworth goes to the window and, seeing bees in the hedge, reveals her enthusiastic nature in a short lyrical effusion. Budd, the police superintendent, is matter of fact; when asked his opinion, he clears his throat on the first beat of the bar and sticks always to usual cadences. The Vicar is bland, in rhythm, harmony and expression. Lady Billows is Wagnerian. When in the midst of her May Day speech she drops her notes, she continues to peal out the clichés, however mixed: "Patriotism is not enough. . . . Keep your powder dry and leave the rest to Nature! . . . Britons rule the deep!"

Such scenes raise a problem in the opera's stage and musical direction, the same problem posed by Mozart's *Cosi fan tutte:* are these people real or caricatures? Should the opera be played as farce or comedy? In farce the characters, either at the end of an act or of the opera, merely take up new positions for the next situation. In comedy, which has a more serious purpose, some character, however comic the events and attitudes, must be changed inwardly by them.

In *Albert Herring* the problem comes to a head in the opera's musical
Threnody climax, the Threnody or choral lament, sung by Lady Billows, her committee of five, Mrs. Herring, Nancy and Sid when they have reason to believe that Albert, missing for twenty-four hours, is dead. It is the most extended musical piece in the opera. Each character in turn has the solo line while the other eight repeat the equivalent of a ground bass:

> In the midst of life is death,
> Death awaits us one and all:
> Death attends our smallest step,
> Silent, swift and merciful.

At the end all repeat their solo lines and close with a majestic coda. It is a beautiful piece of music, but should it be sung straight or for laughs? If straight, then some easy laughs in the early scenes must be sacrificed in order to establish Lady Billows and the others as real people, capable of real grief.

On this point Britten is not altogether helpful, partly because his parodies are so successful—more successful perhaps than his music for Albert, Nancy and Sid—and partly because he himself sometimes cannot refrain from the easy laugh. There are three references, for example, to *Tristan:* when Sid spikes the drink, when Albert drinks it and later when he recalls the taste of it. At the banquet, whenever anyone mentions *Foxe's Book of Martyrs,* there is a delicious shiver on the gong, and the children's chorus of welcome, shown in rehearsal, is too conventionally funny to be real. In fact, the entire banquet scene (Act II, Scene 2) is farce.

Opposed to this is the opera's structure. In each act the place of greatest significance, the final scene (though not necessarily the final line) is given to Albert. In the first, after Lady Billows and her committee have retired, following their announcement of his selection to be King of the May, he knuckles under to his "Mum" and agrees to go through with it. In the second, after the banquet, in a long, interrupted soliloquy, he decides to go out on the town; and in the last he politely but firmly orders the committee and his mother out of the shop. Despite the social parody, the opera's focus is on Albert and the change taking place within him. Comedy, therefore, not farce.

That is not altogether surprising. Britten never presented himself as an Offenbach, and the opera's theme also occurs in two of his tragic operas, *Peter Grimes* and *Billy Budd.* In all three, Britten portrays an individual, in a small, enclosed community, coming into conflict with society. Neither Grimes nor Budd achieves a sure enough command of himself to survive the experience, and for each the opera ends in death. In *Albert Herring,* as befits a comedy, Albert thumbs his nose at the Threnody and survives with a life made better.

THE BEGGAR'S OPERA

A new musical version of John Gay's ballad opera (1728), realized from the original airs, in three acts. World premiere, Cambridge, England, May 24, 1948; American prem., New York, March 24, 1950. Music by Benjamin Britten.

For the story and background of John Gay's opera, see the synopsis of Kurt Weill's *Die Dreigroschenoper*. Britten's version is quite different. Whereas Weill used none of the original ballads, Britten used sixty-six out of the sixty-nine, believing "the tunes to which John Gay wrote his apt and witty lyrics are among our finest national songs."

Britten, while reorchestrating the ballads, kept close to their modal origins and preserved thirty-six of them in their original keys. Those that he changed he rescored to fall into two groups: Polly, Macheath and their love, gravitating around B flat major; and Newgate prison, around E minor and A major. He also provided an overture. In sum, the result is almost an original creation.

The orchestra requires a flute (doubling piccolo), oboe (English horn), clarinet, bassoon, horn, two violins, viola, cello, double bass, harp and percussion. As always with Britten, the individual qualities of the instruments are used skillfully to underline any references to urban and natural sounds and to emphasize the changes in mood. Throughout, whereas Weill put drama and acting first, Britten put music and singing—and despite the fantastic success of Weill's version, Britten's has been frequently performed in the smaller opera houses of England, Germany and Italy.

THE LITTLE SWEEP
from
LET'S MAKE AN OPERA

An opera in one act, being the last part of an Entertainment for Young People, *Let's Make an Opera*. World premiere, Aldeburgh, June 14, 1949; American prem., St. Louis, March 22, 1950. Music by Benjamin Britten; libretto by Eric Crozier.

As the title suggests, *Let's Make an Opera* is a didactic entertainment to introduce people to opera. In its first part, mostly a play, Mrs. Parsworthy entertains a group of children by describing how her grandmother as a girl in 1810 rescued an eight-year-old chimney sweep from his oppressive employers and returned him to his home. The children, excited by the story, decide to make it an opera for the Christmas holidays.

They persuade a composer, Norman Chaffinch, to write the music; they audition an employee of the local building office for one of the adult roles; and with the aid of a friend, Mr. Harper (the conductor), they rehearse the audience in four songs that it will sing as the overture, finale and interludes between the opera's three scenes. During the course of all this, which can be more or less extended or even rehearsed at other times and places, the audience learns much about an opera's structure.

The opera itself, *The Little Sweep* (43 min.), is sometimes given separately or with only a short introduction. At least some part of the audience, however, needs to be rehearsed in the four Audience Songs in order to carry the rest along. The orchestra required is a string quartet, piano (four hands) and percussion (single player). Even this can be reduced to piano and percussion. The six adult roles (two of them can be doubled) need professional singers; the seven children's parts vary from difficult to relatively easy. The music is not continuous; between the twenty-four numbers there are brief patches of dialogue.

The work however presented has been very successful, not only in England but all over the world. In the United States in 1976–77, with seventy-three performances it ranked eighth among the contemporary operas (*post*–Puccini) most frequently performed. The secret of its success seems twofold: the sentiment of children rescuing a chimney sweep is prevented from becoming too sweet by the historical fact of child abuse in the trade; and the audience, with its four songs of differing character, is directly involved in the singing. That, perhaps more than anything else, seems for many persons to release the musical spirit of opera.

BILLY BUDD

Opera (revised version) in two acts. World premiere (first version, four acts), Covent Garden, London, Dec. 1, 1951. American prem., on NBC television, Oct 19, 1952; on stage, Bloomington, Indiana, Dec. 5, 1952. First performance of revised version, BBC radio, Nov. 13, 1961; on stage, Covent Garden, London, Jan. 9, 1964. First Amer. perf. of revised version, in concert, New York, Jan. 4, 1966; on stage, Chicago, Nov. 6, 1970. Music by Benjamin Britten; libretto by E. M. Forster and Eric Crozier based on the story by Herman Melville, 1819–91, first published 1924.

PRINCIPAL CHARACTERS

Edward Fairfax Vere, Captain of H.M.S. *Indomitable*	tenor
Billy Budd, foretopman	baritone
John Claggart, Master-at-arms	bass
Red Whiskers, an impressed man	tenor
Donald, a sailor	baritone
Dansker, an old seaman	bass
The Novice, a young sailor	tenor
Squeak, a ship's corporal	tenor

Except for the Prologue and the Epilogue, in which Captain Vere is an old man recalling what happened, the action takes place on board H.M.S. *Indomitable* in 1797 when Vere was about forty. The *Indomitable* was a seventy-four-gun ship-of-the-line corresponding roughly to a cruiser or small battleship.

The year 1797 was a bad one for Britain. Napoleon, triumphant in Italy, had forced Austria to make a separate peace, leaving Britain to fight alone against France, and for a time Britain seemed likely to lose its strongholds in the Mediterranean and Caribbean and suffer an invasion of Ireland. In addition, in April and May 1797, there occurred at Spithead and the Nore two of the most famous mutinies in British naval history.

At Spithead, the protected waterway leading from Portsmouth to Southampton, the entire Channel fleet had struck, demanding fair wages, better food and medical service, some security against embezzlement of wages and some shore leave at the end of a voyage. The men's organization was admirable; their mutiny, restrained. Through their leaders they declared that they would put to sea if the enemy was sighted, but otherwise not until their demands were met and guaranteed by an act of parliament. Within a week the cabinet had acquiesced. Even so, it required a personal visit of the elderly naval hero Lord Howe, rowed from ship to ship with George III's pardon in his hand, before the men would return to work.

The subsequent mutiny at the Nore, the anchorage of the North Sea fleet in the Thames estuary, was very different: far more political, far less well organized and controlled. There were incidents of disrespect for the flag, advocacy of French revolutionary doctrines about the rights of man, and threats to blockade London. When the leaders began to quarrel among themselves, important groups of sailors returned to work or, in the phrase of the day, resumed their loyalty. The rest were severely disciplined and one leader, Richard Parker, hanged.

Shortly thereafter, in the story and the opera, the *Indomitable* under Captain Vere sails from England to join the fleet in the Mediterranean. Not unnaturally, among the officers "Spithead" and "the Nore" are very much in mind.

The story proceeds on two levels, the natural or narrative and the symbolic, and to the second the first is required to make constant concessions. Persons expecting a rattling good story of the sea will be disappointed, for much happens that will seem unreasonable, unnatural. On the other hand, the symbolic story is remarkably clear and concerns problems of everyone's life: the conflict in the world between good and evil, the tension between what is owed to God and what to Caesar, and the difficulties of moral choice. The confined world of a ship allowed Melville to exclude with a show of naturalness all that was extraneous to the symbolic story.

It raised some problems for Britten, however, that determined the kind of opera he composed. With only male voices for two full acts, there was a danger of monotony. Watch how carefully he has structured the drama and casting so that Captain Vere, a tenor, stands out against the ensemble of his officers, baritones and basses. And how Claggart, the villain of the piece and a heavy bass, has important scenes chiefly with tenors.

Similarly, because male voices in their lower ranges have less penetrating power than tenors or female voices, the orchestration had to be light and transparent. Since strings more than woodwinds or brass tend to cover voices, Britten used the strings relatively little. The first trumpet and first desk woodwinds have larger parts, and the tuba and trombones are prominent. This emphasis gives the opera a special sound and one appropriate to a martial story.

Yet despite the transparent orchestration, the orchestra is more important than in many of Britten's operas. One reason may be the simplicity of the opera's diction. The inarticulate seamen speak simple words, the orders they obey are brusquely stated, and only Claggart in what serves as his Credo has an extended passage of poetic diction. In the story, Melville in his own voice constantly embroiders the scenes he unfolds. Here that role is performed by the orchestra, chiefly through recurring motifs and rhythms.

The differences between the original four-act and revised two-act version of the opera, with one exception, are not great. Acts I and II were joined, and III and IV. The exception is the former finale to Act I, a Captain's muster in which Vere appeared on the quarter-deck, addressed the men on the need to fight the French and was cheered with excitement by the crew. In the revised version Vere's popularity with his men is merely referred to, and he makes his first appearance aboard the *Indomitable* alone in his cabin. The synopsis is of the revised version.

ACT I (82 min.)

PROLOGUE (5 min.)

The music starts quietly, creating an atmosphere of doubt and unresolved tension (by pitting the key of B flat major against B minor). The curtain rises, and a light shines on Vere, an old man looking back "To fathom eternal truth." He has seen much good and evil, "and the good has never been perfect." (A muted trumpet trills beneath short, anguished phrases on the woodwinds, a motif that will be associated with Billy Budd's stammer.) "There is always some flaw in it, some defect . . . so that the Devil still has something to do with every human consignment to this planet of earth." Passionately he cries, "What have I done? . . . So much is confusion. I have tried to guide others rightly, but I have been lost on the infinite sea. . . . Who has blessed me? . . . Who saved me?" He recalls: "In the summer of 1797, in the French wars. . . ." His voice fades, the light on him dwindles to blackout, the music quickens, and lights go up on H.M.S. *Indomitable*.

SCENE 1 (On the main and quarter-decks—31 min.)

Early morning. A party has gone in the ship's boat to a passing merchantman to impress additional sailors.

Aboard the *Indomitable* a gang is holy-stoning the main deck, directed by the First Mate, who with a rope's end strikes a laggard (whip crack in the orchestra). Another gang arrives under the Second Mate, and he, too, strikes a man. Vignettes of ship life alternate with **chanteys** the sailors' chantey, "O heave! O heave away, heave." (Variations on the chantey recur throughout the opera, often suggesting the idea of mutiny, real or suspected.)

The Bosun comes with a gang for the halyards and is accidentally bumped by a young sailor, the Novice. "Sway, and sway!" chant the sailors hoisting. As they run off, the Novice falls, and the angry Bosun assigns him to Squeak, a ship's corporal (on a warship a member of ship's police) for a flogging. "Not that! Not that!" cries the Novice. "O heave!" sigh the sailors.

The press gang returns from the merchant ship *Rights o' Man* with three men. Two officers with John Claggart, Master-at-arms (ship's police officer), prepare to muster them into the crew. Claggart asks the particulars: name, age, etc. The first man, Joseph Higgens (Red Whiskers) protests but gives in to Claggart's bullying (the underlying music is scored "slow and fierce"). The second man offers no resistance. The third is Billy Budd.

He seems the perfect recruit, young, healthy, handsome, eager—until in trying to say the word "foundling" he stammers badly (muted trumpet trill with anguished woodwind phrases as in the Prologue). "Always some flaw," comment the officers, yet adding with a pun, "A pretty good find." Claggart (accompanied, as often, by trombones and tuba) expands on it: "a find in a thousand, your honor . . . a king's bargain." They assign Budd to the foretop.

At the thought of being up in the sky Billy bursts into song (with his phrases set off by fanfares on the strings): "Billy Budd, king of the **aria**   birds! . . . Goodbye to the old life, don't want it no more. Farewell to you old comrades. . . . Farewell, *Rights o' Man!*" He means his former ship, but the officers take it as a protest against impressment and naval discipline. They clear the deck of sailors, order Budd below and instruct Claggart to watch him.

Alone, Claggart expresses his contempt for the officers: have I never studied men, and man's weakness? Have I not apprenticed myself to **arioso**   this hateful world, to this ship, accursed ship? Summoning his corporal, Squeak, he orders him to watch and even to harass Budd. "Oh, what a ship," he murmurs as Squeak runs off. "One piece of dirt after another."

A sailor approaches, saluting. The flogging is done. The Novice, "only a boy," cannot walk. "Let him crawl," says Claggart, going. The Novice enters (saxophone tune over bass clarinet and cello) supported **Novice**   by a small group of sailors. "I'm done for!" gasps the Novice. "Yes," sigh the others, "lost for ever on the endless sea. . . . We're all of us lost, on the endless sea." (Though doleful, the lyricism of this set number is a deliberate respite from the preceding tension.)

Billy and an old sailor, Dansker, watch the Novice being led off. Billy is shocked by the flogging, as is also Red Whiskers, but they forget it as Dansker and another sailor, Donald, begin to tease them. **quartet**   Donald, pulling Red Whiskers' beard, refuses to call him anything but "Whiskers," and Dansker christens Billy Budd "Beauty." Billy doesn't mind. They are interrupted by whistles signaling the changing of the watch. (In the opera's original version, these led to the Captain's muster.)

Claggart passes and orders Billy to remove his colorful neckerchief. "This is a man-o'-war," not a merchant ship. Billy complies good-naturedly, and Dansker warns him to stay clear of Claggart, whom he calls "Jemmy-Legs." Billy asks, "What's the Captain like?"

"Starry Vere we call him," says Donald. (Melville offers a long, literary explanation of the name. Symbolically the sailors mean he is like the stars: you can take your bearings from him; he's honest-dealing, a **finale**   good man.) As sailors gather round the quartet, singing enthusiastically of Vere, Budd catches their excitement and his voice rises above theirs: "Star of the morning. Leading from night, leading to light. Starry, I'll follow you." The Bosun, discovering them on deck, orders them below. The curtain falls for twenty-one measures.

SCENE 2 (14 min.)

Evening. A week later. Vere's cabin.

Vere is alone, reading. "Plutarch, the Greeks, and the Romans **arioso**   . . . may their virtues be ours, and their courage!" Thinking, he adds passionately, "O God, grant me light, light to guide us all."

The cabinboy admits two officers summoned for a glass of port with the Captain. They toast the King, discuss the war with France, **duet**   and then toast "The French! . . . Down with them."The conversation turns to French doctrines and the mutinies at Spithead and the Nore, particularly the Nore, "the floating republic!" (i.e., all assume that a ship must be run as a monarchy). Vere grows agitated in **arioso**   speaking of the Nore: there was "the infamous spirit of France . . . who has killed her king and denied her God. . . . We must be on guard."

One officer mentions the "young chap who shouted out 'Rights o' Man,'" but Vere says quietly, "That's nothing. I've noted the fel-

low . . . just youthful high spirits." Below decks the men sing, and
chantey   their voices sound quietly in the cabin. Vere is moved to
sympathy for them, "some torn from their homes." But the officers add
nervously, "more reason we should watch them."

A report of Cape Finisterre sighted, enemy waters, ends the meeting.
Vere resumes reading but soon puts down the book to listen to the men
singing.

INTERLUDE (Based on chanteys—3 min.)

———

SCENE 3 (29 min.)

Same evening. Crew's quarters.

The watch with Billy, Donald, Red Whiskers and Dansker is off
chantey   duty and singing chanteys: "Blow her away!" and then
"We're off to Samoa by way of Genoa. . . ."

Billy, noting Dansker has stopped singing, discovers that the old
man wants a chew of tobacco, and offers to give him a plug. He disappears to his kitty bag to get it. "He's a good cuss is Billy," says Donald.
"He's too good," says Dansker. "There's his whole trouble."

From offstage comes the sound of Billy's stuttering. "Billy's a-stam-
mer," says his friends. Suddenly, the stammer over, he appears pulling
fight   Squeak into the light. He found him at the kitty bag. Squeak
pulls a knife, but Billy succeeds in knocking him down just as Claggart
appears with his corporals.

Asked by Claggart, "How did this start?" Dansker puts it simply.
"Billy went to his bag. Squeak there. . . . Billy floor'd him. That's all."
Claggart orders Squeak to be put in irons and compliments Billy,
"handsomely done, my lad. And handsome is, as handsome did it,
too." Then ordering "Lights out" he turns. A boy stumbles against
him. Claggart with his stick savagely strikes the boy: "Look where you
go." The men sling their hammocks, the lanterns are turned low, and
offstage voices fade away quietly, singing "Over the water . . . carry me
home."

Claggart, alone, in the light of the companionway, sings his Credo
Credo   (much of it to a trombone solo over a double bass and sus-
tained woodwinds): "O beauty, a handsomeness, goodness would that
I never encountered you . . . that I lived . . . in that depravity to

which I was born. There I found peace of a sort . . . established an order such as reigns in hell. But alas! The light shines in the darkness, and the darkness comprehends it and suffers . . . I am vowed to your destruction. I will wipe you off the face of the earth! . . . I am stronger than love. So may it be! . . . If love still lives and grows strong . . . what hope is there . . . I will destroy you."

(Some critics and stage directors view the drama as primarily sexual: Claggart lusts for Budd and out of frustration and self-hate sets out to destroy him. This is to declare the one percent, if it exists, the ninety-nine. The few clues in Melville that may point this way have been weakened or eliminated in the opera. Britten and Forster mean the drama to be entirely religious.)

The Novice (saxophone) comes down the companionway. Claggart stops him. The flogging truly has broken the Novice's spirit. Under the implied threat of another he will do "anything, anything." Claggart **duet** shows him some gold coins. The Novice is to use them to compromise a sailor. Who? Billy Budd. Not that one, pleads the Novice. Why? asks Claggart. "He's good." At the word Claggart strikes the boy, who, whimpering, takes the money. Claggart goes. Alone, the Novice moans, "it's fate . . . fate. I've no choice . . . may God forgive me."

He goes to the hammock where Billy is sleeping (a rocking accompaniment of solo cello over two bass clarinets). Billy wakes slowly. "It's a-dreaming that I am. Fathoms down, fathoms. . . ." He is equally slow to catch the drift of the Novice's whispered remarks: "pressgangs **duet** are unfair . . . you were pressed . . . others, too . . . a gang of twenty or thirty . . . they want a leader . . . look at the coins . . . yours . . . if you'll lead us." Billy's protest is stopped by his stammer. In rage he clenches his fist, and the Novice flees.

Dansker comes out of the darkness: "Heard your stammer, saw the Novice slipping away." Billy tells what happened, and Dansker falls silent. When Billy offers him tobacco, Dansker says, "I want nothing o' yours, Baby, nothing, nor your youth, nor your strength, nor your looks, nor your goodness. For Jemmy-Legs is down on you!" The duet that follows is in the form of passacaglia with the phrase "Jemmy-Legs **duet** is down on you!" as the bass figure. Billy sings of his happiness on the ship: he is doing well; up soon for promotion; everyone likes him, even Jemmy-Legs. But Dansker repeats heavily, "Jemmy-Legs is down on you."

ACT II (76 min.)

SCENE 1 (21 min.)

Some days later. On deck.

The air is grey with mist. A few men are at work. Vere and his officers are on the quarter-deck. They regret the mist. Some battle action would help morale.

Word comes that Claggart wishes to speak to the Captain, and Vere orders him to the quarter-deck. Claggart starts ponderously, "Duty impels me . . ." and Vere grows impatient. Suddenly, as the mist lifts, there is an excited cry of "Enemy sail!"

The officers hurry forward, Claggart descends to the main deck, and the crew prepares for action. "This is our moment," the men sing, "the moment we've been waiting for." (The battle ensemble is pure action and should be very exciting. Much depends on the stage director's abil-
ensemble ity to bring the different groups of the ship's company, marines, powder-monkeys, etc., onto the stage in such a way that their jobs are made clear to the audience. The scene is in three parts: expectation, a choral prayer for wind, a shot fired and subsequent frustration.) After the test shot is fired and falls short, it is evident that the French frigate is out of range and pulling away. The wind dies, the mist returns. "Back to foil us," says Vere. "The mist creeps in to blind us." The crew's disappointment is palpable. The officers fear for morale. Claggart returns to his interview. Vere calls him up: "Now be brief, man, for God's sake!"

Claggart, referring to Spithead and the Nore, describes how a seaman bribed a young novice with coins to join a mutiny. He shows the coins and names the man: William Budd. "Nay, you're mistaken," says Vere. "Your police have deceived you." When Claggart persists, Vere
duet grows angry: "There's a yard-arm for a false witness." To get at the truth he decides to confront Budd with Claggart and sends a boy to bring Budd "aft to my cabin." After he has interrogated Budd, he will bring in Claggart.

Gazing after the French frigate, a simple, clear enemy, Vere no longer can see it. "O, this cursed mist," he cries. His officers come forward. "Yes, sir, it's got us." "Disappointment, vexation everywhere," says Vere. "Confusion without and within. O for the light, the light of clear heaven to separate evil from good!"

INTERLUDE (3 min.)

The symbolic mist is a phrase of fourteen notes slowly rising through four octaves. As the notes are sustained by the instruments sounding them, they overlap, and the phrase is indistinct, blurred and dissonant. Gradually the symbolic mist lifts, the rising phrase becomes clearer and finally breaks into a clear day: a bright trumpet followed by trombone in little fanfares with the notes sharply sounded. These carry into the start of the next scene. (Persons with sharp ears and long aural memories will recall that such fanfares accompanied Budd's introductory aria, "Billy, king of the birds." Thus the mist is evil and Claggart; clear day is good and Budd.)

SCENE 2 (23 min.)

Minutes later. Vere's cabin.

Vere is alone and without confusion over the moral issue. "John Claggart, beware! . . . The boy whom you would destroy, he is good; **arioso** you are evil. You have reckoned without me. . . . The mists are vanishing [rising phrase clearly played] and you shall fail."

Billy is admitted and enters the cabin radiantly, expecting a promo- **duet** tion. He is so excited he can't stop chattering. Vere finally says firmly, "You must forget all that for the present . . . we want to question you." He calls in Claggart, who solemnly accuses Budd of mutiny.

"William Budd," says Vere, "answer!" But the stammer overtakes Billy. He cannot get the words out. In a response of physical anguish his fist shoots out and strikes Claggart on the temple. Claggart falls, and quickly dies. Vere, kneeling beside him, looks up at the motionless sailor: "Fated boy, what have you done? God help us all." He orders Billy into a stateroom at the back and sends the cabin boy for the officers.

Alone, he repeats "the mists have cleared," (but the rising phrase beneath, all blurred, shows that he means it in a double or new sense). In the greatest agitation he sees how complicated the issue has become: "Beauty, handsomeness, goodness coming to trial. How can I condemn him?" (In a purely moral world he cannot.) "How can I save him?" (In the world of men, on ship, in wartime, he cannot.) "It is not his trial, it is mine, mine, mine. It is I whom the Devil awaits!"

He calls in his officers for a drumhead court. The three officers react **trio** variously with pity, anger and a desire to seek justice through a trial. They prepare the cabin to serve as a court and call in Budd. Vere is the only witness and tells what happened. Billy passionately denies any intent to mutiny. He bore Claggart no malice: "I tried to an- **court martial** swer him back. My tongue wouldn't work, so I had to say it with a blow, and it killed him." He knows of no reason why Claggart should accuse him wrongfully. The officers turn to Vere, but he says only, "I have no more to say." Billy, sensing the trial has gone against him, cries out three times, "Captain, save me." But Vere says nothing.

Billy is sent back to the stateroom while the court deliberates its ver- dict. The officers feel "We have no choice": the verdict must be death. But they appeal to Vere, "Before we decide, help us." He replies, "Do not ask me, I cannot." The verdict is guilty, the sentence, death. The court adjourns, leaving Vere alone.

(By this point some part of any audience will conclude that Vere is unnatural, inhuman, literally monstrous. They are not altogether wrong. The story's symbolism is badly warping natural, human behav- ior. For an enjoyable evening, however, cling to the symbolism.)

Vere begins his chief aria: "I accept their verdict . . . I who am **aria** king . . . of this floating monarchy have exacted death. But I have seen the divine judgment of Heaven. I've seen iniquity over- thrown. . . . And I am afraid. Before what tribunal do I stand if I de- stroy goodness? . . . I [who am] captain of the *Indomitable* lost with all hands on the infinite sea." He goes into the stateroom to explain the verdict to Budd and the reasons for it.

INTERLUDE (3 min.)

Melville did not put into words what Vere told Budd, nor did For- ster in the opera (and where such angels draw back, this fool will not rush in!). Britten sets the interview as a slow sequence of thirty-four chords. They are distinguished by their dynamics, ranging from triple *forte* to triple *piano,* and by their color, being scored, except for the sec- ond and sixth for the entire orchestra, for choirs of instruments: wood- winds, brass, horns and strings.

SCENE III (12 min.)

On the gun deck, shortly before dawn the next morning.

Billy is in irons between two cannon. He is half-asleep, and the accompaniment alternates a gently rocking phrase (viola over double bass, both muted) with very quiet fanfares (piccolo) reminiscent of "Billy, king of the birds." Later, Billy's phrases are accompanied by the cello and bass clarinet.

He sees the moon and thinks of his execution. But, half-dreaming, **aria** he muddles the picture. "I'm sleepy and the oozy weeds about me twist." (The words are taken from the poem "Billy in the Darbies" [slang for manacled] with which Melville ends his story.)

Dansker, evading the sentry, steals in with a mug of grog. He reports a movement afoot to rescue Billy. The men hated Jemmy-Legs (evil) and love Billy (good). Billy emphatically forbids an attempt at rescue. He asks about the day. It will be "fair," says Dansker. "We'd have caught that Frenchie on a fair day," says Billy. "O cursed mist! Maybe you'll still catch her."

The chaplain came by, Billy says. He was kind. Then more forcefully: "But I had to strike down that Jemmy-Legs. It's fate. And Captain Vere had to strike me down. Fate. We're both in sore trouble, him and me . . . and my trouble's soon ending, so I can't help him longer with his. Starry Vere, God bless him . . . help him, all of you." Dansker goes.

Alone, Billy sings ecstatically: "Farewell to ye, old *Rights o' Man!* . . . Farewell to this grand rough world! Never more shipmates, no more sea. But I've sighted a sail in the storm, the far-shining sail that's not fate. And I'm contented, I've seen where she's bound for. She has a land of her own where she's bound for. She has a land of her own where she'll anchor for ever. . . . Don't matter now being hanged. . . . I'm strong, and I know it" (accompanied by the chords of the Interlude and so part of what Billy learned in his talk with Vere), "and I'll stay strong . . . that's all . . . and that's enough." (The chords grow quieter.)

INTERLUDE (2 min.)
———

SCENE 4 (7 min.)

The main and quarter-deck, at four o'clock in the morning.

The crew musters in silence and in perfect order. Billy is marched in (his fanfares on trumpets) by a Marine guard. The First Lieutenant reads the pertinent Article of War and pronounces the sentence: "death by hanging from the main-yard." Billy cries out, "Starry Vere, God bless you!" and is marched offstage to the main-mast.

Vere removes his hat, and all faces turn slowly upward to follow Billy to the main-yard. There follows a moment of silence, and then **chorus** begins a dull, angry groan of revulsion (fugal chorus on a variation of the "O heave" chantey) from the crew. They sing a wordless, dark vowel (*ur* in purple), and the sound grows steadily as the whole wedged mass of faces slowly turns in rebellion to the quarter-deck. Vere stands motionless, but the officers, increasingly fearful, cry "Down all hands. Down!" The men, obeying from force of habit, slowly disperse, and the deck gradually empties while the light slowly fades.

EPILOGUE (5 min.)

Vere, as in the Prologue, is an old man and the music full of doubt as he recalls the incident on the *Indomitable*. "I could have saved him," he concludes. "He knew it, even his shipmates knew it. . . . O what have I done? But he has saved me and blessed me and the love that passes understanding has come to me."

Quietly he repeats the image with which he had tried to explain to Billy the conflicts between the human and the heavenly world (the underlying harmony is the Interlude's succession of chords): "I was lost on the infinite sea, but I've sighted a sail in the storm, the far-shining sail, and I'm content. I've seen where she's bound for. There's a land where she'll anchor for ever."

GLORIANA

Opera in three acts. World premiere, Covent Garden, London, June 8, 1953; American concert prem., Cincinnati, May 8, 1956; American stage prem., San Antonio, June 6, 1984. Music by Benjamin Britten; libretto by William Plomer, based on Lytton Strachey's *Elizabeth and Essex,* 1928.

This opera, a celebration of England's great queen, Elizabeth I, was composed on the command of Elizabeth II as part of her Coronation ceremonies. The premiere resulted in a scandal. Many of the courtiers, forced to attend, apparently were bored by the music and felt that the new Queen and perhaps themselves, too, had been insulted by the portrayal of Tudor royalty and aristocracy. They spoke out vehemently against the opera in their salons, gossip columns and letters to the editors and succeeded in attaching to it the stigma of failure. Though later more musically sophisticated audiences seemed to enjoy the opera, Covent Garden soon retired it. No German house took it up, and in the United States it apparently had only the single concert performance in Cincinnati.

For a time it languished unperformed. Then in London it was given in concert to honor Britten's fiftieth birthday, Nov. 22, 1963. Three years later Sadler's Wells staged it with success, and in 1968 it had its German premiere, also with success. Yet its progress is still slow for an opera that seems in so many ways to be one of Britten's finest: in its melodies, its ensembles, its ballets and choral music.

Musicians have raided it for excerpts, however, and concert and ballet audiences probably have heard more of the music than they are aware. There are the two "lute songs," sung in the opera by the young impetuous Essex to the aging Queen. The first is "Quick music's best when the heart is oppressed," and the second, to a poem written by the historical Essex, "Happy, happy were he."

Then there are the "courtly dances" that in the opera, separated by singing, occur in the following order: Pavane, Galliard, Lavolta, Morris Dance, March and Coranto. In the United States, at least, these may be most familiar in an arrangement by the lutenist Julian Bream.

Finally, there are the six "choral dances" to which the citizens of Norwich offer their homage to the Queen in a Masque. These are sung a cappella and danced by figures for Time, his wife Concord, country girls, rustic swains and fishermen. Ballet companies as well as glee clubs and choirs have adopted them. Singers in particular find them a joy, for the pieces not only sound well but are fun to sing.

The opera is less tightly constructed than usual with Britten, chiefly because of the greater amount of pageantry. Each scene is a unit with its own prelude and displays a different aspect of Elizabethan life. Six of the eight are dominated by Elizabeth and the final part of the last scene, serving as an epilogue, sums up her achievement as Queen.

The story takes place in England in the later years of Elizabeth's reign, 1558–1603, when her chief troubles were a rebellion in Ireland led by Tyrone and in London the ambition of her greatest noble, Robert Devereux, Earl of Essex. He had achieved fame in 1596 with the sack of Cadiz, displaying before all of Europe England's power on land and sea. He was twenty-nine at the time and the Queen sixty-three, and in her increasing age, weakening skills and slightly declining popularity he imagined himself mounting higher and higher—even, perhaps, to the throne. In the troubles in Ireland he saw a chance to increase his fame, popularity and power.

ACT I (44 min.)

SCENE 1 (20 min.)

Outside a tilting ground. Essex (tenor), hearing the crowd cheer Lord Mountjoy (baritone), grows envious and, when Mountjoy appears, insults him. They start to fight, but the entrance of the Queen (soprano) stops them. She asks Sir Walter Raleigh (bass) for his opinion of the two, and he replies: "The blue fly and the bee: 'Buzz,' quoth the blue fly, 'Hum,' quoth the bee, 'How can this busybody take precedence of me?' " The Queen more kindly orders the two lords to be rec-
chorus   onciled, and as they kneel before her, the courtiers sing in admiration, "Green leaves are we, Red rose our golden Queen."

SCENE 2 (24 min.)

An apartment at Nonesuch Palace. The Queen is alone with her minister, Cecil (baritone), with whom she discusses the duel, confessing that she likes Essex's spirit. Cecil warns her to be careful, and they discuss the political situation. She allows Essex to interrupt, dis-
lute songs   missing Cecil. Essex, after singing two songs, asks to be

sent to Ireland, mixing his remarks about his admiration of her as a queen with admiration of her as a woman. Though she enjoys the flattery, she warns him, "Blow not the spark to flame." Dismiss-
prayer ing him without promising the appointment, she considers her position and prays for God's help to "rule and protect my people in peace."

ACT II (48 min.)

SCENE 1 (17 min.)

The Guildhall at Norwich. The Queen is on progress, attended by
choral dances Essex, Cecil, Raleigh and Mountjoy. The citizens present their Masque while Essex fidgets and wonders about Ireland. The Queen, by giving all her attention to her people's efforts to please her, charms them.

SCENE 2 (10 min.)

At night in the garden of Essex House in the Strand. Mountjoy and
duet Essex's sister, Penelope Rich (soprano) have an assignation. (Historical note: after Lord Rich's death, Penelope married Mountjoy.) They hide to avoid being seen by Essex and his wife (mezzo-soprano). He complains bitterly that the Queen does not advance him, but Lady Essex advises caution. The lovers, revealing themselves, urge Essex to
quartet consider that the Queen is old while they are young and fit "to rule the land."

SCENE 3 (21 min.)

At night in the great room in the Palace of Whitehall. Dancing.
courtly dances Lady Essex, on her husband's wish, is wearing a very splendid dress, and the Queen on seeing it is put out. She suggests that the ladies, heated by dancing, change their undergarments, and they leave to do it. The dancing, meanwhile, continues. Lady Essex returns in a very plain dress, her other having mysteriously disappeared while she changed. Everyone suspects a trick, and the Queen enters in the dress. It is too short for her, and she looks grotesque. She parades around the room and stopping before Lady Essex, remarks, "It becometh not me, I have it in mind it can ne'er become thee." (Note: The Queen played such a trick on a Lady Mary Howard.) She stalks out,
quartet and Essex, Penelope Rich and Mountjoy console Lady Essex, "Good Frances, do not weep."

The Queen returns in state and announces that she is appointing Essex to be Lord Deputy in Ireland. His anger at her instantly dissipates as the crowd cheers and the Queen invites him to dance the Coranto with her.

ACT III (45 min.)

SCENE 1 (20 min.)

The Queen's anteroom in Nonesuch Palace. At the back a curtain. Early morning. The ladies in waiting discuss the news from Ireland. Essex has done badly: time and money wasted and only a truce with Tyrone. Suddenly Essex rushes in, demanding to see the Queen. The ladies protest that she is not dressed. Essex thrusts them aside, sweeps back the curtain and reveals Elizabeth in her dressing gown and without her wig. The astonished Queen waves her ladies away and asks Essex, "What brings you here?" He protests that his efforts to defeat Tyrone were undercut by enemies at home. But for her sharp questions he has no answers. When he tries to recall their previous intimacy, she sends him away.

Cecil enters, and she confesses that she has failed with Essex. He is untrustworthy and must be watched. "It is I who have to rule!"

SCENE 2 (10 min.)

A street in the City of London. Between five verses sung by a Ballad Singer (bass), the means through which news then often was spread, Essex's followers try to incite the people to revolt. The citizens refuse to stir, and the City Crier in the Queen's name proclaims Essex a "traitor."

SCENE 3 (15 min.)

A room in the Palace of Whitehall. Essex has been found guilty and condemned to death, but Cecil warns the Councilors that the Queen may delay the execution. She enters and, given the death warrant, says, "I will not sign it now! I will consider it." When Cecil speaks of the need to act quickly, she cuts him off and dismisses everyone.

Alone, she paces about. "I am, and am not; freeze, and yet I burn." Lady Essex, Penelope Rich and Mountjoy are shown in, and they ask for Essex's life. Lady Essex pleads for him for his children's sake, and Elizabeth promises that the children will be safe. Penelope Rich pleads, but too forcefully, insisting on his rank and talents. Elizabeth angrily dismisses the three of them and signs the warrant.

Without a break, in an epilogue, the Queen stands alone in a strong **epilogue** light against ,an indiscriminate background. Time and place fade, and episodes of her reign are intimated in wisps of dialogue and declamation. Finally, facing the audience directly, she says: "When I have to answer the highest Judge, I mean to plead that never thought was cherished in my heart that tended not to my people's good. I count it the glory of my crown that I have reigned with your love, and there is no jewel I prefer before that jewel." Offstage a chorus sings, "Green leaves are we, Red rose our golden Queen. . . ." As the sound fades, the Queen slowly is enveloped in darkness.

The final scene because of its shift to spoken rather than sung words for the Queen often has been criticized as anticlimactic and unmusical. On the other hand, it is very theatrical. Could Britten have achieved in music quite the same sense of the reign passing rather than merely the person?

THE TURN OF THE SCREW

Opera in a prologue and two acts, sixteen scenes. World premiere, La Fenice, Venice, Sept. 14, 1954; British prem., London, Oct. 6, 1954; American prem., New York, March 19, 1958. Music by Benjamin Britten; libretto by Myfanwy Piper, after Henry James's story, published in 1898.

THE CHARACTERS

The Prologue	tenor
The Governess	soprano
Miles ⎱ young children in her charge	treble
Flora ⎰	soprano
Mrs. Grose, the housekeeper	soprano
Peter Quint, a former manservant	tenor
Miss Jessel, a former governess	soprano

Except for the prologue, without time or setting, the action takes place in and around Bly, a country house in the east of England, in the middle of the last century.

The opera is a small masterpiece. "Small" because as a chamber opera it is short (105 minutes in two acts of almost equal length), it requires only six singers (with the tenor taking two parts) and an orchestra of only thirteen (with eighteen instruments; see below). And a "masterpiece" because it is brim full of attractive music, all of which is apt to its purpose and interrelated in a most intriguing fashion.

Like the James horror story from which it is drawn, the opera does not pretend significance: its only purpose is to give the audience an enjoyable shudder. James, using the traditional pattern of such stories, places a number of guests at an English country house around a fire and then has one, to cap the stories of the others, produce an old manuscript, from which he begins to read. Britten reduces this introductory scene to a single man who, as if musing alone before a fire, begins the opera: "It is a curious story. I have it written in faded ink, a woman's hand. . . ." These prologues, besides setting the story in the past, also invest its events with doubt. Both James and Britten present the story as merely what the woman, a governess, *said* took place.

In her youth, on her first job, she had gone down to a country house to take charge of two orphans, a boy and girl aged ten and eight. The house and grounds, "Bly," were beautiful, the children charming, and her only worry for a time was the insistence of her employer, the children's uncle, that he was not to be bothered about anything, however important. She was to manage. Then one day a letter came from the boy's school stating, without explaining, that he was "an injury to his friends" and was not to return at the end of the holiday. The governess, distressed but mindful of her orders, did not inform the uncle and decided for the moment to do nothing. She would keep the boy at Bly and instruct him herself.

Soon thereafter she began to see a strange man about the house—on the tower, by the window—and from her description of him the housekeeper, an illiterate woman, identified the man as Peter Quint, a former valet at Bly who sometime before had died in an accident. Almost immediately the governess sees still another apparition, this time of the children's previous governess, Miss Jessel, who also has died. According to the housekeeper, both Quint and Miss Jessel while alive were evil and taught the children evil ways, and the housekeeper, though she herself cannot see the ghosts, is fearful.

The governess continues to see the ghosts and soon is convinced that the children, too, see them and even communicate with them—though neither child ever speaks of them directly. The ghosts, the governess believes, are trying to dominate the children and to lead them further into evil. She determines, though uncertain how to proceed, to fight for their souls. Her failure with the girl and her success with the boy, though he gives his life for her achievement, is the story.

The horror is in the evil, which neither James nor Britten specify. As James described his purpose: "Only make the reader's general vision of evil intense enough . . . and his own sympathy (with the children) and horror (of their false friends) will supply him quite sufficiently with all the particulars. Make him *think* the evil, make him think it for himself, and you are released from weak specifications."

In pursuing this plan James had, in one respect, an advantage over Britten. Working with a reader's imagination, James could keep the reality of the ghosts ambiguous, so that at the story's end—as the ultimate turn of the screw—a reader can wonder if the ghosts were ever real, wonder if the governess perhaps was not merely an extremely neurotic woman who frightened a child to death with hysterical charges that he was communicating with the dead. In transferring the story to the stage, however, Britten had either to make the ghosts visible to the audience, as they are to the governess, or to signify their invisible presence onstage by some effect of evil resulting from it. The latter course, however, meant abandoning the crux of James's story, the unspecified evil, rather than losing only the final subtlety. In preference, therefore, Britten and his librettist, Myfanwy Piper, made the ghosts real, not only visible but audible and, further, gave them a scene together in which the governess and her imagination are not present. In this respect at least, Britten's opera is quite different from James's story.

But what Britten may have lost in ambiguity, he gained in other respects with sound, a resource unavailable to James. In the opera Quint appears to the ethereal tone of a celesta and Miss Jessel to a quiet shiver on a gong. But the eeriness of these sounds, which Britten applies sparingly, is the least of what the music adds. More important is its ability to suggest and to reinforce the emotions of the characters: the children's high spirits, the boy's sudden shift to melancholy, the governess's serenity as she enjoys the garden at Bly and then her agitation as she sees an apparition on the tower of the house. "Who is it? . . . Who? . . . Who can it be?" With small skips in pitch and rhythm, the music magnifies her astonishment and first stab of fear.

Sound also can provide an excellent medium for joining the many

short episodes with which James built toward his climax, and here, too, though some values were lost in the story's transfer to the stage, other new values were gained. With James, the episodes frequently have a double effect delivered in the last line or word of a chapter: as when the governess (and the reader), spying from a window at dead of night, expects to see a ghost on the lawn but sees instead the boy—and then realizes from the direction and intensity of his gaze that the ghost is in the tower directly over her head. This particular kind of shock, punctuated for a reader by the sudden expanse of white page before the next chapter begins, is difficult to reproduce in a theatre. But with music Britten could do something different. Deliberately retaining the story's narrative character, he constructed the opera in sixteen scenes (see below): each has a title, like chapters in a book, and each is concerned with a single event—an instant in the screw's turn. These scenes, which with stage lighting fade in and out, he has joined with interludes of music in the form of a theme and fifteen variations.
The Theme:

Probably most operagoers who have not studied the score will recognize the theme when it is first stated—immediately after the prologue—and then begin to lose it by the second or third variation. They may find it again as it is sung by the ghosts in their conspiratorial scene, but then, gripped by the drama of the opera's final scene, they probably will fail to realize that the finale is a passacaglia (as so often in Britten's operas) built on the theme's first six notes. No matter. The music, cast in this form so perfect for this story, will work on their subconscious. Later, on rehearings, they can gradually discover how each successive scene or variation, though sounding entirely fresh and spontaneous, proves to be linked with everything else in the score.

Another virtue of the opera's construction is the precision and economy with which each scene is presented—and dismissed. With only 105 minutes for a prologue, sixteen scenes, a theme and fifteen variations, Britten has no time for padding. Several of the variations are stated in less than twenty bars.

The sound generally is pointed and individual rather than massed.

The sparsity of instruments seems to have inspired Britten to draw from each its unique qualities. A churchyard scene is drenched in bells; another in a music room is built entirely, and most amusingly, around a piano. In combination, too, the scoring is imaginative. One of the loveliest variations uses only harp, horn, celesta and gong.

The orchestra is always subordinate, however, to the words, for Britten wants these understood. To that end also he has kept the vocal line relatively simple, allowing the words to fall into their natural patterns and to shape the melodic phrases. There are no great leaps of pitch, repeated words or grand arias. Rather, Britten has pushed recitative and aria toward each other to a point where the distinctions between them have all but disappeared.

But he has not eschewed melody, in the common sense, altogether. He has set the children's nursery rhymes just as children, exceptional children, might sing them; he has also melodized several schoolroom aids for recalling the rules of Latin grammar, and with one of these he has deliberately used melody to give it importance. It is a nonsense poem in which each line begins with the same Latin word, "malo." Its purpose is to remind students that ablatives of "place where" and of "comparison" do not need prepositions:

Malo—I would rather be
malo—in an apple tree (not "in" malo)
malo—than a wicked man (not "quam malum")
malo—in adversity

Like everything else in the opera, the tune Britten has given this mnemonic is related to the theme (above). Accompanied always by the English horn, it is also extremely melancholy, and when the boy first sings it, early in the opera, it suggests in him a spiritual sickness. The governess, and the audience with her, is startled. In the final scene, as the governess sings it over his dead body as a sort of epitaph, it is truly haunting. Once heard in the opera, most persons cannot forget it—a success for which James, working in a different medium, might have tipped his hat to Britten.

Aside from its story, *The Turn of the Screw* offers an unusual chance to relish the sound of individual instruments. It is not just that the orchestra is small, seventeen instruments and a variety of percussion; it is also the clarity with which Britten projects the sounds, the aptness with which he selects them for dramatic purposes and even the intellectual play with them. The opera on several rehearings, particularly if followed on a recording without the distraction of the stage, can be the equivalent of a course on instrumentation.

In the scenario which follows, those instruments which dominate a scene are indicated. The orchestra consists of a flute (doubling piccolo and alto flute), oboe (doubling English horn), clarinet (doubling bass clarinet), bassoon, horn, harp, piano (doubling celesta), two violins, viola, cello, double bass and percussion. Note how Britten often uses the sound of a variation to prepare for the coming scene. This looking forward rather than back (but not always, see Variation XIV) helps to keep the story moving. And note how he never repeats the dominant instruments of one scene in the next.

ACT I (52 min.)

Prologue (the Narrator). The Governess is hired; entirely solo piano. Theme.

Scene 1: The Journey. The clickety-clack of the railroad taking the governess to Bly. Timpani.

Variation I. The theme restated, slightly elaborated.

Scene 2: The Welcome. The children and Mrs. Grose greet the Governess. Her arrival, solo violin.

Variation II. Theme in the bass under phrases associated with the children.

Scene 3: The Letter. Miles is dismissed from school. The Governess tells Mrs. Grose; celesta (associated with Quint) followed by long passage for viola.

Variation III. Oboe alternating phrases with the flute; later, clarinet has rising runs, and bassoon, a faint reiterated note. The sound of a summer evening with bird calls.

Scene 4: The Tower. The Governess enjoys the peace at Bly; oboe, flute, clarinet and bassoon as before. The reiterated note is her frustrated desire to have her absent employer know how well she is doing. She sees Quint on the tower; celesta. "Who can it be?" woodwinds, in their low, hollow registers.

Variation IV. Strings pizzicato, piano, and double bass, percussion. Theme in the bass.

Scene 5: The Window. The children play. The Governess sees Quint at the window; celesta. Mrs. Grose describes Quint to the Governess; cello.

Variation V. Starts with bassoon and viola; later, piccolo prominent.

Scene 6: The Lesson. Miles's Latin lesson. Piccolo continues under mnemonic about nouns ending in "is." Miles sings "malo" mnemonic; English horn.

Variation VI.

Scene 7: The Lake. Flora and the Governess at the lake. Flora's lullaby to doll, harp and muted strings (harmonics) with interspersed phrases for oboe and bassoon. Miss Jessel appears, soft gong.

Variation VII. Celesta, harp, gong with theme stated by horn.

Scene 8: At Night. Quint, unseen, calls to Miles; celesta. Builds to a sextet (the only scene in which all six characters appear) under which horn and woodwind state theme. Ends with timpani, as Scene 1 began.

ACT II (53 min.)

Variation VIII. Between rolls by orchestra, passages for, in order: clarinet, two violins, flute, viola and cello, harp, horn muted, double bass and bassoon, oboe, and timpani.

Scene 1: Colloquoy and Soliloquy. Quint and Miss Jessel. In their duet they sing the theme. The Governess's soliloquy, "lost in a labyrinth," strings.

Variation IX. Bells. The theme as "changes" for church bells.

Scene 2: The Bells. In the churchyard. Miles "challenges" the Governess.

Variation X. The theme in the bass.

Scene 3: Miss Jessel. The Governess attempts to confront Miss Jessel. The Governess's phrases introduced by a flute run; Miss Jessel sings to a bassoon triplet over chords of harp and double bass. The Governess writes the letter to her employer. English horn, horn, viola, cello. She reads it over to herself; harp.

Variation XI. Dialogue of bass clarinet and alto flute with an occasional ping of glockenspiel.

Scene 4: The Bedroom. Miles evades the Governess's questions. Governess talks to bass clarinet and alto flute; Miles, to harp. English horn sounding "malo" song. Quint introduced by ping of glockenspiel. Ends with the candle suddenly extinguished and Miles saying, " 'Twas I who blew it." English horn dominating with "malo."

Variation XII. Strings pizzicato, long-held wind chords under Quint's voice, side drum with brush.

Scene 5: Quint. English horn, "malo." Miles, urged by Quint, steals the Governess's letter.

Variation XIII. Piano, strings and bassoon, bass clarinet.

Scene 6: The Piano. Piano. Part of the fun is the initial classical style turned demoniacal.

Variation XIV. Miles triumphant, banging the piano with full orchestra in best twentieth-century toccata style.

Scene 7: Flora. Flora defeats the Governess. Gong starts swelling chords for Miss Jessel. Piccolo adds shrillness to Flora's "I can't see anybody."

Variation XV. Between rolls in the orchestra, full-force cadenza for piccolo and one for timpani.

Scene 8: Miles. Mrs. Grose leaves with Flora and the Governess turns to Miles. Passacaglia begins in the bass: timpani, double bass (pizzicato) and harp. Coda to the opera, "malo" with full orchestra.

NOYE'S FLUDDE

The Chester Miracle Play set to music. World premiere, Orford Church, Orford (near Aldeburgh), June 18, 1958; American prem., New York, March 16, 1959. Music by Benjamin Britten. The play's text is from *English Miracle Plays, Moralities and Interludes,* ed. by Alfred W. Pollard. To it Britten had added three hymns (composed by others but rearranged) and a chorus for the animals as they march to the ark.

The play, which tells the story of Noah and the flood, is taken from the Chester Cycle, one of the four collections of English medieval plays known by the names of the towns in which they probably were performed; the others are York, Coventry and Wakefield (sometimes called the "Towneley" Cycle). The plays, which reached their fullest development in the fifteenth and sixteenth centuries, were performed generally on the great festival days of Corpus Christi, Christmas, Whitsuntide and Easter and were designed to illustrate for the illiterate the biblical stories and legends of the saints. The town government supervised the productions and assigned the individual plays to the various guilds, which performed them on large carts that could be pulled from one open square to the next. The typical play was short, somewhere between 180 and 800 lines, written in varied metres, sometimes rhymed, sometimes alliterative, sometimes both. The text of this play dates from the late sixteenth century. In the history of drama the plays are notable for the introduction of comic episodes such as Noah's difficulties with Mrs. Noah.

Though Britten assiduously avoided the word opera in any connection with the piece and in the score suggested that for its presentation "some big building should be used, preferably a church—but not a theatre," it is included here because it meets a general definition of opera: a staged drama in which the accompanying music is at least as important as the drama's words and actions; and also because in the last twenty years it has provided many persons with a great musical and even religious experience.

Britten's purpose with *Noye's Fludde* was to involve an entire community, old and young, professionals and amateurs, in music-making and in the worship of God. He was himself a practicing Christian, had been a conscientious objector in World War II, and his music in all forms demonstrated a concern for moral and religious questions.

hymn As the piece generally is given in a church, the audience is a congregation and starts the performance with the hymn, "Lord Jesus, think on me." During the last verse Noah walks through the congregation to a platform stage in the chancel. He kneels, and from the heavens sounds God's Voice (spoken), charging mankind with sin, specifically denial of God's primacy; and prophesying as judgment the destruction of all the world except Noah, who has been righteous. He is to build a ship of 300 cubits, and as the specifications continue God's Voice fades and the words are taken up by Noah (bass-baritone). At the end he rises, calling to his family to come and build a ship. His three sons (boy trebles) and their wives (girl sopranos) come running with tools and start to work. But Mrs. Noah (contralto) and her friends, Gossips (girl sopranos), sit to one side drinking and mocking the others even as the hull is completed and the mast stepped.

kyrie Noah calls to his wife to board, but she will not and in the heavens again God's Voice resounds, promising rain for forty days and forty nights. Barely has its echo died away when a warning wave rolls by, and the animals (children) marching two by two, in seven groups varied by kind and size, come through the congregation singing (and if very young children, squeaking), "Kyrie, Kyrie, Kyri' eleison" (KEER.ee.AY, KEER.ee.AY, keer.ee' ay.LAY.ee.ZON!—Lord, have mercy!)

When all are aboard, Noah calls again to his wife, but she laughs at him. So he sends his sons, who pick her up and thrust her on board. Her friends, the Gossips, run off screaming, and the rain begins to fall.

A great storm blows up (over a passacaglia) with terrifying waves;
storm   the Ark quakes and rolls, the rigging flaps, and the animals begin to panic. With Noah and his family they all sing the seafarers' hymn, "Eternal Father, strong to save . . . O, hear us when we cry to
hymn   Thee, for those in peril on the sea." When the storm continues, the congregation joins them for the hymn's second and third verses. The storm then slowly subsides, and all the creatures in the Ark go to sleep.

When the rain has ceased Noah, looking out a window, dispatches a raven (mimed role) in search of land. It flutters this way and that (cello), and then flies off. When it does not return, Noah surmises that somewhere the land is dry. He sends off a dove (mimed role; recorder), the most meek and gentle of the birds, and it returns to him bearing in its beak a branch of olive. "It is a sign of peace," cries Noah. "Ah Lord, honored must Thou be."

God's Voice calls quietly, urging Noah and all the others to leave the Ark, to go out on the earth and to multiply. The animals two by two
alleluia   descend from the ship singing "Alleluia!" and at the end are joined by Noah and his family. God's Voice, saying that his anger now is stilled, promises a rainbow stretching from heaven to earth as a sign of the covenant of peace between him and his creatures. Behind the Ark a huge rainbow spreads above the stage. Noah and his family
hymn   begin the hymn "The spacious firmament on high . . . publishes to every land the work of an almighty Hand." The sun, the moon and stars appear. On the second verse the animals join the hymn, and on the third, the congregation. After the final "Amen" God's Voice calls tenderly, "My blessing, Noah, I give thee heare . . . For vengeance shall no more appeare. . . ."

In accordance with Britten's purpose of community involvement the cast is, or can be enormous. The Chester play refers to forty-nine species of animal, and at the premiere of this work Britten had thirty-five (in pairs) subdivided into seven groups. This made a total cast of three adults and eighty-three children of all ages—not including members of the congregation.

And Britten did not stop with the singing. He scored the piece for an orchestra of ten professionals—two violins, viola, cello, double-bass, treble recorder, piano (four hands), organ and timpani—to which at least the following number of amateurs should be added: strings, twenty-five; recorders, twelve; bugles, eight; percussion, six; and hand-bells, six. And within the limits of orchestral balance, the more the better.

He has scored for the amateurs so that even relative beginners can play. The second violins, for example, do not go out of 1st position, and the third violins have long passages on open strings. The recorder players must manage only slow chromatic scales and trills.

One lucky amateur will have the opportunity to play an instrument that Britten invented for the piece: Slung Mugs. These are cups or **slung mugs** mugs of varying thickness and size—to make a kind of scale—tied by their handles to a string stretched between two boards. When hit with a wooden spoon, in conjunction with a note sounded on the piano, they reproduce perfectly the plop of a raindrop.

It is hard to overstate the success—and importance—of the work, not in the repertories of the world's great opera houses but in the many festive performances (In the U.S.A. in 1976–77, eighty-two) created by communities working together, much in the spirit of the original medieval players, in churches large and small. As one Englishman put it: "To sit in Orford Church, where I had spent so many hours of my childhood dutifully awaiting some spark of divine fire, and then to receive it at last in the performance of *Noye's Fludde,* was an overwhelming experience."

A MIDSUMMER NIGHT'S DREAM

Opera in three acts. World premiere, Aldeburgh, June 11, 1960; American prem., San Francisco, Oct. 10, 1961. Music by Benjamin Britten; libretto adapted from Shakespeare's play, *c.* 1595, by Britten and Peter Pears.

THE CHARACTERS

Oberon, King of the Fairies	counter-tenor (or contralto)
Tytania,* Queen of the Fairies	coloratura soprano
Puck (also called Robin Goodfellow)	boy acrobat, speaking role
Theseus, Duke of Athens	bass

THE CHARACTERS (continued)

Hippolyta, Queen of the Amazons, betrothed to Theseus	contralto
Lysander ⎱ in love with Hermia	tenor
Demetrius ⎰	baritone
Hermia, in love with Lysander	mezzo-soprano
Helena, in love with Demetrius	soprano
Bottom, a weaver	bass-baritone
Quince, a carpenter	bass
Flute, a bellows-mender	tenor
Snug, a joiner	bass
Snout, a tinker	tenor
Starveling, a tailor	baritone
Cobweb ⎫	
Peaseblossom ⎬ Fairies	trebles
Mustardseed ⎪	
Moth ⎭	
Chorus of Fairies	trebles or sopranos

* This spelling, not Titania, appears in the quarto edition, 1600, published in Shakespeare's lifetime, and, used throughout the opera, changes the pronunciation of the first syllable from the more usual "tea" to "tie": tie' TAN. ee' yah.

The action takes place in a wood near Athens and in the palace of Duke Theseus. Neither Shakespeare nor Britten specifies a time. Theseus and Hippolyta are classical figures, but Athens was a duchy only in the thirteenth and fourteenth centuries. No matter. The wood, the fairies, the workmen (Shakespeare's "rude mechanicals," Britten's "rustics"), and the creative imaginations are all English.

Inspired perhaps by Tytania's cry of "Music, ho!" musicians in every century have been drawn to the play: it seems so very musical in its lyrics, its contrasting worlds of fairy and human, and among the humans the further contrast of those at court, who speak poetry, and the uneducated rustics, who speak prose. But the plot with its three strands of fairies, lovers and rustics is complicated, and one operatic version, Richard Leveridge's *The Comick Masque of Pyramus and Thisbe* (1716), presented only the rustics and their play; another, John Christopher Smith's *The Fairies* (1755), omitted the rustics altogether; and the most successful settings, Purcell's *The Fairy Queen* (1692) and Mendelssohn's *Overture* and *Incidental Music* (1827 and 1843), confined themselves to incidental music.

Britten preserved the three strands, fairies, lovers and rustics, and succeeded chiefly through the skill with which he and Pears restructured the play and through the clarity of his musical organization.

Cutting the play's 2,136 lines roughly by half, he and Pears concentrated the action, except for the final scene, entirely in the wood. They cut out two minor characters, Egeus, father of Hermia, and Philostrate, Theseus' master-of-revels; reapportioned some of the lines among characters and gave some of Puck's lyrics to the chorus of fairies. But except for adding one line—"Compelling thee to marry with Demetrius"—to explain why Hermia and Lysander are fleeing Athens to evade its laws, all the words are Shakespeare's.

The cutting and rearrangement, however, has shifted the focus of the play from the lovers to the fairies. The story, though it still ends at Theseus' court with the presentation of the workmen's play, no longer starts there with the quarrel between Hermia and her father over whom she will wed; it now starts in the wood with the quarrel between Oberon and Tytania over her page. The runaway lovers are not discovered in the wood by Theseus and Egeus and ordered back to Athens; they return of their own accord as a result of their dreams. And finally Theseus, favoring Hermia's choice of Lysander, no longer overrules an angry father who is present, but merely accepts what was accomplished in the wood by the fairies, the creatures of the night. Power has shifted from Theseus to Oberon, from the humans to the fairies and from man-made decisions to the magic of dreams and sleep.

Similarly, though in this respect of little significance, all the scenes of the workmen that formerly took place in Quince's house in Athens now are in the wood.

The changes played to Britten's strength. He had a constant interest in night, sleep and dreams (e.g., *Serenade,* 1943, *Nocturne,* 1958, and *War Requiem,* 1962), and with the wood and fairies emphasized he could expand the magic qualities of sleep and dreaming to permeate the opera. This allowed him to press further an idea that Shakespeare suggested: the quarreling lovers in their dreams work out their aggressions and confusions so that with the new day they can start a more harmonious life. Similarly Oberon, "King of Shadows," whose quarrel with Tytania has disrupted the seasons, reconciles himself and her through her dream experience. While the rustics, except for Bottom, who cannot make head or tail of his dream, remain impervious to it all: simple, blessèd people going through life on goodwill and humor alone.

In his orchestration Britten has made a sharp distinction between the fairies, lovers and rustics. The fairies generally are accompanied by harps, harpsichord, celesta and percussion; the lovers, by woodwind and strings; and the rustics, by the bassoon and lower brass. He continued the scheme for their vocal timbre and range: the rustics, all male, are predominantly low-voiced, bass or baritone; the lovers, male and female, middle-voiced; and the fairies, high-voiced with the unique timbre of children's voices for all but Tytania and Oberon. Tytania is a coloratura soprano.

The casting of Oberon, the opera's most important role, posed, and still poses, a problem. Britten composed it for a counter-tenor, a rare male voice, and one which in its high, sexless tone disturbs many persons because it seems unnatural. It is also relatively weak, unable to fill a large hall or even to hold its own at all times against a coloratura soprano. As an alternative Britten suggested a contralto. Some productions, lowering the vocal line an octave, have used a baritone.

The opera with its large cast of principals, chorus, onstage band and orchestra of about fifty, depending on the number of strings, needs a medium-sized theatre of about 2,000 capacity. If larger than that, the children's voices may fail to project.

ACT I (The wood, in deepening twilight—49 min.)

Prelude: The Wood. The act has six scenes introduced, connected and closed by the sound of the wood at night softly breathing, stretching, yawning and accommodating itself quietly to the comings and goings of the fairies and mortals. The curtain parts on the wood, breathing: a series of chords played tremolo by the strings with between them alternate up and down slides or *portamenti.*

The Fairies. Tytania's fairies enter first, "Over hill, over dale . . ." and **chorus** are interrupted by Oberon's servant Puck (generally drum and muted trumpet), whom they fear. (In Britten's fairy world there is bad as well as good; Oberon can be cruel and Puck, malicious.)

From opposite sides Oberon and Tytania enter, "Ill-met by moon-**duet** light. . . ." Their quarrel has upset the rhythm of nature. "Do you amend it then," urges Oberon and, pointing at her page, "Give me that boy." But Tytania refuses. "His mother was a votress of my Order." Surrounded by her fairies, she sweeps out.

Oberon orders Puck to bring him the herb (generally celesta and glockenspiel) whose juice "on sleeping eye-lids laid, will make a man or woman madly dote upon the next live creature that it sees. . . ," Puck flies off, Oberon departs (solo violin), and the wood breathes.

Lysander and Hermia. The lovers enter, fleeing "the sharp Athenian law" that would compel Hermia to marry Demetrius, as her father wishes. They plan to go to Lysander's aunt, who lives beyond the reach of Athenian law. (With the two sets of lovers Britten had a problem: how to set Shakespeare's verbal sparring which, when spoken, was bright and witty, but set to music might be dangerously slow and long. To achieve speed he set the dialogues mostly as melodic recitative, gathering it only occasionally into a node of lyricism and ensemble. **duettino** The first of these nodes follows.) The lovers plight their troth: "I swear to thee . . ." and continue on their way. The stage empty, the wood breathes.

Oberon, Demetrius and Helena. Oberon, musing on the herbal potion, enters and hides (declares himself invisible) as Demetrius comes on, pursued by Helena.

"I love thee not," says Demetrius, "therefore pursue me not." Helena, out of breath, panting, insists, "I am your spaniel . . . I will fawn on you." But Demetrius, loving Hermia, runs off, leaving Helena to follow if she can. Oberon, pitying her, promises to use the potion to help her.

Puck flies in with the herb, and Oberon sings, "I know a bank where the wild thyme blows. . . . There sleeps Tytania." He will streak her **aria** eyelids with the herb's juice and "make her full of hateful fantasies." Then he orders Puck to take some of it and annoint Demetrius' eyes so that when he wakes he will look first on Helena and madly dote on her. Puck will know the man "by the Athenian garments he hath on." They go out; the wood breathes.

The Rustics. They gather to discuss the play, "the lamentable comedy and most cruel death of Pyramus and Thisbe," that they hope to perform before Duke Theseus tomorrow evening following his wedding with Hippolyta. Quince is in charge, but Bottom is very bossy and wants all the parts. Quince, however, is firm, and, the parts assigned, the men go off to learn them. The wood breathes.

The Four Lovers and Puck. Lysander and Hermia, exhausted and hav-**duettino** ing lost their way, lie down to sleep. "Good night, sweet friend; thy love ne'er alter till thy sweet life end." "Amen, amen, to that fair prayer."

Puck enters and, seeing Lysander in "Athenian garments," takes him for Demetrius and anoints his eyelids. He flies off as Demetrius runs in, followed still by Helena. Demetrius, still searching for Hermia, goes off, and Helena, seeing Lysander, wakes him. He at once declares his love for her. She is first incredulous, then angry and runs off, followed by Lysander. Hermia,waking from a dream in which a serpent ate her heart away, looks for Lysander and not finding him runs deeper into the wood calling his name. The wood breathes, and above its *portamenti* Tytania enters singing, "Come, come, now a roundel and a fairy song."

aria   *The Fairies.* Tytania, her aria ending, settles for the night and orders her fairies, "Sing me now asleep." Four of them, Cobweb, Peaseblossom, Mustardseed and Moth, sing "You spotted snakes with **lullaby**   double tongue . . . come not near our Fairy Queen." The others add, "lullaby, lullaby . . ." and the fairies, leaving one as a sentry, slip away.

Oberon enters stealthily, evades the sentry and approaches Tytania. Gently he anoints her eyelids: "What thou seest when thou dost wake, do it for thy true love take." He slowly disappears, and the lights fade on the sleeping Tytania as the wood breathes.

ACT II (The wood, with Tytania asleep—49 min.)

The Prelude: Sleep. Like the previous act this is framed by a motif—sleep—from which much of the music is developed. The curtain parts on Tytania asleep, and the motif is sounded: a calm succession of four chords.

Strs. (muted)   Brass (muted)   W.W.   Harps, Perc., etc.

Note that they are scored for muted strings, muted brass, woodwinds, and harps with percussion. The different timbres and harmonics provide a basis for variations. The prelude continues, presenting three tiny variations on the motif, in each of which the order of muted strings, muted brass, woodwinds, and harps with percussion is maintained. A fourth variation is started but interrupted at the second chord by the rustics' bassoon and, later, lower brass.

The Rustics and Puck. Bottom is full of ideas. The play needs several prologues to explain that Pyramus does not really die, that the lion is not real, and that the man with the lantern represents the moon. All agree, and the rehearsal begins with Bottom mispronouncing "odorous" savors as "odious." Then Flute, playing Thisbe, says the part, "cues and all," in one rush.

Puck, entering, listens as they go back to start again. As the script requires, Bottom leaves the wall where he awaits Thisbe in order to investigate a noise, and while he is gone, Puck gives him an ass-head. When he reappears on cue, the others are terrified and flee: "Bless thee, Bottom; thou art translated."

Bottom, Tytania and the Fairies. Alone in the dark wood, Bottom sings to keep up his courage, and awakes Tytania who loves him instantly. He, however, is more concerned with how to get home, until she orders Peaseblossom, Cobweb, Moth and Mustardseed to wait on him. "Hail, mortal, hail," they greet him. Flattered, he has a word for each, and each for him, except Moth whose first word is twice cut off by Tytania interrupting. (Unfortunately for Moth, Shakespeare, after including him at the start of the scene, unaccountably dropped him. Britten, however, needs the voice onstage for the quartet of fairies and used the ruse of interruption as a way to avoid the creation of non-Shakespearean lines.) "Come," calls Tytania, and sits Bottom beside her. "Wilt thou have some music?" "Let's have the tongs and the bones," says Bottom.

dance   The fairies, with soprano recorders, cymbals and wood blocks, play a tune while Bottom dances. Tiring, he yawns, and Tytania urges him, "Sleep thou, and I will wind thee in my arms. . . . How I dote on thee!" They sleep.

interlude   The motif of four chords returns beneath Tytania's "How I dote on thee!" and are followed, as a minute orchestral interlude, by three variations in quickening tempo.

Oberon, Puck and the Lovers. Puck points proudly, "See, see, my mistress with a monster is in love," and Oberon is pleased. The night grows darker, concealing Tytania and Bottom, and Hermia runs in pursued by Demetrius. She will have none of him; she wants Lysander, and in search of him she runs off. Demetrius lies down in despair and sleeps.

Oberon whispers to Puck, "Thou hast mistaken quite." He sends him to find Helena and, to cure the mistake, anoints Demetrius' eyelids. Puck returns, and after him Lysander and Helena.

He woos her, but she reminds him of his love for Hermia. Demetrius awakes and falls madly in love with Helena, which after his previous rejection of her she cannot believe. Hermia enters, delighted to find Lysander and astonished to discover that he no longer cares for her. Helena thinks the other three have combined to deride her, and she accuses Hermia of betraying their friendship. The men try to calm her but are themselves close to fighting. Angry, Helena says to Hermia, "Fie, fie, you counterfeit, you puppet, you!" "Puppet?" gasps Hermia, sensitive about her short stature and outraged by the personal remark

quartet All four now furiously quarrel (considered by some the best quartet since *Rigoletto)* until Lysander and Demetrius go off to fight, and tall Helena flees pursued by short Hermia.

Oberon in a rage shakes Puck, "This is thy negligence. . . ." He orders him to separate Lysander and Demetrius and to exhaust them by leading each about the wood. Then, when Lysander sleeps, Puck should anoint his eyelids so that on waking Lysander will see Hermia.

Puck separately brings each of the four to sleep within sight of the **chorus** others. The fairies sing above them (melody harmonized to the four-chord sleep motif): "On the ground, sleep sound; He'll apply to your eye, Gentle lover, remedy." Puck anoints Lysander's eyelids, and he and the fairies creep out, leaving visible onstage four sleeping figures. (Comment for intermission: throughout, the two ladies are constant in their loves; the two men, changeable.)

ACT III (49 min.)

SCENE 1 (19 min.)

The wood, early next morning. Tytania with Bottom, and the four lovers lie asleep.

Prelude: Waking. With dawn the wood awakes, and soon, all those asleep. Whereas the music for the night with its supernatural happenings was chromatic, for rational day it is diatonic, open and clear, a string ensemble with as an inner voice a rising pizzicato figure for violas that also by inversion descends.

The Fairies. Oberon, gazing on Tytania, says to Puck, "Her dotage now I do begin to pity. And now I have the boy, I will undo this hateful imperfection of the eyes." He wakes Tytania: "Be as thou wast wont to be" (celesta). She looks with amazement at Bottom still sleeping and still with the ass-head, which Puck now removes. She calls, "Music,

dance   ho!" and to express their reconciliation she and Oberon dance a sarabande and slowly exit dancing (English horn, clarinet and piccolo predominate). The waking music returns.

The Lovers. In the distance sound the horns of Duke Theseus' hunting party. Demetrius wakes and, looking on Helena, loves her. Lysander wakes and, seeing Hermia, loves her. Helena sings, "I have found De-**quartet**   metrius like a jewel, mine own and not mine own." All four repeat the sentiment in a fugato quartet, concluding: "Why then we are awake; let's go, and by the way let us recount our dreams." Waking music returns briefly.

Bottom. He wakes answering his cue in the play, the moment at which **Bottom's dream**   he was translated by Puck. He looks for the others. "God's my life. Stolen hence and left me asleep." Musing on his dream, which he cannot fathom, he decides it will make a good ballad. He will call it *Bottom's Dream* because it hath no bottom" (stated over four-chord sleep motif), and will sing it in the play. He goes in search of his fellows. They enter from the other side.

The Rustics. When finally they meet up with Bottom, he is full of his adventure but has even more important news: "The Duke hath dined, and our play is preferred." (Because of Britten's restructuring of Shakespeare, the chronology here requires a little willing suspension of disbelief.) Excitedly they all exclaim: "Ev'ry man look o'er his part. Let Thisby have clean linen; let not the Lion pare his nails; eat no onions, no garlic. . . ." And they hasten away.

INTERLUDE (2 min.)

A transformation scene to Theseus' palace, starting musically on the hunting theme (horn calls) and leading into a sumptuous march to which Theseus and his court enter.

SCENE 2 (Theseus' Palace—28 min.)

Theseus, Hippolyta and the Lovers. Theseus and Hippolyta look forward to the consummation of their marriage. The lovers enter, kneel and ask for pardon, which Theseus grants, freeing Hermia from her father's order that she must marry Demetrius, not Lysander. The lovers, Theseus decrees, will celebrate their weddings together with the royal couple. But now to hear the Rustics' play.

The Play. (14 min.) The Tedious Brief Scene of Young Pyramus, and his Love Thisby; very Tragical Mirth. (In Shakespeare the play is a parody on romantic theatre; in Britten, on nineteenth-century romantic opera. Britten's spoof is very comic and also extremely well organized. In fourteen minutes it presents fifteen tiny operatic numbers.) At the play's end, at the request of Theseus, instead of an Epilogue the **dance** Rustics present a Bergomask dance, then withdraw.

Theseus. It is midnight. "Lovers to bed, 'tis almost fairy time . . . to bed." All go out.

The Fairies. They pass through the rooms of the palace, blessing it: "We Fairies . . . following darkness like a dream, now are frolic; now not a mouse shall disturb this hallow'd house." Puck enters, followed **chorus** by Oberon and Tytania, and all sing: "Now until the break of day, through this house each fairy stray. . . ." (The rhythm constantly throws a musical accent on the line's weak beat, contributing perhaps to the feeling of other-worldliness.) Puck ends the opera with an appeal for applause: "Give me your hands, if we be friends. . . ."

THREE PARABLES FOR CHURCH PERFORMANCE

Britten composed his parables, *Curlew River, The Burning Fiery Furnace* and *The Prodigal Son,* in sequence between January 1964 and June 1968. In style and sound they are much alike, and yet wholly individual. They are not a trilogy. Unlike Puccini's *Il Trittico* they never were intended for performance on the same night. In any event, at roughly seventy minutes each, they are too long for that. Yet they are related, and they seem to benefit from performance in a cycle, on successive nights or weeks. Then the sound lingers, the concept carries over and the similarities and differences among the parables become clearer and seem to strengthen them. The audience, reassembling, becomes the congregation that Britten imagined, and the works' religious qualities are more fully released.

The seed from which the parables sprouted was a performance of the Japanese Nō play *Sumidagawa,* which Britten saw in Tokyo in 1956. The play tells of a madwoman who searches for her child and is led to his grave by a ferryman. "The whole occasion made a tremendous impression on me," Britten wrote later. "The simple, touching story, the economy of style, the intense slowness of the action, the marvelous skill and control of the performers, the beautiful costumes, the mixture of chanting, speech, singing which, with the three instruments, made up the strange music—it all offered a totally new 'operatic' experience.

"There was no conductor—the instrumentalists sat on the stage, as did the chorus, and the chief characters made their entrance down a long ramp. The lighting was strictly non-theatrical. The cast was all male, the one female character wearing an exquisite mask which made no attempt to hide the male jowl beneath it."

The impact of the experience remained, and Britten cast about for ways of achieving in Western terms the same "intensity and concentration." Medieval religious drama in England, he decided, "would have had a comparable setting—an all-male cast of ecclesiastics—a simple austere staging in a church—a very limited instrumental accompaniment—a moral story." So, with the Japanese play as a distant model, he and his librettist, William Plomer, created the three parables for church performance.

All three begin with monks singing a plainsong hymn as they enter the church and proceed through the congregation to the playing area, generally a low platform erected in the chancel. Their Abbot announces their purpose: to present a moral tale as an instruction for the congregation in God's grace. Some monks don simple costumes and masks—the cast is all male; others, the instrumentalists, who are never more than nine, take positions at the side of the platform, in full view. The instruments vary slightly among the parables, but those common to all three are flute, horn, viola, double bass, harp, percussion and chamber organ. There is no conductor. At the story's conclusion the monks leave the church singing the same plainsong hymn with which they had entered.

In each parable the plainsong hymn is the germ of the music throughout. Its intervals and sequences constantly reappear. Britten has scored with the reverberation of a church in mind, and except for moments of deliberate confusion the voices and instruments can be heard clearly, often singing and playing unaccompanied. Much depends therefore on individual skills and, lacking a conductor, on cooperation. Performances seem either to succeed exceptionally well or to fail dismally; there is no middle ground of routine. *Curlew River* generally is thought to be the most intense, the most interesting musically, and the most difficult to project; *The Prodigal Son,* the most conventional, musically and theatrically. But as yet there is no critical agreement on which of the three is the best, or why; suggesting perhaps that an individual's response to the religious as well as the musical idea determines the judgment.

CURLEW RIVER

Parable for Church Performance. World premiere, Orford Church, Orford (near Aldeburgh), England, June 12, 1964; American prem., Caramoor (in Katonah), New York, June 26, 1966. Music by Benjamin Britten; libretto by William Plomer, distantly based on the Japanese Nō play *Sumidagawa*.

The instruments are: flute (doubling piccolo), horn, viola, double bass, harp, chamber organ, and percussion consisting of five small untuned drums, five small bells, and one large tuned gong.

The Curlew is a river in the fen country of East Anglia, England. It is also a saltwater sea bird, slightly larger than a gull. The action takes place in a church in early medieval times.

PRESENTED WITHOUT INTERMISSION (70 min.)

The monks enter singing the plainsong hymn:

Te lú - cis   an - te   ter-mi - num, Re - rum Cre - á - tor, pó -sci - mus,
For light before the end, Creator of all things, we entreat you,

Ut pro tú - a cle -   mén-ti - a,   Sis práesul — et cu - stó - di - a.
So that by your indulgence, You will be (our) leader and guard.

After the instrumentalists have gone to their instruments, the Abbot addresses the congregation: ". . . The Brothers have come today to show you a mystery: how in sad mischance a sign was given of God's grace. . . . Attend to our mystery."

The three monks who are to play the Ferryman (baritone), the Traveller (baritone), and the Madwoman (tenor) are ceremonially cos-**robing** tumed (to a march based on the hymn played heterophonically, i.e., instruments simultaneously sounding simple and decorated versions of it); the other monks, as Pilgrims, take seats in what will serve as the Ferryman's boat as he takes them across the river to pray at a grave that is almost a shrine.

The ferryman starts the parable by introducing himself—"I am the Ferryman"—to his characteristic instrument, the horn, loud and bossy. (A minor "mystery" of the parable is how, under the influence of the Madwoman, the Ferryman's latent sensitivity is stimulated and with it that of the horn.) "Today is an important day," he says, for "a year ago today there was a burial; the river folk believe some special grace is there. . . . Mark this well!" He sits in his boat.

The Traveller approaches. His instruments are the harp in sweeping arpeggios over a heavy tread in the double bass. He asks for a place in the boat to cross the river. The Ferryman agrees but asks, "What is that strange noise up the highway there?"

It is the Madwoman, preceded by the sound of her flute (flutter-tongued to suggest madness) and crying, "You mock me, you ask me whither I go, whither I go." (The wide range of her cries contrasts sharply with the narrowness of the others' speech-song.) She comes into view crying, "Let me in! Let me out!" The Pilgrims and the Ferryman are eager to see her, and he delays the boat's departure.

After taking a few steps this way and that, and falling to the ground, she describes herself: "Near the Black Mountains there I dwelt . . . my only child was lost, seized as a slave by a **Madwoman's narrative** stranger . . . he was taken eastward . . . eastward I wander on, on, in longing for my son." (It is the equivalent of an operatic mad scene. But unlike, say, Donizetti's *Lucia di Lammermoor,* which used an echoing flute, here the emotion is suggested, not by scales and trills, but by the slightest change of pitch up or down at the end of the phrase.) She asks for a place in the boat, but the Ferryman, backed by the Pilgrims, refuses unless she entertains them with a song.

She is indignant; she is a noblewoman. She reminds them of a rid-

dle: "Birds of the Fenland, though you float or fly, wild birds, I cannot
riddle understand your cry. Tell me does the one I love in this
world still live?" Turning, she watches a flight of birds. "What are
those birds?" she asks the Ferryman. "Common gulls," he says. "Curlews of the Fenland," she insists, connecting the migratory flight with
the loss of her son. Her yearning for him has moved the others, and
when she repeats her request to the Ferryman, they urge him to take
her aboard. He agrees, and the boat sets off.

During the crossing (long, slow glissandi on the double-bass, viola
and harp) the Ferryman tells the story of the shrine. A year ago a
stranger crossed the river, a Heathen, who had with him a gentle
Ferryman's narrative boy, a Christian. The boy plainly was dying, and the Heathen soon abandoned him. The boy came from
the Black Mountains where he had lived alone with his mother, and
after his death and burial the river folk came to think he was a saint
and believe "his spirit has been seen." "Kyrie eleison," sing the Pilgrims.

The boat lands, and all but the Madwoman, who sits weeping, go
ashore to pray at the boy's grave. "Come along there," says the Ferryman. . . . "You must be soft-hearted to weep at my story." But after
questioning the Ferryman further, she is sure the child was hers, and
so, too, are the Pilgrims.

Rising, she sings her despair, confusing her child with the curlews
overhead: "Where shall I turn. . . . Chain on my soul, let me go!"
Full of sympathy, the others lead her to the grave. But she cannot pray,
only weep. Gently the Ferryman interrupts her: "This is not
right. . . . *Your* prayer is best to rejoice his young soul." As the
others sing a hymn, "Custodes hominum," she gazes into the distance
and repeats her riddle: "Birds of the Fenland . . . does the one I love
in this world still live?"

From the grave, joining in the hymn, sounds the voice of the child's
spirit. "I thought I heard the voice of my child," cries the Madwoman.
"Say your prayer alone, lady," urges the Traveller. "Say it alone," says
the Ferryman. To give her privacy they and the others withdraw
slightly.

Above the grave appears the boy's spirit, seen by all. "Go your way
in peace, mother. The dead shall rise again, and in that blessed day we
grace shall meet in heaven." All cry "Amen!" and the Madwoman
three times repeats "Amen! Amen! Amen!"—and in that moment is
released from her madness.

She kneels, and the Pilgrims surround her. Hidden from view she, the Ferryman and the Traveller resume their monks' habits. The Abbot addresses the congregation: ". . . We have shown you here how . . . a sign was given of God's grace. . . . In hope, in peace, ends our mystery." The monks go out singing "Te lucis ante terminum, rerum Creator, poscimus. . . ."

THE BURNING FIERY FURNACE

Parable for Church Performance. World premiere, Orford Church, Orford (near Aldeburgh), England, June 9, 1966; American prem., Caramoor (in Katonah), New York, June 25, 1967. Music by Benjamin Britten; libretto by William Plomer, based on the Bible, Old Testament, Daniel, 3.

The instruments are flute (doubling piccolo), horn, alto trombone, viola, double-bass, harp, chamber organ and percussion consisting of five small untuned drums, an anvil or untuned steel plate, lyra glockenspiel, whip, and tuned wood blocks. For a march about the church the double-bass player shifts to a Babylonian drum, the chamber organ player, to cymbals, and the harpist to a little harp.

The action takes place in Babylon in the 6th century B.C. when Nebuchadnezzar was king (c. 605–562).

PRESENTED WITHOUT INTERMISSION (64 min.)

The monks enter singing the plainsong hymn:

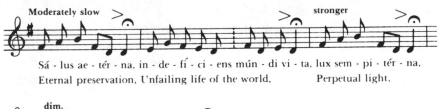

Sá - lus ae - tér - na, in - de - fí - ci - ens mún - di vi - ta, lux sem - pi - tér - na,
Eternal preservation, Unfailing life of the world,   Perpetual light,

et re - dém - pti - o   vé - re nó - stra,
And truly   our redemption

After the instrumentalists have gone to their instruments, the Abbot addresses the congregation: the purpose of the mystery is to show "steadfastness" in the faith under "testing," "God give us all," the monks intone, "the strength to stand against the burning, murderous world!"

The Abbot, who plays the court astrologer (baritone), and the monks who play Nebuchadnezzar (tenor), Ananias or Shadrach (baritone), Misael or Meshach (baritone), and Azarias or Abednego (bass) **robing** are ceremonially robed while the instruments replay the hymn heterophonically, i.e., simultaneously sounding simple and decorated versions of it. Other monks take their places as courtiers, and a Herald (baritone) starts the drama.

By royal command the Babylonian court has assembled to honor three Jews advanced by Nebuchadnezzar to rule three provinces. The courtiers exclaim joyously, and when a flourish proclaims the arrival of the King, they greet him with the royal anthem. He enters with his Astrologer. Nebuchadnezzar announces the appointments, receives the **naming** pledges of the three Jews to serve him faithfully and bestows on them their new Babylonian names: Shadrach, Meshach, and Abednego.

The feast in their honor is served, but they politely refuse what is offered to them. At first their abstinence is concealed by the entertainment. Three acolytes, two singers and a tumbler, present (chiefly to flute and wood blocks) three riddles: the waters of Babylon ran **entertainment** dry . . . the hanging gardens grew like mad . . . and the people ate the figs, melons, and grapes . . . do you know why? Because someone monkeyed with the water supply . . . because the gardens got all the water . . . and because the Babylonians are greedy pigs. If pigs had wings, then pigs would fly above Babylon. Babylon, goodbye. (The riddles' cheeky modern tone and obscure relevance, if any, seem out of place. Dramatically the scene's bright lack of seriousness increases the menace of what follows.)

The Astrologer points out to the King that the three Jews have refused to eat or drink the feast in their honor. Nebuchadnezzar reproves them, gently at first and then with increasing irritation. With one voice (they are never separate personalities) they excuse themselves: "Partaking is forbidden by the laws of Israel, by the sacred laws of Israel."

As the Jews withdraw slightly, the courtiers divide, some angry at the Jews—foreigners!—while others urge patience. The Astrologer triumphantly turns on the King: "I warned you, I warned you the stars were against you. This rash innovation, invasion of immigrants, puts Babylon in danger." Nebuchadnezzar is appalled. "The stars against me! . . . What must I do?" The courtiers rise and flee in panic. "Merodak!" (mer.OH.dak), says the Astrologer portentously, "Mero-dak!" cries the King, hastily following the courtiers.

The three Jews are left alone. "Names cannot change us. What we are we remain. . . . Help us, Lord, help us in our loneliness." Calmly they lie down to sleep.

The Herald comes forward. By royal decree a golden image of Merodak, the great god of Babylon, will be erected and all must fall down and worship it or be cast in the burning, fiery furnace.

The threw Jews pray aloud, "Lord, help us in our loneliness," and between their lines the instruments one by one "warm up" for the procession in honor of Merodak. In order, viola, flute, glockenspiel, harp, horn, trombone, Babylonian drum, and small cymbals.

The procession begins and winds out through the congregation and **march** back to the playing area. (Musically the march is developed out of the previous "warm up" phrases; dramatically, it is a superb pre-amble to the raising of the image.)

The golden image is set up, and the Babylonians all kneel before it, worshiping (with lovely growling phrases), "Mer . . . OH . . . dak!"

The Astrologer draws the King's attention to the three Jews: they do not worship Merodak. Nebuchadnezzar calls them before him, and though they are polite, they are also firm: "We will not serve thy God. . . ."

Nebuchadnezzar orders them to be thrown into the furnace, and ev-eryone expects to see them burn instantly in the sevenfold heat. In-stead, they see among the Jews, who are singing their Lord's praises, an **miracle** Angel (boy treble) whose voice (always on the vowel "o") floats above those of the three Jews.

The King is amazed and because of the heat approaches the furnace carefully. He calls to the Jews to come out and after examining them dismisses his Astrologer. "Hear my decree," he cries. "There is no god except this God, the God of Shadrach, Meschach, and Abednego. Down with Merodak"—and the golden image shatters.

The King and his courtiers join the three Jews in the Benedicte, "O ye Winter and Summer, bless ye the Lord. . . . Praise him and magnify him forever."

The monks help their brethren to put off their costumes and resume their habits, and the Abbot reminds the congregation: "Friends, remember! Gold is tried in the fire, and the mettle of man in the furnace of humiliation. . . . So ends our mystery." The monks go out singing "Salus aeterna, indeficiens mundi vita. . . ."

THE PRODIGAL SON

Parable for Church Performance. World premiere, Orford Church, Orford (near Aldeburgh), England, June 10, 1968; American prem., Caramoor (in Katonah), New York, June 29, 1969. Music by Benjamin Britten; libretto by William Plomer, based on the Bible, New Testament, St. Luke, 15: 11–32.

The instruments are alto flute (doubling piccolo), trumpet, horn, viola, double bass, harp, chamber organ and percussion consisting of five small untuned drums, small Chinese cymbal, one large tuned gong, wood blocks and a gourd rattle. A small group that plays onstage as servants has a small drum, a pair of small cymbals, tambourine, sistrum (jingle rattle) and a small bell-lyra.

In the gospel Jesus tells the parable without specifying its time or setting. The word "prodigal" means given to reckless, wasteful spending.

PRESENTED WITHOUT INTERMISSION (68 min.)

The monks enter singing the plainsong hymn:

After they have reached the acting area and sung their "Amen," from the back of the church a mocking voice calls "Amen!" It is the Abbot (tenor) disguised as The Tempter. Walking forward through the congregation, he announces: "I bring you no sermon. What I bring you is evil. You are about to see a country patriarch, a father with his family. . . . See how I break it up! See how . . . see how." Through his phrases the monks chant, "Deliver us, O Lord, from the evil man. . . . Let not the ungodly have his desire. Amen."

While the monks who are to play the Father (bass-baritone), the Elder Son (baritone) and the Younger Son (tenor) are ceremonially **robing** robed for their parts, the instrumentalists review the plainsong hymn heterophonically, i.e., simultaneously sounding simple and decorated versions of it.

Father, Elder and Younger Sons. (Throughout the parable the alto flute, gentle and pastoral, is associated with the Father, the country patriarch; the double bass, sturdy and sometimes angry, with the Elder Son; the softer viola with the Younger Son; and the horn with work in the fields.) The Father praises the Lord: "All of us are His. . . . Our life we maintain by love and toil. . . . Sin is for idle hands . . . to the fields." Addressing first the Elder and then the Younger Son, he sends them off with the Servants to work. The Elder Son and Servants go willingly, singing. (There are more choral passages in this parable than in the others.) The Younger Son follows slowly, silent, alone.

The Tempter and the Younger Son. The Tempter stops him: "Have you not had enough of this quiet life?" Overriding the young man's protests, he continues, "I am no stranger to you. You know me very well. I am your inner voice, your very self. . . . Imagine what you are missing . . . before it is too late . . . while you are young. Imagine!"

The ideas (to vivid harp accompaniment) fall like rain on parched earth. To himself the Younger Son wonders aloud: "How can he be informed of my most secret longings. . . ."

"Act out your desires," cries the Tempter. (The trumpet flashes in. It is associated with the son's discontent, his eagerness for experience and, later, with the temptations of the city.)

The Younger Son and the Father. The son, approaching his father, speaks of his discontent. "While I am living here, life is passing by. . . . If I could have my portion! If I could have it now!" The Father is reluctant: "Think of the dangers of the journey. . . . You might learn little save what is bad." But finally he agrees. "To content you I will give you your portion."

Full Family and Servants. The Elder Son and Servants return from the fields, and the Father announces the departure of the Younger Son. The Servants clothe him in a robe symbolic of his portion. The Elder

Son protests: "No word of this was uttered to me. He will go jaunting while I stay and work." The Father urges, "Son, be calm. He will be wiser for his journey." The Younger Son starts out (his trudging step suggested by the gourd) against a background of his Father's blessing, the Servants' good wishes and his brother's grumbling.

The Tempter and the Younger Son. Their voices merge but not quite in unison, the Tempter's always slightly ahead. "Free. At last you are free! At last I am free!" (As before, the vivid harp gradually gives way to the flashing trumpet.) They arrive at the City.

The Temptations of the City. Urban Parasites swarm around the young man, welcoming him to the City. Distant Voices (offstage) suggest the pleasures of drink, and the Tempter and the Parasites urge the young man to try it. He does, to excess, and as the price pays a third of his robe. Next, the Distant Voices (offstage) suggest the delights of the flesh—and the young man pays another third. Finally, he is introduced to gambling (two tuned wood blocks and one high-pitched untuned block in accompaniment) and loses all that he has left. "Now you have nothing," says the Tempter, "you are nothing."

"Where are my friends?" asks the young man. Turning to the Tempter he asks, "Now where do I go?" "Fool," replies the Tempter. "After plenty comes poverty. Now you must pay."

There is famine in the land, and beggars appear: "We are starving." "Am I brought down to begging?" asks the son. "Yes, begging!" says the Tempter. "But how am I to live?"—"Go and work as a swineherd. . . . You might get the leavings." The young man, gasping "No . . . no," falls to the ground.

The Tempter turns to the congregation. "I have broken up that family before your eyes. See how . . . see how. . . ." Bowing, he leaves the stage.

The Younger Son. In the dust he reviews his life. "With joy I sowed, my harvest is despair . . . even my father's servants can eat. The end is bitterness; this is the end" (solo viola accompaniment).

Rising, he starts his journey home (gourd): "I will arise and go, I will go to my father and I will say to him, 'Father, I have sinned against God and against you. I am no more worthy to be called your son. . . . Let me only be one of your servants. Let me work for hire.' "

At Home. His father, embracing him, orders the Servants: "Bring my best robe for him. . . . Kill the fatted calf. Let us eat and be merry. . . . For this son of mine was dead and is alive again, was lost and is found."

The Servants, dancing about father and son, rejoice. "O sing unto the Lord a new song, for He hath done marvelous things." But in the midst of the festival the Elder Son enters: "Stay! What does this mean? . . . The waster is back, wearing my father's best robe . . . (and the) fatted calf. You never gave me so much as a kid to feast with my friends." The Father answers the complaint by saying, "You are my right hand. All that I have is yours. . . . Let us all share this joy. For thy brother was dead and is alive again, was lost and is found." And the brothers are reconciled in the joy of "was dead and is alive again, was lost and is found."

The monks put off their costumes, and the Abbot explains the parable to the congregation: "More joy shall be in heaven over one repenting sinner than over ninety-nine with nothing to repent." The monks join him in concluding, "Remember the story of the Prodigal Son. Remember his Father's forgiveness." And they go out singing, "Jam lucis orto sidere, Deum precemur supplices. . . ."

It is not clear in the gospel exactly to whom Jesus addressed this parable: to "publicans and sinners" or to "Pharisees and scribes." Was his purpose chiefly to illustrate for sinners the extent of God's forgiveness or to warn the Pharisees against self-righteousness? The story itself does not resolve the ambiguity. For obvious reasons the parable always has been popular with big sinners. But to many little sinners, struggling to do good, the Father's treatment of the Elder Son seems unjust, a failure in love—assuming, perhaps falsely, that justice is an equality in love (whether of Father or State) that must lead to an equality in treatment. Britten and Plomer kept both strains of the story and risked losing that part of any audience that instinctively sides with the Elder Son. Prokofiev and the choreographer George Balanchine made a different artistic decision. In their ballet *The Prodigal Son* they cut out the Elder Son altogether, allowing a scene of forgiveness untroubled by issues of fairness—simpler, more theatrically successful but less intellectually stimulating.

OWEN WINGRAVE

Opera in two acts, nine scenes. World premiere on television, BBC–London, N.E.T.–New York, May 16, 1971. European stage prem., London, May 10, 1973; Amer. stage prem., Santa Fe, Aug. 9,

1973. Music by Benjamin Britten; libretto by Myfanwy Piper, based on the short story by Henry James first published, 1892.

This opera, shorter than the one-act *Elektra,* is Britten's most direct attack on the use of violence in human affairs. Like some persons in all ages he did not believe in the effectiveness of violence in achieving an end or that it could be used without self-corruption. But he carried his dislike of it further than most, not only in his works, such as *Our Hunting Fathers* and *War Requiem,* but in his life, for during World War II, perhaps the most righteous of recent wars, he was a conscientious objector.

In *War Requiem* he states most powerfully the waste, the pity, the corruption of war, but it attacks violence less directly than *Owen Wingrave* because about an event unmistakably over. Those prone to violence are always willing to lament the fallen—the military are very good at funerals—and the community, in common regret for the past, is reunited. But in *Owen Wingrave* the argument turns on future actions, where any divergence from majority opinion seems divisive, a threat to the community's security. Britten puts onstage characters who represent all those who live by, profit from or secretly enjoy violence, the largest part of any audience. The characters are not an attractive group, and audiences as a rule do not enjoy such self-confrontation. For this reason, regardless of its music, the opera is unlikely ever to be popular.

The action takes place in the late nineteenth century when Britain's most recent major war was the Crimean, often said by historians to have been unnecessary. Owen Wingrave is an Englishman, raised to be a soldier, who repudiates his family heritage and training and in triumphing over the violent streak in himself, which is in all men, loses his life. James made it a ghost story, using the ghosts to symbolize what cannot easily be shown: the internal streak of violence. But he told it without much passion. Britten's music adds passion.

Composed for television, the opera has several scenes which pan in and out or superimpose. In staged productions these have worked equally well with lighting. The reader should imagine a fluid production in which the camera or spotlight constantly reinforces the musical focus on this or that character.

ACT I (63 min.)

A prelude (3 min.) scans the ten portraits at Paramore, the family
prelude   home of the Wingraves, one of England's staunchest military families. Clearly the pressures on the present Wingrave to continue the family tradition will be great.

The most important of the portraits is the fifth, a double portrait of a
Colonel Wingrave of a previous century and of his son, a boy. They are
the ghosts of the house. According to legend the boy, though provoked
by a friend, refused to fight, and his father, watching from a window,
legend   saw. He marched his son to the boy's bedroom and, calling
him "coward," struck him on the head. The blow proved fatal, and the
boy was taken from the room to be readied for burial. The next morning when the household assembled, expecting the father to toll the funeral bell, he could not be found. He was looked for vainly until it
occurred to someone that he might perhaps be in the room from which
his child had been carried to burial. He was found dead on the floor, in
his clothes, as if he had reeled and fallen back, without a wound, without a mark, without anything in his appearance to indicate that he
had either struggled or suffered. Since then no one has slept in the
room, and sometimes at night the Colonel and the boy can be seen
walking into it.

From the ten portraits the camera shifts to the eleventh Wingrave,
Owen. He is at a tutor's house in London where he is cramming for the
examinations to enter a military school. The day's lesson finished,
Wingrave (baritone) lingers to tell the tutor, Coyle (bass-baritone),
that he has decided against soldiering; and he asks Coyle to break the
news to the family, specifically to his maiden aunt, Miss Wingrave
(dramatic soprano), who is in London. Coyle attempts to dissuade
Owen but agrees to talk to Miss Wingrave. "What will they say at
Paramore?" he muses after Owen goes. "Soldiering's their life, and
their religion, Owen their hope, heir to the Wingrave flag of glory."

An interlude follows a sequence of brilliant flags. Then two scenes
flags   develop simultaneously: in a town house, Coyle and Miss
Wingrave, who talks of duty, obedience, sacrifice; in Hyde Park,
Owen, reading Shelley's *Queen Mab* and musing on war. The Horse
Guards ride by. Miss Wingrave talks of "the glory and pride of En-
gland"; Owen imagines the troops in disaster, "false plumes and pride,

obedience that ends in destruction and murder." It is not the possibility of defeat but the soul's corruption that he finds abhorrent. An interlude follows of old, tattered flags while Wingrave reads from Shelley: "War is the statesman's game, the priest's delight, the lawyer's jest . . . [the] trade is falsehood."

Coyle reports his lack of success to Owen. Both he and Mrs. Coyle (soprano), though not agreeing with Owen's ideas, respect him enough to listen to him sympathetically. The Wingrave family, Coyle warns, will not, and Owen must face them at Paramore.

Another cramming student, Owen's friend Lechmere (tenor), reveals in his comments that he understands little of the deeper issues. For him the surface excitement of the military life, the flags with which the statesmen, priests and lawyers entice the country's youth into servitude, is enough. His response to violence is more violence: "revenge."

At Paramore besides his aunt Owen faces his grandfather, General Sir Philip Wingrave (tenor), Mrs. Julian (soprano), a widow, and her daughter Kate (mezzo-soprano). Mrs. Julian's brother had been engaged to Miss Wingrave, and when he and Julian were killed in battle, the Wingraves gave the widow and her daughter a home. Mrs. Julian serves as an unofficial housekeeper at Paramore, and Kate, all have assumed, someday will marry Owen.

His reception at Paramore is frigid, and in a succession of vignettes pressure is put on him to change his mind. Finally Coyle, Mrs. Coyle and Lechmere are brought down to make a last appeal. Owen admits to Coyle that the week has been frightful. Pointing to the portraits he says, "We're tainted all. I've roused up all the old ghosts. . . . They won't let me alone."

The family and guests sit to dinner (finale, Act I) where Owen's decision—in his presence—is discussed. Each of the cast's eight characters has a moment of isolation (camera or lighting focus) in which he **dinner party** or she sings his subconscious thoughts. When Mrs. Coyle, attempting to calm the General, says "Ah, Sir Philip, Owen has his scruples," the word becomes a club with which the family beats him: "Scruples, scruples, scruples. . . ."

Provoked, Owen stands. "Yes, and more—I'd make it a crime to draw your sword for your country, and a crime for governments to command it." Sir Philip in fury rises, "There is no more to be said," and ends the dinner.

ACT II (43 min.)

The act begins with a prologue (5 min.) in which a ballad singer is heard alternately with a distant chorus and trumpet. The ballad, telling
ballad the story of the Wingrave who killed his son and himself died so mysteriously, is mimed in slow motion.

After the refrain is repeated the last time, "Trumpet blow, Paramore shall welcome woe," the scene fades to Owen and Coyle before the portrait of the Colonel and his son. "The bully and the boy," Owen calls them, "walking, walking . . . forever in each other's company," and he shows Coyle the haunted bedroom.

The family's discussion of Owen continues, and he is summoned to a final confrontation with Sir Philip. The General's words can be half-heard throughout the house, and upon emerging Owen makes no secret of them: he is disinherited. Mrs. Julian, whose financial security had rested on Kate's marriage to Owen, weeps (can a stockholder in a munition company want any war to end?). Kate, out of spite, flirts with Lechmere who, uncomprehending, responds. To Miss Wingrave Owen now is a nonperson, and only the Coyles, before going to bed, attempt a word of sympathy.

Left alone, Owen gazes at the portraits: "Now you may . . . turn your faces to the wall. . . . I was surrounded with love . . . spoiled with admiration, but all for the image they made of me. . . . In peace
peace aria I have found my image." In this, the longest solo musical passage (5 min.) of the opera, he describes peace as strong, "passionate, committing—more than war itself." Addressing the portraits, he cries triumphantly, "I am finished with you all."

But at that moment the ghosts of the old man and the boy appear, walking up the stairs to the bedroom. (And the opera moves beyond an external confrontation between pacifist and militarist to the interior struggle of man to control the violent streak with which he is born.) "Ah," cries Owen, "I'd forgotten you! . . . Tell him," he calls to the boy, "his power has gone, and I have won." The ghosts disappear into the room, and Owen sinks exhausted into a chair.

Kate comes downstairs and, calling him "coward," goads him into sleeping in the haunted room. When she suggests that he will not remain the night, he cries, "Then lock me in." They stop outside the door, and he says, "The anger of the world is locked up there, the horrible power that makes men fight: now I alone must take it on."

Later that night Lechmere rouses the Coyles. He saw Kate lock Owen in the room and is fearful. He urges Coyle to go to Owen. But they are already too late. There are terrible cries from Kate who, anxious, had returned to unlock the door: "Owen you've gone . . . gone with the old man and the boy." Everyone, even Sir Philip, is drawn to the haunted room, where Owen lies dead on the floor.

The ballad singer's voice and offstage chorus close the opera: "He did not change, nor did he yield, a soldier on the battle-field. . . . Trumpet blow, Paramore shall welcome woe!"

The opera succeeds best in medium-sized rather than large opera houses. Though using a full orchestra, Britten has scored lightly—there are many instrumental solos—in order to allow the words to be understood. On the whole the music is sparse rather than lush, and the vocal line declamatory rather than lyric. The interest lies chiefly in the music's organization, an area in which Britten has always excelled.

The source of much of the music is in the prelude that scans the ten portraits. It starts with a three-bar rhythmic figure, percussive and martial—the Wingraves and violence—that is interrupted by a short theme for Owen—three accented rising notes for brass, followed by a longer, smoother descending phrase—after which the three-bar rhythmic figure returns. Then the camera or spotlight focuses on the first picture. Each portrait is examined to a short cadenza on a different instrument, and the camera or light moves to the next portrait over the martial rhythmic figure on a solo drum. The instruments in order are: bassoon, oboe, horn, clarinet, trombone and piccolo (Colonel and boy), trumpet, woodwind, trombones, woodwind and all wind instruments (Owen's father). All the cadenzas have been uneasy and incipiently violent, and they are followed, as the camera or light shifts to Owen in the first scene, with a cadenza for him on the horn—his theme of before extended—that is vigorous and yet warm and peaceful.

DEATH IN VENICE

Opera in two acts. World premiere, Aldeburgh, June 16, 1973; American prem., Metropolitan, New York, Oct. 18, 1974. Music by Benjamin Britten; libretto by Myfanwy Piper, based on Thomas Mann's novella *Der Tod in Venedig,* 1912.

This was Britten's last opera, and though composed primarily for small theatres and using only a small orchestra, it requires a large cast of soloists, chorus and dancers. It also needs an outstanding singing-actor for the leading role (tenor) and much rehearsal, for its seventeen scenes—Act I, 7 scenes, 81 min.; Act II, 10 scenes, 64 min.—are swiftly paced and often complicated. In addition, the story is very cerebral, much of it taking place in soliloquies. For all these reasons the opera is likely to remain a work for special occasions.

Its strengths, however, are considerable, particularly its musical and dramatic organization, which are close to perfect. Chiefly because of them, even in large houses the opera can generate an extraordinary intensity.

Its story, leaving aside the fascinating question of what was gained and lost by the transformation into musical drama, proceeds simultaneously on several levels: the physical, the psychological, the artistic, the metaphysical and the mythological. These levels, of course, are not truly divisible, but for clarity's sake pretend that they are.

At its simplest, the physical, the story goes: it is the year 1911, and Gustav von Aschenbach, a distinguished German novelist living in Munich, feels out of sorts. His wife is dead, his daughter married, and he decides on a vacation in Venice. There to his surprise, to his chagrin, he finds himself falling in love with a fellow guest at his hotel, a boy. He cannot bring himself to speak to the boy, but he follows him about and, despite warnings of a cholera epidemic, stays on in the hotel. One day he eats a rotten strawberry washed in the lagoon waters and soon after dies. He and the boy have never spoken, and the boy has no interest in him.

Now, as a psychological tale: Aschenbach, a distinguished German novelist, starts for a vacation in Venice. On the way he sees an elderly fop, rouged and wrinkled, trying to associate with a group of young men. The man's antics disgust him. Later on the beach, examining his feelings for a boy who fascinates him, he recognizes in himself a homosexual streak. Though the discovery rattles him, he is too honest to deny it. Alone in the world, he gives in to his desire to be close to the boy. He dyes his hair, rouges his cheeks, becomes the man who so disgusted him. Remaining in Venice he dies.

As an allegory about artistic creation: Aschenbach, though at the height of his powers, suffers from writer's block. The words no longer come. Inspiration is lacking. He finds it in Venice in the boy's beauty, and the words again flow—until he realizes that it is not the boy's abstract beauty that inspires him but the boy's particular body. Starting with lust he allows himself to become corrupted—in order to keep the boy in the hotel he does not warn the boy's mother of the cholera—and loses the ability to write.

The same idea is expressed metaphysically in the terms of Plato's two dialogues, *Symposium* and *Phaedrus,* to which Aschenbach constantly refers. Eros or love, as Plato used the term, begins with the natural attraction exercised by a beautiful body; it then progresses, if it has found a worthy subject, to admiration for and attraction by the beauties of the mind and character. Thence it advances to the contemplation of Beauty in general, the Form of Beauty, which is imperfectly mirrored in material objects, and so to the Form of Good, of which Beauty is only one manifestation. This is the ladder of idealism which Aschenbach thought he was scaling until at the very close of Act I he blurts out at the boy's back, "I—love you," and realizes the truth. Then, in Act II when joy has dissolved in corruption, he soliloquizes in the opera's most extended aria: "Does beauty lead to wisdom, Phaedrus? Yes, but through the senses. . . . And senses lead to passion, Phaedrus, and passion to the abyss."

Lastly, the idea is expressed mythologically in a conflict between Apollo and Dionysus for Aschenbach's soul. Aschenbach's view of classical Greece opposed Apollo, representing order and clarity, to Dionysus, representing chaos and confusion. In this view Dionysus, unlike Apollo, was not native to Greece but a god whose cult, imported from the East, swept through Greece like a plague—just as the cholera has come to Venice from the East. As an artist Aschenbach considered himself a servant of Apollo, imposing form on disorder, and as he watches the boys at play on the beach, he imagines their sports to be games held in honor of Apollo. He even hears Apollo's voice: "He who loves beauty worships me. . . ." (The scene is long, 17 min., and sometimes slightly cut.) But then he recognizes his love for the boy as sensual, and in Act II he has a dream in which the voice of Dionysus demands entry into his soul. The voice of Apollo cries, "No," but when the half-naked boy appears in the dream, Aschenbach capitulates to Dionysus: "Do what you will with me."

All of these levels interlock so that Dionysus, the alien god in classical Greece, is also in part the cholera, the streak of repressed sexuality, rhapsodic rather than controlled writing, and a flawed application of Platonic idealism.

In the opera's final tableau Aschenbach sits in his chair on the beach, dying and aware of his failure as a man and an artist. Before him the boy moves to the water's edge in a series of arabesque poses reminiscent of the bronze Mercury by Giovanni da Bologna. To Aschenbach's failing vision he seems a messenger beckoning to Plato's "vast sea of beauty" where all experience is embraced and the Good finally becomes clear. Yet it is also the sea of death, he knows, to which his love of the boy's beauty has led him.

Britten cast the boy and his family, his mother and two sisters, as dancers. They never speak or sing but make their presence felt, even in a crowd, by their dancers' movements. The family is Polish and the boy's name Tadzio, short for Thaddeus. Aschenbach hears it first, however, as Adziù, a name from the East, like Dionysus. Tadzio's music, too, has an Eastern sound: bright, rhythmic and rather remote, chiefly a vibraphone over harp, gong and a variety of drums. Throughout the opera his music does not change or develop, just as he does not. He merely is.

Aschenbach's music on the other hand is constantly changing. At the opera's opening, where he describes himself in his first soliloquy, it is warm (strings), proud (trumpets) and, when he talks of his inability to write, troubled (piano, harp). As he moves through the opera, the themes and sounds become distorted, thicker and more dissonant. In the final tableau, however, against Tadzio's bright, cool sound, Aschenbach's returns to its original clarity and warmth, as if stating that death will cleanse him of corruption.

The soliloquies in which Aschenbach examines his feelings and ideas are set as recitative accompanied by piano. They are often signalled by his taking his notebook from a pocket to jot down a thought. As his detachment lessens, however, as he becomes more embroiled with his passions, his ironic observations become fewer and shorter. The piano, as the instrument of self-examination, also accompanies his final aria: "Does beauty lead to wisdom, Phaedrus?"

Beside Aschenbach the only important singing role is a Traveller (bass-baritone) who constantly reappears in guises realistic and symbolic. In Munich, as a Traveller who sings of an exotic land, he puts the idea of a trip into Aschenbach's mind. On the way to Venice he is the Elderly Fop, then an old gondolier, the hotel manager, the hotel barber, the leader of a troupe of players and the voice of Dionysus. In each guise, by ordinary actions he leads Aschenbach to death.

His opening phrase in Munich, "Marvel's unfold," D-C-E-D#, becomes a motif, usually growled on the tuba, that represents the advancing cholera. But the plague, too, is symbolic. Just before Aschenbach blurts out "I—love you" at the close of Act I, there is an orchestral outburst built on the cholera motif, suggesting that Aschenbach's emotional world already is sick.

The opera is filled with such highly organized details. In performance, before an audience that has not studied the score, most of them must be conveyed by acting. For this reason a good singing-actor for Aschenbach is absolutely necessary and a small house better than a large.

THE CRUCIBLE

An opera in four acts. World premiere, New York City Opera, New York, Oct. 26, 1961. European prem., Wiesbaden, Nov. 3, 1963. Music by Robert Ward; text by Bernard Stambler, based on the play by Arthur Miller first performed at Wilmington on Jan. 15 (New York, Jan. 22), 1953.

In his play *The Crucible,* Miller used the Salem witchcraft trials of 1692 as an allegory to probe the problems of individual conscience and guilt by association that for many persons dominated life in the United States during the McCarthy era, roughly 1948–57. At the height of that period, May 1953 to October 1954, following Senator McCarthy's unproven charges that communists had infiltrated the United States government, 6,926 "security risks" were "separated" from their government jobs. Very few of these were even charged with subversion, and not one had committed any crime or breach of duty for which he was brought to trial in a court of law.

The witchcraft trials at Salem in 1692 followed one in Boston three years earlier in which four children seized with convulsions accused an old woman of bewitching them. The woman confessed her guilt, was tried, condemned and executed, all according to established legal procedures. For still another hundred years most men, including scientists, would believe that certain phenomena were the result of witchcraft.

At Salem, children first and then adults accused each other of witchcraft and were tried before a court appointed by the Colonial Governor. The public frenzy infected the proceedings and soon nineteen persons had been hanged, two dogs executed and one man pressed to death. Then, with 150 persons awaiting trial and 200 more accused, public opinion began to right itself.

The legal issue of guilt turned on the weight to be given "spectral evidence." The alleged victims claimed that they were attacked by spirits in the likeness of some person they identified. Was the mere allegation sufficient to convict the accused? If so, once accused who could escape hanging? In Europe the best legal opinion, available in New England, held that such "spectral evidence" by itself was insufficient to convict, yet the court at Salem in its excitement required nothing more.

As public opinion beyond Salem turned against the court, thirteen Puritan ministers condemned the use of spectral evidence, and the Governor thereupon ruled against its admission. The remaining cases collapsed; the accusations were dropped and indemnities granted to the bereaved families. Four years later Samuel Sewall, one of the judges on the court and later chief justice of Massachusetts, rose in his church to make public confession, desiring "to take the blame and shame" of the mistaken court procedure at Salem.

In the transformation of *The Crucible* from play to opera, its focus on the intellectual themes of individual conscience and guilt by association inevitably blurred: words can treat such concepts more precisely than music. On the other hand, music can reinforce a drama's pace, subtly quickening the march to the climax; it can, with ensembles, more directly depict unity or conflict between characters; and with all the resources of an orchestra it can increase the pitch, color and volume with which a story is told. The chief virtues of Ward's score lie in these areas, which are essentially atmospheric and structural. The opera's tension, for example, is very well paced, constantly accelerating up to and through the court scene that closes the third act and then in the fourth, the calm after the storm, allowing the individuals to make their statements.

The opera, in four acts (110 min.), needs only a small orchestra but requires sixteen soloists, a chorus of six girls and extras. The action takes place in Salem in 1692, the first three acts in a ten-day period in the spring and the fourth, in the fall.

ACT I (31 min.)

In the Reverend Parris's house his daughter Betty lies immobile, as she has done since he caught her in the forest with his niece Abigail Williams and other girls dancing to the songs of Tituba, his Negro slave. Abigail (soprano) warns him that the townspeople are whispering of witchcraft, and he angrily demands the truth about the dancing and about her abrupt dismissal from the service of his neighbors, the Proctors.

Thomas and Ann Putnam, entering, report that their daughter Ruth also lies immobile, and they have sent to Beverly for Reverend Hale, an expert in witchcraft. Giles Corey, Rebecca and Francis Nurse enter. Rebecca, a grandmother, urges patience with adolescent girls, but old Corey is flippant about their "flying." When Putnam grows angry, Corey accuses him of starting a witch hunt in order to obtain his neighbors' land. John Proctor (baritone) enters and berates Putnam for summoning Reverend Hale without first consulting others. The argument ends with the departure of Corey and Proctor.

Those remaining start a psalm for God's help, and Betty, moaning on her bed, suddenly attempts to fly from the window. Reverend Hale (bass) arrives and questions Tituba who, under the intensity of his interrogation, breaks down and confesses witchcraft. Betty promptly recovers, and all resume the psalm with thanksgiving. Above their chorus, however, Abigail, envious of the attention given to Tituba, insists that she, too, contracted with the Devil but now has repented. "I kiss thy hand, sweet Jesus," she cries ecstatically, "take me, take me up to Thee, my God."

ACT II (27 min.)

A week later. In the kitchen of the Proctors' farmhouse he and his wife discuss the witchcraft trials. Elizabeth (mezzo-soprano) urges him to inform the court that Abigail has told him privately that the accusations are fraudulent. He is reluctant because Abigail justly can charge him with seduction and, further, he has no witness to her statement. Elizabeth sees his reluctance as evidence of a continuing interest in Abigail.

Their servant girl, Mary Warren (soprano), returns from court. She is upset by her part in the accusations, which now have led to a sentence of hanging and, she reports, to an accusation against Elizabeth Proctor. Elizabeth thinks instantly of Abigail and again urges Proctor to tell what he knows.

Reverend Hale enters with John Cheever, an official of the court, and Cheever reads Abigail's accusation against Elizabeth: attempted murder, with the Devil's assistance, by sticking a pin into the heart of a poppet (a doll).Cheever sees a poppet on the mantel with a pin in it, but under questioning Mary Warren states that the poppet is hers and that Abigail saw her make it and insert the pin. Nevertheless, because of the formal charge Elizabeth is taken to the jail for interrogation. Proctor, alone with Mary, swears that together they will tell the court the truth. Mary is afraid, and she warns Proctor that Abigail, who has told her all, will accuse him of seduction. He will be charged with lechery and his testimony disbelieved. In any event, he insists, he will tell the truth.

ACT III (26 min.)

SCENE 1 (6 min.)

Two days later. At night in the woods near Reverend Parris's house. By moonlight Abigail comes out to Proctor. She is amorous; he, preoccupied and serious. He urges an end to pretense and her accusations; she asks for love and Elizabeth's place in his life. When he refuses both, she exits, threatening, "If your sniveling Elizabeth dies—remember it is you who kill her."

SCENE 2 (20 min.)

Next morning. The courtroom at Salem. Proctor and Mary enter, resolved to tell the truth. Abigail leads in her girls, and "the crowd parts like the sea for the Chosen People."

Judge Danforth (tenor) calls the first witness, Giles Corey, who again charges Putnam with prompting the accusations in order to have the accuseds' lands forfeited and put up for sale. Putnam, he says, stated as much before others, but he refuses to name them for fear they will be the next to be accused. He is ruled in contempt of court and sentenced to "heavy persuasion" (torture by increasing weights on the body) until he reveals the names.

Proctor, offering Mary Warren's deposition on the poppet, is quickly drawn into the interrogation of her. To discredit Abigail, who pretends a seizure caused by Mary and the Devil, he reveals that Abigail is no virgin child but his former mistress dismissed by Elizabeth as a whore.

Judge Danforth promptly has Elizabeth brought from jail and, without allowing her to communicate with anyone, asks the cause of Abigail's dismissal: was it laziness? Elizabeth hesitates. Was it lechery with Proctor? After an agonized moment Elizabeth stammers, "No." She is led away, and Abigail and the girls sing that Mary Warren in the form of a yellow bird is attacking them. Mary, to save herself, joins the girls and accuses Proctor of persuading her to contract with the Devil to upset the court. Reverend Hale is disgusted, but Danforth and the spectators howl that Proctor is "the Devil's man."

ACT IV (26 min.)

Several months later; before dawn, in the town jail. Tituba and Sara Good, the first two women accused and now crazed by months of imprisonment, sing softly of the Devil.

Abigail, having bribed the warder Cheever, urges Proctor to escape with her. But he merely shakes his head and without a word shuffles back into the darkness. Tituba and Sara Good resume their song.

Danforth, Parris and Hale enter, arguing. Parris and Hale want to delay the executions. Abigail has fled, and without an accuser the cases fail. The court is now the accuser, says Danforth. If Proctor confesses, he can escape hanging.

Proctor and Elizabeth are allowed to converse. He wants to confess and live, and she, though she tries not to influence him, also wants him to live. Joyfully he announces that he will confess.

Rebecca Nurse is brought in and in Proctor's presence refuses to confess. She will not damn herself with a lie. Proctor now refuses to sign his confession: it is enough to make it privately; a public, signed confession will shame his sons for life. Told that he will be sent to the gallows, he tears up the paper and follows Rebecca Nurse. Hale pleads with Elizabeth to change Proctor's decision. She refuses: "He has found his name and his goodness now—God forbid I take it from him."

TROUBLE IN TAHITI

Opera in prologue and seven scenes (45 min.). World premiere, Brandeis University, Waltham, Massachusetts, June 12, 1952; English prem. (on BBC television), London, March 17, 1968; continental European prem., Vienna, May 22, 1969; English stage prem., London, February 17, 1970. Music and libretto by Leonard Bernstein.

PRINCIPAL CHARACTERS

Dinah, a suburban housewife in her early thirties	mezzo-soprano
Sam, her husband, same age	baritone
The Trio, a Greek Chorus born of the radio	soprano, tenor,
commerical of the early 1950s.	baritone

Place, "Any American city, and its suburbs;" Time, "Now."

With a light touch Bernstein treats a serious subject, the failure of a marriage. Sam and Dinah are losing the ability to communicate as they pursue success at its most banal, "wine in the soup, two-door sedan and convertible coupe, and a little white house in. . ." Well, any suburb of the 1950s.

The opera's title is taken from a movie Dinah sees one afternoon and which she describes in an aria to the audience, recognizing that the trouble in Tahiti is "twaddle" compared to the situation in her own life. Yet, in recounting the "terrible, awful movie," she again succumbs to its manipulations, responding more fully to its artificialities than to the realities of her home. Her aria, for musical characterization, humor and sadness, is one of Bernstein's best.

The opera has had an unusual history. Despite success at its premiere, as part of a festival at Brandeis, it was overshadowed two nights later by the even greater success of Marc Blitzstein's adaptation of Kurt Weill's *The Threepenny Opera*. The following November it had a television production, but more significantly, in the spring of 1955, a run of 48 performances on Broadway. Thereafter it played steadily in small theatres and music schools, partly because it required only five singers and an orchestra (expandable) of twenty—though all must be expert.

When in 1983 Bernstein, with Stephen Wadsworth as librettist, produced the opera *A Quiet Place,* it served as a sequel to *Trouble in Tahiti,* which was played as a prologue. Later, in a revision of *A Quiet Place,* the prologue was incorporated into Act II as a flashback. Neither way was to the earlier work's advantage.

Bernstein, in his jazzy manner, pokes fun at the Trio's radio background with its smooth, smooth style, and also at his two principals: Dinah for her response to the movie, and Sam for his fatuous self-satisfaction. But even as he mocks the couple's shallow values, he mourns their marriage, neatly balancing satire and sympathy. That balance may save the opera from dating, a frequent fate of satire; for spousal inability to communicate is a subject always timely.

The music, except for a few bars of talk in the final scene, is continuous, and each scene, owing to Bernstein's skill in shifting mood with a flick of a clarinet or stab on the double bass, fades swiftly into the next. Most scenes, as well as the arias, are organized strophically, with returning vocal and orchestral phrases, of which the most important textually are always heightened melodically. Throughout, the opera is exceptionally clear and strong in structure, melody, and rhythm.

PROLOGUE (3 min.)

The Trio, to the side of the stage, huddle around a studio microphone: "Mornin' sun kisses the windows, kisses the walls. . . of the little white house in. . . Ozone Park. Suh.bur.bee.ah!"

SCENE 1 (4 min.)

Inside the house at breakfast. Sam and Dinah's nine-year-old son has left for school, and they remain at table in silence. Argument sputters, each accusing the other of small failures. Then, in a shift of mood, each privately yearns for their lost sympathy. The Trio sings: "Mornin' sun says a good mornin': Have a good day." And Sam and Dinah return to hostility: He can't attend their son's school play, for he has the finals of his handball tournament; and she needs money to pay her analyst. Giving it to her, he leaves for the office, while she stares with hate at the money in her hand.

SCENE 2 (9 min.)

At Sam's office, on one side of the stage. With charm he dodges a request for money, and is pleased with himself; the Trio croons, "Sam you're a genius." Next he is generous to a friend needing a loan, and the Trio sings his thought, "Oh, Sam you're an angel." Fade out on the office and fade in to the other side of the stage.

SCENE 3 (8 min.)

The psychiatrist's office, with Dinah on the couch. She recalls how life had seemed a garden gone to seed until she heard a voice calling to her, offering a love that would lead her and the singer "to a quiet place." As she starts a second verse, the scene fades into Sam's office where he is asking his (invisible) secretary if he ever had made a pass at her. When she rather thinks he did, he blusters, and claims mistake; and the scene fades back to Dinah, who begins to weep as she recalls, to the melody of "love will lead us to a quiet place," that her garden vision had not come true.

SCENE 4 (6 min.)

On the street. Dinah and Sam unexpectedly meet. Each lies, pretending an engagement; then, with backs to each other, they have a long moment of introspection, both ending, "Can't we find the way back. . ." But they separate.

INTERLUDE (2 min.)

The Trio: "Lovely day. . . Lovely life. . . Oodles of culture over T-V; Book-of-the-Month Club; musical tea; It's a wonderful life!"

SCENE 5 (4 min.)

At the gym. Sam has won the handball tournament. In the locker-room, in a three-stanza aria, he sings robustly: "There's a law about men;" some never can win. Starting a second verse while taking an imaginary shower, he booms: "There's a law about men;" some will never be trim; and finally, in an excited variation of the first two, "The winner is born a winner!" Blackout.

SCENE 6 (5 min.)

Hatshop. Dinah describes to the (invisible) milliner the movie she has just seen. And though it was a lot of "escapist Technicolor twaddle," she warms to the memory of the island maiden in her sarong, and still more to "the handsome American." But a legend says that if rain falls on the wedding day, then the white man must be sacrificed. And sure enough, no sooner married than a fierce storm breaks; but the couple, oblivious to wind and rain, sing a ballad, "Island Magic," even as the natives drum for the sacrifice. At the very last moment, the U. S. navy parachutes in, a thousand strong; and all ends happily with a great Rhumba version of "Island Magic," so beguiling and melodic that onstage the Trio is lured into joining the chorus. Coming suddenly to her senses, Dinah rushes home to prepare dinner.

SCENE 7 (8 min.)

The little white house. Twilight. Sam doesn't want to go in, but recognizes "There's a law." A man has to pay for what he gets in life.

The Trio softly sings: "Evenin' shadows. . . the odor of cooking." And lights reveal Dinah and Sam before the fire with their after-dinner coffee. She knits, he reads; they are bored and tense.

They try to talk of their troubles, but fail. The Trio soothingly sings of "sharing, smiling, confiding, loving." And Sam and Dinah try again. In desperation he suggests a movie, one just opened, something about Tahiti. And she goes to get her hat.

When she returns they have a closing duet of introspection in which each privately longs to return to the quiet place. But neither knows how to go, or if an answer can be found there. Meanwhile, there is the other magic of "the Super Silver Screen," and as they go out slowly, the Trio intones: "Island Magic."

SUSANNAH

Musical drama in two acts. World premiere, Tallahassee, Florida, Feb. 24, 1955. European prem., by New York City Opera, Brussels, June 24, 1958. British premiere, London, July 27, 1961. Music and text by Carlisle Floyd; the story tangentially related to that told in the Apocryphal Book of Susanna.

PRINCIPAL CHARACTERS

Susannah Polk, "goin' on nineteen"	soprano
Sam Polk, her brother, "in his thirties"	tenor
Olin Blitch, an evangelist	bass-baritone
Little Bat McLean	tenor
Four Church Elders and their wives	

The action takes place in New Hope Valley, Tennessee, in "the present."

From the time of its New York City premiere, September 27, 1956, in the United States *Susannah* has been one of the most frequently performed of contemporary operas. Its story of mountain valley intolerance is very direct and its music, though not using folk material, is perfectly attuned. Few operas match so perfectly story, diction and music.

In the synopsis descriptions of place and character in quotation marks are taken from the vocal score prepared by Floyd.

ACT I (42 min.)

"OPENING MUSIC" (3 min.)

A prelude of three parts: raw, jagged chords suggesting conflict (Act I, Scene 3, the Elders discover Susannah bathing in the creek), a lyric, broad lament implying tragedy (Act II, Scene 3, Susannah's aria, "Come back O summer"), and a coda of dying phrases leading into:

SCENE I (8 min.)

Mid-July. The Monday night square dance in the yard of New Hope Church. Early evening; oil lamps in the trees. Susannah, prettier than the other girls, her eyes bright with dancing, is the center of attention though unaware of it.

The Elders' wives discuss the hot weather and the new preacher, **square dance**   Olin Blitch, expected in the morning. When even their husbands are attracted to Susannah, the wives, lead by Mrs. McLean, disapprove of her pretty face, dress and manner. But what can you expect, says Mrs. McLean, of a girl raised by a drunken brother.

A stranger enters, "a tall, powerfully built man in a plaid shirt and a ten-gallon hat." The dancing stops. He is Olin Blitch, and he promises powerful preaching to save the lost. "Immediately assuming the role of moral arbiter for the community," he urges the dancers to continue. His eye is caught by Susannah, and Mrs. McLean describes the Polks to him: "Susannah and Sam is evil, I say." "I'll pray for her soul tonight," says Blitch. Joining the dancers, he works his way to her square.

SCENE 2 (13 min.)

Later the same evening. The yard and porch of the Polk farmhouse. Susannah enters followed by Little Bat, the McLean's son. He is "a shifty-eyed youth, not too strong mentally." He "worships" Susannah but glances about furtively, afraid of her brother.

She assures him that Sam never hurt anyone. Looking up into the **aria**   sky she sings, "Ain't it a pretty night!" At the end of her "aria" Sam enters. He is "the uncomprehended poet and recluse . . . gentle by nature and tragically passive, until the one thing of beauty left in his life is attacked." At the sight of him Little Bat runs off, while Susannah starts chattering about the dance. She requests the "Jay-bird" song, and she and Sam sing it together, ending in a hop-skip around the yard. Laughing and out of breath, they sit on the porch step and sigh **song**   together, "Ain't it a pretty night."

SCENE 3 (4 min.)

Following morning. The woods close to the Polk farm. Offstage Susannah's voice humming the "Jay-bird" song.

The four elders enter looking for a creek with a pool suitable for baptisms. Suddenly they see it and in it Susannah bathing, naked. They freeze, their faces registering shock, then lust and finally outrage.

Slowly they back off chanting, "She must be brought to repentance, All the valley must be told." The sound of her voice follows them off.

SCENE 4 (5 min.)

Evening. Same day. Picnic supper at the church, to which every family has contributed a dish of food. Yet the atmosphere is "hushed and foreboding."

The wives comment smugly on Susannah's wickedness, and one Elder, quoting Blitch, says, "She's gotta make a public confession or out o' the church she goes." "An' out'n the valley, too, maybe," says another.

Susannah enters quietly, carrying a covered dish. "Field peas," she says. "I picked an shelled 'em this evenin' an cooked 'em jest a bit ago."

"Susannah," says Elder McLean, "you ain't welcome here." Gradually she realizes that no one will speak to her. Backing away, she puts her hand to her mouth, and runs. Mrs. McLean says, "I wouldn't tech them peas o' her'n."

SCENE 5 (9 min.)

A half-hour later. At the Polk farm. Susannah is seated on the porch step, her head in her hands. Little Bat creeps in. Hearing him, she rises. "I had to come to tell y'," he says, and she asks, "What have I done?" In a tone "with certain mysterious relish" he describes the Elders discovering her in the pool. She interrupts: she has done no wrong; they were wrong "to come a-spyin'." Little Bat goes on to say that the valley has been told and, watching her carefully, "They's more what you don't know."

Susannah "looks at him squarely," and he cowers, his demeanor beginning to suggest duplicity and guilt. He moves away from her, and she stalks him. Terror covers his face. Susannah continues to move toward him, and then Little Bat breaks, screaming and wringing his hands. In hysterical tones he insists that they made him say it. When she shakes him—"Tell me! Tell me!"—he confesses "with an almost luxurious abandon" that he told them that she had let him love her up in the worst sort of way. "It's a lie," she protests (the orchestra swells with phrases that will reappear in her lament), and he agrees. But he was scared. "Git out," she screams. "Don't never come back." And he runs off, blubbering.

Susannah turns, and her brother Sam is on the porch. He has over-heard Little Bat's story. Running to him, she looks intently in his face and asks, "What's it all about, Sam?"

Gently he replies: "About the way people is made, I reckon, an how they like to believe what's bad." She asks what to do, and he says, "nothin'." Time alone will tell. "Meantime, there'll be a lotta bad things. They'll turn this valley into hell." Susannah waits for some-thing more, for something helpful, then begins to weep. Suddenly with desperate intensity she says, "Sing me the 'Jay-bird' song."

ACT II (51 min.)

SCENE 1 (9 min.)

Friday morning, four days later. At the Polk farm. Susannah sits on the porch step, staring straight ahead; behind her Sam leans against the post, watching her sadly. The scene should establish "an atmosphere of static helplessness."

Without turning Susannah asks, "How long's it gonna last, Sam?" He does not know: so long as the people want a public confession. But there's nothing to confess, she cries. He agrees, and she wonders if per-haps she is full of sin. She shudders to think of the dirty gestures the men now make at her. "What have I done to deserve it?" Sam can say only, "We gotta have faith."

After a pause he says: the new preacher must be powerful, for a lot of people are getting baptized. In the store, says Susannah, the preacher spoke to her kindly and wanted her to come to the meeting tonight. To her distress Sam urges her to go. She should show that she's not afraid, and he has to be away overnight tending his traps. She'd be safer at the church than alone for so long at the farm, though he will leave her a gun. Reluctantly she agrees to go. At the scene's end she is staring again before her, and he is watching her sadly.

SCENE 2 (11 min.)

Evening. Same day. Interior of the New Hope Church. The meeting. Susannah sits alone on the last bench, a small, huddled figure. The collection is being taken. "The scene in no way should be a parody but, instead, at all times should aim at projecting the tension, effrontery and, above all, the terror implicit in the revival meeting of this nature."

The people sing, "Are you saved from sin, ready to meet your Lord?
gospel hymn   Has His blood made you free from the avenging
sword?" Blitch, shouting above their voices, urges them, "Dig deep,
brethren. . . . Rember the widder's mite." Accepting the collection he
prays before his sermon: "Send down the tongue of fire upon the heads
of the damned till they won't find no peace 'cept in Thy cleansin'
blood." Amen, say the Elders.

Blitch begins his sermon "half spoken, half sung, gradually using
more vibrato, working into a full singing voice." He tells a story about
sermon   a man who was good but not "saved" and so he died
"scared to death an' his soul went to eternal fire." And many more will
join him unless they come forward now. "Tomorrow might be too
late."

Blitch nods to the choir, which begins a quiet hymn, "Come, sinner,
tonight's the night." Above the voices he calls for sinners to come
forward. "Immediately after the 'call,' one or two boys and girls in
the "call"   their early teens shyly, with terrified eyes, leave their
seats and trance-like walk down the aisle and kneel at the altar." Blitch
lays his hands on their heads, throws back his own, and with closed
eyes, speaks with the Almighty.

After a number have gone up to him, "the exodus to the altar
ceases," and with a wave he stops the choir. "There's one in our midst
tonight who pays no mind to the wooin' o' God in her heart." The
congregation as one body turns to stare at Susannah.

The choir resumes "Come, sinner" as Blitch concentrates his attention on her. "Slowly into his eyes and face comes an expression of intense desire bordering on lust." His voice, reflecting his feelings,
becomes cajoling. Susannah stares at him, transfixed. Slowly she rises,
moves into the aisle and starts forward, her face expressing fear, bewil-
derment and protest. As she stops before him, he smiles triumphantly,
and the spell for her is broken. Screaming "no, no," she rushes from
the church. Blitch, recovering quickly, delivers the benediction.

SCENE 3 (13 min.)

An hour later. At the Polk Farm.

Susannah sings a mountain lover's lament: "Come back, O summer,
aria   come back, blue flame. My heart wants warmin', my baby a
name. Come back, O lover, if jes' fer a day. Turn bleak December once
more into May."

From the darkness a voice compliments her singing. It is Blitch. He has come to talk about her soul. "The Lord would 'a told me," she says, "if I'd done somethin' wrong." She accuses the Elders of making up tales and Little Bat of lying. Blitch is impressed, but as Susannah continues describing the loneliness and misery of the week, he insists it is the sin in her heart. "It ain't! It ain't," she cries, her body wracked with sobs.

Blitch "obviously fighting himself" approaches her and puts his hand on her shoulder. She is too inert and spent to react, and the rest of the scene is "weighted with exhaustion and defeat." He speaks quietly of his own loneliness and on discovering that her brother is away leads her into the house.

SCENE 4 (8 min.)

Next morning. Saturday. Interior of New Hope Church. Blitch is praying, stripped of his bravado and evangelical trappings: "a man terrified by his own image of God."

He begs forgiveness of his sin against God and Susannah: "Return, O Lord . . . and let this cup, if it be Thy will, pass from me."

The Elders and their wives enter; also Susannah, who sits unobtrusively at the back. He has called them, Blitch explains, to right a wrong. We have been in error, and Susanah is innocent. He and the Elders should ask her pardon. Elder McLean asks, "How you know she's innocent?" And Blitch without hesitation says that the Lord spoke to him in prayer. "The devil works in queer ways," says Mrs. McLean, and she and the others leave the church, saying that they'll see Blitch at the baptism.

Alone with Susannah, he pleads, "I tried." "Yeah," she says, "I heard y'." When he promises to make it up to her, she asks flatly, "How?" As she starts out, he calls after her, "Please try an' fergive me." She turns: "Fergive? I've forgot what that word means." In anguish Blitch falls to his knees, "O Lord, if it be Thy will, let this cup pass from me."

SCENE 5 (10 min.)

Evening. Same day. At the Polk farm. Susannah stands stiffly by a porch post. The curtain rises to her lament, now played by the orchestra in rigid tempo and without expression, reflecting the change that has been working within her throughout the day.

Sam enters and quickly senses that something is wrong. "Everything! That's what!" she answers him angrily. Her voice charged with fury she describes how she went to meeting "like you asked me to" and how Blitch followed her home and took her in the house. "Why? Why? 'Cause I was tired!" When Sam explodes: "The bastard!" She says harshly "An' where was you, Sam? Where was you?" Sam thinks of Blitch, "the hypocrite," even now baptizing people in the creek. "I'll kill him," he cries wildly. "That'd do a lot of good," says Susannah, entering the house to prepare supper.

From the distance comes the sound of the choir singing "Come, sinner," and Sam takes down his gun and disappears in the direction of the pool. From inside Susannah calls him to supper. Coming out to find him, she realizes what is going to happen, hears the shot and falls to her knees, sobbing, "Lord, I never meant to do it."

Little Bat runs in shrieking that Sam has killed the preacher. After the shot everyone saw him run from the bushes. And now the people are going "to get" Susannah, because they say she put Sam up to it. In the distance voices merge in a chant, "Git out'n the valley, Susannah. Git out! Git out tonight!" A mob led by the Elders marches onstage, and their voices are deafening.

The Elders charge her with the death of the preacher, her friend. Susannah begins to laugh, and the people move toward her. "Git out," she cries. "You cain't run me off my place." They hesitate, then advance again. Rushing into the house, Susannah gets a gun and faces them down. After they leave, she sees Little Bat lingering behind.

Putting down the gun she calls sweetly to him, "Come an' love me up some. Come on. Don't be afraid." Tentatively he reaches out, puts an arm behind her—and she slaps him viciously across the face. As he runs off, wailing, she bursts out laughing.

"When he is gone, her strident laughter vanishes as quickly as it began. She turns around, straightens her body in the doorway and remains standing there, an inviolably strong and inexorably lonely prisoner of self-imposed exile."

DER JUNGE LORD
(The Young Lord)

Comic opera in two acts, six scenes. World premiere, Berlin, April 7, 1965; American prem. (in English), San Diego, February 13, 1967; British prem., London, October 14, 1969. Music by Hans Werner Henze; libretto by Ingeborg Bachmann from a fable "Der Affe als Menshe" ("The Monkey as a Man") in Wilhelm Hauff's *Der Scheik von Alexandrien und seine Sklaven (the Sheik of Alexandria and His Slaves)*, published in 1827.

PRINCIPAL CHARACTERS

Sir Edgar	mute
His secretary	baritone
Lord Barrat, his nephew	high tenor
Begonia, his Jamaican cook	mezzo-soprano
Baroness Flora Grunwiesel (Greenweasel)	mezzo-soprano
Luise, her niece and ward	soprano
Ida, Luise's friend	light soprano
Wilhelm, a student, who loves Luise	lyric tenor

The action takes place in the small, picturesque town of Hüldsdorf-Gotha in 1830.

Though entitled a comedy, the opera frolics only on the surface; beneath is a dark joke of universal application, a cold, cerebral examination of human nastiness. Depending greatly on how it is staged, the opera can be a playful satire, a parody with some disturbing ideas, or a vision of humanity so profoundly unattractive that many persons would rather not see it. Henze and his librettist deliberately have kept the point of view uncertain.

ACT I (59 min.)

SCENE 1 (The Town Square—20 min.)

The town eagerly awaits the arrival of an English Lord, said to be very grand and rich, who has rented the large house on the square. The ladies and gentlemen of the town, the bourgeoisie, promenade around the square, the common people stand about in groups, and to one side the schoolmaster tries to keep his children's chorus in order. To the front, the mayor, the magistrate, the comptroller, and the town's leading professor fuss over the mayor's speech: should he address the Lord as Sir Edgar? Can the familiar first name be proper?

While promenading with Baroness Grunwiesel, Luise and her friend Ida move sufficiently ahead to be able to talk of Wilhelm, the student whom Luise loves. He stands by himself, gazing at her, and she feels ready "to die." The schoolmaster rehearses the children in their cantata of welcome, but soon they are drowned out by a military band that arrives with brasses blaring. Then suddenly there is the clop-clop of horses' hooves. In the stir of excitement and craning of necks Luise and Wilhelm exchange a few words.

A carriage draws up, its door opens and a goat clambers out. The mayor in his astonishment drops his speech. More pet animals and two grooms emerge. The adults are flabbergasted; the children, delighted. A second carriage draws up. Expectations rise again, only to fall as a servant, a Turk, steps out, followed by two more grooms, a British butler and a Creole cook, Begonia. She takes command, issuing orders.

A third carriage draws up, and plainly from the servants' demeanor it contains Sir Edgar. The Turk opens the door, and a man of about thirty-five descends. The mayor begins his speech, but the man turns his back to him in order to help from the carriage an elderly man of about sixty. The ladies of the town display their French: "Quelle dignité! Quelle élégance!" The schoolmaster struggles to get the children started in their chorus, and the military band bursts into a march (from Mozart's *Abduction from the Seraglio*). The mayor, signaling for silence, begins: "We are honored. . . ."

The younger man, Sir Edgar's secretary, interrupts firmly: Sir Edgar appreciates the charming welcome but is tired from the journey and wishes to retire. When the mayor attempts to say more, he is again cut off by the secretary while Sir Edgar smiles wanly.

Rain begins to fall, and umbrellas go up. The commotion ends the town's greeting. Sir Edgar's entourage sweeps him into the house, leaving the mayor to mutter to his colleagues, "He didn't bother to say one word!" "To me," says the magistrate, "this is an affront!" (dieses ist ein Affront).

INTERLUDE (2 min.)

SCENE 2 (The Baroness's Drawing-room—17 min.)

The Baroness is receiving the ladies of the town, among whom are her best friends Frau von Hoofnail and Frau Harethrasher. The only man present is Monsieur La Truiaire (mute), the music, dancing and deportment instructor. As the scene opens Luise is at the piano, and he is turning the pages. Finally, after a few stumbles she finishes the *romanza* and rises with becoming modesty. The Baroness kisses her approvingly on the brow, and the ladies decorously applaud. (Notice how smoothly Henze passes from piano recital to opera. He gives the scene, in which no man's voice is heard, a special "salon" quality partly by scoring prominently for piano, high strings, celesta and harp.)

The Baroness speaks proudly of Luise. Sir Edgar, when he arrives, cannot help but be impressed by her. Luise gasps her disbelief: he is so learned and so old. The Baroness ignores her. Sir Edgar, of course, will wish to talk on intellectual subjects, and she has ready a new book from Paris. The ladies chatter complacently. Their circle is so refined: they were the first in town to know when to serve punch or champagne, how to sip tea without a sound and how to eat asparagus.

Amid reproving glances a parlormaid runs into the room. Sir Edgar's servant, the Turk . . . she is all aflutter. The Baroness chides such foolishness and orders the Turk shown in. He hands her a note. Sir Edgar, she reads, regrets that. . . . Almost fainting she gasps, "it is an affront" (das ist ein Affront!). The Turk, bowing, departs, and the ladies flock to the Baroness with smelling salts.

But the Baroness, scorned, erupts with rage. Who is this man who dares to remain always at home and to receive no one? What evil has he done that he must hide so continually in his house? The ladies are beginning to support her indignation when Ida, feigning innocence and with girlish coloratura, reminds them that he came with a letter of introduction from Prince Henry (Prinz Heinrich). For a moment the ladies hesitate: Prince Henry. . . . But the Baroness rallies them with a sneering reference to Sir Edgar's "stinking" Turk. Triumphantly she concludes that Sir Edgar is no lord at all: the man is an impostor! (dieser Mensch ist unmöglich). Though Ida and Luise think it unlikely, the ladies are convinced.

INTERLUDE (3 min.)

SCENE 3 (The Town Square—17 min.)

A small travelling circus is performing in the square. There is a fire-eater, a dancing ape, a lady tightrope walker and a juggler. When the last act is finished, the leader Amintore La Rocca (tenor), a Neapolitan, presents the artists for their bows, and the spectators applaud.

The doors of Sir Edgar's house open, and surrounded by his secretary, butler and Turk, he comes out to watch the show. The common people are pleased; the bourgeoisie, not. They mutter that he never comes out to go to church or to pay a call, only to watch a tightrope dancer. When he gives a child a sweet, the child's father confiscates it and slaps the child. The children, who are prepared to like the strangers, are confused.

The mayor and his colleagues approach Sir Edgar to make conversation but are dismissed by the secretary, their proffered hands unshaken. Sir Edgar wants only to see the show. When the performers pass their hats, the townspeople drift off as if they had not been watching. Sir Edgar, however, gives each performer a purse. In gratitude they repeat the finale.

The mayor now announces that in as much as the circus has no license, it must leave the town—at once. The tightrope walker bursts into tears. Through his secretary Sir Edgar, much to the approval of the common people, offers to buy the license. When the mayor starts to find objections, Sir Edgar invites the troupe with its animals to shelter in his house. All go in. The common people are favorably impressed; the bourgeoisie, not. They complain that Sir Edgar is arrogant and prefers mountebanks to solid burghers. With slaps they warn the children against him.

The square clears and for a long moment is empty. Twilight spreads, and to an accompaniment of sinister drumming two men sneak in. Stealthily they paint the word SHAME (Schande) on Sir Edgar's house, and sneak out.

ACT II (78 min.)

SCENE 1 (The Town Square—24 min.)

A winter evening. Fresh snow has turned the square into a fairyland. The Turk enters with a load of parcels. Suddenly he is surrounded by children pelting him with snowballs. "Unreasonably frightened," he rushes furiously at the children, trips, and getting up flees into the house.

A lamplighter enters. While he is at work, there issue from the house "frightful screams, horrible, inhuman, and then a more articulated but strange sort of singing." The lamplighter, alarmed, goes off for help. (By this point the stage director should be making clear to the audience what line he is taking with the opera. How viciously do the children pelt the Turk? How painful are the screams? Is Sir Edgar, who refuses the normal courtesies to the townspeople and who uses his servants as bodyguards, a genial eccentric or a thug?)

Wilhelm enters and waits under a tree for Luise. She comes, and during their love duet (8 min.) there are more screams from the house, but the lovers are too engrossed to notice. Finally a scream more terrible than others penetrates to Luise, and with a shudder she suggests, "it is cold." They walk away.

The lamplighter returns with the four city fathers, and townspeople drawn by the screams gather before the house. More screams, and the mayor, urged by the others, knocks on Sir Edgar's door. It opens, revealing the Turk, the butler and the secretary. On the mayor's demand to see Sir Edgar, they smile faintly and step aside. Sir Edgar appears with a whip in hand.

The mayor asks for an explanation, and the secretary answers. Sir Edgar's nephew, the young Lord Barrat, recently came from London and is learning German from Sir Edgar in order to be able to speak to the townspeople in their own language. The townspeople express their pleasure. German is not an easy language, observes the secretary, and beatings sometimes are necessary. A good sharp rap, says the town magistrate, never hurt anyone; the language is difficult but culturally very rich, says the pedagogue; and the mayor asks Sir Edgar's pardon. The secretary adds that when Lord Barrat has mastered some passages from the best German writers, then Sir Edgar will hold a reception to introduce him to the ladies of the town. The townspeople are delighted and with expressions of goodwill withdraw. Sir Edgar watches them go, smiling faintly. (The scene is the longest and most static in the opera. When combined with the long interlude that follows and the static opening of the next scene, it may be a miscalculation theatrically, for within the sequence the audience's attention often flags.)

INTERLUDE (6 min.)

SCENE 2 (Sir Edgar's house—23 min.)

The servants are preparing for the reception. Begonia brings in a large plate of cookies and in an aria chatters about her recipe. The secretary jokes with her.

Led by the Baroness, the ladies and gentlemen of the town arrive. The young ladies are eager to meet Lord Barrat. He enters with Sir Edgar and is dressed in the latest Paris fashion, with spectacles, gloves and a flamboyantly cut suit. Beside him the young men of the town look provincial. The baroness declares herself charmed—what chic! What elegance!—and tells Luise to offer him a cup of tea. When Luise brings him one, he drains it in a gulp and tosses the cup and saucer over his shoulder. For a moment everyone is aghast. Then Lord Barrat kisses the hands of the Baroness and Luise, and the tension resolves. Hesitantly at first, the other young men fling their cups over their shoulders. When Lord Barrat, whose conversational German extends only to a few quotations, snatches the Baroness's fan, the other ladies rush to have their fans taken.

Only Wilhelm is not impressed. The secretary leads him to Sir Edgar, who tries to interest him in some rare books. But Wilhelm's eye is on Luise, and when he sees Lord Barrat fingering her shawl, he goes to her and cries angrily, "That's enough from this presumptuous person!" Luise bursts into tears, and Sir Edgar, signaling his secretary, collects Lord Barrat and withdraws, bowing on all sides.

Luise faints, and the Baroness urges Wilhelm to depart at once. The other girls follow Luise's example, and the young men hurry to their aid. Wilhelm leaves angrily: "Have you lost your senses?" (Some stage directors make the opposition between Wilhelm and Lord Barrat very direct: reason versus unreason.)

INTERLUDE (3 min.)

SCENE 3 (Ballroom in the Town's Casino—22 min.)

The doors open into side rooms, where guests are assembling. In the ballroom footmen light the candles, and Luise enters alone. (The scene, which not only ends but summarizes the opera, begins with a recitative and aria [8 min.] for Luise and progresses through a duet, trio and quintet to the extended ensemble of the ball. The somber tone, despite the attempted gaiety, appears at the start of Luise's aria. In the six bars before the aria begins a six-note passacaglia theme is stated. It then is repeated twenty-eight times before leading into the dances, waltz and polka, which end in a rout.)

Luise, alone, tries to sort her feelings for Wilhelm and Lord Barrat. She cannot, and yet she realizes that tonight she must decide.

Lord Barrat enters and gives her a rose. Taking it back, he scratches her hand with the stem, drawing a few drops of blood. They converse but at cross-purposes, for his German still is restricted to aphorisms and social phrases.

Wilhelm enters, angry and loving, but Luise in her confusion will not leave Lord Barrat. The Baroness comes in, delighted to see Luise and Lord Barrat together, and attempts with a gesture to drive Wilhelm away. Ida and other guests enter. Wilhelm worries about talk of a betrothal to be announced, Ida tries to comfort him, the Baroness is sure that the betrothal will take place, Luise is resigned to it, and Lord Barrat repeats his phrases.

The guests gather for the dance, and most of the young men are wearing glasses, gloves and Parisian-cut trousers. A waltz begins. After a few bars Lord Barrat begins to behave oddly, and the young people try to imitate his steps and actions. Soon they are drinking out of bottles, eating with their gloves on, licking their lips and wiping their mouths on the back of their hands. Lord Barrat, abandoning Luise, snatches a trumpet (from the onstage band) and blows wild dissonances.

The secretary says soothingly, "Youth will behave badly," and the older people echo him. Lord Barrat hits the trumpeter on the head with the trumpet, and the Baroness suggests that he is in a trance with happiness. It is time for Sir Edgar to announce the betrothal.

Lord Barrat dances faster and faster, until Luise calls out that she cannot go on. He must have pity. But he only increases his pace until finally, dropping her to the floor, he runs around the room alone, upsetting tables, knocking over candles and colliding with everyone. The ladies scream.

In the semidark the servants right the chairs and relight the candles. Sir Edgar, whip in hand, approaches Lord Barrat, who tears off his glasses, gloves, wig, coat and shirt, and lo! he is the dancing ape from La Rocca's circus.

At a sign from Sir Edgar he leaves the room and is followed out by Sir Edgar surrounded by the Turk, the secretary, and the butler.

Wilhelm runs to Luise: "You've been dreaming, a terrifying dream." "Ah, no," she says, embracing him, "I have not been dreaming." The others gasp, "An ape! An ape!" (Der Affe). As they contemplate where their foolishness has led them, the curtain descends. (Is the opera perhaps an allegory of how middle-class Germans in the 1930s came to accept Hitler? An attack on middle-class values in general? Sometime within the five years following the opera's premiere, Henze became a Marxist and in an interview announced, "I feel opera is finished. Of course, the basic idea of putting drama to music is not finished. . . ." But apparently opera as commonly understood was a manifestation of middle-class values and therefore doomed.)

THE BASSARIDS

Opera seria in one act. World premiere (in Ger. trans.), Salzburg, Aug. 6, 1966; American prem. (in Eng.), Santa Fe, Aug. 7, 1968; British prem. (radio), Sept. 22, 1968, (stage), Oct. 10, 1974. Music by Hans Werner Henze; libretto by W. H. Auden and Chester Kallman, based on *the Bacchae* of Euripides

PRINCIPAL CHARACTERS

Cadmus, Founder and retired King of Thebes	baritone
[Semele, his deceased daughter, and mother, by Zeus, of Dionysus. Semele died before giving birth, but the child was saved by Zeus.]	
Autonoe, daughter of Cadmus, unmarried	soprano
Agave, daughter of Cadmus, widow of Eichon, and mother of Pentheus.	soprano
Pentheus, present King of Thebes	baritone

Dionysus, (also Voice and Stranger), son of
  Zeus and Semele, the new God.   tenor
Tiresias, a blind seer.   tenor
Beroe, nurse to Semele and later to Pentheus   alto
Captain of the Guard   bass

People of Thebes; "Maenads," also known as "Bacchae," a chorus of women who worship Dionysus; "Bassarids," a chorus of men and women who worship Dionysus. ["Sown Men." Cadmus, in founding Thebes, killed a dragon, and on a God's advice sowed its teeth, which flowered into armed men. He threw a stone among them, and they fought until only five survived, establishing the noble families of Thebes. Agave's husband, Eichon, was a "Sown Man," and in the opera there are occasional references to these heroes.]

The action takes place in legendary times in the courtyard of the Royal Palace at Thebes and on Mount Kithairon.

The opera, which runs just short of two hours without break, builds steadily to a climax, with much the same power as Richard Strauss' one-act *Elecktra*. And just as with that opera one need not be familiar with the underlying Sophoclean play, so here one need not know *the Bacchae* of Euripides. Auden and Kallman, using the play as a base, built from it their own, rather different drama.

The people of Thebes are disturbed by the growing cult of a new God, Dionysus, coming from Asia with rites said to be ecstatic and liberating. Many Thebans already believe, and to honor Semele and her immortal son, keep a flame burning on her tomb. Others, hearing reports of rites that lead to singing, dancing, and more orgiastic mysteries, oppose the introduction of the new cult.

Cadmus, the old king, grown fearful and unsure, could not settle his mind about Semele's lost child. If his grandson is a God, then to deny him worship is to court a God's vengeance. But if he is not, to permit worship is to irritate the true Gods, who will retaliate. Unable to decide, Cadmus abdicated in favor of his other grandson Pentheus, who for the week since has been immured in the palace, thinking.

Pentheus rules against Godhead for his cousin, and as his first act of kingship has his Captain of the Guard read a proclamation forbidding belief that Semele had a son by Zeus. Emerging from the palace, Pentheus himself extinguishes the altar-flame on his aunt's tomb. Cadmus is horrified, but Pentheus' mother Agave and his aunt, Autonoe, approve: Of course Semele claimed her lover was a God!

From offstage a sensuous Voice calls people to Mount Kithairon to dance and discover new delights. Agave and her sister are first fascinated and then entranced by the voice, and with half the city dance away to the mountain.

Pentheus orders his Captain of the Guard to take a troop and arrest the people on Mount Kithairon, even his mother Agave. While the guard gathers, Cadmus urges his grandson to take care; offended Gods will punish. But Pentheus is scornful. The true God does not punish; Cadmus as King encouraged worship of superstitions, not Truth. As Cadmus retreats to the palace, Pentheus sends off the guard: "Return with all you can find, and kill those who resist."

Alone with his nurse Beroe, he confides to her his inmost thoughts: God is one, not many; without gender or appearance; statues are only misleading shadows of an invisible ideal, the Good. Pentheus is a pre-Platonist, which his people are not. He will allow them, he tells Beroe, to worship the old Gods until they can learn about the Good; but he will not permit them to introduce into the city the worship of the Ungood. Offstage Bassarids sing of Dionysus, and Pentheus angrily equates the God with license to do "the forbidden, shameless thing." From this moment, Pentheus swears, he will live without wine, meat, and women. He, who had been a seeker after truth, exalting reason, is now so sure of knowing truth he will impose it by force on others.

The guard returns, and its Captain reports. Though they heard singing all around them, they could capture only Agave, Autonoe, Tireseas (who blindly follows any new trend), a young Stranger (Dionysus), and a few male Bassarids. All except the Stranger appear to be in a trance. Pentheus questions his mother about the mountain, "What did you see there?" But she replies incoherently, while the Bassarid prisoners, much to Pentheus' irritation, hum contentedly. He sends his mother and aunt into the palace, and contemptuously dismisses Tiresias, ordering as the seer's punishment that his house be razed. He then turns to the Stranger, brushing aside Beroe who, having recognized the young man as Semele's child by Zeus, tries to warn Pentheus that he is dealing with a God. The Stranger, asked about Dionysus, tells of his delight in worshiping Dionysus and predicts Pentheus, too, will soon follow the God.

Pentheus explodes: "Lies, lies!" and orders the Captain to take the man away: "Lay whips to his pampered flesh. Out of my sight. Anathema!"

Darkness falls, the earth quakes, and on Semele's tomb the altar-flame leaps up. Statues fall, prison walls crack, the imprisoned Bassarids escape to the hills, and before Pentheus suddenly appears the Stranger. To the King's question, "Who set you free?", he replies, "Dionysus." He talks insinuatingly of the God's mysteries and advises that if Pentheus will look in Agave's mirror, he will see them. [An Intermezzo (see below) originally followed here, displaying onstage the vulgar decadence that Pentheus imagines.] Intrigued, he resolves to see the mysteries for himself, but the Stranger warns that believers will kill him. He must go disguised as a woman, and Pentheus, at first resisting, but already half entranced, finally agrees, because: "I would see." While he is in the palace, putting on his mother's dress, Beroe pleads for his life: "Spare him, Dionysus." But the God is implacable; and soon he leads the disguised Pentheus out of Thebes.

On the mountain he hides him in a pine tree, and then calls on his Maenads, the women's chorus, which includes Agave and Autonoe, to hunt down the intruder, to kill the non-believer. The women, worked into a frenzy, and with Agave in the lead, find Pentheus and tear him to pieces.

Dionysus leads his worshipers back to Thebes, Agave cradling what she thinks is the head of a lion cub in her arms. Slowly Cadmus talks her out of her trance and makes her recognize what she has done. Autonoe, meanwhile, bleats that she was not responsible: Agave, the stronger-willed, "clawed first." But when Autonoe tries to hide herself among the women of Thebes, they refuse to shield her. The guard carries in a bier, and the Captain reports that they have gathered as much of Pentheus as they could find. Agave, still holding his head, totters and sinks on the palace steps, while Beroe, gently taking the head from her, places it on the bier. Agave, accepting responsibility for her act, stands, looks on her son's corpse, and gives orders for his funeral.

Dionysus leaps on Semele's tomb: "I am Dionysus. Had all shown wisdom and acknowledged my Godhead, Thebes would now be happy. But some failed. . ." He banishes Cadmus, Agave, and Autonoe to separate exiles, with Beroe voluntarily joining Agave. Then he orders the royal palace burned.

As Agave departs, she turns to the God, and through him speaks to all on Olympus: "Rape, torture and kill while you can: one Tartarus [place of punishment] waits for you all."

Ignoring her, Dionysus calls to his followers; "Down slaves, Kneel and adore." And in a closing chorus, as he disappears though his Voice remains, rising above theirs, the Bassarids sing, "We kneel and adore!"

Auden and Kallman were quite clear on what they did not want for their drama: "That Gluck-y Greekiness which permits itself to be staged by combining the Modern Dance with the side-views of a Grecian Urn." They imagined a setting of universal time, with costumes from different periods. Pentheus would be a medieval ascetic; Agave, a French Second Empire sensual sceptick; Tiresias, a Victorian clergyman, and Cadmus, clothed as one who had known the legendary Gods. Thus could the drama "escape further from the neo-Classical plaster-casts."

In addition, they and Henze included an Intermezzo, *The Judgement of Calliope,* in the scene where the Stranger entrances Pentheus. As the King gazes in a mirror, behind him plays out what he sees: Olympian Gods in a vulgar frolic, with Agave and Autonoe, in "Marie Antoinette" shepherdess costumes, sporting lewdly with the Captain of the Guard. Pentheus sees what he expects to see and subconsciously perhaps would like to share. But in the opera's revised version (1992) the Intermezzo was dropped, and is now usually omitted, quickening the opera's pace.

The pivotal scenes of the underlying play are those of the opera: the earthquake freeing the imprisoned followers of Dionysus, the God establishing his hypnotic dominion over Pentheus, his humiliation of Pentheus, Agave entering with her son's head in her arms, her detoxication by Cadmus, and the exile of the Theban royal House. In the play Euripides, less interested in the fate of individuals than in the demonic breakdown of a community, presents chiefly Pentheus, Dionysus, and the women's chorus. Pentheus represents reason, Dionysus emotion, each pushed to an extreme, and revealing the limits of reason; for ultimately life is not logical but emotional. At the same time, he gives the women's chorus lyrical odes expressing the peace, joy, and ecstasy of total surrender to the God. But he makes plain that such emotionalism, carried to Dionysiac extremes, is mere brutality. For Euripides, Dionysus is a God to fear, not to admire.

Auden and Kallman take much the same view: "To a Platonic idealist Dionysus must seem like the enemy itself, an image of all those irrational physical passions that he considers the main obstacle to the good life. Our Pentheus goes to his downfall not so much because of his arrogant behavior toward others as because of his ignorance of his own nature." He is, in the librettists' post-Freudian world, a victim of his repression.

Henze, however, was a generation younger than Auden and Kallman, and he saw the play, and opera, somewhat differently. When he staged a production of it in Dresden (1997) he put Pentheus and The Theban guards in Nazi-style uniforms, shifting sympathy to Dionysus and his young followers as the bringers of a new freedom into a stuffy world of order, law, and proper behavior. But then, part of the greatness of the play and the opera lies in the ambiguity with which either may be read.

Henze's music for the opera, for a large orchestra, is masterly. At its most basic, in Henze's words, "There is one set of ideas [forthright, sturdy] for the chaste, rationalist world of Pentheus; another, very sensual, for the World of Dionysus. I release them against each other equally armed."

Further, he and the librettists structured the opera so that the music could be a symphony in four movements. The first resembles a sonata-form built on the contrasing themes and sound of Pentheus and Dionysus; the second, a scherzo and trio built of a suite of dances; the third, an adagio and fugue; and the fourth a vast passacaglia. Probably only professional musicians will hear the underlying forms or even where the movements begin and end; but onstage the first ends as Agave and Autonoe dance out of Thebes to the mountain; the second, as the Stranger sings of Naxos and his first meeting with the God, and predicts that Pentheus soon will worship him; and the third, with the death and dismemberment of Pentheus.

Henze's choral writing for the Bassarids, one of the opera's great virtues, represents a solution to a difficult problem. As the librettists observed in a Note, *Why Rewrite a Masterpiece?* ". . . Nor could the mass reaction to Dionysus—which obviously interested Euripides more than the personal tragedies of Pentheus, Agave and Cadmus—be kept in the foreground of an opera without its teetering over into oratorio." They decided, therefore, to treat "the important chorus role as a perpetual background to an individualized dramatic action," and thus "to preserve the essential ritualized atmosphere of a work dealing with the nature of a God." To that end Henze marvelously wove the choral odes, onstage and off, into an aural tapestry against which the figures play out their scenes. The effect is often very beautiful, and *The Bassarids* does not teeter into oratorio.

Its start in life was slow, partly perhaps because its premiere production at Salzburg, by most reports, was a poor one. After a flurry of premiers in European and American cities, it all but disappeared. Recently, however, the number of productions has risen, and increasingly it is hailed as a masterwork of the second half of the twentieth century.

POSTCARD FROM MOROCCO

Opera in one act (90 min.). World premiere, Minneapolis, October 14, 1971. English prem. London, July 28, 1976; continental European prem., Karlsruhe, April 22, 1979. Music by Dominick Argento; libretto by John Donahue.

PRINCIPAL CHARACTERS

A Lady with a Hand Mirror ⎱	
An Operetta Singer ⎰	coloratura-soprano
A Lady with a Cake Box	soprano
A Lady with a Hat Box ⎱	
A Foreign Singer ⎰	mezzo-soprano
A Man with Old Luggage ⎫	
First Puppet ⎬	lyric tenor
An Operetta Singer ⎭	
A Man with a Paint Box (Mr. Owen)	tenor
A Man with a Shoe Sample Kit ⎱	
Second Puppet ⎰	baritone
A Man with a Cornet Case ⎱	
A Puppet Maker ⎰	bass

Argento, an American, has composed a notably varied list of works, many touching on a theme of identity and its discovery. In the 1970s he focused four on it, following *Postcard from Morocco* with *From the Diary of Virginia Woolf* (1975), which won that year's Pulitzer Prize and is a song cycle for mezzo-soprano and piano of eight excerpts from the writer's diary. Two years later he produced a monodrama (45 min.), *A Water Bird Talk,* adapting for tenor and orchestra (twelve) the tragicomic monologue by Chekhov, *On the Harmfulness of Tobacco.* In Argento's work the singer, lecturing on the habits of water birds, reveals the bleakness of his own life. And in 1979, he offered a full-length opera *The Voyage of Edgar Allan Poe,* on the poet's last days of madness. Yet the four works, as their forms suggest, are quite different.

In *Postcard from Morocco* the setting is "like a memory (1914), like an old postcard from a foreign land showing the railway station of Morocco or some place, hot and strange, like the interior of a glass-covered pavilion or spa." The "Algerian orchestra" of eight players [piano dominant] is onstage, behind "cardboard ferns,' ostensibly entertaining the seven travellers who await a train—but in many productions the orchestra is put in the pit. Within the opera there are puppet plays and a short concert to divert those waiting who include, besides the seven singers, two mimes and a number of cut-out figures, some of which occasionally change position.

Critics call Argento's musical style "eclectic," meaning he draws on any that seems right for the moment, jazz, Gregorian chant, folk song, a quotation from Wagner, or serialism; and in this opera, besides some Wagnerian and serialist touches there are others recalling Stravinsky and Britten. Because of his skill in joining styles in unexpected ways, Argento's music is often tartly surprising; it also is rhythmically strong and melodic. He treats the human voice not as another instrument of the orchestra, but gives it prominence, gracing it with melodic phrases, encouraging it to express emotion, and seldom obscuring it. With Argento words count, and the music responds to them.

In *Postcard from Morocco* nothing that happens onstage is quite clear. Events proceed as in a surreal dream, a sequence of encounters, confidences, confrontations, interspersed with entertainments that in some mysterious way relate to the characters' past and to their future. As the opera begins, the seven singers—note only one has a proper name—idle and bored with waiting for the train, begin to pick on one another. Each wonders what the others have in their boxes or valises, and it soon seems likely that everyone's luggage conceals personal identity, which none wants to reveal. Whether out of fear or shame, each will refuse to open his or her bag. Yet, starting with the "mirror" Lady, each has an aria that reveals some quirk of personality. She, for example, likes her hand mirror (a powder box) because "you can peek over your shoulder at people." The "Old Luggage" Man, on the other hand, confesses he never packs anything of value and travels with an old suitcase to discourage thieves.

Meanwhile there has been an entertainment. Two Puppets have put on a show about building a ship, perhaps a Flying Dutchman's ship, or a Roman or Greek ship. But the show had ended abruptly with one puppet slapping the other, shocking the onlookers. A foreshadow perhaps?

The "Hat" Lady then seems to find relief from boredom by warbling meaningless syllables as if she imagined herself some glamorous foreign singer (flamenco and Arabic touches). Meanwhile, the others, oblivious to her, continue their questions about each other's luggage.

The station's orchestra as entertainment offers a six-minute *divertimento,* announced by poster as "Souvenirs de Bayreuth"—the sort of salon music, played at "tempo di Fox-trot," that used to be heard at teatime in hotel palm gardens. Wagner lovers will recognize **interlude** themes, chiefly the spinning song from *The Flying Dutchman,* the Valhalla motif from the *Ring,* and the Bridal Chorus from *Lohengrin.* After the spinning song the drummer suddenly awakens and delivers a forty-five-second cadenza for percussion, in which he is to feature "clichés of the period (1914-1920)."

The "Shoe" Man boasts of his bag's capacity to carry sample shoes, but when one lady, eager to see a sample, tugs at his bag, he slaps her hard. The puppets?

In contrast, two singers appear on the bandstand, their voice recalling those of the "Mirror" Lady and the "Old Luggage" Man, and they sing a parody of a Viennese operetta's love duet. In its midst Mr. Owen, the Man with a Paint Box, starts conversing with the "Cake" Lady, and soon they are joining the operetta singers. Their quartet, the opera's happiest sequence, leads Mr. Owen to kiss his Lady gently. She looks at him suddenly, as though the quartet and kiss had not occurred; but he is moved by their memory to a soliloquy in which he reveals how as a child he was called to sail away on a magical vessel, and though he hurried to do it, somehow the opportunity was lost, the promise not fulfilled.

The "Shoe" man leads the others in prodding Mr. Owen to show them his paint box. But he declines. In their eagerness and curiosity, or perhaps meanness, they jostle him, knock his glasses to the ground, and his paint box falls open. Empty. He screams like a train whistle, and the others begin to re-sing their arias in a long crescendo.

Finally, they leave Mr. Owen alone, his paint box lid still flapping open. After an orchestral interlude, perhaps the composer's elegy for him, Mr. Owen summons from the puppets his childhood's magical ship. From below its decks, as in Wagner's *Flying Dutchman,* the chorus responds. "Set sail!" cries Mr. Owen, and in Argento's words: "Another Dutchman is born and—if only in a swan-drawn boat or in a ship of one's own making—a new voyage begins."

Mr. Owen's triumph? Or failure? Undoubtedly one reason performing artists, including stage designers, like the work is the latitude of meaning allowed in its presentation. But always at its center must be sympathy for Mr. Owen, for so the music says.

SWEENEY TODD
THE DEMON BARBER OF FLEET STREET

Musical Thriller in two acts, with prologue and epilogue. World premiere, New York City, March 1, 1979; British prem., London, July 2, 1980. Music by Stephen Sondheim; book by Hugh Wheeler, from an adaptation of old sources by Christopher Bond.

PRINCIPAL CHARACTERS

Sweeney Todd (formerly Benjamin Barker)	baritone
Anthony Hope, sailor	tenor
Beggar Woman	soprano
Mrs. Lovett, baker of meat pies	mezzo-soprano
Johanna, ward of Judge Turpin	soprano
Tobias Ragg, assistant to Pirelli	tenor
Pirelli, an Italian barber	tenor
The Beadle [a minor court official]	tenor
Judge Turpin	baritone
The people of London	

Setting: London, Fleet Street and environs in the nineteenth century.

The happy surprise of *Sweeney Todd,* musical thriller, has been its flexibility; clearly its book and music are sufficiently strong to survive quite different treatments, both musical and in staging. In its world premiere, this story of a barber's revenge, after false arrest and deportation so a lecherous judge might have the barber's wife, was played as an episode of England's Industrial Revolution. To portray London, a large Broadway stage was rebuilt as an iron foundry, with its back wall open to a large mural of the grimy city and its factory whistle frequently piercing eardrums; and the common people were portrayed as helpless prey to capitalist predators, even as they themselves were infected by capitalist ethics. The orchestra numbered 26 (11 strings), the chorus, 18, and the principals' voices all were amplified. The show, running 557 performances, spawned two national touring companies, a third for London, and impressed many musicians.

Several opera impresarios, admiring the music and clever lyrics, soon produced the work with operatic voices, usually unamplified, and for a richer, fuller sound with a chorus enlarged to 32, and orchestra to 52, with additions mostly in the strings. Others took the work the other direction, into smaller theatres, reducing the chorus to few or none, by having the principals sing the lines, and the orchestra to few or none by using synthesizers capable electronically of creating any sound needed. With the latter, the sound to some ears was harsh and metallic, but not inappropriate to an industrial age story. Conversely, the unamplified voices in these chamber productions made the characters more human, and to many persons, more sympathetic.

Such changes are not uncommon in shifting a Broadway show to an opera house, whether large or small. Sondheim, for example, following Broadway tradition had not orchestrated the score himself, but given Jonathan Tunick a vocal score with piano accompaniment and ideas of orchestral coloring. Tunick then had orchestrated the work for the specific Broadway house (a bad one acoustically), and later reorchestrated it differently (nine players, with only three strings) for a London theatre in 1993. Thus when David Krane, for a New York production in 1989, reduced all instruments to three synthesizers, he was not vandalizing a composer's work but continuing the tradition in which it was composed.

In other ways, too, subsequent productions often have continued Broadway custom. In programs the chorus may be called "the company," and instead of scenes, there may be a list of "musical numbers," reflecting the work's origin as a sequence of songs. These traditions are followed here. The numbers' timings are approximate, to the nearest half minute, and do not include occasional spoken dialogue. Sondheim estimated that the first act was 80% music, and the second, somewhat less.

PROLOGUE (3.5 min.)

1. "The Ballad of Sweeney Todd" (3.5). At a burial in London the company sings "Attend the tale of Sweeney Todd, the Demon Barber of Fleet Street." The refrain, beginning "Swing your razor wide, Sweeney!" is set to the opening notes of the judgment day hymn, *Dies Irae,* and the motif will resound in all five of the ballad's reappearances. Now, at its climax, a figure rises from the grave: Todd! Who promises the story.

ACT I (59 min.)

2. "No Place Like London" (3.5) Todd and Anthony Hope, the sailor who saved his life, arrive in London. A beggar woman asks for alms, but as she looks at Todd, "Hey, don't I know you," he rejects her, explaining to Anthony that London "is a hole in the world like a great black pit, and the vermin of the world inhabit it." [Note: the ease and speed with which Sondheim in these early scenes moves from one to another and within them changes mood were virtues to those who heard an opera in the music.)

3. "The Barber and His Wife" (2.5). Todd tells of a barber and his wife, who was beautiful and desired by a judge, "a pious vulture of the law." The judge had the barber arrested and sent overseas. But when Anthony asks if the wife then succumbed, Todd dismisses him, growling again about London's vermin.

4. "The Worst Pies in London" (2.5). Mrs. Lovett greets Todd to her shop with an account of hard times: To get meat into her pies, she's had to imitate her competitor Mrs. Mooney who's been "popping pussies in her pies." But Mrs. Lovett confesses, "them pussy cats is quick," and "Well, pity a woman alone and with limited wind."

5. "Poor Thing" (3.5). When Todd asks about an empty apartment above, Mrs. Lovett explains it is haunted. And she tells of Benjamin Barker, barber, falsely arrested and deported because a Judge and his Beadle lusted after Barker's wife. Later when the Beadle told the wife the judge had repented and wished to see her, she went to the Judge's house, where a party was in progress. And there, while the Beadle held her on a table, the Judge raped her. When Todd, in anguish, asks if no one would help her, Mrs. Lovett names him: "Benjamin Barker." "Not Barker!" he tells her. "Todd now. Sweeney Todd." Answering his questions, Mrs. Lovett reports his wife took poison, and the remorseful Judge has raised Barker's baby daughter, Johanna, as his ward. When Todd, though penniless, vows vengeance on the Judge and Beadle, Mrs. Lovett, to help him to a livelihood, produces his old razors: "You can be a barber again."

6. "My Friends" (2.5). Todd to his razors: "You shall drip rubies." Holding the largest aloft, he cries, "At last my arm is complete again."

7. Company and "The Ballad" (2): "Lift your razor high, Sweeney!"

8. "Green finch and linnet bird" (2.5). From an upper window in a house, a girl with yellow hair sings to birds in a street-seller's cages, comparing her lot to theirs.

9. "Ah, Miss" (2.5). Anthony, on the street, is smitten. From the Beggar Woman asking "Alms, alms" (he gives some coins), he learns the house is Judge Turpin's and the girl, his ward Johanna.

10. "Johanna" (2): Anthony promises himself and her window, he "will steal" her.

11. St. Dunstan's Market Place; Pirelli's Miracle Elixir (4). Tobias, Pirelli's assistant, tries to excite the crowd, including Todd and Mrs. Lovett, to buy bottles of Pirelli's lotion for baldness. (In some productions this crowd scene is cut.)

12. "The Contest" (5.5). Pirelli appears, claiming to be the King of Barbers. Todd proposes a contest: Let each shave a man, and let the Beadle declare the quickest, smoothest shave. They begin, but Pirelli, in a parody of Italian tenors, carols away, and while he is holding a long note, Todd shaves his man, and is named the winner. The contest repeats, this time pulling a tooth. Again Pirelli sings too high and long, and Todd wins. The Beadle promises to stop by Todd's shop for a shave.

13. Company and "The Ballad" (0.5): "Sweeney pondered and Sweeney planned. . ."

14. "Wait" (2): Mrs. Lovett urges Todd to be patient, tries to distract him by suggesting flowers for the shop: "Can't you think of nothing else? Always brooding. . ."

Before the next musical number, Anthony appears in the shop, announcing he has plans to elope with Judge Turpin's ward and needs a place to hide the girl until they can marry. Todd and Mrs. Lovett suggest the shop. As he departs, Pirelli enters, with Tobias. He has recognized Barker-Todd and is planning blackmail. Todd, sending Tobias downstairs with Mrs. Lovett, kills Pirelli.

15. Three Men of the Company and "The Ballad" (0.5): From the side of the stage: "His hands were quick, his fingers strong. . ."

16. Judge Turpin's house. "Mea culpa" (3.5). The Judge, looking through a keyhole, watches Johanna undress while flagellating himself to orgasm, all the time moaning of sin and deliverance. (This song was cut before the Broadway premiere but some later productions have restored it.) The Judge, entering Johanna's room, tells her that to protect her from a sailor who has been seen lurking about the grounds, he will marry her.

17. The next day. "Kiss me" (1.5). In Johanna's room, she and Anthony plan to elope. Which leads into a quartet:

18. "Ladies in their sensitivities." (4). On the street the Beadle urges the Judge to have a shave before the wedding, recommending Sweeney Todd; and the two start for Todd's shop. Meanwhile, within the Judge's house Johanna fiddles about what day of the week she should marry Anthony and what she should wear; and instead of leaving at once, they kiss. And the two duets continue simultaneously.

Meanwhile, Mrs. Lovett, leaving Tobias downstairs, goes up to the shop and is aghast to hear Todd has killed Pirelli. She thinks better of it, however, when upon opening the chest where the body is hid she discoves in Pirelli's purse a large sum of money. The Judge rings the shop bell, and she hastens down.

19. "Pretty Women" (5). Todd has the Judge in the barber's chair and is relishing every last moment of the Judge's life by ironically joining him in a song about the attraction of pretty women. Then, just as Todd lifts the razor, Anthony bursts in, blurting that Johanna will elope with him. The Judge, leaping from the chair, runs out, followed by Anthony.

20. "Epiphany" (3.0). Mrs. Lovett, hurrying upstairs, tries to soothe Todd, who alternates fury with keening for his lost daughter Johanna and his wife Lucy (her name sung to the same motif as the Beggar Woman's "Alms, alms"). Longing for vengeance, Todd has a madman's epiphany, equating himself with God. He will avenge himself on all men, kill all who sit in his chair: "Come on, come on, Sweeney's waiting."

21. "A Little Priest" (7). The practical capitalist Mrs. Lovett wonders what they can do with the bodies. Put them in her pies: that would "save a lot of graves; do a lot of relatives favors." They discuss the various body flavors, priest, poet, politician. Beadle would be greasy; "stick to priest." After all, says Todd, in the world outside "it's man devouring man," so "who are we to deny it in here?" (The duet's position poses a question: did Sondheim miss the act's natural climax by not ending with Todd's "Epiphany?" Or did he wisely balance the melodrama with a dose of comedy? And does his decision mark a difference between opera and musical comedy?)

ACT II (43 min., not including spoken dialogue)

1. "God, That's Good" (6.5). Mrs. Lovett, with her new pies, has prospered, placed tables out of doors, and taken on Tobias as a waiter,

one of whose jobs is to shoo away the Beggar Woman. The crowd exclaims on the delicious pies, while upstairs Todd demonstrates for Mrs. Lovett his new barber chair that will tilt and send a victim straight through the floor to the oven. But at the moment, she is more interested in serving customers.

2. "Johanna" (5.5). Anthony, searching the streets for Johanna, sings of her. So, too, in the barber shop does Todd, as he dispatches two more customers to the oven. While outside the Beggar Woman babbles of "the Fiend," of the "City on Fire," of "Mischief," and of "Alms, alms." By scene's end Anthony has located Johanna in Fogg's Asylum for Lunatics, but with no way to release her, heads for Todd's shop.

3. "By the Sea" (3.5). Mrs. Lovett, in a parody of English music hall songs, tells Todd of the life she wants for them. Plainly, she cares more for him than for his homicidal obsession, and more for him than he, for her.

4. Wigmaker Sequence, including Quintet from the Company and "The Ballad" (3.5). Anthony and Todd plot to free Johanna from the Asylum by having Anthony pose as a wigmaker come to cut her hair for a wig. The quintet sings, "Sweeney'd waited too long before." Not now. He writes a letter to the Judge, telling him to come to the shop to find his ward, and sets off to deliver it.

5. "Not While I'm Around" (4). Tobias affectionately advises Mrs. Lovett that no harm can come to her "while I'm around." She is moved, and offers him a candy, which she takes from Pirelli's purse. Tobias, recognizing the purse, freezes. She, seeing that he has almost guessed what happened, sweetly promises to look out for him, and without saying what she and Todd have been doing offers to let Tobias help with the baking. He is thrilled by the honor. While she is showing him the oven, she hears the harmonium in her parlor, and leaves him.

6. Parlor Songs (4), a parody of Victorian music in the home. The Beadle is playing and singing, "Sweet Polly Plunkett lay in the grass." He has come because of neighbors' complaints of odors from the bakehouse and must investigate. Mrs. Lovett manages to hold him at the piano until Todd returns, then suggests that before inspecting the bakery he have a shave; and he and Todd go upstairs. To cover any sound, she accompanies herself at the harmonium. Todd dispatches the Beadle, and the corpse hurtles down to the oven, landing at Tobias' feet. He shrieks and runs to the cellar. Mrs. Lovett tells Todd to "look

after the boy:" he has guessed their secret. Black out.

7. Final Sequence (13.5). (Though the many short episodes with their twists and turns, advance the story, there is no comparable advance in the music, for Sondheim here, in the Broadway tradition, begins to rely almost entirely on music already heard—reprises. Question: Another difference between opera and musical comedy? Mozart, for instance, closed *The Magic Flute* with new music, as did Verdi in *Aida*.)

Much hurry-skurry around London as Anthony brings Johanna, disguised as a sailor, to the shop. Todd and Mrs. Lovett search for Tobias, without finding him. Johanna hides as the Beggar Woman enters the shop; then in comes Todd, and with the Judge at the door, to be rid of the beggar he kills her, sending her body through the floor. Then, getting the Judge into the chair by describing Johanna downstairs making herself pretty, he dawdles while reprising "Pretty Women" with the Judge until, revealing himself as Barker, he cuts the man's throat. Discovering Johanna in the shop, he almost kills her, for in her disguise he sees only a sailor, an unwanted witness; but Mrs. Lovett downstairs screams, the factory whistle blows, and in the confusion Johanna escapes. Todd goes down to Mrs. Lovett at the oven. She tries to keep him from looking at the Beggar Woman's face, but Todd recognizes his wife Lucy. Holding her body, crying her name, he accuses Mrs. Lovett of lying to him about his wife's death. She replies: She said nothing of dying, only that the wife took poison; but anyway, it was for his good: "Could that thing have cared for you like me?" Seeming to agree on the practicality of the lie, he waltzes Mrs. Lovett around to "By the Sea," and pops her into the oven. Meanwhile, Tobias, his hair turned white, emerges form the cellar and seeing Todd's razor on the floor, picks it up, and slashes the barber's throat. Anthony, Johanna, and police enter to discover a boy gone mad turning the meat grinder.

EPILOGUE (3 min.)

8. The Company and all principals. "Attend the tale of Sweeney Todd!" Todd's last comment, "To seek revenge may lead to hell," and Mrs. Lovett's, "But everyone does it, and seldom as well;" then together, "as Sweeney."

THE LIGHTHOUSE

Chamber opera in a prologue and one act. World premiere, Edinburgh, Sept. 2, 1980; continental European prem. (in Ger.), Salzburg, March 27, 1983; American prem., Boston, Nov. 3, 1983; Australian prem., Perth, Feb. 14, 1985. Music and libretto by Peter Maxwell Davies.

CHARACTERS

Sandy, also Relief Officer One	tenor
Blazes, also Relief Officer Two	baritone
Arthur, also Relief Officer Three and the Voice of the Cards	bass

Time of action: December, 1900. Place, for the Prologue: A Court of Enquiry in Edinburgh, aboard the lighthouse relief ship, and outside the lighthouse door; for the main scene, within the lighthouse.

It is a mystery and a fact that in December 1900, a lighthouse relief ship, landing at a light on an island in the outer Hebrides, found the lighthouse deserted. Food for the three keepers was on the table, each bed made, and the lighthouse door open. The light, though out, was in working order with its reflectors polished and the oil reservoir full. But the keepers had vanished.

The last time the light was seen by a passing ship was on a night following a fierce storm. But the next night, calm and clear, another ship noted with surprise that the light was out. The only plausible explanation seems that during the storm one keeper had gone down to the jetty, and been washed away; and the other two, hearing his cries, had rushed to his aid and similarly been swept away. But no one knows.

After the incident an automatic light, not needing keepers, was installed and worked perfectly for eighty years. Then, it "went dark," on the night of this opera's premiere.

Davies, taking the single fact of the men's disappearance, has weaved around it a story that leaves open several possibilities, allowing an audience to choose. In any staging, the lighting is a major feature. The beam from the lighthouse must be perfectly timed to the music, and at times other lights, real or imagined, but seen by the three characters, must overwhelm the audience.

Davies used an orchestra of 12 players, 24 instruments, and drew from them extraordinary sounds. The instruments are the common woodwinds, brass, and strings, with a variety of percussion, but they are played in unusual ways, at extremes of their registers, with many slides and overtones, and in unusual combinations. Part of the opera's fascination is its eerie sound, well contrasted in its main scene with three 1900-style songs by the keepers, a bar-room ballad, a parlor love song, and a Protestant revival hymn.

Equally intriguing is the story Davies draws from the personalities he has bestowed on his three keepers. As in a murder mystery, clues as to what may have happened are dropped almost from the start, and at the end what any listener thinks *really* happened may depend on the number of clues picked up and the weight given to them.

Though the three keepers have seven roles to sing, their characters throughout remain true to their vocal range, that is, the tenor, whether Relief Officer One or Sandy, tends to be conciliatory; the baritone, Officer Two or Blazes, more aggressive, especially in his dislike of the bass; and the bass, Officer Three, the Voice of the Cards, or Arthur, domineering and religious—though to Blazes, Arthur is a hypocrite.

A word about Arthur's individual form of religiosity. As his revival hymn reveals, he is fascinated by the story of the Exodus and by a particular part of it: Moses's order to the Levites, while the Jews were in the Sinai desert, to slay 3,000 of their bretheren who had worshipped the golden Calf (Exodus: 32:25-30). This order, which Moses said came from God, has been called by political scientists the first revolutionary purge, and has been used by many later revolutionaries to justify killing those who disagree with their aims. The Puritans of seventeenth-century England cited it to justify beheading Charles I, and some Protestants in the late nineteenth century used it to support a doctrine of blood atonement for major sins, such as adultery; that is, God's forgiveness could be had only by the spilling of blood, literally. Arthur, as Blazes senses, is a man of violence who, consciously or not, likes the story because it permits violence in God's name. Although the opera is in two parts, and Davies expressly allows an intermission, if wished, after the Prologue, it is usually played without break, running in all about 73 minutes.

PROLOGUE—The Court of Enquiry (28 min.)

The scene opens in the Court of Enquiry, in Edinburgh, moves aboard the lighthouse relief ship, to the steps leading to the lighthouse door, and back to the courtroom.

The three Relief Officers, singing as one, from the front of the stage address the audience: "From the records. . . [we] went to the lighthouse with relief and provisions."

Throughout the scene a solo horn acts as interrogator (sometimes placed in the audience, the better to simulate questions put to the singers, whose answers reveal the question).

Officer One, singing over an accompaniment of bass, clarinet, cello, double bass, and timpani that suggests swirling water, replies: "Our passage was difficult. . . a sudden eddy. . . against the gale. . . we heard the foghorn, but it seemed to come from all over. . ."

Three "whooping glissandos" on the bass clarinet, followed by a "growl tone," change the scene to shipboard where Officers Two and Three shout orders. Then a sudden calm, with gull-like cries frrm the piccolo. Officer Three, "The calm is more nerve-wracking than the storm." Then Officer One cries, "Look out ahead," and sees three lights, a triangle of white lights, but loses them in the mist.

The interrogating horn asks Officer Two if he saw the lights. "No, Sir. . . but I heard the fog horn." The solo horn turns to Officer Three, who says, "there is no foghorn there, but we all heard it."

The Officers, in turn, describe their landing at the lighthouse jetty. Officer One saw beneath it "three black selkies" [seals] staring at them, "cold as the sea, remote." [In Scottish lore the spirits of drowned men can return as seals.] Officer Two saw "no selkies" but perched on the rail, watching them, "three great scarfs [cormorants], black as a hole." Three saw "no scarfs," but crossing their path "three black gibbies [male cats]. . . not the lighhouse tabbies we had seen before, but wilder, sinewy beasts."

A change in lighting puts the three Officers at the lighthouse door. Unable to imagine why no keeper greets them, they advance slowly. Black rats scuttle over their feet, as Officer Two's voice rises to a shriek.

The interrogating horn brings back the courtroom, and Officer One describes the table set for three. The horn asks about an overturned chair and a broken cup, and in their accounts the men differ slightly. Officer One states the chair's back leg was broken, and Three, its front; Two says the smashed cup was on the floor, and Three, on the table. Then speaking together, they offer their opinion: One keeper, who overturned the chair and broke his cup, was suddenly called by another to aid the third who was in trouble on the jetty, "and then they all three were swept away."

They come forward, as at the opening, to address the audience: "The Court of Enquiry" recorded "an open verdict." It was hard to find replacements for the three keepers, for now the lighthouse had a bad name. So, an automatic light was installed, and the house boarded up. The prologue ends with a phrase first sounded on the flute, and later sung by the men: "The lighthouse is now automatic." The musical phrase repeats the rhythm of the words, over and over, while the light flashes in time with it, growing ever stronger. Curtain, or continuing (in flash-back) directly on.

THE CRY OF THE BEAST (45 min.)

———

Within the lighthouse. The three keepers are at table. They have gone longer than usual without relief, and tension is rising.

The act opens with the trumpet sounding the phrase: "The lighthouse is now automatic." Arthur (bass) speaks first, intoning a grace on their meal. The familiar words irritate Blazes (baritone), who points out they have no wine, and the bread is oatcakes. Even so, observes Sandy (tenor), they are lucky, for they have been stormbound for weeks. When Arthur pompously reproves Blazes for lack of faith, and urges all to pray for deliverance, Blazes bursts out: "Arthur, you're a sinner same as Sandy and me, who uses the Book to justify the Beast in him, and to put us in our place. So enough of this holy talk." Sandy, the peacemaker, suggests a game of cribbage to Blazes: "I know it's too sinful for Arthur, but he can say a prayer for us."

Meanwhile, Arthur, murmuring self-righteously, goes to light the lantern, not yet automatic. [Its musical phrase, therefore, here is different, less powerful, less definite, and played on Glockenspiel, celeste, and guitar.]

During the cribbage Arthur's voice in the loft becomes the Voice of the Cards, predicting dire events in apocalyptic language. [Davies has said: The opera's structure "is based on the Tower of Tarot, whose number symbolism is present in the structure of all the music, and which erupts into the surface of the opera in the form of the words sung by Arthur during the card game, representing the Voice of the Cards. On this level the game of crib is transformed into a play of fate with Tarot cards, summing up all the power of their baleful influence." Thus far, no convincing explanation of Davies's meaning has been discovered, but happily the opera can be enjoyed without one. Take the Voice of the Cards as Arthur in the loft musing to himself.]

The game ends with Sandy accusing Blazes of cheating, though neither takes the charge seriously. Meanwhile Arthur, down from the loft, talks of their slide into depravity. Blazes again rails at Arthur, but Sandy calms him by suggesting a song; and Blazes agrees to sing if the others, in turn, will follow.

His song is accompanied by fiddle, banjo, and bones, the last being the nineteenth-century American and British equivalent of castanets. Used mostly in minstrel shows, it typically consisted of two animal **Blazes's Song** ribs clacked in rhythm. In thirteen rollicking verses Blazes describes his youth as an urban tough, cynically recounting a series of horrifying episodes; and by its end he has described murdering a woman for her money and allowing his father to be hanged for the crime.

Sandy sings next, a Victorian parlor song, "Oh, my love, I dream of you, Your hair of gold, your eyes so blue," and is accompanied by **Sandy's Song** a cello and out-of-tune piano. Lost in memory, he repeats the song, while the other two, with all three unaware of colleagues, interject phrases from it, as if their memories also had been stirred. The conjunction of some of the phrases, now not in exact order, is disturbing, suggesting to the alert in the audience that the song is perhaps not quite what it seems. At its end Blazes comments: "You're a dark hourse, Sandy. God knows what you've been up to;" and Arthur, "I don't know what your song means, but I disapprove."

Arthur's eleven-verse song has a typical Salvation Army accompaniment of clarinet, horn, trumpet, trombone, and tambourine. And he begins with the construction of the Golden Calf: "This be thy **Arthur's Song** God, oh Israel, made with a graving tool. . ." and by the third verse, "The Golden Calf will save you From all adversity." After which Blazes and Sandy dutifully add, "Praise, praise."

Verses four through six tell of the Lord in wrath ordering Moses to destroy the Calf. In the last of these verses Arthur makes a significant but common mistake: He has the Lord, not Moses, order the Levites to slaughter all who had worshipped the Calf. Sandy and Blazes, "Praise, praise."

Verse seven, "There died about three thousand. . . Ere Moses deemed this was enough Atonement to the Lord," is Biblically correct. But thereafter Arthur begins his own prophecy: "Though the Calf was ground to dust. . . The Calf will rise again. . . And will return, a raging bull, Wreaking blind destruction." Sandy and Blazes, "Praise, praise."

Arthur closes in two verses, rejoicing God has set man against brother "to guard against"' the Calf's return; and ending: "So praise the Lord in all His works, Who purges from His herd All who sin against Him, In thought, or deed, or word." Blazes approves, "Well done, Arthur;" but Sandy, to himself remarks, "Preserve us from both the Golden Calf of his imagination and his jealous God."

Quietly Sandy observes the mist has thickened, "Time to start the foghorn;" and Arthur goes to the loft. As the foghorn starts to sound, the orchestral horn has whooping slides up the scale, and the trombone down. Then the tempo slows, horn and trombone cease, and the upslides transfer to the flute, while in the loft Arthur begins to mutter to himself about "The cry of the beast across the sleeping world. One night, that cry will be answered from the deep."

Downstairs Blazes, following several bars from an in-tune piano, begins to see ghosts in the shadows, the face of the woman he murdered. She stares at him; she touches him; blood from her head runs into his eyes. His father and mother appear at the door. They touch him, they curse him and call him to come; they have a boat down on the jetty.

Then Sandy, initially to guitar and cello, sees ghosts of his song. People from his boyhood. Faces. His sister. Was his dream of love for her? No. She turns away. Then, "Him. That boy at the manse." In panic, he bleats: "No. I didn't, we didn't. That preaching minister and that damned prying schoolteacher. I must go with him, the boy. . ."

Blazes quietly remarks, "The room is full of ghosts, called out by the foghorn." And Sandy, in horror, says, "They want us; they need us. They have to take us back. . . into the blackness."

Arthur comes down from the loft, "singing a crazed hymn" which begins to one of Davies's most interesting orchestral directions: "Plastic soap dish scraped round inside rim of tam-tam to produce a 'howl' resembling electronic 'feedback'." Arthur sees the Beast, called from his grave, coming to claim those marked with his sign. "We are snared in a trap between the claim of the Beast and the wrath of the avenging God. Call on all your ghosts. . . to defend us from the might of the Beast." While singing this, he gradually assumes characteristics of the Beast, whose three eyes, flashing red and white lights, come ever closer, in a blinding dazzle. Blazes and Sandy fall in behind him and all three start for the door, bellowing a crazed hymn of winning grace by going to fight the Antichrist.

As the flashing lights blind the audience, the keepers reach the door, and "in a thrice" all is calm, the lights normal, and the three keepers have become the Relief Officers. Behind them the eyes of the Beast are seen to be the lights of the Relief ship. Officer One says, "We had to defend ourselves;" Two, "They were crazed, run amok;" and Three, "Explanations will be difficult. . ." They decide to say, "The men have disappeared—perhaps lost to sea, swept away." They tidy up the house, and leave.

The light dims. Three keepers enter. They are "obscure and phantasmal," and they sit at the table in the same positions as Arthur, Sandy and Blazes in the opening scene. "Arthur" starts to say grace, and "Blazes" scornfully remarks, "There isn't any fruit of the vine; it's tea. And no bread." Sandy says, "Just go on keeping the Beast from the door. . ." The orchestra picks up the musical phrase from the Pologue: "The lighthouse is now automatic." And the light comes on stronger and stronger, as the phrase repeats louder and louder. Sudden blackness.

The opera's ambiguity, though based on a historical event, is surely part of its appeal. At the end of any performance no audience will wholly agree on what happened onstage. Did the Relief Officers kill the keepers? How much was real? Was it a reenactment by ghosts in a lighthouse now automatic and without keepers? And the staging allows still further scope for difference. One German production, at Gelsenkirchen (1984), seemingly contrary to the text, yet reportedly with success, aligned Sandy and Blazes in a homosexual relationship against Arthur. Doubtless, one reason for the great number of productions, more than eighty in the opera's first fourteen years, is the latitude it offers stage and lighting directors. Another is the musical characterization of the three keepers, so clearly projected in their songs. And a third, the audience's delight in the weird sounds drawn from a small orchestra. An eerie thriller is good entertainment.

SATYAGRAHA

Opera in three acts. World premiere, Stadsschouwburg Theater, Rotterdam, Sept. 5, 1980; American prem., Lewiston, N. Y., July 29, 1981. Music by Philip Glass; text by Constance De Jong, adapting verses from the *Bhagavad-Gita.* Sung in Sanskrit.

PRINCIPAL CHARACTERS

Mohandas K. Gandhi	tenor
Prince Arujna ⎱ mythological characters	baritone
Lord Krishna ⎰ from the *Bhagavad-Gita*	bass
Miss Schlesen, Gandhi's secretary	soprano
Kasturbai, Gandhi's wife	alto
Mr. Kallenbach, European co-worker	baritone
Parsi Rustomji, Indian co-worker	bass
Mrs. Naidoo, Indian co-worker	soprano
Mrs. Alexander, European friend	alto

NON-SINGING ROLES

Leo Tolstoy	presiding figure	Act I
Rabindranath Tagore	"	Act II
Martin Luther King	"	Act III

The *Bhagavad-Gita,* the "Song of the Lord," is a philosophical dialogue embedded in the *Mahabharata,* a Sanskrit epic and holy book of Hinduism. The speakers are Prince Arujna and Lord Krishna, debating action on the eve of the three-week battle of Kurukshetra, an episode in a dynastic struggle between cousins. Arujna is anguished to see in the opposing army many of his friends, family, and teachers. But Krishna persuades him to fight by instructing him in spiritual wisdom and the means of obtaining union with God—one of the chief doctrines of the *Gita* being selfless action performed with inner detachment from its results. This idea Gandhi incorporated into his doctrine of political action through non-violence.

For him the *Gita* was sacred text, and in his writings he said of "Satyagraha," or "holding to the truth," as he developed the concept in his twenty-one year campaign (1893-1914) to lessen racial discrimination in south Africa: "Satyagraha is soul force pure and simple, and whenever and to whatever extent there is room for the use of arms or physical force or brute force, there and to that extent is there so much less possibility for soul force. . . In Satyagraha there is not the remotest idea of injuring the opponent. Satyagraha postulates the conquest of the adversary by suffering in one's own person."

There were, in 1893, a collection of laws in South Africa discriminating against immigrants from India. Gandhi, a young barrister who had practised in London, arrived in South Africa expecting to be treated as he had been in England. Instead, on his first railway journey, because of his Indian color and features, the conductor ordered him out of the first class carriage to which his ticket entitled him. Refusing to comply, he was put off the train. Sitting through the night in a railroad station, he debated a return to India, but decided to stay. Thereafter, he spoke often against the injustice of the laws; and when he could, acted, without violence. One of his first victories, won by petition to a court, was the right to wear an Indian turban while arguing his case. Later he came to think of Krishna's advice to Arujna as a rule for living: "Hold pleasure and pain, profit and loss, victory and defeat to be the same: then brace yourself for the fight. So will you bring no evil on yourself." And after twenty-one years of peaceful protest, publicity, and marches, he and his fellow Indian immigrants forced the state to reverse its policy and change the laws.

The opening scene, which serves as a prologue, includes, along with Gandhi, the mythological characters of Arujna and Krishna on the eve of the battle. Thereafter each scene presents a picture of an event of Gandhi's activities in South Africa. The events are not presented chronologically, but rearranged as if a single day in history, dawn to night. Further, Glass makes no effort to individualize the real people; with the exception of Gandhi they are simply voices on stage. Because the text's language is Sanskrit, because much onstage movement is in slow-motion, and because the scenes are tied only loosely by narrative, the audience surveys the sequence of pictures much as one might view pictures in a gallery. Yet the music and the idea of non-violent political action bind the parts and bring them to a climax in the third act, which presents the five-day March of Protest to Newcastle that led ultimately to the repeal of many discriminatory laws.

Each act has a historical figure presiding silently over the events. In Act I, Leo Tolstoy (1828-1910), who, for the last twenty-five years of his life, was a religious inspiration to many, and who corresponded with Gandhi. In Act II, Rabindranath Tagore (1861-1941), Bengali author and in 1913 the first Asian to win the Nobel Prize for Literature. His writings are permeated by a love for all people and a consciousness

of God; and he, too, wrote frequently to Gandhi. And in Act III, showing Gandhi's influence in years to come, Martin Luther King, Jr., (1929-
1968), whose doctrines and civil rights marches in the United States
owed much to Gandhi.

Unlike *Einstein on the Beach* (see Chap. 6) which used the Philip
Glass Ensemble of seven, for this work Glass, as requested in the commission, scored for a more conventional orchestra of 54: a full string
section, woodwinds in threes, and electric organ, but no brass, percussion, or amplification. Yet the orchestra, partly because he scored little
for individual instruments, mixing their timbres as does an organ, produced a sound recalling that of the electronic Ensemble. He also in-
sured, for some ears, a slight Indian tint to the music by using only
instruments that could be found in some form in India. And further,
unlike *Einstein, Satyagraha* calls for operatically trained singers, nine
soloists and a chorus of forty. With it Glass took several long steps
toward opera as the term usually is understood.

Nevertheless, with all its text taken from the *Gita* and sung in Sanskrit, it has been described as "more mystery than opera," "a Hindu
cantata," "a ritual celebration of a way of thinking and of acting." Undoubtedly Glass, his librettist DeJong, an American novelist, and their
American stage designer Robert Israel, conceived of their work as a
moral or even religious experience for the audience; and surely that
was how many received it. They left the theatre exalted and, like the
common people of India, ready to call Gandhi "Mahatma," or "Great
Soul."

ACT I (44 min.)—TOLSTOY

SCENE 1 (19 min.): The legendary Kuru Field of Justice

Dawn on the battlefield, which is also a South African plain. To the
back of the stage, on a truncated pyramid, Tolstoy at his desk. On either
side of the stage, an army; before them, in chariots and resplendent
armor, Arujna and his cousin Duryodhana, and between them, and down-
stage, Krishna. As daylight breaks, Arujna's army is seen to be manned
by Indians and his cousin's by Europeans, their weapons are everyday
objects. Gandhi, in his traditional white robe, appears upstage center
and walks down between the armies. He has a solo (5 min.), "I see
them here assembled. . ." Arujna joins him (duet, 5 min); Krishna joins

(trio, 5 min.), and then, in a brief choral section, the two armies. Gandhi closes the scene singing alone (in Sanskrit): "Hold pleasure and pain, profit and loss, victory and defeat to be the same; then brace yourself for the fight. So will you bring no evil on yourself."

Musically, the scene is built on 143 repetitions of a four-chord progression: F minor, E flat, D flat, C. The opening fourteen statements are in arpeggios of eighth notes (like the accompanying figure of Beethoven's "Moonlight" sonata, first movement). But the number of notes varies, bar to bar, from five up to nine, changing accent. Then follow sixteen measures of F-minor scales, up and down, while above them sustained notes outline the initial chord sequence. And, with such slow, gradual changes, so on throughout the scene, giving rise to the term "minimalist" music. Some listeners find the slow changes mesmerizing; others, boring. One of the latter, a critic for the New York *Times,* reported the score "carries Minimalism to what one must fear is a musical dead end." Yet more than 10,000 persons sold out five performances in Brooklyn in 1981; and in Stuttgart in the opera's first two seasons (prem. in 1984), it had more than thirty performances.

SCENE 2 (12 min.): Tolstoy Farm (1910)

Mid-morning. Singers, Gandhi, Miss Schlesen, Kasturbai, Mrs. Naidoo, and Kallenbach. Following Tolstoy's example Gandhi creates a collective farm where Indians living and working together can create a community. Tolstoy, as before, sits on a truncated pyramid to the rear. Work on the farm drew the Indians into the Satyagraha idea: "a fight on the behalf of Truth consisting chiefly in self-purification and self-reliance." And the scene, like the first, is built on repetition of chords presented in slow variation.

SCENE 3 (12 min.): The Vow (1906)

Noon. An outdoor public meeting. Singers: Parsi Rustomji, Miss Schlesen, Indian crowd (full chorus). The British government had proposed a law requiring every Indian man, woman, and child, to register, be finger-printed, and carry a residency permit at all times; police could invade homes to inspect permits, and violations of the law could be punished by fines, jail, or deportation.

Parsi Rustomji explains the law to the Indians, stressing the importance of opposition, and offering a resolution stating that all would resist it unto death. For such an undertaking, such a responsibility, a vow before God was needed. Slowly the Indians take the vow, standing as they do. The scene ends with a coda of fifty alternations of chords of F and E-flat, with the timing, scoring, and figuration slowly shifting.

ACT II—TAGORE

Throughout this act, in place of Tolstoy, Tagore presides, from a wicker chair on the truncated pyramid to stage rear.

SCENE 1 (15 min.): Confrontation and Rescue (1896)

Stormy day, 2 p.m. Singers: a chorus of angry European men on a street in Durban and Mrs. Alexander, the wife of the superintendent of police. The men wait for Gandhi who is returning from a visit to India. They are angry, for in speeches there he criticized South Africa's laws, bringing the world's attention to them. The men mutter and complain, and when Gandhi appears they begin, with slow-motion gestures, to throw mud and stones at him. Approaching from the other direction is Mrs. Alexander. She sees what is happening, and opening her umbrella she walks at Gandhi's side, leading him to safety.

SCENE 2 (14 min.): Indian Opinion (1906)

Late afternoon, 5 p.m., and a burning, orange sun. In one of the movement's communal residences which houses the press that prints the weekly *Indian Opinion*. The paper, which refused all advertisements, depended entirely on subscribers and volunteer workers and reportedly was read by 20,000. Kallenbach and Miss Schlessen sing: "You should embrace action for the upholding, the welfare of your own kind. Whatever the noblest does, that too will others do."

Everyone works at a job, and Kasturbai, Mrs. Naidoo, and Parsi Rustomji sing: "If I were not to do my work, these worlds would fall to ruin." The large wheel of the press begins to turn; a paper is printed; and they all leave, while for two minutes, over the same progression of chords repeated some twenty times, the press continues to turn by itself. The miracle of machinery. Curtain.

SCENE 3 (20 min.): Protest (1908)

An outdoor field, at twilight. Singers: Gandhi and a large crowd of Indians. The Government was jailing movement leaders who lacked certificates of registration, and the Indian community arranged to be arrested in droves and fill up the jails. The Government thereupon offered a compromise: If the majority of Indians voluntarily registered, the Government would repeal the registration act. After debate, the Indians accepted the proposal and registered; then the Government reneged. The Indians then issued an ultimatum: If repeal was not forthcoming, they would burn their cards and accept the consequences. At the last moment the Government sent its refusal to Gandhi who was conducting a prayer meeting with some 2,500. He reported the refusal, and everyone present threw his or her certificate into a cauldron, which was then fired and the cards burned as the whole assembly rose to its feet, cheering. Through the scene Gandhi sings a long prayer, quoting the Lord: "I love the man who has no expectation. . . who hates not nor exults. . ." And the chorus responds: "Hold pleasure and pain, profit and loss, victory and defeat to be the same. . ."

ACT III (30 min.)—KING

Throughout the Act, played as a single scene—New Castle March (1913)—King in shirt-sleeves (or sometimes his image on a film), stands behind a podium with microphones on the truncated pyramid. Setting: dusk to night, with stars, on the mythological battlefield that is also a South African plain.

The Government once again had broken its promise, and Gandhi's response was to organize a march that might pull all 80,000 Indian workers out on strike. As always, the march was to be non-violent, one aim being to fill the jails to overflowing. And ultimately the march achieved its objective: repeal of the discriminatory laws.

Much of the action is played in slow motion. The marchers gather and Gandhi reviews them, even as police arrive, slowly raising their bludgeons while Indians slowly fall beneath the blows. The leaders are arrested and led off to jail, and the march moves on, leaving Gandhi alone on stage except for the distant presence of King.

Gandhi's final aria, the opera's longest (8 min.), is a rising white-note scale (starting on E), in quarter notes, over a recurring progression of minor chords. He sings five stanzas, each with six scales, separated by an orchestral passage, in all, thirty repetitions of the scale. And the piece, in Glass's fashion, does not so much end as simply stop. Towards the end of it Gandhi sings Krishna's promise: "Whenever the law of righteousness withers away and lawlessness arises, then do I generate myself on earth. I come into being age after age and take a visible shape and move a man with men for the protection of good, thrusting the evil back and setting virtue on her seat again."

This ending, and the feel of the music, a rising scale, is upbeat, hopeful. Yet in the Brooklyn production, surely with Glass' approval, at the end, in slow motion, King is shot, slumps, and falls across the podium. Downbeat. At the Brooklyn performances this ending caused argument: Was it a denial of the message of Satyagraha?

AKHNATEN

Opera in three acts, with prelude and epilogue. World premiere, Staatsoper, Stuttgart, March 24, 1984; American prem., Houston, Oct. 12, 1984; British prem. London, June 17, 1985. Music by Philip Glass; libretto by Glass, in collaboration with Shalom Goldman, Robert Israel, and Richard Riddell. Sung partly in Egyptian, Akkadian, Hebrew, and the language of the audience.

PRINCIPAL CHARACTERS

Akhnaten, King of Egypt (c. 1372-1354 BC and often known as Ikhnaton)	counter-tenor
Nefertiti, his wife	alto
Queen Tye, his mother	soprano
Aye, his father-in-law and advisor	bass
Horemhab, a General and future King	baritone
High Priest of Amon	tenor
Six daughters of Akhnaten and Nefertiti }	three sopranos three altos
A Scribe, who narrates part of the story (in the language of the audience)	

Setting: Egypt at the close of the Amenhotep or XVIII dynasty. Ramses II, of the XIX dynasty and Pharaoh of the Exodus, reigned 1292-1225 BC.

Glass frequently has spoken of his three operatic "portraits" of men whose ideas have changed the world, Einstein, Gandhi (*Satyagraha*), and Akhnaten, as a "trilogy" or "triptych" that might be performed "within the same week;" and so when the Stuttgart Opera, in June of 1990, offered two such cycles of the *Philip Glass Trilogy,* it matched his intent. The company, however, placed last the first opera composed, *Einstein,* confusing the display of Glass' developing musical style, for in the succeeding operas he moved far toward a more conventional approach. On the other hand, the order allowed the noted stage designer and director, Achim Freyer, to move from the most historically based of the three, Gandhi in *Satyagraha,* through the more loosely structured, legendary "portrait" of *Akhnaten,* to the wholly abstract *Einstein,* suggesting the stage picture in these operas is more important than the music.

Whether the works truly are sufficiently related to form a musical trilogy or even are operas in the traditional sense, with music dominant, are questions for the future. It may be that Glass and his collaborators have created a new form of visual drama, with emphasis on lighting, color, and movement, and in which music is merely auxiliary. Meanwhile, it seems true for most persons that what dazzles the eye will close the ear, sometimes for long periods. In many of today's works what happens onstage, with shifting platforms, soft or blazing lights, and marvelous transformations grabs attention from the ear. And possibly that is intended. Significantly, *Akhnaten,* though successful in its first production in the United States, in London with the same stage pictures revised and improved, became for several years a smash hit.

Much is still unknown about the historical Akhnaten. Representations of him show a shrunken body, large head, and signs of hermaphrodism in breasts and thighs, and documents reveal an intense, personal vision of God. But beyond that the opera's view of him runs counter in some respects to what scholars report. Glass paints him as a pioneer, who first gave the world the idea of monotheism, God [Aten] as a wholly abstract idea, secularly represented by the sun-disc with radiant, life-giving beams. Akhnaten's "Hymn to the Sun" has survived, and Glass has it at the center of the opera (sung in the language of the audience). But while scholars acknowledge Akhnaten tried to substitute a form of monotheism for the polytheistic cults of Amon, and so was viewed by the priests of Amon as a heretic, they deride the idea, which Glass seemingly accepts, that Akhnaten was a great religious visionary who influenced Moses, and subsequently, Christianity. It seems, the scholars say, Akhnaten's God was not wholly abstract but was the sun, of whom Akhnaten claimed to be the physical son. Nothing abstract there. Akhnaten's recent biographer, Donald Redford, describes the King as poetic, artistic, fanatic, shallow, un-intellectual and a poor executive. Under him the Egyptian Kingdom, as Glass shows, all but collapsed; but what Glass shows less well is how it promptly returned to its former religion, dominion, and prosperity under Akhnaten's successors. It is questionable, at least, whether Akhnaten's vision and reign changed the ideas of his world, much less ours, or whether Glass's portrait of him is credible.

The opera's three acts offer pictures from different periods of Akhnaten's seventeen-year reign: Act I, the first year, his father's death and his succession and coronation; Act II, from fifth to fifteenth years, his destruction of the temple of Amon, his monogamous love for his wife Nefertiti (ignoring his children by his mother), his creation of a new city, Akhetaten, dedicated to Aten, and finally, his Hymn to the Sun; and Act III, the seventeenth and last year, his isolation, the revolt of the people led by the priests of Amon, and the destruction of the city Akhetaten; a scene in which modern sightseers visit the ruins of the city; and in an epilogue, the ghosts of Akhnaten and his family seen departing the city, figures of the past.

The score calls for a large chorus and orchestra, including electric synthesizer. For a recording the Stuttgart company provided 65 singers and 59 players, but because Glass omitted all violins, typically a quarter of the latter, the orchestra is on a grander scale than its number suggests. Its sound, lacking violins, often is sombre, but brightened at times by flute, bells and trumpet, instruments which in this opera Glass uses more individually than usual. Akhnaten, for instance, is always accompanied by a solo trumpet, and his every appearance, even if silent, is announced in the orchestra by the trumpet.

The Scribe or narrator speaks in the language of the audience, though his text, like that of all the sung passages, is drawn from the monuments, inscriptions and letters of Akhnaten's period, or close to it. The vocal passages, except for the Hymn to the Sun, are sung in the appropriate language, Egyptian, Akkadian (Egyptian of diplomatic correspondence), and Biblical Hebrew. Glass and Goldman aimed, they have said, "to recreate the rhythms and cadences of the languages of a long-forgotten era," though they have no similar thrust for the music. Nevertheless the ancient languages serve to distance the audience from the pictures they watch, just as did the Sanskrit in *Satyagraha* or the numbers and syllables (see Chap. 6) in *Einstein*. Here the Scribe sets the scene and the characters sing words that, except in the Hymn and (for a few) in the Hebrew of the Psalm that follows, carry no meaning. And in several instances the characters are directed merely to vocalise, "no words being necessary." Hence an increase in the dependence on mime; on sight, not sound.

To many persons the stage pictures of the Houston-New York-London production were stunning, projecting a strong sense of sun, sand and water in an eternal setting. Throughout the opera to one side of the stage two farmers slowly threshed wheat; on the other a mason made bricks of mud; and to the back a group of wrestlers periodically changed positions. When Akhnaten ordered his city built, his people, using the sand and water onstage, constructed a row of tiny houses across the stage front; and when the priests of Amon destroyed Akhnaten's city, they trampled these houses, returning them to desert.

Glass always has dodged politely the question of which set of visual images he preferred, the Stuttgart or the Houston-New York-London production. But he has said this much: "The 'funeral image,' for example, did not appear in either production to the extent I would have liked." Clearly, he wants it stressed.

ACT I (46 min.)—YEAR 1 OF AKHNATEN'S REIGN

PRELUDE (11 min.)

Following an orchestral prelude the curtain rises on the city of Thebes. The Scribe sets the historic background: Akhnaten's father, Amenhotep III, has died and the priests of Amon lead the funeral procession and rites.

SCENE 1 (9 min.)

The Funeral. A cortege enters, led by two drummers followed by the priests and Aye, the dead King's advisor. To cellos alone, the dead King comes, "holding his head in his hands;" and as he departs, the chorus sings a last salute. (This funeral music was used by Jerome Robbins as the climax to his ballet, *Glass Pieces,* danced first by the New York City Ballet, May 12, 1983. Robbins preceded the *Akhnaten* excerpt with two works, *Rubric* and *Facade,* from Glass's recording, *Glassworks.*

SCENE 2 (17 min.)

The Coronation of Akhnaten. After the funeral procession has passed, he is left onstage with attendants who dress him for the coronation, a scene of mime followed by a trio for the High Priest, the advisor Aye, and the general Horemhab, who hail Akhnaten as their new King. As he is crowned (mime), the Scribe recites his titles, and the chorus ends the scene with a hymn.

SCENE 3 (9 min.)

The Window of Appearances. A balcony of the palace used for state appearances. Coronation music returns, this time colored by bells, whose sound permeates the scene. Akhnaten, his mother Queen Tye, and his wife Nefertiti appear on the balcony. He sings first, joined soon by his mother, and later by Nefertiti. They praise God's power of regeneration in all nature. It is a "hymn of acceptance and resolve and, in spirit, announces a new era." The women retire, leaving Akhnaten on the balcony, and the act closes with him gazing at the now distant funeral cortege "floating on barques across a mythical river to the Land of the Dead."

ACT II (44 min.)—YEARS 5 TO 15; THEBES AND AKHETATEN

SCENE 1 (13 min.)

The Temple of Amon. The priests sing a hymn to Amon. After which a group who worship Aten, led by Akhnaten and Queen Tye, gather and attack the temple (while singing a vocalise, without words) and destroy its roof, allowing the sun of Aten to pour in. The music is full of trombones and tuba.

SCENE 2 (10 min.)

Akhnaten and Nefertiti. Warm strings, warbling flute and soft trombones lead to a duet. The text is recited first by the Scribe (in English) and then sung by the principals (in Egyptian): "I breathe the sweet breath which comes forth from thy mouth. . . Give me thy hands, holding thy spirit, that I may receive it and may live by it." At the scene's close, behind the couple, appears the funeral procession "in a later stage of its journey, this time ascending on wings of large birds to the heavenly land of Ra."

SCENE 3 (8 min.)

The City of Akhetaten, "the horizon of Aten," and Celebration Dance. The Scribe opens the scene with a long speech (no music) taken from the surviving boundary markers of the city, which gradually rises behind him. The dance, after a fanfare of brass, follows, with musicians (triangle, wood block, and tambourine) onstage. And the movements and sounds are to contrast in their lightness with the heavier rituals of Amon.

SCENE 4 (14 min.)

Akhnaten's Hymn to the Sun. The introductory music recalls his coronation, and alone onstage he sings his Hymn (whose text was found in Queen Tye's tomb): "Thou dost appear beautiful, On the horizon of heaven, oh, living Aten. . . Thou sole God, There is no other like thee. . . There is no other that knows thee, Save thy son, Akhnaten. . ." At its end, he leaves the stage deserted, and a chorus offstage sings, in Hebrew, verses from the Biblical Psalm104, which Glass and his collaborators think reflect the spirit if not the full substance of the Hymn.

ACT III (37 min.)—YEAR 17 AND THE PRESENT; AKHNATEN

SCENE 1 (12 min.)

The Family. A divided stage. To one side Akhnaten and his six daughters. As they sing to each other "a sweet, wordless song," they reveal a family self-absorbed, isolated from the world. The scene shifts to outside where the people, led by priests of Amon, grow restless as the Scribe reads letters from allies abroad that complain of the King's failures in administration. With the scene again on Akhnaten, now with only his two eldest daughters, in his ignorance of what is about to happen he seems still more isolated and withdrawn.

SCENE 2 (8 min.)

Attack and Fall. Brass fanfares. The general Horemhab, the advisor Aye, and the High Priest of Amon, push to the front of the crowd and lead an attack on the palace, capturing Akhnaten and his family. The text, sung in Akkadian, is taken from tablets of the period: "Let the king care for his land. . ."

SCENE 3 (7 min)

The Ruins. The Scribe, speaking over music, describes the rebuilding of Amon's temple and how the new king has brought prosperity to the country. Behind him the city of Akhetaten appears in the ruin it is today. Modern tourists wander about, snapping photographs, and one group stops to hear the Scribe, now a Tour Guide, read from a guide book of the city that was. (This scene often strikes some in the audience as inartistic, jarring in its clash of culture and over-cute in its transformation of the Scribe into Tour Guide.)

SCENE 4 (11 min.)

Epilogue. The tourists leave. Ghosts of the principals roam through the ruins of the city. Akhnaten, Queen Tye, and Nefertiti sing a wordless song, while the others remain silent. Gradually, they realize they are dead, and now figures of the past. They see the funeral cortege of Akhnaten's father moving across the background, and forming one of their own, they move off to join the other "still on its jouney to the heavenly land of Ra." There is a long orchestral close.

THE GHOSTS OF VERSAILLES

Grand opera buffa in two acts. World premiere, Metropolitan, New York, Dec. 19, 1991; radio broadcast prem., Jan. 4, 1992; television prem., Sept. 24, 1992; revival at the Metropolitan, April 3, 1995; Chicago, Oct. 14, 1995; Bloomington, Indiana, April 19, 1997 (shortened version). Music by John Corigliano; libretto by William M. Hoffman, suggested by Beaumarchais' play *La Mère coupable.*

This "grand opera buffa," perhaps the first to combine "grand opera" and "buffa," was commissioned by the Metropolitan in 1979 in hope of performing it in the company's centennial season, 1983-84. But because of a laggard muse the composer was slow with the music, and the opera did not arrive onstage until 1991. Even so, the Metropolitan in its programs referred to it as its "centennial opera," and so it is generally known.

For that celebratory purpose it was a superb success. In its first season at the box office it had seven sold-out performances, and then over radio and television was heard and seen by millions more, becoming one of that year's best known theatrical events. Three years later, in revival at the Metropolitan and in a season at the Lyric Opera, Chicago, it did equally well, and an opera that many persons assumed was too big, too expensive, too spectacular ever to enter the repertory seemed about to do so, especially after a tightened, shortened version of it played in Bloomington, Indiana.

The opera, taking place in the palace of Versailles and in the present (the ghosts are from 1793), is, indeed, on a scale that is "grand." For its two acts (92 and 82 minutes), it requires twelve principal singers and thirty more named soloists. Besides the pit orchestra, the first in the Metropolitan's history to use a synthesizer, it calls for another on stage, as well as a marching, Arabic wind band, and it uses choristers and supers by the dozens. For the finale to Act I, a reception at the Turkish Embassy, as done at the Metropolitan and Chicago 120 persons were onstage, including an automaton representing the Turkish Ambassador, Pasha Suleyman, that though seated and cross-legged was thirty-feet tall and cradled a singer in the crook of his arm. Inside it five stage-hands worked his eyes, hands and feet, and at the close of the scene his turban exploded with fireworks.

This was, however, only one small part of the visual spectacle. Seldom has the Metropolitan's stage machinery been put to such continuous use: Scenes faded into scenes, ghosts floated through the air, characters arrived by balloon, and the lighting throughout was atmospheric. If, as many say, the trend in opera in the century's last quarter has preferred spectacle over music, *The Ghosts of Versailles,* might be an example.

About the quality of its music, from the start there has been argument. It can hardly be discussed, however, without some understanding of the very elaborate plot. The opera opens in the present, with the ghosts of Louis XVI and his court assembling in the theatre at Versailles to hear a new opera by Beaumarchais (music by Corigliano). Beaumarchais is in love with Marie Antoinette, who has been unable emotionally to adjust to her death by guillotine in 1793. Whereas the other dead in a ghostly way seem content, she grieves; and to win her love and free her from depression Beaumarchais plans to introduce her into his opera, in which she will escape from the Revolution, and thus history will be changed: "I'll make you live again." Such, he believes, is the power of art.

There are many complications to his opera's intrigue, most turning on the fate of her diamond necklace, which will be used to buy her freedom. During the course of events Beaumarchais loses control of his characters, Figaro, Susannah, Rosina, Almaviva, all older now than in Mozart or Rossini, and nearly loses the Queen to the machinations of his villain, Bégearss. In the end, moved by Beaumarchais' love for her, Marie Antoinette realizes that she must die, as history requires, and she mounts the scaffold as the people of Paris sing the "Marseillaise." Her death, however, releases her to love Beaumarchais in their ghostly world. And so, in a pun no worse than many in the libretto, she has her cake and eats it, too.

The opera thus takes place in three worlds, which constantly overlap and merge, the after-world of the ghosts, the artistic world of the Beaumarchais opera (titled *A Figaro for Antonia*), and the historical world of the French Revolution. The interaction of the three, as characters pass from one to another, presents any stage director with as many difficulties as opportunities, not least "traffic control" keeping the strands of plot clear.

For the composer the three worlds offered a chance for musical differentiation. The ghostly world is full of eerie sounds, many of them created on the synthesizer; the operatic world, Figaro and the Almavivas, imitates Mozart and Rossini; and the historical world, with touches like the "Marseillaise" has a more romantic, nineteenth-century style. The potential contrasts played to Corigliano's strength, which lay in allusion, parody and pastiche. But a difficulty may be that on third or fourth hearing the joke wears thin. Corigliano's imitations of Mozart and Rossini are not so fine as their originals; and neither are his imitation of Iago's crede from Verdi's *Otello* or his borrowings of mood, tone, and style from the final trio in Richard Strauss' *Rosenkavalier.* On the other hand, he does succeed, after several hours of comic run-a-round, in making the opera's final scenes moving.

The question remains, however, can this "grand opera buffa," which reputedly cost several millions to put on the stage, have any future, or is it already a dinosaur. One company that attempted to find the answer, the Indiana University School of Music, produced a cut-down version that apparently had been approved and perhaps edited by the composer and librettist. Scenes reportedly were tighter, particularly the opera's opening, establishing more quickly the relationship between Beaumarchais and the Queen. The entertainments at the Turkish Embassy were reduced, and even the long solo, composed originally for Marilyn Horne, was cut, though allegedly only for lack of a sufficiently talented singer. And the opera within the opera, Beaumarchais's *A Figaro for Antonia,* which inevitably plays often at stage rear, was projected into the auditorium over microphones. The opera had a success. What lies ahead for it, however, is still a question, for in the long run operas survive not because of their scenery or spectacle, but because musicians are impressed by their music; and Mozart, Rossini, Verdi and Strauss are still—no shame to Corigliano—more impressive than anyone's parodies.

NIXON IN CHINA

Opera in three acts (in some productions Act III is presented as Act II, scene 3). World premiere, Houston, Oct. 22, 1987; European prem. Amsterdam, June 2, 1988; British Prem., Edinburgh, Sept. 1, 1988; Australian prem. Adelaide, Feb. 29, 1992. Music by John Adams; libretto by Alice Goodman.

PRINCIPAL CHARACTERS

Richard Nixon, President of the U. S.	baritone
Pat Nixon, his wife	soprano
Chou En-lai, Premier of the People's Republic of China	baritone
Mao Tse-Tung, Chairman of the Chinese Communist Party	tenor
Chian Ch'ing (Madame Mao)	soprano
Henry Kissinger, U. S. Secretary of State	bass

Chinese secretaries, guides, guards and people; as well as dancers and chorus of the ballet *The Red Detachment of Women*.

Time and Place: Peking, China, Feb. 21-27, 1972.

This opera, in its first five years, achieved great celebrity, for except for one or two by Philip Glass none recently has been launched with greater commercial success and publicity. In its first year, besides gathering a huge number of puff and critical articles, *Nixon in China* played in Houston, New York, Washington, Amsterdam, and Edinburgh; and thereafter, in Germany and Australia. Since then, however, though its title remains embedded in the public's mind and though a recording has brought it many supporters, its annual number of productions has dropped to one or none—a fate not unusual for operas based on living persons. And in 1987, the year of this one's premiere, all the principals might have attended except Mao, who had died in 1976, and his wife, who was in prison.

Perhaps the mortality rate of operas on living persons is high because nothing is staler than yesterday's news. But in this case there is something more: The greatest event of Nixon's presidency, the Watergate scandal that forced his resignation, is not in the story, neither mentioned, nor foreshadowed—Joan of Arc without the stake. Yet his trip to China and his interview with Mao were momentous events, with important repercussions and a place in history, and possibly that place, with its impact on events, is itself an obstacle for an audience, for ultimately the opera is not about real people but about the characters created by the composer and librettist. Still, just as no one today worries that Verdi's King Philip and Don Carlo, or his Simon Boccanegra, have little resemblance to their historic originals, the passing of time may favor *Nixon in China*.

The opera's structure is unusual, its climaxes often becoming introspective soliloquies rather than extroverted arias or grand choral finales. The first act, though ending in general euphoria at a public reception, has its true climax earlier in the lengthy toasts proposed by Premier Chou and President Nixon; Act II closes with Madame Mao's statement of her philosophy, with the chorus echoing her. And the final act presents the Goodman-Adams view of Nixon, Mao, and Chou—a nervous, naive innocent, a self-taught, practical revolutionary, and an exhausted idealist—through their recollections of their past. Some persons have found the act tedious, for nothing happens, beyond the expressions of thought, but others hear in it some of the opera's best music, particularly Chou's closing aria.

Two bits of history crucial to the opera need repeating, for those who may be only dimly aware of them. Nixon's trip to China was momentous, in part, because Republicans in the United States had for so long vilified Democrats for "losing China" to the communists that no Democrat leader dared to open relations with Communist China. The act required a Republican president, and courage, for Nixon could not know in advance how his country and party would respond to his trip to China. Hence his concern in Act I with how the news of it would be received back home.

Madame Mao, at the time of Nixon's visit, was famous for her interest in the arts. She had been an actress, "Lan P'ing," in Shanghai, quit the stage in her mid-twenties to join the Communists in retreat in Yenan, ingratiated herself with Mao, and became his fourth wife. Fifteen years later she took a lead in the Cultural Revolution (1966-1976), becoming one of the "Gang of Four" and intent on reforming the arts. She produced five idealogically-pure ballets in which a heroic woman became a leader, among them *The Red Detachment of Women,* and decreed that only eight "model works" of music, including her ballets, could be studied in schools or performed in theatres. For nearly ten years, until Mao's death in 1976, eight hundred million Chinese could hear or study only the eight works—probably the most severe censorship of music ever experienced by a human society.

Adam's orchestra calls for 34 players, 39 instruments, and among the latter four saxophones, two pianos, and a synthesizer. His music is rhythmically strong but, to some ears, at times rhythmically and melodically monotonous. One problem may be the verse to which it is set. Whole scenes are written in iambic tetrameter, "The people are the heroes now, Behemoth pulls the peasant's plow. . . :" or, as in the chorus and dialogue of the ballet, in a "tumbling" verse of short lines, "Strike the first blow/ For Chairman Mao/ And overthrow/ The tyrant, and/ Share out the land." A good nineteenth-century Italian libretto would have varied the verse forms more frequently, allowing, even demanding, a greater variety of rhythm and melody. On the other hand, librettist and composer do achieve a distinctive voice for each character, so that Nixon's nervous agitation contrasts clearly with Chou's calm, Madame Mao's aggressive certainty with Mao's greater detachment.

The music's style can be most easily heard in the opera's first three minutes, before voices enter. There are 159 measures of rising scales. The first thirty of these, played on violins, violas, and keyboards, repeat an eight, all-white-note scale of A minor, to which gradually are added, first by woodwinds, other scales played at about a seventh of the speed, while beneath them bass instruments sound the fundamental tones. Soon other instruments enter with different figures, and the complications of the scales increase until the chorus enters and the scales become accompaniment.

ACT I (63 min.)

SCENE 1 (19 min.)—Airport at Peking; Nixon's arrival

A cold, clear morning. The airport is deserted; no planes are landing. The music reflects the quiet. A guard of Chinese troops march in, and circle the field singing "The Three Main Rules of Discipline and the Eight Points of Attention." Their voices rise as they frequently repeat: "The people are heroes now/ Behemoth pulls the peasant's plow. . ."

An American jet lands, *The Spirit of '76;* Chou En Lai and a small group of officials step forward to greet the President. The plane's door opens, Nixon appears at the top of the ramp, followed by Mrs. Nixon in a scarlet coat.

They descend, exchange pleasantries with the Chinese, and Nixon has what a more traditional opera might call his "entrance aria," though here a long, interior reflection. He worries how the picture of what is **Nixon's aria** happening will be received: "News, news, news has a kind of mystery. . . We live in an unsettled time./ Who are our enemies? Who are/ our friends?. . . It's prime time in the U.S.A./ Yesterday night. They watch us now;/ The three main networks' colors glow. . ." Then he grows nervous: "The rats begin to chew the sheets. . . Nobody is a friend of ours. . . We must press on." His Secretary of State, Kissinger, interrupts to say that Chairman Mao wishes to meet him, a gesture until this moment only hoped for, and now confirmed.

SCENE 2 (25 min.)—Mao's study

Walls lined with books, many of them showing signs of use and bookmarks. Mao sits in an upholstered armchair; behind him, on straight chairs, sit three secretaries (contraltos), who translate and record. As Nixon, Kissinger, and Chou enter, photographers slip into the room, snapping pictures. Until these depart, the statesmen talk of books, Kissinger remarking that while at Harvard he assigned Mao's writings. When the photographers leave, the conversation turns to politics, and it soon becomes clear that Mao is both more cultivated and smarter than Nixon or Kissinger, who cannot follow all his references.

Mao's view of the United States is that it sends China missionaries and businessmen who "crucify us on a cross of usury;" after which "come the Green Berets,/ insuring their securities." His vision for China is of "Platonic men freed from the caves. . . of industry borne on the wind."

Ignoring the barbs, Nixon rejoins that "this leap forward to light" is the common first step. "Let us join hands, make peace for once./ History is our mother, we/ Best do her honor in this way."

Mao retorts: "History is a dirty sow;/ If we by chance escape her maw/ She overlies us."

Even so, Nixon insists, for peace "We still must seize the hour and seize the day;" and Mao and Chou are impressed. The interview ends well; Mao even remarks in his ironic fashion that Nixon's *"Six Crises* isn't a bad book." And the scene ends with the secretaries recording and repeating Mao's words, "Founders come first, then profiteers." [The scene has intriguing conversational gambits, and some critics feel Adams' orchestration here is too heavy, obscuring the words.]

SCENE 3 (19 min.)—Great Hall of the People.

Evening of the first day, February 21st. Premier Chou is entertaining the Americans; nine hundred communist party members are present, and the mood is warmer than at the airport. Mao evidently has spoken in favor of Nixon's visit.

Late in the evening Premier Chou rises to toast his guests. He gives a long speech, reviewing China's recent history, ending: "All patriots were **Chou's toast** brothers once:/ Let us drink to the time when they/ Shall be brothers again."

Nixon rises, and in his more agitated style, suggests the moment has come to "Start a long march on new highways,/ In different lanes, but **Nixon's toast** parallel. . . The world watches and listens. We/ Must seize the hour and seize the day."

More short toasts, during which Pat Nixon murmurs, "Have you forgotten Washington?" Chou grasps the reference: "Washington's birthday!" And all around the hall party members toast Washington, Mao, the U.S.A., and "Washington's birthday!." The excitement swiftly builds musically; Kissinger remarks, "You won't believe how moved I am;" and Nixon, "It's like a dream."

ACT II (49 min.)

SCENE 1 (21 min.)—Pat Nixon on a sight-seeing tour

Another cold day. Mrs. Nixon has shaken the hands of the employees at the Peking Hotel and now is on her way to see a commune, the Summer Palace, and the Ming Tombs. She reflects that by nature she neither is full of hope or regret. Her family was poor, and she had no time for trivialities. Her guides, three contraltos (who also sang Mao's secretaries) approve her behavior. At the commune they show her a prize pig, and she scratches its ear; then they point to "children having fun."

At the entrance to the Summer Palace Mrs. Nixon pauses in the gate of Longevity and Good Will for an impromptu speech, foreseeing a **Mrs. Nixon** time "when luxury dissolves into the atmosphere," and everywhere, "the simple virtues root and branch." Her vision speaks for many Americans, a longer life, with greater comfort, and surrounded by a large family. The Chinese applaud politely.

At the Ming Tombs, the guides speak with pride of the carvings and regret for the men who made them, who "dug their own graves," with only "two bowls of rice a day." Mrs. Nixon remarks, "It sounds like you remember them;" but the libretto suggests "she is thinking about her bath and the outfit she will wear to the ballet" in the evening. [Critics do not agree on this treatment of Mrs. Nixon, some seeing "a caricature," and others, a fair and complimentary reflection.]

SCENE 2 (29 min.)

At the ballet, *The Red Detachment of Women*. Madame Mao sits between the President and Mrs. Nixon; Chou on the President's right; Mao is not present, nor is Kissinger.

The ballet begins, revealing three beautiful young women chained to
ballet posts, their landlord's victims. The two less beautiful step from the posts and begin to dance while the paragon remains chained. Three contraltos describe how landlords oppress the poor.

The landlord's overseer, Lao Szu (sung by Kissinger), full of lust and breathing heavily releases the loveliest girl; but she, after embracing her two friends, seizes the whip from Lao Szu, beats him to the ground, and escapes. "Doesn't he look like you know who!" whispers Mrs. Nixon to the President. [As many have complained, the caricature of Kissinger throughout this scene, seems to belong to a different sort of opera.]

The beautiful girl is recaptured by the landlord's mercenaries, tortured by him and whipped to death, or seemingly so, by Lao Szu. The scene so upsets Mrs. Nixon that she runs onto the stage, but is held from actual interference by the President. The scenario calls for a tropical storm, and the Nixons, onstage, are drenched.

As the rain stops, a Party Representative enters, finds the girl, and is able to revive her. The clouds part, the sun shines, and a detachment of the Red Women's Militia enter to a jaunty chorus, "Strike the first blow, etc." The Party Representative gives the beautiful girl a rifle, and she joins the militia.

The scene shifts to the landlord's house. Lao Szu sings of how he likes to hang around the rich and powerful to collect a few crumbs, "Loose change." Nixon, still onstage, hands him a coin, "You're talking like a real pro."

Embarrassed, Lao Szu orders the serving girls to dance. Actually, they are the Women's Militia in disguise, and the chorus, singing as if the voice of the beautiful girl, exult, "Revenge is mine."

"That is your cue," cries Madame Mao. The girl hastily pulls out a pistol and fires two shots. (Lao Szu has disappeared). In fact, it was not her cue, and for a moment everyone stops, stunned. "Forward Red Troupe," cries Madame Mao. "Fix bayonets." Soon the red flag flies over the landlord's house, The granary is opened, and distribution begun to the peasants.

The scene ends with Madame Mao's aria of self-revelation: "I am the **Madame Mao** wife of Mao Tse-tung. . . When I appear the people hang upon my words. . . I speak according to the book." The people rejoice, "Joy, joy, joy." And in exaltation she repeats, most often, "I speak according to the book," which is taken up by the chorus.

ACT III (33 min.)

The last night in Peking. The six principal characters retire for the night. Onstage there are six beds in a row, though the audience should imagine the Nixons and Kissinger in their rooms in the Peking Hotel, while Mao and his wife, and Chou are in their separate homes. The thoughts of all six, however, interweave (as if they were in fact all in the same room), so that there are soliloquies and dialogues, as each recalls what brought him or her to this moment. (Again, no agreement among critics, some thinking the scene displays Adams' inability to rise to the complications and inwardness of the scene, while others, comparing it to its predecessors, find it "more richly inventive in melody, freer in rhythm, subtler in harmony, more fanciful in texture.")

Kissinger continues to be the butt of scorn. He scratches his neck, his nose, his ear; asks Chou "Where's the toilet," and disappears, for good.

Nixon is very tired; his wife looks "fragile and heavily powdered;" Madame Mao seems smaller, and Chou is exhausted; but Mao appears full of youth and the hope of revolution.

Nixon and Pat recall California (pianos), which leads them to think of World War II, and in snatches of dialogue he recalls his service in the South Pacific, the poker games, the men who called him "Nick," a hamburger stand he one time set up, what he had learned from it all.

Mao and his wife recall how she came first to Yenan. As he puts it, when "that tasty little starlet came/ To infiltrate my headquarters." Their dialogues display his vigor, his patience, his zeal. When Chou says to him, "In Yenan we were just boys." He replies, "Revolution is a boys' game."

Chou has the final aria [and many persons believe the opera's most beautiful]. "I am old. . . How much of what we did was good?/ Every-
Chou's aria   thing seems to move beyond/ Our remedy. Come, heal this wound. . ." The only answer to the mysteries of life seem to lie in "work." "Outside this room the chill of grace/ Lies heavy on the morning grass."

PART THREE

Compendium and Glossary

"Successes are made by the public, not by the critics."

HUGO VON HOFMANNSTHAL

(In a letter to Richard Strauss, July 23, 1911)

"Make the theatre what it should be, a place of, at once, ecstasy, entertainment, and moral and political enlightenment."

ANDREW PORTER

(In an article dated August 6, 1984)

COMPENDIUM AND GLOSSARY

of composers, a few others, and terms pertinent to
Twentieth Century Opera

Adorno, Theodor W. (1903-1969)—Professor of philosophy at the University of Frankfurt, Germany. The chief musical theorist supporting ideas of the "Second Viennese School," atonal and serial composers, in opera chiefly Arnold Schoenberg and Alban Berg. Adorno's writings, though often obscure in meaning, were very influential in mid-century; perhaps less so later. Admiring Marx and Freud, he wrote of popular music as a commodity whereas avant-garde music, by resisting tradition and concerning itself with human alienation and fragmentation of culture, demanded a more critical, interpretative, self-reflective mode of reception. His best known book is *Philosophy of New Music* (1949). He famously castigated Kurt Weill for abandoning German avant-garde music in his later, "Broadway" works, ranking him as no more a musician than Cole Porter. As for jazz, Adorno thought it merely part of the entertainment industry, not an art. Strangely, he himself was similarly dismissed by Schoenberg, who in 1949 wrote a friend about *Philosophy of New Music*: "The book is very difficult to read, for it uses this quasi-philosophical jargon in which modern professors of philosophy hide the absence of an idea. They think it is profound when they produce lack of clarity by undefined new expressions. . ."

Atonal music. Music without reference to key, the succession of notes or chords not establishing any predominance among them. Schoenberg was composing in this style as early as 1910. One problem of it is that if all notes are of equal importance, none will sound more "at home" than any other, and so creating a sense of closure, cadence, becomes difficult. See discussion of serial music in Chap. 1, p. 11 ff.

Auden, W[ystan] H. (1907-1973). English poet, who later became an American citizen. He had a great love of opera and, with his collaborator, Chester Kallman, became one of the century's great librettists, the equal perhaps of Hugo von Hofmannsthal, who wrote six librettos for Richard Strauss. Auden and Kallman's best known operas are: *The Rake's Progress* (Stravinsky, 1951), *Elegy for Young Lovers* (Henze, 1961), and *The Bassarids* (Henze, 1966); and translations of Mozart's *Magic Flute* (1956) and *Don Giovanni* (1960), Weill's *Seven Deadly Sins* (1958) and *Rise and Fall of the City Mahagony,* (1960). Auden alone wrote *Paul Bunyan* (Britten, 1941) and narrative links in verse for the thirteenth-century liturgical drama *The Play of Daniel,* widely performed by the New York Pro Musica.

Avant-garde (Fr.). Those artists who either are, or feel they are, or are said to be, leaders in charting new paths for their art. They and their supporters often display a self-righteous tone in their preachings, scorning predecessors. The more aggressive are not satisfied that their new style is later in time, different, and acknowledged to be interesting and, perhaps, beautiful; it must be declared better artistically because more daring, and morally because more authentic, more truthful.

Barber, Samuel (1910-1981). American composer, with a lyrical, romantic style predominantly tonal in harmony. His two best-known operas are *Vanessa* (1958), with a libretto by Gian Carlo Menotti, and *Antony and Cleopatra* (1966), after Shakespeare's play. The first, after a premiere and several seasons at the Metropolitan, has had a moderate success in the United States; but *Antony and Cleopatra,* commissioned by the Metropolitan to open its new house, failed, in part because of a ludicrously extravagant production by Zeffirelli. After two seasons it disappeared from the Metropolitan, and has not yet returned. Revised by Barber in 1975, and partially rewritten by Menotti, it has had several productions in smaller houses but still without real success. Yet everyone agrees it has some lovely music, especially the final scene for Cleopatra, composed for and sung at the premiere by Leontyne Price.

Beeson, Jack (1921-). American composer. His operas include *Hello Out There* (1954), *The Sweet Bye and Bye* (1957), *Lizzie Borden* (1965), and *Captain Jinks of the Horse Marines* (1975). With a straightforward, lyrical style, he creates characters and supports them with atmospheric music, happily employing any style from the American past, evangelical hymns, folk songs, dances, and jazz, His operas have played steadily in the United States.

Berio, Luciano (1925-). Italian composer interested in combining layers of meaning and layers of music, the latter achieved by the use of tapes and by reworking music already heard. His four operas are *Opera* (1970), *La vera storia* (1982), *Un re in ascolto* (1984), and *Outis* (1996). The first has been described as offering three accounts of death, while in the last the hero, "Outis," whose name is taken from the *Odyssey* and means "no one," dies at the beginning of each of five scenes. Plainly, to Berio sequential logic is unimportant; but what he intends with any work is not clear, though the stage spectacle often is dazzling.

Birtwistle, Harrison (1934-). English composer, whose operas are the one-act *Punch and Judy* (1968), and full-length *The Mask of Orpheus* (1986) and *Gawain* (1991). Birtwistle is drawn to ritualized dramas, for the most part slow-moving, without narrative logic, and composed in a dissonant style. In *The Mask of Orpheus,* which features loud brass, shrieking winds, and startling percussion, he includes electronic music composed on a computer. His first opera, *Punch and Judy,* the simplest to produce, has had the most productions. It tells a story, based on its puppet original, which aims to start adults thinking. Like a man, the puppet Punch is capable of conflicting emotions. Does he achieve what he wants? Does he know what he wants? Do his violent acts spoil the tenderness sought? Seemingly: Yes, and No.

Boulez, Pierre (1925-). French conductor and composer, famous for his conducting of Wagner's *Ring* (Bayreuth, 1976) and of Berg's *Wozzeck* and *Lulu.* In his own music he favors Berg's atonal, serial style, but carries its techniques further, into all aspects of the music. In his conducting he tends toward swift tempos and clarity of texture; but to some ears he lacks romantic fervor. He once declared that any composer "outside the serial experiments has been useless," and another time, that all opera houses should be "blown up"—apparently furious that audiences still preferred *Rigoletto* to *Wozzeck.* In French music circles he holds a position of great power and by some is much resented.

Brecht, Bertolt (1898-1956). German poet, playwright, librettist. His most famous operatic works are those he (often aided by Elisabeth Hauptmann) wrote for Kurt Weill, *Aufstieg und Fall der Stadt Mahagonny* (1928), *Die Dreigroschenoper* (1930), *Happy End* (1929), *Der Jasager* (1930); and the ballet-cantata, *Die sieben Todsünden* (1933).

Busoni, Ferrucio (1866-1924). German-Italian composer. Of his five operas, all in German, three sometimes are still produced: *Arlecchino* (1917), *Turandot* (1917), and *Doktor Faust* (1925), the last based on a German puppet play. Scholars find the works interesting, but audiences have not warmed to them. In *Doktor Faust,* the most frequently revived, the chief trouble seems to lie in the pacing; scenes, improperly climaxed, go on too long.

Chamber Opera. Any opera with a small cast, chorus (if any), and orchestra. Britten's *Turn of the Screw* is typical, with a cast of seven, no chorus, and an orchestra of 13 players, 18 instruments. Peter Maxwell Davies' *The Lighthouse* is another, with three singers playing seven roles and an orchestra of 12 players, 24 instruments. At what point an opera's cast and orchestra become too large for "chamber" status is arguable. But probably R. Strauss' *Ariadne auf Naxos,* with a cast of fifteen (depending on how roles are doubled), and an orchestra of about 35 players no longer meets the definition. In the twentieth century, as money for opera dwindled, the number of chamber operas increased.

Cherau, Patrice (1944-). French stage director, whose production of Wagner's *Ring* at Bayreuth (1976) raised a storm and greatly strengthened a new style of "concept" staging. To heighten his view of the work's political message, oppression of workers by the middle class, he set the operas in the midst of the nineteenth-century industrial revolution, with the opening scene not at the bottom of the Rhine but on a hydroelectric dam. Where Wieland Wagner (q.v.) in his abstract style had stripped away details, Cherau, in support of his concept, added them. The dwarf Alberich, for instance, in seeking love from a Rhinemaiden (at the dam) put his head up her skirt; and throughout Cherau staged the works with scenes and gestures of startling sex and violence. And to achieve some of Brecht's "alienation" of the audience, he had the scenery visibly changed by stagehands. After Cherau's *Ring,* concept stagings, in which the director's ideas sometimes countered the composer's, became common; and contemporary reference seemed often the chief, or only goal sought.

Copland, Aaron (1900-1990). American composer. His skills, though great, flowered more in orchestral than in vocal music, and of his theatrical works his ballets, *Billy the Kid* (1938), *Rodeo* (1942), *Appala-*

chian Spring (1944), and *The Pied Piper* (Clarinet Concerto, 1951) have been far more successful than his two operas, *The Second Hurricane* (1936), and *The Tender Land* (1954).

Corsaro, Frank (1924-). American stage director, who has worked much since the late 1950s in opera. In the United States he is often associated with the New York City Opera, and in England, since 1983, with Glyndebourne. His staging of Janáček's *Makropoulos Affair* (1970) at the City Opera is an early example in United States opera, pehaps the first, of using projections on backstage screens in connection with action. He is noted for motivating singers to act, and one of his great achievements, aided by the soprano Patricia Brooks, was a City Opera *La Traviata* (1966), in which with startling realism an old opera became new. In the United States, at least, his work is so widespread and copied that his contribution to opera can be easily overlooked. In both New York and Glyndebourne he has worked often with the children's writer and illustrator Maurice Sendak as scenic designer.

Countertenor. A male voice with a range higher than tenor and reaching easily into that of the female mezzo-soprano. It was lost for many years through lack of use and only reemerged in the 1950s with the work of Alfred Deller. It is used often for seventeenth-century castrato roles, such as in Handel's operas, or in modern operas with roles written for it, notably Oberon in Britten's *Midsummer Night's Dream,* the Voice of Apollo in Britten's *Death in Venice,* and the title role in Glass's *Akhnaten.*

Dallapiccola, Luigi (1904-1975). Italian composer, with a serial style more lyrical than most. He composed three operas: *Volo di notte (Night Flight,* after the novel by Antoine de St. Exupéry), 1940; *Il Prigrioniero,* (radio) 1949, and (stage) 1950; and *Ulisse* (1968). Of these the most performed was the one-act (46 min.) *Il Prigioniero,* which despite a cast of five (one singer taking two roles) and an offstage chorus is almost a monodrama in which the Prisoner's thoughts are externalized. The setting is Philip II's Spain, though audiences understood the Inquisition to be a symbol for Fascist oppressions in Europe; and the drama focuses on the Prisoner, who believes, after talks with his Jailer and the Grand Inquisitor (who are the same), that he soon will be freed. At the opera's end he realizes that as his final torture he has been tricked into hope. Dallapiccola uses a large orchestra, stressing brass and bells, and employs three twelve-tone rows, which he defined as prayer, hope, and freedom. For a bleak subject in a severe style the opera in its first twenty-five years was remarkably successful, especially in Europe where it still has an occasional revival.

Davis, Anthony (1951-). American composer with an eclectic style that includes improvisation, jazz, and contemporary pop. His first opera, *X, The Life and Times of Malcolm X* (1986), in twelve scenes recounts the life of Malcolm X, the assassinated black leader (1925-1965). His most recent, also based in history, is *Amistad* (1997), about a slave uprising (1839) on the Spanish slave ship *Amistad* and its outcome in the U. S. Supreme Court with the slaves represented by former U. S. President John Quincy Adams.

Debussy, Claude (1862-1918). French composer, whose lone opera *Pelléas et Mélisande* (1902), is sometimes said to be the first of the twentieth century. As a reaction to Wagner and romantic, realistic music drama it was very influential, setting Maeterlinck's symbolist (q.v.) play almost word for word and in a declamatory style rarely mounting to melody. The orchestra carries much of the interplay between musical motifs, which represent the play's themes as much as its characters, and the orchestral writing is notable for its clarity, color, and ability to shift constantly as the text demands.

Delius, Frederick (1862-1934), English composer, noted for an ethereal quality to his music. He inclined to a declamatory style, stronger in creating atmosphere than character, and weak, perhaps, in handling action. He wrote several operas, of which the most performed is *A Village Romeo and Juliet* (1907). In six scenes, it tells of the children of two Swiss farmers who contest title to a field. The protracted battle ruins the patriarchs, but their children fall in love and, symbolically denied a return to the field of their childhood, at the opera's end consummate their love in a river barge, which they deliberately sink. The interlude sometimes played between scenes five and six, "Walk to the Paradise Garden," used to appear on concert programs. It was composed five years after the opera, using themes from it.

Diaghilev, Serge (1872-1929). Russian impresario (q.v.), whose taste influenced the development of twentieth century opera, ballet, and scenery.

Among the composers he employed were Debussy, Falla, Milhaud, Poulenc, Prokofiev, Ravel and Stravinsky; and among the singers, notably Chaliapin, whom he introduced to the West in one of its first hearings (1908) of *Boris Godunov.* Stravinsky's *Oedipus Rex,* at its premiere performance in Paris, 1927, was dedicated to Diaghilev.

Diva (It.). "Goddess." A term of opera buffs to celebrate a favorite female singer. Among devotees enthusiasm can be shown by inventing other similar terms: Joan Sutherland, for some, became "La Stupenda," and Leontyne Price, "La Leonessa."

Dodecaphonic music. Twelve-note music. See the discussion of serial music, Chap. 1, p. 11 ff.

Egk, Werner (1901-1983). German composer. Of his seven operas the best-known is *Der Revisor* (*The Inspector General,* 1957), based on Gogol's play about official corruption in a small Russian town whose Mayor and citizens mistake a penniless civil servant for a powerful Government Inspector.

Einem, Gottfried von (1918-1996). Austrian composer, with a romantic style giving prominence to the orchestra. His first of seven operas was *Dantons Tod* (*Danton's Death,* 1947) and his fourth *Der Besuch der alten Dame* (*The Old Lady's Visit,* 1971), based on Friedrich Durrenmatt's satire of a town's corruption through its lust for money.

Electric guitar. See the discussion in the opening pages of Chap. 6.

Enescu, George (1881-1955). Romanian composer, who worked mostly in Paris. His lone opera, *Oedipe* (1936), based on the plays of Sophocles, is considered his masterpiece and, after a long period of neglect, is now more performed.

Envelope shaping. A term for amplified or electronic instruments. Every note sounded has a period of initiation or attack, continuation, decay, and cutoff or ending. The timbre is much affected by what are called the starting transients, the combination of harmonics that sound for only the first fractions of a second as a note is started. On a guitar, for example, these differ depending on whether the string is struck with a finger or a plectrum. On a graph the lifetime of a note is shaped like the outline of a flat-topped hill or the flap of an envelope. By changing the shape of the envelope, particularly the harmonic starting transients, the note's timbre can be changed.

Epic theatre. A type of dramatic presentation associated with Bertolt Brecht and aiming, often by an episodic style, to appeal more to reason than emotion, to reduce the audience's sympathy and identification with the characters—Brecht's "distancing techniques" or "alienation" of the audience. Epic theatre is apt to use several forms of narrative at once, projections, films, etc. and to stress the drama's social and political background. Brecht's librettos for Kurt Weill are examples, as, even more, is Zimmermann's *Die Soldaten,* discussed in Chap. 6.

Expressionism. Originally a term for painters in revolt against Impressionism and attempting to express what was within them rather than what they saw around them. In theatre and opera it came to mean a style of production in which scenery, lighting, and costume attempted to make exterior the character's inner feelings. It has been particularly associated with German theatre in the era of the two World Wars. Berg's opera *Lulu,* based on Frank Wedekind's plays is an example; but any production employing unrealistic scenery, tilted walls, exaggerated costumes, spot-lighting, owes something to expressionist techniques.

Falla, Manuel de (1876-1946). Spanish composer, whose chief operas are *La vida breve* (*A Brief Life,* 1914) and *El retablo de maese Pedro* (*Master Peter's Puppet Show,* 1923). The first, in two acts, from which two dances often are extracted, tells of a gypsy girl, betrayed by her lover, who dies of a broken heart. The second, running only thirty minutes, is based on an incident from *Don Quixote,* in which the knight watches a puppet show and, confusing play with reality, attacks the puppets. Though seldom performed, the opera is charming. Falla's one-act mime-ballet *El amor brujo* (*Love the Sorcerer,* 1915), with songs for mezzo-soprano and its "Ritual Fire Dance," is sometimes performed on opera programs.

Fauré, Gabriel (1845-1924). French composer who, apparently inclined by temperament to short works, composed only one opera, *Pénélope* (1913), based on Homer. Seldom revived but much admired, it has a prelude that sometimes appears on concert programs, attractive dances, and a clarity and economy of texture which, though Fauré uses motifs somewhat à la Wagner, is essentially a French musician's reaction against what was considered Wagnerian excess.

Feedback. A term of electronic music. It is a self-perpetuating signal in the amplification system, occuring when the loudspeaker emits a sound sufficiently loud to reactivate the microphone, which then starts another electric signal through the amplifier to the loudspeaker. The result is a howl or whistle that feeds on itself until the cycle is broken, generally by reducing or cutting off the electric power to the amplifer. Sometimes a player can break the cycle simply by interposing his body between the loudspeaker and microphone. Unwanted feedback is the curse of electronic music. Peter Maxwell Davies, in his opera *The Lighthouse* (1980), scores for "a plastic soap-dish scraped round the inside rim of tam-tam to produce a 'howl' resembling electronic 'feedback'."

Fiasco (It.). In operatic language a big failure. In nineteenth-century Italy a fiasco was the bulb-shaped wine bottle that needed a straw basket in order to stand upright on a table. The glass bottles or "flasks" often were odd-shaped because of some defect in the blowing; hence the figurative meaning of a failure.

Film music. A branch of operatic music that can rise to more than mere "movie music." Two great composers for films are Bernard Herrmann (1911-1975) and Erich Korngold (1897-1957). Herrmann's most notable scores were composed for Alfred Hitchcock's *Psycho* and *Vertigo;* Korngold's, for *Captain Blood* and *The Sea Hawk.* Both men also composed operas, a form in which Korngold (q.v.) had the greater success. See also Rota and Walton.

Follow-spotlights. These can be subtle or, as in a nightclub, the prime or only source of light. For many years they were used chiefly in musical comedies or nightclubs where emphasis was on the glamor of the artists rather than on their vocal skills. In any audience there will be some for whom this form of lighting contributes to the excitement; and others who, in many operas, find it arbitrary and out of style. With the rise in opera of expressionistic stagings the use of follow-spots became much more common.

Fuzz box. An electronic effect. By deliberatly distorting the amplitude of the electric signal, it is possible to distort the ultimate sound. Different boxes distort in different ways, but in general a fuzz box is an attempt to put harshness to use.

Giannini, Vittorio (1903-1966). American composer, teacher. He wrote eight operas, of which the most successful was *The Taming of the Shrew* (1953), based on Shakespeare. Giannini had a gift for melody, a sure theatrical sense, and a conservative style. For thirty years, starting in the mid-1930s, he was an important figure in American opera.

Ginastera, Alberto (1916-1983). Argentine composer who succeeded with three operas: *Don Rodrigo* (1964), which two years later the New York City Opera used to open its new house at Lincoln Center; *Bomarzo* (1967), which played happily in the United States, though banned in Buenos Aires until 1972; and *Beatrix Cenci* (1971), commissioned to open the opera house at Kennedy Center, Washington, D.C. He supposedly said that sex, violence, and hallucination are the roots of opera, and he offers these in abundance; but he also supports them with carefully constructed, theatrical music

Hamilton, Ian (1922-) Scottish composer. His three best-known operas are *The Catiline Conspiracy* (1974), *The Royal Hunt of the Sun* (1977), and *Anna Karenina* (1981). He also composed, for the 400th anniversary commemoration of Sir Walter Raleigh's attempt to plant an English colony on Roanoke Island, North Carolina (1584), *Raleigh's Dream* (1984). An hour's meditation on failed ideals, in a prologue and eight scenes, for its special occasion it was highly successful. Hamilton, always his own librettist, has a musical style emphasizing tonal structure, a vocal line that is sometimes difficult but usually rewarding, and an orchestral accompaniment that responds to the text and is often lyrical.

Hartmann, Rudolf (1900-1988). German stage director, associated particularly with the works of Richard Strauss and the Munich opera. He had created at Bayreuth, on the invitation of Wieland Wagner (q.v.), the festival's first post-war production of *Die Meistersinger,* but his orthodox approach to scenery and staging, while successful, was not what W. Wagner sought, and he was not asked back. So he made the

Munich opera in the 1950s and 60s a rival to Bayreuth for productions of Wagner, and though the trend was against him, he was noted for keeping to the composer's conception of the work.

Hauer, Josef Matthias (1883-1959). Austrian composer, whose eccentricities somewhat obscured the value of his work, including two forgotten operas. He claimed to have invented the system of twelve-tone music before Arnold Schoenberg and published a book asserting precedence. Schoenberg grew irritated, retaliated publicly, and Hauer began to use a rubber stamp, which said (trans.): "Josef Matthias Hauer, the spiritual begetter of twelve-note music, and, despite many bad imitators, still the only one who understands and knows how to use it."

Hindemith, Paul (1895-1963). German composer, who became an American citizen in 1946 and taught at Yale University 1940-1953, where he had great influence. His three best-known operas are *Cardillac* (1926), *Neus vom Tage* (*News of the Day,* 1929), and *Mathis der Maler* (1938). His last opera, *The Long Christmas Dinner* (1960), about the continuity of family life, sets a libretto by Thornton Wilder. Both *Cardillac* and *Mathis der Maler,* the latter loosely based on the life of the painter Matthias Grunewald, primarily concern the problems of an artist in a hostile world; *News of the Day* (late 1920s) is a satire on current social behavior, chiefly divorce, journalism, and celebrity. Hindemith's music is always well constructed, usually highly contrapuntal, and perhaps a trifle rigid and lacking in lyricism.

Hofmannsthal, Hugo von (1874-1929). Austrian poet, dramatist, librettist, particularly associated with Richard Strauss, with whom he created six operas and part of a seventh: *Electra* (1909), *Der Rosenkavalier* (1911), *Ariadne auf Naxos* (1912, rev'd 1916), *Die Frau ohne Schatten* (1919), *Die ägyptische Helena* (1928), *Arabella* (1933) and *Die Liebe der Danae* (completed by J. Gregor, 1944). Hofmannsthal brought to Strauss, and the few others for whom he wrote, an established reputation as a poet and dramatist; among his other works, in 1920 he founded with the producer Max Reinhardt the Salzburg Festival, which annually performs his play, *Jederman* or *Everyman.* In stimulating Strauss, von Hofmannsthal raised the position and craft of librettist, creating a new balance of words to music that only recently has been questioned by such composers as Philip Glass, who sometimes replace words with syllables, numbers, or stage pictures. W. H. Auden and Chester Kallman, who sought to continue the Hofmannsthal tradition, dedicated to him the libretto of their opera with Henze, *Elegy for Young Lovers* (1961).

Hoiby, Lee (1926-). American composer, whose best known opera is *Summer and Smoke* (1971, based on the Tennessee Williams play). The work is lyric, suffused with emotion, and often interweaves music with spoken dialogue; it is said to be the first opera based on a Williams play.

Honegger, Arthur (1892-1955). Swiss composer. His best-known stage work, *Jeanne d'arc au bûcher* (*Joan of Arc at the Stake,* 1938, text by Paul Claudel) is an oratorio or mystery play rather than an opera, in part because the lead character and a great many others only recite, never sing; yet it often has been performed in opera houses. The action is dreamlike, occurring in Joan's mind as, about to die, she reviews her life. In the final scene, of childhood, the Virgin appears to her, and Joan, faith restored, dies with courage. The role has attacted many actresses, among them Vera Zorina, Ingrid Bergman, and Mia Farrow; and at the premiere was played by Ida Rubinstein, the dancer-mime for whom, in 1928, Ravel composed *Boléro.*

Impressario (It.). From "impresa," meaning "enterprise" or "undertaking," usually in a business sense. In the early nineteenth century for instance, the seal of the most important theatre in Venice was inscribed: "Impresa del Gan Teatro La Fenice." In the arts, an impresario is one who contracts with artists and puts on a show; more specifically, the director of a travelling ballet or opera company. Some of the greatest of the twentieth century were Serge Diaghilev, Max Reinhardt, Sol Hurok, and Florenz Ziegfeld. Each influenced contemporary taste in design, color, staging, music and dance.

Intendant. Though the word may originally have been French, it is used today mostly in German-speaking countries to mean the administrative director of a theatre or opera house.

Intermezzo (It.). Originally a short, light or comic play or opera inserted between the acts of a serious work. More recently it has come, at least in opera, to be an orchestral passage, sometimes of considerable length, between scenes. It can represent a passage of time, a change of mood, thoughts occurring to a character, or be merely delightful. It goes by many names: interlude, divertimento, entr'acte, or in Philip Glass's *Einstein On the Beach,* "knee plays."

Joplin, Scott (1868-1917). American composer. Joplin is best known for his ragtime piano works, such as "Maple Leaf Rag" and "The Entertainer." His lone opera, *Treemonisha,* a mixture of ragtime, barroom waltz and ballad, and operetta arias, did not receive a full staging until 1972, though Joplin had tried to win a production of it by publishing a piano score in 1911 and some vocal excerpts in 1913 and 1915. After his death his orchestration for the opera was lost and starting with what remained, twenty-seven "numbers" without connecting music, has been reconstructed. The opera tells of a Negro community near the Red River in Arkansas, where a schoolteacher helps her people to overcome superstition through education. The effect of the opera, however, is less serious than joyful, and despite defects of structure and pacing, at the end, triumphant.

Karajan, Herbert von (1908-1989). Austrian conductor and opera director. Artistically one of the best and administratively the most powerful conductor of the second half of the twentieth century, surpassing for longevity of reign even Toscanini or Mahler in the century's earlier years. In 1967 Karajan established the Easter Festival at Salzburg, of which he was the chief conductor and artistic director until 1988. While there he had a hand in all aspects of productions, with the Berlin Philharmonic as his orchestra (1950-1989), and his pick of singers and designers. His productions were lavish, financed largely by his television appearances and recordings, which were commercially very successful, and still are. His favored stage designer was Günther Schneider-Siemssen and for costumes, Georges Wakhévitch.

Korngold, Erich Wolfgang (1897-1957). Austrian-American composer, whose life and works roughly divide on the year of his migration to the United States, 1934. Before then he was a Viennese composer with a romantic, lyric style, set off by a remarkable gift for orchestration. After that, while continuing occasionally to compose in classic forms—concertos, symphonies—he created 18 film scores for Hollywood (chiefly for

Errol Flynn costume dramas), which were outstanding for their melodies, rich textures, and orchestration. In his Viennese years he composed five operas, of which the two most frequently performed are the one-act *Violanta* (1916), a Renaissance drama of love, sex, and violence, and the three-act *Die tote Stadt* (*The Dead City,* 1920), a dreamlike story of a man's love for his dead wife and his ultimate escape from the past through an affair with a woman who resembles her. Korngold's lush, melodic style fell out of fashion with the rise of the Second Viennese School (q.v.), and in his later years he was no longer thought a "serious" composer and his music of whatever sort ignored. In the century's final quarter, however, his operas have had several revivals.

Krenek, Ernst (1900-1991). Austrian composer who emigrated to the United States in 1938. Despite a flourishing career in Austria as a composer, with World War II fashion seemed to pass him by, and in America success came mostly as a teacher. His one well-known opera, in title at least, is *Jonny spielt auf* (*Jonny strikes up [the band],* 1927), in which the hero is a Negro jazz violinist and his friend Max, a parody of Arnold Schoenberg. Audiences of the 1920s, titillated by the use of saxophones, banjo and drums, found the mixture of jazz and twelve-tone music amusing; but the opera seems to resist revival, perhaps because to ears familiar with jazz Krenek's seems tame, even misunderstood.

Legge, Walter (1906-1979). English record-company executive, music administrator and writer. He was responsible, chiefly at EMI, for many of the best operatic recordings of the century, among them: A *Die Meistersinger,* live from Bayreuth 1951; the Callas-di Stefano-Gobbi *Tosca,* conducted by De Sabata, 1953; a *Così fan tutte,* conducted by Karl Bohm, and a series of Viennese operettas with his second wife Elisabeth Schwarzkopf and Nicolai Gedda. As a young man he had worked as a music critic and later as an assistant to the conductor Thomas Beecham; after World War II he created the Philharmonia Orchestra and Chorus in London. Among recording executives he set a high standard for knowledge of music and taste.

Lieberson, Goddard (1911-1977). American record-company executive. Lieberson in his early years worked as a musical journalist and became a composer of some note, one of his later works, composed for son Peter, also a composer, being *Piano Pieces for Advanced Children or Retarded Adults* (1963). He joined Columbia Records in 1939 and worked his way up to presidency; from which position he successfully launched the long-playing record, recorded most of the works of Copland, Schoenberg and Stravinsky, and started a series of "original cast" albums of Broadway musicals. By his taste and understanding of both Broadway and "serious" music, he made Columbia a positive force in the art. His wife was the ballerina-actress, Vera Zorina.

Ligeti, György (1923-). Hungarian composer. Better known for his orchestral works, Ligeti's lone opera, much talked about though less often seen or heard, is *Le grand macabre* (*The Great Figure of Death*), first performed in Stockholm in 1978. The opera is surrealistic, anti-rational; searching for exact meaning is unrewarding; it opens with an overture for twelve tuned motor horns. It is a comedy, perhaps. Death comes to Breughel Land to end the world and kill everyone. He enlists as his aide a Common Man, who is always drunk. The appointed hour strikes, but the next morning everyone awakes with a hangover; and Death expires of shame. But was he Death? Ligeti does not say. There is a lot of song, talk, and nonsense requiring a large cast, a huge, skilled orchestra, and sophisticated stage machinery to fly characters in and out. Because expensive to produce, the opera may continue to be more talked about than seen or heard.

Maestro (It.). "Master," one skilled in his art. Most musicians of any nationality (except French) are delighted to be addressed by this title; the French prefer "Maître."

Mahler, Gustav (1860-1911). Austrian composer and conductor. In opera his fame rests on ten years (1897-1907) as director of the Hofoper (now Staatsoper) in Vienna and, perhaps only in the United States, on two years (1908-1910) at the Metropolitan, New York. He transformed the Vienna Opera and its audience from a nineteenth century house, dominated by singers and an audience that arrived late, left early, and talked through all but the favorite numbers into one where the music and drama came first. He insisted on dimming the house lights, banned late-comers and loud-talkers, restored cuts in Wagner's operas, greatly improved the orchestra, and created a company of first-rate singers rather than local favorites. He modernized the repertory, performing works by Puccini, Pfitzner (q.v.), and Zemlinsky (q.v.), and had a hand in every aspect of a production, preferring as his stage designer, Alfred Roller (1864-1935). In sum, he made the Vienna Opera the leading house and company of the world, giving it a reputation that still clings a century later.

Martinů, Bohuslav (1890-1959). Czech composer, who worked in almost every form, and with success. Among his sixteen operas the two best known are *Julietta* (1938) and *The Greek Passion* (1961), though *Comedy on the Bridge* (1937, rev'd. 1950) and *Mirandolina* (1959) press close. Martinů's style is eclectic, perhaps reflecting his many years spent in forced and voluntary exile from Prague. The opera *Julietta* concerns the conflict between dreams and reality, and its meaning is ambiguous; it has been called, in *Kobbé's Opera Book,* "the lurching of a mind between sanity and madness; it is pure schizophrenia." In contrast, *The Greek Passion,* based on Nikos Kazantzakis' novel *Christ Recrucified,* recounts the failure of Greek villagers, reenacting the passion, to put its message into practice; and the music here is dramatic and reminiscent of the Greek Orthodox Church. The *Comedy on the Bridge* satirizes the absurdities of war, while *Mirandolina,* in Martinů's words, is "a light, uncomplicated thing, with something of Goldoni." In his variety of subjects and musical styles Martinů reflects the diversity of twentieth century opera. One mystery of his career is why his operas, performed widely elsewhere, are less often heard in the United States.

Matthus, Siegfried (1934-). German composer. Two of his operas, unalike in structure and orchestration, have made a strong impression in Europe and the United States: *Judith* (1985) and *Die Weise von Liebe und Tod des Cornets Christoph Rilke* (*Cornet Christoph Rilke's Song of Love and Death,* 1985). The first, based on a play by Friedrich Hebbel and the Old Testament, tells the story of Judith and Holofernes, two strong characters. After he rapes her, she kills him, but then, more neurotic than the Biblical Judith, kills herself. Why? Because she had responded sexually to the rape and so killed him less for patriotic reason than personal revenge, the right deed done for the wrong reason. Hence, suicide. Matthus accompanies the story with a large orchestra playing all out. His other opera, *Cornet Rilke,* based on poems by Rainer Maria Rilke, requires an ensemble of only eleven players, with no strings (except for an electric bass guitar), four flutes, two harps, a horn, and three players for a variety of percussion, in whose use Matthus is a master. With these forces he effectively tells a story of young love and a life wasted in war.

Messiaen, Olivier (1908-1992). French composer, organist and teacher. From 1931 until death he was organist at La Trinite, in Paris, and taught in various schools, including the Paris Conservatoire (1941-78). Among his pupils were Pierre Boulez (q.v.) and Karlheinz Stockhousen (q.v.). Messiaen composed only one opera, *Saint François d'Assise* (1983), briefly described in Chap. 6. He has often experimented with styles, adopting Greek and Asian rhythms, serial techniques, and bird songs. His music often develops a religious, ceremonial atmosphere, which he wants matched by shifts in color of lighting and design. He is often said by admirers to be the greatest French composer since Ravel; but some cheeky people say, "No, since Poulenc;" and one, the critic Andrew Porter, called *St. François* "an unseemly, self-indulgent, bombastic work, musically unchaste, indecent" (article dated May 5, 1986.)

Milhaud, Darius (1892-1974). French composer, who from 1940 until his death spent much of his time in the United States teaching at Mills College, Oakland, California, and in Aspen, Colorado. His great work is *Christophe Colomb* (1930), an opera conceived on such a vast scale it is almost never performed. In contrast is *Le pauvre matelot* (*The Unfortunate Sailor,* 1927), which although in three acts lasts only forty minutes, and needs only four singers and thirteen instruments. It tells of a faithful Wife who has waited fifteen years for the return of her Sailor-Husband. He comes, a wealthy man, but to test his wife he masquerades as a friend of the Husband who, he reports, is poor. To have money to rescue her Husband, the Wife murders the rich "friend." Milhaud tells the story tersely, with touches of folk song, such as "Blow the man down."

Musgrave, Thea (1928-). Scottish composer, conductor, teacher, residing since the 1970s in the United States and working chiefly with the Virginia Opera Company, Norfolk, Virginia. Musgrave has composed nine operas on a variety of subjects. Five of them are *The Voice of Ariadne* (on a Henry James story, 1974), *Mary, Queen of Scots* (1977), *A Christmas Carol* (after Dickens, 1979), *Harriet, the Woman called*

"Moses" (about the slaves' underground railroad to freedom, 1985), and *Simon Bolívar* (1995). And to a remarkable extent she has been able to accomodate her style to the needs of the subject. For *Harriet,* about a courageous Negro slave, Musgrave weaves into her score references to spirituals and gospel music; whereas in *Mary, Queen of Scots,* a historical drama on a grand scale, she attempts a Verdian sweep. Possibly *The Voice of Ariadne,* because a chamber opera in three acts requiring only eight singers and small orchestra, is the most frequently performed. Based on James' *The Last of the Valerii,* it concerns a husband who falls in love, or believes he does, with the voice he imagines of Ariadne (pre-recorded on tape) calling to Theseus. His wife manages to merge herself with Ariadne in his mind and so restores their love. The opera thus becomes a psychological struggle between ideal and real love, and in several scenes lends itself to fanciful stagings. Its chief virtue, perhaps, is the poetic aura Musgrave gives it.

Neo-classical. A vague term to denote those composers who claim to be in revolt against the excesses of nineteenth-century romanticism. In opera it means, roughly, music of emotional restraint, textual clarity, marked rhythm, with an air of simplicity, the opposite of the romantic style, (say, Wagner), in which the whole orchestra often unites to blare out the big tune. Practitioners usually claim they are returning to the roots of music, in form, structure, and orchestration. An example is Stravinsky's *The Rake's Progress,* structured in the pre-Wagnerian style of individual "numbers" (q.v.), connected at times by recitative or even spoken dialogue, rather than being declamatory and through-composed.

Nielsen, Carl August (1865-1931). Denmark's most famous composer whose operas are, *Saul og David (Saul and David,* 1902), and *Maskarade* (1906). The first is tragic, the second, comic, with a climax at a masked ball, ending happily in "a gallop," a quick, lively dance. Both operas, with *Maskarade* the leader, are much performed in Denmark but, lacking good translations, seldom elsewhere. In 1995 the Sarasota Opera Company, in Florida, met the problem head-on, presenting *Maskarade* in Danish (with supertitles) and selling out all eight performances. The opera's attractive overture sometimes appears on concert programs.

Nono, Luigi (1924-1990). Italian serialist composer, married to Arnold Schoenberg's daughter, and as a Marxist interested in politics. His lone opera, *Intolleranza 1960,* tells of an unnamed Migrant Worker, oppressed by an industrial society, tortured by its police, and killed when its dam, built to provide hydroelectric power, breaks and sweeps all away. The opera includes political tracts, often spoken, but also music of considerable power. It was premiered at the Biennale, in Venice, 1961 and caused a riot, probably more because of its politics than music. It had only a few other productions, but because of the scandal of its initial reception, its name is well known.

Number. In an opera score it is the individual piece, aria, duet or chorus, printed as a unit, with its own beginning, middle, and end. In the early nineteenth century this was the typical structure of an opera, and scores would list the aria, duet, etc. by number in a table of contents. Thus, in *La Traviata* (1853) the brindisi or drinking song is No. 3, and the finale to the opera, No. 19. Then if a "number" proved popular, the publisher would issue it separately, under its number, as sheet music for voice and piano, or, in arrangements, for harp, flute, or any other instrument for which there was demand. Composers, however, soon began to cut short individual endings, merging one number directly into the next, so that the score had no obvious breaks of spoken dialogue or recitative. And by the time of *Falstaff* (1893), Verdi's last opera, most scores were "through-composed." Nevertheless, in most twentieth-century operas beneath their apparent seamless flow can be found the old, basic structures of opera, aria, duet, chorus; only the arithmetic number and opening and closing bars have been banished, not the structural substance. Stravinsky, in his neo-classical *The Rake's Progress,* deliberately revived the old "number" style, and gave each piece, aria, duet, etc., its own very plain beginning and end.

Opera (It.). Today there are as many definitions of opera as persons interested in the art. One, much favored in view of the present diversity of works, is merely: "Anything performed in an opera house." Yet, more can be said. Though opera may be the joining of all arts, visual and aural, for a work to be an opera, music must be first in importance; what stimulates the imagination should come primarily through the ear. Said differently, the work's drama and climax must be in the music, not in the spoken dialogue, the lighting, stage pictures, or operation of stage machinery. One difference between traditional Broadway musical comedy and opera, for instance, is that in opera the climax is in the music, and presented often to new music. Verdi in *Aida,* for example, offers three new melodies in the final eight-minute scene, all designed to lead the ear and imagination to new thoughts. Whereas in the typical Broadway musical, the composer in the last eight minutes begins to reprise music already heard, and the audience, sensing the show is over, though the curtain still up, starts to shift its feet, gather coat and hat, and prepare to exit, humming.

Penderecki, Krzysztof (1933-). Polish composer, conductor, teacher, who gathered international acclaim for his *Threnody for the Victims of Hiroshima* (1960), his cantata *St. Luke's Passion* (1966) and for his first opera *The Devils of Loudun* (1969), based on Aldous Huxley's novel. Three subsequent operas had less success, *Paradise Lost* (after Milton, 1978), *Die shwarze maske* (*The Black Mask,* 1986), and *Ubu Rex* (1991). In his early works he was an avant-garde composer, famous for his tone-clusters, sometimes brutal orchestration, and harsh vocal line. In *The Devils of Loudun,* in which a Vicar of the Catholic Church in 1634 is brought to the stake by church politics and false accusations of traffic with the Devil, some of the stage pictures of torture and the stake are horrifying, and the musical accompaniments exceedingly graphic, enough so to turn some in the audience against the work. In later operas Penderecki moved somewhat away from such sensationalism and composed music more tonal in structure, but seemingly with less power. He seems to thrive on grand subjects that are bloody, searing, and painful.

Pfitzner, Hans (1869-1949). German composer, conductor, teacher. His masterpiece is a three-act opera *Palestrina* (1917), presenting a view of that sixteenth-century Roman composer that also throws light on Pfitzner's life. It tells of Palestrina's effort to continue and revive the polyphonic tradition of church music which seems threatened by new trends in Florence. He is visited by a Cardinal who asks him to compose a new mass in the old style and so influence the Roman Catholic council of Trent, in final session, to declare for the Church in favor of the polyphonic style. Palestrina at first declines, but then composes his famous *Missa Papae Marcelli,* strains of which run through the opera. In Pfitzner's life he opposed the new modernism in music, twelve-tone and serial, and his opera carries on the romantic tradition of Wagner. Thus he saw himself in a position not unlike Palestrina's, and hoped with his opera to win a similar victory for the conservative cause in twentieth century music. The opera is a huge work, its second act portraying a session of the Council of Trent, with bishops, cardinals, and papal nuncios abounding; in the third act the Pope appears to thank Palestrina for the mass; and there are frequent angelic and human apparitions as well as a full angelic choir. The opera has been repeatedly performed in Germany; somewhat less elsewhere.

Pizzetti, Ildebrando (1880-1968). Italian composer, teacher, scholar, journalist. Though many persons saw in him the leader of the generation after Puccini, his grasp on the role was never firm. He started as a modernist, but followed its tenets only a little way, and to some ears seemed to stall in a dead end of his own creation. He eschewed melody except where the text gave a character a song, and developed a style of declamation that followed closely the rhythms and accents of Italian. A flaw was a tendency at times to monotony; on the other hand his choral writing was always successful. Generally, the two best of his fifteen operas are said to be *Fedra* (1915) and *Dèbra e Jaéle* (1930), but his *Assassinio nella cattedrale* (1958) is also admired and, because based on T. S. Eliot's play *Murder in the Cathedral,* is possibly the most widely performed. Its two acts are connected by an intermezzo representing Thomas Becket's Christmas Sermon in the cathedral. It opens and closes with sung fragments connected by an orchestral interlude that seems to resolve Becket's moral and philosophical dilemmas and lead to his acceptance of martyrdom.

Pountney, David (1947-). English stage director. Best known for his work over many years with the English National Opera, London. Elsewhere, he has staged the Rotterdam premiere of Philip Glass's *Satyagraha* (1980) and in New York, the Metropolitan premiere of Glass's *The Voyage* (1992). He generally favors a strong, expressionistic style that includes many of Bertolt Brecht's "distancing techniques," with emphasis on social and psychological themes. Sometimes, however, most often with nineteenth century opera, these same techniques seem to lead him astray. Thus, in his *Traviata* for the ENO (1988) he played down the nobility of Violetta's decision in order to stress the hypocritical double-standard of a male-dominated society. To this end he set the opera in a brothel, and in justification offered in the program a long note on Victorian attitudes toward prostitution. But neither setting nor note were apt to the Parisian *demi-monde* of the 1840s or to Verdi's attitude toward his characters. Pountney more often succeeds with twentieth century operas such as *Wozzeck* or *Doktor Faust.*

Reimann, Aribert (1936-). German composer, whose opera *Lear* (1978), based on Shakespeare, was composed for the baritone Dietrich Fischer-Dieskau and widely performed. Its style is predominantly serial, and the orchestration, though seldom obscuring the voices, is full of tone clusters and percussion, heavy and dissonant.

Resphigi, Ottorino (1879-1936). Italian composer. Several of his seven operas hang on the edge of the repertory, in part because of their orchestration. Two of the best known are *La campana sommersa (The Sunken Bell,* 1927), and *La fiamma (The Flame,* 1934). The first tells of a bellmaker who leaves his mortal wife for an elf who is able to cure his illness. But when the first wife kills herself, out of guilt he rejects the second. The opera, with fine music for the fantastical world, and beautiful scoring throughout for bells, projects an artist's conflict between inspiration and everyday life. The second, *La fiamma,* is a story of witchcraft set in seventh-century Ravenna, when that city was under Byzantine rule; it is strong in dramatic expression, archaic atmosphere, and choral climaxes.

Reverberation. In a good concert hall the sound comes at the audience directly from the stage and by reflections from the walls, floor, and ceiling. The reflections, because they must travel farther, reach the ear momentarily later than the sound from the stage. The slight delay gives the sound richness; if too long delayed the reverberation becomes an echo and is confusing. The most common method for achieving reverberation is mechanical rather than electric. The electric signal, by a crystal, is turned into a sound wave at one end of a long steel spring. The sound wave travels relatively slowly down the spring, where it is converted by another crystal back to an electric signal. But within the spring there have been innumerable reflections of the sound wave backward and forward from the ends, and the overall result picked up electrically is a sound of reverberation. This "spring" form of enhancing reverberation is often used on guitars, organs, synthesizers.

Rihm, Wolfgang (1953-). German composer, whose chamber opera

Jakob Lenz (1979) has had success. With thirteen scenes running seventy minutes, and an orchestra of eleven, it presents the fate of Lenz, German dramatist, friend of Goethe, and author of *Die Soldaten* on which Zimmermann based his opera (See Chap. 6). Lenz, a schizophrenic unable to reconcile the world's horrors with its beauties, ultimately went mad; and the opera's focus is steadily on him, with only minor notice for two friends who try but fail to save him. The music is atonal, expressionistic, alternating moments of lyricism with the jagged lines and cries of incipient madness, through which, from time to time, rise strains of a country waltz and old chorale tunes. The effect overall is poetic and moving.

Ring modulator. An electronic box that by combining the overtones or harmonics of two notes—i.e. two electric signals—can create a complex chord. Its simplest and most common use is to double the frequency of a single note, allowing the instrumentalist to add in perfect synchronization to his melodic line its counterpart an octave higher.

Rota, Nino (1911-1979). Italian composer and conservatory director, at Bari, who composed many film scores, among them *La dolce vita* and *Il gattopardo* (*The Leopard*), and ten operas of which one, *Il cappello di paglia di Firenze* (*The Florentine straw hat,* 1955), had a great success. Set in Paris in the 1890s, it's a farce of perpetual motion, a lot of run-around-nonsense started by a horse eating a straw hat. The music is only slightly more modern in style than Rossini, whom it often delightfully parodies, including the obligatory storm scene, here slyly combined with Wagner's "Ride of the Valkyries."

Sallinen, Aulis (1935-). Finnish composer, whose operas include, *The Red Line* (1978), *The King Goes Forth to France* (1984), and *Kullervo* (1988). The first is possibly the most frequently performed. A grim story of life on a farm in the Finnish backwoods in 1907, the year of the first election under universal suffrage, the conflicts of politics as well as the solitude and dangers of nature have a part, the "red" line symbolizing both the mark on a ballot and a throat ripped by a bear. Sallinen's style is frequently tonal, sometimes lyrical, and in the political scenes full of contrast.

Second Viennese School. A short-hand way of referring to Arnold

Schoenberg (1874-1951) and his two chief disciples Alban Berg (1885-1935) and Anton Webern (1883-1945). These three, in a time of swiftly shifting styles of composition, held consistently to Schoenberg's development (out of Wagner's chromaticism in *Tristan und Isolde*) first of atonal music, roughly 1908-1914, and then of serial or twelve-tone music in which each note in the twelve-note chromatic scale is of equal importance. See the discussion in Chap. 1, and above, Adorno.

Schreker, Franz (1878-1934). Austrian composer of nine operas, whose career was closed by Nazi anti-semitism and dislike of his increasing adherence to avant-garde, "decadent" techniques. His second opera, *Der ferne Klang* (*The Distant Sound,* 1912), much performed until 1933, has recently had some successful revivals. It is a fanciful story of an artist who insists on achieving fame before marrying the woman he loves. She, while waiting, becomes a high-class whore in Venice (second act), sinks to a street prostitution (third act), but at the end the artist, reconciled, dies in her arms, planning a new last act to his opera (fragments of which resemble *Der ferne Klang*). The score is lushly orchestrated and skillfully mixes exotic settings with touches of realism.

Serial music. See discussion in Chap. 1.

Sessions, Roger (1896-1985). American composer and teacher, known mostly for his instrumental works, wrote two operas, the one-act, relatively tonal, and small-scaled *The Trial of Lucullus* (1947, to a libretto by Brecht), and the full-length, twelve-tone and highly complicated *Montezuma* (1964, to an original libretto by Antonio Borghese). The second, dealing with Cortes's conquest of Mexico and clashes of culture, calls for twenty-two soloists, a large chorus for Indians and Spaniards, a hugh orchestra and an onstage band. Perhaps these are reasons enough to explain its few performances, but in addition, opinion of its worth is very divided. Despite the color of Aztec costume and ritual many consider the opera, because of its somewhat inept libretto, heavy orchestration and often ugly vocal lines, a long bore; others, including many musicians, think it the greatest of American operas.

Shostakovich, Dmitry (1906-1975). Russian composer, whose career in opera was blighted by Soviet politics. Under the pressure of Stalin's disapproval in 1936, expressed after seeing a performance of *The Lady*

Macbeth of Mtsensk District (1934), Shostakovich turned his genius to orchestral and chamber music, and their gain was opera's loss. His first opera, indebted musically to Berg's *Wozzeck,* was *The Nose* (1930), based on Gogol's short story satirizing civil servants, government officials, and police. His second, *Lady Macbeth,* which in 1963 resurfaced, revised and titled *Katerina Ismailova,* tells of the bored wife of a provincial merchant who takes a factory hand as her lover. Together they kill her husband, but the body is discovered, and they are sent to Siberia. On the way, he promotes another woman in his affections, whom Katerina kills, and then drowns herself. The opera mixes satire and realism in an odd way but said to be very Russian. The police, for instance, are ludicrous; the final scene, on the steppes, tragic.

Still, William Grant (1895-1978). American composer, whose best-known opera is *A Bayou Legend* (1974). He composed in a traditional style, tonal, melodic, mildly dissonant, and was admired for his use of Negro motifs in his music and for excellent orchestration. The latter may owe much to his work in jazz, particularly for the bandleader Paul Whiteman.

Stockhausen, Karlheinz (1928-). German composer. Of his generation he is the outstanding composer continuing to work in the techniques of the Second Viennese School (q.v.); and like its leader Schoenberg, he is a master of self-explanation and advertisement as well as one of the twentieth century's most important musicians. He is started on a seven-opera cycle titled *Licht* (*Light*), with an opera for each day of the week. To date three have been completed: *Donnerstag* (*Thursday,* 1981), *Samstag* (*Saturday,* 1984), and *Montag* (*Monday,* 1988). For each, besides music, he provides libretto, choreography, stage direction and gestures. At performances of *Donnerstag* at Covent Garden in 1985, according to Andrew Porter's report: "The soloists—singers and instrumentalists—had each an individual microphone, and over forty more microphones were used in the pit and on the stage and the side stages. Loudspeakers ringed the theatre. Stockhausen, with assistants, sat in the center of the house, a thirty-six channel mixer before him and a twenty-four channel mixer beside him, to control balances, dynamics, and timbres. The 'sound perspectives' were exquisitely fashioned. . ." Indeed, many critics report that Stockhausen's sounds are very beautiful. But where will *Licht,* or its parts, play? Yet this question was asked, in the nineteenth century, of Wagner's four-opera *Ring,* which now plays in many theatres.

Strehler, Giorgio (1921-1997). Italian stage director. Fully contemporary, able to use every trick of modern theatre, he was yet a humanist who saw plays and operas as an expression of humanity. He had great success with twentieth-century operas, but even more remarkable, because perhaps more difficult, he was able to revive many nineteenth-century operas, sometimes in modern trappings, without violating the composer's intent. Two examples from Verdi, widely seen, were his *Simon Boccanegra* (1971), stressing for Boccanegra the freedom of the sea against the onshore tensions of statesmanship, and *Macbeth* (1975), which Strehler thought Verdi saw as a play of power and crime, but even more of solitude: "the drama of two lonely people who never meet on the same ground, who sink into the void of madness. . ." Lady Macbeth into "infantile" madness, "a reversion to childhood," and Macbeth into "progressive self-destruction." In 1995, emphasizing the composer's primacy in opera, Strehler said, "The greatest director of *Don Giovanni* will never be the equal of Mozart;" adding, "There is a diabolical danger in the craft of interpretation, to believe that we are as capable, or even better than Mozart or Shakespeare." See Sutcliffe in bibliography.

Surrealism. In drama and opera a style of presenting the subconscious, as if in a dream, with scenes often out of order and strange contrasts. It began in France in part as a response to Freudian psychoanalysis, and because dealing with the subconscious surrealistic scenes often pervade stories of the insane. An opera using such techniques is Poulenc's *Les Mamelles de Tirésias* (1947); and see the introductory paragraphs to its synopsis. Another is *Postcard from Morocco* (1971).

Symbolism. A form of theatre and opera close to expressionism (q.v.), but more poetic and without the latter's exaggerations and frequent violence. Symbolism began in the theatre with the dramas of Maeterlinck, which rejected realism, and in opera with Debussy's *Pelléas et Mélisande,* based on Maeterlinck. Typically, in symbolist dramas the characters are primarily projections of the poet or musician's self, with little life of their own; for example, Bartok's *Duke Bluebeard's Castle,* in which as Judith opens doors in the castle she sees different aspects of

Bluebeard's personality. Plays or operas with artists as the main character often are treated in a symbolist style.

Taylor, Deems (1885-1966). American composer, critic, radio commentator. During the late 1920s and 30s he was the country's outstanding opera composer, with two works commissioned by the Metropolitan and played there with success. These were *The King's Henchman* (1927, libretto by the poet Edna St. Vincent Millay) and *Peter Ibbetson* (1931, after George du Maurier's novel). After World War II both, perhaps because in a style bred of Wagner, Debussy, and Puccini and lacking true individuality, began to seem out of date, and have seldom been revived. Taylor also composed several orchestral suites, of which *Through the Looking Glass* (1922) for fifteen or twenty years was much performed.

Timbre. Tone quality pecular to each instrument, produced largely by the strength or weakness of its notes' overtones or harmonics. To many ears, the cello has a soft and rich "brown" tone, and the trumpet, bright "scarlet." Because electronic instruments, through treble boost (q.v.), can change the strength or weakness of the overtones, they can imitate any instrument's timbre.

Toscanini, Arturo (1867-1957). Italian conductor, of enormous prestige and power. In opera his chief work was done at La Scala, Milan, and the Metropolitan, New York. At La Scala he became the artistic director in 1898, staying until 1903, when he walked out in disgust at the audience's attempt to force an encore. He returned in 1906, but left again in 1908 to join the Metropolitan where he stayed until 1915. In both houses he greatly raised the standard of performance. He was again at La Scala, 1920-1929, leaving after a conflict with Fascist officials. He conducted at Bayreuth 1930-1931 and at Salzburg 1934-1937, but left both on political grounds. Thereafter, he did not conduct opera except in concert, radio, or recorded performances. Because he had played in several orchestras under Verdi, as well as consulting with him before conducting the Italian premiere of the *Pezzi sacri,* he had strong ideas on conducting Verdi; and though lacking such personal contact with Wagner, he was equally strong in conducting him. Puccini, he knew personally and after Puccini's death arranged for the completion of *Turandot* (1926) by Franco Alfano. After the 1920s his taste did not incline to contemporary music, and he conducted very little of it.

Treble boost. An electronic device. The same note, say middle C, will have a different timbre (q.v.) when played on an oboe, trumpet, or guitar because the intensity or loudness of the note's overtones or harmonics vary among the instruments. It is a reason instruments can be identified by sound alone. Treble boost, generally worked by a pedal switch wired to the instrument, allows the player to increase the intensity of the electric signal's harmonics as much as thirty-five times, changing the note's timbre.

Tremolo. The amplitude of the electric signal, which determines the ultimate sound's loudness, is made to increase and decrease slightly *without* varying the pitch. It adds "liveness" to the sound, but to most ears less than does vibrato (q.v.). The two terms are often confused, to the extent some guitars have a "tremelo arm" or "tailpiece," that because it varies the pitch is in fact a "vibrato arm."

Verismo (It.). Lit., "realism." A style of opera that flourished during the first quarter of the twentieth century, mostly in Italy and with an early example Mascagni's *Cavalleria Rusticana* (1890). Its hallmarks are violence, passion, sensationalism, springing usually from jealousy and ending in death. Reacting to the previous generation's addiction to historical dramas, verismo composers often featured working-class characters. One of the style's best works, because more inspired, better orchestrated, and more carefully wrought than most, is Puccini's *Il tabarro* (*The Cloak,* 1918); and a later example is Menotti's *The Medium* (1946). But many operas have veristic touches.

Vibrato. Used as a term of electronic music. The electric signal's frequency, its number of vibrations per second, is made to increase and decrease slightly. This causes the ultimate sound to rise and fall slightly in pitch, just as any string player can do acoustically by rocking the finger on the string. Vibrato in excess becomes a wobble in pitch; if just right—tastes vary—it gives a rich, full-bodied sound. It also helps to "sustain" the sound. Being able to flick vibrato on or off mechanically, by pressing a foot or hand lever wired to the instrument, has advantages for a player though subtleties of shading may be harder to control.

Wagner, Wieland (1917-1966). German stage director, grandson of

Richard Wagner. With his brother Wolfgang he revived the Bayreuth Festival after World War II, and in his designs for the operas abandoned the romantic, realistic style until then employed, substituting bare stages, tilted discs, less movement and gesture, and much more subtle lighting. With lighting freed from illuminating tables, chairs and fancy costumes onstage, it could be used to create the opera's essential mood, to act on the subconscious emotions of the audience. His ideas of abstraction, stripping away irrelevant details, despite opposition from traditionalists, were generally thought successful and were much copied, though often in weak versions. Many of his productions ran counter to usual stagings. For an *Aida* in Berlin (1961) though the Triumphal Scene is usually set in daylight, he put it at night, with torches, reminiscent of Nazi Nuremberg rallies; and the Tomb scene, which Verdi wanted dimly lit, he flooded with light on a theory that the dying lovers were moving to an eternal day. His most successful non-Wagnerian production, again reversing usual staging, was a *Salome* for Stuttgart (1962). Throughout the opera, including her dance, *Salome* for long periods was kept motionless while John the Baptist was sent constantly striding about the stage. At each new production many of the audience were outraged, many entranced.

Wah-wah effect. An electronic term and similar to treble boost. Depending on how far a pedal is depressed, different filters are activated and higher, middle, or lower harmonics of a signal will be boosted. A single note or chord can be passed from a guitar's twang to an oboe's whine, to a trumpet's brassy clarity, and back.

Walton, William (1902-1983). English composer. Though his fulllength opera *Troilus and Cressida* (1954, rev'sd, 1976) had little success, his one-act "extravaganza" *The Bear* (1967), after a farce by Chekhov, had much. It tells of a widow, faithful in mourning, who suddenly succumbs to a virile creditor of her deceased husband. The music is witty, the orchestration light and delightful. Walton also composed for films, with three of his most famous scores for the Olivier-Shakespeare *Henry V, Hamlet,* and *Richard III.* In addition, with great success, he composed coronation marches for George VI and Elizabeth II, *Crown Imperial* and *Orb and Sceptre.*

Webber, Andrew Lloyd (1948-). English composer, whose musical theatre works have found enormous success, chiefly *Jesus Christ Superstar* (1971), *Cats* (1981), and *Phantom of the Opera* (1986). The last, partly because of its title, has led the public to call him an opera composer; and the *Phantom,* though a pastiche of styles, and without the individual stamp that, say, Sondheim achieves, is a full-length musical thriller with solos, ensembles, and lots of creepy music. Essentially, however, it may not be an opera because the climaxes are more in the stage spectacle than in the music.

Weisgall, Hugo (1912-1997). American composer, teacher, whose work is praised by critics, but scorned by the public. At the premiere and few performances of his opera *Nine Rivers from Jordan* (1968), the audience's haste to leave the theatre was brutal. Even his supposed masterpiece, *Six Characters in Search of an Author* (1959), at its premiere lost half its audience, and on two repetitions did little better. In forty years it has had two professional, two school productions. Even his most recent opera *Esther* (1993), initially more successful, had its first revival canceled. Weisgall is a high-minded composer; *Nine Rivers* discusses such problems as individual versus collective guilt. His style is largely atonal, hard to sing and play, and without concessions to attract an audience. His operas doubtless repay study and rehearing, but without some quality to cajole people to listen, their future seems dim.

Wilson, Robert (1941-). American stage designer and director, whose beautifully lit, abstract, stylized stage pictures, with movement often in slow motion, has greatly influenced multi-media stagings. His most revolutionary operatic work, with Philip Glass, was *Einstein on the Beach* (1974), and the two presently are perfecting a new multi-media work, *Monsters of Grace* (1998). Wilson has designed and directed some nineteenth-century opera, notably a *Zauberflöte* (1991) for the Bastille Opera, Paris, and a *Lohengrin* (1998) for the Metropolitan, New York.

Wolf-Ferrari, Ermanno (1876-1948). Italian composer of Venetian background, best-known today for a one-act farce *Il segreto di Susanna* (1909), in which Susanna's secret is that she smokes cigarettes; and her problem is that her husband, detecting a scent of tobacco in the house, suspects she has taken a lover. Until World War II Wolf-Ferrari was also known for settings of two Goldoni plays, *Le donne curiose* (*The Inquisitive Women,* 1903) and *I quatro rusteghi* (*The Four Boors,* or as sometimes retitled, *The School for Fathers,* 1906). Both are comic, in a light, well-orchestrated style. He also composed in a verismo style the highly-melodramatic *I gioelli della Madonna* (*The Jewels of the Madonna,* 1911), which is set in the Neapolitan underworld where passions are volcanic.

Zandonai, Riccardo (1883-1944). Italian composer, who developed a style orchestrally rich and theatrical. Of his thirteen operas the two most successful, and still occasionally revived, are *Francesca da Rimini* (1914) and *I cavalieri di Ekebù* (1925). At his best, often in quieter moments, or when composing for women's voices, he can be affecting; at his worst, in battle scenes, or where men's voices dominate, the music tends to rant and roar.

Zarzuela (Sp.). A theatrical work mixing singing, dancing, and talk. Over three centuries, gaining and losing popularity in Spain, the form has often changed its style. In the twentieth, influenced by Lehár and the Viennese tradition, it became more like an operetta, and in this style Amadeo Vives (1871-1932) had a continuing success with his *Doña Francisquita* (1923), as did also Manuel Penella (1880-1939) with *El gato montés* (1916).

Zeffirelli, Franco (1923-). Italian stage director and designer. In the 1950s he seemed unable to put a foot or hand wrong and in a realistic style did memorable work, particularly in nineteenth-century romantic opera. But then he became increasingly interested in spectacle, and in1966 created a hugely overblown production of Barber's *Antony and Cleopatra* to open the Metropolitan's new house at Lincoln Centre; and thereafter the disease, like malaria, seemed to return periodically. In 1985 he produced a *Tosca* at the Metropolitan in which he overwhelmed Scarpia's "Te Deum" in Act I by parading behind him a vast collection of brightly-robed ecclesiastics and choirs; and in Act III, to create two scenes where Puccini had one, he spoiled some fine atmospheric music by raising huge, visible stage elevators. But the majority of the audience loved it.

Zemlinsky, Alexander von (1871-1942). Austrian composer and conductor, whose sister married Arnold Schoenberg. Though an admirer of Schoenberg, Zemlinsky did not adopt atonality or serialism, but maintained an eclectic, late-romantic style, fitfully lyric and highly theatrical. Of his nine operas the best-known are *Eine florentinische Tragödie* (*A Florentine Tragedy*, 1917) and *Der Zwerg* (*The Dwarf*, 1922), both one-act, both based on stories by Oscar Wilde, *A Florentine Tragedy* and *The Birthday of the Infanta*. The first offers a Renaissance love triangle in which an elderly husband, by killing his wife's lover with bare hands, rearouses her sexual interest. The second recounts how a dwarf at the Spanish court, a poet, in love with the Infanta, and unaware of his deformity, dies after she reveals it to him. Zemlinsky's music all but disappeared in the Nazi era and after the War, but recently much of it has been revived, including the operas.

A SHORT BIBLIOGRAPHY
of Books pertinent to Twentieth Century Opera
published in the century's last quarter

Books are listed alphabetically by author's last name, or where merely edited, by title. Some composers have entries by last name which refer to the authors of books about them.

Ardoin, John. *The Stages of Menotti* (New York: Doubleday, 1985). Includes a Chronology of works, compiled and annotated by Joel Honig.

————*The Callas Legacy: The Complete Guide to her Recordings on Compact Discs,* 4th ed., fw'd by Terence McNally (London: Duckworth, 1995).

————*Callas at Juilliard: The Master Classes* (New York: Knopf, 1987).

————*The Callas Legacy, A Biography of a Career,* rev'd ed. (New York: Scribner's, 1982).

Ashbrook, William, and Harold Powers. *Puccini's* Turandot, *The End of the Great Tradition* (Princeton, 1991).

Auden, W. H. and Chester Kallman. *Libretti and other Dramatic Writings by W. H. Auden, 1939-1973,* ed. Edward Mendelson (Princeton: Princeton, 1993), a vol. in *The Complete Works of W. H. Auden.* Besides libretti, it includes essays on the operas' origins and interpretations, with many observations by Auden and Kallman.

Banfield, Stephen. *Sondheim's Broadway Musicals* (Ann Arbor, Mich., 1993). Through *Into the Woods* (1987).

Berg, Alban: See Carner, Jarman, Perle.

Bernstein, Leonard: See Burton, H. and Burton, W. W.

Birkin, Kenneth. *Richard Strauss,* Arabella (Cambridge: Cambridge, 1989); a "Cambridge Opera Handbook."

Bordman, Gerald. *American Operetta* (New York: Oxford, 1981).

Boulez, Pierre. *Orientations—Collected Writings* (London: Faber, 1986). Reprints his essays on *Wozzeck* and *Lulu* (completed) as well as on *Pelléas* and Wagner.

Bowen, Meirion. *Michael Tippett* (London: Robson, 1981, 1998); "Contemporary Composers" series.

Brett, Philip. *Peter Grimes* (Cambridge: Cambridge, 1983); a "Cambridge Opera Handbook."

Britten, Benjamin. *Letters from a Life, Selected letters and diaries of Benjamin Britten,* 2 vol.s, ed. Donald Mitchell and Philip Reed (London: Faber, 1991).

The Britten Companion, ed. Christopher Palmer (London: Faber, 1984).

Britten: See Brett, Cooke, Headington, Herbert, Howard, Kennedy, Mitchell, Whittall.

Burton, Humphrey. *Leonard Bernstein* (New York: Doubleday, 1994).

Buron, William Westbrook. *Conversations about Bernstein* (New York: Oxford, 1995).

Carner, Mosco. *Alban Berg, The Man and the Work,* 2nd ed., rev'd (New York: Holmes & Meier, 1983).

Clarke, David. *Language, Form and Structure in the Music of Michael Tippett* (New York: Garland, 1989).

A Confidential Matter, The Letters of Richard Strauss and Stefan Zweig, 1931-35, trans. Max Knight, fwd., Edward E. Lowinsky (Berkeley: California, 1977).

Conrad, Peter. *A Song of Love and Death, The Meaning of Opera* (New York: Poseidon, 1987).

Cooke, Mervyn, and Philip Reed. *Benjamin Britten, Billy Budd* (Cambridge: Cambridge, 1993); a "Cambridge Opera Handbook."

Corsaro, Frank. *Maverick: A Director's Personal Experience in Opera and Theater* (New York: Vanguard, 1978).

Dahlhaus, Carl. *Foundations of Music History,* trans. J. B. Robinson (Cambridge: Cambridge, 1983).

Davenport-Hines, Richard. *Auden* (New York: Pantheon, 1995).

Daviau, Donald G. and George J. Buelow, The Ariadne auf Naxos *of Hugo von Hofmannsthal and Richard Strauss* (Chapel Hill, N. C.: North Carolina, 1975).

Davis, Peter G. *The American Opera Singer, The Lives and Adventures of America's Great Singers in Opera and Concert from 1825 to the Present.* (New York: Doubleday, 1997).

Debussy, Claude. *Debussy Letters,* ed.s François Lesure and Roger Nichols (London: Faber, 1987).

DeJong, Constance, and Philip Glass. *Satyagraha, M. K. Gandhi in South Africa, 1893-1914* (New York: Standard Editions, 1980). The libretto and a history of the politics underlying the events in South Africa.

Douglas, Nigel. *The Joy of Opera* (London: Deutsch, 1996).

———*Legendary Voices* (London: Deutsch, 1992; New York: Limelight, 1995).

———*More Legendary Voices* (London: Deutsch, 1994; Limelight, 1995).

Drew, David. *Kurt Weill, A Handbook* (Berkeley: California, 1987).

Ewans, Michael. *Janáček's Tragic Operas* (London: Faber 1977).

Forsyth, Karen. *Ariadne auf Naxos by Hugo von Hofmannsthal and Richard Strauss, Its Genesis and its Meaning* (New York: Oxford, 1982).

Fuegi, John. *Brecht & Company, Sex, Politics, and the Making of Modern Drama* (New York: Grove, 1994. See his essay in *The New Orpheus,* "Most Unpleasant Things with *The Threepenny Opera,* Weill, Brecht, and Money."

Glass, Philip. *Music by Philip Glass.* with additional material by Robert T. Jones (New York: Harper, 1987); in England titled *Opera on the Beach* (London: Faber, 1988). Focuses chiefly on *Einstein, Satyagraha,* and *Akhnaten.* See also, DeJong, Page, Redford.

Gobbi, Tito. *Tito Gobbi, on his World of Italian Opera* (New York: Franklin Watts, 1984).

Griffiths, Paul. *Stravinsky* (London: Dent, 1992); "Master Musicians Series."

———*Oliver Messiaen and the Music of Time* (London: Faber, 1985).

———*Igor Stravinsky,* The Rake's Progress (Cambridge: Cambridge, 1982); a "Cambridge Opera Handbook."

———*Peter Maxwell Davies* (London: Robson, 1982); "Contemporary Composers" series.

Hartmann, Rudolf. *Richard Strauss: The Staging of His Operas and Ballets,* (New York: Oxford, 1981).

Headington, Christopher. *Britten* (London: Eyre Methuen, 1981); "Composer as Contemporary" series.

Henze, Hans Werner: See Auden, Porter.

Hines, Jerome. *Great Singers on Great Singing* (New York: Doubleday, 1982, and Limelight, 1984).

Hinton, Stephen. *Kurt Weill,* The Threepenny Opera (Cambridge: Cambridge, 1990); a "Cambridge Opera Handbook."

Hirsch, Foster. *Harold Prince and the American Musical Theatre,* fwd.s.

by Prince and Stephen Sondheim (Cambridge: Cambridge, 1989); "Directors in Perspective" series.

Horowitz, Joseph. *Understanding Toscanini, How He Became an American Culture-God and Helped Create a New Audience for Old Music* (New York: Knopf, 1987).

Howard, Patricia. *Benjamin Britten,* The Turn of the Screw (Cambridge: Cambridge, 1985); a "Cambridge Opera Handbook."

International Dictionary of Opera, 2 vol.s, ed. C. Steven LaRue (Detroit: St. James, 1993).

Janáček, Leoš. *Intimate Letters, Leoš Janáček to Kamila Stösslová,* ed. and trans. by John Tyrrell (Princeton: Princeton, 1994).

————*Janáček's Uncollected Essays on Music,* ed. and trans. by Mirka Zemanova (New York: Marion Boyars, 1989).

Leoš Janáček, see Ewans, Tyrrel.

Jarman, Douglas. *Alban Berg,* Lulu (Cambridge: Cambridge, 1991); a "Cambridge Opera Handbook."

————*Alban Berg,* Wozzeck (Cambridge: Cambridge, 1989); a "Cambridge Opera Handbook."

Kennedy, Michael. *Britten* (London: Dent, 1981); "Master Musicians" series.

————Richard Strauss (London: Dent, 1976); "Master Musicians" series.

Leinsdorf, Erich. *The Composer's Advocate, A Radical Orthodoxy for Musicians* (New Haven: Yale, 1981): "To discover the composer's grand design. . . [is] the conductor's mission." (63).

————*Cadenza, A Musical Career* (Boston: Houghton Mifflin, 1976). He withdraws from a Bayreuth production of *Tannhaeuser* (1972) that misconceives the composer's purpose. (276-280).

Lindenberger, Herbert. *Opera, The Extravagant Art* (New York, Cornell, 1984).

Mascagni, Pietro. *Mascagni, An Autobiography,* ed. and trans. by David Stivender (White Plains, N.Y. : Pro/Am Music Resources, 1988).

Minturn, Neil. *The Music of Sergei Prokofiev* (New Haven: Yale, 1997).

Mitchell, Donald. *Benjamin Britten:* Death in Venice (Cambridge: Cambridge, 1987); a "Cambridge Opera Handbook."

The New Grove Dictionary of Opera, 4 vol.s, ed. Stanley Sadie (London: Macmillan, 1992).

The New Kobbé's Opera Book, eds. Lord Harewood and Antony Peattie (New York: Putnam's, 1997).

The New Orpheus, Essays on Kurt Weill, ed. Kim H. Kowalke (Nw Haven: Yale, 1986). Including essays on *Down in the Valley, Street Scene,* and *Threepenny Opera* (See John Fuegi).

The Operas of Benjamin Britten, ed. David Herbert, intro. Hans Keller (New York: Columbia, 1980). Librettos, with illustrations of sets, costumes, and first productions.

The Oxford Dictionary of Opera, 3rd ed., eds. John Warrack and Ewan West, (Oxford: Oxford, 1996).

Paddison, Max. *Adorno's Aesthetics of Music* (Cambridge: Cambridge, 1993; pbk, 1997). See Adorno in Compendium.

Page, Tim. *Music From the Road, Views, and Reviews, 1978-1992* (New York: Oxford, 1992). Interviews with Glass and Bernstein; reviews, among many, of *Postcard from Morocco, Saint of Bleecker Street, Sweeney Todd,* and *Death of Klinghoffer.*

Perle, George. *The Operas of Alban Berg;* vol. 1, *Wozzeck,* vol. 2, *Lulu* (Berkeley: California, 1980, 1985).

Porter, Andrew. *Musical Events, A Chronicle, 1983-1986* (New York: Summit Books, 1989).

———*Musical Events, A Chronicle, 1980-1983* (New York: Summit Books, 1987).

———*Music of Three More Seasons, 1977-1980* (New York: Farrar, Straus, Giroux, 1978).

———*A Musical Season, A Critic from Abroad in America* [1972-1973] (New York: Viking, 1974). These chronicles with commentary, a remarkable history of music for the years covered, are well-indexed, and offer reports on most contemporary operas and composers, often with information not easily found elsewhere, e.g. Argento, Floyd, Henze.

Prokofiev, Sergei. *Selected Letters of Sergie Prokofiev,* ed. Harlow Robinson (Boston: Northeastern, 1998).

———*Prokofiev by Prokofiev, A Composer's Memoir,* ed. David H. Appel, trans. Guy Daniels (New York: Doubleday, 1979).

Prokofiev: See Minturn, Robinson.

Puccini: See Ashbrook, Weaver.

Ravel, Maurice. *A Ravel Reader: Correspondence, Articles, Interviews,* ed. and trans. Arbie Orenstein (New York: Columbia, 1990).

———*Ravel Remembered,* ed. Roger Nichols (London: Faber, 1987); "Composers Remembered" series.

Redford, Donald B. *Akhenaten* [sic], *The Heretic King* (Princeton: Princeton, 1984).

Robinson, Harlow. *Sergie Prokofiev, A Biography* (New York: Viking, 1987).

Rodgers, Richard. *Musical Stages, An Autobiography* (New York: Random House, 1975).

Rosen, Charles. *Arnold Schoenberg* (New York: Viking, 1975); "Modern Masters" series.

Sachs, Harvey. *Reflections on Toscanini* (New York: Grove, 1991).

————*Music in Fascist Italy* (London: Wiedenfeld, 1987).

————*Toscanini* (Philadelphia: Lippincott, 1978).

Schmidgall, Gary. *Literature As Opera* (New York: Oxford, 1977).

Schoenberg: See Rosen, White, P.

Smith, Patrick J. *A Year at the Met* (New York: Knopf, 1983).

Solti, Georg, with Harvey Sachs. *Memoirs* (New York: Knopf, 1998). "We conductors. . . are there to serve with the best of our abilities the wishes of the composers, who are the creators." (208). See Sutcliffe.

Sondheim: See Banfield, Hirsch, Zadan.

Steane, John B. *Singers of the Century* (Portland: Amadeus, 1996).

Stravinsky, Igor. *Stravinsky in Pictures and Documents,* ed.s. Vera Stravinsky and Robert Craft (New York: Simon and Schuster, 1978). See also, Auden, Griffiths, Walsh.

Strauss, Richard: See Birkin, *Confidential Matter,* Daviau, Forsyth, Hartmann, Kennedy.

Sutcliffe, Tom. *Believing in Opera* (London: Faber, and Princeton: Princeton, 1996). A book celebrating not composers but stage directors, such as Peter Brook, Patrice Chereau, David Pountney, and Peter Sellars. "Any theory of decorum and duty owed to the original composer and librettist is pointless." (15). See Leinsdorf, Solti; and in Compendium, Hartmann and Strehler.

Sutherland, Joan. *The Autobiography of Joan Sutherland: A Prima Donna's Progress* (New York: Regnery, 1998).

Thomson, Virgil. *Music With Words, A Composer's View* (New Haven: Yale, 1989).

————*A Virgil Thomson Reader,* intro. John Rockwell (Boston: Houghton Mifflin, 1981).

Thomson: See Tommasini.

Tippett, Michael. *The Operas of Michael Tippett,* ed. John Nicholas (London: Calder, and New York: Riverrun, 1985); chiefly the libretti; an "English National Opera Guide." See also Bowen, Clarke, White, E. W., Whittall.

Tommasini, Anthony. *Virgil Thomson: Composer on the Aisle* (New York: Norton, 1997).

Trauber, Richard. *Operetta, A Theatrical History* (New York: Doubleday, 1983).

Trotter, William R. *Priest of Music, The Life of Dimitri Mitropoulos* (Portland: Amadeus, 1995).

Tyrrell, John. *Janáček's Operas, A Documentary Account* (London: Faber, 1993).

———*Czech Opera* (Cambridge: Cambridge, 1988).

———Leoš Janáček, *Kát'a Kabanová* (Cambridge: Cambridge, 1982); a "Cambridge Opera Handbook."

Vishnevskaya, Galina. *Galina, A Russian Story,* trans. Guy Daniels (New York: Harcourt, 1984). An artist's life in Soviet Russia, and abroad.

Volkov, Simon. *Testimony: The Memoirs of Dmitri Shostakovich,* as related to and ed. by S. V., trans. Antonina W. Bouis (New York: Harper, 1979; Limelight, 1984).

Walsh, Stephen. *Stravinsky:* Oedipus Rex (Cambridge: Cambride, 1993); a "Cambridge Music Handbook."

Weaver, William. *Seven Puccini Librettos,* trans. by W. W., (New York: Norton, 1981). Includes Italian on opposite page and the stage directions: *Bohème, Tosca, Butterfly, Tabarro, Angelica, Schicchi, Turandot.*

Weill: See Drew, Hinton, Kowalke.

White, Eric Walter. *Benjamin Britten, His Life and Operas,* 2nd ed. (Berkeley: California, 1983).

———*A History of English Opera* (London: Faber, 1983).

———Tippett and his Operas (London: Barrie and Jenkins, 1979, 1981).

White, Pamela C. *Schoenberg and the God-Idea: The Opera* Moses und Aron (Ann Arbor: UMI Research Press, 1985).

Whittall, Arnold. *The Music of Britten and Tippett: Studies in Themes and Techniques,* 2nd ed., (Cambridge: Cambridge, 1990).

Zadan, Craig. *Sondheim & Co.* 2nd ed. rev'd (New York: Harper, 1986). Through *Sunday in the Park with George.*

INDEX

Page numbers in *italic type* at the start of an entry indicate where the opera's synopsis may be found. The first paragraph of the synopsis will give the dates of the opera's premieres in Europe and America (also in England and the United States when different as well as the opera's librettist and source.

For composers, birth and death years are given in parentheses.

Abduction from the Seraglio. See *Entführung aus dem Serail*

Abravanel, Maurice, 428

Acoustic guitar, 72-73

Adami, Giuseppe, 152, 153, 163, 178

Adams, John (1947-   ), 622, 623
Opera, see *Nixon in China*

"Adoration of the Magi" (Bosch), 473

Adorno, Theodor W., 429
compendium and glossary on, 633

"Affe als Mensch, Der," 577

Ägyptische, Helena, Die (Strauss), *214-217*, 7, 198, 210, 218, 643; psychiatry and marriage counseling, 215; Preface to opera, 217

Agon, 43, 48

Agostini, Philippe, 398

Aida (Verdi), 5; inspires Puccini, 33; night music compared with *L' Enfant,* 274; compared with *Porgy and Bess,* 385; new melodies in final scene, 652; Weland Wagner staging changes, 661

Akhnaten (Glass), *613-619,* 79-80, 81; countertenor role, 637

"Ain't it a pretty night," 571

A Kékszakállú Herceg Vára. See Duke Bluebeard's Castle

Albert, Eugen d' (1864-1932), 4

Albert Herring (Britten), *499-503,* 14; typical twentieth-century comedy, 10, 503; chamber opera orchestration, 500; transformation of source, 500-501; characterization, 502; compared with *Cosi,* 502; "Threnody," 502

Alfano, Franco (1876-1954), completes *Turandot,* 41, 178, 179, 659

Alexander Nevsky (film), 59, 62

Amahl and the Night Visitors (Menotti), *472-477,* 465; visual source 294, 473; casting problems, 474; carol, 476; shepherds' dance, 476

Amelia al Ballo (Amelia Goes to the Ball) (Menotti), *455-456,* 457

Amistad (Davis), 638

Amor brujo, El (Falla), 640

Amore delle tre melarance, L' (Gozzi), 333

Amour des trois oranges, L' (Prokofiev), *333-341,* 64, 65, 69, 244;